INTRODUCTION TO
MARKETING
MANAGEMENT
Text and cases

INTRODUCTION TO MARKETING MANAGEMENT

Text and cases

STEWART H. REWOLDT
Professor of Marketing

JAMES D. SCOTT
Sebastian S. Kresge Professor of Marketing

MARTIN R. WARSHAW
Professor of Marketing

All of the
Graduate School of Business Administration
The University of Michigan

 Revised Edition · 1973

RICHARD D. IRWIN, INC. *Homewood, Illinois 60430*
IRWIN-DORSEY LIMITED *Georgetown, Ontario L7G 4B3*
IRWIN-DORSEY INTERNATIONAL *London, England WC2H 9NJ*

Revised Edition

First Printing, February 1973
Second Printing, January 1974
Third Printing, July 1974
Fourth Printing, April 1975
Fifth Printing, June 1975

ISBN 0-256-01442-6
Library of Congress Catalog Card No. 72–90532
Printed in the United States of America

To Allison, Sara, and Alice

Preface

This text is designed for a first course in marketing management. It introduces students to the approaches and problems of marketing decision making under conditions of uncertainty. The point of view taken is that of a marketing manager responsible for the planning and execution of a complete marketing program. It recognizes that marketing planning must be accomplished in the light of a changing economic, social, and legal environment which poses many constraints and requirements for the marketing manager. The text draws upon economics, the behavioral sciences, and quantitative analysis wherever these are helpful in the solution of marketing problems. No one of these "orientations" to the teaching of marketing management predominates. Rather, all are utilized in order to provide the student with all the tools available to a present-day marketing manager.

In general, an analytical rather than a descriptive approach is taken; only essential descriptive material necessary to marketing decision making is provided. The text material focuses on basic concepts and methods of analysis. By applying these to the analysis of cases the student will come to appreciate their relevance and value. The student learns marketing decision making by making marketing decisions. There is no other way to train marketing managers that works as well.

The 34 cases included present fundamental issues in marketing management. Of these 34 cases, 20 are completely new while 14 cases have been carried over from the first edition. These provide students valuable experience in exercising their analytical powers and their judgment; they develop the student's capacity to make decisions. The cases follow each major section of text material and are designed to deepen and extend the student's understanding of the challenge the marketing manager faces in carrying out his responsibilities. Additional factual background about marketing and the environment in which it is carried on is also gained from case study.

This revised edition is divided into seven parts as was the first edition. Part I, which introduces the student to marketing management, has been expanded, however, to emphasize the role of marketing planning as a prelude to the development of a marketing strategy. Part II, which stresses buyer behavior as the prime determinant of basic marketing strategy, has been extensively revised, not only in terms of coverage of behavioral concepts, but also in how these concepts can provide a better understanding of buyer behavior in both the consumer and industrial markets. Parts III through VI deal with the major decision areas of marketing management—product strategy, distribution strategy, promotional strategy, and pricing strategy. Part VII is composed of a series of longer cases which can be used to integrate the strategies discussed in each of the marketing management decision areas into an overall marketing program for the firm.

Introduction to Marketing Management is shorter than some texts. It is intended for a one-semester course; hence, coverage has been limited to essentials. It is assumed that where greater depth of coverage is wanted this will be accomplished by personal input of the teacher, the use of additional readings, and the assignment of cases from other readily available sources. Our aim has been to design the book so that it is flexible and can be used in a variety of situations.

This revised edition is the by-product of the teaching experience of the authors at both the graduate and undergraduate level. Since we have all taught the introductory marketing management course at the University of Michigan, we have had an opportunity to test both the text material and cases in the classroom and to revise these materials in the light of this experience. Our thinking about the content of this revision has been much influenced by discussions with our faculty colleagues about ways in which the first edition could be improved. We have also received extremely valuable input from our students, from the many teachers who adopted the first edition, and from the intensive review of the first edition commissioned by our publisher. We wish to express our sincere appreciation for all of these contributions.

We are indebted to the Graduate School of Business Administration of the University of Michigan, and particularly to its Bureau of Business Research for financial support for the collection of the case materials included in this volume. The cases were collected by several individuals working on research assignments under the supervision of the authors or of certain of our colleagues. The index of cases at the end of the book lists each of the case authors and faculty supervisors. To each we extend our hearty thanks.

Special acknowledgement is due to Professor Charles N. Davisson, our colleague at Michigan, for permission to use the Advanced Technologies, Inc., case which was written under his direction and funded by his research grant. We also wish to single out another Michigan colleague, Professor Joseph W. Newman and the Board of Trustees of the Leland Stanford Junior University for permission to use the Falstaff Brewing

Corporation (B) case. Special thanks are due to the Stichting Bedrijfskunde (Foundation for Business Administration), Rotterdam, and the Program for International Business, Graduate School of Business Administration, the University of Michigan, for permission to use the Dutch Food Industries (A and B) cases, which were gathered in the course of a cooperative research project. We are most grateful for the support received from the Stichting Bedrijfskunde and especially from its former Dean, Professor Dr. Hein J. Kuhlmeijer of the Netherlands School of Economics, Rotterdam, for research support resulting in the collection of the cases dealing with the *U. K. Monopolies Commission* v. *Procter & Gamble and Unilever,* and the *Shell International Chemical Company* and for permission to use these cases in this text.

We are also indebted to the many business executives who cooperated with us in our case research activities and shared their experiences in order to provide a realistic learning experience for students. Although these individuals must go unnamed in order to protect confidential information, we nevertheless deeply appreciate their unselfish contributions.

Finally, we are indebted to our wives for their substantial contribution in providing encouragement when difficulties were encountered and in furnishing an environment conducive to the authorship task.

Ann Arbor, Michigan
January 1973

STEWART H. REWOLDT
JAMES D. SCOTT
MARTIN R. WARSHAW

Contents

part three
Product strategy   229

part four
Distribution strategy 333

8. The distribution structure 335

Exchange and market intermediaries: *Exchange without intermediaries. The wholesaler and exchange. Number of transactions and marketing costs.* Channels of distribution: *Major channels—Consumer goods. Major channels—Industrial goods. Use of higher cost channels. Use of multiple channels.* The retail structure: *Classification of retail establishments. Forces influencing the retail structure. Retailing in the future.* The wholesale structure: *Basic types of wholesale middlemen. Size and importance of wholesale trade.*

9. Distribution policy decisions 358

Degree of directness: *Nature of the product. Characteristics of the market. Characteristics of the manufacturer. Nature and availability of middlemen.* Selectivity in channel selection: *Illustrations of the above policies. Wisdom of restricting distribution.* Legal aspects of restricted distribution: *Legal status of exclusive dealing. Legal status of territorial protection. Justification of legal restraints.*

10. Physical distribution 390

Reasons for renewed interest: *Rising costs. Cost-saving potential. Promotional potential. Implications.* Systems analysis: *Systems terminology and logic. A physical distribution system. Implications.* Designing a physical distribution system: *The distribution audit.* Alternate systems design: *Hypo Company. Decision I: Number of distribution points. Optimizing number of distribution points. Decision II: Customer service level (CSL). Decision III: Warehouse replenishment time. Decision IV: Selective stocking. Total system optimization.* Inventory management. Location decisions. *Single-plant relocation. Multiple-facility location. Warehouse location and relocation.* Managing the physical distribution function.

part five
Promotional strategy   471

11. Promotional strategy decisions   473

Determination of basic promotional strategy: *Promotion involves communication. How communication works. Determining the promotional mix. Promotional methods. Choice of promotional methods.* Advertising: *Appraising the opportunity to make profitable use of consumer advertising. When should advertising receive main emphasis in the promotional mix? Other problems of advertising management.* Personal selling: *Factors influencing the use of personal selling. When should personal selling receive main emphasis? Other problems of sales force management.* Dealer promotion: *When should dealer promotion carry the main burden? When advertising is emphasized, how necessary is dealer promotion? When retail personal selling is emphasized, how necessary is dealer promotion? Methods of encouraging dealer promotion. Consumer promotions.* Determining the promotional mix: *Adaptive Planning and Control Sequence (APACS).*

12. Determining the promotional appropriation   506

Theoretical analysis of the problem. Common approaches to determining the appropriation: *Percentage of sales. All available funds. Competitive parity. Research objective. Advertising as an investment. Research to determine expenditure levels. Relation of communication objectives to sales results.*

13. Brand strategy decisions   534

Family brands versus individual brands: *Generalized preferences for family brands. Semantic generalization and family branding. Factors influencing choice of family versus individual brands. Summary and conclusions.* Company name combined with individual brand. Promotional implications of brand-quality-price relationships. Whether to manufacture under distributors' brands: *Distributors' brand policy. Manufacturers' brand policy. Mixed-brand policy. Decision-theory approach to mixed-brand policy choice. Evaluation of decision-theory approach.*

CASES FOR PART FIVE

part six
Pricing strategy

14. Price determination

Introduction: *Price versus nonprice competition. Special importance of pricing decisions.* Pricing and the competitive environment: *Implications.* Pricing objectives. Setting the basic price for a new product: *Demand estimation. The role of costs.* The interactive approach: *Break-even analysis.* Pricing strategy. Price redetermination: *Motivation for redetermination.* Pricing a new addition to the product line: *Cost interdependence. Demand interdependence. Implications.*

15. Price policies

Introduction: *Basic policies. Variable versus nonvariable price policies.* Price variation: *Goals of price variation. Implementation of price variations.* Discount policy: *Quantity discounts. Trade discounts. Trade discount strategy. Promotional discounts and allowances.* Price variation—legal issues: *The Robinson-Patman Act. Implications for discount administration.* Geographic pricing policies: *Geographic pricing—legal constraints.* Resale price maintenance: *Implementing a policy of resale price maintenance. Implications.*

CASES FOR PART SIX

part seven
Integrated marketing programs

CASES FOR PART SEVEN

part one

MARKETING PLANNING
AND STRATEGY

THE MARKETING FUNCTION in the business enterprise embodies many diverse activities, but the heart of marketing is marketing planning and marketing strategy. The marketing manager, in developing his marketing plan, works with those marketing variables over which he has a significant measure of control, such as the product, distribution, price, and promotion, including personal selling and dealer promotion. He attempts to design and implement a marketing strategy that will most efficiently achieve the goals of the company. He must do this with full awareness of the many constraints which limit his freedom of action. Above all, he must design his plan so that it is consistent with buyer behavior in the market he intends to serve.

Part One of this text introduces the student to marketing management and to marketing planning and marketing strategy. Part Two focuses on buyer behavior. It takes an intensive look at buyer behavior and approaches to understanding buyer behavior. Parts Three through Six deal with the major decision areas of marketing—product strategy, distribution strategy, promotion strategy, and price strategy. Part Seven attempts to integrate strategies discussed in each of these decision areas into an overall marketing program for the firm.

1

Marketing and marketing planning

THIS CHAPTER presents an overview of marketing and marketing planning. It attempts to answer such questions as: (1) What is marketing? (2) What is marketing planning? (3) What are the essential elements of a marketing plan? (4) How is a marketing plan developed? (5) What sort of marketing organization is necessary to implement the marketing plan?

What is marketing?

Marketing is not easy to define. No one has yet been able to formulate a clear, concise definition that finds universal acceptance. To the extent that a common view of marketing does exist, that view is usually based on the assumption that economic activity can be broadly divided into

FIGURE 1–1

three primary categories—production, marketing, and consumption. Goods and services must first be created—on the farm, in the factory, or in the shop. Before consumption can take place, these goods must be made available to consumers. Making the goods available is assumed to be the role of marketing. If the role of marketing is so perceived, marketing can be defined as "those activities involved in getting goods and services from producers to consumers."

3

This definition sees marketing as essentially a bridge between two other, perhaps more basic, economic functions. Its only purpose is to make it possible for the utilities created by the production process to meet the ultimate economic purpose of serving the consumption process.

This is a limited view of the economic role of marketing. It does recognize the need for such marketing functions as personal selling and advertising, necessary to persuade potential buyers to purchase, and

FIGURE 1–2

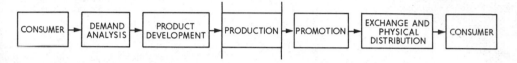

physical distribution to get products into the hands of consumers. However, it implicitly assumes the existence of a product before the role of marketing gets underway. It also takes it for granted that a demand for things which are produced exists in the marketplace and that marketing effort can successfully convert this demand into sales. This is a most unrealistic view of what marketing is all about.

In the progressive business firm, marketing is a broad and pervasive function, affecting all aspects of the business operation. It both begins and ends with the consumer. Because the basic purpose of business is to serve the welfare of consumers, it is essential that business operations be geared to this end. Relating business activities to consumer wants is accomplished through marketing. It is the role of marketing to identify consumers, to determine their wants and the manner in which they prefer these wants to be satisfied. Through demand analysis the consumer's wants are studied, measured, and understood. His behavior as a buyer is observed so that a marketing program may be devised which is consistent with that behavior. Such demand analysis is the function of marketing research activities.

Once consumer requirements and preferences are known, marketing plays a role in guiding the development of a product or service along lines consistent with consumer demand. The basic objective of the product development process is to translate consumer requirements into a physical product or a useful service. Other business functions also play a role in product development. However, it is the particular role of marketing to assure adaptation of the product or service to consumer needs and preferences.

In the case of a product, production is the next step after product development. Again, marketing has an influence. Through the information gathered about demand, product specifications are set, production schedules are determined, and inventory levels are planned. Once a product exists, consumers must be informed of its availability and its ability to serve their needs. It is through promotional activities (advertising, personal selling, etc.) that this communications function is accomplished. Informing consumers, of course, is the most commonly recognized marketing activity. It should be remembered, however, that it is only part, albeit an important part, of the total marketing process.

At some point, an exchange of the product for (usually) money must occur. The product, furthermore, must be made available where the consumer requires it. It is the role of marketing to perform these functions of exchange and physical distribution. Marketing does not end when the consumer receives the product, but it continues until his satisfaction with the product is assured. Common tools used in assuring such satisfaction are warranties, service facilities, and service contracts. These, too, are a part of the marketing process.

The broad scope of marketing poses a difficult problem of definition. In order to be sufficiently comprehensive to include all marketing activities, a definition of the marketing function must be either broadly worded or long and detailed. Perhaps the best definition of marketing that has been formulated is the following:

Marketing is the process in a society by which the demand structure for economic goods and services is anticipated or enlarged and satisfied through the conception, promotion, exchange, and physical distribution of such goods and services.[1]

A typical reaction to so broad a definition of marketing is likely to be, "But what else is there to business management? Doesn't this definition encompass all business functions?" No, not really. The underlying problem is that marketing *pervades* all other business functions and is intermingled with them. It has not proven possible, in framing a definition, to make this distinction fully clear.

In recent years there has been a trend among business firms to adopt what is known as "The Marketing Concept." Although this term has been loosely used and means somewhat different things to different people, it generally implies customer orientation of the total business firm. The implication of this concept is that the fundamental purpose of business activity is the satisfaction of consumer wants. It follows from this that a prerequisite to rational business activity is knowledge and understanding of consumer behavior. The function of marketing is to study and interpret consumer needs and behavior and to guide all business activities toward the end of consumer satisfaction. In doing this, marketing gets involved in all business functions. Successful imple-

---

[1] "Statement of the Philosophy of Marketing of the Marketing Faculty," The Ohio State University, College of Commerce and Administration (Columbus, 1964), p. 2.

mentation of the marketing concept is possible only if management perceives marketing as an all-pervasive business activity.

Synergism and marketing

Synergism is a popular word in business management literature. It is defined by Webster as: "Cooperative action of discrete agencies such that the total effect is greater than the sum of the two effects taken independently." [2] Nowhere in business management is synergism a more important concept than in management of the marketing function. The effectiveness of action taken with regard to one controllable variable depends greatly on what is done with regard to others. For example, the effectiveness of advertising depends on the adequacy of distribution of a product. Even favorable responses to advertising appeals cannot lead to consumer purchase if the product is not available in the marketplace. Personal selling can have its effectiveness blunted if advertising has not been used to lay the groundwork for the approach of the salesman. A price cut may fail to have the hoped-for effect if it is not promoted effectively. In short, the total effect of marketing effort is very much a function of the integration a firm manages to achieve in developing and carrying out its marketing program.

The concept of synergism applies not only to the marketing function but to the total operation of a business. The marketing concept involves the orientation of the entire business to the needs of the consumer. This means, for example, that production must be integrated with marketing requirements and that finance must provide the capital resources required to serve these consumer needs. It is the special role of marketing not only to assure that the marketing function is so oriented but also to guide the other business functions in serving the same goal.

Current trends in business are complicating this integration process. Firms are becoming larger and more complex, thus increasing the magnitude of the task. Product lines are broadening and diversifying, making it more difficult to achieve an optimal overall approach to the market. The growth of so-called "conglomerate" firms represents an extreme illustration of this problem.

Approaches used to achieve synergism in business vary widely. In the small enterprise, important decisions are usually made by one man. This in itself provides some measure of an integrative approach. As a firm grows in size, effective integration usually requires more and more committees and staff meetings. At some level of size, these somewhat casual approaches to integration no longer are adequate, and

---

[2] *Webster's Seventh New Collegiate Dictionary.* Copyright © 1963, by G. & C. Merriam Co., Springfield, Mass.

achievement of this goal becomes a difficult and perplexing thing. In the large firm, achievement of the synergistic effect is accomplished by more formal planning. Although planning is important to the small firm, it is indispensable to the large one. In the smaller firm, close interpersonal contact overcomes some defects in organization; ability to change course quickly overcomes some inadequacies in planning.

Marketing planning

Marketing planning is a subfunction of business planning. An inevitable result of the complex business environment in which change is the order of the day is the need for both short-range and long-range planning. A business firm, in order to survive and prosper, must know where it is going and how it is going to get there. It needs clearly defined goals and a well-thought-out course of action to achieve these goals. Without them efficient employment of resources is not possible.

A business firm may have many goals, either implicit or clearly stated. It may choose to maximize long- or short-range profits, to achieve steady but not necessarily maximum growth, to provide maximum security for management personnel, to maximize dividend payments to stockholders, and so on. The merit of these or other goals is not at issue here. What is at issue is the fact that these goals must be known before marketing planning can proceed. Planning for marketing activities must be consistent with the overall goals of the company.

The role of marketing planning is a special one in overall business planning. Marketing is the major link between the business firm and its environment. In order to achieve the orientation of the business firm to its market, marketing must study and interpret consumer needs and then guide the firm in serving those needs. In a rough sort of way, a marketing plan can be thought of as a company's battle plan. It surveys the environment, isolates marketing opportunities, and states the courses of action to be followed in taking advantage of those opportunities. Other parts of the overall business plan (for example, those relating to production and finance) are more in the nature of support plans— things which must be done to carry out the marketing plan which has been agreed upon. Obviously, however, no part of the overall plan for a business is independent of the other parts.

Because the marketing plan must be consistent with and serve a particular company's objectives, the marketing planning process and the resultant marketing plan will differ from one firm to another. Nonetheless, an in-depth look at the marketing planning process in one company that has adopted the marketing concept will reveal some practices that have general applicability.

The marketing planning process

The marketing planning process as it is carried out in the General Electric Company is outlined in Figure 1–3. The process as a whole is visualized as beginning with and ending with the customer. The whole process rests on the study of the customer, as carried out through marketing research activities. Such research activities are the first step undertaken—to determine who and where the customer is; what he needs, wants, and will buy; where and how he will buy; and how much he will pay. The next step is formulation of the master marketing plan. Note that this plan is based upon general management's overall plans for the business. This means, of course, that the master marketing plan must be consistent with the short- and long-range goals of the company as a whole.

The company objectives must be translated into marketing objectives. These are indicated in Figure 1–3 as being stated in terms of volume, position (market share), profit, gross margin, and budgets. Then, and

FIGURE 1–3
The General Electric marketing planning process

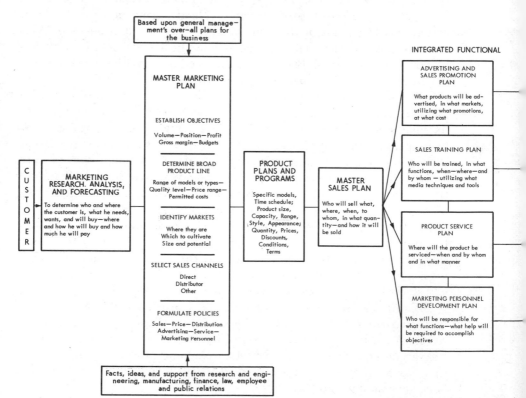

only then, can the product line to be offered by the company be determined. This clearly implies that the product line is considered a controllable variable—something that can be manipulated in order to achieve agreed-upon objectives. At this stage in the planning process, products are specified only in very broad terms, such as the type of product, the overall range of models, the general quality level, the price range, and permitted costs. The details are to be worked out later.

The next step in formulating the master marketing plan is seen as identifying markets. This step is a logical outgrowth of the previously made market studies and the decisions which have been made about the product line to be offered. Given these two types of information, markets can be identified as to where they are, which to cultivate, and their size and potential. Knowing the markets to be served, distribution channels can be selected. It is now possible to formulate basic policies concerning sales, price, distribution, advertising, service, and marketing personnel. Again, these are broad in concept and are to be refined later with regard to specific products.

Now that the master marketing plan has been structured (or, in a sense, now that the company has decided what business it is going

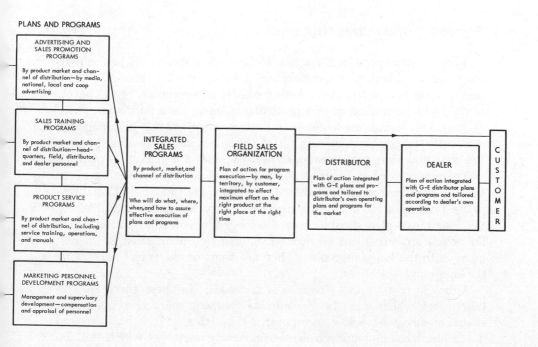

Courtesy of General Electric Company

to be in), it is time to construct plans and programs by products. Decisions must be made as to specific models, time schedules, product size, capacity, range, style, appearance, quantity, prices, discounts, conditions, and terms. In essence, these are the product strategy decisions discussed in Chapters 6 and 7.

The next step in the General Electric Company's marketing planning process is to develop a master sales plan (a subplan of the marketing plan) to determine how the things it has been decided to produce are to be sold to the markets that have been discovered. This, in their words, means deciding "who will sell what, where, when, to whom, in what quantity—and how it will be sold." The master sales plan is now broken down to its several integral parts—advertising and sales promotion, sales training, product service, and marketing personnel development. These plans are then converted into concrete programs, which in turn must again be put together into an integrated sales program to achieve the desired synergistic effect. The plans must now be implemented through the field sales organization, distributors, and dealers. As a result of this planning process, the customer is more likely to receive the product he needs and wants, and the company is more likely to achieve the profit it seeks.

Anatomy of a marketing plan

There is an important distinction to be made between marketing planning and a marketing plan. Marketing planning is a continuous function and is never completed. A marketing plan is an expression of the output of the planning process as of a particular moment for a particular period of time. Our discussion to this point has emphasized the planning process, with particular emphasis on the steps involved in that process. We shall now shift our attention to the structure of a marketing plan.

There is a trend in business toward formal, written marketing plans. Usually both long-range and short-range plans are prepared. The appropriate time span for marketing plans will vary with each industry, but the long-range plan should cover the longest predictable period ahead for which objectives can be defined. Short-range plans must be in harmony with the long-range plan. They are steps on the way to achieving the long-range objectives.

Although no one plan structure is necessarily the best, there are certain things which must be encompassed in any marketing plan. The structure discussed below incorporates these things. It is built around the controllable and uncontrollable marketing variables which will be discussed more fully in Chapter 2. These are integrated with other factors to form a plan structure that has wide applicability.

General structure of a marketing plan

An appropriate skeletal structure for a marketing plan might appear as follows:

I. Situation analysis
    a. Demand
    b. Competition
    c. Distribution structure
    d. Marketing law
    e. Nonmarketing cost
II. Problems and opportunities
III. Marketing strategy
    a. Objectives
    b. Methods
        1. Product strategy
        2. Distribution strategy
        3. Price strategy
        4. Promotion strategy:
            a) Advertising
            b) Personal selling
            c) Sales promotion
IV. Marketing tactics
    A. Who
    B. What
    C. When
    D. Where
    E. How

The situation analysis

Basic to marketing planning is an understanding of the environment in which marketing effort is to be expended. The environment determines not only what must be done, but what it is possible to do. Situational variables are multitudinous in number. One useful way of classifying them is the one suggested in the outline.

The purpose of the situation analysis is, in a sense, to take a picture of the external environment for marketing planning. It cannot, however, be a still picture that merely depicts what exists at the time it was snapped. It must be a moving picture that reveals trends and helps us to forecast what the environmental situation will be throughout the planning period. It is really the future situation in which we are most interested.

Demand is the most significant situational variable because it is least known and least predictable, yet has the greatest effect on what can or cannot be done in marketing. This means that marketing research is a very important tool in the marketing planning process. Demand must be understood both quantitatively and qualitatively. We need estimates of total potential demand, the distribution of demand, and so on. In addition, the marketing plan should include information on buying motives, buying practices, and the like. The other situational factors included in the outline (competition, distribution structure, marketing law, nonmarketing cost) must be similarly analyzed and the pertinent information recorded.

Problems and opportunities

The next phase of the marketing plan is a listing of problems and opportunities which are uncovered by distilling the information gleaned from the situation analysis. Sometimes it is hard to tell which facts constitute problems and which facts constitute opportunities. In the early 1960s, automobile manufacturers noticed that economy compacts that had been introduced several years earlier were not selling well. However, compact cars with sporty features, such as bucket seats, were doing well. For example, the sporty Monza model of the Corvair line went from 4.8 percent of total Corvair sales in 1960 to 71.5 percent in 1962.

Marketing research conducted as part of a situation analysis by Ford Motor Company revealed several important changes taking place in the

FIGURE 1–4
Population count and percentage change by age groups, 1960 to 1970

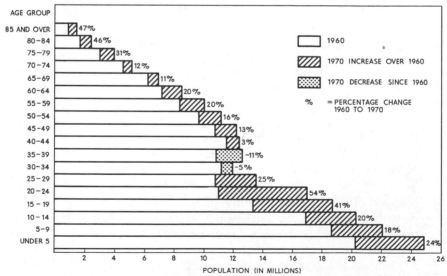

Source: U.S. Bureau of Census, *Current Population Reports*, Series P–25, No. 241 (January 17, 1962), Series II Estimates.

automobile market. First, a major change was occurring in the age makeup of the population of the United States, as shown in Figure 1–4. In the 1960–70 decade, there would be a tremendous increase in the 15–19, 20–24 and 25–29 age groups, while the over-30 age group would grow much more slowly. Younger buyers could therefore be expected to be a more potent factor in automobile demand in the future than in the past. Younger buyers have different tastes in automobiles, these tastes tending more toward the sporty than toward the staid models.

A second significant market fact bearing on automobile demand was the anticipated growth in college enrollment, which was expected to almost double in the 1960–70 decade (from 3.6 million to 7 million). People who have attended college behave differently in the purchase

FIGURE 1–5
New-car buying rate increases with educational level

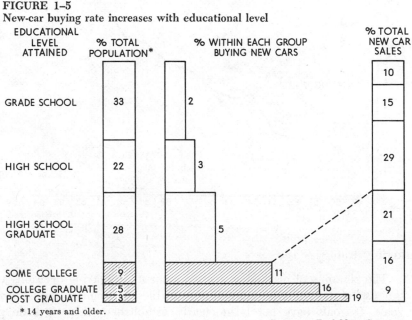

* 14 years and older.

Courtesy of Ford Motor Company

of automobiles from those who have not attended college. For one thing, they buy more automobiles. The 17 percent who have attended college account for 46 percent of total new-car sales, whereas the 83 percent with a high school education or less account for 54 percent (see Figure 1–5). Furthermore their tastes are more sophisticated and tend more toward sporty vehicles. Most sports cars, domestic and imported, are purchased by people with some college education.

A third important market fact was the trend toward multiple car ownership (see Figure 1–6). This trend reduces the domination of the all-purpose family vehicle and opens a market for more "personalized" transportation.

These three facts about the market uncovered in a situation analysis were dominant factors leading to the introduction of the Mustang by the Ford Motor Company. The success of this car entry is well known.

FIGURE 1–6
Multiple car owning spending units, January, 1949–65

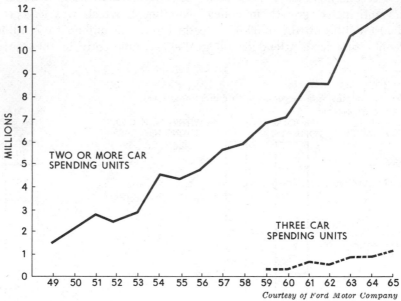

Courtesy of Ford Motor Company

Marketing strategy

The planning of marketing strategy consists of making decisions about the use of controllable marketing variables to achieve predetermined goals. If goals have not been clearly established, there is little point to planning. If you don't know where you are going, any road will take you there, and there is no meaningful basis for choice between one route and another. Therefore, the first step in planning marketing strategy is to establish goals.

In order to be useful, goals should be reasonably specific, and performance in achieving them should be measurable. A goal of maximizing profits does not fit these criteria when the achievable maximum is not known. Growth is not a meaningful objective unless expressed as a specific growth rate which is either achieved or is not. The most common ways of stating marketing strategy objectives are: (1) sales volume, expressed in either dollars or units; (2) market share, expressed as a percentage of the total market for a product or service; and (3) profit, expressed as a return on investment. These objectives are concrete, and the degree to which they are achieved can be calculated.

The heart of the marketing plan is the section on methods of strategy. Here decisions are made about the manner and extent of use of each controllable marketing strategy variable and how these variables should be meshed together into a total strategy. How this is done will be discussed in Chapter 2. Again, decisions should be reasonably specific and should be consistent with the kind and amount of resources available. Plans must be consonant with budget considerations, and often must be modified to fit budget constraints.

Marketing tactics

A marketing strategy program still is not an action program. Many details remain to be worked out. Specific responsibility for carrying out individual portions of the strategy must be assigned. Those to whom responsibility is assigned must be instructed as to just what they are to do. Time schedules must be planned and carefully integrated. Decisions must be made about the allocation and sequencing of marketing effort. Specific procedures must be agreed upon. This is the tactical part of the plan. Although not very glamorous, it is essential to the successful implementation of the marketing program.

Marketing planning in the future

Forecasting the future is an imperfect art at best. It is difficult to foresee the many events that will shape the future, but some are already on the horizon. Forecasting the future of marketing and deriving its effect on marketing planning is perhaps more difficult than forecasting in many other fields, because marketing is shaped in such large measure by the environment in which it is practiced. However, although there is uncertainty concerning what the future will bring, it is becoming increasingly apparent that marketing planning is going to become more complex to encompass more variables than it has in the past. The development of marketing to date, and its present methods of operation, are not as well suited to the environment in which they will probably have to operate in the future as they should be. Because marketing and marketing planning must of necessity reflect this environment, basic changes in marketing planning will have to take place.

When the marketing concept was introduced in the early 1950s, a quiet revolution began in the world of marketing. One implication of the marketing concept (see Chapter 2) is that demand is essentially an uncontrollable variable and that business can maximize profits by adapting its activities to demand as it exists in the marketplace. This, it was held, was far less costly and more efficient than trying to get consumers to buy whatever business chose to produce.

Simple as the marketing concept sounds, it brought great changes to marketing. The most visible change was a great increase in expenditures for marketing research. If business were to adapt to consumer demand, it must know and understand that demand. Companies that already had marketing research departments expanded them, and companies that did not have them established them. Another change was an increase in the status of marketing and a substantial broadening of its role. Previously, the highest ranking marketing officer was usually the sales manager. Now companies named vice presidents for marketing and gave them more authority and wider responsibility than sales managers had usually possessed. They began to play a role in product development, corporate planning, and long-range marketing planning, as well as in personal selling, advertising, and distribution.

Present day marketing, because the marketing concept demands it, has come to place great emphasis on research related to buyer behavior. Buyer behavior research is focused heavily on the needs and wants of consumers, including economic, psychological, and social needs, and on how consumers behave in the marketplace in satisfying their needs. The emphasis has been on individual needs and has not usually taken into account the needs of society as a whole (societal needs). The reasoning behind this approach is that consumers make purchase decisions on the basis of individual, not societal, needs.

The need for changes in marketing planning

Concern for the environment in which we live has long been voiced by some environmentalists, but the general public and marketing executives have been slow to recognize these increasingly serious problems. Beginning in the mid-1960s concern about air and water pollution, waste disposal, auto safety, preservation of the landscape, and so on has grown rapidly. The trend is likely to continue and governments are becoming increasingly responsive to such societal needs. Much new legislation to protect the environment and foster attention to other societal needs has already been passed, and much more is likely to be enacted in the future.

Strong and growing concern about societal needs, as distinct from individual needs, is certain to complicate the marketing planning process in the future. As pointed out earlier, present day marketing planning reflects, and is shaped by, individual needs. Societal needs have been generally ignored. This orientation in marketing planning is basically incompatible with the increasing concern for societal needs. Marketing is not going to find it easy to adapt to the new world in which it must operate in the future.

The problem of adaptation

For marketing planning to adequately reflect societal needs will be difficult for several reasons. First, it involves a new way of thinking for marketing managers. Humans are slow to change their way of thinking and their approach to problem solving. It took 20 years for the marketing concept to have a widespread effect on marketing planning, and in some industries and some countries it has had little impact at all.

A more basic obstacle to effective marketing planning lies in human nature itself. Consumers, unfortunately, are basically selfish. They pay lip service to societal needs, but their purchase behavior generally does not significantly reflect such considerations. They are, of course, hopeful that others will exercise concern for societal needs, but the average consumer continues to give primary emphasis to individual needs in making his own purchase decisions. Such seems to be the nature of man.

Several illustrations will make this point clearer. In the purchase of automobiles, many consumers still place great emphasis on styling, status value, personal comfort, and high performance. A particular model's contribution to air pollution, for example, and its road safety character- istics play, at best, a minor role in purchase decisions for automobiles. There is evidence that automobile choice criteria are changing, but the change is slow. Although everyone professes concern about auto safety, less than 30 percent of all drivers use their seat belts, and a much smaller percentage use shoulder harnesses. Another illustration is the failure of lead-free gas to gain widespread acceptance among motorists.

A firm faces another basic dilemma in its marketing planning. If it tries to adapt its marketing strategy to societal as well as individual needs, it runs a high risk of deterioration of its competitive position and profit return. Ironically, firms that ignore societal needs and stress only individual needs stand a good chance of being more successful in the marketplace than companies which try to be responsible citizens. This dilemma has international dimensions. If, for example, the United States imposes strong environmental controls, and Japan does not (until recently, Japan virtually ignored environmental problems), the United States will be at a competitive disadvantage in relation to Japan in international markets. This means that neither individual companies nor individual countries can act entirely independently in forcing an increas- ing recognition of societal needs in marketing planning.

According to Feldman, "Marketing emphasizes material consumption and ignores considerations of societal benefit when circumstances suggest this course of action is no longer suitable. In that sense, the present marketing system is an anachronism."[3] It is very true that marketing planning has not kept pace with the changing conditions in the environment in which it must operate in the years ahead. Inevitably, marketing planning in the future will be much more complex than it has been in the past. There will be many more variables to be considered in the situation analysis, and many more constraints imposed by marketing law. The resultant marketing strategy must strike the right balance between its reflection of individual and societal needs.

Marketing organization

A business firm is a combination of men, money, plant, and equipment so coordinated that they can fulfill an economic objective. The active ingredient in this combination, of course, is people. The other resources are inert and are effective only if people make them so. Basically, therefore, company objectives are accomplished through people. In order to achieve these objectives, the activities of people must be coordinated. This is the function of organization planning. An organization is simply a means for carrying out tasks necessary to achieve a predetermined goal. In the case of a marketing organization, the goals are those incorporated in the marketing plan.

Marketing planning and marketing organization have something of a chicken and egg relationship. As stated, a marketing organization is a means for carrying out the marketing plan. Therefore, the plan should determine the organization structure. On the other hand, an organization is needed to carry out the ongoing marketing planning function. Most marketing planning is, in fact, done within established organization structures. The answer to this dilemma, as usual, is that the marketing plan and the marketing organization must reflect and adapt to each other. The result is that they are more or less simultaneous activities, and each is continually prompting changes in the other.

Implications of marketing concept

Implementation of the marketing concept is intended to achieve customer orientation of the business firm. This objective is simple in statement, but to accomplish it is far from easy. Such accomplishment

---

[3] Lawrence P. Feldman, "Societal Adaptation: A New Challenge for Marketing," *Journal of Marketing*, Vol. 35 (July 1971), p. 57.

requires a proper state of mind on the part not only of top management but also of all key executives. It requires a concern with ends external to the company, such as service to consumers, rather than allowing internal considerations to dominate decision making. It requires an organization that makes possible effective coordination and integration of all business activities.

Organization is a key factor in implementation of the marketing concept, and implementation of this concept is a key factor in overall business success. A consequence of these basic facts is an increasing concern with organization structures, particularly for marketing. Much experimentation has been going on with regard to organization for marketing in recent years. There is a strong feeling among students of marketing that while the perfect answer has not yet been found, improvements have been made.

To illustrate the nature of the changes that have been taking place in marketing organizations and to suggest the reasons for them, let us take a look at a hypothetical pre-marketing-concept organization of a typical marketing department and compare it with what such a department might look like today. Of course, the appropriate organization structure varies widely by type of industry. Therefore, let us assume we are talking here about a company in the consumer packaged-goods field—a food company, say. For such companies, marketing tends to be the dominant business function. This adds piquancy to their problems of marketing organization.

Pre-marketing-concept organization

Until relatively recently a typical organization structure for a food company was likely to have some resemblance to the organization depicted in Figure 1–7. Sales was recognized as a major function and

FIGURE 1–7
A pre-marketing-concept organization structure

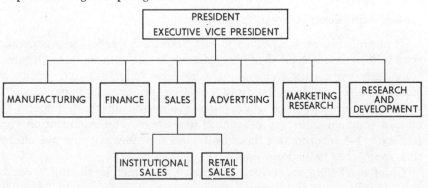

was likely to be headed by someone with the title of sales manager. If the company sold both through retail stores to ultimate consumers and to the institutional market (hotels, restaurants, and so on), there might be a separate sales organization for each of these markets. Advertising was a separate and distinct function from sales and probably was headed by an advertising manager, an executive on a par with the sales manager. The director of marketing research reported to neither the sales manager nor the advertising manager, but operated independently of both. Manufacturing, finance, and research and development were separate functions and had no direct ties to marketing activities.

Several things in particular should be noted about this type of organization structure. There is no provision in the marketing structure per se for integration of marketing activities. Sales, advertising, and marketing research are seen as separate activities. If there is to be integration, it must come through the actions of top management or through informal contacts of the executives heading each activity. If top-management people have marketing backgrounds, a fair measure of integration might be achieved. If they do not, such a result is unlikely.

There is no provision in the organization structure itself for coordination of marketing and nonmarketing activities. If production reflects marketing requirements, this is again a result of action by top management. This is true likewise for finance and research and development. There is no clearly defined route for information about the environment to be processed and translated into a marketing strategy. Again, this must happen by chance or through the coordinating efforts of top management.

There is nothing about this organization structure to assure achievement of a synergistic effect. The several business functions are fragmented and insulated from each other. If there is any marked degree of achievement in implementing the marketing concept, it is in spite of, not because of, the organizational structure.

A post-marketing-concept organization structure

It is probably presumptuous to talk about any particular organization structure as being typical of the post-marketing-concept era. Organizational structures vary tremendously both by industries and within the same industry. Still, to be fully effective, an organizational structure must make provision for achieving a synergistic effect, and to do this certain common traits are beginning to emerge. The organization chart in Figure 1–8 incorporates these traits, but this does not rule out alternative approaches to the same end.

Chief marketing executive. Note that the chief marketing executive

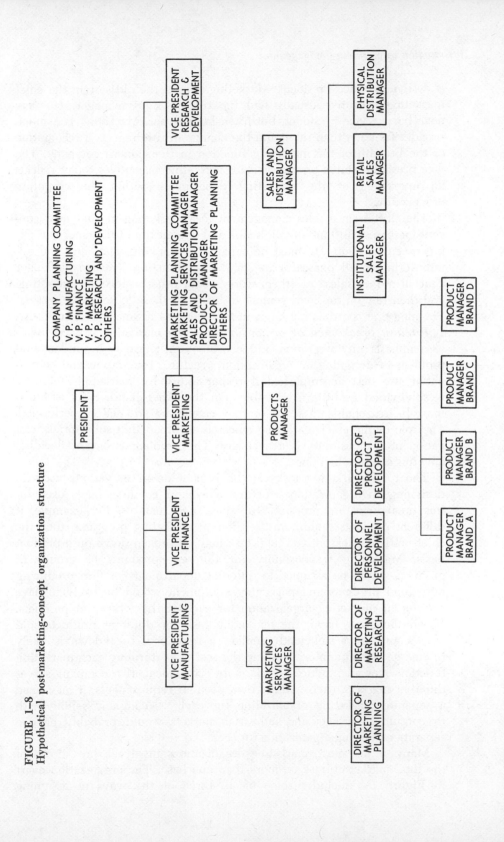

FIGURE 1–8
Hypothetical post-marketing-concept organization structure

is designated Vice President, Marketing. Under the old system the chief marketing executive usually had the title of sales manager. He may have been a vice president, but often he was not. Marketing is a much broader function than sales, and the change in title reflects a recognition of the breadth of the marketing function in the modern company. The vice president status typical of chief marketing executives today reflects an upgrading of the marketing department within the corporate organization.

The shift from a sales management to a marketing management concept increases substantially the scope and complexity of the chief marketing executive's job. He must be capable of thinking, planning, and administering in all phases of the marketing function. He can no longer concentrate on sales, let others worry about other aspects of marketing, and then rely on top management to bring all these loose ends together. Planning and coordination have, in fact, become his major responsibility.

Primary breakdown of responsibility. The marketing concept, with its emphasis on integration and coordination, presents a fundamental problem in designing an organization structure. Integration and coordination are best accomplished if responsibility for marketing activities is subdivided as little as possible. On the other hand, tasks assigned must be reasonable in scope or they cannot be adequately performed. The role of the chief marketing officer is so broad that substantial delegation of responsibility is a necessity. The problem is one of deciding how this can best be done.

The total marketing task can be broken down in various ways in designing an organization structure. The most common bases used for this breakdown are products, functions, and markets. For example, if different products require vastly different marketing programs, then the chief marketing executive's total task may be broken down on a product basis. Marketing responsibility for different products or groups of products would be assigned to different departments. A firm producing both food products and packaging equipment would be likely to have a different marketing organization for each of these types of products. If, on the other hand, the marketing task for different products sold by a company is sufficiently similar, a functional breakdown is likely to emerge. This permits spreading the cost of performing each marketing function over all products and is more economical. If a company serves different markets, each with its own peculiar requirements, it may need a separate marketing organization for each. A company selling both to consumer markets and industrial markets would probably have a separate marketing organization for each.

Many, if not most, marketing organizations involve a breakdown of the total marketing task on more than one base. The organization chart in Figure 1–8 includes some of all three of the ways of assigning responsibility just discussed. The division of responsibility among the marketing services manager, the products manager, and the sales and distribution manager is a functional one. The product managers responsible for individual brands have responsibilities assigned on a product basis. The existence of an institutional sales manager and a retail sales manager, each in charge of a sales force, represents a breakdown on a market basis.

The organization chart presented in Figure 1–8 is a consequence of major trends affecting organization for marketing in the past 15 years. The separation of marketing services from line sales and distribution activities is a way of focusing more attention on these service activities and improving performance in regard to them. Grouping them together under a marketing services manager who is responsible for their integration and coordination reflects a recognition of the need for synergism in marketing. The use of product managers has become a major approach to assuring that there is integration of all marketing activities associated with a particular product. How each of these departments operates to further the accomplishment of an integrative marketing program will now be explained.

Sales and distribution manager. The closest thing to the general sales manager of the pre-marketing-concept era included in Figure 1–8 is the sales and distribution manager. He is responsible for all field sales operations. His duties are complex, including all aspects of sales force management: recruitment, selection, training, supervising, and so on. These duties have here been broadened further to include physical distribution (discussed in Chapter 10). There is logic in combining responsibility for these two functions. The service that salesmen can render customers is very much a function of delivery dates, adequacy and location of inventory, means and times of transportation, and so forth. The physical distribution system must be so designed that it gives full support to sales requirements.

This organization chart, assumed to be for a food company, includes separate sales forces for institutional and retail sales. This separation may or may not be justified. It is based on the assumption that the sales requirements for these two markets are substantially different, that the salesmen who call on one type of customer would not be effective in making calls on the other. Because these customers overlap geographically, this involves duplication in market coverage and adds to costs. If the increased revenues generated by this specialization of salesmen does not justify this cost increase, then a common sales force would be preferable.

Marketing services manager. It was rare to find a position such as marketing services manager in a pre-marketing-concept organization. Staff functions in marketing were often organized on a helter-skelter basis, and no overt attempt was made to provide for integration and coordination. Today, this position is commonplace in marketing organizations. Its existence is evidence of a determined effort to develop integrated marketing programs. The specific marketing functions assigned to the marketing services manager vary widely, and usually the number is greater than the four included in Figure 1–8. Only the most common are shown there.

Marketing planning is and should be a top-management function. The chief marketing executive has overall responsibility for marketing planning and probably spends the better part of his time on this function. The role of the director of marketing planning is to assist in this activity and to put together the detailed long and short range marketing plans. He accepts the goals and broad strategy which have been agreed upon by top management and designs a detailed marketing plan consistent therewith. He coordinates the planning activities of all marketing organization units, particularly the product managers, and attempts to assure integration and consistency in the plans they devise. In short, the marketing planning department is concerned with the mechanics and coordination of marketing planning; it is not a policy-making unit.

Marketing research is a key function in a market-oriented firm. It is the basic tool for obtaining the information about demand essential to the planning and execution of marketing strategy. Without the information it provides, goals cannot be set and choices among different strategies cannot be made. To obtain, process, and disseminate this information is the assignment of the director of marketing research. He is also usually charged with the task of measuring market performance, providing the feedback of information essential to modification and restructuring of marketing strategy. The information-gathering role of the marketing research department is important to all organizational units within marketing, and all of them can be expected to utilize its services. The director of marketing research must work closely with the directors of marketing planning and product development. The product managers need marketing research information for decision making. The sales and distribution manager requires data on market potential in order to assign salesmen, set quotas, and allocate stock. It is not surprising that marketing research departments have been growing faster than any other unit in the marketing organization.

Responsibility for personnel development on a companywide basis is likely to be centered outside the marketing department. However, there is usually a personnel development department within marketing as well. Its role is the initial and continuing development of all marketing personnel. In a changing environment, nothing is more crucial to a company's long-run success. One of the implications of the marketing concept is the need for broad-gauged marketing personnel. Narrowly trained personnel greatly complicate the task of developing and executing integrated marketing programs.

Chapters 6 and 7 describe the product development function and the important role of marketing with regard thereto. Even if a company has a "new products" division organized separately from marketing, the marketing department is likely to require a director of product development. His role is concerned with the marketing aspects of product development and liaison with the nonmarketing departments also involved in product development. In a consumer packaged-goods company, particularly a food company, product development is often more a marketing task than a technological one. In such a case, the basic function of the product development department is to translate consumer wants into a product that adequately serves those wants. Then, its role becomes one of assuring that the product keeps pace with changes in the market.

Products manager. Although a few companies have employed the product manager concept for many years, there has been a great surge in its popularity since the advent of the marketing concept. The use of product managers is an attempt to cope with the complexities of modern marketing through the use of decentralization.

The product management concept is simple. A product manager is assigned to each product or group of products. It is his task to plan for the marketing of that product and to see that his plans are implemented. In so doing he works closely with other organization units. He draws heavily on the staff services available in the marketing services department and works with and through the sales and distribution department in implementing his plans. The products manager who oversees the work of product managers for specific products integrates and coordinates their activities.

The product management concept is too new for uniformity in its application to have been achieved. There seem to be three basic types of product management organization.

1. Product managers with primarily advertising and sales promotion orientation. This type predominates among consumer companies, such as Procter & Gamble, where advertising is a large and critical part of the marketing program. Product managers work directly with advertising agencies. There is probably no separate advertising department in the firm.

2. Product managers with primarily customer service and customer relations responsibilities. This type is most common among firms selling to the industrial market.

3. The most comprehensive (and most rare) kind of product manager can probably be more correctly called a general manager. He is found in large companies in charge of a product division. He is

responsible for all manufacturing as well as marketing, with supervision from above.[4]

The product managers in Figure 1–8 are the first of these types. It is for this reason that advertising does not appear as a separate function under marketing services. This is not to imply that the job of these product managers is limited to advertising and promotional strategy, but only that this is the major part of what they do. They are concerned with marketing planning for their products in the broadest sense. It is just the nature of things that marketing strategy for consumer packaged goods involves heavy emphasis on advertising and promotion.

The status of product management in marketing organizations is ambiguous. *Printers' Ink* makes the following comment about the product manager:

How does he operate? Some of the confusions about the PM system can be laid to the lack of sufficient experience with it. For example, 60 percent of the consumer companies choose to designate their PMs as line executives, when in fact some of them exercise little line control and actually perform planning and advisory duties usually designated as staff. Probably the most realistic approach to the question of line or staff designation is offered by those two out of ten consumer companies that reported they make no distinction—for they most clearly suggest the fluidity of the situation.[5]

If the status of product managers is unclear, the objective sought by companies who use this organizational concept is not. They hope by this means to assure integrated and coordinated marketing planning and strategy for each product and for the company's entire product line. Although the concept originated among consumer packaged-goods companies, it has now spread to companies of all types.

Marketing planning committee. The hypothetical marketing structure of Figure 1–8, as discussed to this point, reflects a heavy emphasis on the achievement of integrated and coordinated marketing effort. In spite of this emphasis, there is a strong likelihood that this goal will have been less than perfectly achieved. To aid in its accomplishment, the establishment of a marketing planning committee is suggested. The purpose of the committee is twofold: (1) to aid the marketing vice president in the formulation of broad marketing policy and strategy, and (2) to improve coordination among the several organization units which make up the marketing department. It is a way of achieving a two-way flow of information, both up and down the organizational ladder, on a face-to-face basis. Each executive is kept aware of what others are doing and thinking, and why.

---

[4] "Why Modern Marketing Needs the Product Manager," *Printers' Ink*, Vol. 273 (October 14, 1960), pp. 25–30.

[5] Ibid., p. 30.

The makeup of the marketing planning committee will vary greatly from firm to firm. Almost invariably, however, it will include the executives who report directly to the vice president and are in charge of major marketing functions. The director of marketing planning should be included because of his detailed knowledge of the marketing plan and his need fully to understand company goals and overall strategy. Others can be brought in when their knowledge is relevant to the topic under consideration.

Company planning committee. The purpose of the company planning committee is to coordinate companywide efforts to achieve the company's goals. The marketing concept specifies customer orientation of the entire business, not just of the marketing department. This is one approach to stimulation of coordinated effort toward this end.

Review and modification

No amount of planning is likely to produce the perfect marketing program, nor is any organization likely to implement it faultlessly. Perhaps this is particularly true of marketing programs because of the rapidly changing environment in which they operate. There is need for continuous review and modification. It is the rare marketing program that achieves its full measure of success from the beginning. Rather, most successful marketing programs become such through evolution over time. Therefore, a marketing program must have built into it procedures for review of performance.

What should be reviewed? The nature of marketing in such that anything short of an all-encompassing review is likely to be unsatisfactory. The success or failure of a marketing program depends in large part on the interaction of activities and people. Hence a review of any one part of that program is likely to be inconclusive even though it might be helpful in a limited way. A full-scale review must reconsider goals, strategy, and tactics as well as the organization structure.

Review of goals

Perhaps the best place to start a review of company and marketing goals is with a determination of whether or not they were achieved. Failure to achieve stated goals may be the result of one or more of the following: (1) the goals were unrealistic, (2) the wrong strategy was employed, (3) the right strategy was employed, but not successfully implemented. Marketing goals are usually stated in terms of sales volume, market share, or profit contribution. It is possible that specific goal choices did not properly anticipate demand conditions, competitive activity, actions of government, changes in production capacity, and so on. Should this be the case, goals must be revised before marketing strategy performance or organizational effectiveness can be determined.

Unfortunately, if goals are achieved or exceeded, the correctness of the stated goals is not proven. Goals can be set too low as well as too high. The stated goals, even though achieved, may not be the ones most important to a company's long-run success. Many corporation executives have recently come to the conclusion that they have placed too much emphasis on the profit goal and have not been sufficiently concerned with their total contribution to society. This has led them into programs to recruit and train the underprivileged, help secondary schools upgrade vocational education, and undertake other public-spirited activities even at the expense of immediate profits. It is not clear, however, that such moves are necessarily inconsistent with maximization of long-term profit.

Review of strategy and tactics

A review of marketing strategy and tactics can be done only on the basis of originally stated or revised goals. But here again attainment of goals doesn't prove correctness of the strategy. For example, a high-cost strategy may have been employed when one of lower cost would have been equally successful. In this case attainment of goals stated in terms of sales volume or market share is an insufficient measure of strategy performance.

The measurement of specific elements of marketing strategy is a difficult one for two reasons. It is difficult because integration of marketing activities in order to achieve a synergistic effect makes it hard to measure the effect of any one activity by itself. The end result achieved is always a function of total marketing strategy. It is also difficult because of the inadequacy of measurement tools. For example, the effectiveness of advertising is very hard to gauge. We measure exposure to advertising, recall, and so on, but not net contribution to sales success. Quotas used in the measurement of salesmen's performance are far from perfect, often being based on inadequate data. Hence, a lot of judgment must be used in evaluation of marketing strategy and tactics.

Review of marketing organization

The same limitations on evaluation, in terms of goal achievement mentioned in connection with marketing strategy, apply to reviewing the effectiveness of the marketing organization. Another complication exists in the fact that goals stated in the marketing plan are too broad for use in evaluation of specific organization units. The sales manager (or products manager, etc.) is not by himself responsible for achieving a specific share of market. This is the function of the entire marketing department. Therefore, the sales manager must be judged against some sort of subgoal. These subgoals might be such things as number of new accounts gained, increase in average order size, sales against quotas which take into account other marketing effort, and so on. A major problem exists in setting subgoals which are fully consistent with, and whose achievement leads to, accomplishment of the more general goals.

The marketing audit

Auditing of accounting and financial operations is traditional in the business world. Some marketing experts are now suggesting that a similar formal, periodic review and evaluation be made of marketing operations.[6] Probably this is a good idea, but many questions remain about appropriate procedures, measurement tools, scope of the investigation, and so on. In essence, this would merely be a more formal review and evaluation than the one discussed above. Such an audit would be a far more difficult task than are audits of accounting and financial operations. Quantitative measures in marketing are both less developed and harder to apply. Judgment would be an extremely important ingredient.

Oxenfeldt describes the marketing audit as follows:

A total evaluation program for the marketing effort can be termed a marketing audit. The term is employed here to denote a systematic, critical, and unbiased review and appraisal of the basic objectives and policies of the marketing function, and of the organization, methods, procedures and personnel employed to implement those policies and to achieve those objectives. Clearly, not every evaluation of marketing personnel, organization, or methods is a marketing audit; at best, most such evaluations can be regarded as parts of an audit. The total audit includes six separate aspects of marketing activities that should be appraised: (1) objectives, (2) policies, (3) organization, (4) methods, (5) procedures, and (6) personnel.[7]

Whether it is called a "review" or a "marketing audit" is not important. What is important is recognition that integrated marketing programs evolve into success stories out of such careful attention.

Conclusion

Successful marketing depends on more than effective product policy, distribution policy, advertising policy, personal selling policy, and pricing

---

[6] See A. Shuchman, "The Marketing Audit: Its Nature, Purpose, and Problems," American Management Association Report, No. 32 (1959); R. Ferber, and P. J. Verdoorn, *Research Methods in Economics and Business* (New York: Macmillan Co., 1962), chap. 2.

[7] Alfred R. Oxenfeldt, *Executive Action in Marketing* (Belmont, Calif.: Wadsworth Publishing Company, Inc., 1966), p. 746.

policy. It requires that these controllable variables be so integrated that the overall result is more than the sum of its individual parts. This, in turn, is made possible by (1) marketing planning that achieves a synergistic effect and (2) effective implementation of the marketing plan through a vital and viable marketing organization. In the last analysis, success of a free enterprise economy depends on its ability to out-perform other economic systems. High performance of a free enterprise economy depends, to no small degree, on efficient marketing.

Questions

1. In what ways is marketing different from selling?
2. The marketing concept implies orientation of the business firm's total operation to the needs, wants, and desires of the consumer. What are the implications of this concept for consumer welfare?
3. By what means can marketing become more responsive to societal, as distinct from individual, needs?
4. The planning and execution of marketing strategy has·been described as a "synergistic" process. What does this mean?
5. What is the relationship between marketing planning and corporate planning?
6. Figure 1–3 outlines the marketing planning process as it exists in the General Electric Company. Which part of this outline would also be encompassed in General Electric's sales plan? What is the essential difference between a sales plan and a marketing plan?
7. Discuss the role of marketing research in the marketing planning process.
8. Why must a situation analysis precede the planning of marketing strategy?
9. Discuss the ways in which implementation of the marketing concept affects the problem of developing a marketing organization.
10. The primary breakdown of tasks in planning a marketing organization is sometimes on a product basis (for example, General Motors) and sometimes on a functional basis (for example, Figure 1–8). What determines which type of organization structure is best?
11. The brand management type of organization is rapidly growing in popularity. How do you explain this trend?
12. If a marketing plan fails to achieve its objectives, it should, of course, be reviewed to determine what went wrong. What sequence of steps do you recommend for such a review?
13. Write a job description for the vice president, marketing, in a large consumer packaged-goods company. Reference to Figure 1–8 may be helpful.

2

Development of
marketing strategy

IN CHAPTER 1 the overall approach to marketing planning was discussed. The approach was general and each element in a marketing plan was discussed only briefly. The heart of marketing planning is the formulation of a marketing strategy. Marketing strategy is the "action plan" that the marketing manager intends to follow. It is based on the situation analysis and the company's objectives. It is the way in which these objectives are to be achieved.

Marketing strategy often must be different for various segments of the market. We shall first consider the planning of a marketing strategy for a total market which is assumed to be relatively homogeneous. Then we shall consider the topic of market segmentation.

Marketing strategy

In the planning of marketing strategy, the marketing manager must make decisions about how he will employ the marketing tools he has at his disposal to achieve a predetermined goal. The variables the marketing manager works with in planning strategy are of two types: controllable and uncontrollable. He can decide, for example, whether he will or will not use advertising, how much, and what kind. He must make similar decisions about the product line, distribution, pricing, sales promotion, and the use of personal selling. He can weave these together into an overall marketing program in an infinite number of ways.

In planning his strategy, the marketing manager faces certain constraints which are inherent in the environment within which his strategy must be employed. For example, he is faced with certain characteristics of demand as they exist in the marketplace. His strategy must be appropriate to these demand characteristics or it cannot be successful. Competition is a fact of life that has a heavy influence on what he can and cannot do. Many legal considerations constrain his efforts. He must adapt his strategy to the needs and operations of the distributors and dealers through which his product will be sold. Production capabilities of his company may either limit his sales opportunities or suggest the desirability of changing his strategy to achieve greater volume.

FIGURE 2–1
Controllable and uncontrollable variables in marketing

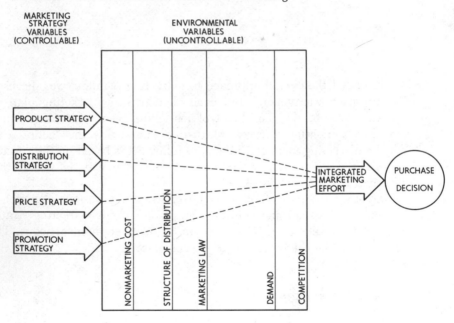

In essence, marketing strategy consists of manipulating those variables the marketing manager can control and adapting optimally to those variables he cannot control, to most effectively attain his objective. Those variables he can control are, for his purposes, the relevant marketing strategy variables. The uncontrollable are environmental variables. They, in a sense, limit the strategy choices available to him in trying to achieve a favorable purchase decision by the consumer. Figure 2–1 attempts to portray this approach to achievement of an integrated marketing effort.

Environmental (uncontrollable) variables

There are many uncontrollable variables that condition marketing strategy. Only the most basic, and each rather broadly defined, are discussed here.

Demand. A demand for goods and services is not created, in a basic sense, by marketing activities employed by sellers. Demand is a resultant of consumer needs and goals. It is colored by established consumer buying patterns. It is constrained by such basic forces as income, norms of acceptable behavior, and time pressures under which consumers operate. Demand may be latent and its existence unknown. Marketing strategy can be employed to convert it into effective demand by offering a product or service in a manner consistent with underlying demand forces.

Many social critics assign great powers to marketing, particularly to advertising, to influence consumer behavior.[1] It is claimed that sellers are able, through modern marketing methods, to induce consumers to buy products they neither need nor want. This would seem to be something of an exaggeration. The Ford Motor Company had little success in building demand for the Edsel and Du Pont could never make Corfam profitable. Campaigns to get people to stop smoking have not had the hoped-for effect on the demand for cigarettes. The marketing of goods and services would be a far easier task if a significant control over demand were possible.

Marketing actions can modify and channel demand. However, the cost inputs required to produce basic changes in demand can be very high. It is usually more efficient, in planning marketing strategy, to adapt to demand as one finds it. If a firm's objective is to maximize profits, demand can best be considered an essentially uncontrollable variable.

Competition. The present state of competition, the expected future state of competition, and anticipated retaliatory moves of competitors necessarily affect the planning of marketing strategy. A competitor may so dominate a market that gaining a satisfactory market share is impossible, or is possible only at too high a cost. There may be so many competitors that market-share opportunities are limited. If a competitor is employing a particular marketing strategy, this may suggest that it is wise to vary one's own strategy to avoid direct confrontation in the market.

The formulation of marketing strategy requires prediction of retaliatory moves of competitors. If our firm does this, how will competitors respond? How long a time period before this response becomes effective?

---

[1] See Vance Packard, *The Hidden Persuaders* (New York: David McKay Co., Inc., 1957), and John Kenneth Galbraith, *The New Industrial State* (Boston: Houghton Mifflin Co., 1967).

How can we alter our strategy to minimize our competitors' ability to respond? Expected profitability to the Ford Motor Company of varying its product offering by introducing the Mustang would very likely have been less if General Motors could have been expected to introduce a comparable car within six months instead of two years. In some instances, the mere threat of retaliation is sufficient to cause a particular marketing strategy not to be employed. The uncertainty surrounding competitors' possible responses greatly complicates strategy planning. In short, marketing strategy planning must take into account the nature and extent of competition, both present and future, in determining the optimal course of action to be followed.

The distribution structure. Most sellers must reach the market with their products through the existing distribution structure. The distribution structure in the United States is described in Chapter 8. There are certain types and numbers of agent middlemen, wholesalers, and retailers, and they interrelate in certain ways. To distribute some products—automobiles, for example—a firm may set up its own dealership network; but this is a very costly, and often totally inappropriate, move for other sellers. Even automobile companies sell replacement parts through independent automotive wholesalers and repair shops.

Marketing strategy plans must take into account such matters as: (1) the existence or nonexistence of appropriate distribution channels; (2) a firm's ability to gain access to those channels; (3) ability of the demand for the product to support the cost of distribution through the chosen channels; (4) the intra- and interchannel competition that the product will face; (5) trends in institutions in the channels that may affect the marketing of the product; and (6) requirements placed by the channel on such other marketing functions as advertising, personal selling, and sales promotion.

The problem of gaining acceptance of a product by channel institutions is a very real one. Most such institutions are swamped with offers of new products by manufacturers. Profitable operation for the channel institution depends on choosing from this total offering those products which will contribute most to profits within the confines of limited capacity of the channel. Products whose demand is uncertain or limited are avoided. Products that will merely divert demand from existing products and not increase total sales are likewise avoided unless a demand for choice among consumers requires that they be carried.

Marketing law. Legal constraints have been imposed upon sellers in order to protect the public interest. For example, a seller may decide that he can best maximize profit by selling to each of several segments of the market at the maximum price that market segment is willing to pay. This enables him to capture more revenue from those who are willing to pay an above "average" price and to earn still additional profit from those willing to pay a minimum price that is "below average" so long as that price covers incremental costs. However, the Robinson-Patman Act (discussed in Chapter 15) prohibits discrimination in price among buyers whenever such discrimination may serve substantially to lessen competition. This constraint upon the seller's freedom of action forces him to find alternative means of maximizing profits. One possibility is to offer different models of his product, each with features intended to appeal to a different market segment, and to follow a different pricing policy with each model.

A seller may wish to improve the quality of the selling effort devoted to his product by distributors and dealers. He may decide to accomplish this objective by getting these middlemen to agree not to carry competing products, but to devote all their selling efforts to his products. This constitutes what is known as an "exclusive dealing" contract. Section 3 of the Clayton Antitrust Act (discussed in Chapter 9) prohibits such contracts if they might tend substantially to lesson competition. The so-called Truth-in-Packaging bill (discussed in Chapter 7) placed certain constraints upon package design and information included on the package. The Food, Drug, and Cosmetic Act (also discussed in Chapter 7) places many restraints upon marketing practices for foods, drugs, and cosmetics. Recent automotive safety legislation has forced automobile manufacturers to modify automobile design and to add additional safety features.

Nonmarketing cost. In planning marketing strategy, such nonmarketing costs as production and overhead costs place limits on the strategy that can be contemplated. For example, if per unit production costs for a product are $100, to which overhead and marketing costs must be added, pricing strategy must involve a per unit price sufficiently above $100 to cover these several types of cost. An increase in production or overhead costs for a product through time may force a change in marketing strategy, perhaps in the direction of reduced emphasis on price and more emphasis on other variables in the marketing mix.

Marketing strategy (controllable) variables

In formulating his marketing strategy, the seller manipulates the variables over which he does have control so as to arrive at the optimum strategic approach to his market goal. These controllable variables we have broadly classified as: (1) the product, (2) distribution, (3) price, and (4) promotion. Before attempting to compose these variables into a general marketing strategy for several different types of products, a brief word of explanation about each is in order.

Product. If one accepts the narrow and unrealistic view of marketing mentioned early in Chapter 1, namely, that marketing consists only of those activities involved in getting goods and services from the producer to the consumer, the product involved would have to be considered an uncontrollable variable in the planning of marketing strategy. In reality, the product is one of the major controllable variables the marketing manager has to work with and, in many cases, his most effective. The product can be modified in many ways better to achieve a marketing goal. It can be changed in quality, size, shape, color, variety, and in other ways.

A company is in business to serve the needs of consumers; it is not in business to sell any specific product. If consumer needs can be better served by dropping a product from the group offered by a particular firm, it can be dropped. If a new product would contribute favorably to the firm's achievement of its objective, it can be added.

Distribution. The planner of marketing strategy has many choices to make with respect to distribution policy. He must choose the geographical area in which he will market his product, and those areas he will not enter. He must decide the types of retail outlets in which he wants his product carried and the number of such outlets needed in each portion of the market. He must determine whether it is better to sell directly to retail outlets or to work through wholesalers. If he elects to sell through wholesalers, he must decide what type of wholesalers and how many. How shall he work with the institutions through which he has chosen to sell to assure their effectiveness? How much control over the efforts of middlemen should he try to exercise? These and many other decisions must be made with regard to the distribution variable.

Price. The price at which a product is offered is controllable within limits. A seller may elect to compete on a price basis and set his price low in relation to the prices of competitors. Conversely, he may strive for a high-quality image and foster this image with a high-price policy. Discounts may be utilized to vary price with quantities purchased or to achieve different prices for different classes of trade.

A seller's control over price is by no means absolute. The range of price options available in planning marketing strategy is constrained by cost considerations. Demand factors and competition determine what the market will accept. Further constraints are to be found in marketing law and trade custom.

Promotion. Marketing managers may elect to utilize promotional tools in various amounts and in various combinations. They may choose to use advertising as a major method of communication with consumers, or they may use it only as a supplement to other forms of communication. They may choose from among various types of media (for example, television, radio, newspapers, and magazines), and they have many specific choices available within each of these media categories. The opportunities for choice extend to appeals to use in the advertising, amount and type of copy, layout and artwork, and so on.

As with advertising, the marketing manager may elect to utilize more or less personal selling, to direct it at different market targets, to use it in various ways, to employ various appeals. In some cases he has an open choice between the use of advertising and personal selling in his planning of strategy; in other cases circumstances force him in the direction of the use of one or the other.

Sales promotion is another variable in promotional strategy which may take a great variety of forms and be used in varying amounts. It consists of such things as window and interior displays, consumer contests, free samples, cents-off offers, and many other activities. For some products, sales promotion is heavily relied upon in marketing strategy; for others, it is a minor or nonexistent element.

Comparative marketing strategies

Formulation of marketing strategies is more an art than a science, and creativity is an important ingredient in success. Still, because marketing strategy is molded in large measure by uncontrollable forces in the environment surrounding the marketing of a product, certain strategy patterns tend to be associated with certain types of products. Marketing strategies generally employed with some products, say, consumer durables, are substantially different from those generally used for other products such as, for example, food products. Within a given product class there are often differences in the strategies followed by different companies, but it is still possible to talk of a particular overall marketing strategy as being generally typical of a certain type of product. For example, a strategy of intensive distribution (selling through as many retail outlets as posssible) is typical of food products, whereas consumer durables usually are sold through a smaller number of selected retail outlets.

The remaining chapters of this book are concerned with the many concepts and problems involved in the planning of marketing strategy. At this point we are in a position to deal only with broad profiles of marketing strategy. A comparison, however, of the general marketing strategies appropriate to different kinds of products will provide an overview of what is to follow and will serve as a framework on which to hang the discussion of individual strategy variables in marketing.

Chosen for comparison of typical marketing strategies are four different products: automobiles, automotive parts, life insurance, and bread. One of these is a high-priced consumer durable, one is a replacement component, one is an intangible product, and one is a basic staple.

Figure 2–2 is a very simple decision matrix for planning a marketing strategy profile for each of these products. Our objective, a very limited one, is to indicate the relative importance of each of the marketing strategy variables in the overall marketing plan. Another way of stating it is: How can we best allocate our resources of time, effort, and money among these five variables for each product in order to achieve the best possible marketing strategy for that product? Our purpose in doing this is not to derive the only feasible strategies, or necessarily even the best ones, but rather to highlight the differences in marketing strategies for different products. In the process of doing this, we shall also focus on the factors which cause these differences.

FIGURE 2–2
Marketing strategy planning matrix

Marketing strategy variables	Automobiles	Automotive parts	Life insurance	Bread
Product				
Distribution				
Price				
Promotion				
Advertising				
Personal selling				
Sales promotion				

Using a rating scale of 0 to 5, let us assign "importance values" to each variable. The most important variable for each product will automatically be given a rating of 5, and then the others can be rated in relation thereto. For each product a marketing strategy profile will be suggested, and then the rationale for the suggested profile will be offered.

Strategy profile: Automobiles

This profile suggests that the most important strategy variable for automobiles is the product. To be more accurate, it is the image of the product among consumers that is the key to success, not the physical attributes of the product itself. The automobile is an important and a high-cost purchase. The typical consumer will spend considerable time comparing various makes and models. Unless the product fully meets his needs as he sees them, he probably will make an alternative choice. Another way of putting it is: If the product is unsatisfactory to the consumer, manipulation of the other variables cannot be expected to overcome this defect. When Ford Motor Company was unable to overcome the bad product image of the Edsel, they dropped this product from their product line. Chrysler Corporation did the same for the

DeSoto. Pontiac Motors Division, on the other hand, drastically restyled its product during the 1950s and substantially increased its market share. The success of the Mustang in 1964 was undoubtedly due primarily to the strong appeal of its unique design.

The 2 rating for distribution is subject to challenge. The rating reflects what would seem to be a reasonable answer to this question: If a company already has distribution of its products in all areas (the near normal state for automobiles), can it expect substantially to increase its market share by adding more dealers? Because of the importance of the purchase of an automobile, consumers will normally go to great effort to view those they consider to have favorable product images. No one buys a Ford rather than a Chevrolet because the Ford dealer is several blocks closer. If it is a choice between spending a limited sum of money either on improving the product or on increasing the number of dealers by a small percentage, usually the product improvement would promise the greatest return. Consumer concern for postpurchase service may be the best grounds on which to challenge this view. Easy access to a dealer is more important for service than it is for initial purchase.

FIGURE 2–3
Marketing strategy profile: Automobiles

Controllable variables	*Importance value*
Product......................	5
Distribution..................	2
Price........................	2
Promotion	
Advertising................	3
Personal selling............	1
Sales promotion.............	2

The 2 rating for price is based on what is thought to be a realistic situation, namely, that it is a small price difference only, say, $25, that can usually be considered in planning marketing strategy. Ford could surely outsell Chevrolet if it could sell its cars at 50 percent of the Chevrolet price, but cost considerations prohibit this. The decision is more likely to be of the sort suggested by this question: Should we limit product features or reduce quality and drop our price by $25? A well-conceived product improvement would normally be expected to have a greater effect on sales than would a small price reduction. As a matter of fact, keeping prices down by limiting product features is what Henry Ford did in the days of the Model T. This enabled Chevrolet to emphasize product refinements, at higher prices, and become the leading seller of automobiles.

Advertising is rated at 3 because of its importance in establishing a desirable product image. It is doubtful that even extensive and highly skilled advertising could compensate for an unsatisfactory product. However, given an attractive product, advertising can do much to mold the consumer's image of that product. The status value of the Cadillac owes much to skillful advertising.

The low rating of 1 for personal selling will be hard for many to accept. Personal selling comes into play at the retail level for automobiles, and the low quality of this selling effort has long been of concern to both automobile buyers and manufacturers. One might take the view that if this selling effort has been so bad, and car sales have continued to rise dramatically over the years, it cannot be a very important factor. Surely it is unlikely to offset the depressing effect on sales of a poor product. On the other hand, we have little real evidence of what personal selling can do, because it has so rarely been used effectively in the sale of automobiles.

Sales promotion is given a rating of 2. Such things as effective product display, contests for both dealer salesmen and consumers, banners, gift offers to consumers to build showroom traffic, etc. are effective sales strategy elements for automobiles. Even entering cars in racing events could probably be considered as sales promotion.

Strategy profile: Automotive parts

For automotive parts, distribution is the most important variable. The purchase of such parts by the ultimate consumer is tied to his purchase of a repair service. He really has no demand for automotive parts as such. His demand is for a properly functioning vehicle, and he purchases a repair service to achieve this goal. In seeking out a repair service, he is governed by such things as past experience with the repair outlet, the outlet's reputation for quality service, convenience of location, etc. With these things governing his choice, he almost implicitly agrees to accept whatever brand of replacement parts the repair outlet chooses to install. If the repair outlet carries Brand A parts in stock, he accepts Brand A. If the outlet carries Brand B, that is the brand he receives and accepts.

FIGURE 2–4
Marketing strategy profile: Automotive parts

Controllable variables	Importance value
Product	1
Distribution	5
Price	1
Promotion	
Advertising	1
Personal selling	3
Sales promotion	1

The moral to be drawn from this pattern of buyer behavior for automotive parts is this: Sales can best be maximized by assuring that a manufacturer's brand of parts is stocked by as many repair outlets as possible. Where his brand is not stocked, there is no chance of a sale. Where it is stocked, his probability of a sale is determined by the number of substitute brands also carried. However, because of usually insignificant brand preference for automotive parts among car owners, the repair outlet has little incentive to stock multiple brands.[2]

The low rating of 1 on the product variable reflects the fact that there is little opportunity for product differentiation. The design of the part is largely determined by its function, and aesthetics are usually unimportant because the part is hidden from view. Quality, of course, must be adequate to gain and maintain acceptance in the repair trade.

Price competition is not strong for automotive parts except within the do-it-yourself market served by such outlets as Sears Roebuck, Montgomery Ward, and Western Auto. The product is usually a small part of the total repair cost; hence, price differences to the ultimate consumer are small even if differences in parts prices are large percentagewise. Because a high margin to the repair outlet, even if it means a higher list price for the part, is important in inducing the outlet to stock a particular brand, there is little incentive for manufacturers to compete on a price basis.

There is some, but not heavy, advertising of most replacement parts to the ultimate consumer. Advertising cannot develop a brand preference of significance for such a product or change the consumer's willingness to accept what the repair outlet offers. Therefore, it is much better to utilize funds to expand distribution rather than to advertise. What advertising to the consumer is done is usually done to help achieve distribution. The repair outlet would rather carry a known than an unknown brand, other things being equal.

Personal selling is rated as high as 3 for one reason only: It is an important tool in gaining and holding distribution. The various services provided by personal selling are important to the repair outlet in choosing which brands to stock.

Sales promotion activities are normally minimal in the marketing of automotive parts, except on TBA type items. Therefore, they receive only a 1 rating here. They are quite heavily relied on, of course, in the marketing of repair services which would include the installation of parts.

Strategy profile: Life insurance

Life insurance is an "intangible" product—one cannot see, feel, or taste it. The need for it, although real, is elusive. It is not likely to be within the awareness span of the average consumer. Rather, this need must be pointed out, explained, and demonstrated. Because this can be done most effectively by personal selling, a value of 5 is assigned to this variable.

---

[2] Because of greater brand preference among so-called TBA items (tires, batteries, accessories), these comments do not apply to this group of products.

Product variation is possible for intangible products. In the case of life insurance, variations are possible in coverage, terms, service, and so on. However, because the product is intangible, it is somewhat difficult to communicate these differences to consumers. Here again there is dependence on personal selling. In fact, the differences in the quality of personal selling are likely to be far more important than the differences in the product offered.

Distribution (in the case of life insurance, the number of agents) is very important to success in the marketing of life insurance. Dealing with the right agent is more important to most people than having the name of a particular insurance company on the policy. Although unknown companies might be rejected, the typical consumer has no strong preference among larger, better known companies. Rather, if he has confidence in the agent he will accept the insurance company the agent represents. Hence, it becomes very important in planning marketing strategy for life insurance to devise means to secure an adequate number of qualified agents.

FIGURE 2–5
Marketing strategy profile: Life insurance

Controllable variables	Importance value
Product	2
Distribution	4
Price	2
Promotion	
Advertising	3
Personal selling	5
Sales promotion	1

For most life insurance companies, price is not heavily emphasized in marketing strategy. Competition tends to be more on a nonprice basis. It is difficult for the consumer to compare prices because of the intangible nature of life insurance. Lower priced life insurance, such as that sometimes sold by mail, has not been overly successful.

Advertising of life insurance is not an effective substitute for personal selling but can be an important supplement to it. Advertising conditions consumers to the approach of the agent and makes them more willing to accept his statements. It is likely that personal selling would be less effective if advertising did not pave the way for it. Also, advertising can be very helpful in lining up agents, thus gaining better distribution.

Sales promotion activities are virtually nonexistent in the sale of life insurance because they serve no useful purpose. In the sale of other types of insurance—automobile insurance, for example—bumper stickers and the like are employed.

Strategy profile: Bread

Bread is a product in the basic staple category. It is purchased frequently, without much planning or forethought, and usually in connection with the purchase of other food items. If we focus on plain white bread and disregard specialty breads, or the quality bread offered by small bakeries, there is only limited brand preference. The typical consumer will choose from the brands offered in the outlet she has entered for food shopping. She will not make a special effort to go to another outlet to acquire a particular brand. Consequently, breadth of distribution is essential to achieving maximum sales of this product.

Plain white bread is a relatively homogeneous type of product. There is little opportunity for product differentiation. Probably the most desired product characteristic is freshness, and this is likely to vary among brands over time. Product appeal can be enhanced more effectively by rapid stockturn than by varying the physical attributes of the product.

Because ordinary white bread is a largely homogeneous product class, even small price differences can have a drastic effect on demand. Therefore, price competition is severe among brands carried within a particular retail outlet. Although distribution is the most important variable in overall bread marketing, price becomes the dominant variable once adequate distribution is gained. The average housewife is well aware that small price differences "add up" on basic staples.

FIGURE 2–6
Marketing strategy profile: Bread

Controllable variables	Importance value
Product	1
Distribution	5
Price	4
Promotion	
Advertising	2
Personal selling	1
Sales promotion	1

For the adult bread market, advertising is of limited value. It ranks far below distribution in importance. For the market influenced by children, advertising can be, and has been, effectively used to mold a differentiated product image. Perhaps childrens' requests for a particular brand of bread result in a fairly long-run family habit of buying a particular brand. It surely will not do so, however, if distribution is inadequate or price is out of line.

Personal selling, in the case of bread, serves mainly two major objectives—first, to gain distribution; second, to gain more or preferred shelf space. As these two purposes are already reflected in the high rating for the distribution variable, personal selling is rated a lowly 1 in our strategy profile.

There is little sales promotion used in the marketing of plain white bread. There is some use of special display stands, window and in-store banners, etc., but sales promotion ranks far below distribution and price in importance.

Variation in strategy profiles

The objective in discussing the broad marketing strategy for each of these four products *has not been to establish agreement* as to the best marketing strategies to utilize. The planning of marketing strategy is too much of an art for such agreement to be expected or achieved. Rather, the objective has been to point out how marketing strategies vary for different types of products and to indicate the sorts of things that produce these variations. The differences in "importance values" we have assigned can be seen in Figure 2–7. The variables assigned

Figure 2–7
Variations in marketing strategy profiles

Marketing strategy variables	Importance values			
	Autos	Auto parts	Life insurance	Bread
Product...................	[5]	1	2	1
Distribution..............	2	[5]	[4]	[5]
Price.....................	2	1	2	[4]
Promotion				
Advertising.............	3	1	3	2
Personal selling.........	1	3	[5]	1
Sales promotion.........	2	1	1	1

high values (either a 4 or a 5) are marked so as to call attention to the differences which have been highlighted in the discussion above.

Variations in the constructed profiles are depicted in yet another way in Figure 2–8. Although these profiles are not necessarily those others might devise, it is unlikely the marked differences among them would be much diminished if any or all of them were redesigned. It is not likely that bread will ever be marketed in a manner similar to automobiles, nor can the marketing plan developed for automotive parts be used as a guide to the marketing of life insurance.

Basic cause of variation

All five of the environmental (uncontrollable) variables influence the planning of marketing strategy. In a specific situation, any one of them can have the dominant influence on a firm's marketing program. As a generalization, however, it is correct to say that the demand variable is the most basic factor influencing what is done in marketing. The

FIGURE 2–8
Variations in marketing strategy profiles

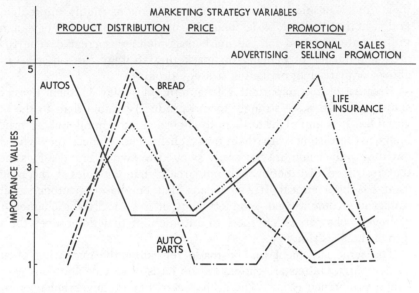

other environmental variables (competition, the distribution structure, marketing law, and nonmarketing cost) have somewhat less across-the-board significance. In fact, they themselves are much influenced by the demand variable.

Demand has several other characteristics that make it a special case among the environmental variables. The present state of demand cannot be known as can the state of other variables. The present distribution structure exists and can be observed. Marketing law, although often ambiguous, is known in general outline. Nonmarketing costs are often observable and can be calculated. The present state of competition is relatively well known, although future competitive moves may be highly uncertain. On the other hand, we still know very little about underlying demand factors that influence purchase. In spite of much valuable research related to buyer behavior in recent years, the consumer is still an enigma, a "black box" into which we cannot see.

The demand factor is even less predictable than the other variables, due largely to our limited knowledge of it. The competition factor may be almost as hard to predict. The other environmental variables, however, tend to change more slowly and therefore at least the near future can be more clearly seen. Distribution structures evolve slowly, and new legislation affecting marketing is often years in the making. In the long run, nonmarketing costs are closely tied to labor costs. Although not easy to predict, a certain pattern of advance has been established over time. Consumer behavior, however, remains highly unpredictable, and if it is the most basic influence upon marketing strategy, a most unfortunate situation for the marketing planner is created. The fundamental influence of demand on marketing strategy can be seen in the above comparison of marketing strategy profiles.

Because of the important role automobiles play in their lives, consumers respond more strongly to the product variable than to the other variables. It is important to them to choose an automobile whose product image is consistent with their own self-images. Hence, they will seek out the product and are not easily swayed to switch brands. This means that restricted distribution will not greatly hamper sales if the product itself has high appeal. It also means that emphasis on other variables cannot overcome a weak product. Thus, it is basically the characteristic of buyer behavior with respect to automobiles that determines the pattern of their distribution.

The same statement can be made regarding the marketing of automotive parts. Outlets are chosen on the basis of service and convenience. Brand preference is low. These characteristics of buyer behavior make breadth of distribution of prime importance in marketing strategy.

Because life insurance is an intangible, and because the consumer's need for it is often not clearly or fully perceived, personal selling is the dominant strategy variable. Should people perceive their life insurance needs as clearly as their automobile needs, and possess the same strong brand preferences, the appropriate strategy pattern would change substantially.

The strategy profile for plain white bread derives primarily from the fact that consumers perceive such bread as a largely homogeneous product. Hence, they will not go out of their way nor pay a price premium for a particular brand.

What is true of marketing strategies for these four products is true of marketing strategy generally. *Appropriate marketing strategy is primarily a function of buyer behavior.* It will, as a matter of fact, become increasingly evident to the student as he proceeds through this text that almost everything done in marketing is based fundamentally on facts or assumptions about buyer behavior.

Because of this singular importance of demand in the planning of marketing strategy, it is singled out in this text for first and more intensive treatment than the other environmental variables. The next three chapters focus upon it. Attention is given to the nature of the demand for goods and services and causal factors that produce changes in demand. Subsequent chapters will then incorporate this knowledge of demand into the decision-making process in planning marketing strategy.

Alternate marketing strategies

The task of developing a marketing strategy to this point has been oversimplified by assuming that the firm is following what has been termed a strategy of undifferentiated marketing.[3] This is a strategy in which the firm seeks to attract as many buyers as possible from the mass market with essentially one product and one marketing program. Although all markets are composed of prospects who differ from one another in certain respects, given this strategy the firm assumes that the market is of a relatively homogeneous nature and concentrates on what is similar among the prospects rather than upon what is different. In years past a strategy of undifferentiated marketing was the rule rather than the exception. The great marketing programs of the pre-World War II era in the cigarette, soft drink, and soap industries were illustrative of this approach.

When an increasing number of firms in an industry follow a strategy of undifferentiated or mass marketing, the result can be increasing competition, declining market shares for each firm, and a concomitant reduction in profits. In addition, those customers who are not served well by the standardized approach may seek goods and services more to their liking elsewhere. Often such specialized offerings come from smaller domestic or foreign firms who see, in the filling of specialized needs, a way of gaining market entry.

Excessive competition in the mass market has led to attempts by firms to gain a competitive advantage over their rivals by engaging in a strategy of product differentiation. In utilizing this strategy the marketer attempts to promote product differences, either real or imaginary, to the typical consumer in the group of potential buyers for his product.[4]

The success of a strategy of product differentiation is highly dependent upon some unusual aspect of the marketing strategy mix. Whether it be a unique product or package design, utilization of special channels of distribution, or the creation of a catchy promotional theme, the difference is what counts.

The past 25 years have witnessed rapid population growth both in this country and abroad. With this growth has come the increasing recognition that the market is not a homogeneous mass of prospects, but rather a set of submarkets each of which may be composed of potential customers who have certain characteristics of a demographic

---

[3] Philip Kotler, *Marketing Management: Analysis, Planning, and Control,* 2d ed., (Englewood Cliffs, N.J.: Prentice-Hall, Inc., 1972), p. 182.

[4] See Wendell R. Smith, "Product Differentiation and Market Segmentation as Alternative Marketing Strategies," *Journal of Marketing,* July 1956, pp. 3–8.

or behavioral nature in common. A marketing strategy which attempts to reach these submarkets rather than the total market is an alternative to product differentiation and has been termed a strategy of market segmentation.[5] Market segmentation is "based upon developments on the demand side of the market and represents a rational and more precise adjustment of product and marketing effort to consumer or user requirements."[6] In contrast to a strategy of product differentiation, market segmentation recognizes the diversity of demand and attempts to adapt to it by better meeting the needs of part of the market.

Requirements for segmentation

If a manufacturer elects to follow a strategy of market segmentation he must be able to divide the market into identifiable subsets each of which shares some common characteristic. Thus there is a measurability requirement attached to the segmentation strategy. The variables to be measured may be concerned with geography, demography, or some aspect of consumer behavior. Regardless of the market characteristic or characteristics upon which segmentation is to be based, without the ability to identify segments and to measure their various dimensions, little progress can be made.

Even if a subset of the market is readily identifiable and measurable it must be reachable by the manufacturer. This "reachability" includes both the promotional as well as the physical distribution aspects of the marketing strategy mix. It does little good to identify and measure a segment of the market if no channels of distribution are available to reach its occupants or if no economic way exists to communicate with them.

Third, the subset of the market must be of sufficient size, in terms of purchasing power, to offer a profit potential consonant with the extra effort required to design and implement a unique marketing strategy.

Cost-benefit tradeoff. Following a strategy of market segmentation is neither easy nor inexpensive. A great deal of expertise is required in the area of market research as well as in marketing strategy design. Economies of scale are lost as the firm tailors its marketing mix to the needs of a smaller audience group in each of several different market subsets.

On the other hand, the benefits to be derived from a segmentation strategy may be considerable. The manufacturer is closer to each of his submarkets and can react more rapidly to changing tastes or consumption trends. He can compare the effectiveness of different strategy vari-

---

[5] See R. William Kotrba, "The Strategy Selection Chart," *Journal of Marketing,* July 1966, pp. 22–25.

[6] Smith, "Product Differentiation."

able mixes and can experiment in a submarket with less risk than in the mass market. The manufacturer can design his offerings to meet the needs of his customers more closely and in so doing may capture a larger share of each of the submarkets which he is attempting to serve.

As more and more firms find that the payoff from segmentation strategy is highly favorable, the move toward seeking competitive advantage through adapting to the needs of submarkets is accelerating. At present it appears that the question facing most marketing managers is not whether or not to engage in segmentation strategy, but rather on what basis or bases should the market be divided.

If the preliminary situation analysis indicates that a segmentation strategy is desirable then two questions must be answered. These are: (1) Which bases for segmentation are most likely to provide identifiable, reachable, and substantial submarkets? and (2) What marketing strategy is most likely to gain maximum results from each target segment?

Bases for market segmentation

The number of variables which might be used for market segmentation is almost limitless. To help the marketing manager with the selection process these variables have been classified into categories such as geographic, demographic, psychographic, and buyer behavior.[7] These categories and typical breakdowns associated with each are illustrated in Figure 2–9.

As seen in the figure the demographic variables include such dimensions as age, sex, family size, income, occupation, education, family life cycle, religion, race, nationality, and social class. The geographic variables are those which pertain to region, climate, size of city, county, and whether the location of the potential customer is in an urban, suburban, or rural area.

Segmentation bases which are of a demographic or geographic nature are easy to understand and data collection and analysis are usually straightforward. For example, suppose a beer manufacturer were interested in applying a segmentation strategy. Market research indicated that the sales of his product were strongly correlated with such demographic variables as age of head of household and level of income. In addition, beer sales appeared related to the geographic variable which described the population density. Given this information, the market for this manufacturer's beer might be segmented into 36 submarkets as illustrated in Figure 2–10. Each submarket might then be evaluated

---

[7] Kotler, *Marketing Management*, p. 170.

FIGURE 2–9
Major segmentation variables and their typical breakdowns

Variables	Typical breakdowns
Geographic	
Region	Pacific; Mountain; West North Central; West South Central; East North Central; East South Central; South Atlantic; Middle Atlantic; New England
County size	A; B; C; D
City or S.M.S.A. size	Under 5,000; 5,000–19,999; 20,000–49,999; 50,000–99,999; 100,000–249,999; 250,000–499,999; 500,000–999,999; 1,000,000–3,999,999; 4,000,000 or over
Density	Urban; suburban; rural
Climate	Northern; southern
Demographic	
Age	Under 6; 6–11; 12–17; 18–34; 35–49; 50–64; 65+
Sex	Male; female
Family size	1–2; 3–4; 5+
Family life cycle	Young, single; young, married, no children; young, married, youngest child under six; young, married, youngest child six or over; older, married, with children; older, married, no children under 18; older, single; other
Income	Under $5,000; $5,000–$7,999; $8,000–$9,999; over $10,000
Occupation	Professional and technical; managers, officials and proprietors; clerical, sales; craftsmen, foremen; operatives; farmers; retired; students; housewives; unemployed
Education	Grade school or less; some high school; graduated high school; some college; graduated college
Religion	Catholic; Protestant; Jewish; other
Race	White; Negro; Oriental
Nationality	American; British; French; German; Eastern European; Scandinavian; Italian; Spanish; Latin American; Middle Eastern; Japanese; and so on
Social class	Lower-lower; upper-lower; lower-middle; middle-middle; upper-middle; lower-upper; upper-upper
Psychographic	
Compulsiveness	Compulsive; noncompulsive
Gregariousness	Extrovert; introvert
Autonomy	Dependent; independent
Conservatism	Conservative; liberal; radical
Authoritarianism	Authoritarian; democratic
Leadership	Leader; follower
Ambitiousness	High achiever; low achiever
Buyer behavior	
Usage rate	Nonuser; light user; medium user; heavy user
Readiness stage	Unaware; aware; interested; intending to try; trier; regular buyer
Benefits sought	Economy; status; dependability
End use	(Varies with the product)
Brand loyalty	None; light; strong
Marketing-factor sensitivity	Quality; price; service; advertising; sales promotion

Source: Philip Kotler, *Marketing Management: Analysis, Planning, and Control*, 2d ed., 1972, p. 170. By permission of Prentice-Hall, Inc.

in terms of market potential and strategy could be devised to reach those segments most likely to produce the most profitable sales volume.

Psychographic variables are those which describe the personality traits of potential consumers such as degree of compulsiveness, gregariousness, autonomy, and so forth. A more complete array of these variables and their typical breakdowns are illustrated in Figure 2–9. The use of these variables to isolate segments of the market is very difficult. Although it is true that certain products or certain brands have specific images, there is little evidence available to support the hypothesis that specific personality types are attracted to a given product "image." Perhaps when personality measurement techniques are devised which can isolate more

FIGURE 2–10
Segmentation of beer market by two demographic and one geographic variable

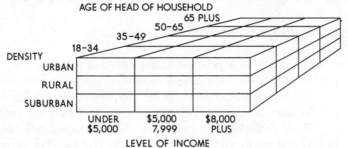

Source: Adapted from Philip Kotler, *Marketing Management: Analysis, Planning, and Control*, 2d. ed., 1972, p. 171. By permission of Prentice-Hall, Inc.

effectively specific personality types, some meaningful experimentation can take place. Until such time as test results indicate how to use psychographic variables successfully for commercial market segmentation, "psychosegmentation" must remain for most marketers a laboratory curiosity.

The use of the buyer behavior variables for segmentation purposes has been more successful. The usage rate, readiness stage, benefits sought, end use, and brand loyalty dimensions have proved to be useful means of identifying submarkets in each of which consumers behave in a unique manner. For example, the behavior of consumers who are heavy users of a product type and have strong brand loyalties is different from the behavior of infrequent users who show little or no loyalty to a given brand.

Closely allied to consumer reaction to a specific brand is consumer sensitivity to the various elements in the marketing strategy mix. Marketing factor sensitivity is the name given to the variable which can be used to segment a market on the basis of how consumers react to product quality, service, advertising, and other aspects of the sales promotion program. Using this basis the manufacturer might identify a market segment composed of consumers very sensitive to price, and another segment in which potential buyers were concerned with quality and service.

Two versions of the product might be designed and an economy priced model would be marketed by means of a strategy mix which emphasized price. Retail outlets would be discount stores or basement departments of leading department stores. In contrast, a more costly version of the product would be directed to the market segment in which consumers emphasized quality and service. The marketing strategy mix would be varied accordingly, with greater emphasis placed on gaining distribution through full service, quality retail outlets.

Selecting a marketing strategy

Facing the alternatives of a product differentiation strategy and one of market segmentation, the marketing manager must decide which strategy is best suited to the attainment of the objectives of his firm. To aid in this decision process it has been suggested that six factors be considered.[8] These include: (1) size of market, (2) consumer sensitivity, (3) product life cycle, (4) type of product, (5) number of competitors, and (6) typical competitor strategies.

Size of market. If the total number of buyers for a given product type is small, then segmentation strategy becomes less feasible simply on the basis of cost. Regardless of bases used for isolating submarkets, unless these submarkets are substantial, the marketing manager would be well advised to pursue a product differentiation strategy.

Consumer sensitivity. If consumers appear to be sensitive to real or imagined product differences, then a product differentiation strategy may be the preferred one. On the other hand, if the product category is dull or uninteresting, a segmentation strategy under which the product or promotional mix is aimed at the needs of a smaller group of prospects may offer better chances for success.

Product life cycle. If a product is being introduced into a market in which similar type products have existed for some time a segmentation strategy may provide an opportunity to gain a competitive advantage by supplying a specially designed offering to a selected market segment or segments. On the other hand, if new product introduction is at a time when the market is just becoming familiar with the generic product

---

[8] Kotrba, "The Strategy Selection Chart," pp. 22–25.

type then a product differentiation strategy which attempts to build primary demand is preferable.

Type of product. If a product is a distinct item such as an automobile, significant changes can be made in its design or performance. Such a product lends itself to a strategy of market segmentation. If a product is of a commodity type such as gasoline or sugar, consumers are less likely to perceive differences among offerings by various manufacturers. Thus each manufacturer would be advised to engage in a strategy of product differentiation in which promotion and/or distribution can be used as the means of gaining selective demand for his output.

Number of competitors. The greater the number of firms selling the same product, the more difficult it becomes for any one firm to differentiate its offering from that of its competitors. Thus, for each firm in the industry a segmentation strategy directed at those customers which are the most likely prospects for its product line is preferable. In contrast, given a few firms in the industry, a product differentiation strategy may prove both effective and less costly.

Typical competitor strategies. The general consensus of students of the subject is that it is difficult to counter an industrywide segmentation strategy with one of product differentiation. On the other hand, when competitors are engaging in product differentiation the firm which engages in market segmentation may gain a considerable competitive advantage.

Utilizing the six factors briefly discussed above, a Strategy Selection Chart has been devised.[9] This chart is illustrated in Figure 2–11. It has been suggested that use of this chart will aid the marketing executive in deciding whether a market segmentation or product differentiation strategy will be most suited to the marketing of a specific product.

Two products were chosen to illustrate the application of the chart. The *X*'s indicate the judgment rankings for rocking chairs while the *O*'s indicate those for flyswatters. The profile of *X*'s or *O*'s can then be examined to see if they indicate a strategy of differentiation, segmentation, or a combination of the two. As an aid in evaluating products, the continuum for each selection factor is divided into ten sectors. The values in the sectors containing judgment ranking marks can be summed and averaged to obtain a strategy selection value for each product appraised.

For example, in the illustration the *X* values for rocking chairs average out to 7.16 while the values for flyswatters average 4.16. As a midpoint value would be 5.5, the chart indicates that a segmentation strategy would be more suitable for rocking chairs, while a differentiation strategy would be preferable for flyswatters.

[9] Ibid., pp. 22–25.

FIGURE 2–11
The Strategy Selection Chart

	APPLY PRODUCT DIFFERENTIATION	STRATEGY SELECTION FACTORS	APPLY MARKET SEGMENTATION
	Strategy emphasis should be on promoting product differences		Strategy emphasis should be on satisfying market variations
MARKET FACTORS	Narrow	Size of Market	Broad
		O (3) · X (6) — scale 1 2 3 4 5 6 7 8 9 10	
	High	Consumer Sensitivity to Product Differences	Low
		O (4) X (5) — scale 1 2 3 4 5 6 7 8 9 10	
PRODUCT FACTORS	Introduction Stage	Product Life–Cycle	Saturation Stage
		O (6) X (7) — scale 1 2 3 4 5 6 7 8 9 10	
	Commodity	Type of Product	Distinct Item
		O (3) X (8) — scale 1 2 3 4 5 6 7 8 9 10	
COMPETITIVE FACTORS	Few	Number of Competitors	Many
		X (4) O (6) — scale 1 2 3 4 5 6 7 8 9 10	
	Differentiation Policy	Typical Competitor Strategies	Segmentation Policy
		O (1) X (9) — scale 1 2 3 4 5 6 7 8 9 10	

Source: R. William Kotrba, "The Strategy Selection Chart," *Journal of Marketing*, July 1966, p. 25. Reprinted by permission.

Conclusion

It is the role of marketing, more than of any other business function, to assure that economic resources are allocated effectively to serve consumer needs and wants. If marketing does not perform this role well, the business firm will not attain its objective of maximizing profits. Consumers, too, will lose. Economic resources will have been consumed, yet consumer needs and wants will not have been fully met. Thus, society has a high stake in the skill with which marketing executives perform the marketing task. The heart of this task is the planning of marketing strategy. This is the focal point of the chapters which follow.

Questions

1. Construct a marketing strategy profile for each of the following products, indicating the relative importance of the six controllable marketing variables. Explain your reasoning.
   a) Electronic computers.
   b) Encyclopedias.
   c) Chewing gum.
   d) Men's suits.
   e) Deodorants.

2. Generally speaking, marketing strategy for intangible products places more emphasis on personal selling than does marketing strategy for tangible products. Why?

3. Buyer behavior in the purchase of television sets has changed substantially over the last ten years. How has this affected marketing strategy for this product?

4. People in different age groups have different buyer behavior patterns. In the case of life insurance how should marketing strategy for the over-35 age group differ from the strategy used for the 20–25 year age group?

5. Should the development of new products be considered a marketing function or should responsibility for this function be assigned elsewhere in a business firm?

6. Some critics of marketing argue that marketing strategy, because it is based on buyer behavior, takes advantage of consumer weaknesses. They suggest that marketing strategy should be based on what is best for people. For example, automobile advertising should stress safety, durability, and economy rather than styling and horsepower. Do you agree?

7. Why should demand be considered an uncontrollable rather than a controllable variable in planning marketing strategy?

8. Why do different companies in the same industry, selling comparable products, often use different marketing strategies?

9. Why has marketing management moved from strategies of undifferentiated marketing to those involving product differentiation?

10. What is meant by a strategy of "market segmentation" and how does such a strategy differ from one in which product differentiation is emphasized?

11. Compare and contrast demographic segmentation bases with bases of a psychographic or behavioral nature.

12. What factors should be considered by management in deciding whether or not to engage in a segmentation or differentiation strategy?

13. Can you envision a situation in which a mixed strategy of differentiation and segmentation might be utilized? Explain briefly.

cases for part one

CASE 1–1

Pop-Tent (A)*

Marketing program for a new product

Some years ago, Henry Stribley and William Moss, of Ann Arbor, Michigan, were considering the question of how they should market a new type of tent which they had designed and were producing. The tent was called "Pop-Tent" and was based on a new conception of tent design which enabled the tent to be packed in a compact, light, and easily portable package and which made it possible for the tent to be erected in 90 seconds without the use of a center pole or ropes.

The idea for "Pop-Tent" had been developed three years earlier by these two men. Mr. Stribley, a retired garage owner, conceived the basic idea and designed the mechanical parts with the assistance of Mr. Moss, then an artist on the *Ford Times,* a publication of the Ford Motor Company. Originally, the purpose had been to design a portable duck blind for hunting. The first design was based on the principle of an umbrella and employed a center pole. However, after building a prototype, it was decided that the design was impractical. The blind weighed too much, was too difficult to erect, and was too bulky. From this original design, it was decided that fiber glass rods could be sewn into the cloth itself instead of the ribs, struts, and center pole of the umbrella design—these glass rods being under tension, and thus holding the tent in shape. A locking hinge was also designed and perfected so that the rods could be folded into a compact package.

On the basis of their new design, another prototype was built, and it met their fullest expectations. The inventors soon realized they "had something." Going beyond the duck blind, they now designed a large size for tenting and camping purposes and applied for patent and trademark protection. (The name "Pop-Tent" was adopted because it was descriptive of how the tent erected—it just "popped-up.")

In the final design, the camping size was sufficiently large so that

---

* Written by Ross. J. Wilhelm, Professor of Business Economics, Graduate School of Business Administration, The University of Michigan.

it could sleep two adults on the floor in sleeping bags and perhaps a child on either side of each adult. While the height in the center of the tent was only 58 inches, this was not felt by the designers to be a serious disadvantage.

The inventors then arranged for several prototypes of the new size to be built, and instead of having them made in the usual khaki color, they had them made in various attractive colors.

There probably has been no new product in recent history which received as much free publicity as did Pop-Tent. Its new igloo or dome shape, plus its attractive colors and inherent product appeals, made it a natural for inclusion in articles and features in magazines and other media on new items in the tenting-camping field. At the same time, the Ford Motor Company, as part of its promotion of station wagons, was emphasizing outdoor camping and vacation trips in station wagons, and the company included illustrations of Pop-Tents in its promotional literature.

By the spring of the year, when the final design of Pop-Tent was completed, the promoters had received a two-page color spread in the *Ford Times,* which then had a circulation of 3 million customers of the Ford Motor Company; had been on the front cover of *Popular Mechanics* with a full story with pictures inside; had a three fourths of a page picture story in *Life;* and Pop-Tent had been shown on numerous TV shows in the Detroit area in addition to mentions in other news stories and features. In most of the stories, the names and address of the inventors were mentioned, along with the fact that they were intending to market their product in the near future at a retail price of about $125 for the tent and $87.50 for the duck blind. On the basis of these stories, about 100 inquiries and actual orders had beeen received from prospective customers. While such publicity could not be bought outright it was "guesstimated" that comparable advertising would have cost over $100,000 to obtain.

By the fall of the same year, the inventors had felt that it was necessary for them to start producing so as to be able to capitalize on the free publicity which had been received. A second feature article which had been promised in the *Ford Times* precipitated the decision to go into actual production. The inventors felt, and the *Ford Times* made it known, that this second feature depended on the inventors having the product available for sale.

As a result, a decision was made to produce 500 sleeping tents and 500 duck blinds, with Mr. Stribley putting up the money. Since these men did not have any production experience in the tenting field, they jobbed out the production. They contacted a major tent producer in St. Louis, who agreed to produce the tent, and they obtained the glass rods and hinges from Michigan manufacturers. The final cost of the

Pop-Tent was $48 delivered to Ann Arbor, and the duck blinds cost $34 each. In specifying how the tent and blind were to be made, the inventors placed great emphasis on top quality, and the final product was made out of expensive, long-staple Egyptian cotton and had a sewn-in vinyl floor. It was because of this emphasis on quality and the inherent appeals of the product that the inventors felt they could get the prices they had originally set. They did not feel they could go much beyond these retail prices, however. They also knew that in the sporting goods trade, and on items of this type, retailers were accustomed to receiving a 40 percent markup, wholesalers 16⅔ percent and manufacturers' agents 10 percent. As a result, they were considering the possibility of marketing their products by mail order, selling directly to consumers rather than going through the regular channels which took such a large proportion of the final selling price. Further, neither of the principals wanted to invest much more money or time in the product if they could avoid it. It just was not available.

At this time, the highest price tent being sold by Sears, Roebuck mail-order department was a four-wall tent which could hold four cots, enabled a person to stand up at full height anywhere in the tent, had screens built into all of the walls, had a canvas cover for a porch, a canvas floor, and sold for about $120. Other tents could be obtained at prices ranging from just below $20, the actual price depending on the size, screens, presence or absence of canvas flooring, height of the walls, and other such features. There were no other tents on the market which were as easy to erect or transport as was the Pop-Tent.

CASE QUESTION

What steps should Messrs. Moss and Stribley take to market their new products?

CASE 1–2

Da-Roche Laboratories, Inc.*

Strategy for marketing a new antibiotic product

In February of 1969, the officers of Da-Roche Laboratories, Inc. met to discuss the company's sales and advertising plans to launch their

---

* Written by Kenneth L. Bernhardt, Assistant Professor, Georgia State University, Atlanta.

new product, Dapper-Diaper. The focus of the meeting was the strategy to be used in the marketing of the new product which had recently been approved by the Food and Drug Administration (FDA). They were particularly interested in the possible methods of promoting the product and in the channels of distribution to be used in distributing Dapper-Diaper.

BACKGROUND

Da-Roche Laboratories, Inc., was established in Jackson, Michigan, in 1964 to develop and market a new antibiotic baby product, Dapper-Diaper. Dapper-Diaper was composed of an aqueous solution of the antibiotic neomycin sulfate which was placed in a ten-ounce aerosol can. Neomycin inhibited odors in the animal kingdom, and Mr. Roy Crutchfield thought that the antibiotic could be used to eliminate odors from baby diapers. Dapper-Diaper kills bacteria which cause the decomposition of urea and thereby prevents ammonia from forming in diapers.

Da-Roche Laboratories convinced selected doctors to do some initial testing of its new product and the results were very encouraging. Doctors discovered that when sprayed on diapers in the diaper pail, it solved the odor problem. In addition, if sprayed on a clean diaper before it was worn by the baby it appeared to stop or prevent diaper rash on the baby.

GAINING FDA APPROVAL

With a great deal of encouragement from the doctors involved in the initial testing of their new antibiotic product, Mr. D. R. Wiley, then president and general manager of Da-Roche Laboratories, along with Mr. Crutchfield and Dr. John B. Holst, the company's consulting M.D., went to Washington and informed the FDA that they had discovered a new gift to mothers which they wished to begin marketing immediately. The FDA did not agree and told the Da-Roche personnel that they would have to do studies to show that the product actually did what it claimed to do, and at the same time show that there were no harmful side effects from using the antibiotic product.

Thus, while they thought they could go through the Food and Drug Administration (FDA) for approval of a new cosmetic-type product, the Da-Roche executives discovered that they had actually created what was termed a new drug which had to be approved by the New Drug Division of the FDA.

Although the one active ingredient in "Dapper Diaper" was neomycin sulfate which had been known and widely used for about 15 years as one of a number of antibiotic products, the ingredient had never been mixed with water and other chemicals and placed in a pressurized spray can for sale over the counter. It appeared that it was due to the packaging and marketing plans for the new product, rather than its active ingredient, that it was declared a new drug, subject to FDA jurisdiction.

Consequently, what started out to be a new cosmetic product which would not have had to prove that it did any good as long as it did not do any harm, ended up being a new drug under FDA regulations. Consequently, both the efficacy of the product and the absence of any harmful effects had to be proven to the satisfaction of the FDA committee of doctors. This effort required approximately four years and the expenditure of nearly one-half million dollars in testing costs alone.

Three basic steps had to be taken to get the required certification by the Federal Food and Drug Administration. First, research of all the available literature was undertaken to see what kinds of problems should be researched in experimental situations. Animal testing (toxicity) was next conducted, including autopsy reports of white mice to be sure there were no harmful effects from continued use of the new product. The third step in the testing procedure involved clinical tests on infants using a placebo (the product minus the active ingredient) with double blind and double blind crossover techniques whereby aerosol spray cans labeled X and Y were tested both for safety and for efficacy. The doctors and nurses involved in these clinical observation studies did not know which cans contained the aqueous solution of neomycin sulfate and which contained the placebo, in order to insure their objectivity throughout the duration of the study. Culture studies of diapers and the babies' skin were made and it was found that the bacteria which produced odor and diaper rash were gradually eradicated in the diaper with no effect on the resident flora (normal balance of bacteria) of the babies' skin. An example of this type of study is explained in Exhibit 1.

Finally, at the end of 1967, after 30 visits to Washington and 25 label changes, the FDA approved Dapper-Diaper for over-the-counter sale. Since the machinery for producing the new antibiotic had been purchased and inspected about one and one-half years before the FDA approval had been received, Da-Roche was now able to begin production immediately.

DISTRIBUTION

The original plan was to obtain distribution in Michigan and then use the capital generated by sales in this area to expand into adjacent markets. This plan was to be repeated until Dapper-Diaper was distributed throughout the United States. To obtain regional distribution as fast as possible, Da-Roche hired a broker's broker. This man had formerly sold to brokers and he was well acquainted with the food

EXHIBIT 1

OAKWOOD HOSPITAL
OAKWOOD HOSPITAL CORPORATION

18101 OAKWOOD BOULEVARD
DEARBORN, MICHIGAN

DEPARTMENT OF NURSING
OFFICE OF THE DIRECTOR   February 11, 1969   PHONE LOgan 5-1000

Mr. Roy Crutchfield
Mr. Darrell Wiley
533 Hupp Avenue
Jackson, Michigan

Gentlemen,

In answer to your request, I am enclosing the report of a seven month controlled study conducted at Oakwood Hospital using Dapper-Diaper, formerly Diaper Dan, a new antibiotic diaper spray containing Neomycin Sulfate 0.14%. This study was undertaken to evaluate Dapper-Diaper as a safe and effective product in the control of diaper rash and diaper odor.

Oakwood Hospital is a large general hospital with 458 beds, 84 bassinets, an approved Obstetric and Gynecology residency and a yearly newborn census of over 4,000 babies. It ranks third in the entire metropolitan Detroit area for new births. Each obstetrical wing has its own nursery making it an ideal arrangement for a controlled newborn study.

This study was conducted from May 1, 1965 to November 30, 1965. During this time there were 2,407 births at Oakwood Hospital; 976 of these babies were assigned, at random, to the study nursery and the remaining 1,431 babies were admitted to the nurseries serving as controls. On admission to the nursery each baby was given a phisohex bath. The babies admitted to the study nursery were diapered with diapers sprayed with Dapper-Diaper. All other routines remained the same. The babies in the other nurseries were diapered with diapers laundered in the same manner but without the addition of Dapper-Diaper.

Neomycin Sulfate is well established as a safe and effective drug. Sensitivities to this drug have been reported as very infrequent. The purpose of Neomycin in Dapper Diaper is to halt or suppress the formation of urea splitting bacteria which may result in the production of ammonium hydroxide. Under the proper conditions its presence will cause diaper rash.

From the results of our seven month study Mrs. P. M. Holton, obstetrical supervisor, and I can support the claims of this product on the basis of the following conclusions:

    a. There was not one single case of diaper rash seen in the babies treated with Dapper-Diaper.

    b. The same incidence of diaper rash (10 to 12%) remained in the control nurseries.

    c. The diaper odor in the soiled diapers was completely eliminated.

    d. There were absolutely no adverse skin reactions seen in the babies treated with Dapper-Diaper.

I was greatly impressed with this product and feel that it would be effective in the control of one of the most common and irritating pediatric problems, diaper rash.

Sincerely,

E. J. Alban Jr. MD

E.J. Alban Jr. M.D.

EJA/da

and drug brokers in Michigan and knew what it would take to get them to handle the company's product. The brokers, in turn, sold to large wholesale drug companies such as McKesson-Robbins and Hazeltine-Perkins, and to large grocers such as A & P, Kroger, Food Fair, and even to smaller "Mom and Pop" stores in some areas. The brokers also sold to some discount chains such as K-Marts. It was felt that established brokers would be much more effective in bargaining with large accounts than salesmen from a new, unfamiliar company.

By March 1, 1968, the new product was on the market in many of these retail outlets, and a concerted effort was being made to get every drugstore in Michigan to carry the product as well. This objective was pursued by sending a free sample can of Dapper-Diaper to every major druggist in the state of Michigan. While this plan entailed giving away free more than 2,000 full-size cans of Dapper-Diaper, it also allowed Da-Roche to claim that its product could be found in every major drugstore in the state of Michigan. At the same time, it acquainted all of Michigan's druggists with the new product. By June, brokers had managed to obtain distribution in 80 percent of the stores in eastern Michigan but distribution in the western part of the state was much slower with only about 20 percent of the stores stocking Dapper-Diaper.

PRICING

It was estimated that if the same amount of neomycin as was contained in one ten-ounce can of Dapper-Diaper were to be bought by prescription, it would cost from $5 to $8. After talking with retailers, brokers, and doctors, it was decided that the "suggested retail price" of Dapper-Diaper would be $1.98. The Da-Roche executives, however, expected that it would sell between $1.60 and $1.70 within four to six weeks after introduction. And, in fact, it was selling for $1.69 in Kroger and other supermarkets as of April 1, 1968. The product sold as low as $1.39 in some stores, and the average retail price was about $1.80.

COST

The average retail price allowed the company enough margin to promote the product properly. The average retail price was about six times the cost of goods sold, which was normal for the drug industry. After discounts and allowances to wholesalers and retailers, the proceeds to the company were about $1.00 per can. Administrative and overhead costs were $100,000 per year exclusive of marketing costs.

MARKET POTENTIAL

In determining the size of the total market of Dapper-Diaper, Da-Roche executives first found out that there were approximately 8 million babies in diapers in the United States. (There were 350,000 babies in the company's initial marketing area.) A ten-ounce can of Dapper-Diaper was expected to last one month. Da-Roche executives reasoned that they would be able to get 10 percent of the total market to use Dapper-Diaper, resulting in sales of 9.6 million cans per year.

USE OF PERSONAL SELLING THROUGH ETHICAL CHANNELS TO GET INTENSIVE DISTRIBUTION

The original strategy called for personal selling through five detail men. These men were to call on people in all medical professions to explain the benefits of the new product, how it was used, and where it could be obtained. In addition, small-size free samples were left with the doctor so he could recommend the product to a patient and be able to give her a ten-day supply of Dapper-Diaper as well.

Da-Roche's executives were immediately faced with the problem of how to get the detail men in to see a doctor, especially since they represented a new company with only one product. To solve this problem, the five detail men were each given an hourglass which was timed for three minutes. The detail men then went into the doctor's office and started the sand in motion, asking for three minutes of the doctor's time. Only the essential facts were given to the doctor in the three minutes, after which some free samples were distributed and the detail men attempted to leave. At this point, Da-Roche executives declared nine out of ten doctors asked for more information about Dapper-Diaper before the detail man could leave. The following points were made about the new baby product: It is certified by the Federal Food and Drug Administration; it is an antibiotic; its active ingredient is neomycin; it is sold over the counter (no prescription needed); it is safe, because it is made from one of the most nearly perfect drugs known; and it is time saving, economical, easy to use, and it really works.

The use of detail men was selected over consumer advertising for the initial promotional job, because the Da-Roche executives believed that if the product was recommended by doctors, women would surely use Dapper-Diaper and tell their friends about it, too. This would give the new product the most desirable kind of promotion possible—word of mouth.

Another consideration which favored personal selling over consumer advertising, was the fact that during the first week of February, when promotion of Dapper-Diaper by the company's detail men was first begun, distribution of the product was just beginning too. If consumer advertising had come in at the same time, the Da-Roche executives believed that much of it would have been wasted because the product was not yet available. It was felt that by April 1, 1968, this problem would be remedied and a consumer advertising campaign could be launched at that time. With only a limited amount of money available for advertising, it was important that distribution be achieved before the advertising commenced, in order that the advertising would not be wasted.

DAPPER-DIAPER CONSUMER ADVERTISING CAMPAIGN

To be consistent with their intensive distribution policy within the introductory selling regions, the Da-Roche executives had planned a consumer advertising campaign which was to begin April 1, 1968. They believed that by waiting until April 1, they could be sure that Dapper-Diaper could be readily available to most stores by the time the consumer advertising campaign would begin. Discussion with brokers, people in the trade, and Da-Roche's agency, the La Vanway agency in Jackson, Michigan, resulted in an advertising budget of $50,000 for the first 13 weeks. After that time, advertising would be budgeted at 25 percent of net sales. It was decided that to get maximum reach and frequency, the company should use half- and whole-minute radio spots, with some ten-second ID's; ID's and whole minutes on television, with some advertising in trade journals and newspapers. The first 13-week advertising schedule can be found in Exhibit 2.

In anticipation of the FDA's approval of the new use for Dapper-Diaper which was expected in the near future, the company's advertising was based largely on the diaper and not exclusively on the narrower diaper pail use for which the product was currently certified by the FDA. A baby wearing a top hat, which appeared on the can, became known as "The Happy Baby" and was used in the company's introductory advertising campaign. All advertising carried the line, "Do your baby a favor, ask your baby's doctor."

PROTECTION FROM COMPETITION

It was hoped that eventually Dapper-Diaper would become almost a generic name, since it would be the first on the market and likely enjoy the status of being the only such product for at least one more year. This protection, it was felt, would be afforded by the patent which was pending on the new product, the trademark and copyrighted Dapper-Diaper name, and the fact that any competitor would have to do extensive testing of the type that took Da-Roche four years, in order to get its product approved by the FDA as a new drug.

PURSUING NEW USES

While Da-Roche was still in the process of introducing Dapper-Diaper into its first region which included all of Michigan and part of Ohio and Indiana, it was also engaged in more clinical testing. The product, as of February 1969, had received FDA approval only as a diaper pail spray. Knowing that it had no harmful effects on babies and that it

EXHIBIT 2
Advertising—first 13 weeks

Television

150 Minutes and ID's on WXYZ-TV (7) Detroit
150 Minutes and ID's on WNEM-TV (5) Flint-Saginaw-Bay City
150 Minutes and ID's on WILX-TV (10) Jackson, Lansing, Battle Creek
150 Minutes and ID's on WOOD/TV (8) Grand Rapids, Battle Creek, Kalamazoo, Muskegon

Radio

260 Minutes, 30's and 10's on CKLW, Detroit, etc.
200 Minutes, 30's and 10's on WTAC, Flint
260 Minutes, 30's and 10's on WILS, Lansing
270 Minutes, 30's and 10's on WKNX, Saginaw
245 Minutes, 30's and 10's on WIBM, Jackson
260 Minutes, 30's and 10's on WKFR, Battle Creek
280 Minutes, 30's and 10's on WKLZ, Kalamazoo
250 Minutes, 30's and 10's on WLAV, Grand Rapids
260 Minutes, 30's and 10's on WTRU, Muskegon

Newspaper

7 ads in each of the following newspapers:
Detroit News and *Detroit Free Press* (if operating—interim papers, if not)

Ann Arbor News	*Bay City Times*
Flint Journal	*Grand Rapids Press*
Kalamazoo Gazette	*Muskegon Chronicle*
Saginaw News	*Ypsilanti Press*
Pontiac Press	*Lansing State Journal*
Battle Creek Enquirer News	*Port Huron Times Herald*
Benton Harbor-St. Joseph Herald Press	*Holland Sentinel*
Midland News	*Monroe News*
Owosso Argus-Press	*Adrian Telegram*

---

would inhibit bacteria growth which caused ammonia burn or diaper rash, Da-Roche was seeking FDA approval to promote Dapper-Diaper as a diaper spray as well. For this new purpose the product would be sprayed on a clean diaper before it was to be worn by the baby. Much of the extensive testing which had already been conducted by Da-Roche, indicated that when diapers were sprayed in the diaper pail, the diapers became clinically clean prior to washing and helped inhibit the growth of ammonia-producing bacteria, preventing odor and diaper rash.

Dr. J. D. Holst, M.D., Da-Roche's medical liasion with the FDA, explained that with the tests that had already been done, it would only require about six months of tests to return to the FDA requesting permission to use a broader label describing Dapper-Diaper as a diaper spray as well as a diaper pail spray. This additional use for the product could then be promoted by the company's detail men in talking to doctors and in the company's consumer advertising. Thus, while at the time of introduction Dapper-Diaper was only an antibiotic diaper pail spray which would limit the number of bacteria to control odor, its rash-prevention benefit was a by-product which the Da-Roche executives believed might soon become an equally important use for the new product.

Beyond the one new use of Dapper-Diaper in controlling ammonia burn, the nature of the product itself and the way in which it worked suggested a variety of entirely new uses for which the new product might be equally well suited. The active ingredient, neomycin, was extremely effective in reducing or completely eliminating bacterial odor, and for this reason it might be used for eliminating all odors caused by organic decomposition. Examples would include a garbage pail or pet spray.

CONSIDERATION OF A FULL BABY PRODUCT LINE

Da-Roche executives also considered introducing companion products, such as baby powder and paper diapers, which would help better entrench the company as a producer of a more complete line of baby products and perhaps speed the translation of the brand name Dapper-Diaper into almost a generic concept. Another advantage would be that these companion products, as they were developed, could be promoted along with the Dapper-Diaper spray by the company's detail men as they called on doctors and left free samples and literature.

RESULTS, APRIL 1968–JANUARY 1969

The company ran into significant problems as Dapper-Diaper was being introduced. A batch of 180,000 three-ounce cans to be used as samples and distributed to doctors was not approved by the FDA. A change in the can design had resulted in values which did not fit properly. The company therefore had to use trade cans for samples to distribute to the doctors and, due to the greater cost of the full-size cans, a smaller number of samples was distributed.

After a product had been distributed to the retailers and had been on the shelf for a short period of time, problems with the full-size can became evident. Some of the ingredients in the product were interacting with the can, causing the can to rust. As the can rusted, the pressure in the aerosol leaked out, making it impossible to get the product out of the aerosol can. The company replaced bad cans, as they were found, with good ones, but then even the good ones turned bad. Finally, the source of the problem was discovered and a change in Dapper-Diaper's formulation had to be developed. Da-Roche then had to get FDA approval on the new formulation and on the new can. In effect, the company had to start all over.

THE PRESENT SITUATION

In January 1969, the company finally received approval from the FDA to again begin marketing Dapper-Diaper. Da-Roche executives were now considering several alternative ways of marketing the product. First, they could follow exactly the same strategy that they followed with the initial launching of the product. This would entail both detail men and consumer advertising with distribution through drugstores, supermarkets, and discount stores.

A second alternative was to take a marketing approach similar to that used for ethical drugs. Thus, the company could use established outlets that do not require the high cost of familiarizing people with the product. Instead, detail men would be used to encourage doctors to recommend the product, and people would therefore become familiar with the product through their doctor's recommendation. This would eliminate the need for a significant amount of consumer advertising required to support a product which is to be distributed through supermarkets and discount stores.

Da-Roche's executives came upon a third alternative after reading an article in *Time* magazine. The article quoted the president of The American Diaper Service Association describing the smell of the diaper pail as diaper services' biggest single problem. The urea content of a new baby's urine is not very heavy, but as the baby gets older, the urea gets heavier. Therefore, after the baby gets about three months old, the smell in the diaper pail significantly increases. Diaper services supply pails with neoprene bags, and therefore the diapers cannot be soaked. The diapers are usually picked up only once a week so there are 50 to 100 by that time. Mothers, therefore, began to buy diapers and wash them themselves three to four times per week.

The Associated Diaper Services of America and the other trade organization, The National Institute for Diaper Services, have members who make 83 million contacts per year where money changes hands. With the help of these two associations, Dapper-Diaper could be made known to millions of women through diaper service distributors. Da-Roche executives felt that either of the diaper services could sell 2 million cans per year with a minimum of effort. The company executives stated that Da-Roche would be very profitable at that volume.

Da-Roche executives had also made contact with a manufacturer of institutional clothing. This company sold very high quality sleeping garments for babies and mentally retarded children in hospitals and training schools; and other garments for hospitals, penitentaries, and other institutions. The manufacturer would distribute Dapper-Diaper along with his other products. As the institutions have a large problem with odor, Da-Roche's executives thought that this method of distribution would yield a large market.

Da-Roche executives were also considering one further alternative. A cosmetic broker—the best known in the country—with offices in Dallas, New York, and Chicago, had become interested in Dapper-Diaper. This broker employed over 100 people and distributed products of such well-known companies as Schick, Alberto-Culver, Revlon, and Tampax. The broker told Da-Roche's executives that if they could give him $1 million for advertising, he could guarantee them $3 million in sales with the company's present label (Dapper-Diaper had still not been approved for anything except use as a diaper pail spray).

CASE QUESTION

What marketing strategy should be used to reintroduce Dapper-Diaper, the new product that had just been approved by the Food and Drug Administration?

CASE 1–3
Wolverine World Wide, Inc.: Hush Puppies*
Marketing strategy for Hush Puppies brand shoes

During the spring of 1968, the director of marketing for Hush Puppies at Wolverine World Wide, Inc., was reviewing past marketing strategies as an aid to formulating marketing plans for 1969. Increased competition, rising raw material costs, and a stabilized demand in the past two years made him wonder what changes, if any, might be appropriate in the Hush Puppies marketing program.

Wolvering World Wide, Inc. first started in 1883 as the partnership of Hirth and Krause, a wholesaler of hides, shoes, and leather supplies. Shoemaking and tanning operations were first begun in 1903. Wolverine, for many years, specialized in the tanning of unusual leathers, enabling the company to occupy a niche for itself in the competitive cowhide field. The firm's main product from the 1920s through the 1950s, when it was called Wolverine Shoe and Tanning Company, was shell

---

* Written by Kenneth L. Bernhardt, Assistant Professor, Georgia State University, Atlanta.

horsehide. This was an extraordinarily stiff and strong leather in which the company had a competitive advantage due to the special triple-tanning process which the company had developed. This tannage was highly acid resistant, which was a significant advantage around the farm where there were lactic and other acids. Shell horsehide, a natural leather, dried soft, stayed soft, and was the second toughest leather in the world after kangaroo leather. The company considered itself as selling leather and not just work shoes.

In the late 1930s, the company became concerned about their raw material supply. Horses were becoming more and more scarce (there were 26 million horses in the United States in 1910 and only 4 million in 1950), and the company realized that they could not make shoes out of tractors. Further, the company believed that its success would be linked to the development of other unusual leathers.

It was about this time that a new opportunity presented itself to the company with the introduction, by the meat packing houses, of prepackaged sliced bacon. Previously, bacon was sold with the skin on it. After hand-skinning the bacon, people just threw away the rind. The prepackaging made available large quantities of bacon rind from which the company was able to develop a suede pigskin leather suitable for a line of work gloves. This was the beginning of Wolverine's entry into the pigskin business. The company soon turned its attention from smoked bacon rinds to large-scale processing of "green" (unsmoked) pigskin.

Pigskin possesses certain outstanding qualities. It wears exceptionally well and is highly resistant to deterioration from perspiration. It cannot be damaged by moisture and humidity. Another important characteristic is the fact that pigskins are available in large quantities, as some 70 million pigs are slaughtered each year in the United States alone. Of course, not all this pigskin is acceptable for tanning purposes by shoe manufacturers.

Unfortunately, however, the pig is not easy to skin. With horses and cows, the skin fits loosely, like a coat, and is very easy to remove, much as a banana is peeled. On the other hand, skinning a hog is somewhat like peeling an apple; the hide is bound tightly to the animal by a layer of fat. A highly trained workman requires more than a half hour to "slay" or skin a hog. This is an obvious production bottleneck, when large packing houses process 600 or more animals each hour.

During World War II, the war production board encouraged packers to develop new ways to produce pigskin as a leather source. Wolverine, due to its experience in tanning unusual leathers, was selected to process this pigskin output into work shoes.

Following the war, the pork packers returned to producing bacon. Wolverine, confronted with a diminishing supply of horsehides, bought several units of a wartime mechanical pigskinner and set out to perfect a new pigskinner that satisfied the requirements of both shoemakers and packers. After seven years of research and upwards of $2 million in expenditures, the company developed a unique and highly efficient machine for effectively skinning pigs at the packing plant without damaging the skins. Twenty packers were induced to install the perfected skinning machines in their pork processing operation. Wolverine now had the first and only volume pigskinner.

The company could now produce a skin uniform in size and about two feet square from each side of the animal. The machines, which were owned by Wolverine and cost $15 thousand to $18 thousand each, could remove pig hides at the rate of about 460 an hour. Another equally expensive unit called a flushing machine removes all excess fat remaining on the skin.

However, the company still had a problem. The only shoes that Wolverine was making at the time were work shoes, and while pigskin made very comfortable footware, its lightness worked against it in the work-shoe field. In appraising markets, Wolverine decided that the greatest potential lay in easy-to-care-for leisure shoes. Leisure shoes look attractive with a brushed finish, the best finish for pigskin. Brushing pigskin eliminates surface marks and permits distinctive colors. It also leaves the tiny bristle holes in the leather unblocked, giving the shoes natural ventilation.

In 1957, Wolverine had 30,000 pairs of men's shoes made in the new pigskin leather. The soles were cemented to the uppers, not sewn, as was the practice with most shoes. There was one basic pattern in 11 different colors including scarlet, canary yellow, and kelly green. These shoes were offered to the trade to retail for $7.95, and were distributed nationally through the work-shoe salesmen who generally sold in small rural towns.

A big turning point came in 1958, when Wolverine changed advertising agencies and employed MacManus, John, and Adams, Inc. The agency had done no shoe advertising previously, and Wolverine thought that the new agency would therefore be willing to take new approaches and try new ideas in promoting this brand-new product. The first thing the new agency did was to set up a market test. One hundred pairs of shoes were given to consumers, with a follow-up study being done eight weeks later. At the end of the study the researcher told the consumers that the company needed the shoes back, but if they wanted to keep them, they could upon payment of $5.00. Overwhelmingly, the consumers wanted to keep the shoes. Of course, the company let them keep them without paying the $5.00.

With strong encouragement from the consumer test, the agency then attacked the problem of what to call the shoes. The only "Hush Puppies" that people had ever heard of at the time was a corn fritter which people in some southern states threw to their barking dogs with the command, "Hush, puppies." Several of Wolverine's executives liked the name and thought it appropriate to give this name to a comfortable shoe that is kind to the feet and hushes that special kind of "barking dog," one's tired feet.

An outside marketing research firm was commissioned to conduct the name study. Interviews were held with 300 people in Los Angeles and Chicago testing six potential names: Swash Bucks, Lazers, Breathers, Slow Pokes, Ho-Hums, and Hush Puppies. Swash Bucks and Lazers were the best liked names. The Hush Puppies name had a high association with food and dogs and was the least desirable name. The agency wanted the company to change the name, but the Wolverine sales manager was insistent that Hush Puppies was the name that should be used, and he won out. To go along with the name, a logo was prepared to help create an image for the shoes. A sad-eyed, droopy-eared basset hound was created for this purpose.

The agency and company then set out to reintroduce the new men's leisure-time shoes. Up until this time Wolverine had sold only 30,000 pairs of the Hush Puppies, an extremely small proportion of the total men's shoe market of 200 million pairs per year. This market was, at the time, a relatively stable market, with the men buying an average of only 1.3 pairs of shoes per year and owning an average wardrobe of only 2.5 to 3 pairs of shoes. Research has indicated that men dislike shopping for shoes and feel little need for owning several pairs, which helps explain the lack of growth in the industry.

INITIAL MARKETING STRATEGY

Wolverine's problem of introducing Hush Puppies was also intensified by the company distribution network in 1958. The company had 57 salesmen who had been selling shell horsehide work shoes and boots, calling on outlets in the small towns and villages of the United States—rarely, if ever, setting foot in the big cities or the growing suburbs. The work shoes and boots were sold primarily to farmers—a main copy point was their stout resistance to "barnyard acid"—whereas the market for Hush Puppies was in the cities and suburbs. A plan to gain new distribution was then worked out.

The company's sales manager was told that the Board of Directors would approve an advertising budget of 17 percent of anticipated sales, if the sales manager could open 600 new accounts in 35 cities in 6 weeks. The 35-city plan resulted from an idea to advertise in the 35 cities in which the *This Week* Sunday supplement to newspapers was distributed. This was a large amount of advertising, relative to the industry average of 1.5 percent of sales, and the sales manager accepted the challenge. So in August 1958, all of the company's salesmen were pulled in, literally "transferred" for at least a month, and sent to the 35 cities for a concerted sales drive on Hush Puppies.

It was decided to spend the entire advertising budget in one full-page, four-color advertisement in *This Week* magazine, distributed in 35 leading cities of the country. The extra incentive for the retail stores was that their name would be prominently listed in the Sunday supplement newspaper ad if they ordered the minimum specified assortment of Hush Puppies shoes.

The salesmen were trained by the sales manager on the sales pitch to be used. Each salesman got the highlights of the consumer acceptance study. He carried samples of the shoes in all 11 colors. He used a demonstration kit showing how the "Breathin' Brushed Pigskin" leather resisted soil, rain, and stains, and he carried a preproof of the color ad showing how the store's name would be handled.

The Wolverine salesmen received orders from 600 major retail accounts—all new—in three weeks, and the ad was run at the end of August. The copy in the ad was unusual compared with normal shoe industry advertising. The shoes were shown on people's feet, and both feet were shown. Previously, most shoe ads had shown just one shoe, so it could be pictured as big as possible, usually against a solid colored velvet or other elegant background.

The ad ran on Sunday, and most retailers sold out their complete stock in a few days. One hundred twenty thousand pairs of Hush Puppies were sold at a retail price of $7.95. Another ad was immediately authorized for the Christmas gift season, again with the dual objectives of 1) selling the concept of leisure shoes, and 2) using dealer listing to gain better distribution in the large markets. It was felt that *This Week* supplement could best satisfy these objectives because of its high impact and penetration into a large number of homes in each city. The Christmas ad was even more successful than the initial ad in August.

CHANGES IN MARKETING STRATEGY, 1959–1963

For 1959, the strategy continued, but expanded into over 50 additional markets covered by *Parade* magazine. The advertising was scheduled for late spring to give the Hush Puppies salesmen time to cover their newly expanded territories, opening up more new retail accounts. Another men's style was added and sales tripled. Promotion effort and sales results both continued to grow. *Family Weekly* Sunday newspaper supplement was later added plus the *Sunday Group* and independent newspapers. By 1961, Hush Puppies was the most heavily promoted brand of shoe in the United States. The advertising budget, by this time, had leveled off at 7 percent of sales, which was four times the industry average. Demand continued to be greater than capacity, but

Wolverine kept on advertising and adding new dealers through the listings. The Sunday supplement promotions were run four times per year: at Easter, at the end of May, in August, and in December. The salesmen would send in a report by telegram on Monday and would file a full report on the promotion's success on Friday of the same week.

The company followed a selective distribution strategy, protecting their dealers so that a proper amount of inventory would be stocked. The price was increased to $9.95 as Wolverine needed a larger margin to support plant expansion and other growth programs, including the largest advertising expenditure for a single brand in the shoe industry. Also, dealers would be more interested in adding the Hush Puppies line if higher margins were offered. All outlets maintained the suggested retail price.

During this period, Wolverine expanded its product line. In 1960, golf shoes were introduced. The total golf shoe market had been about 100,000 pairs per year, but in its first year 94,000 pairs of Hush Puppies golf shoes were sold. In 1961, women's shoes were designed and, by 1963, Hush Puppies were available in styles for the entire family and age spectrum from five years old up.

Until 1963, Wolverine continued to sell Hush Puppies shoes faster than they could ship them, with pairage volume showing great increases (see Exhibit 1). Total company sales increased from a plateau of $11 million to $33 million during this period, with profits increasing by an even greater percentage. Selected financial statistics are in Exhibit 2.

Up to this point, no one in the company knew the real consumer marketing reasons why sales were increasing this rapidly. The main problems executives had been concerned with centered around how to get more pigskin, more tanning, and more production out of the factories, which were working three shifts a day. There had been no time to think about who was buying Hush Puppies or for what reason. The marketing executives thought that the buyers were from the lower middle class, with emphasis among those people, such as service station attendants, who were on their feet much of the day.

In 1963, the company, in conjunction with its advertising agency, designed a consumer research study to find out more about Hush Puppies' consumers, and about what people's experience with Hush Puppies had been. Twenty thousand screening interviews were conducted, followed by one thousand in-depth interviews. Some of the results are shown in Exhibits 3 and 4. The study showed that 61 percent of

EXHIBIT 1
Pairs of Hush Puppies sold (in 000s)

1957	30
1958	301
1959	1,000
1960	1,500
1961	2,600
1962	4,900

EXHIBIT 2
Wolverine World Wide, Inc: Selected finanical information

	Sales (000's)	Profits (000's)	Percent of profits	Assets (000's)	Share-holders' equity (000's)	Earnings per share
1956	$11,313	$ 251	2.2	$ 6,394	$4,750	$.09
1957	10,925	125	1.1	6,692	4,200	.05
1958	11,376	341	2.9	6,496	4,387	.13
1959	15,264	591	3.9	8,025	4,742	.24
1960	17,929	658	3.7	9,895	6,159	.22
1961	23,992	1,218	5.1	12,428	7,069	.40
1962	33,231	1,945	5.9	14,375	8,561	.64

Source: Wolverine World Wide, Inc. Annual Report, 1968.

the adult population was aware of Hush Puppies, but only 10 percent of the population had bought a pair. The buyers had higher than average income and education, and their occupation generally was as a professional or skilled worker. The company, for the first time, really knew who was buying Hush Puppies. When they asked these people why they bought Hush Puppies, comfort kept coming back, followed by light weight and long wear. The company could now plan marketing strategy based on knowledge of both buyers and nonbuyers.

MARKETING STRATEGY, 1963–1966

Armed with the information about the consumer, the company was now better able to plan its marketing strategy. To increase the reach and frequency against the new target market, the company began using television in 1964. The *Today* and *Tonight* programs, whose viewers closely matched Hush Puppies' new target market, were tested and subsequently added. This was designed to increase brand awareness and emphasize the comfort theme. It also gave the advertising program some continuity, instead of only the four "waves" per year provided by the Sunday supplement advertisements. Specific advertising objectives were set, and progress was measured. Magazines were added to the media plan to even more effectively reach the newly defined target audience. The following is a list of magazines which were used: *Good Housekeeping, Parents, Jack and Jill, Esquire, Playboy, True, Mademoiselle, Glamour, Redbook, Seventeen, Ebony, Sports Illustrated,* and *Family Circle.*

The company continued to use *Family Weekly, This Week, Parade,* and other Sunday supplements at the beginning of each season to introduce the new styles and to provide a promotional peak for retail tie-in advertising.

EXHIBIT 3
1963 consumer research on Hush Puppies' buyers

	Percent in United States	Percent of Hush Puppies' buyers
Sex		
Men..............................	48	43*
Women...........................	52	57*
	100	100
Household income		
Under $3,000......................	20	7
$3,000–$5,000.....................	19	13
$5,000–$7,500.....................	22	31
$7,500–$10,000....................	21	28
Over $10,000......................	18	21
	100	100
Occupation (head of household)		
Professional/technical/merchants/ official/proprietor..................	19	30
Skilled/foreman/craftsman.............	15	20
Sales-clerical........................	10	20
Unskilled/operatives..................	20	11
Farmer............................	6	1
Service............................	5	6
Others............................	25	12
	100	100
Education (head of household)		
Grade school.......................	33	8
High school........................	46	52
College............................	21	40
	100	100
Age 18 years and older		
Under 25 years.....................	14	9
25–34 years........................	20	25
35–44 years........................	21	34
45–54 years........................	18	21
55 and over........................	27	11
	100	100

* Many of these were purchased for others. (See Exhibit 4.)

The consumer study also resulted in a change in Hush Puppies' copy strategy. The 1964 ads stressed the comfort of Hush Puppies, and in 1965 the theme, "Hush Puppies make the sidewalks softer," was created and used to illustrate and communicate this comfort.

The company's distribution structure now included 15,000 retail accounts consisting of 60 percent shoe stores and 40 percent department

EXHIBIT 4
Person for whom Hush Puppies were purchased by men versus women

	Percent of total buyers	*Percent of men buyers*	*Percent of women buyers*
For self only...............	46	66	32
For self and others..........	18	12	22
For others only.............	36	22	46
	100	100	100

stores (which did 60 percent of the total shoe volume). The company maintained its selective distribution policy which was somewhat unusual in the shoe industry, where it was common for a company to have several different labels for their shoes, giving each retailer an exclusive franchise for one of the labels. Another unusual aspect of Hush Puppies' distribution strategy was that some of their biggest competitors were also their biggest customers.

Wolverine had maintained the same $9.95 price from 1959 until 1965. At that time, rising costs forced an increase to $11.95. It was not felt that this increase would hurt sales as the company still had no strong competition in the quality, lower priced, leisure shoe market.

The company's strategy continued to be successful. Sales grew from $39 million in 1963 to $55.4 million in 1965. Profits nearly doubled. The company had gone from sixty-third in the industry in 1958 to sixth in the industry at the end of 1965. Eighty-four percent of the adult population was now aware of the brand name and 22 percent of them had now purchased at least one pair.

PRESENT SITUATION

By the beginning of 1968, things had changed considerably. Hush Puppies sales were down from the 1966 level, and total company profits were down 40 percent. Selected financial information for this period is included in Exhibit 5. Increased competition and rising raw material costs were known contributors to the present financial situation. The management reviewed recent research to find other causes of the leveling off of sales and to find ways to change the marketing strategy to renew the company's growth.

By early 1967, 88 percent of the adult population was aware of the Hush Puppies name and 40 percent had purchased at least one pair (see Exhibit 6). Thus, the percentage of the population which had purchased at least one pair of Hush Puppies had increased sharply in the past few years, and the company management and the advertising agency were concerned with market saturation and what marketing strategy to use to expand sales and profits.

Introduction to marketing management

EXHIBIT 5
Wolverine World Wide, Inc: Selected financial information

	Sales (000's)	Profits (000's)	Percent of profits	Assets (000's)	Share-holders' equity (000's)	Earnings per share
1963..........	39,021	2,527	6.5	19,180	10,424	$ .84
1964..........	49,083	4,148	8.5	25,080	13,690	1.37
1965..........	55,357	4,797	8.7	28,266	17,280	1.59
1966..........	55,813	3,796	6.8	35,393	19,567	1.26
1967..........	54,839	2,857	5.2	38,295	20,916	.95

Source: Wolverine World Wide, Inc. Annual Report, 1968.

EXHIBIT 6

	Percent 1967	Percent 1965	Percent 1964	Percent 1963
Awareness of Hush Puppies brand name (total unaided and aided) Have heard of Hush Puppies.....................	88	84	67	61
Have not heard of Hush Puppies.....................	12	16	33	39
Base: Total respondents........	(1,234)	(17,685)	(70,420)	(68,409)
Prior purchase of Hush Puppies (1967 compared with prior years) Have purchased Hush Puppies.....................	40	22	15	10
Have never purchased Hush Puppies.................	60	78	85	90
Base: Total respondents..........	(1,234)	(14,855)	(47,181)	(41,729)

EXHIBIT 7
Composition of total franchise (by new, repeat, and former customers)

	Percent in 1967	Percent in 1965	Percent in 1964
New buyers in past year....................	21	30	33
Former buyers, bought in past year...........	16	34	34
Former buyers, prior years but not in past year...............................	63	36	33
	100	100	100
Base: Total buyers........................	(492)	(3,850)	(10,789)

EXHIBIT 8
Occasions or purposes for which Hush Puppies are worn (1967 new buyers in past years versus other buyers in 1967 study, in percent)

	Men buyers			Women buyers		
Occasions	New in past year	All others	Differ-ence	New in past year	All others	Differ-ence
Grocery shopping............	90	54	36	85	66	19
In-town shopping.............	81	48	33	71	44	27
Evening out at friends.........	78	47	31	51	38	13
A PTA meeting..............	52	29	23	43	27	16
At regular work..............	51	33	18	57	41	16
Church.....................	35	19	16	25	12	13
A wedding..................	13	8	5	6	4	2
Don't know/no answer.........	4	28	24	1	27	26
Base: Total buyers...........	(83)	(126)		(79)	(204)	

EXHIBIT 9
Hush Puppies' product image—Feb. 1967 (men only)

WHY PURCHASED: (MAJOR REASONS)

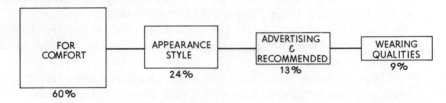

WHY NOT PURCHASED: (MAJOR REASONS)

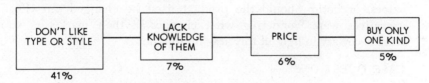

Exhibit 7 revealed another related problem. Fewer former buyers were continuing to buy new pairs. Exhibit 8 showed one possible reason why. Previous buyers who had their Hush Puppies for over one year were not wearing them for as many or as dressy occasions as new buyers. One of the product's advantages, its resistance to wearing out, was apparently hurting repeat buying. The older pairs were being used for painting, mowing the lawn, etc. The shoes were being downgraded in their usage. However, because the shoes were not worn out, the owners were not buying new pairs.

EXHIBIT 10
Hush Puppies' product image—Feb. 1967 (women only)

WHY PURCHASED: (MAJOR REASONS)

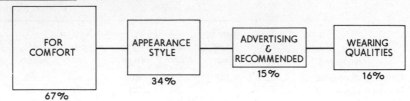

WHY NOT PURCHASED: (MAJOR REASONS)

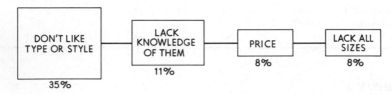

The executives also reviewed the reasons why people purchased and did not purchase Hush Puppies. This information is in Exhibits 9 and 10. Comfort continued to be the outstanding reason for purchase, but dislike of style was the most important reason for not purchasing Hush Puppies.

After reviewing this information, the executives were trying to find good solutions to the problems they faced. They wondered if they should change the copy approach from the present "comfort" appeal. Should the media strategy be changed, dropping the Sunday supplements, magazines, or both? Should the product itself be changed? In effect, the executives were wondering what changes in their marketing strategy were necessary in light of this new information.

CASE QUESTIONS

1. Evaluate the initial marketing strategy for Hush Puppies shoes and the changes that were made up through 1963. In your opinion, what factors account for the success achieved by the brand during this period?
2. What changes in marketing strategy were made during the period 1963–1966? Were these modifications sound?
3. What is your diagnosis of the reasons for the leveling off of sales subsequent to 1966? In view of this analysis, what changes, if any, would be appropriate in planning marketing strategy for 1969?

part two

BUYER BEHAVIOR

BUILDING an effective marketing strategy requires identification of the target market for the product and an understanding of the behavior of prospective buyers as they make their purchasing decisions. Since the identification of market targets has been discussed in the previous chapter, this section begins with a consideration of certain fundamental concepts essential for an understanding of how and why people buy. Initially, attention is focused upon a study of the purchase of consumer goods. A simple model of the consumer buying process is employed to help identify key factors influencing the purchase decision. Buying behavior results from the interplay of the consumer's personality and the environment in which he lives. What are the key elements in the consumer's personality which are relevant in making purchasing decisions? How do environmental factors influence the choice? These are the questions which are analyzed in depth in Chapter 3 and the first half of Chapter 4.

Although the initial explanation of the buying process is relatively simple, it is recognized that consumer purchasing behavior is actually very complex. In the last half of Chapter 4, therefore, a comprehensive model of buyer behavior is presented, in which the simplifying assumptions of the previous discussion are removed and a closer approximation of reality is achieved. The points in the model at which marketing strategy may influence buyer behavior are also given careful consideration.

Attention is then turned to an analysis of buyer behavior in the purchase of industrial goods. What is the character of the industrial market? How does industrial buying differ from consumer purchasing? How is it similar? What models are available to help in understanding the decision? These are the topics covered in Chapter 5.

3

Concepts of buyer behavior

PREVIOUS CHAPTERS have emphasized the importance of using buyer behavior information in planning marketing strategy. This approach appears logical since the fundamental purpose of business activity is the satisfaction of the wants of consumer and industrial buyers. In recognition of this point, progressive firms have adopted "The Marketing Concept," which implies the consumer orientation of the entire business firm. As a means of achieving such an orientation, it was shown that the process of planning marketing strategy requires understanding of and adaptation to the environment in which the product is to be sold. It was demonstrated that the demand variable is the most basic environmental factor influencing the character of effective marketing strategy.

How to get buyer behavior information into marketing decisions

Granted that buyer behavior information is important for effective marketing decision making, the problem is how to insure that such information is actually used in planning marketing strategy. This problem is critical, according to Newman, because of the substantial progress that has been made in recent years in developing new and more powerful concepts and tools for use in gathering information.[1] It relates not only to the use of buyer behavior information, but also to other data potentially helpful in planning, executing, and monitoring marketing programs.

While better research tools are now available to supply information

---
[1] Adapted by permission from Joseph W. Newman, "Put Research into Marketing Decisions," *Harvard Business Review*, March–April 1962, vol. 40, no. 2, pp. 105, 107–10.

that will help executives in understanding and solving their problems, not enough is known about how to put them to work effectively in the decision-making process. Among the impediments to progress, Newman lists (1) the limited backgrounds of certain marketing executives; (2) the fact that some business executives see research as a threat to their personal status and therefore resist its use; (3) the absence of systematic planning in some organizations; (4) the inability of some executives to make productive use of specialists from such varied disciplines as psychology, anthropology, sociology, semantics, economics, mathematics, and statistics; and (5) the isolation of some marketing research departments from management. If we are going to correct this situation, according to Newman, we first must do two basic things:

1. Think more specifically in terms of an ongoing process of decision making which requires a flow of inputs.
2. See research as the systematic application of a variety of concepts and methods which can be useful in generating these inputs.

Stated differently, "The main point is that research is not simply a matter of having a survey done from time to time, as has been so typical in the past. Instead, it should be a continuous program designed to help management set its objectives, plan for its accomplishment, implement the plans successfully, and evaluate the outcome so that still better programs may be undertaken in the future." In short, one way to get buyer behavior information into marketing decisions is through the development and use of a marketing information system. Such a system would also help to insure that other types of essential data would be available for use by marketing executives in planning, execution, and control.

Concept of a marketing information system

A firm's *marketing information system* consists of "A structured, interacting complex of persons, machines, and procedures designed to generate an orderly flow of pertinent information, collected from both intra and extra-firm sources, for use as the basis for decision making in specified responsibility areas of marketing management."[2]

The components of a *marketing information system* are visualized in Figure 3–1.[3] This diagram shows the marketing information system

---

[2] Samuel V. Smith, Richard H. Brien, and James E. Stafford, eds., *Readings in Marketing Information Systems* (Boston: Houghton Mifflin Co., 1968) p. 7. This source is recommended for those wishing additional background on marketing information systems.

[3] Adapted from Philip Kotler, *Marketing Management: Analysis, Planning, and Control*, 2nd ed., 1972, pp. 294–96. Reprinted by permission of Prentice-Hall, Inc., Englewood Cliffs, N.J.

as the connecting link between the environment and the marketing executive. The system generates a *marketing data flow* concerning the noncontrollable variables in the environment. The marketing information system converts this flow of data into a *marketing information flow* which is made available to marketing executives for use in planning, execution, and control. Using this information, the executives then develop *marketing plans and strategies* which result in a flow of information back to certain elements in the environment.

FIGURE 3–1
Components of the marketing information system

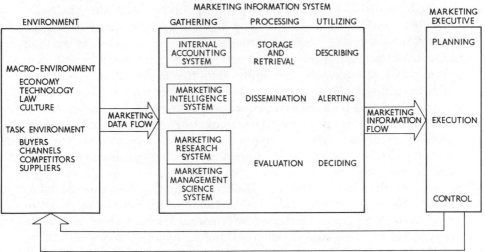

Source: Adapted from Philip Kotler, *Marketing Management: Analysis, Planning and Control* 2d ed. 1972, p. 295. Reprinted by permission of Prentice-Hall, Inc., (Englewood Cliffs, N.J.

As Figure 3–1 indicates, a marketing information system includes four subsystems: (1) the *internal accounting system* which provides measures of current activity and performance, (2) the *marketing intelligence system* which gathers information on developments in the environment and makes it available to executives, (3) the *marketing research system* which gathers, evaluates, and reports information required by executives for problem solving, planning, and the development of marketing strategy, and (4) the *marketing management-science system* which assists executives in analyzing complex marketing problems and operations often through the use of analytical models.

Only a limited proportion of the number of companies in the United States have advanced marketing management systems designed to provide the executives with the types of information described above. Nevertheless, it is clear that a carefully designed marketing information system may provide executives with important data on the qualitative and quantitative aspects of demand which is required in planning marketing strategy.

Even where sophisticated marketing information systems are available, however, there is still a problem in getting executives to integrate the resulting flow of data into the decision-making process. Especially, we are concerned at this point in how to get marketing executives to seek and use the best information on demand which it is profitable to secure. How can this problem be dealt with? Present and future executives are more likely to utilize demand information effectively if they have a personal understanding of the new concepts, skills, and methods available to marketing researchers today. According to Newman, the problem of supplementing limited backgrounds will require several measures: (1) Such information may be provided to existing executives through specially designed management development programs; (2) Management can bring into the organization researchers who have up-to-date technical backgrounds, and who are qualified by training and skill to be effective educators, as they work with key executives from day to day; (3) The marketing managers of tomorrow (today's students) may be supplied with the necessary background through electing well-planned courses in the various business schools that prepare students for marketing careers.[4]

One of the objectives of this book, accordingly, is to provide background on new concepts, skills, and methods which may be made available through a modern marketing information system to help the executive in his planning and decision-making activities. Our understanding of the prospective buyer has been vastly improved in the past 25 years through research, making wider use of concepts and research methods adapted from psychology, sociology, and cultural anthropology (the behavioral sciences). Likewise, substantial progress has been made in expanding the theoretical structure that helps us to understand buyer behavior. A number of models of buyer behavior have resulted, which help to identify both the internal and external variables acting upon the prospective buyer. As a means of providing this essential personal knowledge, accordingly, we shall now turn to a discussion of certain fundamental concepts that help us to understand buyer behavior.

Consumer goods

In considering the problem of buyer behavior, it will be helpful to discuss the factors that influence the purchase of consumer goods separately from those resulting in the purchase of industrial goods. Con-

---

[4] Adapted by permission from Newman, "Put Research into Marketing Decisions," pp. 110–11.

sumer goods are those destined for use by ultimate consumers or house-holds, and these goods are in such form that they can be used without commercial processing. Industrial goods are products destined to be sold primarily for use in producing other goods or rendering services, as contrasted with goods destined to be sold primarily to the ultimate consumer.[5] Since executives responsible for purchasing industrial goods are professionals who make their decisions in the context of a complex organization, the factors that influence their buying actions tend to differ considerably from those that influence the buying behavior of the ulti-mate consumer. Accordingly, we shall deal with consumer buyer be-havior first and then turn to a consideration of the behavior of the industrial buyer in Chapter 5.

As a means of organizing our discussion, it will be helpful to conceive of consumer buyer behavior essentially as a decision-making process, although it will be recognized that experience leads the consumer to make many purchases by habit, as a means of conserving time and energy. We shall then discuss some of the key concepts which help the marketer to understand buyer behavior and which are useful in guiding research designed to assist executives in deciding how best to influence purchase through product changes, price changes, and promo-tional effort.

Consumer behavior as a decision process

In analyzing consumer buying behavior we can distinguish two broad types of approaches: (1) problem-solving behavior involved in the pur-chase of major items, such as a color television set, or innovations, such as Kellogg's Pop Tarts (a product introduced in 1964 consisting of a tender pastry crust with a flavorful fruit preserve filling); and (2) habitual brand choice which is characteristic of repeat purchases of well-known low-priced products such as cigarettes or coffee. While it is recognized that a considerable portion of buying is done on the basis of habit, we shall give emphasis to the problem-solving (or decision-making) type of behavior which is involved in the buying of innovations or of infrequent, major purchases. The factors influencing choice in such situations are more complex and merit careful analysis. Behavior in-volved in the first purchase of a new type of product, moreover, provides helpful background in understanding the formation of habits which pre-dominate as consumers gain experience with a product such as Pop Tarts and the item appears regularly on the housewife's shopping list.

In the purchase of an innovation or a major item such as a color

---

[5] Reprinted by permission from *Marketing Definitions,* compiled by the Committee on Definitions, American Marketing Association, Ralph S. Alexander, Chairman (pub-lished by American Marketing Association, 1960), pp. 11, 14.

television set, accordingly, we can distinguish the following stages in the decision-making process: (1) recognition of a problem (felt need); (2) the search for alternative solutions to the desire; (3) evaluation of alternatives (brands); (4) purchase decision; (5) postpurchase feelings and evaluation. With this decision-making process in mind, let us consider certain key concepts which will help us to understand the behavior of the prospective buyer.

Relation between the individual and his environment

The problem with which we are concerned is why some consumers buy a particular brand, why others do not, and how nonusers can be led to switch to it. It will help us to understand such behavior if we start with the following simplified equation:

$$B = f(P,E).$$

That is, any given type of behavior (such as the purchase of an RCA color television set) is a function of the interplay between the consumer's personal makeup, P (personality) and his perception of the environmental situation (E). Thus, any given brand is one possible choice which the consumer might make among other brands in the same category, and even among other kinds of products. Allowing for external situational influences which might have a bearing on buying behavior, we can understand the consumer's decision if we can assess the hold the brand has on its current consumers as well as the appeal it might offer to its most likely prospects. We can do this by relating the consumer's perception of the brand to his "needs."

In our analysis, therefore, we shall deal first with the individual consumer and his "needs" and "attitudes." We shall then consider the influence of the consumer's perception of the environment upon his buying behavior.

The individual consumer

Basic needs or motives

The starting point in the purchase decision-making process is the recognition of a need (or a buying motive). Motives are "all those inner striving conditions variously described as wishes, desires, needs, drives, and the like. . . . . Formally, then, a motive is an inner state that energizes, activates, or moves (hence 'motivation'), and that directs or channels behavior toward goals. . . . Hunger, the quest for power or status, the desire to land on the moon or to own a new car—all these are motives according to this definition." Goals, in turn, may be thought of as "the object, condition, or activity toward which the motive is directed, in short, that which will satisfy or reduce the striving."[6]

Motivational theory received its greatest impetus from Freud. Nearly all theorists who have worked with clinical data have accepted part of the Freudian scheme but have rejected other portions.[7] One of the more recent theories is that developed by Maslow, who has integrated most of the leading approaches to motivation into an overall scheme designed to conform to the known facts—clinical and observational, as well as experimental. He refers to his synthesis as a "holistic-dynamic theory." It is especially interesting to marketing people, since it is based primarily upon a study of normal people rather than the abnormal subjects who have been the concern of most other theorists.

Maslow classifies motivational life in terms of fundamental needs or goals, rather than in terms of any listing of drives in the ordinary sense of instigation (the "pulls" rather than the "pushes"). He lists the following five levels of needs, arranged in order of their basic importance to the individual:[8]

1. The physiological needs—for example, to satisfy hunger and thirst.
2. The safety needs—for example, security, order, and stability.
3. The belongingness and love needs—such as affection and identification.
4. The esteem needs—such as prestige, success, and self-respect.
5. The need for self-actualization—to do what one is best fitted for, for example.

Also identified are two classes of cognitive needs, which are not definitely located in the need hierarchy but which are believed to exist perhaps as a function of intelligence and of gratification fairly high up the scale of lower order needs:

6. The desire to know and understand (an essential precondition to the satisfaction of basic needs).
7. The aesthetic needs—for example, the craving for beauty.

Maslow believes that the five basic needs develop in such a way that the most important—that is, the physiological needs—must be satisfied before the safety needs, which are next in importance, can fully

---

[6] Reprinted by permission from Bernard Berelson and Gary A. Steiner, *Human Behavior* (New York: Harcourt, Brace & World, Inc., 1964), pp. 239–40.

[7] See D. C. McClelland, *Personality* (New York: Dryden Press, 1951), pp. 388–410, for a brief summary of Freud's motivational system, an evaluation of his conceptual scheme, as well as contributions of other scholars to motivational theory.

[8] Adaptation of "The Basic Needs," pp. 80–101 in *Motivation and Personality* by A. H. Maslow. Copyright 1954 by Harper & Row, Publishers, Inc. Reprinted by permission of the publishers.

emerge in a person's development; and so on up the ladder from the lower needs (most important) to the higher needs (least important) in the hierarchy.

For example, he explains that the physiological needs are the most prepotent of all needs.[9]

What this means specifically is that in the human being who is missing everything in life in an extreme fashion, it is most likely that the major motivation would be the physiological needs rather than any others. A person who is lacking food, safety, love, and esteem would most probably hunger for food more strongly than for anything else. . . .

It is quite true that man lives by bread alone—when there is no bread. But what happens to man's desires when there is plenty of bread and when his belly is chronically filled? *At once other and (higher) needs emerge* and these, rather than physiological hungers, dominate the organism. And when these in turn are satisfied, again new (and still higher) needs emerge, and so on. This is what we mean by saying that the basic human needs are organized into a hierarchy of relative prepotency.

Maslow explains that the need hierarchy is not as rigid as may be implied by the above explanation. While most people feel the needs in about the order indicated, there may be exceptions in individual cases. Also, it would be a mistake to conclude that each need must be satisfied 100 percent before the next need emerges. Instead, most members of our society who are normal are partially satisfied in all their basic needs and partially unsatisfied in all their basic needs at the same time. A more realistic description of the hierarchy would be in terms of decreasing percentages of satisfaction as we go up the hierarchy of prepotency. To illustrate, it is as if the average citizen is satisfied perhaps 85 percent in his physiological needs, 70 percent in his safety needs, 50 percent in his love needs, 40 percent in his self-esteem needs, and 10 percent in his self-actualization needs.

According to Maslow, these basic needs are neither necessarily conscious nor unconscious. In the average person, however, they are more often unconscious than conscious. Moreover, these needs must be understood not to be *exclusive* or single determiners of certain kinds of behavior. For example, one may make love not only for pure sexual release but also to convince oneself of one's masculinity, to make a conquest, to feel powerful, or to win more basic affection.

One of the problems encountered in the use of the above list of motives is that we can all think of other needs that do not fit neatly into the seven classifications listed above.[10] For example, what about

---

[9] Ibid., pp. 82, 83.

[10] This discussion is based upon James H. Myers and William H. Reynolds, *Consumer Behavior and Marketing Management* (Boston: Houghton Mifflin Co., 1967), pp. 89–91. Used by permission.

the desire for maturity among young people? Where does simple hedonism (seeking pleasure, avoiding pain) fit? Also, what about instrumental needs—the desire for goal objectives which help us perform various tasks such as mowing a lawn, washing dishes, or getting to work on time?

Another difficulty is to fit the purchase of each product neatly into a single motive category. Consider the following examples:

1. A man buys an expensive Omega wristwatch for a combination of instrumental and esteem needs.
2. A couple joins a country club to satisfy both belongingness and personal interest needs (tennis, golf, swimming).
3. A girl joins a "Great Books" discussion group both to satisfy the desire to know and to belong (her friends have joined).

Then too, different motives can lead to identical buying behavior and, conversely, entirely different buying decisions can be traced back to identical motivations. Three neighbors might satisfy their safety needs in three different ways, as follows: One might install seat belts in his automobile, another might buy accident insurance, and a third might commute to work by train rather than drive his own car.

The purchase of a color television set, however, might be made by one family primarily to satisfy the desire for entertainment of the husband and wife; by a second family mainly as a means of keeping three small children entertained and quiet during the preparation of dinner or while the father is relaxing after the evening meal; by a third family because others in their social group have purchased color television sets and they feel a need to take similar action to maintain their status (desire to maintain prestige in eyes of others).

It is evident that the marketing executive cannot infer motivation directly from behavior. Also that behavior cannot be predicted in a simple way from motivation. Realization of these complexities has led to the use of research as an aid to gaining an understanding of this important influence upon buying behavior. The task of finding out why people buy, however, is not an easy one. Often people will not, or cannot, explain their actions. Let us examine this problem briefly and indicate some of the approaches which may be taken to deal with it.

Motivation research. In discussing the basic needs that motivate human behavior in all phases of living, Maslow made the point that these motives are more often unconscious than conscious. While this may not be equally true when we restrict our analysis to buying behavior, the problem of getting behind the superficial reasons people give in response to direct questions about their buying motives has long been recognized. Smith clarified the problem by discussing three levels of awareness in the range from consciousness to unconsciousness.[11] The first level deals with conscious and public material which consumers are willing to discuss with an interviewer. A man's desire for a shirt with a collar that won't wrinkle and buttons that won't come off is a typical example.

The second level includes material rarely discussed—that is, motives only slightly outside awareness (preconscious level). Examples would be the desire to impress one's neighbors with an expensive color television set, moving to a better neighborhood as a means of social climbing, driving a high-powered car at high speed in order to let off aggressive impulses, drinking a Coke as a reward after frustrating circumstances, and smoking cigars to feel more masculine. People tend to conceal these motives behind a mask of rationalizations, intellectual discussions and half-truths. They insist that they buy the new television set because the old one had a flicker, move into the high-toned neighborhood because a home in that location represents a better investment, drive fast in order to save time, drink the Coke because it "tastes good," and smoke the cigar because it has a pleasant aroma.

The third level deals with material which is unanalyzed by the individual and not discussed with other people (unconscious level). It includes motives which are not consciously recognized by the consumer and which often would create anxiety if they came into consciousness. Examples of material at this level are the origin of some "common colds" in the need for attention and the loss of security; bargain hunting as the need to outsmart others and to express aggression toward a substitute for the bad, refusing mother; chronic psychogenic constipation as a symbol of withholding from the world (not giving); homosexual and Oedipus tendencies; and numerous personal experiences, sexual and otherwise.

It was to gain access to material in the preconscious and unconscious levels of awareness that marketers turned to the research methods of the behavioral scientists. The methods most commonly used are the informal, qualitative interview, and projective techniques.

The informal, qualitative interview (depth interview) is described as casual, conversational, and free-flowing. The respondent is encouraged to talk at length in the subject area of interest and to express whatever thoughts or feelings come to mind.[12] Generally, there is no list of questions which must be asked in a prescribed way. The emphasis is on

---

[11] From G. H. Smith, *Motivation Research in Advertising and Marketing*, an Advertising Research Foundation Publication (Copyright 1954 by McGraw-Hill Book Co.), pp. 19–21. Used with permission of McGraw-Hill Book Company.

[12] Adapted by permission from Joseph W. Newman, *Motivation Research and Marketing Management* (Boston: Division of Research, Graduate School of Business Administration, Harvard University, 1957), p. 406.

letting the respondent lead the way in order to find out what is important to him and why and to allow opportunity for unanticipated responses to be made. Interviews may run for one or two hours.

From this description it is clear, of course, that the qualitative interview is *not* psychoanalysis. If such interviews are properly conducted and skillfully interpreted, they offer a potentially rewarding source of hypotheses based upon material from the preconscious level of awareness. Forgotten experiences which have been deliberately submerged are not likely to be tapped. Because of the relatively high cost per interview, and the fact that neither questions nor interpretation are standardized, the qualitative approach is most useful during the exploratory stage of a research project.

Projective techniques have two principal characteristics: (1) Their specific purpose is not apparent. (2) The projective device is ambiguous—i.e., it contains no specific meaning; it can be interpreted in different ways. The object is to find out what meanings the respondent will read into it. The underlying assumption is that in responding promptly, the consumer will reveal something of himself—his thoughts, feelings, values, and needs. The main principle which is assumed to be at work is that of *projection,* or the unconscious imputation to others of the characteristics of oneself. Free association may also come into play, so that the resulting chain of thoughts is related in meaning and revealing about the respondent.

Projective devices may serve two main objectives: (1) to learn of the important ideas and feelings people have toward the product or brand under investigation; (2) to learn something about the personality characteristics of the consumer.

The kinds of projective techniques commonly used in motivation research are word association, incomplete sentences, narrative projection, cartoons, requests for descriptions of others, and picture responses (adaptations of the Thematic Apperception Test).[13]

Skillfully designed projectives, properly administered, are helpful in approaching difficult topics and may secure motivational material of considerable depth. Even where material desired is at the conscious level, they are more likely than direct questions to produce full and valid responses. Where unstructured stimuli are used, the problem of interpretation will require about the same degree of skill as does the qualitative interview. This type of projective is most useful at the exploratory stage of research. Where more structured types of projectives are used, they are suitable for testing hypotheses during the second phase of the project, since they lend themselves to sampling on a nationwide scale.

---

[13] For a discussion of projective techniques, including examples, see ibid., pp. 424–40.

As soon as promising hypotheses are developed, direct questions may also be devised to help test these ideas during the second phase of research. Indeed, there is no point in using a projective device to test a motivational hypothesis where a direct question can be devised which would do the job equally well. The direct question is usually less costly to administer and the resulting findings easier to interpret.

Then, too, the very open research approaches (such as the qualitative interview) tend to be strongest where those which restrict response (the direct question) are weakest, and vice versa. Benefits may therefore be realized by combining these various approaches in a motivation research project and from using other techniques of a more intermediate character as well.

One of the criticisms of motivation studies employing behavioral science techniques relates to the size and composition of the sample of consumers interviewed in such research. Clearly, this is an important matter which must be handled on a sound, scientific basis. During the exploratory stage of research, when hypotheses are being sought, much benefit may be derived from a relatively small number of interviews using the informal qualitative approach or carefully designed projective techniques. If the findings are labeled "hypotheses" and are treated as such, the requirements of sound research are met.

In the second stage of the research project, however, these hypotheses should be subjected to careful testing by appropriate procedures. Well-designed, direct questions or carefully prepared projective techniques, or both, may be used at this stage. At this point, however, the sample should be representative of the consumers who make up the market for the brand and should be large enough to yield a satisfactory degree of accuracy. This is essential so that the findings may be projected to that consumer population with which the seller is concerned.

Where the nature of the product and the nature of the marketing mix permit, it is good practice to incorporate the findings of a motivation research study in an actual selling or advertising campaign and conduct a test to determine the relative effectiveness of the new appeal as compared with that previously used. Validation tests of this sort, if properly conducted under favorable circumstances, may provide a much needed measure of the value of motivational studies.

Attitudes

While it is true that the consumer's motives tend to activate behavior which results eventually in a purchase, the previous discussion indicates that behavior cannot be predicted in a simple way from motivations. Other intervening factors internal to the individual also come into play, factors that tend to influence the consumer's perception of the various goal objects (products, brands) which may be utilized to satisfy his desires. These intervening variables include the consumer's attitudes, self-image, and traits (habits). Let us turn to a consideration of the consumer's values or attitudes.

As mentioned earlier, the consumer purchase decision process begins with the identification of a need to be satisfied. After the desire has been aroused, the next step is to evaluate different products or services as ways of satisfying this need. The decision to buy a particular product or service is then followed by the choice of the brand or the selection of the supplier of the service. Consumer attitudes play an important part in the process of evaluation of both (1) alternative products or services as means of satisfying the desire, and (2) the choice of the brand to be purchased or the supplier to be patronized. Thus, attitudes directly affect purchase decisions.

"Attitude is the predisposition of the individual to evaluate some symbol or object or aspect of his world in a favorable or unfavorable manner. Opinion is the verbal expression of an attitude, but attitudes can also be expressed in nonverbal behavior." Attitudes have two important dimensions: (1) an "affective, or feeling, core of liking or disliking"; (2) "cognitive, or belief, elements which describe the object of the attitude, its characteristics, and its relations to other objects." Included in the latter would be evaluative beliefs which attribute to the object good or bad, desirable or undesirable, qualities. "All attitudes thus include beliefs, but not all beliefs are attitudes."[14]

Attitudes also have a third dimension which is important for marketing—an implied readiness for some kind of action toward the object of the attitude. For example, if a consumer has a favorable attitude toward Coca-Cola, there is an implication that this individual is more likely to buy this brand than alternative competing brands. This action tendency suggests a relationship with the motivational factors discussed previously and is an important consideration in understanding the buying process.

How are attitudes formed? To a very considerable extent they are learned in the process of interaction with other people. Factors which tend to develop and change attitudes may include the following: (1) In the satisfaction of his basic desires, the individual will develop favorable attitudes toward people and objects which satisfy his needs and unfavorable attitudes toward those which block attainment. (2) Attitudes are based in part upon the kind and amount of information which the individual receives and upon the nature of the source of this information. (3) Many attitudes held by individuals come either directly or indirectly

[14] Adapted by permission from D. Katz, "The Functional Approach to the Study of Attitudes," *Public Opinion Quarterly*, vol. 24 (Summer 1960), pp. 163–204. For a broader *concept of* "attitudes" see McClelland, *Personality*, chap. 8.

from the groups of which he is a member—for example, family, work, and social. (4) Personality factors (such as intelligence, appearance, activity levels, withdrawal tendencies, and dominance) have some effect upon attitudes. (5) Actual experience with the object—favorable or unfavorable—will have a profound effect upon attitudes toward it.[15]

Evidence on the relationship between consumer attitudes and their buying decisions comes from the work of the Survey Research Center of The University of Michigan. The Center has been making surveys of consumer finances since 1946. The information is secured through annual personal interviews with the head of each spending unit in a national sample of dwelling units selected by area probability sampling to represent the population of the United States. Through these surveys, data are gathered on consumer attitudes; income; ownership, purchases, and purchase plans of automobiles, durable goods, and houses; assets; debts; and personal characteristics. Our special interest is the Center's studies dealing with the measurement of consumer attitudes and their relationship to spending.

Two measures of attitudes toward spending are used by the Center. The primary measure is an index of consumer attitudes based upon answers to six attitudinal questions: (1) whether the family is better or worse off than a year earlier; (2) its personal financial expectations for the coming year; (3) its one-year expectations regarding business conditions; (4) its longer range economic outlook; (5) its appraisal of buying conditions for household goods and clothing; and (6) price expectations. The six components of the index have equal weight.

A second measure of attitudes toward spending is an index of buying intentions. Data have been collected on expressed intentions to buy houses, cars, and durable household goods; to make home improvements or repairs; and to make major nondurable goods expenditures. Only plans which respondents rated as having at least a fair chance of fulfillment were considered.

To what extent do consumer attitudes influence spending? According to Katona, a graphical comparison of disposable consumer income, consumer attitudes and durable goods sales over an eight-year period leads to the following conclusions:[16]

Sometimes attitudes change autonomously and indicate changes in demand for consumer durables which cannot be explained by changes in income or other traditional financial data; sometimes attitudes are influenced by past developments in incomes, production, sales, and the like, and do not contribute

[15] Adapted from D. Krech, R. S. Crutchfield and E. L. Ballachey, *Individual and Society* (Copyright 1962 by McGraw-Hill Book Co.), chap. 6. Used with permission of McGraw-Hill Book Company.

[16] From George Katona, *The Powerful Consumer* (Copyright 1960 by McGraw-Hill Book Co.), pp. 52–53. Used with permission of McGraw-Hill Book Company.

significant new information. It seems probable that the former is the case when the impending changes in economic trends are substantial.

It is always possible to translate a graphical presentation of correspondence between sets of data . . . into an algebraic equation. Thereby a measure of the degree of correspondence is obtained. . . . It may be reported that a substantial proportion of the fluctuations in expenditures on durables is explained by the fluctuations in the index of consumer attitudes. The contribution of changes in the income level to the explanation of fluctuations in sales is very much smaller.

Thus, on the basis of six years of study of changes in consumer attitudes, this conclusion emerges: Changes in consumer attitudes are advance indications of changes in consumer spending on durable goods and make a net contribution to the prediction of such spending after the influence of income has been taken into account.

The work of the Survey Research Center deals with the relation of consumer attitudes to primary demand—i.e. to the purchase of *alternative* types of products such as automobiles, durable goods, and houses. Let us now consider the relationship between attitudes and the purchases of individual brands. A study by Seymour Banks provides interesting evidence on this point. Banks collected data from a representative panel of 465 housewives in Chicago during the period April–June. Each respondent was interviewed twice, the second interview coming three weeks after the first. During this three-week period, respondents reported purchases weekly by mail. The first interview was used to obtain information on brands on hand, preference statements for brands, and a statement of purchase intentions for seven classes of household products. The products used were scouring cleanser, coffee, ice cream, peanut butter, potato chips, mayonnaise and salad dressing, and catsup.

During the second interview, preference statements were collected again for brands of scouring cleanser and coffee. In addition, the respondents were asked to give preference scores on the product attributes of these brands. Also, if the housewife had failed to buy according to her stated intentions, she was asked why.

A brief summary of the results is as follows:[17]

1.   It was found that brand preference was almost identical with purchase intention; about 96 percent of the panel included their most preferred brands in their purchase intentions.

2.   Preference for brands was a good predictor of purchases; the average coefficient of correlation between preference for a brand and the relative share of purchases obtained by that brand was 0.918 for the seven product classes. Last purchase made and statements of purchase intentions were even better predictors of relative brand purchase by the panel.

---

[17] Reprinted by permission from Seymour Banks, "The Relationships of Brand Preference to Brand Purchase," *Journal of Marketing*, vol. 15 (October 1950), pp. 145–57, published by the American Marketing Association.

3. Preference was a fairly good predictor of purchase for the individual panel member as well as for the entire group. Only 15 percent of the group who stated brand purchase intentions bought brands entirely different from those mentioned. However, another 15 percent performed only partially on their brand purchase intentions. There was much greater variance quantitatively between predicted and actual purchases.

4. As predictors of the number of units to be purchased, the panel fared poorly. Overall, they bought 61.4 percent more units of the seven product classes than they expected. The biggest error was for ice cream; the panel's members bought 2.6 times the predicted amount; the best job of quantitative prediction was for peanut butter, in which they exceeded their predictions by only 12.4 percent.

These findings suggest that brand preference is a good predictor of actual buying behavior for products of the type studied—i.e., convenience goods of low unit price which are purchased frequently. Failure to make intended purchases was explained by price reductions on competing brands, item out of stock, and desire for change. Variations in the actual amounts purchased as compared to expectations are probably explained, in part, by the impulsive nature of the purchasing of certain products, such as ice cream.

Additional evidence is reported by Alvin A. Achenbaum in discussing an attitude measurement system developed by the marketing research department of Grey Advertising, Inc., over a period of eight years. This system was designed to measure attitude as a predispositional response—one that is indicative of future behavior. According to Achenbaum:[18]

. . . we start with the point of view that attitudes reflect needs or motivation and are predictive of behavior. There is a growing abundance of marketing data which suggest that this is a tenable point of view. . . .

In our own work, we have found in every study we have done—and there has been not a single exception—that there is a very direct relationship between attitudes and usage behavior. [Figure 3–2] shows four random examples from the 25 studies we conducted. As can be seen, the more favorable the attitude, the higher the incidence of usage; the less favorable the attitude, the lower the incidence of usage.

In an effort to inject dynamism into the analysis, we also looked at the relationship with regard to former triers and never triers of the product.

In [Figure 3–3] can be seen that the inverse relationship is true for former users. As we would expect, the more unfavorable people are toward a product, the more likely they are to stop using it. The interesting thing is that if you look at people who have never tried the product, their attitudes tend to fall in a normally shaped curve [see Figure 3–4].

---

[18] Reprinted by permission from Alvin A. Achenbaum, "Knowledge Is a Thing Called Measurement," in *Attitude Research at Sea*, Lee Adler and Irving Crespi, eds., published by American Marketing Association, 1966, pp. 112–14.

FIGURE 3–2
Relationship between attitudes and usage for selected brands of consumer products

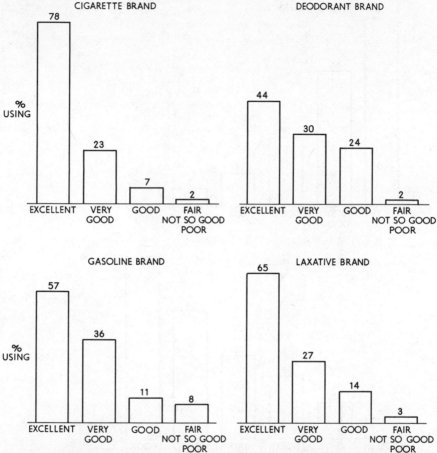

Source: Reprinted by permission from Alvin A. Achenbaum, "Knowledge Is a Thing Called Measurement," in *Attitude Research at Sea*, Lee Adler and Irving Crespi, eds., published by American Marketing Association, 1966, p. 113.

While the above evidence shows that there is a direct relationship between attitudes and usage behavior, Figure 3–4 calls our attention to the finding that the following percentages of "never users" had favorable attitudes toward the product: 14 percent, excellent; 29 percent, very good; 45 percent, good. Why haven't these people purchased the brand? There are a number of possibilities. (1) Considerable time may elapse between the formation of a favorable attitude toward a brand and the date when an actual purchase decision is made. Thus, advertising and word-of-mouth comment may lead a consumer to form a favorable attitude toward the Toyota compact automobile in September, but

FIGURE 3–3
Relationship between attitudes and usage for a dental product

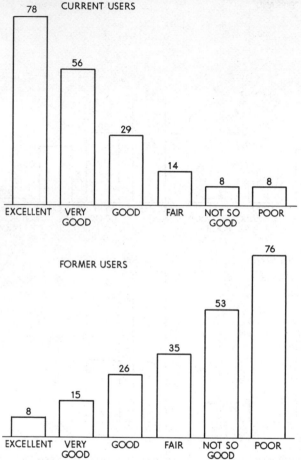

Source: Reprinted by permission from Alvin A. Achenbaum, "Knowledge Is a Thing Called Measurement," in *Attitude Research at Sea*, Lee Adler and Irving Crespi, eds., published by American Marketing Association, 1966, p. 113.

the consumer may then own a year-old Volkswagen which he does not wish to trade in until it is three years old. (2) Lack of money may lead the consumer to purchase a less expensive brand which is his second choice, rather than the more expensive brand which he really prefers. (For example, he may buy a Panasonic color television set at a lower price than he would have to pay for the RCA model that he really prefers.) (3) The preferred brand (e.g. Maxim freeze-dried coffee) may be out of stock when the housewife goes to make a purchase and she may, therefore, accept a substitute which does not rate as high

FIGURE 3–4
Relationship between attitudes and usage for a dental product

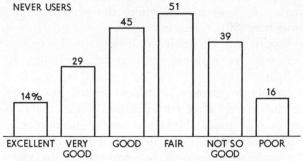

NEVER USERS

Source: Reprinted by permission from Alvin A. Achenbaum, "Knowledge Is a Thing Called Measurement," in *Attitude Research at Sea*, Lee Adler and Irving Crespi, eds., published by American Marketing Association, 1966, p. 114.

on her preference scale, rather than seek the desired brand in another store. (4) Attitudes may be more favorable to a competing brand than to the one "never tried." For example, a portion of the 45 percent who rated the brand "good" may rate a competing brand "excellent," and some of these may buy it when a purchase decision is finally made. (5) Other inhibiting forces such as social influences and time pressure may also prevent the purchase of the preferred brand. In recognition of the fact that a number of forces other than consumer attitudes influence the purchase decision, Howard has suggested the measurement of intention (to buy) as an intervening construct in explaining buyer behavior.[19]

Attitude change. The previous discussion has indicated that consumer attitudes have an important influence on the purchase decision. If this is the case, the question then arises as to how the firm can lead prospective buyers to adopt more favorable attitudes toward the type of product he manufactures (for example, air conditioners) as well as to his own brand, as opposed to competing brands (for example, Frigidaire versus General Electric).[20]

There are two basic approaches to this problem. One is to undertake research by which to determine current desires and attitudes of prospective buyers toward the product and the brand. Once this information is known, the firm may redesign its product so that it more adequately conforms to these desires and preferences. The firm may also modify its promotional approach in the light of this information.

[19] The relationship between the constructs of attitude, intention, and purchase are discussed in Chapter 4. (See also John A. Howard and Jagdish N. Sheth, *The Theory of Buyer Behavior*, New York: John Wiley & Sons, Inc., 1969, pp. 132–33.)

[20] Based upon Myers and Reynolds, *Consumer Behavior*, pp. 165–66.

A second method is to attempt to change the consumer's desires and attitudes toward the product and the brand. This is a more difficult task than the first, but it is necessary where the product represents an innovation, as was true with television when it was first introduced commercially after World War II. Such would also be the case where a product used primarily by women, such as hair coloring, is first marketed for use by men.

If the marketer wishes to change attitudes toward his brand, his approach should be chosen only after consideration of the factors which influence the formation of attitudes: biological needs, information, group affiliations, personality, and experience. Analysis indicates that certain of these attitude-forming factors cannot be changed by the marketer. Certainly this is true of basic needs, personality characteristics, and group affiliations. Under certain circumstances, experience of consumers with the brand may be changed. For example, people who have never used it may be given free samples for trial—provided the item is a consumable product of low unit price subject to repeat purchase (for example, toothpaste). If the product is superior, and its want-satisfying qualities may be evaluated through usage, experience with a free sample may indeed modify consumer attitudes toward the brand. Distribution of free samples, however, is not suitable for all types of products.

Of the various attitude-forming factors, therefore, the possibility of changing the information which the consumer has about the brand is often the most effective approach. The effective use of communication through personal selling, promotion, and publicity, therefore, is worthy of careful study.[21] While space does not permit a discussion of this topic here, we shall deal with the subject of building an effective promotional mix by which to influence consumer desires and attitudes in Chapter 11. Crane summarizes a discussion of this topic, however, as follows:[22]

Attitudes are not easy to change. First, because there seems to be a tendency to restore balance when it is upset and, second, because there is a tendency to avoid an upset by avoiding exposures to messages inconsistent with the existing attitude structure. Accidental exposure does occur, however. A communicator who knows existing attitude structures and the ways in which people react to their upset, can choose the method and point of attack most likely to produce, in the end, the new attitude structure most favorable to his objectives.

---

[21] For an interesting discussion of five broad strategy alternatives which advertisers may use to change attitudinal structures, see Harper W. Boyd, Jr., Michael L. Ray, and Edward C. Strong, "An Attitudinal Framework for Advertising Strategy," *Journal of Marketing*, April 1972, vol. 36, no. 2, pp. 27–33.

[22] Reprinted by permission from E. Crane, *Marketing Communications* (New York: John Wiley & Sons, Inc., 1965), p. 66. See this source for a discussion of ways to change attitudes through communications.

Attitude measurements.[23]   A wide variety of methods is available for the measurement of attitudes. Here we shall limit our discussion to identifying certain of the more important approaches. Those interested in more background should consult the reference listed in footnote 23.

Projective techniques and qualitative interviews, discussed earlier, are useful in the determination of attitudes as well as motives. In addition, attitude scaling can be used to determine the position of an individual with respect to a topic, event, retail store, or brand. It can also be used to chart the entire population, or some subgroup, to determine distribution of spread of opinion about some topic. For example, what percentage of teen-age boys are hi-fi enthusiasts?

The following are some of the more useful attitude scaling techniques:

1.   Continuum of feeling (for example, from "extremely important" in steps to "of no importance"; from "extremely good" to "extremely bad"; from "extremely sure" to "not sure at all").

2.   Paired comparisons—items, colors, products, brands may be presented in pairs to consumers for comparison.

3.   Rank order—the investigator may present all items to be compared (for example, alternative advertisements) at once and ask respondents to rank them in the order of their preference.

4.   Statement selection or sorting—attitudes may be measured by having individuals respond to verbal expressions about a given topic, for example, "Almost every advertisement is honest." When a large number of such statements have been developed for a given topic, as, for example, government regulation of advertising, attitudes may be measured through several alternative approaches: (*a*) Thurstone scaling—statements are sorted into piles ranging from "most favorable" to "most unfavorable"; each statement is then assigned a point value; consumers are then asked to select statements with which they agree; attitude scores for each individual are then calculated. (*b*) Likert scaling—a scale indicating strength of agreement ("agree very strongly," "agree fairly strongly," etc.) is presented. Each respondent rates each statement according to how strongly he agrees or disagrees; the score for each is determined from both the direction and strength of the respondent's feelings toward the various statements.

5.   Osgood Semantic Differential—pairs of words, or statements of opposite meaning which might describe a product are presented to respondents (for example, ball-point pens might be rated as slow-fast, loose-tight, faddish-conservative, simple-complex). The respondent rates each of several products on each dimension by placing a check at the

---

[23] This discussion based on Myers and Reynolds, *Consumer Behavior*, pp. 150–57. Used by permission. See also, J. P. Guilford, *Psychometric Methods* (New York: McGraw-Hill Book Co., 1954), and C. E. Osgood, G. J. Suci, and P. N. Tannenbaum, *The Measurement of Meaning* (Urbana, Ill.: University of Illinois Press, 1957).

place on a line which indicates his feelings. The average of the checks is plotted as a profile for each product.

According to Myers and Reynolds, attitude scaling techniques constitute a very powerful means of acquiring insights into the minds of consumers, and they are widely used in marketing studies today.

Cognitive dissonance[24]

We have previously noted that attitudes (brand preference) directly affect purchases. Once a purchase decision has been made, however, there is evidence which suggests that this action may itself also influence preference for the brand purchased and hence subsequent buying behavior. This idea is suggested by the theory of cognitive dissonance.

The theory holds that the individual—the consumer—strives toward consistency within himself. His attitudes, values, and beliefs are ordered into clusters that are internally consistent, and consistent with his behavior. Prior to making any major decision, such as the purchase of a new color television set, the consumer is faced with the necessity of choosing between two or more alternatives—for example, Zenith or RCA—both of which have attractive features. Unfortunately, after making the decision the consumer is often faced with uncertainty as to the wisdom of his choice. He may wonder if he shouldn't have purchased an RCA television set instead of a Zenith.

These doubts that remain after purchase are identified as states of "cognitive dissonance" by Festinger. Even the worst of alternatives has some positive features, and the moment a decision is made, the positive features of the rejected alternative and the negative features of the selected alternative are dissonant with the individual's action. The feeling of inconsistency or dissonance is uncomfortable and demands reduction. According to Festinger, therefore, when there is cognitive dissonance (i.e., perceived incongruity) between the person's own attitudes and his behavior, the person may tend to reduce the dissonance by appropriate changes in attitudes. In addition, the person will actively avoid situations and information which would be likely to increase dissonance.[25]

An interesting survey testing the reactions of smokers and nonsmokers to the U.S. Surgeon General's report linking cigarette smoking to various illnesses, including cancer, illustrates the behavior of consumers when cognitive dissonance exists. The survey was made by Kassarjian and Cohen three months after the release of the Surgeon General's report.

---

[24] This section is based upon H. H. Kassarjian and Joel B. Cohen, "Cognitive Dissonance and Consumer Behavior," reprinted by permission from *California Management Review*, vol. 8, no. 1 (Fall 1965), pp. 55–64. Copyright 1965 by the Regents of the University of California.

[25] For additional background, see L. Festinger, *A Theory of Cognitive Dissonance* (Stanford, Calif.: Stanford University Press, 1957), chap. 1, pp. 1–31.

Personal interviews were conducted with a probability sample of residents of Santa Monica, California. Since there had been wide dissemination given to the Surgeon General's findings in mass media of communication, cigarette smokers were in a state of dissonance. Smoking behavior is clearly dissonant with the need to survive or stay healthy. Accordingly, respondents were asked questions to test hypotheses concerning their reactions in reducing dissonance.

The results were as follows: (1) Among respondents who were smoking at the time of the study, 75 percent stated that they had made no serious attempt in the previous year to stop smoking, while about 25 percent had made one or more serious attempts at dissonance reduction in this manner during the same period. (2) The confirmed smoker appears to be behaving consistently with his belief system by continuing to smoke. He has justified his rationality either (*a*) by disassociating his responsibility over the decision; (*b*) by denying, distorting, misperceiving, or minimizing the degree of health hazard involved; (*c*) and/or by selectively drawing out new cognitions and new information that will reduce the inconsistency of his behavior and achieve consonance in his own cognitive world.[26]

Note that one method of reducing dissonance is selective exposure to new information that tends to support the individual's behavior. In another study, 125 male residents of Minneapolis were interviewed to determine the extent to which they selectively exposed themselves to information about the cars they owned. Sixty-five were new-car owners, and the rest owned cars three or more years old. Results of the experiment indicated, as dissonance theory would predict, that new-car owners recalled reading significantly more advertisements of their own car than did old-car owners. When offered information about different makes of cars, a few more new-car owners than old-car owners elected to read about their own make. The difference was not statistically reliable, but it was in the expected direction.[27]

In contrast, Engel interviewed two groups of consumers in Ann Arbor, Michigan, to test the hypothesis that more recent purchasers of Chevrolets read advertisements featuring this brand than those who have not bought new Chevrolets.[28] On the basis of unaided recall, 42 percent of new owners mentioned they had seen the Chevrolet dealer's advertisements while only 23 percent of the nonowners had. When the "recognition" approach was used in checking readership, however, no significant

---

[26] Kassarjian and Cohen, "Cognitive Dissonance," pp. 55–64.

[27] D. Erlich, I. Guttman, and P. Schonbach, "Postdecision Exposure to Relevant Information," *Journal of Abnormal and Social Psychology,* vol. 54, 1957, pp. 98–102.

[28] Reprinted by permission from James F. Engel, "Are Automobile Purchasers Dissonant Consumers?" *Journal of Marketing,* vol. 27, no. 2, April 1963, pp. 55–58, published by the American Marketing Association.

difference was found as between new owners and nonowners. Checks to determine whether new Chevrolet owners were dissonant, however, were negative. There was little indication of anxiety by Chevrolet owners following a purchase decision. This raises a question as to whether dissonance may be expected to occur following a consumer's free choice among alternative brands which may appear to the individual to be almost equally attractive.

There is also a problem of research methodology involved in this type of study. Did the buyer notice more ads for his chosen brand *after* the purchase than before he was faced with the necessity for making the decision? Such a research design would appear to be needed to discover the existence of dissonance. A single cross-sectional study design does not adequately demonstrate the existence of dissonance.

Judging from the evidence presented above, we cannot be sure that cognitive dissonance occurs in every buying situation. Better methods of measuring the occurrence of this phenomenon are needed to resolve the question. In the meantime the study on cigarette smoking, and other experiments, tend to support the theory of cognitive dissonance in other areas. There is enough evidence from such studies to suggest that cognitive dissonance may occur in certain types of buying situations, if only we could measure it. Where it does exist, the consumer's efforts to reduce dissonance may tend to strengthen preference for the brand purchased.[29]

Learning

After a need is recognized, alternative products and brands are evaluated, and a purchase has been made, the consumer arrives at one of the most significant aspects of the entire sequence. It is with the use of the brand that some degree of satisfaction of the initial need will be experienced. If the consumption of the brand leads to gratification of the initiating needs, then "reinforcement" will occur. If the same need is aroused at some later date, the consumer will tend to repeat the purchase of the same product and brand. We have described here the process of "learning," which is defined as any change in behavior which results from experience or practice in similar situations (as opposed to changes due to physiological variations such as growth, deterioration, hunger, fatigue, effects of alcohol, or sleep).[30]

We are especially interested in the influence of the learning process upon attitudes toward both alternative types of products and brands,

---

[29] For suggestions as to the circumstances under which dissonance reduction may be useful in increasing the repurchase probability of a purchased brand, see Sadaomi Oshikawa, "Can Cognitive Dissonance Theory Explain Consumer Behavior?" *Journal of Marketing*, vol. 33, October 1969, pp. 44–49.

[30] Berelson and Steiner, *Human Behavior*, p. 135.

i.e., upon brand preference. If Brand A is purchased and yields a high degree of gratification upon usage, then when the same need arises at a later time, the consumer will have an increased tendency to purchase Brand A once again. Each succeeding time that Brand A is purchased and gives satisfaction, additional reinforcement occurs, thus further increasing the probability that Brand A will be selected in the future when the same need arises again. The increasing likelihood that the purchase of Brand A will be repeated is *learning*. Reinforcement is necessary for learning to take place.

Note that the increase in the probability that Brand A will be purchased is related to the number of times the brand has been purchased, has gratified the need, and hence has provided reinforcement. Accordingly, the opportunity for experience, or learning, to influence brand preference tends to be greater for products which are purchased frequently than for those purchased only occasionally, or those purchased once in a lifetime.

It is also important to note that reinforcement depends upon the degree to which the felt need of the consumer is gratified. This underscores the importance of product development and product improvement activities in planning the marketing mix. If the firm decides to produce a product capable of satisfying an important consumer need, and individualizes its brand in ways important to the user, then gratification of desire and reinforcement should follow purchase of the brand.

It is clear from the above discussion that learning theory helps us understand consumer buying behavior. Indeed, theories of stimulus-response learning are an important element in the Howard model of consumer behavior, which is discussed in the next chapter. Still another approach views learning as a probabilistic process, under the assumption that the best predictor of future buying behavior is the sequence, rhythm, and frequency of past purchasing behavior. As an example, Kuehn has developed a mathematical model describing brand-shifting behavior as a probabilistic process and incorporating the effects of past purchases and time elapsed between purchases. This model was tested through empirical research using sequential purchase data from 600 Chicago families over a three-year period. Although space does not permit a discussion of this approach here, it is worthy of careful study.[31]

Conclusion

Buyer behavior information has been shown as an important input for use in planning marketing strategy. Initially, we have limited our

---

[31] See Alfred A. Kuehn, "Consumer Brand Choice as a Learning Process," *Journal of Advertising Research,* vol. 2 (December 1962), pp. 10–17.

analysis to the purchase of consumer goods, but will deal with industrial goods in a later chapter. Consumer buying behavior is treated as a decision-making process involving: (1) recognition of a problem (felt need); (2) the search for alternative solutions to the desire; (3) evaluation of alternatives (brands); (4) purchase decision; (5) postpurchase feelings and evaluation.

In seeking to understand those aspects of the individual consumer's psychological makeup that are relevant for the buying decision, we discussed the concepts of motives, attitudes, cognitive dissonance, and learning. Research methods used to identify the motives that activate the buying process and to measure the attitudes which consumers have with respect to alternative brands have been briefly described and illustrated.

It is recognized, of course, that the purchase decision is also influenced by cultural and social forces in the prospective buyer's environment, as well as by certain factors in the external situation which may facilitate or inhibit the purchase. These influences will be discussed in the following chapter. A comprehensive theory of buyer behavior will also be introduced which serves to tie together both the internal and external variables influencing the buying process.

Questions

1. Distinguish between consumer goods and industrial goods. Into which classification would you place the following products?
   a) A computer manufactured by General Electric.
   b) Smith-Corona typewriter ribbons for portable typewriters.
   c) IBM typewriter ribbons used primarily on office typewriters.
   d) Champion spark plugs (1) sold as original equipment to automobile manufacturers and (2) sold through service stations for replacements.
   e) Bayer aspirin (1) distributed through drug stores and (2) sold to hospitals for patients under treatment there.
2. What needs might the following products or services satisfy? (Use Maslow's list in responding.)
   a) Simba—a new soft drink by Coca-Cola.
   b) *Book of Knowledge* encyclopedia.
   c) Sidewinder General tire (patented puncture sealing).
   d) State Farm Life Insurance.
   e) Panasonic complete stereo system (phonograph and twin speakers).
   f) Dale Carnegie course.
3. Do the needs satisfied by the following products fit into Maslow's seven categories? If not, what new classifications would you suggest?
   a) Ski-Doo Snowmobile ("Makes fun no problem").
   b) Goodyear Polyglas winter tire ("wide, deep tread; is built to keep its grip longer").

    c)   Hormel chili ("It's not exactly tame!").

    d)   Polaroid color camera ("under $50"), ("The 60-second excitement"), (grandfather taking pictures of grandchildren during family outing).

    e)   Right Guard antiperspirant ("When underarm wetness shows up, do you cover up? Check wetness with new Right Guard antiperspirant").

4. *a)*   Give examples of purchases (other than those mentioned in the text) that may satisfy more than one need.

    b)   Illustrate how a given need (for example, belongingness) may be satisfied by purchasing several different products or services.

5. *a)*   In motivation research, what consumer research techniques may be used to get information at the preconscious level of awareness?

    b)   Through what stages should motivation research be carried before substantial sums of money are invested in advertising and promotional efforts? Why?

6. Distinguish between motives and attitudes. How do attitudes affect the purchase decision?

7. To what extent do consumers' attitudes influence purchase decisions:

    a)   Of alternative types of products (for example, color television versus outboard motorboats)?

    b)   Of alternative brands (for example, Maxwell House, Chase & Sanborn, or Hills Bros. coffee)?

8. *a)*   What approaches may be taken in attempting to change consumers' attitudes toward a manufacturer's brand?

    b)   What factors should be considered in deciding which of the approaches identified in (*a*) should be used in a specific instance? Apply these factors to the following situations:

      (1) At one time, Kroehler furniture was purchased primarily by the "common man"—the upper-lower and lower-middle-class families. After having consumer research done by a consultant, the firm wished to modify the brand image so that its line would also appeal to the upper-middle and upper classes.

      (2) Clairol had long sold hair coloring to women successfully. In a recent year the firm introduced Great Day hair coloring for men. Clearly the firm faced a problem in overcoming longstanding attitudes of men believed to be unfavorable to such a product.

9. *a)*   Explain the concept of cognitive dissonance. Give an example to illustrate your explanation.

    b)   In what types of buying situations is cognitive dissonance likely to be of significance?

    c)   What may a manufacturer do to help consumers reduce cognitive dissonance involved in the purchase of his brand?

10. *a)*   What is the definition of learning?

    b)   How does this concept help us to understand consumer buying behavior?

4

Consumer buyer behavior

IN THE FIRST PART of this chapter we continue our discussion of basic concepts by tracing the influence of the environment upon buyer behavior. In the second part we turn to a consideration of a comprehensive model of buyer behavior which ties together the behavioral, situational, and economic variables influencing the buying process. Such a model has potential value in (1) helping the executive understand consumer behavior and the points at which marketing effort may influence the buying process, and (2) facilitating the planning, execution, and analysis of research designed to aid the executive in planning marketing strategy.

Influence of environment upon consumer behavior

In our discussion of buying behavior up to this point, we have focused attention upon the individual consumer. Drawing upon psychology and social psychology, we have traced the influence of motives, attitudes, cognitive dissonance, and learning upon buying decisions. But the individual consumer lives in an environment which exerts important cultural and social influences upon his behavior. Indeed, both motives and attitudes of the consumer are patterned by the culture and the social institutions in which he lives. Accordingly, to assist in explaining certain uniformities in motives and attitudes of consumers which influence their buying behavior, we shall now draw on the fields of anthropology and sociology for a number of helpful concepts relating to the cultural and social influences. We shall consider, first, the concept of *culture*.

Cultural influences

According to Kroeber, "the mass of learned and transmitted motor reactions, habits, techniques, ideas, and values—and the behavior they induce—is what constitutes *culture*." It is all those things about man that are more than just biological or organic and that are also more than merely psychological.[1] It is the man-made part of the environment; the total way of life of a people; the social legacy the individual acquires from his group.[2]

The culture into which a consumer is born, accordingly, provides a good many ready-made solutions to problems growing out of the geographical, biological, and social environment in which he lives. These ready-made solutions are provided in the form of cultural patterns relating to the ideology, role definitions, and socialization procedures of the society in which he lives. These cultural patterns are transmitted to individuals through social institutions, such as the family, school, church, and social class, by means of language, parent's attitudes and behavior, reading, and public school instruction, among others. The end results of this learning process are found in the individual's organization of ideas and values, role perceptions and performance, and maintenance and development conceptions (i.e., need patterns and associated goal objects). Stated differently, the cultural patterns which consumers learn influence their ideas and values, the nature of the roles they play, and the way in which they carry them out, as well as the manner in which their needs and desires are handled.

The influence of culture upon attitudes is illustrated by studies of the correlation between the attitudes a man holds and the religious, ethical, political, and economic institutions under which he lives. For example, it has been found that Jewish college students hold the most liberal attitudes toward the concept of a personal God, toward war, and toward birth; Protestants are intermediate; and Catholics are the most conservative.[3]

An example of the influence of our Early American heritage upon beliefs and attitudes, and hence upon buying behavior, is found in the motivation study dealing with coffee.[4] In the findings it was pointed out that strong remnants of puritanical attitudes are still alive in the American consumer, and they influence his feelings toward coffee. He enjoys coffee but is at the same time convinced that coffee has many

---

[1] A. L. Kroeber, *Anthropology* (New York: Harcourt, Brace & Co., 1948), p. 8.

[2] Clyde Kluckhohn, *Mirror for Man* (New York: Premier Books, 1957), p. 20.

[3] Adapted by permission from D. Krech and R. S. Crutchfield, *Elements of Psychology* (Copyright 1958 by Alfred A. Knopf, Inc.), p. 674.

[4] Adapted by permission from Joseph W. Newman, *Motivation Research and Marketing Management* (Boston: Division of Research, Graduate School of Business Administration, Harvard University, 1957), pp. 214–18.

drawbacks. Thus, he is caught in a coffee conflict. Contributing to this conflict is a punishing attitude toward pleasure, especially sensory pleasure. Any feeling of "sinning" usually is followed by an expectation and fear of "punishment," although the "sinner" may not always be aware of this. According to the consultant, therefore, one of the major tasks of the coffee industry is to help in changing the image of coffee from that of a sinful and escapist beverage to that of a positive and life accepting one.

The same motivation study also provides an illustration of a situation in which the image of the product has lagged behind cultural changes. Since World War II, according to the report, people have become aware of several cultural changes with which coffee has not kept pace: (1) a desire for more gracious living; (2) Americans are moving away from earlier restrictions imposed on enjoying sensory pleasures; (3) a new kind of individualism which has as its goal the expression of one's personality by more individualized consumption, appreciation, and enjoyment of differences and variety. Attitudes toward coffee have lagged behind these trends. The image has become too utilitarian; coffee is related more to nutritional than emotional health; and coffee drinking has become routinized. Hence, there is a need to emphasize the pleasure rather than the utility to be derived from coffee, to stress its sensory pleasures and make it more of a beverage for emotional health.

Culture provides patterns that guide individuals in the satisfaction of their biological needs. Thus, the child learns the diet pattern of his culture, modesty and hygiene of elimination, proper conduct in sexual affairs, patterns of propriety in dress. The requirement for food, for example, is met in every society. But the specific foods which an individual regards as acceptable are determined by his culture. The Chinese, for instance, dislike milk and milk products, while dairy products make up an important part of the American diet.

Culture not only patterns the ways in which people satisfy their needs but also creates desires which exert a strong influence upon their buying behavior. The learned desires of certain consumers for cigarettes or alcohol, for example, may be just as compelling as their requirements for food. So too, the desires for a late-model automobile or television set, which are learned from the American culture, may occupy a position high in the list of products wanted by a newly married couple—perhaps even ahead of the need they may feel for a home of their own.

It is helpful to recognize, also, that within a complex, heterogeneous culture, such as that found in the United States, subcultures exist which are especially relevant to the understanding of buyer behavior.[5] Such

---

[5] For a discussion of subcultural groupings and their significance for marketing strategy, see Thomas S. Robertson, *Consumer Behavior* (Glenview, Ill.: Scott, Foresman and Co., 1970), pp. 102–15.

subcultures may be defined in terms of region, rural or urban residence, ethnic background, or religion, among other factors. Those identified with a subculture tend to think and act alike in certain respects, and this has important implications on their "life style."[6] Recognition of this point has led to experimentation with market segmentation as a means of developing effective marketing strategy adapted to market targets believed to have special promise.

Influence of social class

In addition to being molded by culture, the attitudes and needs of the consumer are patterned by the *social class* to which he belongs. Even though American political ideology is based on the concept that "All men are created equal," studies of many communities in all the regions of the United States clearly demonstrate the presence of a well-defined class structure. This structure is not an abstraction invented by the social scientist, but it is regarded as real by the people in each community and is referred to by them in explaining different ways of thinking and acting among their neighbors and acquaintances.

Pioneering research dealing with the existence of social class in America and how it may be measured was done during the early 1940s by Warner and his associates. This work was done in small communities located in New England (Yankee City), the Midwest (Johnson City), and the Deep South, among others. Warner conceived of social class as "two or more orders of people who are believed to be, and are accordingly ranked by the members of the community, in socially superior and inferior positions."[7] Associated with this definition are the ideas that the individual must participate in the social interaction of the class and must be accepted as a peer by its members. After considerable investigation, Warner and his associates came to the conclusion that a family's position in the social structure of a community is determined by the following criteria: occupation, amount of income, source of income, house type, neighborhood, and education.[8] Further analysis indicated that the accuracy of prediction of social class would not be

---

[6] Life style reflects the overall manner in which people live and spend time and money. It may be measured by (1) the products a person consumes; (2) the person's activities, interests, and opinions. See Jerry Wind, "Life Style Analysis: A New Approach," in *Combined Proceedings 1971 Spring and Fall Conferences,* Fred C. Alvine, ed., American Marketing Association, 1972, pp. 302–5.

[7] Reprinted by permission from W. Lloyd Warner and Paul S. Lunt, *The Social Life of a Modern Community* (New Haven, Conn.: Yale University Press, 1959), pp. 81–91.

[8] Adapted from W. Lloyd Warner, Marchia Meeker, and Kenneth Eells, *Social Class in America* (Torchbook edition), pp. 11–15, 31, 35, 174, 181. Copyright 1919 by Science Research Associates, Inc., Chicago. Copyright © 1960 by Harper & Row, Publishers, Inc. By permission of Harper & Row.

seriously affected by eliminating amount of income and education from the list of criteria, but that some adjustment was desirable to reflect the influence of ethnic and religious factors. Under Warner's approach, individuals are classified as to social class by other people who know them.

Using this research design, Warner identifies six social classes as follows:

Upper-upper (1.4 percent): Members of "old families," the aristocracy of birth and inherited wealth, born into their positions of prestige, with enough wealth to maintain a large house in the best neighborhood.

Lower-upper (1.6 percent): Similar to the upper-upper in costly homes in the best neighborhood and in design for living, but lacking in distinguished ancestry. While their incomes average somewhat larger than families in the upper-upper class, their wealth is newer and it is not inherited.

Upper-middle (10.2 percent): Respectable, achieving, solid citizens of high moral principles and personal integrity; moderately successful business and professional men and their families. Their incomes average somewhat less than the lower-upper class, and these incomes are derived predominantly from salary rather than from invested wealth. Some education and polish is necessary, but lineage is unimportant.

Lower-middle (28.1 percent): Clerks, white-collar workers, small business-men, schoolteachers, foremen in industry; people who live in small homes on side streets; frequently homeowners.

Upper-lower (32.6 percent): "Poor but honest" workers, usually in semi-skilled occupations, who participate less in the educational and other advantages of our society, and who spend a large percentage of their income on food and shelter. This class and the lower-middle class are closely related in tastes, problems, and beliefs. Together, these two classes are regarded as "the common man."

Lower-lower (25.2 percent): Semiskilled and unskilled workers; families who live in the worst homes in poor neighborhoods, people who are often on relief, who have low incomes, and who are lacking in ambition or oppor-tunity to improve their lot. Believed by classes above them to be lazy, shiftless, and irresponsible, while research indicates that many of them are guilty of no more than being poor and lacking in the desire to get ahead.

Warner's work on social class is regarded as a substantial contribution in the field of sociology, but certain aspects of his research approach have been criticized—notably the use of the "reputational" approach in determining an individual's social class and the subjective judgments involved in evaluating two of the index factors: house type and quality of neighborhood. Then, too, other scholars have claimed that studies made in cities of from 10,000 to 20,000 population cannot be justifiably regarded as representative of the United States as a whole.[9]

---

[9] For an evaluation of the work of the Warner school, see Milton M. Gordon, *Social Class in American Sociology* (Durham, N.C.: Duke University Press, 1958), chap. 4.

Hollingshead has developed an objective system of classification of individuals into five major social classes. Individuals and families are placed in classes through the use of his Index of Social Position. This index is based upon three assumptions: (1) that social stratification exists in the community, (2) that status positions are determined mainly by a few commonly accepted cultural characteristics, and (3) that items symbolic of status may be scaled and combined by the use of statistical procedures, so that the researcher can quickly, reliably, and meaningfully stratify the population.

The three indications of status utilized by the Index of Social Position to determine class position are: (1) the residential address of a household, (2) the occupational position of its head, and (3) the years of school the head has completed.[10]

The social class hierarchy which results from Hollingshead's system of classification is shown in Figure 4–1.

FIGURE 4–1
Social class hierarchy

Class	Description	Percentage
I	"Old families," top business management and professional occupations, high incomes, highly educated, expensive homes, the social elite.	3.4
II	Business managers (but not policy formulators), lesser professionals, (engineers, etc.), often college graduates, socially sensitive, "on the way up."	9.0
III	Employees in various salaried administrative pursuits, small business owners, average incomes, high school graduates, modest homes in "good" areas.	21.4
IV	Semiskilled and skilled manual employees, below average incomes, many are homeowners but live in multiple units, many have some high school but did not graduate, often members of minority ethnic group (Italian, Irish, etc.).	48.5
V	Unskilled and semiskilled, low incomes, no savings, live in old tenement areas, most did not finish grade school, "live today, let tomorrow take care of itself."	17.7
	Total	100.0

Source: A. B. Hollingshead and F. C. Redlich, *Social Class and Mental Illness* (New York: John Wiley & Sons, Inc., 1958), pp. *passim*, chap. 10, Appendix 2. Reprinted by permission.

While Hollingshead's system is simpler and more objective than that of Warner, we do not know whether it provides a better representation of the social class structure in the United States. It was developed 17 years later than that of Warner, however, and it does provide a some-

[10] Reprinted by permission from A. B. Hollingshead and F. C. Redlich, *Social Class and Mental Illness* (New York: John Wiley & Sons, Inc., 1958), p. 66.

what more explicit basis for classifying certain families and individuals notably top business management as opposed to middle management.

Our interest, of course, is in the value of social class stratification to the marketing executive. Because Warner's research had been done in smaller communities, there was concern that the same social class system might not exist in more complex metropolitan centers. If some such system did exist, would the Warner research approach uncover it? Then, too, many marketers did not see the relevance of social class to consumer buying behavior, since previous research in this area had been concerned with broad differences in patterns of living, moral codes, and mental illness, as well as other behavioral science goals.

With this in mind, the *Chicago Tribune* undertook several extensive studies during the mid-1950s exploring social class in a metropolitan city and the relevance of this factor to the individual family's buying behavior. The studies were carried out under the direction of Pierre Martineau, Research Director of the *Chicago Tribune*, and W. Lloyd Warner. In this study, interviewing was done in metropolitan Chicago and involved 3,880 households. In carrying out the research, problems were encountered in relating the occupations of Chicago workers to different social classes, in securing house typings, and in working out a suitable scoring system appropriate for a complex metropolitan society. The data finally used to calculate the "Index of Status Characteristics" were: (1) occupation (weighted by 5), sources of income (weighted by 4), and housing type (weighted by 3). Martineau reported the following conclusions:[11]

1. There is a social-class system operative in metropolitan markets, which can be isolated and described.
2. It is important to realize that there are far reaching psychological differences between the various classes.
3. Consumption patterns operate as prestige symbols to define class membership, which is a more significant determinant of economic behavior than mere income. Income has always been the marketer's handiest index to family consumption standards. But it is a far from accurate index. For instance, the bulk of the population in a metropolitan market today will fall in the middle-income ranges. This will comprise not only the traditional white-collar worker, but the unionized craftsman and the semiskilled worker with their tremendous income gains of the past decade. Income-wise, they may be in the same category. But their buying behavior, their tastes, their spending-saving aspirations can be poles apart. Social-class position and mobility-stability dimensions will reflect in much greater depth each individual's style of life.

---

[11] Reprinted by permission from Pierre Martineau, "Social Classes and Spending Behavior," *Journal of Marketing*, vol. 23 (October 1958), p. 130, published by the American Marketing Association.

It is apparent from the descriptions of social class outlined above that there are significant differences in the standard of living, the ideas and values, the roles (occupational and other), and in the amount and character of the education of the individuals in the different social classes. It follows, therefore, that a child born into an upper-class family would be subjected to training of a different pattern than that given to a child born into a lower-lower class family. Because of the difference in the scale of living (i.e., the amount and quality of goods and services consumed), the needs and desires of the upper-class child would be patterned differently from those of the lower-class child. Differences in social status, prestige, education, and moral values of the upper-class family as opposed to the lower-lower class might likewise be expected to produce different patterns of attitudes, beliefs, and values of the two children.

Because important differences in the attitudes and needs of consumers result from the training which they receive as members of the various social classes, the concept of social class is recognized as an important influence upon consumer buying behavior.

In discussing this influence, Levy describes social class variations as variations in life style. He then identifies broad differences between social classes in the four areas of values, interpersonal relations, self-perceptions, and daily life. He adds that these groups "do different kinds of work, have different types and amounts of financial reward, are evaluated differently along various dimensions of social esteem and importance in the community. As consequences, they think of themselves differently, behave differently, and want differently.[12]

Levy notes that social status appears to affect how people feel about where they should shop. Lower status people tend to prefer local, face-to-face places where they feel they will get a friendly reception, and easy credit if needed. As a result, the same products may be purchased in different channels of distribution by members of different social classes. In the purchase of cosmetics, for example, upper-middle class women are more apt to shop in department stores than are lower status women, who are, in turn, more likely to shop in variety stores. Drugstores seem equally suitable to all. Studies of department stores also show that among the stores available, there are sharp differences in status reputation, and that consumers tend to sort themselves out in terms of where it is appropriate for them to shop.

Interesting background on the importance of social class, as opposed to income as an influence on consumer behavior is provided by Cole-

---

[12] Adapted by permission from Sidney J. Levy, "Social Class and Consumer Behavior," in Joseph W. Newman, ed., *On Knowing the Consumer* (New York: John Wiley & Sons, Inc., 1966), pp. 146–60.

man.[13] He notes that three families, all earning around $8,000 a year, but each from a different social class, exhibit a radical difference in their ways of spending money. An upper-middle class family in this income bracket (for example, a young lawyer and his wife) is apt to be found spending a relatively large share of its resources on housing in a prestige neighborhood, on rather expensive pieces of furniture, on clothing from quality stores, and on cultural amusements or club memberships.

Meanwhile, the lower-middle class family (headed by an insurance salesman or a fairly successful grocery store owner), probably has a better house, but in not so fancy a neighborhood. The family is apt to have as full a wardrobe though not so expensive, and probably more furniture though none by name designers. These people almost certainly have a much bigger savings account in the bank.

Finally, the working class family (with a cross-country truck driver or a highly paid welder as its chief wage earner) is apt to have less house and less neighborhood than the lower-middle or upper-middle family of the same income. But this family will have a bigger, later model car, plus more expensive appliances in its kitchen and a bigger TV set in its living room. This family will spend less on clothing and furniture, but more on food if the number of children is greater. The man of the house also probably spends much more on sports, attending baseball games, going hunting and bowling, and perhaps owning a boat of some description.

Social group

Another way in which the environment exerts an influence upon the individual consumer is through the social groups to which he or she belongs. A *social group* is "a number of persons who communicate with one another often over a span of time, and who are few enough so that each person is able to communicate with all the others, not at second-hand, through other people, but face-to-face."[14] Groups which have an important influence upon the housewife, for example, are her family, circle of friends, neighbors, and clubs, among others. These are known as *primary groups* and are characterized by intimate, face-to-face association over a long period of time. Sociologists have found that such groups tend to develop *norms* as to what the members of the

---

[13] Adapted by permission from Richard P. Coleman, "The Significance of Social Stratification in Selling," in Martin L. Bell ed., *Proceedings of the 43rd National Conference of the American Marketing Association*, December 28–30, 1960 (published by the American Marketing Association, 1961), pp. 171–84.

[14] G. C. Homans, *The Human Group* (New York: Harcourt, Brace & Co., 1950), pp. 1, 123. Reprinted by permission of the publisher.

group should do, ought to do, are expected to do, under given circumstances. These norms are in the nature of shared attitudes and opinions, and as such, influence the behavior of group members. Recognition of this tendency has led behavioral scientists to use the concept of the *primary group* in studies of consumer buying motivation and behavior.

Influence of primary group. The concept of the primary group is recognized as an important intervening variable in a study by Katz and Lazarsfeld dealing with personal influence in the purchase of household goods such as breakfast cereals, coffee, and soap flakes or chips.[15] They asked women who had recently changed from one type of household product to another or from one brand of food to the next, what had made them change. Specific questions were asked which were designed to assess the relative impact of personal contact, and of the mass media like newspapers, radio, TV, and magazines. The source of the personal contact was also determined.

Among the various possible influences which might lead to a change in product or brand, the impact of informal personal advice was found to be greater than the impact of mass media advertisements. And, for products of all kinds, friends and neighbors were named influentials most often, with adult female kin ranking next. The influence of primary groups on buying behavior is thus clearly demonstrated.

Another interesting finding of this study was that the flow of marketing information is horizontal—i.e., within a given status level—rather than vertical. Both advisee and "opinion leader" tended to share the same status position. This finding is contrary to the previous common belief that acceptance of new products tends to move in a vertical direction—i.e., from high to low status levels.[16] It serves to underscore the influence of the primary group upon individual buying behavior.

It is noteworthy that the human group influences the individual in two ways. (1) It is through the primary groups that the culture is transmitted and the personality of the individual is shaped. As a result, continuing influence is exercised over the individual's behavior throughout his life. (2) Personal interactions with members of primary groups influence the individual in his day-to-day decisions. And after the decisions are made, the approval or disapproval of primary group members

---

[15] E. Katz and P. F. Lazarsfeld, *Personal Influence* (New York: Free Press, 1955), pp. 178, 246.

[16] Katz and Lazarsfeld also asked women who had made a recent change in their hairdo, clothes, or cosmetics to tell what brought about this turn in their fashion habits. As with the marketing of products, noncommercial personal influences had greater impact than did salespersons, while magazines had least of all (p. 180). In 6 out of 10 instances, the flow of influence was within the same status group. When influence did cross the status lines, there was evidence of a slight downward flow, predominantly from women of middle status to women of lower status. (Ibid., pp. 180, 330.)

tends to reinforce certain kinds of behavior and discourage other kinds.

Reference groups. Individuals belong to a variety of groups of various kinds, both formal and informal—the family, a fraternity or sorority, a small dinner club meeting once a month, a teen-age gang, a bridge club, and a professional club, among others. Not all of the groups to which the individual belongs exert the same influence over him. Indeed, some groups of which he is not even a member may have a considerable effect upon his attitudes and behavior. As a means of helping to clarify which groups have the greatest influence over the individual, the concept of *reference groups* was developed. Herbert Hyman coined the term "reference groups" to designate the kind of group that an individual uses as a point of reference in determining his own judgments, beliefs, and behavior. Since the concept was originally developed, according to Shibutani, it has been applied in three different types of usage: (1) to designate that group which serves as a point of reference in making comparisons or contrasts; (2) to identify that group in which the actor aspires to gain or maintain acceptance; (3) to specify that group whose perspective constitutes the frame of reference of the actor. Shibutani believes the third usage is the most meaningful one, and thus defines a reference group as . . . "that group whose outlook is used by the actor as the frame of reference in the organization of his perceptual field." [17]

Note that the individual may not be a member of a group which serves as a frame of reference for his judgments, beliefs, and behavior. It may be a group to which he aspires; by adopting its dress, habits, and attitudes he may hope to be invited into membership.

Our interest is in the influence which reference groups may have upon buying behavior. Whether or not reference group influence is likely to come into play depends upon two key factors: (1) the feeling of security or insecurity which the individual consumer feels with respect to potential reference groups; and (2) the nature of the product or brand involved. Individuals enjoying the greatest amount of security, by virtue of their prestige and status within a group, will generally conform (both publicly and privately) to the standards of that group; but they are also the most free to deviate from these standards on occasions when particular circumstances seem to justify such deviations. On the other hand, those with the weakest feelings of security and least status in a group are most likely publicly to conform to its standards on all occasions, even though harboring private opposition and resentment.

---

[17] Reprinted from Tamotsu Shibutani, "Reference Groups as Perspectives," *American Journal of Sociology,* vol. 60, no. 6 (May 1955), pp. 562, 563, and 565 by permission of The University of Chicago Press. Copyright 1955 by The University of Chicago.

Reference group influence is particularly potent in an informational vacuum. Where the individual has little or no knowledge about the attributes of a product, reference group influence is at its strongest. In contrast, when the individual has personal knowledge and experience with the product, the reference group influence is likely to be less relevant.

Then, too, there is evidence that reference group influence on purchasing varies widely from product to product. On this point, Bourne cites evidence from research conducted by the Bureau of Applied Social Research, Columbia, University.[18] This research indicates that buying may be a completely individualistic activity or very much socially conditioned. Consumers are often influenced by what others buy, especially those persons with whom they compare themselves or use as reference groups.

The conspicuousness of the product is perhaps the most general attribute bearing on its susceptibility to reference group influence. Two aspects to conspiciousness help to determine reference group influence: (1) The item must be one that can be seen and identified by others; (2) It must be conspicuous in the sense of standing out and being noticed—i.e., no matter how visible the product is, if everyone owns one it is not conspicuous in the second sense. Also, we should keep in mind that reference groups may influence either (1) the purchase of a product, (2) the choice of a particular brand or type, or (3) both.

The susceptibility of various products and brands to reference group influence is summarized in Figure 4–2. According to the system of classification used in this research, an item might be susceptible to reference group influence in three different ways, corresponding to three of the four different cells in Figure 4–2.

1.   Reference group influence may operate with respect to both product and brand (product+, brand+) as in the upper right cell of Figure 4–2. With respect to cars, both the product and the brand are socially conspicuous. Whether or not a person buys a car, and also what brand he buys, is likely to be influenced by what others do. This is also true for cigarettes and drugs (decisions made by M.D.s as to what to prescribe) and for beer with respect to type (premium versus regular), as opposed to brand.

2.   Reference group influence may operate with respect to product, but not brand (product+, brand—) as in the case of air conditioners, instant coffee, and TV (black and white). Instant coffee is a good example of this type of reference group influence. Whether it is served in a household depends upon whether the housewife, in view of her own

---

[18] Adapted by permission from Francis S. Bourne, "Group Influence in Marketing," in Rensis Likert and Samuel P. Hayes, Jr., eds., *Some Applications of Behavior Research* (UNESCO, 1957), chap. 6.

FIGURE 4–2
Reference group influence (relatively weak [−]; relatively strong [+])

		Weak − [−]	*Product*	*Strong +* [+]	
[+] Brand or Type [+]		Clothing Furniture Magazines Refrigerator (type) Toilet soap		Cars* Cigarettes* Beer (premium versus regular)* Drugs*	**[−] Brand or Type [−]**
[−] Brand		Soap Canned peaches Laundry soap Refrigerator (brand) Radios		Air conditioners* Instant coffee* TV (black and white)	**[+]**
		[−]	*Product*	[+]	

Products and brands of consumer goods may be classified by the extent to which reference groups influence their purchase. (The classification of all products marked with an asterisk (*) is based on actual experimental evidence. Other products in this table are classified speculatively on the basis of generalizations derived from the sum of research in this area and confirmed by the judgment of seminar participants.)

Source: Bureau of Applied Social Research, Columbia University. Reprinted by permission.

reference groups and the image she has of their attitudes toward this product, considers it appropriate to serve it. The brand, itself, is not conspicuous or socially important and is a matter largely for individual choice. In the case of air conditioners, it was found that little prestige is attached to the particular brand used, and reference group influence related largely to the idea of purchasing the product itself. Black-and-white TV, with its antenna often visible from outside the house, also falls in this class. As the saturation point approaches, this product may shift to the "product −, brand −" class, and be replaced by color TV with "color" rather than brand as the element strongly related to reference groups. This transition has now taken place.

3. Where a type of product is owned by virtually all people, reference groups may influence the selection of the brand, but not the product (product−, brand+). In this cell are classified clothing, furniture, magazines, refrigerators (type), and toilet soap. Clothing is a leading example of this type of product. It is socially visible, but the fact that everyone wears clothing takes it out of the area of reference group influence. The type of clothing purchased is, however, very heavily influenced by reference groups, with each subculture in the population (teen-agers, Ivy League collegians, workers, bankers, advertising men, etc.) setting its own standards. Similarly, such articles as furniture, magazines, refrigerators, and hand soap are seen in almost all homes, causing their purchase in general to fall outside reference-group influence. The visibility of these items, however, makes the selection of particular kinds highly susceptible to reference-group influence.

4. Purchasing behavior for "product —, brand —" items is governed by product attributes rather than by the nature of the presumed users. Examples are laundry soap, canned peaches, refrigerators (brand), and radios. In this group, neither the product nor the brands tend to be socially conspicuous. Reference groups, accordingly, exert very little influence over purchasing behavior.

Assuming that a product or brand has been correctly placed with respect to the part played by reference groups in influencing its purchase, how can this help in marketing the product in question? Bourne makes the following suggestions: (1) Where neither product nor brand appear to be associated strongly with reference group influences, advertising should emphasize the product's attributes, intrinsic qualities, price, and advantages over competing products. (2) Where reference group influence is operative, the advertiser should stress the kinds of people who buy the product, reinforcing and broadening, where possible, the existing stereotypes of users. This involves learning what the stereotypes are and what specific reference groups enter into the picture, so that appeals can be "tailored" to each main group reached by the different media employed.

Buying decisions within the family. We have already noted the influence of primary groups upon consumer behavior. The family, of course, is an especially important primary group. Accordingly, let us examine the framework in which buying decisions are made within the family and some of the factors that influence brand choice in this setting. According to Coulson, there are three sources of influence on brand and product choices: the purchaser, the user, and the authority.[19] General areas of prerogative and responsibility relative to the brand decision exist within the family. Some areas are seen as the wife's domain, some as the husband's domain, and some as the child's domain. Usually one person in the family (generally the housewife), but occasionally more than one member, has the assigned job of "purchasing agent" for a particular product class. These roles vary from one product class to another, but they can be determined and described.

Another influencer of product and brand selection is the authority or adviser. He may be the buyer and/or the user, and his role may be more important for some product classes than for others.

In this context, it is clear that the purchasing agent has the strategic role in the brand decision, since she acts as the "gatekeeper" controlling the channel through which products flow from the stores to consumption within the family. In this context, Coulson developed some tentative propositions about how the household "purchasing agent" accommodates

---

[19] Adapted by permission from John S. Coulson, "Buying Decisions within the Family and the Consumer-Brand Relationship," from Joseph W. Newman, ed., *On Knowing the Consumer,* pp. 59–66.

the user and the authority in making her brand decisions. These propositions were based on the results of previous research and also upon a pilot study among 100 housewives in Chicago. The study covered ten product classes that have a high percentage of their sales in food stores. These were: beer, cake mix, candy bars, canned peas, canned spaghetti, chewing gum, cigarettes, cold cereals, deodorants, and margarine. A selection of Coulson's propositions follow:

1. Other members of the family exert considerable influence on the housewife in making brand decisions.
2. In the role of purchasing agent, the housewife knows the family's brand preferences for some product classes better than she does for others.
   a) The housewife is most aware of the brand preferences of her family for products in which the brand name is clearly visible in use (e.g., deodorants, cold cereals), less aware for products in which the brand is not visible in use (e.g., canned peas), and least aware for products in which a substantial change is made in the product (e.g., cake mix).
3. In the role of purchasing agent, the housewife takes into account the family's brand preferences for some product classes more than she does for others.
   a) On products with the brand name clearly visible in use, she is more receptive to the brand preferences of her husband than she is of her children. (If she thinks a brand is not good for a child, she may veto the request.)
   b) The housewife is most receptive to the brand preferences of her family for products in which the brand is clearly visible, and least receptive for products in which there is a substantial change in the product before use. (If the family cannot identify the brand during consumption, the housewife is free to select the brand she desires.)

This study calls our attention to the different roles played in the buying process, distinguishing between users, influencers, and buyers. Let us now turn to the concept of the "family life cycle" and examine the ways in which life cycle position influences consumer behavior.

The family life cycle. The family life cycle describes the orderly progression of stages through which households tend to pass in the United States today.[20] The concept of the family life cycle, which had its origins in sociology, has been studied intensively by the Survey Research Center of The University of Michigan. The center classifies the life cycle into the following stages: (1) The bachelor stage: young, single people; (2) Newly married couples: young, no children; (3) The full nest I and II: young married couples with dependent children, (a) youngest child under six, (b) youngest child six or over; (4) The

---

[20] Reprinted by permission from William D. Wells and George Gubar, "Life Cycle Concept in Marketing Research," *Journal of Marketing Research*, vol. 3 (November 1966), pp. 355–63, published by the American Marketing Association.

full nest III: older married couples with dependent children; (5) The empty nest: older married couples with no children living with them, (*a*) head in labor force, (*b*) head retired; (6) The solitary survivors: older single people, (*a*) in labor force, (*b*) retired.

Our interest is in the influence of position in the life cycle upon buying behavior. A considerable amount of research has been done on this question, and the results are summarized briefly in Figure 4–3, which presents an overview of the life cycle and the changes in income, financial burdens, and purchasing behavior associated with the various stages. As a means of illustrating the influence of the life cycle on buying, let us compare three widely separated stages:

Full nest I, youngest child under six: house purchasing at peak; buy washers, dryers, TV, baby food, chest rubs and cough medicine, vitamins, dolls, wagons, sleds, skates.

Full nest III, older married couples with dependent children: high average purchase of durables; buy new more tasteful furniture, auto travel, nonnecessary appliances, boats, dental services, magazines.

Empty nest II, older married couples, no children at home, retired: buy medical care, products which aid health, sleep, and digestion.

It is clear from Figure 4–3 that the products purchased by households are influenced significantly by the life cycle stage achieved. As an indication of the significance of such information to an individual firm, let us examine data gathered for the Kroehler Manufacturing Company by Social Research, Inc., concerning furniture buying and the life stages.[21]

This study indicates that interest in furniture buying is highest during two separate life cycle stages and that the type of furniture bought is different from one stage to the other. The first high-interest stage is during the early years of marriage, when the couple must acquire enough furniture to satisfy its basic living needs. Here the young family places relatively greater emphasis on sensibility and practicality than on style and beauty.[22]

The second stage occurs, for middle class parents, when their children (especially their daughters) have started to party and date. At that stage attractiveness, reflection of good taste, and compatibility with existing decor becomes more important than sturdiness and low cost. With the peers coming in, the family needs to put up a good front.

Information of this kind is helpful to the manufacturer in designing

---

[21] Adapted by permission from Social Research, Inc., *The Kroehler Report* (Naperville, Ill.: Kroehler Manufacturing Co., 1958), pp. 37–42.

[22] For evidence that newlyweds have priority plans for the acquisition of household durables over time, and the implications of this finding for marketing strategy, see John McFall, "Priority Patterns and Consumer Behavior," *Journal of Marketing*, vol. 33, October 1969, pp. 50–55.

FIGURE 4–3
An overview of the life cycle

Bachelor stage; young, single people not living at home	Newly married couples; young, no children	Full, nest I; youngest child under six	Full nest II; youngest child six or over six	Full nest III; older married couples with dependent children	Empty nest I; older married couples, no children living with them, head in labor force	Empty nest II; older married couples, no children living at home, head retired	Solitary survivor, in labor force	Solitary survivor, retired
Few financial burdens. Fashion opinion leaders. Recreation oriented. Buy: Basic kitchen equipment, basic furniture, cars, equipment for the mating game, vacations.	Better off financially than they will be in near future. Highest purchase rate and highest average purchase of durables. Buy: Cars, refrigerators, stoves, sensible and durable furniture, vacations.	Home purchasing at peak. Liquid assets low. Dissatisfied with financial position and amount of money saved. Interested in new products. Like advertised products. Buy: Washers, dryers, TV, baby food, chest rubs and cough medicine, vitamins, dolls, wagons, sleds, skates.	Financial position better. Some wives work. Less influenced by advertising. Buy larger sized packages, multiple-unit deals. Buy: Many foods, cleaning materials, bicycles, music lessons, pianos.	Financial position still better. More wives work. Some children get jobs. Hard to influence with advertising. High average purchase of durables. Buy: New, more tasteful furniture, auto travel, non-necessary appliances, boats, dental services, magazines.	Home ownership at peak. Most satisfied with financial position and money saved. Interested in travel, recreation, self-education. Make gifts and contributions. Not interested in new products. Buy: Vacations, luxuries, home improvements.	Drastic cut in income. Keep home. Buy: Medical appliances, medical care, products which aid health, sleep, and digestion.	Income still good but likely to sell home.	Same medical and product needs as other retired group; drastic cut in income. Special need for attention, affection, and security.

Source: William D. Wells and George Gubar, "Life Cycle Concept in Marketing Research," *Journal of Marketing Research*, vol. 3 (November 1966), p. 362. Reprinted by permission.

his line to meet consumer desires and in planning his advertising and promotional approaches.

Summary

In the preceding pages we have discussed how the buying behavior of the individual consumer is affected by the cultural and social influences of his environment. We have shown how motives and attitudes are patterned by the culture in which he lives, the social class to which he belongs, as well as by his family and his reference groups. The position of the household in the family life cycle was shown to have significant influence upon the types of products and services which are purchased at any given time.

In addition to these influences, we should note that the consumer is also affected by certain factors in the external situation, such as his income, the proximity of stores to his home, the time of day he shops, the availability of parking space near different stores, the brands carried in the stores of his choice, the exposure of goods through display, and so on. Knowledge of the interplay of the buyer's motives and attitudes with the cultural and social influences in his environment, as well as with these situational influences, is important in understanding why, how, where, and when people buy.

Models of consumer buyer behavior

In the preceding discussion we worked with a simple descriptive model of the consumer buying process to help identify key factors influencing the purchasing decision. Attention was focused upon problem-solving behavior involved in the purchase of major items and innovations. Our explanation considered the psychological makeup of the consumer, the cultural and social influences upon his decision processes, and the influence of external situational forces upon his decisions.

We now have the conceptual background to enable us to understand the more complex theoretical models of buyer behavior that have developed during the past decade. These models tie together in a logical structure a large number of variables known to operate in purchase behavior. Emphasis is on the explanation of the relationships among these variables. Theoretical constructs are defined in such a way as to facilitate measurement through research. A basis is thus provided for formal expression of these models in mathematical terms.

Why do marketing executives and marketing researchers need a theoretical model of buyer behavior? It serves to guide buyer behavior research and improve marketing strategy decisions. A comprehensive theory also provides the "leverage" which makes possible substantial predictions about consumer behavior. It assists researchers in integrating, interpreting, and evaluating the large flow of buyer behavior findings published in research journals in recent years. It aids the executive in interpreting and utilizing the facts coming to him from research. It improves communication and understanding between executives and the marketing research experts who plan and execute studies to assist in decision making.

While several comprehensive models of buyer behavior have been developed, we shall limit ourselves to the discussion of the Howard-Sheth model since it has received wide attention in marketing circles and has been subject to several large scale validation tests. Those interested in learning about other notable comprehensive models should consult the references cited below.[23]

The Howard-Sheth model

The Howard-Sheth model is a general theory of buying behavior designed to apply to most people buying most products.[24] The theory may be used to understand industrial buying as well as consumer purchasing. It attempts to explain brand choice behavior of the buyer over time. It postulates that buying behavior is caused by a stimulus either in the buyer or in the buyer's environment. This stimulus is the input to the system. The outputs are a variety of responses which the buyer is likely to manifest, the most important of which is the purchase of the brand. Accordingly, buying is explained in the context of stimulus-response theory upon which a more elaborate structure has been built. The model integrates ideas from learning theory, cognitive theory, and the theory of exploratory behavior, among others. (See Figure 4–4 for a diagram of this model.)

The central rectangular box isolates the various internal variables and processes ("endogenous variables") which, taken together, show the state of the buyer. The inputs are stimuli from the marketing and social environments. The outputs are a variety of responses which the buyer is likely to manifest, based upon the interaction between stimuli and his internal state.

Beside the inputs and outputs, there is a set of seven "exogenous variables" which affect the internal state of the buyer: importance of

---

[23] See Francesco M. Nicosia, *Consumer Decision Processes* (Englewood Cliffs, N.J.: Prentice-Hall, Inc., 1966), chap. 6; James F. Engel, David T. Kollat, and Roger D. Blackwell, *Consumer Behavior* (New York: Holt, Rinehart & Winston, Inc., 1968), chap. 3.

[24] From John A. Howard and Jagdish N. Sheth, "A Theory of Buyer Behavior," in *Perspectives in Consumer Behavior,* edited by Harold H. Kassarjian and Thomas S. Robertson. Copyright © 1968 by Scott, Foresman and Company. Used by permission.

FIGURE 4–4
A simplified description of the theory of buyer behavior

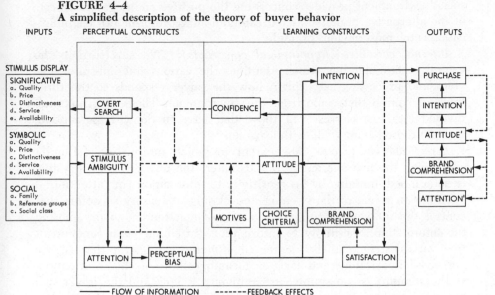

Source: Reproduced by permission from John A. Howard and Jagdish N. Sheth, *The Theory of Buyer Behavior* (New York: John Wiley & Sons, Inc., 1969), p. 30.

purchase, personality traits, social class, culture, time pressure, financial status, and social and organizational setting.

Stimulus input variables.[25]   Let us examine this model more closely, beginning with the inputs shown at the upper left-hand corner of the diagram. Assume that the buyer becomes aware of a need which he expects can be satisfied by the purchase of a brand from a generic product class. Three types of inputs may furnish stimuli designed to influence his choice of an individual brand from among five alternatives that are available. Through their marketing activities the five competitors attempt to communicate information (stimulus display) to the buyer in the hope that it may influence his choice. From the buyer's point of view, these communications basically come by way of either the physical brands themselves (*significative*) or some linguistic or pictorial representations of the attributes of the brands (*symbolic*). Examining an automobile in the dealer's showroom, for example, would communicate "significative" stimuli to the prospective buyer. Likewise, when the prospect reads, views, or hears advertisements for different brands of cars he is receiving "symbolic" stimuli.

A third input is social stimuli; that is, the information that the buyer's

---

[25] The description of the Howard-Sheth model that follows is summarized by permission from John A. Howard and Jagdish N. Sheth, *The Theory of Buyer Behavior* (New York: John Wiley & Sons, Inc., 1969), chaps. 2 and 3.

social environment provides concerning the positive and negative aspects of the alternative brands under consideration. Word-of-mouth communication is the most obvious example.

Internal variables (hypothetical constructs). We now turn to the central rectangular box which identifies the various internal-state variables and processes that explain how the buyer responds to the three types of stimuli that come from the environment. These constructs are divided into two classes: (1) those that have to do with perception, and (2) those having to do with learning.

Perceptual constructs. The extent to which information (stimuli) concerning the five alternative brands enters the buyer's nervous system is determined, initially, by his sensitivity to information (or "attention").

Attention refers to the opening and closing of sensory receptors that control the intake of information, i.e., paying attention to or ignoring the information. Sensitivity to information (attention) is a function of two variables. One is the degree of *stimulus ambiguity;* that is, the perceived uncertainty and lack of meaningfulness of the information. If the stimulus is too simple, its ambiguity is low, and the buyer will not pay attention. If the stimulus is so complex that it is hard to understand, he will ignore it. Only if the stimulus is moderately ambiguous will the buyer be motivated to pay attention and freely absorb objective information about the brand under consideration.

The second variable which governs *attention* is the buyer's *attitude* toward the five brands under consideration. If it is favorable to a given brand, then his interest in information about this brand leads him to pay attention to messages from the input stimuli. If it is unfavorable, then lack of interest leads him to disregard such communication. Since *attitude* influences the degree of interest that the buyer has in getting more information about each of the five brands, and thus influences the *attention* which he gives to input stimuli, this relationship is shown as a feedback effect in Figure 4–4 (indicated by the dashed line).

The buyer not only is selective in the attention he gives to information, but actually distorts it once it enters his mental state. In other words, the meaning of information about the five brands is altered by the buyer through the process of *perceptual bias,* the third perceptual construct shown in Figure 4–4. The amount and character of distortion of this information is influenced by what the buyer already "knows" about the ability of each of the five brands to satisfy his desires (motives). New information tends to be distorted to make it congruent with the buyer's frame of reference. It is significant that information provided by salesmen or by advertising is more likely to be distorted by *perceptual bias* than that coming from the buyer's social environment (family, friends, reference groups).

Overt search is the fourth perceptual construct shown in Figure 4–4. Over a period of time when there are several repeat purchases of a generic product class, there are stages where the buyer *actively* seeks information about the alternative brands which might satisfy his desires (motives). At other times he may passively receive information as he naturally is exposed to it while listening to a news broadcast, driving to work, lunching with friends, watching his favorite television program in the evening, reading the newspaper, or taking part in other activities. The information received in this passive state may or may not arouse his attention and be processed through perceptual bias as described above.

There are a number of reasons why the buyer may actively seek information about the alternative brands which could satisfy his desires (motives). *Overt search* by the buyer may occur if the purchase is important, if the product is one that he has never bought before, if he doesn't have enough information about the different brands to make a choice, if he is uncertain about the ability of the alternative brands to satisfy his desires, among others. Where these conditions exist, the buyer may actively seek information by talking with his friends (social environment), by reading an advertisement, by writing the seller for information, by talking with a salesman, among other possibilities. Since promotional effort by the manufacturer or his dealers has a high probability of influencing the buyer engaged in *overt search,* it is important to distinguish this situation from that where the buyer is passive.

Learning constructs. We are now ready to consider how the buyer makes his brand choice decision, taking into account the modified information which he has stored in his memory or has actively acquired in preparing for making the purchase. The elements of his decision are (1) a set of motives, (2) alternative brands, and (3) choice criteria, by which the motives are matched with the alternatives. (See Figure 4–4.)

Motives are the needs, wants, or desires of the individual that are satisfied in buying and consuming alternative brands in a product class. Motivation is the arousing or energizing element in buying behavior. When the buyer becomes aware of certain needs or desires that may be satisfied by purchasing a generic type of product, he may then actively seek information with which to evaluate these brands, as described above; or, information from the commercial or social environment may stimulate his desires and thus initiate the buying process.

When a need is aroused, a buyer who is familiar with a product class will call to mind several alternative brands (or goal objects) capable of satisfying that motive. These brands constitute the *evoked set* and may represent only a few brands out of the many that are available on the market. *Brand comprehension* is a learning construct which refers to knowledge about the existence and characteristics of the brands in the purchaser's evoked set.

Choice criteria are the buyer's mental rules for matching alternative brands with motives and ranking them in terms of their want-satisfying capacity. Their function is to generate appropriate attitudes toward brands, so that the brand with the greatest favorable attitude is potentially most satisfactory to him. *Choice criteria* are derived from motives as a process of learning. The sources of the learning are: (*a*) actual experience with the brands; (*b*) information about them coming from the commercial and social environment. These criteria are important to the manufacturer, because if he knows them, he can deliberately build into his product and its promotion those characteristics which will differentiate his brand, favorably, from competing brands.

Attitude refers to the buyer's relative preferences for brands in his evoked set, based on his evaluative beliefs about these brands as goal objects.[26] It might be visualized as the place where the connotative meanings of the brands in the buyer's evoked set are compared with *choice criteria* to yield a judgment on the relative contribution of brands toward satisfaction of buyer's *motives*. This judgment includes not only an estimate of the value of the brand to him, but also an estimate of the confidence with which he holds that position. The more confident he is about his estimate, the more likely he is to buy the favored brand.

Intention refers to a buyer's forecast as to when, where, and how he is likely to buy a brand. Although a buyer may prefer Brand A over Brand B, he recognizes that certain situations may arise at the *time* he decides to buy that prevent him from choosing Brand A (*inhibitors*). When he is questioned as to his *intention* to buy the brands that have been rated in order of preference, he will take these *inhibitors* into account in giving his answer. Five types of inhibitory situations are postulated. They are: (*a*) high price of the brand, (*b*) lack of availability of the brand, (*c*) time pressure on the buyer, (*d*) the buyer's financial status, and (*e*) social influences. These inhibitory contingencies may thus lead the buyer to purchase Brand B, for example, when he had previously indicated a preference for Brand A.

Confidence refers to the degree of certainty with which the buyer believes he can estimate the reward from buying a given brand. This certainty may relate to his *brand comprehension*, his *attitude* toward the brand, his *intention* to buy the brand, and his purchase experience with it. Accordingly, *confidence* is treated as a separate hypothetical construct. Also it has great potential for empirical investigation by the

---

[26] Howard's definition is somewhat more restrictive than that of Katz utilized in the discussion of attitudes in Chapter 3. For comments on these differences, see Howard and Sheth, *The Theory of Buyer Behavior*, pp. 128–30.

manufacturer. *Confidence* has a feedback effect upon *motives* since it affects information seeking and processing discussed earlier.

The last of the learning constructs shown in the rectangular box (Figure 4–4) is *satisfaction,* which is a feedback effect coming from previous purchases of various brands in the buyer's evoked set. *Satisfaction* refers to the degree of congruence between the actual consequences from purchase and consumption of a brand, and what was expected from it by the buyer at the time of purchase. If the actual outcomes are adjudged by the buyer to be *better than or equal to* those expected, the buyer will feel satisfied. If, on the other hand, he adjudges the actual outcomes to be *less* than what he expected, the buyer will feel dissatisfied. If the brand proves more satisfactory than he expected, the buyer has a tendency to enhance the attractiveness of the brand. If it proves less satisfactory than he expected, he is likely to diminish its attractiveness. Accordingly, where the buyer has had experience with alternative brands that may satisfy his motives, *satisfaction* is an important learning construct which influences *brand comprehension* directly as well as other variables leading up to the outputs of the buying process.

Output variables. While the act of purchase is the culmination of the processing of input stimuli explained above, there are other types of buyer responses that are important to executives in evaluating past marketing strategy and in planning future programs. As Figure 4–4 shows, there are five output variables: (1) attention', (2) brand comprehension', (3) attitude', (4) intention', and (5) purchase.[27] These variables are operationally well defined and may be used in research designed to measure results of marketing effort.

Attention' indicates the magnitude of the buyer's information intake. *Brand comprehension'* refers to the buyer's verbal statement about his knowledge of brands in a product class. It could vary from the buyer's simply being aware of a brand's existence, to a complete description of the attributes of a brand. *Attitude'* is a buyer's verbal evaluation of a brand's potential to satisfy his motives; his description of the connotative meaning of a brand. *Intention'* is a buyer's expectation, expressed verbally, that, given his information about all the aspects of a buying situation and his predictions about the future states of the environment, he will buy the brand he likes most the next time he is motivated to buy. Finally, *purchase* behavior refers to the overt act of purchasing a brand.

---

[27] Note that all output variables, except *purchase,* are given the same labels as some of the hypothetical constructs described above, but are differentiated from them by the addition of primes. Howard and Sheth explain that the output variables are at least monotonically related to their counterpart hypothetical constructs (internal variables). The essential difference is that hypothetical constructs are more inclusive in meaning, richer in speculation, and add considerably more than the output variables. Ibid., p. 31.

Exogenous variables. As mentioned earlier, there are several influences operating on the buyer's decisions which are treated as "exogenous" in the Theory of Buyer Behavior. No attempt is made to explain their formation and change. Typically, they are assumed to be *constant* during the period of *observation* of the buyer.

Many of these influences come from the buyer's social environment. It is desirable to separate those effects of his environment which have occurred in the past and are not related to a specific decision, from those which are current and do directly affect the decisions that occur while the buyer is being observed. Past influences are already embedded in the values of the perceptual and learning constructs.

These exogenous variables are included in the discussion because (1) they are useful as market-segmenting variables, (2) in setting up controls for research in buyer behavior, and (3) in measuring results of marketing effort.

There are seven exogenous variables shown in Figure 4-5 which are

FIGURE 4–5
Effects of exogenous variables

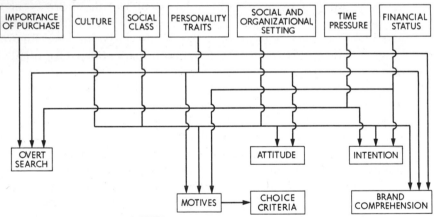

Source: Reproduced by permission from John A. Howard and Jagdish N. Sheth, *The Theory of Buyer Behavior* (New York: John Wiley & Sons, Inc., 1969), p. 92.

believed to provide the control essential to obtaining satisfactory, predictive relations between the inputs and outputs of the system.

1. *Importance of purchase* refers to the degrees of ego-involvement in or commitment to different product classes. It will influence *overt search*—the amount of effort the buyer will devote to obtain the necessary information. It also influences the size of the *evoked set* considered in the buying process.

2. *Personality traits* include those characteristics that account for

differences among people and that are predictive of their behavior. These include such variables as self-confidence, self-esteem, authoritarianism, and anxiety. It is believed that their effect is felt on *motives,* the *evoked set, overt search, attitude,* and *brand comprehension.*

3. *Time pressure* is the inverse of the amount of time the buyer has available to perform the behavior required for the acts of purchasing and consumption. It is the amount of time required to perform these acts, in relation to the time he has allocated to himself for doing them. Time pressure limits overt search and forces the buyer to make his decision based on less complete information. Since some effort is usually required to carry out the purchase act, *time pressure* tends to inhibit *intention* to buy.

4. *Financial status* refers to the funds available for purchasing goods and services during some specified time period. It has important effects upon buying behavior. (*a*) A reduction in income may affect the product class from which the buyer chooses a brand to satisfy his *motives*— e.g., it may lead him to buy less expensive cuts of meats than formerly. (*b*) Limited funds may affect *intention* (to buy) as an inhibiting factor, by leading him to purchase a brand which is ranked as his second or third choice in terms of *attitude.* For example, he may prefer to buy an expensive Mercedes automobile, but limited funds may force him to purchase a Volkswagen instead.

5. *Social and organizational setting* is an exogenous variable that takes into account the influence that groups have on the individual's behavior. Where the problem involves *consumer behavior,* informal social organizations such as the family and the reference group are relevant, as has been pointed out earlier in this chapter. Where we are analyzing *industrial buyer behavior,* then the formal organization is an important influence upon those making procurement decisions. (The character of this influence will be described in the following chapter.) As Figure 4–5 shows, *social and organizational setting* influences the learning constructs of *motives, brand comprehension, attitude,* and *intention.*

6. *Social class* is the second social variable recognized in the theory. This concept has already been explained and methods of classifying people socially have been described. According to Figure 4–5, *social class* influences the buyer's *motives* and *attitude.* Also, some social class sanctions may be regarded by the buyer as a constraint upon his behavior, thus affecting inhibitors and *intention.* Finally, his evoked set is influenced, and so *brand comprehension* is affected.

7. *Culture* is the third social variable included in the model. It consists of patterns of behavior, symbols, ideas, and their attached values. Accordingly, *culture* influences the buyer's *motives, attitude, intention,* and *brand comprehension.*

Decision making process.[28] While the Howard and Sheth Model is complex, an important feature of the theory is that the buyer tends to simplify the buying process, as a result of the learning that comes from past experience and information processing. Past experience includes generalization from similar buying situations and repeat buying of the same product class. Information comes from both the commercial and social environments. The changes in the decision-making process over time are especially significant.

Howard and Sheth classify the buying decision process as (1) extensive problem solving (EPS), (2) limited problem solving (LPS), and (3) routinized response behavior (RRB), depending upon the strength of *attitude* toward the brands in the buyer's evoked set. In *extensive problem solving,* attitude toward the brands is low, because the buyer is unfamiliar with the product class with which he is first being confronted. Brand ambiguity is high, with the result that the buyer actively seeks information. The time interval from the initiation of the decision process until its completion (*latency of response*) is greater than with LPS or RRB. *Deliberation,* or reasoning, will be high, since the buyer lacks a well-defined product class concept. He is also apt to consider many brands as part of the evoked set, his brand comprehension will be extensive, but shallow, on any one particular brand, and stimuli coming from the commercial environment are less likely to trigger any immediate purchase reaction.

When attitude toward brands is moderate, the buyer's decision process can be called *limited problem solving.* Here the buyer is familiar with the product class, but unfamiliar with the brand (brand ambiguity still exists). He is likely to seek information, but not to the extent that he seeks it in EPS. His fact gathering is to aid in comparing and discriminating among different brands. His deliberation is much less, since choice criteria are tentatively well defined. Brand comprehension will consist of a small number of brands, each having about the same degree of preference.

In *routinized response behavior,* the buyer will have a high level of attitude toward brands in his evoked set. Furthermore, he has now accumulated sufficient experience and information to have no brand ambiguity. He will in fact discriminate among brands enough to show a strong preference toward one or two brands in his evoked set. He is unlikely to actively seek any information. Whatever information he passively or accidentally receives will be subject to selective perceptual processes, so that only congruent information is allowed. Very often the congruent information will act as "triggering cues" to motivate him

---

[28] For a very helpful example illustrating how the Howard-Sheth model may be applied in explaining how a typical consumer might react to marketing stimuli for Maxim freeze-dried coffee, see Ibid., pp. 40–41.

to manifest purchase behavior. (Much impulse buying may be explained in this way.) The buyer's evoked set will consist of a few brands toward which he is highly predisposed. However, he will have greater preference toward one brand in his evoked set and lesser towards others.

Validity of the Howard-Sheth model. The Howard-Sheth model provides a framework, portrayed as a flowchart, which explains the interactions of the psychological, socioeconomic, and situational factors at work in consumer decision-making processes. Note that it will provide a satisfactory explanation for behavior in buying frequently purchased products (such as cigarettes) as well as those which are bought at widely spaced intervals (automobiles), or very seldom (pianos). Observe, also, that it can handle different classes of buying behavior such as extensive problem solving, limited problem solving, and routinized response behavior. Remember, finally, that the model can be applied in analyzing industrial purchasing as well as consumer buying.

During an interview with *Advertising Age* in June 1972, Howard mentioned that four years were spent developing the Theory of Buyer Behavior. Then six more years had been used in testing it.[29] Let us briefly review published reports of these validation tests.

The first major test of the Howard-Sheth model concerned a branded grocery product.[30] Faced with the problem of testing the model in its entirety, the authors chose to use an econometric approach. The model was viewed as a system of simultaneous equations, with each endogenous variable serving as the dependent variable in one of the equations. Using this approach, the data from a sample of 693 housewives were analyzed. Both ordinary least squares and two-stage least squares regression analysis were performed. The results, though obviously affected by considerable noise, were generally favorable. The model was useful for organizing this analysis of consumer behavior, but the test put extreme pressure on the data.[31]

The second full model test was in many ways a replication of the first. Data were collected in three waves from a special panel of 200 to monitor the test market introduction of a new frequently purchased product in two cities in Argentina. The form of the model was adapted to the specific situation.

Analysis of these two extensive tests of the model led Lehmann,

---

[29] Reprinted by permission from Stanley E. Cohen, "Ads a 'weak signal' in most buying decisions: Howard," *Advertising Age*, June 12, 1972, p. 3.

[30] Adapted by permission from Donald R. Lehmann, John U. Farley, and John A. Howard, "Testing of Buyer Behavior Models," *Proceedings, 2d Annual Conference, Association for Consumer Research*, 1971, pp. 232, 239.

[31] For further background on this initial attempt to adapt the Howard-Sheth model for a specific empirical test, see John U. Farley and L. Winston Ring, "An Empirical Test of the Howard-Sheth Model of Buyer Behavior," *Journal of Marketing Research*, vol. 7, Nov. 1970, pp. 427–38.

Farley, and Howard to the following conclusions. First, the model seems to have substantial validity. Second, the model is still in need of considerable refinement and subsequent testing.

One possible use of the model is in structuring and analyzing a test market for a new product. In a second article, the above authors discuss their experience in applying the model in the Argentina test market referred to previously.[32] Their comments on this research follow.

1. There were strong implications about how a test market should be configured; what data should be collected, and when.
2. The buyer behavior framework is also appropriate for analyzing the marketing mix in a "roll out," by monitoring the effects of the introduction to see which aspects of the marketing mix are succeeding and which are failing. The brands against which the new brand is making competitive inroads can be identified, and sources of competitive strengths and weaknesses can be isolated.[33] After the initial "roll out," elements of the buyer behavior model can be used to continue to monitor the "life cycle" of the brand to detect any warning signs of decay or competitive inroads, providing a basis for an on-going "marketing information system."
3. Somewhat further in the future is the possibility of evaluating new product ideas in the buyer behavior framework.

Especially significant is the following concluding comment:

Before any of these more advanced applications of the model become feasible, however, massive testing of buyer behavior models is needed. Since much of the advantage of the model, in terms of relevance to advertisers, and much of the weakness, in terms of predictive power, centers on the perceptual variables (attention, confidence, etc.), much of the effort in refining the model must center here. . . . In order to refine the model, a variety of small experiments aimed at refining the definitions of, and studying linkages between, two or three of these variables seems the most useful approach. Yet, in spite

---

[32] Adapted by permission from John U. Farley, John A. Howard, and Donald R. Lehmann, "After Test Marketing, What?" *1970 Proceedings of the Business and Economic Statistics Section,* American Statistical Association (Annual Meeting, Detroit, Dec. 27–30, 1970), Washington, D.C., pp. 293, 294.

[33] Editorial note: *After* test marketing is completed, management decides upon a marketing mix to be used when the brand is introduced to the market. It is assumed that a "roll out" means the introduction of the new brand, area by area, until it achieves national distribution. The authors are suggesting that a buyer behavior framework may be appropriate in measuring the effectiveness of the marketing mix applied in the first areas where it is introduced; aspects of the marketing mix that are failing may then be changed; elements that are succeeding may be continued. In this way the marketing mix used in the first areas where the brand is introduced may be modified in *later* areas to improve effectiveness of the program. This process may be repeated until national distribution is achieved.

of the fact that major aspects of the model are still developmental, the buyer behavior framework provides a useful structure for planning, executing, and analyzing a test market.

A third comprehensive test of the model involved the marketing of a subcompact automobile in 1970, Chevrolet's Vega. Although the results of this research have not been published in the journals as yet, Howard made the following brief comments about it in an interview reported in *Advertising Age*.[34]

"We could see consistent results. Whether it was a car, a breakfast food, or a soap in South America, the same theory operates," he said. . . . The results are consistent with a fair degree of accuracy, given stable market conditions, Professor Howard claims. As more experience develops, he believes it will be possible to adjust the forecasts to take changing marketing conditions into account . . . One surprise, he said, was that the system works better for established products than new ones. The marketer who uses these techniques gets an interesting by-product, according to the professor. He gets exactly the same data on his competitor's product as his own. "That is," Professor Howard said, "you learn exactly how good their ad is."

Relevance for marketing management. At this point it is helpful to inquire, "What is the relevance of the Howard-Sheth model for marketing management?" The model has several uses.

1. It provides a useful service in identifying stimuli acting upon the consumer as coming from the environment (noncontrollable variables) and from the marketing plan (controllable influences). In developing marketing strategy, management should identify which of the following noncontrollable (exogenous) variables are especially significant in their influence upon the consumer: importance of purchase, personality traits, social class, culture, social and organizational setting, time pressure, and financial status. The executive might then ask whether adequate information is available as to the impact of significant uncontrollable variables upon consumer response. Where data are inadequate, then research might be planned to provide missing information useful in executive decision making.

2. The model also helps to identify the points at which the marketing plan applies stimuli influencing the prospective buyer's choice process. The model indicates that the prospect's choice process is influenced by his perception of the characteristics of the firm's brand as compared with competing brands—any one of which might satisfy his desires. Management decisions which change the firm's product, its price, the service available, and its availability may, therefore, influence the

---

[34] Cohen, "Ads a 'weak signal' in most buying decisions: Howard," p. 78. Reprinted by permission of the publisher.

consumer's evaluation of alternative brands and hence his buying decision.

3. The evoked set of brands considered by the consumer when a desire is aroused may be influenced by advertising, personal selling, and information provided through personal contact with the buyer's social groups. Recognition of this important point may be taken into account by management in working out promotional strategy.

4. The model also indicates that advertising, point-of-purchase promotion, or personal selling may stimulate the buyer's motives and thus serve as a triggering cue that starts the buying process. This understanding may be used to identify communication objectives and to decide upon the proper promotional methods to be used to gain the maximum results.

5. The model also explains that the effects of advertising or personal selling may be transmitted to prospective buyers through interaction with members of their social groups. Such knowledge may suggest research to identify which groups influence the prospective buyer and, with such information in hand, may provide a basis for developing a promotional program aimed, in part, at groups which may serve as a channel through which information may flow by personal interaction.

6. The model calls attention to the point that advertising and personal selling may also influence the way in which prospective buyers perceive the firm's brand as compared with alternative brands. Such effort may serve to create not only favorable attitudes toward the firm's brand but also an intent to buy. This identifies another task which may be assigned to advertising and/or personal selling in developing the promotional strategy.

7. The model suggests the wisdom of adapting the marketing strategy to the amount of experience which the typical consumer has had with the brand and hence the complexity of the buying decision. The theory suggests that different strategy is appropriate for products where "extensive problem solving" is involved in the purchase decision, as compared to those where "limited problem solving" or "routinized response behavior" are followed.

8. With knowledge of points in the model at which stimuli from marketing programs may be applied, management may find it useful to undertake research or controlled experiments to develop consumer response curves which describe how prospective buyers respond to changes in product, price, advertising, and personal selling efforts. Such response curves may be helpful in arriving at management decisions as to what strategy moves to make, and in what sequence, in order to maximize sales and profits.

9. Although the model provides a useful structure for planning,

executing, and analyzing a test market, its application by a particular firm is likely to require considerable effort and expense. As is true of all marketing research, therefore, an attempt should be made to estimate the payoff resulting from providing better information for use in decision making. Taking into account the probability that such improved information will actually be secured, the incremental revenue resulting from better data can then be compared with the additional costs and a decision made as to whether it is desirable to undertake the proposed research.[35]

10. One merit of the model is its comprehensiveness. It provides a useful reminder to the executive of the various factors which need to be considered in working out marketing plans to influence consumer behavior. It also helps the executive to understand why consumers behave as they do in the process of buying.

Concluding comments. This model appears to be a powerful tool for explaining consumer behavior, especially for frequently purchased items where past experience is likely to influence future attitudes. While it works better when used to guide research on the marketing of established products, rather than new ones, it has been useful in planning, executing, and analyzing test markets for new brands. There is hope, also, that further developmental work with the model may improve its usefulness in these applications. Results of validation tests of the model are encouraging, but Howard and his associates indicate that further testing is needed before some of the more advanced applications envisioned for the model become feasible. Executives in forward looking firms might do well to encourage their market research people to experiment not only with the applications of the Howard-Sheth model, but also with other leading models of buyer behavior, as a means of evaluating them and of adapting them to their own specific situations.

Conclusion

After concluding our discussion of the influence of environmental and situational factors on buyer behavior, the Howard-Sheth theoretical model was presented to tie together, in a unified structure, the many variables that affect the purchase of a brand. Empirical tests indicate that this model appears to have substantial validity, but it still requires additional development and further validation studies before its full potential can be realized.

---

[35] For a discussion on the cost and value of information, see Joseph W. Newman, *Management Applications of Decision Theory* (New York: Harper & Row, 1971), chap. 2.

Executives and researchers need a theory of buyer behavior to guide them in the development of effective marketing programs. Their interest in a workable theory comes about because it tells them at which points marketing effort may alter the buyer's environment and thus influence his purchasing behavior. Thus, management can change the quality level and characteristics of the product, its price, and its availability in retail outlets where consumers would expect to find it. Equally important, the character of the messages communicated through the sales and promotional programs, as well as the amount of such effort, can also change the symbolic information content of the prospect's environment and may thus influence the buying decision.

With such a theoretical model of buyer behavior in mind, the executive and the market research expert can work together in deciding (1) what information to gather, in order to provide data needed for planning marketing strategy for the year ahead, and (2) what output measurements to secure as a means of evaluating the effectiveness of the program. Weaknesses identified through such audits can then serve as an input in planning improved strategy for the following year. In short, an ongoing program of research which feeds essential information to those responsible for the planning of marketing strategy has the potential of making possible significant improvements in the effectiveness of the marketing effort. Such a research program would constitute part of a modern marketing information system such as that described earlier in this discussion.

An idea of considerable practical value suggested by the Howard-Sheth model is that marketing strategy should be adapted to the amount of experience which the buyer has had with the brand. Entirely different strategies are required for marketing a new generic type of product, where prospects will be involved in *extensive problem solving;* marketing an unfamiliar brand in a familiar product class, where *limited problem solving* is required; or marketing a brand with which the buyer has had considerable experience and which he will purchase following *routinized response behavior.*

Then too, the use of a theoretical model of buyer behavior helps to identify exogenous variables influencing the purchasing process which may be helpful in guiding research designed to determine whether market segmentation is desirable and, if so, on what basis to segment.

Finally, a theoretical model may be of substantial value in planning test market research designed to monitor the effects of an introduction to see which elements of the marketing mix are succeeding, and which are failing. Such research may result in a more effective marketing strategy when the brand is introduced on a nationwide basis, if it is properly conceived and executed.

Questions

1. *a*) What criteria did Warner use to identify a family's position in the social structure of the community in which it lives? What social classes did he identify?

   b) Warner used the reputational approach in classifying families. How did Hollingshead's method differ? What indications of status did Hollingshead use to determine social position?

2. *a*) What criteria were used to determine the Index of Status Characteristics in Chicago by Warner and Martineau?

   b) What conclusions did Martineau reach concerning the value of social class stratification to the marketing executive?

   c) Would segmentation of markets along social class lines be equally significant for the marketing of automobiles, gasoline, beer, coffee, and dietary foods?

3. *a*) Explain briefly the concept of reference groups.

   b) How susceptible are the following products and brands to reference group influence? (Use the following classification system: product+, brand+; product−, brand+; product+, brand−; product−, brand−.)

   (1) automobiles.

   (2) beer (premium versus regular).

   (3) air conditioners.

   (4) radios.

   (5) color television sets.

4. For which of the products listed below does the housewife tend to take into account the preference of other members of the family in making purchases?

   a) Kellogg's Sugar Pops (preferred by four year old son).

   b) My Sin perfume (wanted by 13 year old daughter).

   c) Marlboro cigarettes (preferred by husband; wife likes Kents).

   d) Maybelline eye shadow (requested by 17 year old daughter).

   e) Rival dog food (preferred by Fido).

   f) Betty Crocker cake mix (preferred by 17 year old daughter; mother likes Pillsbury cake mix).

   g) Idahoan instant potatoes (liked by wife; husband likes Maine potatoes boiled and then mashed by hand).

   h) Eckrich frankfurters (preferred by seven year old son, nearest supermarket stocks Oscar Mayer brand).

   i) Dubble Bubble gum (requested by seven year old son).

   j) Crest Mint toothpaste (preferred by 17 year old daughter; mother likes Crest Regular, which is wintergreen flavored).

5. Research suggests that the position of a family in the life cycle is likely to have an influence on its purchasing behavior. Which of the products in column one would the families listed in column two be most likely to purchase?

Products	Life cycle stages
Sleeping pills	Bachelor
Boats	Newly married
Ski equipment	Full nest I
Round-the-world tour	Full nest II
Piano	Full nest III
Automatic washer and dryer	Empty nest I
Bicycle	Empty nest II

6. Using the Howard-Sheth model, distinguish between the following stimulus input variables relating to the Vega compact car that might be perceived by the owner of a four year old Volkswagen: (*a*) significative; (*b*) symbolic; (*c*) social.

7. *a*) Using the same example as in question 6, what variables influence *attention* given to stimulus input concerning alternative brands of compact cars by the owner of the four year old VW?

   b) How might *perceptual bias* of this consumer operate on the information to which he gives attention? Give examples relating to the Vega, using information originating from advertising, a salesman, and a member of one of the individual's reference groups.

   c) Under what conditions might the VW owner undertake *overt search* for information about different brands of subcompacts? Should Chevrolet aim different types of promotional effort at both "active buyers" and "passive buyers"? If so, how might this be done?

8. *a*) Distinguish between *brand comprehension, attitude,* and *intention.* Illustrate, using the VW owner mentioned above as an example.

   b) What *choice criteria* might the VW owner use in ranking alternative brands?

9. In evaluating the effectiveness of the marketing strategy for the Vega during the current year, should Chevrolet executives limit their measurements to the change in units purchased during the current year, as compared with the previous year, expressed as a percentage of total purchases of compact cars in the United States during the same time periods? If not, what other output variables should be measured? Why?

10. The Howard-Sheth model classifies the buying decision process as extensive problem solving (EPS), limited problem solving (LPS), and routinized response behavior (RRB). This is based on the observation that the consumer tends to simplify the buying process, as a result of learning and information processing.

    a) Explain briefly how EPS, LPS, and RRB differ with respect to the following characteristics (use a grid with "characteristics" listed on the left hand margin as row headings and EPS, LPS, and RRB as the column headings):

    (1) Brand comprehension (extent of knowledge about characteristics of brands in the evoked set)

    (2) Number of brands in evoked set

    (3) Level of attitude toward brands

    (4) Amount of overt search

(5) Length of decision time

(6) Amount of deliberation involved

11. Assume that a man in his late twenties, married for two years, with no children receives an increase in salary from $10,000 to $15,000 per year. What would probably be the effect of this change on the internal psychological state of the buyer, and thus upon his buying decisions?

12. At what point in the Howard model (Figure 4–4) may executives apply stimuli through the marketing plan used? In what ways might such stimuli influence the consumer's buying behavior?

13. Why should the marketing plan be adapted to the amount of experience which the consumer has had with the brand? In answering, relate your response to (a) users of Kent cigarettes, and (b) prospective buyers of the Polaroid color camera.

5

Industrial buyer behavior

THE PREVIOUS chapter has dealt with buyer behavior in the consumer market where the purchasing units are individuals who buy goods and services for the satisfaction of their own needs or those of their families. The consumer market is large, varied, and widely dispersed geographically. Because we all participate in the consumer market to some extent, our knowledge of its workings is rather extensive. Any discussion of buyer behavior in the consumer market can be related to concepts which are generally understandable in light of our own experiences with the purchase decision process.

There is, however, another market which is even larger than the consumer market but about which the average person knows very little. This other market is the industrial market and is composed of those individuals and organizations which purchase goods and services necessary for the production of goods and services—which they, in turn, sell or lease to others. Because this market has not received the attention from the press or from marketing writers that has been given to the consumer market, the average college student is somewhat hazy about the industrial market and how it operates. A brief review of the nature, importance, and organization of this vast "other" market will, therefore, precede the discussion of how buyers behave in an industrial, rather than a consumer, setting.

Nature of the industrial market

The industrial market is composed of almost 10 million producer units which buy (or lease) goods and services which enter into or support their productive process. Although this number is small when compared with 200 million individuals organized into approximately 60 million family purchasing units in the consumer market, the 10 million producer units account for a considerably larger volume of sales than do their consumer counterparts. For example, over half of all manufactured goods produced in this country is sold to industrial users. These sales amounted to $325 billion in 1969.[1] In addition, it has been estimated that 80 percent of the total output of domestic farms and mines enters the industrial market. Thus, another $66 billion of sales must be added to the industrial market total.[2]

Of course, one of the reasons for the fact that the industrial market has such large sales volume is that so many transactions are required to convert raw materials into finished products and to make these products available at local outlets. Even though some double counting may occur as goods move through the production and distribution processes, the measurement of value added at each stage in the journey validates the economic contribution of the producer units involved. Suffice it to say that any market employing 50 million people and generating over $600 billion in national income[3] is too large and important to be ignored by any marketing manager.

The industrial market, as commonly defined, encompasses the wide range of industries noted below:

1. Agriculture, forestry, and fishing
2. Mining and quarrying
3. Contract construction
4. Manufacturing
5. Transportation, communication, and other public utilities
6. Wholesale trade
7. Retail trade
8. Finance, insurance, and real estate
9. Services
10. Government—federal, state, and local

Under this broad definition every wholesaler or retailer is an industrial customer, as is any contractor or public utility. In like manner, any governmental entity is considered to be part of the industrial market.

One writer prefers to define the industrial market in a more narrow sense. He views the various purchasing units which lie outside of the consumer market as belonging either to what he calls the producer market, the reseller market, or the government market.[4] Under this

[1] *Survey of Current Business,* February 1970, back cover.

[2] William J. Stanton, *Fundamentals of Marketing,* 3d ed. (New York: McGraw-Hill, 1971), p. 157.

[3] Philip Kotler, *Marketing Management: Analysis, Planning, and Control,* 2d ed. (Englewood Cliffs, N.J.: Prentice-Hall, Inc., 1972), p. 139.

[4] Kotler, *Marketing Management,* pp. 138 ff.

three-market concept, the producer market is defined as synonomous with the industrial market.

Although there is considerable merit in the three-market approach, based on the fact that producer, reseller, and governmental customers may differ widely in terms of buying motives, behavior, and mode of operation, for our purposes in this chapter the broader definition of the industrial market will be used. The industrial market will be viewed as containing all of those customers who are not in the consumer market. By construing the industrial market to be so all-encompassing does not mean that it is homogeneous. Indeed, the opposite is true, and those differences which are found in the industrial market provide many meaningful bases for market segmentation. This process will be discussed later in this chapter.

Regardless of whether one views the government market as a separate entity or a segment of the industrial market, it is an area worthy of brief discussion. The government sector is of special interest simply because it uses such vast quantities of goods and services. The federal government consumes 20 percent of the gross national product, while state and local governmental units use another 10 percent. Thus, almost one third of everything produced in this country each year is sold to some agency of government.

Although government purchases are large, it is not necessarily easy to sell to government. The average marketer finds it difficult to make contact with those persons who influence decisions as to what the government will buy and from whom it will buy. Of course, a great deal of government procurement must, by law, be on a bid basis. Under the bidding system, the government advertises for bids from suppliers stating the specifications of the goods or services desired. The order goes to the lowest bidder who meets the specifications. In a growing number of situations where a good deal of research and developmental work is required or where there is no feasible competition to support a bid procedure, the government will enter into a negotiated purchase contract either on a cost-plus or incentive basis.

The average marketer does not want to get involved in the red tape and other complications entailed by selling to government. Those firms which have taken the time and trouble to develop specialized marketing skills have found the governmental market segment to be extremely profitable.

Classification of industrial goods

Goods sold in the consumer market are often classified in terms of how buyers behave when they seek out these goods. Thus, the commonly used classifications such as convenience goods, shopping goods, and specialty goods refer to the amount of time and effort the average potential buyer will expend in order to find, investigate, and finally purchase a specific item. Such a classification approach has only limited application in the industrial market. Producer units do not shop in the usual sense. In most cases, vendors seek them out.

A more useful way of classifying industrial goods is in terms of how these goods enter the production processes and cost structures of the various producer customers. With this type of information, marketing executives can identify more readily the persons involved in the buying process and can develop a marketing strategy mix to reach these people and to influence them to buy their product. A classification schema which aids in the analysis of the industrial market, in terms of the entry characteristics of specific goods and services, has been suggested by Kotler.[5] In Figure 5–1 below, a wide array of goods and services

FIGURE 5–1
Classification of industrial goods

I. *Goods entering the product completely—materials and parts*
   A. Raw materials
      1. Farm products (examples: wheat, cotton, livestock, fruits and vegetables)
      2. Natural products (examples: fish, lumber, crude petroleum, iron ore)
   B. Manufactured materials and parts
      1. Component materials (examples: steel, cement, wire, textiles)
      2. Component parts (examples: small motors, tires, castings)

II. *Goods entering the product partly—capital items*
   A. Installations
      1. Buildings and land rights (examples: factories, offices)
      2. Fixed equipment (examples: generators, drill presses, computers, elevators)
   B. Accessory equipment
      1. Portable or light factory equipment and tools (examples: hand tools, lift trucks)
      2. Office equipment (examples: typewriters, desks)

III. *Goods not entering the product—supplies and services*
   A. Supplies
      1. Operating supplies (examples: lubricants, coal, typing paper, pencils)
      2. Maintenance and repair items (examples: paint, nails, brooms)
   B. Business services
      1. Maintenance and repair services (examples: window cleaning, typewriter repair)
      2. Business advisory services (examples: legal, management consulting, advertising)

Source: Philip Kotler, *Marketing Management: Analysis, Planning, and Control*, 2d ed., © 1972, p. 141. By permission of Prentice-Hall, Inc.

---

[5] Ibid. p. 141.

sold in the industrial market have been placed in three major categories shown as Type I, II, and III producer (industrial market) goods.

The Type I goods enter the product completely. Thus their costs are assigned directly to the manufacturing process. In contrast, Type II goods are generally large and expensive. They are capitalized as assets and, as they are used up or worn out over time, a portion of their original cost is assigned to the production process as depreciation expense. Type III goods are those which do not enter the production process at all, but which facilitate operations. The costs of such goods (and services) are treated as expenses in the periods in which they are used.

Marketing patterns

The physical nature of an industrial good and the way in which it is used by the buyer have an important influence on the manner in which it is marketed. Over time, therefore, certain patterns of marketing have become associated with classes of industrial goods. It is possible, given these patterns, to describe the nature of the marketing strategy mix used by most sellers of a specific class of industrial raw material, product, or service.

Raw materials. The marketing pattern associated with agricultural raw materials results from the fact that these materials are usually supplied by many small producer units located some distance from the points of consumption. Although the amounts of these materials that can be supplied in total each year are, to a large extent, under the control of man, these quantities cannot be changed quickly. In addition, production is seasonal, and the goods produced are perishable. Thus the marketing strategy mix emphasizes distribution in its broadest sense. Long channels of distribution include specialists who perform the functions of accumulating, sorting, standardizing and grading, warehousing, and transportation.

Because agricultural raw materials are sold on a contractual basis with product specifications clearly stated, price is extremely important. Because the product itself is a commodity which cannot be physically differentiated from the offerings of other suppliers, the seller does not engage in branding, advertising, or other forms of demand creation for his product. Rather, the seller earns patronage by gaining a reputation for meeting his quality and delivery commitments while charging competitive prices over a period of time.

Natural products have their own marketing patterns which are somewhat different from agricultural raw materials, especially in the area of distribution. As supplies of these goods are limited by nature and are usually concentrated geographically, producers tend to be large and few in number. The product is standardized, bulky, generally of low unit value, and costly to transport. As a result, channels of distribution tend to be short—often direct from producer to user. Price is important and influenced greatly by transportation costs, thus placing a premium on locational advantage for the seller. Demand creation opportunities are again limited by the commodity nature of the goods, and emphasis is placed by the seller on consistent quality and service at competitive prices.

Manufactured materials and parts. These items share many of the marketing characteristics of raw materials. They are usually purchased in large quantities, generally on a contractual basis, and in most industries directly from the manufacturer. Smaller users or hand-to-mouth purchasers may avail themselves of industrial distributors or other marketing middlemen. Price and service are still the basic appeals used by sellers; but the products in this category are often less standardized than are raw materials, and thus some opportunity does exist for product differentiation and demand creation activity. Branding, advertising, and personal selling are all utilized by certain manufacturers to gain patronage for their products. Catalogs and trade publications are important sources of information for potential buyers; while, in some instances, promotional messages are directed at the consumer market to create brand awareness for materials and parts which enter a consumer product such as an automobile, a refrigerator, or a piece of wearing apparel.

Installations. These are the large, expensive items of capital equipment which affect the scale of operation of the buyer. The marketing of installations is a difficult and complicated business in which a number of highly qualified salesmen and technicians work with prospective customers over a long period of time. Channels of distribution are generally direct because of the need for close communication between buyers and sellers. Some less costly, standardized installations may, however, be sold through middlemen.

The criteria for purchase considered by the buyer include the nature of the installation and how well it can be adjusted to fit the specific needs of the buyer, the nature of the service offered by the seller—not only presale, but also during installation or construction and postsale follow-up—and the price. It should be noted that the price for installations is viewed by the buyer as having a close relationship to the cost savings which will be provided by the installation over its life. Thus a higher price will be paid to gain even higher cost savings.

In terms of the marketing strategy mix, the product ranks first in importance when selling installations. There is an opportunity, however, for demand creation activity and in this area personal selling is the main vehicle. Trade advertising, catalogs, and direct mail are used to supplement the efforts of the salesmen and to reach those members of the buying team who cannot be reached in person. The highest levels of management are generally involved in the purchase decision for installations.

Accessory equipment. Items of accessory equipment facilitate the production process without changing the buyer's scale of operation. Accessory items are more standardized, generally cost less, and are purchased by lower levels of management than are installations. Although some distribution is on a direct basis, a great deal of accessory equipment is sold through industrial distributors. Markets for these items run across industry lines and, therefore, broader coverage is required than can be attained economically by the manufacturer himself. In addition to the importance of the distribution variable to provide availability, personal selling has a large role to play in the marketing strategy mix. Greater emphasis is placed upon selling skills than technical skills, unlike the situation in the installations market.

Price is also a very important factor and, to gain some freedom from price competition, many sellers of accessory equipment engage in a strategy of promoting product differentiation. Personal selling and advertising are both used to emphasize product advantages and to deemphasize direct price comparisons with competing products.

Supplies and services. Operating supplies of one type or another are used by almost all producer units. Thus broad distribution is a necessity if availability requirements in the market are to be met. Because operating supplies are fairly well standardized, if one manufacturer is not represented in a market because of lack of coverage or because of a stockout, the product of another manufacturer can be substituted quite easily. Although distribution is generally through middlemen, some large buyers are served on a direct basis. In addition to availability, price is an important consideration for the potential user. Catalog listings, advertising to resellers as well as to final users, and personal selling are all utilized to gain sales for the branded or nonbranded goods of selected suppliers.

Services are marketed in ways which are different from those used to sell operating supplies. Because buyers tend to value quality and reputation of the provider of services, price is less important in the seller's marketing mix. What is important is personal selling to explain the capabilities of the supplier and to negotiate a purchase contract. Sales efforts are directed at higher levels of management for services than for operating supplies. Thus personal selling efforts are often supplemented by direct mail or business periodical advertising of a professional nature. The appeals used emphasize quality of performance rather than price.

Nature of demand for industrial goods

Demand for industrial goods and services has several characteristics which differentiate it from demand in the consumer market. These characteristics are an outgrowth of the fact that the demand for industrial goods is derived from the demand for the goods and services of which they are a part. For example, the demand for automobile tires is derived both from the demand for new cars as well as from the replacement needs of those car owners whose tires have worn out. The simple illustration which follows provides a basis for discussion of the impact that derived demand has upon the industrial market and thus upon marketing strategy formulation.

Derived demand. Let us assume the existence of a company which manufactures bottles for sale to the soft drink industry. This company has a factory containing ten bottle producing machines, each with a capability of turning out 100,000 bottles per year. Each machine has a useful life of ten years and their ages are conveniently staggered for this example so that one machine must be retired at the end of each year. The history of the demand for bottles faced by this manufacturer, as well as his own demand for bottle producing machinery for the past five years, is illustrated in Figure 5–2.

FIGURE 5–2
Company demand history for bottles and bottle producing machinery

Year	Bottles demanded	Percent change	Machines demanded	Percent change
−5....	1,000,000	0	1 replacement	0
−4....	1,000,000	0	1 replacement	0
−3....	1,100,000	+10	1 replacement + 1 expansion	+100
−2....	1,300,000	+18	1 replacement + 2 expansion	+ 50
−1....	1,200,000	− 8	0	−100

Changes in demand for bottles, which do not exceed 18 percent in any one year, are translated into very large changes in demand for the bottle producing machinery. These fluctuations which reflect year-to-year changes of as much as 100 percent are typical of demand for capital goods. Sellers of these goods face a feast or famine situation, depending on whether forecasts of future demand for end products in a particular industry are favorable or unfavorable.

In contrast, demand for component parts or operating supplies shows a lesser degree of fluctuation than does demand for capital goods. In addition, demand for these goods is linked to the level of general business conditions rather than to the fortunes of any particular industry or group of industries. Finally, as the production process for these goods is shorter than for capital goods, and because these goods can be more economically stockpiled, estimates of demand for the end product need not be carried as far into the future as would be the case with capital goods.

Demand for component or supply type items is also affected by the inventory-holding policies of the users. Generally, these policies specify that sufficient goods will be purchased and on hand to support a specified number of days of production. Increases in demand for the output of the firm will trigger a need to add to inventories. Conversely, a falloff in demand will cause a moratorium on buying until stocks on hand fall into line with the needs of the production line.

Elasticity of demand. Derived demand and the psychology of the industrial buyer interact to cause unusual things to happen with respect to the influence of price upon quantities of goods and services demanded by industrial users. Let us examine first the impact of price changes on the demand for capital equipment such as expensive, specialized machinery.

Purchasers of such machinery are seeking a way to increase the profitability of their operations. They are, in effect, buying cost-saving capability. When demand for the end product is depressed there is no need to purchase machinery for expansion purposes. Indeed, even the replacement of old machines may be delayed. Facing such a situation, a reduction in price by the seller of capital equipment will have little effect on stimulating sales. This is because the cost of any particular piece of capital equipment typically represents a very small part of the price of the ultimate consumer product. A price reduction which can effect the price of the end product in a price sensitive market may accelerate replacement of existing machinery. The size of the price cut required may be so large, however, that the seller often prefers to redesign the machine to increase its cost-saving potential instead of reducing its price.

In the face of a forecast upswing in final demand, users of capital equipment will add to capacity at prices which allow them profitable operations. Moderately high prices will not deter them from buying, as the profit potential, not the price, is the important consideration. Thus, when viewed from the downside or the upside, derived demand for capital goods is relatively inelastic. Price plays a secondary role in the marketing strategy mixes of sellers of such equipment, while product design to afford cost savings to users, personal selling, and service dominate the strategies of marketers of capital equipment.

Demand for raw materials and component parts, although derived, is more sensitive to price changes than is demand for capital goods. In the short run, demand for these types of goods may exhibit reverse elasticity in that when prices decline buyers may sit on the sidelines until they can determine whether or not the price decline is temporary or a prelude to a continued succession of price reductions. On the other hand, if prices start to rise, buyers may accelerate their purchases to beat what they believe will be even higher prices in the future. Of course, in the long run the laws of economics will prevail, and lower prices will result in larger quantities of materials and parts being utilized, while higher prices will have the opposite effect. When an individual seller in an industry lowers his price, one would expect that his sales would increase at the expense of his competitors. This does not always happen. Industrial customers do not change sources on the basis of price alone. Quality of product and service and the existence of a long-standing relationship between source and user cause demand to be sticky, and a price reduction, even if unmatched by competitors, to be a less effective way of gaining patronage.

As one moves from consideration of capital goods to materials and parts and thence to supplies and services, the sensitivity of demand to changes in price increases. As goods become more standardized and service requirements lessen, more emphasis may be placed upon price in the seller's marketing mix. A price reduction is especially effective when the material or part being sold is important in terms of the cost composition of the finished product of which it is a part. In such a situation, a price reduction may enable the seller of the end product to reduce his price and gain a competitive advantage in his market.

Because demand is different in the industrial market (in that it is derived, it fluctuates, and it is relatively inelastic) as compared to demand in the consumer market, special marketing plans must be developed. Industrial marketers who have borrowed planning processes from the consumer market have, to a large extent, achieved disappointing results.[6]

Extent of demand for industrial goods and services

As noted previously, there are approximately 10 million buying units in the industrial market. This is a relatively small number of potential customers when compared with the 200 million individuals in the consumer market. The market seems even smaller to the average industrial seller who is concerned not with the total industrial market but rather with a smaller segment of the total, composed of buyers for his specific offerings. For example, those sellers of component parts for use in the manufacture of textile machinery may find that the most recent census data indicate that only 560 such establishments exist. Those sellers of

---

[6] B. Charles Ames, "Marketing Planning for Industrial Products," *Harvard Business Review*, vol. 46, no. 5 (September–October 1968), pp. 101 ff.

supplies used by meat packers will discover that their market is limited to approximately 2,700 firms.[7] A major problem facing the industrial marketer is, therefore, the identification and location of those firms which are likely prospects for the goods and services offered for sale.

To aid in the identification and location process, the federal government has developed the Standard Industrial Classification system (SIC) under which all business and governmental organizations are classified in terms of ten groups. Each of these groups is assigned a range of two-digit numbers, as illustrated below:[8]

01–09   Agriculture, forestry, fishing
10–14   Mining
15–18   Contract construction
19–39   Manufacturing
40–49   Transportation and other public utilities
50–59   Wholesale and retail trade
60–67   Finance, insurance, and real estate
70–89   Services
90–93   Government—federal, state, and local
99   Others

A separate two-digit number is then assigned to each major industry within the group, and three- and four-digit numbers are used to identify specific segments within each industry. For example:

SIC 20   Food and kindred products
SIC 201   Meat products
SIC 2013   Sausages and other prepared meat products

While the industrial market is composed of relatively few firms which are potential users of the offerings of specific suppliers, these few firms represent a great deal of purchasing power. An examination of the size distribution of manufacturing establishments, as illustrated in Figure 5–3, shows that less than 11 percent of the establishments employ 75 percent of the persons involved and account for over 80 percent of the value added.

In addition to the concentration of demand within an industry in terms of size of firms, demand in the industrial market is concentrated on a geographic basis. As seen in Figure 5–4, when each state is portrayed with its area in proportion to the value of products manufactured in the state, the middle Atlantic and midwestern states dominate. Industries, other than manufacturing, are concentrated elsewhere. For example, the petroleum industry is heavily concentrated in the southwestern

---

[7] *U.S. Census of Manufacturers: 1967,* vol. I.

[8] *Standard Industrial Classification Manual,* Washington, D.C.: U.S. Government Printing Office, 1967.

FIGURE 5–3
Size distribution of manufacturing establishments in the United States, 1967, by number of employees

Number of employees	Number of establishments	Percent of firms	Percent value added	Percent of employees
1–4.............	117,514	38.4	1.1	1.1
5–9.............	39,343	12.9	1.3	1.4
10–19...........	41,678	13.6	2.7	3.1
20–49...........	48,942	16.0	7.0	8.3
50–99...........	24,923	8.2	8.0	9.4
100–249.........	19,762	6.5	14.9	16.6
250–499.........	7,749	2.5	13.8	14.5
500–999.........	3,450	1.1	13.3	12.8
1,000–2,499.......	1,639	0.5	15.0	13.2
2,500 or more.......	674	0.2	23.1	19.6
Total............	305,680	100.0	100.0	100.0

Source: *U.S. Census of Manufacturers: 1967*, vol. 1.

FIGURE 5–4
An industrial map of the United States showing area of each state in ratio to other states, based on value of manufactured products

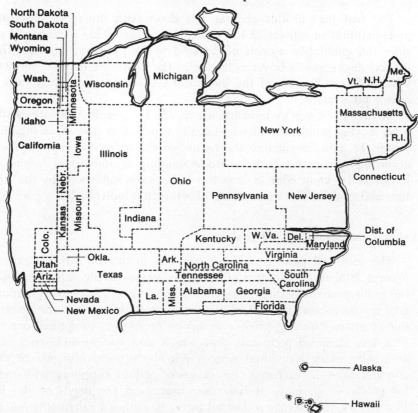

Source: *U.S. Census of Manufacturers: 1963*, vol. III, "Area Statistics," p. 39.

states; shoe manufacturing in New England and St. Louis; ladies' ready-to-wear in New York, Chicago, and southern California; and steel in Pittsburgh and Chicago.

Data are available from governmental or private sources which indicate the extent of activity for most SIC classifications in each of the nation's counties or Standard Metropolitan Statistical Areas (SMSAs). This latter classification is especially important because the SMSAs, which are 230 in number, accounted for about 76 percent of value added by manufacturing in 1967. By utilizing the information on geographic concentration of industrial demand, in conjunction with the SIC system, industrial marketing managers can identify and locate the most likely markets for their offerings. In addition, by noting the type, number, and location of individual firms which are likely prospects, an effective distribution and promotional strategy can be developed.

Buyer behavior in the industrial market

The first part of this chapter has dealt with the more descriptive and quantitative aspects of the industrial market. This section will consider the qualitative aspects of demand in the industrial market—those aspects analogous to buyer behavior in the consumer market, yet somewhat different because of the industrial environment in which such behavior takes place.

Buying decisions in industry are made by people who are paid to solve buying problems and who usually function as part of an organized group. To gain insight into the nature of the industrial buying process, accordingly, requires both an understanding of individual buying behavior and a knowledge of how this behavior is influenced by the structure and goals of the organization of which the individual is a part.

Individual and organizational goals

The idealized picture of those engaged in the industrial purchasing process is that of a group of men dedicated to the advancement of the profit position of their company. They seek to achieve this corporate goal by purchasing goods and services in such a way that the combination of product quality, price, and service received is an optimal one.

A less idealized picture is that which portrays the industrial buyer as a self-seeking individual who is not above accepting gifts or other considerations in exchange for favoring certain suppliers with orders for goods which may, or may not, best meet the needs of the firm. In actuality, the average industrial buyer is neither a calculating machine whose rationality is above question nor is he a totally selfish person always willing to subordinate the needs of the organization to his own. A more honest description is that of a human being who is trying to do a good job for the company but who is also interested in advancing his own career. Thus, the industrial buyer has two goals: to further the interests of his company and to further his own position within the organization.

Sometimes these goals overlap, while other times they may be in conflict. It has been suggested that the organizational-factors model developed in a political context by Thomas Hobbes offers a useful interpretation of the relationship between organizational goals and individual goals.[9] The Hobbesian view is that although each man is "instinctively" oriented toward preserving and enhancing his own well-being, fear of a "war of every man against every man" leads men to unite in a corporate body.[10]

Perhaps if the various blendings of goals were illustrated by a Venn diagram, the marketing implications of these goal relationships might becomes clearer. Such an attempt is made in Figure 5–5 which illustrates

FIGURE 5–5
Individual goals (*I*), group or organizational goals, (*O*), and areas of goal mutuality (*M*) in three situations

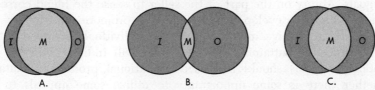

A.   B.   C.

three situations. Situation A is one in which there is a high degree of overlap between individual goals and organizational goals. In situation B there is very little overlap. In situation C there is considerable overlap but still some areas where individual and group goals do not coincide.

In situation A there is a great deal of overlap between individual goals and organizational goals. In such a situation, the use of rational appeals illustrating how the product will help in organizational goal achievement should receive a great deal of acceptance from purchasing personnel. Such is the case when individuals responsible for the buying decision perceive that the best way to achieve their personal ends is

---

[9] Philip Kotler, "Behavioral Models for Analyzing Buyers," *Journal of Marketing*, vol. 29, no. 4 (October 1965), pp. 44–45.

[10] Thomas Hobbes, *Leviathan*,1651 (London: G. Routledge & Sons, Ltd., 1887).

to seek attainment of organizational goals. Thus, promotional efforts which emphasize the congruence of goals should be most effective here. The seller's slogan in situation A might be, to paraphrase a rather famous quotation, "What is good for General Wickets Corporation is also good for its buyers."

In situation B there is very little goal overlap. This is not a desirable state of affairs from the standpoint of the buying organization. If the true nature of the goal relationship is perceived by sellers, then their promotional activity will be directed to stimulation of efforts by individuals to achieve their personal goals even at the expense of corporate well-being.

Situation C is a more normal one. There is a better balance between individual and organizational goals. The area of goal mutuality *M* is larger than the area of either segment *I* or *O*. Given this type of situation, the perceptive seller will depend heavily on rational product arguments but will supplement these appeals with others of a more emotional nature, aimed at the egos of the individuals involved in the buying process.

It must be recognized that goal overlap is a matter of degree. The type of product being purchased, the type of organization being considered, and the relative strength of individual drives to achieve specific goals influence the blend, in a given situation, of individual and organizational goals. Ability on the part of the seller to sense the blend correctly will enable him to develop a more effective promotional strategy. An appraisal of the relative importance to the individuals involved in the purchase process of attaining the two goals will indicate whether the promotional appeals should be based on rational product advantages or whether there is some opportunity to utilize some appeals to the self-interest of the individuals concerned.

Stages in the buying process

The specific buying processes of individual firms or institutions vary widely. For example, no two companies seem to follow the same purchasing procedures. Indeed, within a given firm the purchasing processes appear to vary according to the kind of need being filled or the type of product being sought. In spite of this seeming diversity, investigation of the industrial buying process has indicated that it is, in reality, an orderly one consisting of several clearly defined steps or phases.[11]

A recent study has termed these steps in the industrial buying process "buyphases" and has suggested that for analytic purposes the buying process might be broken down into eight distinct stages which, although

---

[11] John H. Platten, Jr., Scientific American research study, *How Industry Buys.* Copyright © 1950, 1955, by Scientific American, Inc.

generally sequential, may occur concurrently one with the other. These "buyphases" are:

1. The anticipation or recognition of a problem (need) and the awareness that such a problem may be solved by a purchase.
2. The determination of the characteristics and quantity of the needed item.
3. The description of the characteristics and the quantity of the needed item.
4. The search for and qualification of potential sources.
5. The acquisition and analysis of proposals.
6. The evaluation of proposals and selection of suppliers.
7. The selection of an order routine.
8. Performance feedback and evaluation.[12]

Time element. The stages or "buyphases" in the procurement process may take a considerable length of time for their completion. In Figure 5–6 a period of almost four months elapses between recognition of need and delivery of the order. This rather long time was required, although the purchase was for a standard type of item which had been purchased many times in the past.

FIGURE 5–6
A decision network diagram of the procurement process (a straight rebuy: drills)

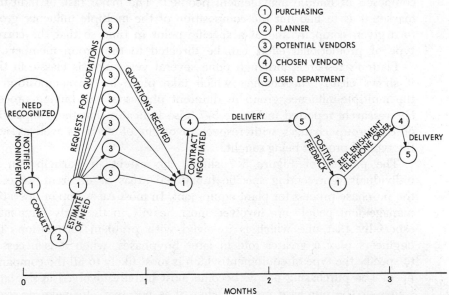

---

[12] Patrick J. Robinson, Charles W. Faris, and Yoram Wind, *Industrial Buying and Creative Marketing* (Boston: Allyn & Bacon, Inc., 1967), p. 13.

The term "straight rebuy" used in the caption for Figure 5–6 refers to a type of buying situation in which there is a recurring or continuing requirement which is handled on a routine basis. Other types of situations may be termed "modified rebuys" or "new tasks," and we shall talk about these a little later in this chapter.

Multiple influence groups

Each buyphase of the industrial purchase process is the responsibility of several individuals performing different functions within the organization. Top management has routinely delegated authority to these persons to make the necessary decisions based on their evaluation of the pertinent factors.[13] Three aspects of the process which have been verified by the research findings of Platten are: (1) that top management rarely takes a direct hand in the buying process, (2) that few decisions are made by individuals and most decisions are group decisions, and (3) the composition of these groups characteristically changes from phase to phase.[14]

These groups of individuals involved in the purchase process are called "multiple purchase influence groups." They are, for the most part, composed of middle management people.[15] The major task of industrial marketers is to find out the composition of the multiple influence group in a given company and at a specific point in time so that the correct type of promotional effort can be directed to the group members.

Platten's research, although done several years ago, is classic in that it shows clearly the changes which take place in the composition of the multiple-influence group in different phases of the buying process. His research, reported in Figure 5–7, also indicates that the composition of the group changes with respect to origin of need as well as with the type of product being sought.

The part A of Figure 5–7 shows the extent of participation by individuals representing specific functional areas at different stages in the purchase process for plant equipment. In most cases, top or operating management people are involved most heavily in the early buyphases, especially that one which is involved with problem recognition. The engineers play a greater role in later buyphases, when it is necessary to specify the type of equipment which is most likely to fill the company's need. The purchasing people become most heavily involved in the latter stages of the purchase process, when it is necessary to make decisions pertaining to source qualification and selection.

---

[13] Platten, *How Industry Buys.*

[14] Ibid.

[15] "Who Makes the Purchasing Decision?" *Marketing Insights* (October 31, 1966), p. 16.

Note, however, that in the initial buyphase for plant equipment the composition of the group may differ in a given company according to the origin of need. For example, as seen in column 1 of part A of Figure 5–7, the participation of top management is heaviest when the purchase motive is to expand capacity. Operating management, on the other hand, is most heavily involved when the purchase motive is to replace old equipment. Given a motive involving a change in production process, it appears that the engineers take on a more important role.

The part B of Figure 5–7 illustrates how industry buys component parts. These are industrial goods which go to make up another product but which retain their physical identity. Note the lesser involvement of top and/or operating management in the earlier buyphases as compared with the extent of their involvement in the earlier phases of the purchase process for plant equipment.

It is generally easier to draw up specifications for component parts and to compare the performance of parts from various sources with respect to these specifications than to perform these tasks with plant equipment. Thus, the multiple influence groups are composed of a greater proportion of engineering and purchasing personnel in the earlier buyphases than was true with major installations of plant equipment.

Types of buying situations

Members of a multiple purchase influence group at a given "buy-phase" may find that their decision making process is a function of the type of buying situation with which they are involved. The degree of newness of the problem, the amount of information required before an acceptable solution can be found, and the extent to which alternative ways of solving the problem are considered, all go to make up or define a specific type of buying situation.

The terms "new task," "modified rebuy," and "straight rebuy" have been suggested as describing three distinct types of buying situations or "buyclasses."[16] The "new task," for example, describes a buying situation in which the problem encountered is a new one, information requirements are high, and the consideration of alternatives is very important.

Those situations characterized by an essentially recurring problem which has certain new aspects, by moderately high information requirements, and by limited importance of considering alternatives may be called "modified rebuys."

Finally, if the problem faced is not a new one, if information require-

---

[16] See Robinson, Faris, and Wind, *Industrial Buying*, p. 25.

FIGURE 5-7
How industry buys plant equipment and component parts (in percent)

In manufacturing industries, personnel with these functions → participate in the percentages indicated at these steps in the development of a purchase. →

	Top management	Operating management	Production engineering	Design and development engineering	Maintenance engineering	Research	Purchasing	Finance	Sales, advertising	Others in company	Others outside company
A. How industry buys plant equipment*											
Motive 1. Who is most likely to initiate project leading to new equipment purchase for:											
a) Replacement of old equipment?	16.7	59.8	22.1	14.1	34.2	8.6	4.8	1.1	0.5	1.2	0.8
b) Expansion of capacity?	64.5	43.9	18.1	17.3	5.0	7.9	3.5	2.4	4.6	1.8	1.3
c) Change in process?	17.9	37.5	33.5	40.1	4.5	31.8	3.2	0.9	1.4	1.7	1.2
d) Production of new product?	41.8	25.8	20.2	40.5	2.6	40.0	3.1	2.0	11.5	1.4	1.3
Kind of equipment 2. Who surveys alternatives and determines kind (not make) of equipment to be used?	10.1	37.1	38.5	45.8	14.9	17.9	6.6	0.5	0.2	2.1	
3. Who specifies as to size, capacity, etc., of the equipment?	10.5	39.8	40.9	38.9	10.9	11.3	2.0	0.5	0.8	2.1	0.8
Make or supplier† 4. Who surveys available makes or suppliers of the specified kind of equipment and chooses suppliers from whom to invite bids?	6.8	23.0	24.5	30.4	11.7	8.0	57.4	1.2	0.1	2.0	0.5
5. Who evaluates equipment offered by suppliers for their accord with specifications?	6.9	30.5	36.2	42.4	16.1	11.9	18.3	0.6	0.1	3.0	0.6
6. Who decides which supplier gets the order?	23.7	38.7	17.1	23.5	8.6	6.2	50.9	1.2	0.7	1.5	1.0

B. How industry buys component parts‡

In manufacturing industries, personnel with these functions → participate in the percentages indicated at these steps in the development of a purchase →

	Top management	Operating management	Production engineering	Design and development engineering	Maintenance engineering	Research	Purchasing	Finance	Sales, advertising	Others in company	Others in outside company
Motive 1. Who is most likely to originate project leading to purchase of a component part:											
a) To take advantage of a price differential?	10.2	24.6	19.0	25.0	7.2	9.8	56.6	2.0	1.6	2.3	0.9
b) As a result of change in design of an established product?	6.4	21.4	30.8	50.4	8.1	16.0	14.9	0.4	3.1	1.9	0.9
c) As a result of a change in production process?	5.5	30.1	48.6	35.4	5.7	15.6	9.0	—	0.5	2.0	1.0
d) For production of a new product?	15.0	23.6	26.2	52.5	4.0	31.3	7.8	0.2	4.3	1.8	1.3
Kind of component part 2. Who surveys alternatives and determines kind (not make) of component parts to be used?	5.3	17.7	29.8	60.9	7.7	22.6	10.2	0.2	0.9	2.0	0.8
3. Who specifies design and characteristics of the parts?	3.7	12.4	27.4	68.2	8.4	20.8	3.5	—	1.3	2.1	1.6
Make or supplier§ 4. Who surveys available makes or suppliers of the specified kind of component parts and chooses suppliers from whom to invite bids?	4.7	12.2	18.0	36.1	6.0	12.0	68.3	1.0	0.6	2.1	0.9
5. Who evaluates component parts submitted by suppliers for accord with specifications?	3.7	14.7	29.1	56.0	8.4	21.3	17.3	0.1	0.2	5.4	0.8
6. Who decides which supplier gets the order?	16.5	26.7	14.7	29.8	5.0	9.9	63.5	1.3	1.0	1.8	1.2

* Example: In industry generally, when it comes to specifying size and capacity of plant equipment, design and development engineers in 38.9 percent of the plants play more than an occasional role.

† Choice of make or supplier limited (due to company preferences or policy in setting up the specifications and characteristics required) to: one make, 11.4 percent; two makes, 11.8 percent; unlimited, 76.8 percent.

‡ Example: In industry generally, projects leading to purchases of component parts to take advantage of a price differential are frequently initiated by design and development engineers in 25 percent of the plants.

§ Choice of make or supplier limited (due to company preferences or policy in setting up the specifications and characteristics required) to: one make, 13.2 percent; two makes, 11.9 percent; unlimited, 74.9 percent.

Source: From the Scientific American research study, *How Industry Buys.* Copyright © 1950, 1955 by Scientific American, Inc. All rights reserved.

ments are minimal, and if there is no consideration of alternatives, then the situation may be termed a "straight rebuy."

The search process

Having considered the impact of the buyphase, the origin of need, and the type of good being sought upon the composition of the multiple-purchase influence group and having noted briefly that the decision process may differ with respect to the nature of the buying situation, we now turn our attention to that part of the buying process known as the search procedure. The search which is conducted by those persons involved at a given buyphase may be for a specific type of good, for selection criteria, or for qualified sources of supply.[17] Figure 5–8 is a schematic representation of one buyer's search for the latter.

An examination of the figure reveals that once a stimulus is received, the buyer may search as many as six different areas in order to gain sufficient information to enable him to solve the problem of where to buy. The marketing implications of understanding the nature of the search process are quite evident. Information input by a prospective seller in any of the six areas can direct the searcher to a specific answer. As there is no way of predicting the sequence of the buyer's search, the seller's best strategy is to make certain that information about his qualifications as a source is well dispersed among the areas most likely to be searched by the prospective buyer. The fact that not all of these areas can be reached by salesmen means that the promotional mix must include advertising, direct mail, and other methods of nonpersonal sales promotion, including the use of catalogs.

Search with learning. Given a sequence of searches by the same buyer (or group of buyers) for a source to supply goods to fill a recurring need, one would expect that with time the search process would become more efficient. Memory would lead the prospective buyer to a source which had performed well in the past. If prior experience with a source had been less than satisfactory, then memory would enable the buyer to start the search process with the most effective route used last time. Figure 5–9 illustrates such a search when learning from past experience is involved.

The Howard-Sheth model of consumer behavior discussed in Chapter 4 is a stimulus-response model involving learning. By substituting the concept of source for that of product, the Howard-Sheth model becomes readily applicable to an industrial buying situation. One value of looking at the industrial buying process, in terms of a learning model, is that the implications of the various buyclasses are readily seen.

[17] See Frederick E. Webster, Jr. "Modeling the Industrial Buying Process," *Journal of Marketing Research*, vol. 2, no. 4 (November 1965), p. 371.

FIGURE 5–8
The process of a buyer's search for a source of supply

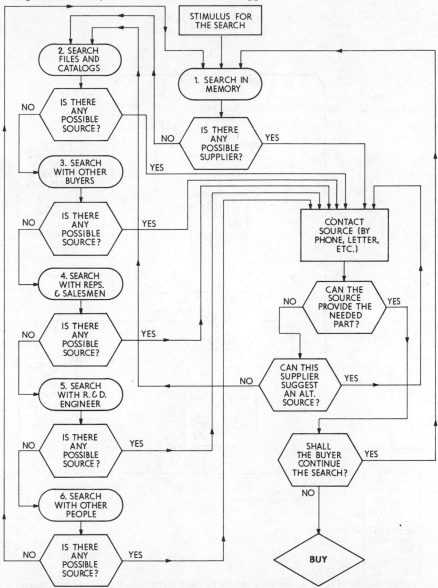

Source: From Patrick J. Robinson, Charles W. Faris, and Yoram Wind, *Industrial Buying and Creative Marketing*, p. 107. Copyright © 1967 by Allyn and Bacon, Inc., Boston. Reprinted by permission of the publisher and the Marketing Science Institute.

FIGURE 5–9
A buyer's search process when learning is involved

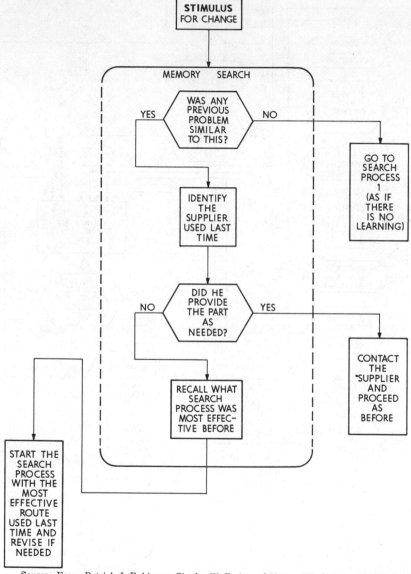

Source: From Patrick J. Robinson, Charles W. Faris, and Yoram Wind, *Industrial Buying and Creative Marketing*, p. 107. Copyright © 1967 by Allyn and Bacon, Inc., Boston. Reprinted by permission of the publisher and the Marketing Science Institute.

For example, the straight rebuy, which generally represents the bulk of a firm's buying transactions, is characterized by behavior which is closely akin to what Howard and Sheth have termed routinized response behavior (RRB). In this type of buying situation a great deal of learning has occurred, very little if any searching is required, and the buyer's response to a need stimulus is largely automatic. The purchasing department has a "list" of approved suppliers, and orders are routinely placed with these firms when needs arise. In many cases, straight buys are made by computers which track stock levels or reorder points.

The modified rebuy situation is one in which changes have taken place with respect to the buyer's requirements and/or some aspect of the nature of supply. Instead of a recurring problem with a "learned" solution, the buyer is faced with the need to have more information, to consider alternative solutions to his problem, and to conduct a search in order to find the best way of solving the problem at hand. Again we see a parallel with what Howard and Sheth have termed limited problem-solving (LPS) behavior.

Faced with this type of a buying situation, the buyer is hopeful that once the problem is solved, sufficient learning will have occurred to shift a modified rebuy back to a straight rebuy, which is easier and more economical to handle. Howard and Sheth would describe the same process in terms of a movement along the learning curve from limited problem solving to routine response behavior.

The sellers who are not active suppliers to the buyer's firm might wish to delay this shift.[18] In fact, they might even develop a strategy of moving buyers from a straight buy situation to a modified rebuy situation. This is because under a modified rebuy these suppliers may be in the "evoked set" of possible alternatives, while in a straight rebuy they may not be considered at all.

Given a new-buy or new-task situation, information requirements are very heavy, and the consideration of many alternatives is necessary. The buyer behavior here is very close to what Howard and Sheth have described as extensive problem solving (EPS) behavior. Very little learning has occurred, and a great deal of ideation is necessary. The process takes time and is expensive because of the information needs and the extensiveness of the search process.

An understanding of the Howard-Sheth model can help the marketing manager to direct the controllable variables of product, distribution, promotion, and price so that they can influence the industrial buying decision most effectively. For example, personal selling and advertising efforts can have a triggering effect in that they increase the potential buyer's awareness of his needs to the point that the buying process

[18] Ibid. p. 28.

starts. Moreover, if the buyer is required to search for clarification of alternatives by seeking additional information from personal or impersonal sources, promotional effort can be directed to these sources so that the information which the seller wants to impart about his offerings is available during the buyer's search.

In those situations where alternatives are known but must be compared, product quality, availability, and price are the important considerations. It is in these areas that the other variables of product design, distribution strategy, and pricing play their roles.

Conclusion

Knowledge of the industrial buying process provides insight as to where promotional effort should be directed with respect to different *phases* of the buying process. The recognition that decision making is carried on by groups of changing composition is a prerequisite to the design of an effective promotional strategy.

Buying decisions also differ with respect to the *kind* of buying situation faced. The amount of information needed by a buyer, the number of alternatives to be considered, and the extent of the search process all influence whether the buyer's behavior will be oriented toward a routinized response or toward what has been termed limited or extensive problem-solving behavior.

Finally, an understanding of the nature of the buying process, be it in the industrial or consumer market, is essential to the development of an effective marketing strategy. The controllable variables of product, distribution, promotion, and price, which were mentioned in Chapter 2, must be blended together in such a way that the product attributes, including quality, availability, and price, place it in competition with other alternatives. In addition, the promotional strategy must be designed to inform potential buyers of the product's existence and to persuade them to buy.

Questions

1. Why does the industrial market have a larger volume of purchases than the consumer market, even though the number of industrial purchasing units is relatively small?
2. How do the producer, reseller, and governmental markets differ? In what ways are they similar with respect to marketing considerations?
3. Why do many businessmen not seek governmental business?
4. Compare and contrast the classification criteria for consumer goods with those suggested for industrial goods.

5. What is derived demand, and how does it affect elasticity of demand in the industrial market?

6. Does the impact of derived demand fall evenly on each category of industrial goods? Explain.

7. What is the Standard Industrial Classification system and how may it be of use to an industrial marketer?

8. Of what value, if any, is a knowledge of the goals of industrial buyers in the formulation of marketing strategy for a line of industrial goods?

9. What is meant by a multiple-purchase influence group? Under what circumstances may the composition of such a group change? Why is the ability to identify the membership of the relevant group so important to an industrial marketer?

10. What assumptions might be made about the composition of multiple-purchase influence groups concerned with buying major plant equipment, as contrasted with groups concerned with the purchase of component parts?

11. How might different types of buying situations be contrasted in terms of the search process required? Explain the implications of search with learning for a seller of a "new" type of industrial product.

12. What is meant by the terms: new task, modified rebuy, and straight rebuy? Relate these concepts to the Howard-Sheth model of buyer behavior.

13. Of what help is a model of buyer behavior in developing a marketing strategy for selling to the industrial market? What is required to adapt a consumer market model to an industrial market model?

cases for part two

Falstaff Brewing Corporation (B)*

Taste and image research

Falstaff Brewing Corporation, a large St. Louis, Missouri, brewer with one of its eight plants located in San Jose, California, had been unable to improve its sales performance in California despite strong retail distribution and heavy promotional efforts there. Falstaff sales were roughly 5 percent of total beer sales in southern California and 10 percent in northern California, but both figures were well below Falstaff's average share of 16 percent for all of its sales districts, which covered half the United States.[1]

Mr. Alvin Griesedieck, Jr., vice president and director of marketing turned to Mr. Willard Evans, the director of market research, for help in determining why Falstaff's California performance was not better. Mr. Evans reasoned that consumer awareness of the Falstaff brand was not a factor. Previous studies showed that many Californians had recently moved from the East and Midwest, often from areas where Falstaff was well established.

While Mr. Evans was considering the California problem, Mr. Hugh Schwartz, executive director of the Institute for Design Analysis in San Francisco, paid him a visit. Mr. Schwartz brought with him a copy of a report on an experimental taste test of eight brands of beer he recently had conducted in the San Francisco Bay Area. The test had been designed to determine the influence of label design on the perceived flavor and difference for certain brands of beer. Mr. Schwartz could not divulge the data in a form which would relate them to specific brands.

---

*Reprinted from *Stanford Business Cases, 1963,* pp. 217–43, with the permission of the publishers, Stanford University Graduate School of Business, © 1963 by the Board of Trustees of the Leland Stanford Junior University. Writen by Milton J. Gaines, research assistant, under the direction of Professor Joseph W. Newman, Graduate School of Business Administration, The University of Michigan.

[1] For additional background see "Falstaff Brewing Corporation (A)" in Joseph W. Newman, *Marketing Management and Information* (Homewood, Ill.: Richard D. Irwin, Inc., 1967), pp. 3–27.

Mr. Schwartz proposed that a consumer taste test between the Falstaff brand and two or three of its leading competing brands be conducted in California. His proposal was accepted and the test was conducted during the spring of 1962.

PLANNING THE TEST

In talking about the test, Mr. Evans commented: "We want to know first whether California beer drinkers actually could taste and logically define differences between certain brands. Secondly, we wanted to learn what they thought an 'ideal' beer should be and how this image compared with the image they had of Falstaff."

With these goals in mind, Mr. Schwartz designed a test to accomplish three objectives:

1. To determine the extent to which consumers can perceive taste differences between Falstaff, Brand A beer, and Brand B beer in a "blind" test in which the brands would be unidentified. Both competitive brands were classified by laboratory technical personnel as having characteristics which differed.
2. To determine consumer impressions or "images" of the taste of the above three brands, plus Brand C and Brand D.
3. To relate the blind taste-test results and the brand taste images to the consumer conception of the characteristics of an ideal beer.

TEST PROCEDURE

The Institute for Design Analysis rented a store in an area of high pedestrian traffic of Oakland, California, in which to conduct the study. It took three weeks to obtain the desired sample of 800 male respondents from pedestrians passing by the store. Mr. Evans had decided that one test location in California was adequate at that stage for Falstaff's purpose. Only male beer drinkers were interviewed, since previously published surveys estimated that they drank 78 percent of the beer sold.

The testing procedure was outlined to the test staff as follows:

In the study we are going to interview 800 male beer drinkers. One of you will be assigned the job of recruiting beer drinkers. Screen out those who drink less than one glass or bottle of beer per week. As the test progresses, you will be required to recruit definite kinds of people. In the beginning, however, all male drinkers will be acceptable.

Under no conditions will we interview anyone under 21 years of age. If there is any question whatsoever, you must request identification in the form of either a driver's license or draft card. Further, we will not interview anyone who is in the slightest bit intoxicated. In this case, let him fill out the background information sheet and then tell him that the quota for his brand is filled. Give him one of our premiums and thank him for stopping in.

There will be four different test locations within the store: the first is a general waiting area; the second where the consumer fills out the background information and ideal beer sheets; the third where the taste test is conducted; and the fourth where the brand-image profiles are administered.

The receptionist will give the letter and the attached background information sheet to the consumer. It will be the receptionist's responsibility to see that the consumer fills out the form correctly and completely.

The background information was used as the basis for assigning 25 percent of the respondents to each of four taste groups so that the

EXHIBIT 1
Description of sample

Sample	I Falstaff and Falstaff	II Falstaff and Brand A	III Falstaff and Brand B	IV Brand A and Brand B	Total
Total interviews.............	198	201	202	199	800
Race: white (percent).........	75.3	75.1	76.2	74.9	75.4
Occupation: white collar......	49	47.5	47.1	47.7	47.9
Age: 40 and over.............	48	49.8	48.1	45.8	47.9
Consumption: 10 and under (bottles, cans, glasses)......	57.6	56.6	61.4	64.2	60
Usual brand					
Falstaff...................	10.6	9.5	10.4	10.5	10.4
Brand A...................	12.1	12.9	12.9	11.6	12.4
Brand B...................	11.6	11.9	11.9	12.6	12

groups were similar in such characteristics as race, occupation, age, weekly beer consumption, and brand preference. (See Exhibit 1.)

Taste Group I................	Falstaff versus Falstaff
Taste Group II...............	Falstaff versus Brand A
Taste Group III..............	Falstaff versus Brand B
Taste Group IV..............	Brand A versus Brand B

The taste test actually was made with 900 respondents, representing an oversample of 100. The extra represented an allowance for unusable responses sufficient to assure that 800 qualified responses had been obtained during the test.

"Ideal" beer

The second part of the questionnaire presented an open-end question which asked the respondent to describe in his own words the taste attributes of an ideal beer.

The respondent then was asked to describe the ideal beer by placing an X in one of seven boxes appearing between each of eight "paired opposite" descriptive phrases. (See below.) The position of an X between the two extremes indicated his feeling as to what the ideal beer should be in regard to the quality concerned.

From previous taste tests, Mr. Schwartz had concluded that certain descriptive phrases were regarded positively, while their opposite phrases were regarded negatively. The rating form was designed so that the "positive" phrases were distributed evenly between the left- and right-hand sides.

Bitter beer	□ □ □ □ □ □ □	Not bitter beer
Good-quality beer	□ □ □ □ □ □ □	Poor-quality beer
Strong alcoholic content	□ □ □ □ □ □ □	Weak alcoholic content
Watery beer	□ □ □ □ □ □ □	Full-bodied beer
Good flavor	□ □ □ □ □ □ □	Poor flavor
Sweet beer	□ □ □ □ □ □ □	Not sweet beer
Has no bad aftertaste	□ □ □ □ □ □ □	Has a bad aftertaste
Light beer	□ □ □ □ □ □ □	Heavy beer

Blind taste test

For the next part of the test, the respondent was directed to the tasting area in the store. The instructions given to the testing staff for the blind taste test follow:

Ask the consumer to sit down. Then explain to him what he is expected to do while tasting the beer. Please read the instructions on top of Form III to the consumer and ask if he has any question about it.

Then serve him one of the beers. In all cases fill the glass completely and in the manner in which you have been instructed. The consumer must fill out the form completely. Do not let him make more than one X for any of the pairs of phrases.

The consumer will never be told the brand name of the beer he is testing. He will never see the bottle from which the beer is poured.

The tester will place the glass in front of a number on the table, indicating that the consumer is rating number 24. The tester will not tell the consumer anything about the beer except, if questioned, to say that the beer is made by a reputable brewery. No other information about the beer will be told to the consumer.

During each test there will be only two numbers on the table. After the consumer has ranked one beer, he will then taste and rank the second. Remember that the respondent must not cross-taste, but must rate each beer by itself. After he has drunk the first beer and rated it, please remove it.

The tester will permit the consumer to drink as much or as little of the glass of beer as the consumer wishes.

The taste test was carefully supervised to control sequence rotation in any pairing of number codes, the freshness of the beer, the temperature at which it was served, and the consistency of pouring methods.

The test staff had purchased the beer from a high-volume retail outlet and a reading of the code indicated that the beer was fresh.

The respondent was served a full glass of one of two unidentified brands. He was asked to taste the beer and then describe it by placing X's appropriately between each of the same paired opposite phrases used to obtain descriptions of the ideal beer. The procedure then was repeated for the second unidentified brand.

The respondent then was asked to indicate by code number which of the two beers he preferred. Following this the respondent was asked to explain in his own words the reasons why he preferred the coded brand.

Taste impression

Upon completion of the blind taste test, the respondent was asked to describe his impression of the taste of Falstaff and each of four well-known competitive brands of beer sold in California by using the same pairs of descriptive phrases used earlier. He was given a separate form for each of the five brands. The testing staff was instructed as follows:

By this time the consumer will be familiar with the taste-rating procedure. However, it is important to ask him to rate even those brands which he might not have tasted, based on his impressions of the beer. Before the consumer leaves, make sure that he has checked one box for each of the five forms. You will also give him the notebook which is his gift and our way of saying thanks for his cooperation.

The entire testing procedure required approximately 20 minutes.

Tabulation of responses

A taste profile was developed for each of the five brands by combining the descriptions given by all respondents. To facilitate the compilation, a number was assigned to each box on the eight-phrase rating forms as follows:

$$1 \quad 2 \quad 3 \quad 4 \quad 5 \quad 6 \quad 7$$
Bitter □ □ □ □ □ □ □ Not bitter

The frequency of response for each box was tabulated and an average was computed for each pair of descriptive phrases. The standard deviation for each average was also computed for use in determining statistical significance.

Brand profiles were computed for the entire sample and for each of the four test groups. The results from each test group were broken down for subgroups based on age, occupation, consumption pattern, and "usual brand." In the report, the data were summarized using averages of all scores for each item or pair of phrases.

FINDINGS

The ideal beer

Responses given most frequently when respondents were asked (in an open-end question) to describe the taste of an ideal beer were "not bitter," "smooth and mellow," "somewhat light," and "very light." (See Exhibit 2.)

EXHIBIT 2
Beer drinkers' descriptions of the characteristics of an ideal beer° (total interviews: 634)

An ideal beer is:	Percent mentioning†
Not bitter	23.5
Smooth, mellow	21
Somewhat light	17.5
Very light	16.6
Distinct malt or hop taste	9.9
Somewhat bitter	6.9
Very tangy	6
Slight malt or hop taste	4.7
No aftertaste	4.7
Somewhat heavy	5
Somewhat tangy	4.6
Somewhat sweet	2.8
Some aftertaste	2.7
Aged	2.1
Very heavy	1.9
Very sweet	1.7
Very bitter	0.6
Miscellaneous taste attributes	17.7
Nontaste attributes	21.6

* Of 800 selected interviews, only 634 respondents actually referred to taste attributes in answering this question.

† 166, or 21 percent of the respondents, did not know or did not answer this question.

The profile of an ideal beer, determined by use of the eight pairs of descriptive phrases, was described by the Institute for Design Analysis as follows (see Exhibit 3):

It was most desired that the ideal beer have good flavor and be of good quality.

It should not be too sweet or bitter . . . nor have a discernible aftertaste.

It should promise some "alcoholic content," but a great amount was not thought desirable.

While the ideal beer was on the light side of the heavy-light continuum, the ideal beer should be full-bodied, not watery.

EXHIBIT 3
A profile of the taste attributes of the ideal beer

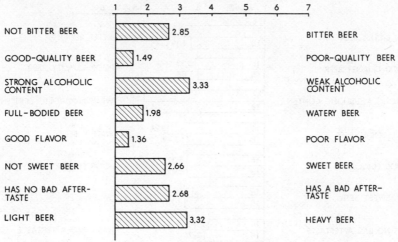

NOT BITTER BEER	2.85 — BITTER BEER
GOOD-QUALITY BEER	1.49 — POOR-QUALITY BEER
STRONG ALCOHOLIC CONTENT	3.33 — WEAK ALCOHOLIC CONTENT
FULL-BODIED BEER	1.98 — WATERY BEER
GOOD FLAVOR	1.36 — POOR FLAVOR
NOT SWEET BEER	2.66 — SWEET BEER
HAS NO BAD AFTER-TASTE	2.68 — HAS A BAD AFTER-TASTE
LIGHT BEER	3.32 — HEAVY BEER

Base: 800 northern California beer drinkers.

The ideal-beer profile did not vary significantly among light, medium, heavy, and very heavy drinkers. There also were no significant differences between white- and blue-collar workers or between those under and over 40 years of age.

While reviewing the test results, Mr. Schwartz and Mr. Evans questioned the advisability or having required all respondents to describe their ideal beer as the first step of the test. They wondered whether this might have influenced responses obtained later by the use of the same descriptive phrases in the rating forms. In other words, the effect might have been to minimize scaling differences for the beers subsequently tasted in the blind taste test. Also, if a respondent liked the taste of a beer in the blind taste test, it was possible that he might tend to describe it in the same terms he used to describe his ideal beer.

The blind taste test

Taste Group I unknowingly compared Falstaff and Falstaff. No respondent recognized that the two servings were of the same beer. Forty-three percent said they preferred the beer when it was served under one of the codes used and 52 percent said they preferred it when served under the other code. The blind-taste profiles of the two servings were almost identical. (See Exhibit 4.) Mr. Schwartz considered that the difference between scores for "light beer" and "heavy beer" was not significant.

EXHIBIT 4
A comparison of the blind-taste profiles of Falstaff (code 16) and Falstaff (code 18)

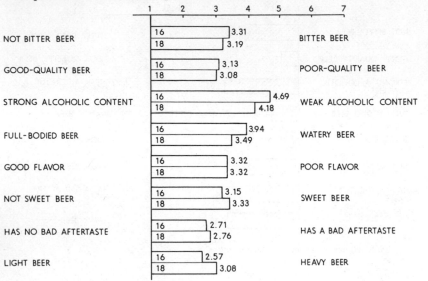

Base: 198 northern California beer drinkers.

The taste profiles for the beers used in Test Groups II, III, and IV also varied only in minor respects, as follows:

Group II, Falstaff versus Brand A—Falstaff was considered a lighter beer, less bitter and with less aftertaste than A. However, these differences were not statistically significant.

Group III, Falstaff versus Brand B—the latter was perceived as a lighter beer, Falstaff as more full-bodied. Again, these and related differences were not statistically significant.

A combining of the results obtained in each blind taste-test group resulted in profiles for the three brands which were almost identical. There were no statistically significant differences.

Blind-taste profiles versus the ideal beer. Since the profiles for the three brands tasted were so similar, they deviated from the ideal-beer profile on the same taste characteristics to about the same degree. (See Exhibit 5.)

Preference in blind-taste comparisons. Additional evidence that the respondents were unable to distinguish taste differences among the beers tested was the fact that no one brand was significantly preferred to the others and the widest range in preference was illustrated by Falstaff versus Falstaff. (See Exhibit 6.)

There were no significant differences in preferences by age, occupation, or consumption pattern of respondent.

EXHIBIT 5
A comparison of Falstaff's cumulated blind-taste profile with the ideal-beer profile
(other brands paralleled this comparison)

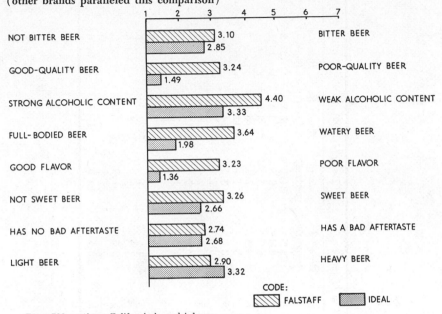

	Falstaff	Ideal	
NOT BITTER BEER	3.10	2.85	BITTER BEER
GOOD-QUALITY BEER	3.24	1.49	POOR-QUALITY BEER
STRONG ALCOHOLIC CONTENT	4.40	3.33	WEAK ALCOHOLIC CONTENT
FULL-BODIED BEER	3.64	1.98	WATERY BEER
GOOD FLAVOR	3.23	1.36	POOR FLAVOR
NOT SWEET BEER	3.26	2.66	SWEET BEER
HAS NO BAD AFTERTASTE	2.74	2.68	HAS A BAD AFTERTASTE
LIGHT BEER	2.90	3.32	HEAVY BEER

CODE: FALSTAFF   IDEAL

Base: 799 northern California beer drinkers.

EXHIBIT 6
Blind taste test: Percent choosing each brand

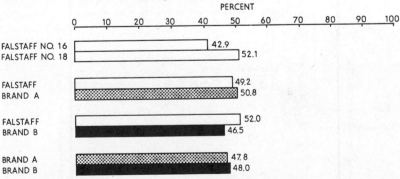

PERCENT

FALSTAFF NO. 16	42.9
FALSTAFF NO. 18	52.1
FALSTAFF	49.2
BRAND A	50.8
FALSTAFF	52.0
BRAND B	46.5
BRAND A	47.8
BRAND B	48.0

Reasons for preferences. After indicating which brand they preferred
in the blind taste test, respondents were asked the reasons for their
preference. Mr. Schwartz noted in the report that ". . . the consumers
used the words selected from the various phrases that they had been
rating." (See Exhibit 7.)
The reason most frequently mentioned for preference was that of

EXHIBIT 7
Reasons for preferring one brand over another*

Reasons for preference	Test I (198)		Test II (201)		Test III (202)		Test IV (199)	
	Falstaff #16 (percent)	Falstaff #18 (percent)	Falstaff (percent)	Brand A (percent)	Falstaff (percent)	Brand B (percent)	Brand A (percent)	Brand B (percent)
Better taste, flavor	26.3	32.3	27.4	28.9	31.0	27.7	27.2	19.1
Full-bodied, not watery	12.6	18.7	11	16.4	19.8	9.4	13.1	15.1
No aftertaste	9.1	6.6	8.5	6.5	5	5.9	6	8.6
Not bitter	8.1	7.6	11.5	6.5	7.4	6.4	6	11.1
Light	8.1	7.6	8	5	1.9	11.9	7	5.5
Smoother	6.6	2.5	5.5	3	3.5	14.4	2.5	7
Not sweet	4.5	3.1	9	8.5	7.9	3.5	4.5	2
Stronger, heavier	2.5	5.1	5.5	5.5	12.9	5.9	7.5	1.5
Good quality	5	3	5	2.5	2.5	12.4	6	4
Sweet	2	1.5	1	1.5	1.5	3.5	2	2
Mild	2.5	1.5	5	3.5	1	0.5	2	3
Heavy alcohol content	1.5	7.1	4	2.5	1.5	1.5	2.5	4
Some aftertaste	1	3	1.5	1	1	2.5	1.5	1
Somewhat tangy	1	2.5	3	5.5	2	1	1.5	—
Light alcohol content	1	1.5	2.5	2.5	1.9	1.9	3	2
Miscellaneous	1	2	1.5	2	1	1	1.5	2
No answer or don't know	26.4	27.9	21.5	26.3	19.9	15.5	21.6	18.5

* Multiple mentions cause totals of more than 100 percent.

better taste or flavor. Next was that the beer was full-bodied rather than watery.

The report pointed out that in Test Group III there were some interesting and significant taste differences mentioned. For example, Falstaff was preferred over B, although B was thought to be lighter, smoother, and of better quality than Falstaff in the image section that follows.

Taste images. This section reported beer drinkers' taste images for Falstaff, Brand A, Brand B, Brand C, and Brand D. The images were obtained from a test in which the brand names were made known to the respondents.

Mr. Schwartz reported the following differences in taste-image profiles (see Exhibit 8):

Not bitter beer/bitter beer: B was thought the least bitter beer, with D second. Falstaff, A, and C were clustered in the middle of the continuum.
Good-quality beer/poor-quality beer: B and D were regarded as being the closest to a good-quality beer. Falstaff was in the middle.
Strong alcoholic content/weak alcoholic content: The image of all five beers was much the same here. There was some indication that B was thought to have the weakest alcoholic content. (Impressions of a stronger or weaker alcoholic content are definitely a function of image only.)
Full-bodied beer/watery beer: All five brands were seen to be in the middle of the range.
Good flavor/poor flavor; not sweet beer/sweet beer: All five brands were close to the middle on both attributes.
Has no bad aftertaste/has a bad aftertaste: B was thought to have the least bad aftertaste, followed by D and Falstaff.
Light beer/heavy beer: B was seen as being lighter than the other four brands.

Interpretation of taste results. Mr. Schwartz interpreted the brand taste-image results as follows (see Exhibit 8):

The image of all five brands was remarkably close. Only B clearly differentiated itself from the other brands. D did this somewhat by paralleling the image of B, yet not with the same image clarity.

The image of Falstaff was much less clear than that of several brands. Falstaff ranked third among the brands on each pair of phrases. Falstaff's taste image was stable and did not vary among different types of beer drinkers.

A and C had almost identical taste images—somewhat heavier, stronger alcoholic beers.

Falstaff blind taste versus brand taste image versus ideal. Falstaff's blind taste-test profile was compared with its brand taste image and the taste profile for the beer. The results of the comparisons as reported by the Institute for Design Analysis follow (see Exhibit 9):

First, Falstaff's blind taste profile and its brand taste image were

EXHIBIT 8
A comparison of the taste-image impression profile of Falstaff and four other brands

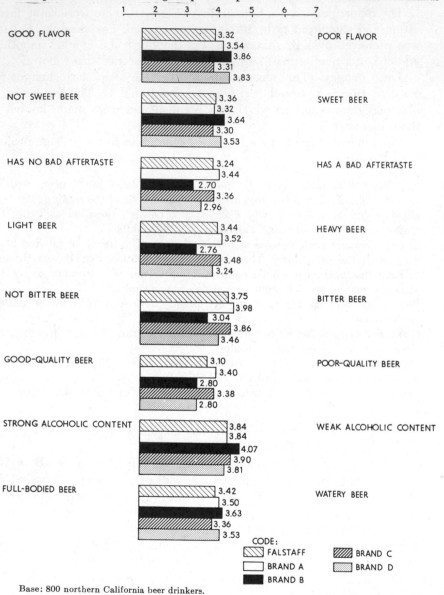

Base: 800 northern California beer drinkers.

EXHIBIT 9
A comparison of Falstaff cumulated blind taste image-impression profile,
and ideal-beer profile°

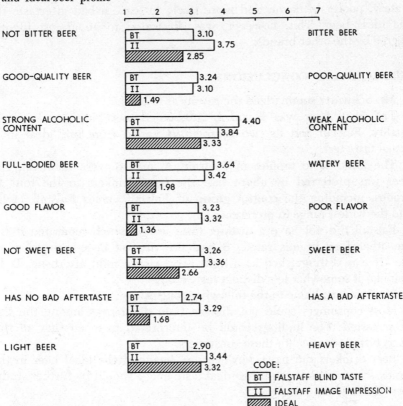

	1	2	3	4	5	6	7	

NOT BITTER BEER — BT 3.10 / II 3.75 / IDEAL 2.85 — BITTER BEER

GOOD-QUALITY BEER — BT 3.24 / II 3.10 / IDEAL 1.49 — POOR-QUALITY BEER

STRONG ALCOHOLIC CONTENT — BT 4.40 / II 3.84 / IDEAL 3.33 — WEAK ALCOHOLIC CONTENT

FULL-BODIED BEER — BT 3.64 / II 3.42 / IDEAL 1.98 — WATERY BEER

GOOD FLAVOR — BT 3.23 / II 3.32 / IDEAL 1.36 — POOR FLAVOR

NOT SWEET BEER — BT 3.26 / II 3.36 / IDEAL 2.66 — SWEET BEER

HAS NO BAD AFTERTASTE — BT 2.74 / II 3.29 / IDEAL 1.68 — HAS A BAD AFTERTASTE

LIGHT BEER — BT 2.90 / II 3.44 / IDEAL 3.32 — HEAVY BEER

CODE:
BT FALSTAFF BLIND TASTE
II FALSTAFF IMAGE IMPRESSION
IDEAL

* Other brands differed similarly from the ideal.
Base: Falstaff blind taste: 799 northern California beer drinkers.
    Falstaff image impression: 800 northern California beer drinkers.
    Ideal: 800 northern California beer drinkers.

well matched on most of the eight characteristics. In four instances,
differences were noted illustrative of contrasts or conflicts between taste
impression and image impressions:

Not bitter/bitter beer: The brand taste image was more bitter than the blind
taste rating.
Strong alcoholic content/weak alcoholic content: In the taste test the beer
was rated as stronger in alcoholic content than it was in the brand taste
image.
Has no bad aftertaste/has a bad aftertaste: In the blind taste test the beer's
"less aftertaste" rating was higher than in the brand taste image.
Light beer/heavy beer: In the blind taste test it was considered a lighter
beer than in its brand image.

Secondly, on four of the image attributes, Falstaff differed significantly from the ideal profile. It was seen as being poorer in quality, more watery, poorer in flavor, and more likely to leave a bad aftertaste than the ideal beer. This, however, was illustrated to an almost identical degree by the other brands.

SUMMARY AND CONCLUSIONS

Mr. Schwartz summarized the results as follows:

The ideal beer was flavorful, full-bodied, not bitter, and of good quality. Falstaff and its two competitors varied from this ideal in the actual taste test.

The blind taste profiles of Falstaff, A, and B were identical. Each beer was preferred by about half the beer drinkers in the four test groups, including the control group of Falstaff versus Falstaff (which had the widest range in preference).

Falstaff did not have a distinct taste image which separated it from the other four brands rated. B had the clearest taste-impression profile—it was distinguished as a light beer with a mild aftertaste. D had a similar if somewhat less distinct taste image.

Mr. Schwartz came to the following conclusions:

Most consumers could not discern taste differences among the three beers tested. The findings could be interpreted to mean that all three beers tasted identical to these consumers.

Beer drinkers did have, however, an image of the ideal beer in their minds. The significance of this ideal taste image should be further studied from the following angles:

1. To determine what consumers mean when they seek "good flavor" and a "full-bodied" beer.
2. To determine if these concepts could be translated into useful marketing devices.

WHAT RECOMMENDATIONS FOR MANAGEMENT?

Mr. Evans reviewed the research report in his effort to determine what recommendation he should make to the marketing vice president as to what should be done to increase Falstaff's share of the California beer market.

CASE QUESTIONS

1. What were the main elements of the research approach?
2. Was the research well designed to accomplish the stated objectives?
3. Evaluate the taste test from the standpoint of experimental design.

4. What was learned from the research?
   a) Did the taste test prove an absence of taste differences between the brands tested?
   b) How much was learned about "ideal beer"?
   c) How much was learned about how Falstaff's image compared with the images of other brands?
   d) How much was learned about why people bought one brand of beer rather than another?
5. Now that the research findings have been reported, what should Mr. Evans do next?
   a) Should he recommend to the director of marketing a marketing program for improving Falstaff's position in California?
   b) Should he propose more research? If so, what? Why?

CASE 2–2

Ford Motor Company (A)*

Marketing strategy for the 1972 Pinto

On January 1, 1971, after four months of sales experience with the Pinto, a new economy subcompact automobile, the Ford Division of Ford Motor Company was faced with the problems of position assessment and strategy planning for the 1972 model year. The Pinto team was comparing the results of the 1971 marketing strategy with those measurable goals that had been established months before, and the beginnings of the new planning cycle were underway. Such things as the need for reidentification of target market segments and the search for appropriate product and pricing policies were under consideration, in light of the continued European and now stronger Asian small car penetration into the domestic market. This penetration had reached an alarming 14.7 percent of all domestic passenger car sales.

After having delved into target, product, and price, the problem of promotion mix also had to be dealt with. In sum, the Pinto marketing team was challenged to offer an overall marketing strategy to the Ford Division for the 1972 model year.

---

* This case was prepared by Jay D. Lindquist, Research Assistant, Graduate School of Business Administration, The University of Michigan.

BACKGROUND

In the early 1960s, the Detroit auto complex had been successful in temporarily stemming the foreign import tide with compact automobiles such as the Ford Falcon and the Chevrolet Corvair. However, continued size and weight increases, coupled with extensive accessory and option availability and attendant price increase, caused this class of vehicle to slowly move out of direct competition with the economy subcompact which it had been designed to combat. In its place, the sporty compact caught the American public's fancy; and from 1964 to 1967, when sales peaked at about 850,000 units or a 10.4 percent share of the market, such cars as the Mustang, Barracuda, and Camaro were the American auto industry's substitute for its lost compact sales.

During this period import sales had continued to rise and in 1966 enjoyed a 7.3 percent share of passenger vehicle sales in the United States. This trend continued upward, and in 1969, 11.0 percent of auto sales were made by foreign vehicle dealers. Concurrently, sales of sporty compacts were on the decline, and by 1969 a little over 650,000 units were sold for a 7.1 percent share of the market. The overall compact, or economy car, segment of total car sales also had been growing through this period, and by the end of 1969 it had reached 19.8 percent of total industry sales.

Ford Motor Company realized that action had to be taken to both stem the tide of the foreign imports and to move swiftly into the potentially profitable economy subcompact arena. In 1969 the Ford Division introduced its "Simple Machine," the Maverick. This vehicle was not a head-to-head match with the average foreign subcompact, but the company felt that it would reach a segment of the market that was interested in economy. Also, the vehicle was thought to have the ability to capture some potential import buyers. Maverick was a sales success but did not seem to stem the flow of imports to any great extent.

In September 1971, Ford introduced Pinto, a true economy subcompact. The vehicle concept and design was a product of extensive consumer research and was intended to meet the import challenge.

THE BUYER IDENTIFIED—PRIOR TO INTRODUCTION

Demographics

The Pinto team first looked at the kind of people who purchased imported economy subcompacts and in particular the Volkswagen (VW) buyer. Exhibit 1 offers some interesting comparative data on purchasers of various size vehicles.

Some of the interesting facts that came to light were that the median age of VW and import buyers was 8 to 9 years less than Maverick

EXHIBIT 1
Demographics of small car buyers, compared with intermediate and average new
car buyers

	Im-ports	Mav-erick	VW	Com-pact	Inter-mediate	Aver-age
Age						
Median..................	31	39	30	42	36	42
Percent 55 and over........	7	11	5	17	18	21
Martial status						
Percent single..............	21	16	27	22	25	18
Education level						
Percent beyond high						
school..................	65	44	60	46	48	51
Income ($1,000)						
Median...................	11.4	11.0	10.7	10.5	11.1	12.1
Multiple car ownership						
Percent that own more						
than one car.............	67	70	65	62	58	62

Source: "Small Car Market Presentation," by R. L. Landgraff.

buyers and 11 to 12 years less than the average compact auto purchaser.
Also, the data indicated that a very low percentage of VW and import
buyers were over 55 years of age. Note was also taken of the income
and education levels of the potential target buyers versus other vehicle
size purchasers.

In sum, the Pinto prospective buyer was seen by the company as
more affluent, younger, and better educated than the typical Ford economy car buyer of the past.

Psychographics

Having examined the demographic characteristics of the VW and
other import segments versus those portions of the buying public who
purchase the vehicle classes shown in Exhibit 1, the Ford Division, with
the aid of its advertising agency, J. Walter Thompson Company, proceeded to attempt to identify buying motivations for various market
segments by vehicle type. Exhibit 2 summarizes the results for selected
significant motivators as identified by marketing research.

Of particular note from the data was the fact that although only
20 percent of the average new car buyers indicated that economy was
a factor, 48 percent of all import buyers interviewed stated that, indeed,
economy was of considerable importance. Ford researchers also noted
that the need to realize value for the money was a significant motivator
for the import group of buyers. Not unexpected was the low concern
for exterior appearance and riding comfort displayed by the import

EXHIBIT 2
New car buying motivations by market segment (by percent)

Market segments	Economy of operation and maintenance	Good value for money	Durability	Exterior appearance	Riding comfort
Imports	48	48	30	10	4
Compact	42	47	14	20	5
Small speciality	12	24	10	56	6
Intermediate	12	30	18	41	13
Standard	15	36	25	24	22
Medium	6	29	28	24	39
Personal luxury	2	12	16	49	35
Luxury	3	14	25	23	48
Average new car buyer	20	34	22	28	19

buyers who were probably strongly influenced by Ford's leading competitor, VW.

Analysis of the data also led to the conclusion that, in some cases, the responses could have been after-the-fact rationalizations to reaffirm purchase decisions already made, rather than true measures of buyer motivation. However, the response differences between import buyers and other passenger vehicle buyers pointed up qualities that a Ford product would have to strive to achieve in order to be successful.

Also, through experience, the Ford Division had learned that the buyer's previous experience with the local dealer, combined with the overall company reputation, could have an effect on purchase intentions that exceeded the product influence.

The data contained in the 1970 research mentioned above was a confirming capstone to the information that had already been gathered by such organizations as *Newsweek, U.S. News and World Report,* J. Walter Thompson, and Ford itself.

Some noneconomic reasons for purchase of imported vehicles were also discovered through Ford sponsored research. They were: (1) dislike of American products, (2) change in life style of young people—a rejection of traditional values placed on "big" American cars, (3) reverse snob appeal of owning an ugly utilitarian product, and (4) belief that foreign car ownership receives more status than domestic car ownership. Ford's market research indicated that these reasons are much less active in the decision process than the rational economic reasons stated previously.

In response to the research facts, two schools of thought developed as to what the specific buyer target segment should be and what should be considered as true major competition. One opinion was that Pinto marketing strategy should be directed primarily toward buyers of domestic or imported subcompacts; the other school advocated a direct focus upon the import market segment. Eventually a compromise was agreed upon, and the result of this "targeting" will be mentioned under the advertising strategy section of this case.

THE COMPETITIVE PICTURE

The primary competitor of interest to the Ford Motor Company was Volkswagen. Other imported vehicles such as Toyota, Datsun, Opel, Volvo, Fiat, and Renault were also in the picture. Of particular interest to the firm were the recent advances made by the Japanese.

Additionally, consideration was given to the American Motors Gremlin, and the Chevrolet Vega. Ford, however, felt that neither of these two vehicles met the import challenge squarely. The Pinto team was also aware of the Lincoln–Mercury Division entry, Capri, and the potential of Chrysler Corporation to either manufacture a subcompact in the United States or to import a foreign competitor such as the Cricket.

Of complementary importance to Ford was the problem of competition with its own products. Because of the lower profit margin in actual dollars per unit sold for Pinto, the Ford Division had to be reasonably sure the incremental sales (noncannibalization sales) would be high enough to justify product introduction. After all, the objective of the division was to maximize overall profits.

As noted in the background discussion, the import economy subcompact was rising in share of the market, and the projection for 1970 was some 13 percent.

To add momentum to this surge, the number of dealerships for imports had reached the level of 12,870 by the end of 1969, and a forecast of some 14,000 dealerships was made for 1970. The greatest increase in this competitive distribution picture was seen to be coming from the Japanese segment of the import, subcompact market.

PINTO MARKETING STRATEGY FOR 1971

Objectives

Two major sales objectives were established: first, that 400,000 units were to be sold; and second, that the Pinto should produce 55 percent incremental sales. Charles W. Richert, light car marketing plans manager, stated that the method used to obtain the 400,000 unit goal was a three-step process. He said that approximately three years prior to the introduction of the new vehicle, the Ford planners established what is termed a "planning volume" which reflects a minimum rate of return per vehicle and a minimum number of vehicles to be sold. As the car comes closer in time to introduction, a consideration of historical records and trends for the Ford Division is examined to assess potential market share for all Ford vehicles. This figure has been around 21 percent in the recent past. From the historical data, a projection of potential sales is made for the new vehicle in its introductory year. These three steps from "planning volume," to historical performance, to sales forecast are also tempered by other factors, such as available plant capacity. Mr. Richert stated that in the case of Pinto the 400,000 unit goal was influenced by production capacity.

No specific communication objectives were established that were of a measurable nature, though product identity (i.e. as an economy subcompact) was to be of importance, along with buying-public awareness of the product name.

The product for 1971

Having the benefit of the research done since 1966, Ford's Pinto was designed to meet the import buyers profile of desires and particularly those desires of Volkswagen (VW) buyers, because of the strong showing of their car.

The major product objectives were:[1]

1. Overall size about the same as the VW
2. Cost of ownership to equal VW
   a) Competitive purchase price
   b) Equivalent fuel consumption
   c) Built-in durability and reliability
   d) Serviceability equal to or better than VW
   e) Less maintenance cost
   f) Competitive parts prices
3. Comfort, convenience, and appearance pluses versus VW
   a) Wide tread and lower height for better stability
   b) Better maneuverability (rack and pinion steering)
   c) Better ventilation and heating
   d) Easier front and rear seat entry and exit
   e) More interior room
   f) Wider option availability
   g) Distinctive modern styling

The ideas of economy, durability, and good value for the money moved throughout the Pinto product objectives in order to properly position the car to meet the target market's goals. (See Appendix 1 for a brief description of major product features.)

The 1971 model Pinto was a two-door sedan with body and frame

---

[1] "Small Car Market Presentation," by R. L. Landgraff.

welded into a single unit. The vehicle had a long hood, short rear deck, and side glass without vents. The interior of the vehicle contained a full-width crash pad and a two-dial instrument cluster. High bucket seats and vinyl trim were standard. The engine was mounted in the front and the Pinto had a conventional drive train and rear wheel drive. A 75-horsepower 1,600 cubic centimeter, 4-cylinder overhead valve engine was standard. (Optional—2,000 cubic centimeter, 100-horsepower engine.) Either a standard four-speed floor-mounted manual transmission or an optional three-speed automatic transmission were available. The product also had a high-level ram-air ventilation system and a good heating and defrosting unit. Rack and pinion steering was used to increase response and maneuverability, and standard manual brake drum brakes were offered (see Appendix 2).

The price for 1971

The pricing strategy for Pinto was to place it as close to the VW Beetle as possible, considering appropriate profit margins. In Exhibit 3 we see the list of various vehicle models that are considered comparable by the Pinto team and their relative 1971 model prices.

EXHIBIT 3
Subcompact base price comparison

Make	Lowest base price model*	Next highest base price model
Pinto	$1,919	$2,062
Vega	2,096	2,196
Gremlin	1,899	1,999
Datsun	1,736	1,866
Fiat	1,555	2,059
Opel	1,878	1,994
Renault	1,799	—
Toyota	1,798	1,918
VW	1,845	1,985

* Some of the vehicles, particularly the Japanese vehicles, include more extras in their base price than do comparable American vehicles.

The Ford Motor Company planned to sell according to "sticker price," as had VW and other import subcompact dealers in the past, rather than the usual discount approach generally followed by American new car dealers.

The distribution for 1971

The car sales programming manager for the Ford Division, J. V. Holbeck, described the general distribution determination process that the company went through for Pinto as follows. He stated that the distribution options considered were those that would key purely on Volkswagen, those that keyed on the total universe of imports, and those that synthesized the two individual options into a compromise third option.

To use the first option, the company would have examined VW's relative share of the market throughout the United States and matched it with Pinto distribution on a share-for-share basis. To follow the second option, the programming group would have considered import dealership distribution and new entries, and historical data on import registration patterns.

The problem of significance that the company would face if it followed either option, stated Mr. Holbeck, was that these approaches would have neglected Ford dealership past performance. That is, dealerships located in areas other than those where the imports are the strongest contribute significant sales volumes in large markets, and this volume consideration would have been neglected in Pinto distribution pattern decisions.

In light of these considerations, the Ford Division looked at both the import/VW potential and dealers' past performance in order to determine the relative emphasis for distribution for Pinto.

Having decided on the overall approach, the programming group then followed a procedure to attain district sales quotas with the actual analysis of data beginning in the summer of 1970. The first step taken was to decide what the total industry potential for all passenger vehicles would be. Such things as the economic outlook, surveys of new car buying intentions, fluctuations in savings rates, and other pertinent data were considered. Next, a look at each of the various car segments was undertaken (i.e. intermediate, compact, subcompact). This was done by examining past history of sales and market shares and market trends. Mr. Holbeck also indicated that extensive market research was done. Next, the potential performance of Ford within each of these segments was assessed; again, past history plus trends were explored to arrive at Ford's potential penetration. Along with these outside factors, such problem areas as production capacity were examined. The final step taken was to allocate Pinto distribution to sales district level and below.

The approach generally could be considered a top-down method, though inputs from the sales force at the district level were solicited by the division. Mr. Holbeck emphasized that the smooth relationship between the division and the sales district allowed for planning of appropriate distribution of Pinto vehicles to meet company goals.

The promotion plan for 1971

Two general categories of efforts were employed by the Pinto team in promoting the vehicle to the buying public. These were broadly classed as advertising and merchandising. According to James Doyle, major market advertising manager, the corporation overall split in advertising dollars versus merchandising expenditure is about 75 to 80 percent versus 25 to 20 percent respectively. The dealer organization which is independent of the Ford Division spends its self-assessed funds on a 90 percent to 10 percent basis for advertising versus merchandising.

The merchandising strategy employed by the Ford Division had a threefold purpose. First, it was to maximize the effectiveness of the contact between the retail organization and the customer. This was carried out through the new-model introduction shows, whose object was to presell the sales organization, salesman training programs, point-of-sale displays, and contest and incentive programs.

The second essential merchandising function was that of communication of the national marketing strategy to the dealers so that their own local programs would fit in. The latter was accomplished mainly through meetings with dealers. The third merchandising function carried out was that which attempted to provide special incentives for buyers to visit dealer showrooms. Here special value vehicles, plus giveaways and contests, were employed. Although the merchandising efforts cited were corporate in nature, they were applied to Pinto. The allocation for Pinto merchandising was approximately $2.5 million.[2]

An example of a Pinto merchandising program was the special key offer. A free do-it-yourself Pinto key was to be made available to all 1971 showroom visitors. People were to register and then receive a free key that had such items on it as a spark plug gap setter, a Phillips screwdriver, and a regular screwdriver. The objective was not only to identify prospects but also to emphasize the simplicity of maintenance for Pinto (see Appendix 3).

The advertising strategy for Pinto had, as its initial constraint, a given dollar budget as specified by the corporate level, based upon field sales objectives. However, the budget was not seen as inflexible in that the corporate structure would approve additional funds for special actions when these actions were deemed necessary. The budget allocated for the advertising phases of the promotional scheme was $10 million.[3]

Fred R. Wuellner, the advertising budget and media analysis manager for the Ford Division, stated that in order to arrive at the budget allocation for Pinto, the overall division profit plan for the 1971 model year was examined, and its objectives were compared to and reconciled with the penetration objectives and field sales objectives for the subcompact. These field sales objectives were compared with those of the other Ford Division vehicles, and the initial portion of the adver-

---

[2] This is not the actual allocation, but is an approximation for the purpose of this case.

[3] This is not the actual allocation, but is an approximation for the purpose of this case.

tising budget assigned to Pinto was close to a straight-line function of its sales objectives versus the other Ford Division cars. Geographical allocation of expenditure was to be based primarily upon sales objectives for the area in question.

Prior to Pinto introduction, the Ford Division had decided to go to a new expenditure plan with regard to advertising. Mr. Wuellner commented that the plan divided the sales year into four specific periods, and further, that the first four months (September to December) were to be termed the "Announcement Period," the next three months—the "Winter Period," the following two months were to be used for special spring sales, and the final two months for clean-up of carry-over sales of Ford Products. The fraction of the budget to be spent in each of the four periods was 42 percent, 26 percent, 24 percent, and 8 percent respectively.

In consonance with the buyer behavior research done and the target segment identification, the Ford Division asked J. Walter Thompson Company to test the impact of various copy headlines on the potential buying public. These headlines were:

1. The little long-distance car
2. The little carefree car
3. Put a little kick in your life
4. The little car for a big country
5. Introducing a little better idea

The advertising agency completed 196 personal interviews with the sample split approximately three to one with regard to male versus female respondents. The sample was taken in Pittsburgh, Cincinnati, Dallas, Miami, and Syracuse. The interviewees were shown several copies of a Pinto advertisement, all of which were identical except for the headline, and they were asked how the ad communicated specific characteristics of Pinto. Exhibit 4 indicates a tabulation of responses.

The following comments from "Research Report—Pinto Headlines" by J. Walter Thompson Co. illustrate the interpretation of the results. (The meaning elicited by each of the five headlines was measured through a combination of open-ended probing and aided descriptive checklists; further, reading interest and personal association comparisons of the five headlines were obtained.)

Findings. The five headlines studied elicited desired meanings—the strong motivating factors in the foreign car segment of the market—in varying degrees. Exhibit 5 groups some of these desired meanings, according to strengths and weaknesses in the image of Volkswagen, and lists the headlines that are seen to communicate these points to the greatest extent in Pinto's favor.

EXHIBIT 4
1971 Pinto—headline research: Interviewee asked to indicate which of the headlines shown most communicates each characteristics (shown by percent)

	Little long distance	*Little carefree car*	*Put a little kick*	*Little car, big country*	*Little better idea*
A small size car..............	17	(35)	3	33	9
Economical...................	(54)	28	1	10	6
A car to complete with VW.....	21	26	4	(28)	18
Well-built and durable........	30	(34)	3	14	16
Safe........................	22	21	1	10	(35)
Young person's car...........	3	22	(67)	4	2
A car for a small family.......	21	24	4	(31)	12
Fun to drive.................	5	21	(69)	4	1
Comfortable..................	(49)	9	2	10	19
A good handling car that holds the road well........	(47)	10	4	21	10
Easy to repair or take care of yourself.................	5	(68)	1	2	16
A kind of sporty car..........	3	18	(72)	3	2
A lot of car for the money.....	21	16	5	22	(26)
A car which may not change its styling for five years.....	14	18	3	7	(42)
Combines the best features of both American and European small cars............	20	18	3	21	(30)
My kind of car	15	26	(27)	11	17
Average...................	21.7	24.6	16.8	14.4	16.3

EXHIBIT 5

In areas where VW is strong	*Most applicable headline(s)*
Economy and durability/reliability	"The little carefree car" "The little long distance"
Ease of maintenance and repair	"The little carefree car"
Youthful, fun car	"Put a little kick in your life"
Value (a lot of car for the money and styling stability)	"Introducing a little better idea"

In areas where VW is weak	*Most applicable headline(s)*
Sporty, spirited car	"Put a little kick in your life"
Comfortable, good handling car	"The little long distance"

Obviously, the choice of headlines depends greatly upon what the *most* desired meanings really are. In addition, it is useful to consider:

—The headlines that elicited the most *broad* variety of meanings were "The little long distance car," and "The little carefree car."
—The most *pointed* headline was "Put a little kick in your life." This headline was strong in terms of eliciting the related ideas of a "young, sporty, spirited" kind of car.

With respect to positioning as the respondent's "own kind of car," "A little kick" is joined by "The little carefree car" in the minds of the *average* prospect. These two are judged to portray the Pinto about equally well in this respect with differences by age group:

—"Little kick" does a strong positioning job among the younger (under 35) group.
—"Carefree" is the strongest among the older (35 and older) group, while being a very strong second to younger group (under 35).

Summary

Most of the headlines studied possess some virtue. However, some stand out with respect to fulfilling the desired qualities of a headline in appealing to the small-car market:

—"Put a little kick in your life" appears to be very strong in eliciting *personal* meanings, especially among the young people, as a sporty, spirited car, and attacks a Volkswagen's weakness in this regard.
—"A little, carefree car" is a little more oriented to older prospects, and elicits the great variety of "economy, reliable, well-built, easy-to-care-for" car characteristics—the traditional strengths of Volkswagen.
—"The little long distance car" shows great strength in communicating economy, comfort, and good handling characteristics . . . thus putting Pinto in a position to attack a VW product's strength—its economy image; and some VW weaknesses—its poor comfort and handling images.
—The line "Introducing a little better idea" has strength aside from the specific meanings it elicits—it gets the person interested without really pinpointing a message. It is more open in its meaning than the other two lines mentioned above.

In summary, the principal marketing product attributes for Pinto are best expressed in "The little carefree car" and "The little long distance car." An outline of the strategy summary can be found in Appendix 4.

With regard to media choice, detailed analysis was performed by Mr. Wuellner and his staff, and the projected fractional expenditure

EXHIBIT 6
Pinto media expenditures (in percentages)*

	1970 September–December period	1971 January–June period
Television	46	50
Radio	6	23
Newspapers	15	12
Outdoor	20	2
Magazines	13	13
	100	100

* F. R. Wuellner, May 19, 1971.

by media vehicle type for the introductory period (September 1970 through December 1970) and for part of the sustaining campaign (January 1971 through June 1971) are shown in Exhibit 6.

STRATEGY RESULTS THROUGH 31 DECEMBER 1970

The buyer of the 1971 Pinto

After four months of experience with Pinto, data from a Ford Division buyer questionnaire were used to determine how well the car had reached the import target market segment and, in particular, the VW portion of the market. This assessment was primarily based upon a comparison of demographic data. Exhibit 7 tells the story.

EXHIBIT 7
Buyer questionnaire (actual)

		1970 new car buyer study	
Buyer demographics	1971 Pinto	VW	Total imports
Median age	33.0	30.0	31.0
Median income ($1,000)	12.5	10.7	11.4
College education*	34.0	26.0	32.0
Technical, managerial*	42.0	44.0	45.0
Male*	70.0	72.0	75.0
Female*	30.0	28.0	25.0
Married*	68.0	73.0	73.0
Married w/2 children*	45.0	40.0	42.0
Multiple car owners*	73.0	65.0	67.0

* By percent.

Because of the tremendous inroads that the Japanese imports were making during this same time period, data from the "1970 National New Car Buyers Study" were combined with selected "Ford Division Buyer Questionnaire" information in order to develop an up-to-date comparative profile of all major foreign competitors that Pinto faced. This information is included in Exhibit 8.

EXHIBIT 8
Buyer demographics (1971 Pinto compared with 1970 Maverick)

	1971 Pinto	1970 Maverick	1970 VW Beetle	1970 Toyota	1970 Datsun	1970 avg. new car buyer
Age						
Median age............	33	34	28	32	31	42
Age 55 and older*......	7	9	5	7	11	21
Income						
Median income........	$12.5	10.5	10.5	12.0	10.8	12.1
Education						
Some college or						
graduates*..........	64	57	60	64	62	51
Sex and marital status						
Male*................	70	67	68	72	78	78
Married*..............	68	67	71	79	75	74
Occupation						
Professional, technical						
and managerial*......	42	42	40	38	44	38
Car ownership						
Multiple car*..........	73	65	66	70	74	62
First new car*.........	31	36	NA	NA	NA	NA
Sample size..............	4,397	5,460	123	175	143	19,652

* Shown by percent.
"Ford Division Buyer Questionnaire," cumulative four months after introduction (Pinto and Maverick). 1970 National New Car Buyers Study" (all other car lines).

A comparison of the demographic profile of the Pinto buyer with buyers of similar vehicles indicated the following:

1. The Pinto had been attracting buyers essentially the same as those who were initially attracted to Maverick.
2. Pinto buyers resemble import buyers in most aspects, with the exception of relative income (see Exhibit 8).

Research has indicated that Pinto buyers are small-car oriented and that the most frequently mentioned makes seriously examined before purchase of Pinto were subcompact vehicles (see Exhibit 9).

Exhibits 10 and 11 also offer interesting insights into the Pinto buyers' reasons for buying and consideration of the vehicle versus other makes. One should note the significant positions of "operating economy" and "within my budget" in the Pinto purchase decision criteria.

Competitive structure and sales results

Although there was some disagreement among Ford executives on primary target vehicle (VW versus Vega, for example) the advent of the General Motors workers' strike did have an impact on the competitive situation. As a result of the strike, Chevrolet was able to manufacture

EXHIBIT 9
Consideration of other makes

Make of car seriously considered	Percent mentions (includes multiple mentions)
Imports	53
Vega	27
Gremlin	7
Total subcompact	87
Maverick	6
Other Ford	6
GM	14
Chrysler and other AMC	2
None	28

"Pinto September Buyer Study," December 1970.

EXHIBIT 10
Reasons for buying

Motivation	Pinto	1969–1/2 Maverick*
Operating economy	66	65
Within my budget	38	52
Styling	23	25
Value for money	21	35
Easy to repair and service	17	n/a
Maneuverability in city traffic	10	8

* Maverick was added to the Ford line in the middle of the 1969 car buying year; hence management referred to the first model as the "one-half 1969" model.
"Pinto September Buyer Study," December 1970.

EXHIBIT 11
Consideration of Pinto

	1971 model owners of		
	VW	Toyota	Vega
Considered buying some other car	42	64	61
Considered buying Pinto	16	24	27
Considered buying Pinto as percent of those considering some other car	38	38	44
Actually shopped Pinto	11	18	19
Actually shopped Pinto or percent of those considering Pinto	69	75	70

and sell only 22,363 Vega sedans, as compared to the Pinto sale of 76,038 units. The ten-week strike did aid Ford in its Pinto introductory period, but to what extent is hard to assess. The other American competitor, the American Motors Corporation Gremlin, sold 39,701 units in 1970.

Of additional interest is that the number of import franchises in the United States rose to 14,056 in 1970, and of this number the increase in VW, Datsun, and Toyota dealers was 50, 242, and 66 respectively. Note particularly the forward thrust of the Datsun marketing organization. (See Exhibit 12.)

Import sales for 1970 totaled 1,230,961 units, up from 1,061,617 units in 1969. The import share of all passenger car sales for 1970 was approximately 14.7 percent. Two factors of major interest, however, discourage the use of this figure for growth projections. They are (1) the previously mentioned GM strike and (2) the delivery difficulties that VW experienced in September (32,000 units) due to the three-week vacation shutdown at the home plants.

EXHIBIT 12
Import new car registration in the United States in 1970

Manu- facturer	1970 registrations	Relative imports 1970	Position by make 1969
Volkswagen.............	569,182	1	1
Toyota.................	184,898	2	2
Datsun................	100,541	3	4
Opel..................	83,189	4	3
Volvo.................	44,630	5	6
Fiat..................	36,642	6	5
Renault...............	19,584	9	10

During the introductory period VW also changed the competitive picture by introducing its lowest priced model for the first time in the United States. This vehicle sold for $1,780. The regular Beetle was priced at $1,899, lengthened three inches, and then renamed the Super Beetle.

Dodge Motor Division of Chrysler decided not to enter the subcompact race with a domestic vehicle in 1970 and, instead, intended to introduce the Japanese-built Mitsubishi "Colt" after January 1, 1971. Also Chrysler Corporation stated that an additional vehicle, an overseas manufactured Chrysler product, the Cricket, was to be introduced in early 1971.

OBJECTIVES ACHIEVEMENT

Sales goals

The goal of 400,000 units for the entire year implied that sales of about 120,000[4] units (based on historical seasonal trends) would have been realistic for the introductory period had the Ford Division concentrated on pushing the Pinto subcompact. However, the initial strategy was to use Pinto to sell up to other Ford vehicles such as Maverick

---

[4] Author's estimate (not an official Ford goal).

and Mustang. There were disagreements among Ford strategists on this policy; however, during the introductory months, the course outlined above was followed. As a result of this general policy there was no waiting period for Pinto deliveries after the first 30 days of availability, and Maverick sales were sustained at a high level. Another factor depressing Pinto sales was the General Motors strike. All new car sales were thought to have suffered from this ten-week production stoppage. Finally, the overall state of the economy during 1970 probably depressed sales possibilities. Therefore, we see that actual Pinto sales were approximately 76,000 units.

EXHIBIT 13
Pinto source of sales (1971 Pinto)

Make	Percent disposed	Percent would have bought
Ford Motor Co.		
Ford.....................	9	1
Torino...................	4	1
Mustang................	8	6
Maverick...............	2	17
Falcon.................	8	1
Other...................	5	2
Total Ford...............	36	28*
GM......................	28	26*
Chrysler.................	6	4
AMC.....................	3	5
Imports..................	27	37
	100	100

* May be affected by GM strike.
Source: "Ford Division Buyer Questionnaire." Survey of 12 major markets. Cumulative sample, four months after introduction.

The incremental sales goal of 55 percent was ambitious, based upon past performance of new products introduced by the Ford Division. Generally speaking, incremental sales of new Ford vehicles have run between 20 and 30 percent. At the end of 1970, Pinto incremental sales were between 30 and 40 percent which was below target, but quite respectable considering historical results. Exhibit 13 indicates Pinto source of sales.

The Ford Division share of the subcompact segment improved from 3 percent during the fourth quarter of the 1970 model year (with Cortina alone) to 15 percent during the first quarter of the 1971 model year. At 15 percent, however, the share of the subcompact segment was considerably below Maverick's 24 percent share of the compact segment during the same time period. Maximum attainable Pinto share was put at 22 percent, assuming year-end stocks of 5,000 to 6,000 units.

Although the full impact of the Pinto and other domestic subcompacts had not been felt by the end of 1970, no appreciable effect on import penetration had been seen to that date.

Additionally, during an interview, Mr. Richert stated that the company noticed that within about one month after the Pinto was put on sale, the subcompact market seemed to be segmenting itself into a luxury subcompact and an economy subcompact segment. The economy subcompact vehicles appeared to be those in the $1,500 to $1,800 class, whereas the luxury subcompact vehicles were in the $2,000 or a little bit higher price class. There, the problem of placing Pinto "reared its ugly head."

Product acceptance

In general, the styling of Pinto was well accepted in relationship to its major competition. On the factors of both overall interior and exterior appearance, the vehicle scored higher (based upon a Ford Feature Rating Study) than its import competitors, VW and Toyota. There were some minor problems found with bumper design, luggage space, and visibility to the rear.

Possibly the most prominent negative product feature, with respect to the competition, was width of product line. Vega offered four styles from a two-door sedan to a light panel truck and VW, Datsun, and Toyota also offered a wide variety of vehicle types to choose from.

The size, weight, and style of Pinto placed it easily in the consumer's mind as an economy subcompact and, therefore, cannibalization of other Ford brands was at an acceptable level.

Price acceptance

The public appeared to accept the pricing strategy for Pinto as reasonable. The use of "sticker price" was supported by Ford dealers. However, the apparent subcompact segmentation mentioned by Mr. Richert placed Pinto somewhere in between the two general price classes that emerged. The impact of this factor, coupled with the VW small-size Beetle priced at $1,780, may have affected the price-oriented subcompact buyers. The influence of these conditions had not been measured by the Pinto team.

Merchandising results

In general the merchandising efforts of Ford Division were successful. Particularly noteworthy was a tie-in with Sears, Roebuck in which Pinto and Maverick automobiles were displayed during the September 16–19, 1970 period in "Pinto Boutiques" located in 196 category "A" Sears stores. Complementing the Pinto were "Pinto Put-On" fashion displays in which "Pinto Maids," provided by Sears, distributed Pinto promotional material to approximately 15 million customers. Each store conducted a registration program in which the winner received the use of a Pinto for one year. Names and addresses of registrants were provided Ford salesmen for follow-up activity.

Also the sales strategy of trading up to other vehicles when Pintos were not in stock hampered Pinto sales merchandising efforts.

Advertising results

From the standpoint of awareness of the Pinto as an entity and of placing it with respect to the remainder of the Ford line, the campaign was successful.

No special actions were taken during the GM strike to take advantage of the situation. The new plan for expenditure of 42 percent of the budgetary allowance was followed, with the exception of an additional dollar increment added by the corporation for Pinto and Maverick promotion in November and December.

From the standpoint of the mechanics of space and time purchase for promotion, no changes were made in network television sequencing because of prior commitments. However, more emphasis than usual was placed upon magazine advertising during introduction, and commitments to other media were delayed until the last moment. There were conflicts of opinion on whether to really push during the strike or to back off. The middle course of no discernible change was finally followed.

After the strike was over, GM started on a reintroduction of Vega, and Ford was faced with the problem of what to do about this in the beginning of 1971.

Another interesting development was the assertion by the Volkswagen dealers in the United States that their sales had been boosted by the influx of domestic advertising dollars into the economy subcompact field.

Strategy considerations for the 1972 model year

Little in the way of concrete decisions about the 1972 Pinto line had been made by 31 December 1970. In general, however, some of the gross considerations that come to the fore as underlying factors were: (1) that a continued inflationary spiral was expected—boosting material costs, (2) labor costs were also on the rise, (3) the Japanese, in particular, had been offering more in the way of extra equipment for the same price as base-line American competitors such as Pinto.

Some of the more specific areas of concern follow.

The target. There still was discussion among Ford executives as to whether Pinto should be aimed at the buyers of domestic subcompacts or import subcompacts. In particular, there was continued controversy over the alternatives of either targeting for the import segment in general or the potential buyer of a specific vehicle make such as the VW, Datsun, or Toyota. Also, the question of whether or not to attempt to woo a specific segment, such as the buyer of a first vehicle or the multiple car owner, was pursued.

Sales objectives. The Pinto team had not developed final sales volume goals for the 1972 model year; however, assessment of the continued upswing of the economy was being undertaken. Pinto penetration was also being considered in light of the strong 1970 showing of foreign competitors—in particular, Volkswagen, Datsun, and Toyota. No definite plans for capacity expansion beyond 400,000 units per year had been arrived at, though such a move was considered feasible, should it be dictated by the sales forecast.

No change in incremental sales goals was being voiced at this time. The obvious questions to be dealt with were what the sales forecast should be for the 1972 model year, and what incremental sales goals would be desirable and/or attainable.

The product. The Pinto team was also wrestling with the question of whether or not Ford should offer additional models of the Pinto in the 1972 model year. In January 1971, there was a proposal under consideration to bring out a "hatch-back" model. Because of the broader lines of most competitors, this question had to be resolved. Another alternative was to offer optional packages of extras, and the Pinto strategists were considering such things as a "rally package" or a "power package" (bigger engine, etc.). Also under consideration was the idea of making a smaller product that could be offered at a more competitive price.

The price. Another important issue under discussion was whether the Pinto should be priced (and designed) to meet the low-priced economy subcompact segment that seemed to be emerging, or whether the Ford Division should raise the vehicle into the "$2,000 plus" price class. This question was being examined because of the middle-ground position of the Pinto early in 1971, with respect to the emerging subcompact segments.

Selling strategy. Also being considered by the Pinto team was the question of whether or not the 1972 model should be used in a selling-up strategy similar to that followed during the majority of the 1971 introductory period. There had been talk already that a "hard-sell" course of action should be followed. Ford executives still disagreed on the "most logical" course of action because of the implications with respect to Ford Division profits versus stemming the import tide.

Promotion. What new merchandising programs could be instituted for the 1972 model year? This was a pressing problem in light of the low level of success of the Pinto key program. Showroom results demonstrated that getting prospects to test-drive the Pinto strongly influenced the purchase decision favorably. The merchandising segment of the Pinto team had been attempting to develop a program to do just that.

Determination of an appropriate budget for merchandising efforts and advertising pursuits was also a problem of significance. The balance between these two efforts, from an expenditure standpoint, had Ford advocates who favored the status quo and those specialists who preferred a change in favor of either of the two areas of endeavor.

The question as to whether the established method of budget determination was sound was also of significance.

There was also the rather obvious question as to whether or not Ford should even continue to manufacture the Pinto line in 1972.

CASE QUESTIONS

1. Evaluate the results of the marketing strategy followed during the introduction of the Pinto subcompact automobile.
2. What changes in marketing strategy for the Pinto, if any, would you recommend for the 1972 model year?

APPENDIX 1

1971 PINTO
MAJOR PRODUCT FEATURES

EXTERIOR

All new 2-door sedan with unitized body featuring long hood, short deck styling

INTERIOR

Two dial instrument cluster with full width crash pad
High back bucket seats

POWER TRAIN

Conventional drive train system: front engine, rear wheel drive
Standard 1600 cc engine, 2000 cc OHC engine optional
Standard 4-speed manual transmission, automatic optional

FUNCTIONAL

Direct Aire ventilation
European design rack and pinion steering
Manual drum brakes

SAFETY

All standard Ford Motor Company safety features including three-point restraint system, collapsible steering column, flashing side marker lights and steering column Ignition lock.

APPENDIX 2

APPENDIX 3

APPENDIX 4

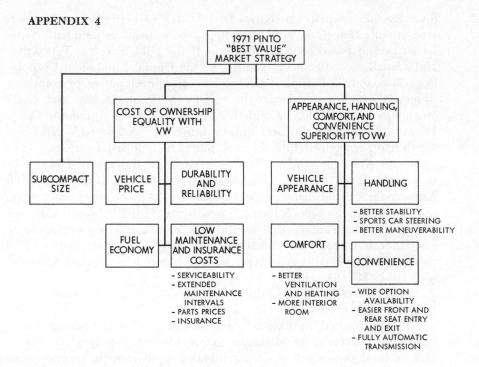

CASE 2-3

Information Control Systems, Inc.—
Automatic Office Division*

Study of industrial buyer behavior

Information Control Systems, Inc. (ICS) of Ann Arbor, Michigan was a computer-oriented firm of modest size which provided both programming and system services to local business, institutional, and governmental organizations. Early in 1968, Bruce E. Shenker, president of ICS, considered several new product possibilities in an attempt to

---

* Written by Jerry Solomon and based in part on a research study by Richard C. Greenough, both MBA students at the Graduate School of Business Administration, The University of Michigan.

diversify the company's activities beyond that of being primarily a service organization. One very promising product was an automatic typewriter system based on a combination of the IBM Selectric Typewriter and a small computer manufactured by the Digital Equipment Corporation. The contribution of ICS would be the development of computer programs which would make the system the most efficient and easily operated one available. By mid-1968, ICS formed the Automatic Office Division to develop further and to introduce "Astrotype," the name which had been selected for the new automatic typewriter system.

Martin Anderson, the marketing manager of the newly formed division, was faced with the task of bringing Astrotype to market. While Astrotype possessed many product advantages over its major competitor, the IBM magnetic tape/Selectric typewriter (MT/ST), the division was at a great disadvantage due to the lack of a marketing organization. Mr. Anderson's problem, therefore, was to develop a strategy and an organization to market Astrotype, so that it could successfully compete with IBM's MT/ST system.

Company background

ICS was formed in 1962 by two computer-oriented undergraduates from The University of Michigan to provide programming services to various local organizations. It experienced rapid growth, increasing its payroll from two to more than eighty employees by 1969. As a corporate organization, it consisted of three separate divisions: Programming Services, Computer Operations, and the Automatic Office Division. Each operated as a separate profit center with responsibility for technical development and marketing.

The product

Essentially, an automatic typewriter reproduces standard or previously typed material on the typewriter without the aid of a secretary. The most sophisticated and widely applicable automatic typewriter then available was driven from a magnetic tape cartridge by an electromechanical logic control unit. Astrotype was a similar system, but was controlled by a miniature computer. It consisted of a central control unit which could operate up to four remote terminals. The keyboards of the terminals were the standard keyboard of the IBM Selectric Typewriter; typing produced copy in the temporary storage of the computer and transferred the copy to tape upon completion of a line. Corrections could be made by backspacing and retyping or by a simple editing procedure. After a correct copy in storage was obtained, typing p (for printout) produced an error-free copy.

Astrotype had several important advantages over its major competitor, the IBM MT/ST. Although it was equally applicable to most business-oriented functions, it was a much less complex system to operate. The editing and correcting procedures, in particular, were much easier to accomplish. In addition, the instruction commands to the control unit were programmed through the standard keyboard of the Selectric typewriter, thereby eliminating the necessity of learning new dials and button settings. The Astrotype system, therefore, required a much shorter training period and could easily be operated by lower skill-level typists. Since the main purpose of the automatic typewriter was to increase productivity and thus reduce the cost of typewritten material, Astrotype's simplicity and ease of operation, combined with its speed and accuracy, afforded it many competitive advantages.

Competitive situation

The IBM MT/ST, as previously mentioned, was the major competitive factor that Astrotype would face when breaking into the market. MT/ST had been on the market for several years and its total sales exceeded 30,000 units. IBM had many marketing advantages, including a strong sales and service organization, extensive research and development resources, and a very favorable corporate image. Prior to the introduction of Astrotype, it had launched a program to establish MT/ST in the market as the original automatic typewriter.

Before bringing the Astrotype system to market, and in order that the company might adopt an appropriate strategy for doing so, Mr. Anderson employed Richard Frost, an MBA student from The University of Michigan, to investigate the characteristics of the purchase process for an automatic typewriter. Because IBM's MT/ST was the only automatic tape-driven typewriter that enjoyed widespread use at that time, it was selected as a basis for the investigation.

Again, the purpose of the study was to help Mr. Anderson uncover a method of capitalizing on the competitive advantages of Astrotype as a product, given ICS's competitive disadvantages in the area of marketing and company image.

THE RESEARCH STUDY

Buyer behavior

In the process of conducting the research, several questions of critical importance were raised. These included:

1. Who initiated the purchase decision and under what motivating conditions?
2. What levels of authority contributed to the purchase decision?
3. Were certain selection criteria more important at particular stages of the decision process?

4. Were certain organizational, psychological, and situational influences more important to the purchase decision than the product characteristics?

The results of the study were outlined by the purchasing process model in Exhibit 1. It was evident from the start that the purchasing process had many of the elements of a "modified rebuy." This was due to the fact that there were a great many similarities involved in purchasing electric typewriters and automatic typewriter systems, and most buyers of automatic systems had, at one time or another, purchased an

EXHIBIT 1

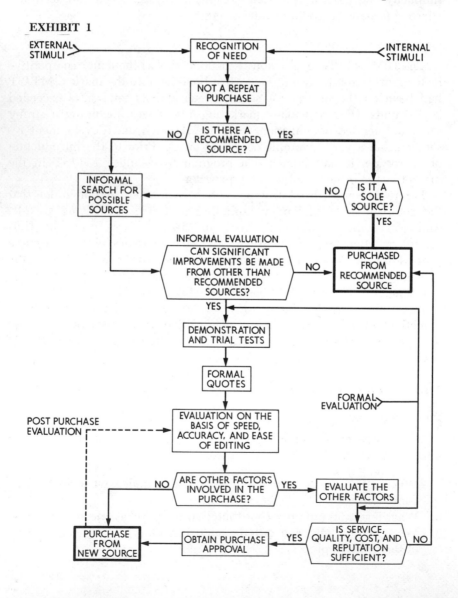

electric typewriter. As a result, the buyer is faced with a recurring problem containing certain important new aspects.

Participation in the purchase decision

The research study indicated that middle-management, and particularly those office managers involved in office supervision, were the prime buying influences in the automatic typewriter market. The purchasing department was rarely involved in the initiation or information-gathering stages, but generally played a secondary role in the purchase, being called on only to complete the necessary documents and procedural functions of the transactions. On several occasions, it was found that because performance advantages for a specific task were being sought, those directly concerned with the benefits (e.g., typists) often participated. Other buyer influences served only limited functions in the purchase process.

Recognition of need

Interviews conducted with firms which had purchased the IBM MT/ST revealed that recognition of the need for an automatic typewriter system occurred at the office supervisory level. Such recognition resulted from either internal or external stimuli. A common example of an internal stimulus was an office cost reduction program which motivated the office manager to seek information about potential cost-saving devices.

In many instances, external stimuli caused a recognition of need. Routine sales calls, advertising, trade show promotions, and personal contact with users often generated interest in the automatic typewriter idea. It was noted, however, that once interest was developed in this manner, the consumer often did not fully appreciate the potential applications of the automatic typewriter and was reluctant to seek out more information.

Recommended source

If a need for the product was recognized and a decision was made to proceed further along the purchase path, the concept of a recommended source became of utmost importance in the decision process. It seemed that because of IBM's reputation it was the first source considered by most potential buyers. Even with no previous experience to rely on, consumers tended to select IBM products. With its low-pressure selling efforts, but widespread and continuous contact with potential customers, IBM had succeeded in securing and maintaining a predisposition toward its products to the extent that other suppliers were often excluded from buyer consideration as possible sources. Those situations in which IBM was perceived as the recommended and often the sole source, thus precluding formal search and evaluation of other sources, are indicated in the model (Exhibit 1) by the heavy line which cuts short the search procedure and leads to purchase from a recommended source.

It is not difficult to understand the cause of this short-circuit process. From the buyer's point of view, the consideration of reliability of the source and minimization of risk was of utmost importance. Purchasing from an unknown supplier put the onus of the decision on the buyer, who was responsible should the product fail to perform. On the other hand, the selection of a well-known source relieved the buyer of a great deal of such responsibility, since he had no way of anticipating the poor performance, based on the supplier's past record.

In general then, risk reduction seemed to be the most powerful purchasing influence in the buying situation. The decision making responded by favoring recommended sources to reduce the risk of making a "bad buy."

Informal search for sources

If and when the decision was made not to go with the recommended source, the buyer typically entered an informal information-gathering stage. Promotional literature and salesmen provided the information input necessary to establish a list of alternative suppliers. Generally, this search of alternatives was followed by an informal evaluation of the proposed sources.

Informal evaluation

If the alternatives which were uncovered by the information search did not differ significantly in performance, the buyer was induced by his biases to remain with the predetermined, recommended source. Conversely, if the recommended source did not meet the performance level of an alternative, middle management decided that more information would be needed before a decision could be reached. As a result, a formal information collection and evaluation procedure was initiated.

It appeared that when such a point was reached, the buying influences began to disregard their perceptual biases toward the recommended source and were indeed willing to include the products of other less known sources in the set of alternatives.

Formal acquisition and analysis of information

At this point in the purchase process, the salesmen of the suppliers were actively sought to provide the additional information which was necessary to the decision process. Demonstrations accounted for the most significant portion of this information, although the use of in house trials was occasionally encountered. During this particular stage, the buying influences consisted mainly of the office manager, the office or secretarial supervisor, and frequently a typist from the staff.

Primary criteria. The primary criteria for evaluation did not involve cost data, but rather focused on areas of performance such as speed, accuracy, and editing ability. Since most systems were similar, with respect to speed and accuracy, the ability to edit became a crucial pre-purchase performance factor.

Secondary criteria. After the alternative systems were ranked according to performance, several other secondary factors such as cost, service, and supplier image were considered.

Although the office managers were conscious of costs, this factor was not as significant as might have been expected, considering the size of the monetary outlay required. The buying influences seemed willing to recommend that the company pay more for a superior system.

Fast and reliable service, when needed, was seen as an important requisite to the full realization of the system's benefits. Generally, buyers felt that service organizations of small suppliers could not retain adequately trained personnel, thereby contributing to the down-time of the system, should it require this service. The ability to service the system was definitely associated with the perceived image of the supplier. In several instances, the expression of a lack of confidence in a small, unknown supplier's service ability was quite severe. Comments were heard from buyers to the effect that they would not sign a contract with such a company due to the inherent service problems, no matter how superior the system was.

The image of a supplier was found to be related to size. Those firms which were large and had an established reputation seemed to create customer confidence. Certainly, company image did not generate sales on its own (except where the buyer did not proceed beyond the recommended source stage), but even at this late stage of the evaluative process, the perception of a supplier seemed to have a strong influence. On occasion the buyer did revert to the original recommended source, despite a heavy preponderance of information that supported the selection of an alternative source.

Purchase

Upon completion of the evaluation and the selection of a product, the proposal for purchase was sent to the management level one step above the office manager. Generally, once the system was selected, the purchase was approved. The purchasing department then took over the procedural phase of arranging delivery dates, payments, and so forth.

An additional note must be made. It was evident that once the system was placed for trial purposes with a company, it was rarely removed.

Upon completion of the trial period, even those who had been initially opposed to this idea were unwilling to part with the system.

Postpurchase evaluation

Within the context of the study, all users but one found that the concept of an automatic typewriter could be applied to their existing office procedures successfully. The users were favorably impressed with the benefits gained via the system, but only rarely was a formal cost/benefit study conducted. Postpurchase evaluation, therefore, was based almost entirely on subjective analysis.

Length of purchase period

The length of the purchase decision process, from the initiation of the contact until the final installation, varied from four to eighteen months. This was in no way an indication of the time period between the recognition of the need and the solicitation of information. Indeed, it was found that in many cases these phases occurred simultaneously (i.e., the need was generated by salesman contact).

CASE QUESTION

Suppose that you have been called in by Mr. Anderson to formulate a marketing strategy for the introduction of "Astrotype." Based upon Mr. Frost's study, what recommendations would you submit?

CASES 2–4

Advanced Technologies, Inc.*

Reappraisal of industrial marketing program

THE COMPANY

John Cambron and John Morley were optimistic when they incorporated their business in October 1967. The new firm, Advanced Technologies, Inc., was the only machine shop in Michigan offering an electron beam welding service to industry.

Advanced Technologies was typical of the many science oriented busi-

---

* Written by Lawrence M. Lamont, Assistant Professor, Graduate School of Business, The University of Colorado while a doctoral student at The University of Michigan under the supervision of Professor Charles N. Davisson.

nesses that had been formed in Michigan during recent years. John Cambron, the firm's president, was a former machine shop owner. He was skilled in the operation of standard machine tools such as lathes, grinders, and milling machines. John Morley, vice president of Advanced Technologies, had technical experience in welding and in the design and construction of welding equipment. He was a former employee of National Electric Welding Machines Co., a manufacturer of welding equipment. This combination of business and technical skills seemed most natural. Both men were convinced that a business offering a capability such as electron beam welding, supplemented with the standard machine shop services, would be in a unique competitive position.

THE SETTING

Advanced Technologies (ATI) was located in Bay City, Michigan, an industrial community having a population of over 50,000. Most of the industry in the region (as well as the state) was geared to the production of motor vehicles, heavy industrial equipment, and electro-mechanical machinery. A number of large corporations had manufacturing plants located within a 250-mile radius of Bay City. In addition, many smaller suppliers of subassemblies and components were nearby. These firms supplied the OEMs (Original Equipment Manufacturers) with fabricated parts, accessories, castings, tooling, and fixtures.

Almost all of the firms involved in manufacturing used one or more of the conventional types of welding in their business. Some of the firms had their own equipment, while others contracted their welding requirements to job shops similar to ATI. Very few of the plants owned electron beam welding equipment.

THE TECHNOLOGY

Electron beam welding is a relatively new technology, developed about eight years ago by the aircraft industry. It is used extensively in defense and aerospace, but has not gained widespread acceptance by the manufacturers of industrial goods and consumer products. Only about 30 electron beam job shops exist in the entire country. Advanced Technologies' nearest competition was located in Cleveland and Chicago.

Although electron beam welders cost in excess of $100,000, the technology is deceptively simple. The process uses a heated filament to generate a high-energy stream of electrons. The stream is accelerated to a high velocity and focused by a magnetic field to a point of high concentration. When the electron beam impacts with the objects to be welded, the energy is converted to heat where it melts the two surfaces and joins them together. The welding process generally takes place in a vacuum chamber to prevent molten metal from oxidizing under the beam and burning up.

Compared to conventional welding techniques such as oxyacetylene, arc, and resistance welding, electron beam welding offers some unique advantages:

1. Electron beam welding joints are straighter and stronger than those produced by other welding techniques.
2. The weld has a minimum concentration of contaminants and stress, which gives the welded joint high corrosion resistance.
3. The weld has a highly uniform surface, giving the welded part an aesthetic appeal.
4. Electron beam welding can be used to weld unusual shapes and thin gage metals with minimum warping and heat distortion.
5. The electron beam makes it possible to weld tool steel and other metals as well as nickel, tungsten, molybdenum, copper, titanium, tantalum, magnesium, and aluminum.

THE PROBLEM

Despite the advantages of electron beam welding, the company was unable to develop enough business to keep the machine running at a profitable level of operation. The situation was critical because the electron beam welder represented an investment of $103,000 or 63 percent of ATI's $164,000 investment in machinery and equipment.

Prices for the service were quoted on a piece basis. Morley figured that for most of the applications the service could be priced so that the welder would generate at least $40 of revenue for every hour of continuous operation. Under these circumstances, the electron beam welder was the most profitable piece of equipment in the shop. The cost to operate the machine was $10 an hour—estimated as follows:

$$\begin{array}{rl} \$ \ .50 & \text{Utilities} \\ 4.50 & \text{Direct labor} \\ \underline{5.00} & \text{Overhead} \\ \$10.00 & \text{Total costs} \end{array}$$

After ATI began business in 1967, it became apparent that some type of marketing effort would be required to reach potential customers. The firm considered hiring a salesman, but because of financial limitations this approach was rejected. In 1969, Cambron and Morley decided to employ a manufacturers' representative on an expense-plus-commission basis to contact accounts in Michigan. The representative they selected had 30 years of experience selling welding equipment and capital goods. He knew most of the customers for welding equipment, including many that were contracting their welding requirements to job shops similar to ATI. This sales arrangement was not successful because the representative had not produced enough sales to cover his expenses.

The company decided to employ the representative only on a commission basis.

THE BUYING PROFILES

The difficulty that ATI had experienced selling the electron beam welding service disturbed Morley and Cambron. Looking back on their first two years of business, they reflected that in selling the service they encountered at least three different selling situations.

Tranco, Inc.

Tranco, Inc., is a large producer of transmissions and gears for motor vehicles and industrial equipment. The company's engineers were designing a transmission for a new line of equipment, and they needed a method to fabricate a high-strength gear. ATI's electron beam welding service was used to weld a two-piece special alloy steel gear for the transmission.

In making the sale, ATI's representative first contacted Tranco's senior staff engineer in the metallurgy department. He explained some potential applications for electron beam welding and left sales literature.[1] Subsequent sales calls were made on Tranco's process and manufacturing engineers who were responsible for making the gear. They gave ATI design prints for the gear and requested welded samples and prices for production volumes. A price quotation was submitted to the buyer in Tranco's purchasing department, and the electron beam welded gears were evaluated by the engineering staff.

Prior to making the decision to award a production order to ATI to weld the two-piece gear, technical personnel from Tranco made a visit to the ATI plant to inspect the electron beam welding equipment and evaluate the firm's ability to handle production quantities.[2] Negotiation with Tranco's purchasing department followed the visit and resulted in a lower price and the award of an order. The sale required about six months from the initial sales call to the first production order. By the end of 1970, ATI expected to weld 5,000 to 10,000 gears which would amount to $7,500 to $15,000 of business; this could reach 60,000 gears and $100,000 by 1972.

One of the key buying influences in the sale was the design engineer. The designer specified the use of a two-piece gear which required

---

[1] The senior staff engineer contacted Tranco's design engineers and told them about the joint strength and design flexibility offered by electron beam welding. The design engineers, in turn, specified a two-piece gear in the transmission design which could be fabricated by electron beam welding.

[2] Five different people visited ATI. They included the facilities engineer, the chief tooling engineer, the manager of corporate metallurgical engineering, a plant metallurgist, and the chief engineer of research and development.

EXHIBIT 1

ADVANCED TECHNOLOGIES, INC.

2490 E. Midland Rd.
Bay City, Michigan 48706
(517) 686-0676
Jan. '69

JOHN CAMBRON   JOHN MORLEY

Machine Shop & Electron Beam Welding Facilities
6400 sq. ft. floor space
16 ft. ceiling height with crane

Equipment

1—6 kw.-52″ × 36″ × 36″ Chamber 150 kv. Hamilton Standard Electron Beam Welder

1—Mass Spectrometer for Leak Detection
1—30″ × 72″ Leblond Lathe
1—16″ × 96″ Leblond Lathe
1—15″ × 60″ Colchester Lathe
1—10″ × 36″ South Bend Lathe

1—36″ Blanchard Grinder
1—6 × 12 Boyar Schultz Surface Grinder
1—K.O. Lee Tool & Cutter Grinder
1—11″ × 40″ Elgin Cylindrical Grinder with I.D. Attachment
1—24″ Heald Internal Grinder
1—Keller-Flex Grinder

1—Sunnen Honing Machine
1—28″ Cincinnati V Ram Shaper
1—16″ Gemco Shaper
1—Excello-6″ Double End Carbide Grinder

1—10″ × 48″ Bridgeport Vertical Mill
1—10″ × 48″ Excello Vertical Mill
1—No. 2 Pratt & Whitney Die Sinker
1—No. 3B Milwaukee Horizontal Mill

1—Bridgeport Cherrying Attachment
2—15″ Rotary Table
1—Hardinge Dividing Head
1—8 × 16 Johnson Cut Off Saw
1—Powermatic Band Saw

1—10 HP-2V Type Worthington Air Compressor
1—Oxy-Acytelene Welder
1—Arc Welder
1—Resistance Spot Welder
2—81 pch. Sets Gage Blocks

a high-strength weld to fabricate. This decision created the application for electron beam welding.[3] However, the product designers in other OEMs were generally not aware of the design advantages offered by electron beam welding, and they were reluctant to specify its use. Part

---

[3] The buying profile for the electron beam welding service is also different from the typical profile for the purchase of welding equipment. In the purchase of welding equipment, the customer usually has a known requirement, and the buying process resolves around whom the firm should buy from. The tool engineer is the procurement arm of production. He specifies the equipment design and plays a key role in the purchase decision. Purchasing also influences the procurement. The buyers evaluate and screen the proposals and negotiate with the suppliers on price, as well as the technical features of the proposal. A purchase requires from three to four months from the recognition of a need.

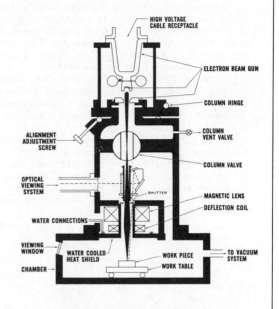

ELECTRON BEAM WELDING

● RESEARCH & DEVELOPMENT ● PROTOTYPE ● EXPERIMENTAL ● PRODUCTION

IN WELDING OF:

- COLD ROLLED STEEL
- TOOL STEEL
- STAINLESS STEEL
- TITANIUM, TANTALUM
- NICKEL, TUNGSTEN
- MOLYBDENUM, COPPER
- MAGNESIUM, ALUMINUM
- DISSIMILAR METALS

ELECTRON BEAM OFFERS:

- MINIMUM HEAT
- MINIMUM DISTORTION
- MINIMUM STRESS
- HIGH PURITY

WELDING FIXTURES:

VERTICAL & HORIZONTAL LATHES
MULTI-SPINDLE LATHES
ECCENTRIC TABLE
STAKING FIXTURE
SPECIAL TOOLING
MASS SPECTROMETER TESTING
ZYGLO TESTING
VAPOR DEGREASING

ELECTRON BEAM WELDING MACHINE
SCHEMATIC — HAMILTON STANDARD
6KW 52" x 36" x 36"

of ATI's service to Tranco included assisting in the design of the gear. They were able to suggest several improvements.

Engineered Fabrications, Inc.

Engineered Fabrications, Inc., is a contract engineering and manufacturing firm already knowledgeable about electron beam welding. The company had previously used ATI's welding service on several small jobs and had requested price quotations for a number of others. Engineered Fabrications had recently been the successful bidder on a contract to produce tantalum beakers for a large manufacturer of synthetic

EXHIBIT 2
Article appearing in *Welding Design and Fabrication*

EB tackles ticklish tasks

Electron beam welding is big in aerospace and defense, but not in consumer product manufacture. Equipment is expensive, and many design engineers aren't aware of EB's potential. In the United States, only 40 or 50 contract welding services are equipped to electron beam weld. Contract shops, which have the equipment and the skill, offer the only practical way for a prospect to learn what EB might do for him.

Assemblies of titanium, the new, hard tool steels, stainless, and plastics or composite materials often must be joined by new methods. EB can join a hardened ball of stainless steel to a hardened shank of tool steel, in diameters from $3/16$ to 2 inches, and shanks from $1/8$ to $5/8$ inch diameter. The parts will not crack with ordinary abuse, and there is no heat zone embrittlement. A factory in Germany makes 3,000 automobile pushrods an hour by this method.

Advanced Technologies, Inc., Bay City, Michigan, is one contract welding service tackling EB jobs from experimental to production runs. The company has a new Hamilton Standard machine and a knowledgeable staff, a combination that makes Advanced Tech ready for anything. EB welding requires unique tools for the work—like a 24-spindle carousel (photo) that can hold 24 parts—a big help for production jobs since EB welds best in vacuum. The spindle can hold fewer larger parts, can move from horizontal to vertical axis and 30° beyond. The machine also has staking fixtures and an eccentric table. Other special tooling has been developed for special parts—like a heat exchanger in which the cap of the watercooling port is EB welded to the base. Both parts are of H-13 (high molybdenum tool steel), and form part of the tooling for a large automotive diecasting die. The electron beam penetrates the $1/4$-inch-thick cap, without distortion or gaps (sketch).

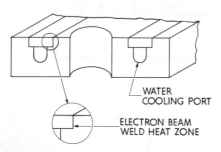

WATER
COOLING PORT

ELECTRON BEAM
WELD HEAT ZONE

Joining a cast steel flange to a precision ground coupling of tool steel shows EB's success in making precise, deep, sound welds without distortion. The coupling is a hemisphere type used in chemical manufacturing. The fixture turns the parts under the electron gun. Weld must be completely sound. There can be no leak around the coupling.

The advantages of electron beam welding—little distortion, depth and speed of welds—depend on the optics of the beam. A high-voltage positive charge on a metal plate with a hole in it, accelerates electrons emitted by a heated filament to high-velocity. The electrons speed through the hole, then coast. What they hit, they heat, which is why one can heat and weld nonconducting materials. The weld itself can be made in a soft vacuum or even in the atmosphere, but high vacuum is ideal. The ATI machine pumps down in $2\frac{1}{2}$ minutes, and, with its 24-spindle carousel, can take on production work. If a vacuum is not practical, the firm will EB weld your job in air.

Source: *Welding Design and Fabrication*, April 1969, p. 112.

diamonds.[4] They were fabricating the beakers using conventional welding techniques, but encountered corrosion problems with the welded joint. Corrosion reduced the life of the beakers and increased the manufacturers' processing costs. Engineered Fabrications subcontracted with ATI to weld the beakers. Electron beam welding produced a high-purity, corrosion-resistant weld resulting in a beaker that had a longer service life.

Through previous contact, ATI had established a working relationship with the chief engineer at Engineered Fabrications. When the corrosion problem occurred, he recognized the possibility of using electron beam welding and contacted ATI. After evaluating a few welded beakers and obtaining a price quotation, the chief engineer made the decision to use the welding service. Only a few weeks were required to make the sale, which was expected to amount to a minimum of $8,000.

The buying process for the welding service is often complicated because some of the parts to be welded are contracted by OEMs to suppliers of subassemblies and fabricated parts. These firms, in turn, subcontract with a job shop to perform the welding, if they do not have electron beam welding equipment. In some of these instances the buying influences are split between the OEM and the first-level contractor.[5]

Bay Chemicals Co.

Bay Chemicals Co., is a large, diversified producer of inorganic and organic chemicals. For some time the company had experienced a corrosion problem with a tank drain that was lined with tantalum. When spot welding was used to seal the liner to the drain, chemical corrosion occurred and the liner had to be replaced every two weeks. ATI electron beam welded the liner to the drain and eliminated a costly maintenance problem.

The sale was made when an engineer from Bay Chemicals' maintenance department talked to John Morley about electron beam welding and brought the drain and liner to ATI's plant to see if it could be welded. The application was successful, and now the engineer periodically brings maintenance problems that can be solved by electron beam welding to ATI. Little or no sales effort is necessary to sell these applications, but they consist only of infrequent one-of-a-kind jobs amounting to $50 each.

---

[4] The beakers were used in the processing of synthetic diamonds. Tantalum was required because the diamonds were manufactured at high temperatures, and it was the only metal that would withstand the heat.

[5] The OEMs design engineers could be influenced to design a part that could be electron beam welded, while the contracting firm helped to select the job shop to perform the welding service.

THE MARKETING PROGRAM

In addition to employing a manufacturers' representative to call on potential customers, ATI designed a sales brochure describing electron beam welding and the other machine shop capabilities. A copy of this brochure is shown in Exhibit 1. The firm was also successful in placing a technical article describing the advantages of electron beam welding in a national trade journal. Reprints of this article (see Exhibit 2) were attached to the sales literature and distributed to potential customers by the manufacturers' representative during sales calls.

In late 1969, Morley and Cambron were concerned about the slow development of the electron beam welding service. Although business had continued to improve, they were still operating well below capacity. While they believed their marketing program was adequate, they wondered what changes, if any, should be made.

CASE QUESTIONS

1. Identify the major problems facing Morley and Cambron.
2. What changes in their marketing program might you suggest as likely to overcome these difficulties?

part three

PRODUCT STRATEGY

MODERN marketing management views the product as a controllable variable in the planning of marketing strategy. Products can be improved to make them more acceptable to the market, new products or services can be added to a company's line, and weak products or services can be dropped. In a sense, product decisions are more basic than decisions about other marketing variables. A product that effectively meets consumer needs reduces problems associated with decisions on distribution, pricing, advertising, and personal selling. A poorly conceived product, on the other hand, creates many problems for other decision areas in marketing.

Demand is increasingly dynamic, and product life cycles are getting shorter. A company that hopes to grow and prosper over the long run must have a capability for product innovation. Marketing management, facing today's market situation, is repeatedly required to answer a very basic question: "What new product or service should we offer?" A company's survival depends on its ability to answer this question correctly. An approach to providing this answer is the subject of Chapter 6.

Sellers face a dilemma with regard to product policy. New products are essential to survival, yet most new products fail in the marketplace. Thus, another requirement for today's business firm is a product development process that maximizes the probability of success. This is the topic considered in Chapter 7.

6

Product choice decisions

PRODUCT decisions are concerned with changes in a firm's product or product line (or service). For our purposes, the term "product" will be thought of in the inclusive sense as being all that the consumer receives when making a purchase. It is not only a physical entity but also a complex of tangible and intangible attributes, including such things as warranties, packaging, color, design, and even psychic stimulation, as well as services. Product policy involves the adjustment of this complex of product variables to the needs and requirements of the market on one hand, and to the capabilities of the firm on the other, along with the attendant activities of procedure and control.

Product decisions may relate to changes in existing products or their use, or to the offering of products or services new to the firm. These decisions are not fundamentally different, for in either case a "new" product emerges. The difference is only in the degree of newness involved. However, the greater the degree of newness, the more uncertain the outcome of the product decision. The focus of this chapter is on decisions concerning essentially new products, but the decision-making process is basically the same, albeit somewhat easier, for modifications of existing products.

Formulation and execution of a product policy requires the making of a great many decisions. Many of these are subsidiary to, or variants of, three very basic decisions. These most basic product decisions are: (1) Should a firm offer a new product? (2) What new product should be offered? (3) Should the new product be developed internally or acquired by merger?

Decision to offer a new product

Not all firms engage in product development. In the array of product policy choices available to a firm, one is the null choice; that is, to stick with existing products in their present form and to forego product innovation. Company management, having observed the high rate of failure among new products, may decide this is the prudent course to follow. Most new products are failures. The record shows that in recent years in the United States, of every three products emerging from research and development departments as technical successes, there is an average of only one commercial success. New product failure rates run as high as 80 percent, and the waste in research and development has been estimated at 70 percent or more.[1] When this high failure rate is considered along with the often high cost of developing and launching a new product, the risks associated with product development appear formidable indeed.

On the other hand, there is risk and potentially high cost associated with not offering new products. All products have a life cycle, although there is substantial variation in life cycles by type and class of products. Products are like people: They are born, they grow (some more than others), and eventually they die (some sooner than others). In contrast with that of people, the average life cycle of products is constantly being shortened. The time scale on most products is being compressed by accelerated research and technology, rapidly changing markets, mass media, and mass distribution. During the last ten years, while new brand introductions more than doubled in the frozen-food and dairy-grocery business, average product life expectancy fell from 36 months to 12 months.[2]

The basic life cycle of new products is illustrated in Figure 6–1. Sales of a successful new product go through a period of growth, reach a peak, and eventually decline. Also significant, from the standpoint of product policy, is the behavior of product margins over the product life cycle. Profits tend to peak, and usually begin to decline, earlier than sales volume. Maximum sales volume is often reached only after competitors have entered the field, price rivalry has become severe, and profit margins have been compressed. To sustain profits, new products may be needed long before sales of established products have begun to fall.

The critical underlying causes of product life cycles are two: (1)

---

[1] "New Products: The Push Is on Marketing," *Business Week,* March 4, 1972, p. 72.

[2] Ibid., p. 72.

FIGURE 6–1
The basic life cycle of new products

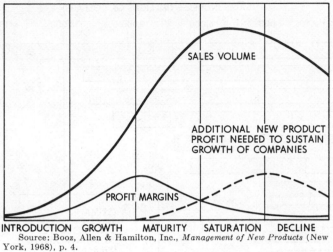

Source: Booz, Allen & Hamilton, Inc., *Management of New Products* (New York, 1968), p. 4.

instability of demand, and (2) instability of competitive position.[3] Consumer demand is unstable because factors which influence it are continually changing. Changes in the geographical and age distribution of the population, in income, in education, in mobility, in taste, and in other factors produce changes in consumer preferences. Competitors change and improve their products, and the company whose product does not change is likely to find its market share declining, even if basic demand conditions remain stable. It, too, must innovate to hold its competitive position.

Does a firm have a real choice insofar as product innovation is concerned? *In the short run*, the answer is yes. Given the substantial costs and high risks associated with product change, plus uncertainty about the present phase and future course of the life cycle of existing products, short-run profits may well be maximized by a decision not to offer new products. On the other hand, *long-run survival of a firm precludes choice* about product innovation. Eventual decline in the market acceptability of virtually all products is certain. "Innovate, or die" is a slogan containing a large measure of truth.

Even if survival over an extended period were possible without product innovation, most firms are not content with mere survival. They want to grow and to prosper. New products are customarily a major

---

[3] For a more extensive discussion of the effect of these factors on product life cycles, see D. M. Phelps and J. H. Westing, *Marketing Management* (3d ed.; Homewood, Ill.: Richard D. Irwin, Inc., 1968), pp. 57–63.

Introduction to marketing management

FIGURE 6–2
Contribution of new products to expected sales growth, 1963–67

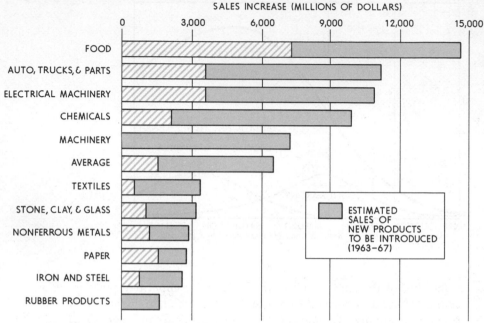

Source: Booz, Allen & Hamilton, Inc., *Management of New Products* (New York, 1968), p. 5.

factor in company growth. Figure 6–2 shows expected sales increases in 11 industries for the period 1963 through 1967 and the portion of this increase accounted for by products first produced during this same five-year time span. Therefore, if a firm desires both survival and growth, its fundamental choices concerning product innovation narrow to two: (1) what (not whether) new products should be offered; (2) whether these new products should be gained through internal development or by external acquisition.

What new products to offer[4]

New products are "new" in varying degrees. They may be minor or major modifications of a firm's existing products. They may be new to the particular firm but not new to the market. If new to the firm, they may be closely related, loosely related, or totally unrelated to the

[4] Assumed in this chapter is complete freedom of choice among a large number of alternative products. This assumption permits consideration of all variables affecting selection of a new product. The choices facing a particular company would usually be more limited. Thus, fewer variables would be involved.

firm's existing products. Or the product may be new to the market, something not previously available in any form to consumers. If a product is both new to the market, so that there is nothing by way of guidance to be found in the experience of others, and also unrelated to a firm's existing products, so that there is little carry-over of experience from these, then the risks of product innovation are great indeed. In order to minimize these risks, yet keep alive the opportunity for survival and growth that accompanies product innovation, a well-formulated "add-and-drop" policy is necessary.[5]

Objective of profit maximization

The most basic goal of business in a free enterprise society is the maximization of long-term profit. Therefore, the basic test to be applied in deciding which new product should be added is contribution to the overall profit position of the firm. Unfortunately, such a test is not easily applied. Profit is a function of many things, such as the nature and extent of demand, the activities of competitors, and costs of production and distribution. Furthermore, when deciding whether to add a new product, it is the future, not the present, condition of such variables which counts. Profit calculations relating to new products must be based on forecasting, an art which mankind has not yet mastered.

In spite of the difficulty of applying a profit test in product choice decisions, a profit calculation cannot be avoided. Any decision to add a new product *implicitly* involves an assumption concerning profitability. Other standards, if used, are at best only substitute ones which are assumed to be correlated with long-term profitability. If initial profit calculations are necessarily very crude, there is opportunity to refine them as the product development process evolves. At this stage, however, we are concerned only with the initial decision of which new product should be selected for development. Refinements of some of the calculations discussed below will be made in the next chapter.

Profitability formula

The total profit directly (but not indirectly) attributable to a new product addition is expressed by the formula:[6]

$$R = D \times (P - C) \times L,$$

---

[5] Although emphasis here is on the adding of new products, decisions to drop existing products are governed by the same factors.

[6] Indirect contributions to a firm's total profits by a new product are discussed later.

in which:

    R = Total long-term net profit in dollars.
    D = Average total unit sales per year.
    P = Average sales price per unit.
    C = Average cost per unit.
    L = Expected life (in years).

Estimate of demand

The existence of an adequate demand for a potential new product is basic to profit opportunity. An attempt must be made to measure the extent of demand, its strength and location, the segmentation which may be present, and other demand variables. For example, a plan to produce a new sports car which is expected to appeal to young people might involve studies of the number of people in the appropriate (for example, 18–30) age group, their geographic dispersion, segmentation by income groups, variations in tastes in car styling, mechanical features, and so on.

Estimates of future demand for established products are difficult to make because of the many factors, both tangible and intangible, which affect sales opportunities. Demand estimates for a projected new product, at the time a decision must be made whether or not to undertake its development, are far more difficult. Just how difficult depends on the nature of the demand determinants (for example, automotive replacement parts versus a new style of clothing). Still, such a decision is implicit in the choice process and, therefore, cannot be avoided.

Management must estimate future market potential for the type of product it expects to add, as well as the share of the market it expects to serve. Because of the uncertainty associated with sales forecasts at this early stage in the product development process, several forecasts, involving various degrees of optimism and pessimism, might be made. Figure 6–3 shows three sales forecasts for a proposed new product—one highly pessimistic, one optimistic, and one considered most likely to occur. This process might be refined by assigning probabilities to the several estimates, thus making possible the derivation of expected values of unit sales for each product under consideration.

Sales of most new products can be expected to grow for a time, gradually achieve more stability, and eventually decline. If the respective sales of several products are to be compared, it is useful to convert sales data to average sales per year over the expected life cycle of the product. Such a figure can be readily calculated and easily fitted into the profitability formula above. The value of this figure, of course,

FIGURE 6-3
Estimates of alternative sales volumes, proposed new product

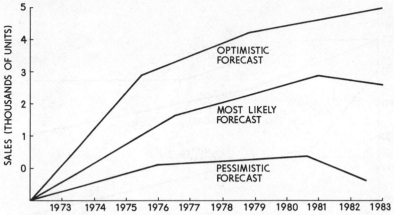

depends on the expected life of the proposed new product as well as on the trend of sales during its time on the market. Expected life is discussed separately below.

Price estimates

Management must have some idea of the price to be obtained for a new product throughout its life cycle in order to estimate a product's profit contribution. Valuable price information can usually be gained from demand studies, for price is basically a demand-determined variable. Needless to say, uncertainties of demand cause uncertainties also in the price estimating process. Price is quite likely to vary through time, by size and type of customer, by markets, and so on. As was suggested for estimates of sales volume, it might be useful for price estimates also to range from optimistic to pessimistic and to attempt to derive the "most likely" behavior of price over the life cycle of the projected product. This approach is illustrated in Figure 6-4.

Price received for the new product and its behavior over the product life cycle is a function not only of demand but also of price strategies followed, activities of competitors, changes in the cost structure, and so on. Obviously, the expected price can only be a "best guess." Again, however, it can be pointed out that such a decision is inherent in the product choice process and must be made regardless of its difficulty. As was suggested for sales volume estimates, it is useful to convert price estimates into an average unit price throughout the life cycle of the product. This value can be inserted directly into the profit formula.

FIGURE 6–4
Alternative price expectations, proposed new product

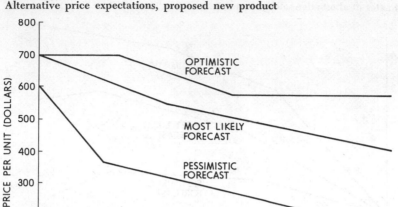

Cost estimates

Price received per unit, less cost per unit, determines the profit contribution of each unit sold. Cost per unit includes both variable and
fixed costs, so the sales forecast must precede any estimate of unit costs.
It is in the area of production and marketing costs per unit that a firm
adding a new product has a major opportunity to influence the volume
of profits that a new product will generate. If it chooses a new product
that "fits" production and marketingwise with its present products, it
can obtain more efficient utilization of resources in two ways. First,
fixed costs are spread over a larger volume of operations, thus reducing
costs per unit. Second, proper fit may have a favorable effect on demand
for both the new product and for existing products, thus increasing
the total scale of operations on which profits depend.

Life cycle estimates

The life cycle of a proposed product may well be the most difficult
variable in the profit formula to estimate. The anticipated time period
may be long and the factors which might affect it (change in consumer
taste, actions of competitors, changes in technology, for example) almost
impossible to predict. Nonetheless, such an estimate is highly relevant
to the decision at hand. Generally speaking, management would want

to avoid products whose life cycles are expected to be short and favor those whose life cycles are expected to be long, other things being equal.

The difficulty of estimating life cycles varies greatly by type of product. In some fields fairly uniform cycles may be observable in past sales. These may then be used as a guide to the expected life cycle of the proposed product. In other fields, no such uniformity in life cycles may be observed. Here, perhaps, some arbitrary time period may be chosen for purposes of the profit calculation. For example, ten years may be established as the maximum time period to be considered. All new products will be judged only on the profits generated in that time span. If the life cycle is expected to be shorter than this, the values of other variables in the formula will have to be higher in order to compensate.

Net revenue

The total long-term net profit in dollars to be expected over the life cycle of the projected product can now be calculated. Because both the length and shape of life cycle curves vary greatly among products, the total profit figure should be converted to "present value" for purposes of comparison. A quick return not only has a higher present value but also a higher probability of being realized because of the greater uncertainty of longer term forecasts.

Compound profitability formula

If a firm is starting operations from scratch with a new product and has no existing products, the above analysis may be sufficient for the product choice decision. Such, however, is rarely the case. Most new products are introduced to the market by going concerns which are already producing and selling one or more products. In this circumstance, it is axiomatic that it is the effect of adding the new product on overall profitability of the firm that counts. If new product sales are entirely at the expense of continued sales of existing products of equal profitability, there is no net gain.[7] When Ford Motor Company introduced the Maverick, its sales were in part at the expense of sales of the standard Ford. Introduction of the Princess telephone by American Telephone and Telegraph Company had an adverse effect on the installation of standard telephones. Conversely, the new product, because it in some way complements existing products, may favorably affect their profitability. A manufacturer of automatic washers who did not

---

[7] This assumes that the present product sales would continue if the new product were not added. If it is likely a competitor will offer a new product which will cut into sales of the existing product(s), this assumption is not valid.

also produce dryers might find it difficult to sell his washers because of the demand among consumers for matched pairs of these products. A manufacturer of a car wax who did not offer a car cleaner might find sales difficult because consumers believe such products "go together" better if made by one company.

Because of such considerations as these, the profitability formula should be expanded as follows:

$$R = [D \times (P - C) \times L] \pm [d \times (p - c) \times l]_1$$
$$\pm [d \times (p - c) \times l]_2 \ldots \pm [d \times (p - c) \times l]_n.$$

This formula recognizes that the proposed product may either increase or reduce the profitability of every other product in a firm's product line, ranging from the product designated as 1 up to product n. The effect on profits may be a result of the influence of the new product on any of the variables involved. The new product may either increase or reduce the demand (d) for an existing product. It may make possible receipt of a higher price (p) or cause a need to lower price. If the new product is wisely chosen, it may well serve to reduce the average cost per unit (c) of producing and marketing present products. The life cycle of existing products (l) may be affected favorably or unfavorably. Any one or more of these effects would cause variation in anticipated overall profits.

Resource utilization: Its relationship to product planning

A business firm employs various resources (inputs) in order to produce revenues (outputs). In the short run, many of these inputs are relatively fixed in amount (for example, plant capacity, size of sales force, and advertising expenditures) and do not vary proportionately with the scale of operations. Profits will be maximized at that point where the marginal cost of the total of inputs is equal to the marginal revenue of the total output. For any *given* scale of operations, profit will be maximized when the ratio of the total output to the total input is greatest. Therefore, if profit maximization is assumed to be a firm's objective, new products should be chosen so as to optimize resource utilization. It should be borne in mind that this concept emphasizes optimum utilization of all resources, employed in combination, rather than the optimum use of each resource.

A great variety of resources is utilized in the average business firm. For purposes of simplicity, these are here divided into production resources and marketing resources. On the production side are such resources as plant, equipment, and technical know-how. On the marketing side are such resources as distribution facilities, the sales force, and established relationships with middlemen. If a proposed product and established products "converge" in production in the sense that they can share use of production resources, then production costs per unit can be expected to decline. Shared use of marketing resources (for example, sale of a new product through an established sales force) will produce the same result. In addition, a good fit marketingwise among products may have a favorable influence on demand.

Production and marketing "fit" is one of the more controllable factors in product planning. An individual firm's influence on demand, price, and the product life cycle is likely to be slight. By assuring that new products have good production and marketing fit, input cost can be minimized and output may also be expanded. Not only does this serve to maximize profits in the short run but it also affects the probability of a firm's survival and growth. The efficient firm has all the advantages in a competitive environment.

Utilization of production resources

Many production resources are employed in the production of revenues, and these vary greatly by industry classification. Among the more important resources employed in production are the following: (1) physical capacity, (2) labor skills, (3) technical know-how, (4) raw materials, and (5) by-products. Some of these are relatively tangible and fairly easy to measure, while others are less tangible and more difficult to measure. Other things being equal, that new product is best which, when added to existing products, provides optimum utilization of these production resources.

Physical capacity. Every manufacturing firm has a certain physical capacity for production in the form of plant and equipment. If this capacity is not fully utilized and sales of present products cannot be increased because of demand limitations, new products which can be manufactured with the same plant and equipment will spread fixed costs and reduce production cost per unit. Even when new production facilities must be created, it may often be desirable, because of the indivisibility of factors of production or in order to obtain other economies of scale, to plan to produce additional products so as to achieve competitive production costs on each product manufactured.

Labor skills. The skills of a labor force are as real an asset as buildings or machinery and often far more difficult to expand or modify. A firm that employs highly paid, and perhaps underutilized, fashion designers, adding a new product for which style is not a critical factor would not be optimizing the use of styling resources. Many technical skills are in short supply and perhaps unavailable to a firm seeking them for the first time. Use of existing skills avoids this problem.

Technical know-how. If technical knowledge built up over many years is transferable to a newly added product, a firm has an advantage not possessed by others. Past production of military electronics gear may aid a firm in turning out civilian electronics ware. Technical knowledge derived from manufacturing stainless steel cutlery may be an asset to a firm which elects to produce stainless steel razor blades. Sometimes technical know-how has been "solidified" by the acquisition of patents on certain processes. Although intangible and difficult to assign a value, technical know-how can be a very real asset. Many companies moving into a new product field have failed because lack of experience in that field caused costly errors to be made.

Common raw materials. If new products can be added which make use of the same raw materials as existing products, several advantages may accrue. First, this may make possible a lower cost for raw materials because acquisition cost tends to be a function of volume purchased. Second, there tends to be a relationship between the use of the same raw materials and common production facilities and distinctive know-how.

By-product factor. The most obvious case of underutilization of resources occurs when potentially valuable by-products of present production activities are not used. The chemical, petroleum refining, and meat packing industries are excellent illustrations of the opportunity to improve the total output-input ratio by finding profitable uses for by-products.

Decision matrix: Utilization of production resources[8]

Isolation of a firm's tangible and intangible resources and the exposure of each new product idea to the light of these criteria is essential to a sound product policy. However, the decision of which new product to choose is complicated by the almost infinite number of product alternatives sometimes available. Management may be in the position of having to select the product that best utilizes company resources out of hundreds or even thousands of possible alternatives. Also, in practice, the number of criteria used in making a judgment may be far in excess of the number employed here. For this decision-making process to be manageable, a practical basis for weighting the several criteria employed, and for assigning an evaluation score to each product considered, is necessary. Then the various alternative choices can be compared. In order to do these things, a reasonably objective evaluation scheme is desirable. This is the purpose of using a decision matrix.

[8] The use of decision matrices for evaluating product choice decisions was suggested by the Van Wart Chemicals, Inc. case in Harry L. Hansen, *Marketing: Text, Techniques, and Cases* (3d ed.; Homewood, Ill.: Richard D. Irwin, Inc., 1967), pp. 517–31.

Product choice decisions are made under conditions of uncertainty. Even for such tangible criteria as, for example, the ability of a proposed new product to use existing plant and equipment, there may be a significant degree of uncertainty. Perhaps the product can be physically produced with these facilities, but there is doubt whether costs will be competitive. Perhaps certain desirable design features cannot be produced if present equipment is used, and modifications in the product will have to be made which may adversely affect demand. On such intangible factors as the application of technical knowledge gained from producing existing products, there may be even less certainty. Thus, there is need to consider the *probability* that a new product will, or will not, produce the benefits expected. A decision matrix facilitates such consideration.

If a proposed product is rated on conformance to each of the suggested criteria, and a probability estimate is assigned each of these ratings, then the "estimated value" of the proposed product for each criterion can be calculated. If these are totaled, an "estimated value" for each new product for total production resource utilization is obtained. The values so obtained for each of the products being considered can then be compared.

Example: Proposed new product "X." Assume a hypothetical new product "X" is under consideration and a decision matrix is used to evaluate its contribution to optimum use of the firm's production resources (Figure 6–5). In constructing the matrix, weights have been assigned to the several relevant criteria discussed above. These weights are based on management's best judgment of the relative importance of conformance to each standard for the particular company. Arbitrary values have been assigned to the possible ratings, ranging from 10 for "very good" down to 2 for "very poor."[9]

Management must now estimate the probability that the proposed new product will qualify for each of the possible ratings on each of the five criteria used in the evaluation. Note that achievement of any particular rating is not a certainty. For example, the illustrative figures included in the matrix (Figure 6–5) for utilization of physical capacity assume a 20 percent chance of a "very good" fit, a 60 percent chance of a "good" fit, and a 20 percent chance of a fit of only "average" quality. This range of possibilities is possible because of uncertainty which exists at this early stage of the product development process. For the second criterion (labor skills) the stated probabilities may reflect uncertainty about the adaptability of the labor force to production requirements of the new product. It is estimated there is a 20 percent chance that the

---

[9] In addition, precise definitions should be framed for each possible rating on each of the several criteria. As these must differ greatly by industry, they are omitted here.

FIGURE 6–5
Decision matrix: Utilization of production resources (proposed new product "X")

Decision criterion	Criterion weight	Very good (10)		Good (8)		Average (6)		Poor (4)		Very poor (2)		Total	Criterion evaluation (total EV × Wt.)
		P	EV	P	EV	P	EV	P	EV	P	EV		
Physical capacity............	0.20	0.2	2.0	0.6	4.8	0.2	1.2	0	0	0	0	8.0	1.60
Labor skills................	0.30	0.2	2.0	0.7	5.6	0.1	0.6	0	0	0	0	8.2	2.46
Technical know-how..........	0.30	0	0	0.2	1.6	0.2	1.2	0.6	2.4	0	0	5.2	1.56
Common raw materials........	0.10	0	0	0	0	0.7	4.2	0.3	1.2	0	0	5.4	0.54
By-product.................	0.10	0	0	0	0	0.1	0.6	0.6	2.4	0.3	0.6	3.6	0.36
Total production resources value......													6.52

labor force will adapt with no difficulty. If so, a "very good" rating would be achieved. However, it is more likely (probability .7) that the labor force will require some, but not expensive retraining (rating: good). It is possible (probability .1) that extensive, and expensive, training will be required (rating: average).

The probabilities decided upon for ratings on each criterion are similarly recorded in the decision matrix. Each probability is multiplied by the respective rating value (ranging from 2 for "very poor" to 10 for "very good") to arrive at the "expected value" (*EV*) for each rating. By adding across, the total expected value of each criterion is obtained. The difference in importance of the several criteria are now taken into account by multiplying the total *EV*'s by the criteria weights. The resulting evaluation scores are recorded in the right hand column. The separate criteria evaluation scores are in turn totaled to obtain the "total production resources" value. The illustration in Figure 6–5 shows a final value of 6.52 out of a possible 10. This is an index number which can now be compared with values similarly derived for other products under consideration. In general, the higher the score for utilization of production resources, the lower production costs per unit can be expected to be.

Utilization of marketing resources

A going concern has marketing resources which, though often less tangible, are no less real than its production resources. These, too, can be underutilized by present products, thus again providing an opportunity for a new product to optimize a firm's input-output ratio. Marketing resources of firms are many and varied. Discussed here are four basic resources which are important in a wide array of product choice decisions. These are: (1) goodwill, (2) marketing know-how, (3) physical facilities, and (4) distribution channels.

Goodwill. In many cases the most valuable asset a firm possesses is the goodwill it has built up among consumers over the years through its present products. If this goodwill could be tapped for the support of a new product without undermining the sale of existing products, it is an underutilized resource just as much as is physical plant operated at less than capacity. General Mills, when it undertook the sale of small household appliances some years ago, did so in part because it felt the goodwill attaching to the General Mills name would help support the sale of appliances. A new Heinz food product probably finds a measure of market acceptance just because of its association in name with products already favored by consumers. A favorable association in the minds of consumers between a new product and existing products can influence the input-output ratio for the entire product line.

This relationship between new and present products can work both ways. The new product may sell better because of its association with present products. On the other hand, and at the same time, existing products may sell better because the new product helps to "round out" the line, sheds prestige on present products (for example, addition of the Continental Mark III to the Ford-Mercury-Lincoln line), or in some other way makes present products more acceptable to consumers. Unfortunately, a negative association between the new and present products in a line will produce opposite, and potentially disastrous, effects. For this reason such product relationships must be carefully considered in product choice decisions.

Marketing know-how. The knowledge management has gained through experience in the marketing of certain types and classes of products is often a very important asset. Knowledge of promotional strategies, pricing, dealer buying practices, consumer purchasing patterns, etc., can be the critical factor determining success or failure of a new product. New products similar in marketing requirements to established products trade on this knowledge, thus greatly increasing chances of success. It is far less risky for Procter & Gamble to introduce a new detergent than, for example, Monsanto Chemical Company to move into this field. Monsanto did introduce a new detergent, "All," which later it sold to Lever Brothers because of the difficulties it experienced in marketing a product with which it was unfamiliar. The rate of failure among new products introduced by firms unfamiliar with their marketing requirements is high.

The fuller utilization of marketing knowledge lowers marketing costs per unit just as does the use of a more tangible asset. Marketing knowledge is often gained only at the very high cost of trial and error. Such knowledge, of course, reduces the chance of future mistakes and, at the same time, helps assure that fuller advantage will be taken of all demand opportunities.

Physical facilities. Perhaps the most obvious opportunity for spreading marketing costs over a greater volume occurs when a new product can utilize physical distribution facilities which may contain excess capacity. Such facilities may be warehouses, truck fleets, retail outlets owned by the manufacturer, and so on. When Standard Brands, Inc., decided to distribute camera film to grocery stores along with its yeast, coffee, puddings, and other products, the dominant motivating factor was excess capacity in the direct distribution facilities which it maintained.

Distribution channels. If the new product can be sold through the same channel of distribution as existing products, it probably can be handled by the same sales force. This will increase average order size and reduce costs as a percentage of sales. If a new channel is required, then possibly an entirely new sales organization will be necessary. Because the cost of this sales force will have to be borne entirely by the new product, distribution costs as a percentage of sales will tend to be high. Also, it is difficult for a firm to break into new channels with a new product. Middlemen are naturally reluctant to add products without an established demand. Normally they already are carrying competitive brands, and they are not eager to assume the risks involved in replacing established products with new and untried brands. Of course, the same factors may apply even to the channels now used for existing products, but at least the innovating firm has an established relationship with its channels which helps in getting its new product accepted.

A strong force favoring new products which can use existing channels is the natural desire of middlemen, other things being equal, to minimize their sources of supply. When the same assortment of products can be acquired from one source as from several, acquisition costs are reduced. If in addition these products are favorably associated with each other in the minds of consumers, perhaps linked by use of a common brand name, the middleman's selling costs may also be reduced. Thus, new products which can use the same channels as existing products are preferred over products which must utilize new channels of distribution.

Decision matrix: Utilization of marketing resources

A decision matrix of the same type used for utilization of production resources is now employed to evaluate the use of marketing resources. Weights are assigned to the four decision criteria, probabilities of various ratings for each are estimated, the estimated values are calculated, adjusted for criterion weight, and summed to determine the total marketing resources utilization value of the proposed new product (Figure 6–6). There is now an objective basis for comparison with other proposed new products.

Summary: Resource utilization

With the aid of a decision matrix, two values relating to the efficiency with which a new product would use the resources of a firm have been arrived at—one for production resources and one for marketing resources. At this point, two pertinent questions arise: (1) What do these values mean? and (2) What does one do with them?

Probably the major value of these figures lies in the analysis that has been necessary in order to derive them. In this process, the potential effects of adding a new product on all operations of the firm have been carefully considered. Problem areas which might have been over-

FIGURE 6–6
Decision matrix: Utilization of marketing resources (proposed new product "X")

Decision criterion	Criterion weight	Very good (10)		Good (8)		Average (6)		Poor (4)		Very poor (2)		Total	Criterion evaluation (total EV × Wt.)
		P	EV	P	EV	P	EV	P	EV	P	EV		
Goodwill..........	0.20	0	0	0.2	1.6	0.5	3.0	0.2	0.8	0.1	0.2	5.6	1.12
Marketing knowledge........	0.20	0.1	1.0	0.5	4.0	0.3	1.8	0.1	0.4	0	0	7.2	1.44
Distribution facilities.........	0.30	0.3	3.0	0.5	4.0	0.2	1.2	0	0	0	0	8.2	2.46
Distribution channels.........	0.30	0	0	0.2	1.6	0.6	3.6	0.2	0.8	0	0	6.0	1.80

Total marketing resource utilizaion value................. 6.82

looked have been thought about by company management. Much of this analysis has been subjective, but often no other approach is possible in the real world.

The value for utilization of production resources and the one arrived at for use of marketing resources are not necessarily equal in significance. Which is more important in influencing the product-choice decision depends on the area in which potential benefits from proper "fit" between new and old products is greatest. A steel company, for example, has high fixed costs of production and, because of fluctuations in the demand for steel, is often faced with excess production capacity. Marketing costs, on the other hand, tend to be more variable. Hence, optimizing the use of production resources through the addition of new products offers the greatest opportunity to reduce average unit costs. A manufacturer of soaps or toiletries would usually have low production costs and high marketing costs. Consequently, a proper marketing fit among its products is of most importance.

FIGURE 6–7
Utilization of company resources

	Value	Weight	Weighted value
Production resource utilization.........	6.52	0.60	3.91
Marketing resource utilization..........	6.82	0.40	2.72
Company resource utilization......			6.63

A value for the utilization of total company resources can be obtained by combining these two figures. In the process, greater weight can be given to optimizing use of resources in the area with greatest potential benefits. For example, if it is desired to give 50 percent greater weight to the use of production resources than to utilization of marketing resources, then a value for efficiency of use of total company resources can be derived as shown in Figure 6–7.

If one new product under consideration utilizes company resources more efficiently than others, this fact has an important bearing on the anticipated profitability of adding this product to the company's line. A good marketing fit, if it produces a carry-over of goodwill from one product to another, may influence demand or price.

The major impact of efficient utilization of production and marketing resources is on cost. Both manufacturing and marketing costs may be reduced because of the spreading of fixed costs which this fit brings about. This cost advantage, in turn, may result either in higher profit margins per unit or in an opportunity to charge a lower price and thus increase the number of units sold. Which of these courses is followed depends on management's decisions on pricing strategy.

A final word of caution is now in order about the interpretation and use of these numbers. The appearance of objectivity such numbers give can be misleading. Underlying them is a great deal of subjective analysis, much of it based on inadequate information. Small differences in derived values are therefore of little significance. Even larger differences should be looked at as only rough approximations. On the other hand, the calculated values constitute a useful tool. Alternative product choices can be ranked in order and sorted and classified as desired. However, their main value continues to be in the analysis required to derive them.

A note about services

In essence, a product is whatever a customer might choose to purchase. Increasingly, consumers are spending more of their incomes on services of all kinds, and such services might very realistically be considered as products.

The decision of what services to offer is not fundamentally different from a decision of what physical product to offer. The same profitability formula used in this chapter can effectively serve as a framework for such decisions. Consideration must still be given to potential demand, the price that can be attained, the cost of providing and marketing the service, and how long demand is likely to continue. Product fit (i.e., capability of providing the service) and marketing fit (i.e., ability to market the service) continue to be important. However, the particular factors to be considered in determining production and marketing fit, and their relative importance, would be different for services than for physical products, in most instances.

These factors would also vary from one type of service to another. Services differ greatly in their nature. The same factors would not be relevant to deciding whether to offer a dry cleaning service, a lawn upkeep service, health related services, a food service, etc. For example, location would be a key factor for some, but unimportant for others.

Internal development or external acquisition

If a decision is made to offer a new product, a firm may, under certain circumstances, have a choice of developing the new product on its own or of acquiring it by taking over a company already marketing such a product. This choice is available, of course, only if the product is one new to the firm but already available in the market. Because relatively few products are truly new to the market, this choice of pathways is a prevalent one. It is a course which has been followed with increasing frequency in recent years. The desire for adding new products has become one of the dominant causes of the so-called merger movement. What is it that causes firms to acquire new products by merger rather than through their own development efforts? Is such an approach to product line diversification good or bad? If good for the firm, is this approach also good for the economy as a whole?

Advantages of acquiring new products by merger

Reduction of uncertainty. Internal development of new products is fraught with uncertainty. Most new products are failures. Costs of development are high as well as difficult to estimate. The employment of sound product development procedures can reduce the risk involved, but even the best such programs do not reduce risk as much as a cautious management might desire. Merger also involves risk, but the sought-after product and its market position are relatively known quantities. The degree of uncertainty is less when a firm acquires a product whose commercial success has already been demonstrated.

Early profitability. The road to commercial success for new products developed internally may be a long one. Technical research and development may take years of effort, and this may then be followed by an extended period of market development. Market growth may be slow in coming, and costly to achieve. Substantial sums may be invested before any return is realized. Acquisition of new products by merger, on the other hand, may mean profitability beginning with the moment of acquisition if due care is exercised to assure that the purchase price is in line with profit opportunity.

Knowledge and experience. When a company by the process of product innovation moves into a new field, it assumes many risks which are associated with lack of experience. Knowledge of markets, particularly of consumer behavior, and the best means to cultivate those markets, comes in large part from marketing experience. Firms lacking such experience operate with a handicap. When new products are acquired by merger, the benefits of experience may also be acquired if knowledgeable personnel come to the new company as a result of the merger. In some cases this knowledge may take the form of patent rights or of research and development experience.

Removal of competitor. When an existing company is purchased to obtain a new product, at least one potential competitor is removed from the market. This can be an important advantage indeed, perhaps one which spells the difference between success and failure. If a firm contemplated adding tomato soup to its product line, acquisition of the Campbell Soup Company would virtually assure market success. When the Gillette Company decided to enter the home permanent field, its acquisition of the Toni Company not only removed the major competitor it would have faced, but immediately made Gillette the major competitive force in the home permanent field. Its later acquisition of the Paper Mate Company did the same thing for ball-point pens.

Market access. An obstacle to the success of new products is the difficulty such products often have in gaining access to the market. If the product is of a type new to the market, there will usually be an understandable reluctance among middlemen to handle it because a new product is an unknown quantity in terms of market acceptance and profitability. New products are risky to middlemen as well as to manufacturers. If the new product is similar to products already carried by middlemen, they may still be reluctant to stock it, but for different reasons. To add a product for which products already carried are reasonable substitutes may increase inventory and handling costs but add little to revenues. Receipts will be increased only if there is a significant brand preference or if there is a demand for variety in the market. In this case it is necessary to weigh the anticipated increase in revenues against the increase in costs. If the comparison is not favorable, the new brand will not be added.

An excellent illustration of the difficulty even a major firm may have in gaining market access is the attempt of Ford Motor Company to gain distribution for the Motorcraft line of replacement automotive parts. All automotive wholesalers already carried comparable parts, under other brands, which would fit all known applications. Brand preference in the repair trade was not strong, being outweighed by patronage considerations. Thus, there was no incentive for middlemen to add the new line either as a supplement or as a substitute for lines already carried. After an extended period of failure to gain acceptance of its new line, Ford solved the problem by acquiring the Electric Auto-Lite Company, which already had a strong distribution network.

Capitalization of development costs. Current accounting practice, because of the risky nature of new product development, is to treat development expenditures as a current expense rather than as an investment to be amortized over the market life of the new product.[10] When a product is acquired by merger, the purchase price is treated as an investment. The difference in effect on short-run profits of this difference in accounting treatment serves to discourage internal development.

Advantages of internal development

Greater profit potential. Although most new products are failures, some new products are very successful indeed. In the long run, profit

---

[10] John A. Howard, *Marketing Management: Analysis and Planning* (rev. ed.; Homewood, Ill.: Richard D. Irwin, Inc., 1963), p. 318.

opportunity tends to be commensurate with risk. In particular, those products which are new to the market have the potential of a high return. On the other hand, if a new product is acquired by merger, acquisition cost can be expected to be commensurate with demonstrated profit potential. A safe return tends to be a smaller return. Few companies that acquired their new products by merger can match the rate of return achieved by such companies as Xerox, IBM, and 3M.

Progressive image. Although an intangible and hard-to-measure factor, the overall image a company projects can be very important to its long-term success. Successful product innovation marks a company as progressive and as a leader in its field. This stimulates interest and confidence in its products. Again, companies like IBM and the 3M Company are good cases in point.

Better resource utilization. Either acquisition by merger or internal development of new products may lead to better utilization of resources. On the average, however, internal development is likely to achieve this objective most effectively. It permits a larger measure of "custom tailoring" of new products so as to optimize resource utilization. When the merger route is followed, often little is contributed to the more efficient use of present assets (plant, equipment, distribution facilities, etc.). Duplicate facilities may be acquired. Often, unwanted products must be accepted in order to get the ones which are wanted. By proceeding carefully in selecting companies for acquisition, these problems can be minimized, but in practice it is rare for them to be avoided altogether.

Clayton Antitrust Act, Section 7. A substantial disadvantage of product line diversification via merger is the danger of violation of Section 7 of the Clayton Act. This act prohibits mergers whose effect might be "substantially to lessen competition." Until 1950, Section 7 of the Clayton Act was relatively ineffective because it prohibited only those mergers which were consummated by stock purchase. A company could expand by purchase of another company's assets unless this violated the Sherman Antitrust Act. However, in 1950, Congress made three major changes in Section 7 (the Celler Antimerger Act). First, it broadened the section's reach to cover corporations acquiring the "whole or any part" not only of the stock but also "of the assets" of another company. Second, it eliminated from the statute the illegality test of whether the acquisition's effect may be substantially to lessen competition between the *acquiring* and the *acquired* company. Finally, Congress struck the prior test of whether the acquisition might restrain commerce "in any community," and substituted as the measure whether "in any line of commerce in any section of the country" the acquisition may substantially lessen competition or tend to create a monopoly.[11] As a result

---

[11] *Report of the Attorney General's National Committee to Study the Antitrust Laws* (Washington D.C.: U.S. Government Printing Office, 1955), p. 117.

of these changes, mergers are much more suspect than formerly and, consequently, a more risky approach to broadening a firm's product line.[12]

In recent years many companies have been ordered by the courts to divest themselves of merger acquisitions. Procter & Gamble Company was ordered to dispose of Clorox Company, General Foods Corporation of its S.O.S. Division, Continental Oil Company of Malco Refineries, Inc., and Ford Motor Company of Electric Autolite Company. The most important test of whether a merger is illegal is the effect of the merger on the share of market controlled by the surviving company. In the *Brown Shoe Company* case the court stated, "The market share which companies may control by merging is one of the most important factors to be considered when determining the probable effects of the combination on effective competition in the relevant market."[13] In ruling against Pillsbury Mills, Inc., the Federal Trade Commission looked at Pillsbury's market position for prepared mixes before and after two challenged acquisitions. Pillsbury increased its share in the Southeast market from 22.7 to 44.9 percent and moved ahead nationally from second to first place, increasing its share from 16 to approximately 23 percent.[14] This fact alone was deemed sufficient to establish a substantial lessening of competition.

Firmer base for long-term growth. Gaining new products via merger is inevitably a somewhat opportunistic approach to product line diversification. Whether or not this route can profitably be followed depends on the availability of firms with desired products whose owners are willing to sell at a particular time, on the ability to succeed against others who might be bidding for these same companies, and on ability to avoid subsequent divestiture under Section 7 of the Clayton Act Internal development of new products is less opportunistic. Properly executed, it contemplates product development as a continuing and permanent function of the firm. Surely this provides a firmer basis for rational long-term growth. It might be said that one of the important benefits of internal development of new products is that a firm exercises and develops its product innovation capability. Over the long term this might be the greatest competitive advantage it could possess.

---

[12] Section 7, in relevant part, now reads: "No corporation engaged in commerce shall acquire directly or indirectly, the whole or any part of the stock or other share capital and no corporation subject to the jurisdiction of the Federal Trade Commission shall acquire the whole or any part of the assets of another corporation engaged also in commerce, where in any line of commerce in any section of the country, the effect of such acquisition may be substantially to lessen competition, or to tend to create a monopoly" (64 Stat. 1125).

[13] 82 S. Ct. 1502 (1962), p. 1534.

[14] FTC Dkt. 6000 (1953).

Product development and public policy

The government has attempted to discourage firms from acquiring new products by merger when the effect might be to lessen competition. Many have felt that the government and the courts have been over-zealous in applying Section 7 of the Clayton Act, ruling out many mergers that would not have affected competition adversely and at the same time denying to business many of the advantages of product line diversification. The effect of mergers on competition is of relevant concern, but there is another possible effect which should also be considered. This is the effect of mergers on product innovation. Unfortunately, the effect of mergers on the pace of product innovation is unclear.

Assume for the moment that *all* firms acquire *all* their new products *only* by the merger route. In this case the market would gain nothing new. Already available products would merely be reassigned among various firms. There would be, in effect, no true innovation. Even the *possibility* of obtaining new products by this means may have some deleterious effects. It reduces the pressure upon management for new ideas and for the development of new processes and techniques. It offers "a way out" to the lethargic, to the company that sat idly by and did not attempt to innovate.

This extreme picture is highly unrealistic. In addition, the circumstances of the individual situation have much to do with the effect of acquisition by merger on product innovation. When Gillette Company acquired the Toni Company and Paper Mate, nothing new became available in the marketplace. On the other hand, innovation may be spurred when a large, well-financed company, acquires a small company, rich in ideas perhaps, but unable to afford the high costs and risks of product development. The acquisition of Philco by Ford Motor Company probably increased Philco's innovation capability. Funds received by small firms when they are bought out by larger ones may be devoted to research and development of additional new products, while the larger acquiring firm fully develops the market for the small firm's past innovations.

Conclusion

Because all products have a life cycle, survival of the business firm depends on the infusion of new products into the market. In a broader sense, the economic welfare of society is based on this same economic function. Long-term growth in man-hour productivity is due primarily to development of new machines and processes, not to people working harder. The affluent society owes its present comfort more to the new products developed by this and preceding generations than it does to attempts to lower production costs. One automatic washing machine is worth, in terms of its effect on our way of living, an infinite number of old-fashioned washboards.

Questions

1. Profit margins usually reach a peak and decline at an earlier point in the product life cycle than does sales volume. Why is this so?

2. A manufacturer of central home heating equipment is considering the possibility of adding a line of electric space heaters selling at $9.95, $14.95, and $19.95. The company's present line is sold through heating contractors and is used both in new home construction and in renovation of older homes. The electric space heaters are portable, and it is thought a large market for them exists among homeowners for supplemental heating, in cottages and resorts, and as a major heat source in parts of the country where central heating is not required.

    What factors should be considered by the firm before committing itself to the manufacture and marketing of these electric space heaters?

3. The National Safety Razor Company is a major producer of safety razors, razor blades, shaving creams, and men's toiletries. Management is now considering a proposal to add a line of electric razors. One executive doubts the wisdom of this move. He points out that the Gillette Safety Razor Company failed in its attempt to introduce an electric razor. The reason for this failure, he says, is that electric razors did not fit well with the rest of the Gillette line. Is this executive's reasoning sound?

4. This chapter emphasized the importance of a good production and marketing fit between a company's present products and a new addition. Yet many companies, particularly the so-called "conglomerates," have in recent years entered businesses completely unrelated to their present businesses. Is a decision to do this necessarily unsound?

5. When deciding to add a new product, is it more important that there be a good production fit or a good marketing fit between present products and the proposed addition? Explain.

6. Business firms have a substantial degree of choice in the amount of emphasis they place on product innovations in planning their long-term marketing strategy. What arguments can you offer in favor of relatively heavy stress on this strategy variable?

7. The rate at which new products are introduced into the market has increased greatly in the last decade. Some observers of this fact view this as evidence of economic progress; others view it as no more than an increase in planned obsolescence, which is wasteful. What is your view? Explain.

8. "When a company produces a wide line of products, management should take care to determine that each product covers its full costs and yields a satisfactory rate of profit." Appraise this statement.

9. "Trolley cars and newsreels. Milk bottles and Mason jars. Argyle socks and blue-suede shoes. Where are they now?

"They're with shaving mugs, soap flakes, Burma-Shave signs, automobile seat covers and 78 rpm records—vanishing from the American scene.

"It's all due to technology and taste. Both are changing more rapidly than ever, causing a fast turnover in the artifacts of everyday life. Change is so fast that yesterday's dream is today's necessity—and tomorrow's fond memory" (*The Wall Street Journal*, February 6, 1968).

The above quotation suggests the importance of an innovation capability to the business firm. By what criteria do you judge whether a firm does or does not possess such a capability? Explain.

10. Discuss the proposition that acquisition of new products by merger, although this course might best serve the interest of the firm, is not necessarily beneficial to the total economy.

7

Product
management
decisions

THE PROCESS of developing a new product is broad in scope. Directly
or indirectly the process must involve all operations of the business
firm—marketing, production, research and development, finance, and
even the legal department. Because of its inherent risk feature, top management is usually intimately involved in it. In order for so complex
a task to be carried out effectively, it is imperative that a sound program
for product development be formulated and then followed.

The most basic and critical decision involved in the product development process is the one discussed in the preceding chapter—selection
of the product which, for the particular firm in question, provides the
best profit opportunity. If this decision has been made wisely, with
due consideration given all variables involved, the remaining steps in
the process are made much easier, and chances of success are greatly
enhanced. Still, much remains to be done and many opportunities for
error remain after this choice has been made.

Product development is, in essence, the process of fitting the proposed
product to the requirements and opportunities of the market. The decision to produce, say, a sports car still leaves unanswered questions about
styling and configuration, size, color, convenience options, the image
to be projected, and so on. An almost infinite number of specific decisions
must be made to provide this market adaptation. If they are made wisely,
the profit opportunity visualized will be realized. If not, the profit opportunity will be lost.

Selection of the best product for development is, as previously explained, a procedure fraught with uncertainty—uncertainty concerning

demand, price, cost, and the product life cycle. In a very real sense, the product development process is a procedure for gradually reducing this uncertainty by increasing the information available to the decision maker.

The product development process

The product development process is not, and cannot be made, uniform for all companies. Each company is unique, and this uniqueness finds expression in differences in goals, requirements, and procedures. Figure 7–1 shows how the product development process might be carried through in a hypothetical firm. Although not necessarily applicable to situations faced by all companies, it will serve as a useful frame of

FIGURE 7–1
Steps in conversion of new product idea into new business

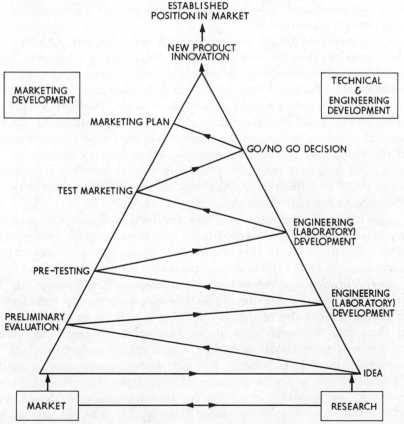

reference for discussion of the types of decisions involved in product development.

Characteristics of product development

An overview of the product development process as depicted in Figure 7–1 reveals certain important characteristics.

Process span. Product development begins with the conception of an idea for a new product and does not end until an established sales position for the new product has been achieved in the market. In a very real sense, a product has not been "developed," nor has a true innovation been accomplished, until that product has been accepted in the market. This achievement marks the adaptation of the new product to the market in an overt, profit-making, sense. It is the point at which the basic objective of new product development, maximization of profits, begins to be realized. In fact, it can be argued that product development doesn't end even here, that it is necessary to continue to change and improve products throughout the total life cycle if profits are to be maximized. However, this process is more commonly referred to as product improvement.

Concurrent marketing and production development. As discussed above, product development involves all operations of a business. Figure 7–1 stresses the concurrency of marketing and technical and engineering development. Technical and engineering development must be geared to marketing requirements as closely as possible. Production must provide the product the market wants, in the right quantities, at the right time. Marketing strategy, on the other hand, must reflect certain realities of the production process. For example, offering many varieties of size, color, and style may maximize sales, but only at prohibitive production costs. Profit is a function of efficiency of the total firm, not maximum efficiency in one part or another.

Concurrent development of a new product, marketingwise and engineeringwise, offers certain economies. Test marketing, for example, provides an opportunity to experiment with production processes so as to eliminate bugs before full-scale production is required.

Interdependence of marketing and engineering development. In Figure 7–1 each of the steps in product development on the technical and engineering development side is related to a step on the marketing side, in the sense that each depends on the other. Perhaps this interdependence is most clearly seen in the case of laboratory research and marketing research. Laboratory research without accompanying marketing research can easily be misdirected and sterile. In a market directed economy, the standards employed in laboratory research should reflect what people want from the product. High quality reflected, say, in durability is not a reasonable standard if consumers prefer low price and are willing to sacrifice quality in order to get it.

Before laboratory testing can be meaningfully undertaken, marketing research is usually necessary. The extent to which this is true, however, varies by products and by the type of standards involved. In many cases, important market standards for a product are already well known (for example, safety and durability of tires, efficacy of drugs, purity of food). Some laboratory testing is often possible without market testing; *complete* laboratory testing usually is not.

The same type of interdependence exists between the other steps in production and marketing development. Essentially, the market testing activities provide feedback which allows engineering development accurately to reflect marketing requirements. The triangular shape of Figure 7–1 is intended to illustrate that product development is a process of merging marketing requirements with technical and engineering requirements through a step-by-step process. Only when such a merger is completed is a successful product innovation possible.

Product development is a cautious process. It is a step-by-step feeling out of the market as the process evolves. Each step taken is intended to reduce further the uncertainty inherent in the product development process by increasing the information available about marketing requirements for the new product. Implicit in the taking of each step, therefore, is the need to decide how much additional market information is worth—in research expenditures, in time, and in relation to the cost of assuming more risk. The cost of reducing risk to zero, if this were possible, would usually be prohibitive. In carrying through this cautious approach, another objective is to retain as long as possible the option of *not* introducing the new product, with a minimal investment loss should this decision be made.

Product development involves the "total" product. There is equal need for development of such things as distribution strategy, promotional appeals, service policy, and warranty policy, as for development of the physical product. In reality, they too are a part of each of the steps. Marketing research, for example, done on the new product is equally relevant to such matters as service, warranty, and so on. In fact, the physical product may even be changed to adapt to such things as distribution strategy and promotional appeals.

Steps in product development

The previous section considered some characteristics of product development as a total process. This section will take a closer look at what is involved in carrying out the specific steps in product development.

New product ideas

Ideas for new products come from many sources—from the market, from production, from home office and research personnel, from salesmen, from other companies, and even from independent inventors. No one knows just where a good idea for a profitable new product might come from. Some sources are more likely to be productive than are others, but no company wants to close off any of them.

Most firms claim to be receptive to new product ideas, but few make an overt attempt to stimulate them or to ferret them out. Rather, this important process is left more or less to chance. This is a mistake. Some sort of organization for seeking out and handling new ideas is required; what form this organization takes is of secondary importance. Unless responsibility is centered somewhere, both the search and the processing will be neglected. Both line and staff personnel are usually fully busy with current operations, and added burdens are neither welcomed nor pursued.

The search for new product ideas can go on in many ways, the most appropriate approach depending on the industry involved. Primarily for industrial goods, but to some extent for consumer goods, call reports of salesmen may be so constructed and analyzed that they reveal consumer problems with present products, comparisons with competing products, unmet needs, and so on. Basic research may turn up many ideas which can profitably be followed up. Even brainstorming sessions may be worthwhile. What is most important is that ideas be actively sought, whatever the methods used.

Preliminary evaluation

The next step in Figure 7–1, preliminary evaluation of new product ideas, is in essence the product-choice decision discussed in the preceding chapter. However, it is usually not feasible to subject every new idea to complete and rigorous analysis. Most ideas are not worthy of extensive consideration. Therefore, some sort of preliminary screening method is usually employed. It is quite customary to have a screening committee, made up of representatives from different functional areas of the business (marketing, production, research and development, finance, and so on) to look over and discuss new product ideas. On the basis of the breadth and background of experience of committee members, these ideas are reviewed. Usually, most are rejected. Those that look most promising are turned over to some sort of new product task force for detailed study. This study might well follow the procedures outlined in the preceding chapter. This group then reports back to the preliminary screening committee, which reports, in turn, to top management.

Engineering development

Those new product ideas which have survived preliminary screening can now be subjected to engineering (laboratory) development to determine if they are feasible from a technical standpoint. Perhaps the idea is "beyond the state of the art" from the standpoint of production capability. If a proposed product cannot possibly be produced, there is no point in going to the market to find out if consumers would purchase it. Also, a more precise concept of what the product might be like and what it is intended to do is usually necessary before a logical pretesting program can be set up. Engineering development, at this stage, is unlikely to be complete, because more market information is required before it can proceed that far.

Pretesting

The fundamental purpose of pretesting is the acquisition of knowledge useful in assuring that the new product properly reflects demand factors. The "pre" in pretesting can mean preproduct, preproduction, premarketing program, and so on. Of necessity, it is a step that must come early in order to provide proper guidance. Because it must come early, it also usually means testing under circumstances which are somewhat artificial and in other ways difficult.

Methods used in pretesting of products are almost infinite in number. It is an area with much room for ingenuity. A few of the more common are: (1) *Consumer panels and juries:* Groups of various sorts and sizes (women's clubs, company visitors, etc.) are asked their opinion of various proposed product features (styling, color, etc.). (2) *Consumer surveys:* Representative samples of consumers may be selected, asked to view and comment on proposed new products. (3) *Field tests:* Tentative versions of new products may be presented to consumers for use in the home and their reactions ascertained. Pillsbury Mills asked housewives to bake two different formulas of cake mix, serve them to their families, and then record their preferences. Chrysler Corporation gave consumers new turbine cars to drive for several weeks and then interviewed them to learn their reactions. (4) *Trade shows:* American Telephone and Telegraph displayed the Princess telephone at the International Home Builders' Show. Five thousand visitors filled out cards giving their impressions of the new phone.[1]

---

[1] *American Telephone and Telegraph Company* case, in M. P. Brown, W. B. England, and J. B. Matthews, Jr., *Problems in Marketing* (3d ed.; New York: McGraw-Hill Book Co., 1961), p. 79.

Many other methods of pretesting are in use. All of them involve certain dangers. It is both difficult and costly to choose representative samples. The consumer's ability to indicate a true preference under artificial conditions is always a source of doubt in the results. Even if consumers have true preferences, it is difficult to conclude what this means in terms of actual sales in the real marketplace. Still, admittedly inadequate information is better than no information at all and usually well worth its cost.

Further engineering development

After pretesting, further engineering development is usually necessary. The product can now be refined to more fully reflect consumer tastes and wants. Alternative production processes can be compared concerning feasibility and cost. Some units of the product must be produced for distribution before the next step in marketing development, test marketing, can be taken.

Test marketing

Test marketing involves the sale of a proposed new product under conditions as near normal as possible in a test market which is as representative as possible of the target market. Sales performance of the product in test markets is observed and measured in order to ascertain what can be expected to be future sales performance in the total market.

The need for preliminary market testing of new products stems from the inherent limitations of pretesting. Pretesting is, as mentioned above, artificial in varying degrees as far as market conditions are concerned. Also, pretesting usually involves only some, and not all, aspects of the new product. A pretesting of Pillsbury Cake Mix, for example, was limited to taste preference between two alternative formulas. It revealed no information on such matters as package design, price, promotional appeals, comparisons with competing products, and so on. Consequently, it left a large measure of uncertainty about future market performance.

Test marketing, too, has limitations. The basic problem of sampling error is an important one. Cost limitations usually prevent use of a truly representative sample of the total market. Usually only one or a few cities are chosen. Also, the cost of arranging for the gathering of maximum information in the test market is high. Expensive store audits and consumer surveys may be necessary to do this. Some companies set up their own test markets and do their own data collection. Others use the test markets of such market research organizations as the A. C. Nielsen Company, which have elaborate facilities for data gathering.

Because of cost, as well as for other reasons, the time that can be devoted to test marketing is usually limited. It is questionable whether sales in a short time period are fully representative of longer term sales experience. The difference between initial sales and repeat sales is particularly critical. Initial sales may indicate a high consumer interest in a new product, but only repeat sales indicate presence of the sort of consumer satisfaction on which long-term success must be built.

Market testing runs the risk of loss of secrecy for a firm's new product plans. This may take away the promotional advantage associated with a dramatic, nationwide introduction. Also, it divulges a company's plans to competitors and may lessen the time it takes for them to retaliate. For such products as automobiles, these two limitations are deemed highly important.

Test marketing of new products provides an opportunity for further experimentation on the production side. The manufacture of limited quantities allows development of production processes and techniques so as to minimize production cost.

The go/no go decision

The process of product development up to this point has been one of gradual and continuous improvement in information available for product decisions. Information seeking can vary greatly in its extent, time consumed, and cost incurred. Throughout this process, management would normally attempt to retain as long as possible the option of going ahead with introduction of the new product or not. At some point it becomes uneconomic to continue to seek information, and a decision must be made to "go" or "not go" with the product in question. Success of the new product at this point is always still uncertain, sometimes highly so. It is a question of weighing carefully the probability of success and deciding whether or not to proceed.

The go or no go decision is a difficult one. Information is never complete. Furthermore, the decision makers have a vested interest in a favorable decision in order to justify the substantial investment that has been made bringing the product to this point. A no go decision is, in a sense, tacit admission that previous expenditures should not have been made. This is a difficult psychological barrier to overcome. An objective approach to this decision would, of course, ignore costs already incurred. These are "sunk" costs. The only relevant decision variables are future revenues in relation to future costs. This relationship determines the expected controllable profit associated with the new product.

The go/no go decision involves, in essence, a careful review and correction of the several variables in the profitability formula developed in the previous chapter.[2] Hopefully, as a result of pretesting and preliminary market testing, demand can now be more accurately defined both qualitatively and quantitatively. Expectations of price behavior, likewise, can now be refined. A recalculation of production and marketing fit, based on expanded knowledge of marketing and production requirements, should allow a refinement of earlier cost calculations. Expected life usually will still be a major uncertainty, but perhaps some estimating improvement is possible here. Effects on these same variables for existing products should now also be better known.

These refinements of the component variables in the profitability formula will now permit a more precise estimate of expected profits associated with adding the new product. A comparison with alternatives available for investment will then allow the go/no go decision to be made.

The marketing plan

The final step in this process, before actual introduction of the new product into the market, is the formulation of a detailed marketing plan. The purpose of such a plan is to give form, direction, and control to the market introduction process. The new product marketing plan must, of course, be integrated with, and fully consistent with, the overall marketing plan of the company.

Actually, development of a marketing plan doesn't start from scratch at this point. Previous steps in the development process are as relevant to this activity as they are to the go/no go decision. Evolution of the marketing plan began with the new product idea and grew with each succeeding step. What remains is to give concrete form and structure to this plan and to fill in the still missing details.

The essential parts of a marketing plan for new product introduction are the same as for the company's overall marketing plan: a situation analysis—facts about demand, competition, marketing law, the available distribution structure, and nonmarketing costs—can be based on information gathered in the earlier steps in production and marketing development. If these steps were well handled, the requisite information will be available. The problems and opportunities this situation provides should also now be known.

What remains is the planning of marketing strategy and tactics. The essence of marketing strategy is the setting of objectives and the determination of methods to be employed to accomplish them. Objectives can be stated in terms of the market(s) to be served—geographical area, income, and age groups, etc.—as well as sales volume in units

---

[2] $R = [D \times (P - C) \times L] \pm [d \times (p - c) \times l]_1 \pm [d \times (p - c) \times l]_2 \ldots \ldots$
$\pm [d \times (p - c) \times l]_n.$

and/or dollars. A specific profit goal is the most important objective to be decided upon.

The methods to be utilized in marketing strategy fall into such categories as product strategy—models, sizes, package design, etc.; distribution strategy—direct versus indirect channels, types of outlets, degrees of selectivity, etc.; price strategy—skimming versus penetration pricing, trade discounts, etc.; advertising strategy—media, appeals, etc.; and personal selling strategy—size and distribution of the sales force, selling methods, and so on. These objectives and methods, when the necessary detailed decisions concerning each have been made, constitute the heart of the marketing plan for the new product.

Before this plan can be implemented, this strategy must be converted into specific marketing tactics—who will do what, when, how, where, and so on. We are now ready to proceed to the final step of actual introduction of the new product into the market. Only when this step is successfully accomplished, and the product has secured an established position in the market, can we consider the product development task completed.

Ancillary product decisions

The term "product" is used in this text to refer to everything the consumer receives when making a purchase. Consequently, product decisions cover a wide spectrum. This has been recognized in the discussion up to this point, but emphasis has been on the physical product and little has been said about some of the special problems associated with such functions as packaging, branding, warranty policy, and service policy. A closer look at these areas is now in order.

Packaging

A package has two major functions: containment and promotion. Containment is essential to efficiency in physical distribution, while the promotional aspects of packaging operate to influence demand. Problems of containment tend to be technical and reasonably objective, such as requirements as to strength and size and resistance to moisture and other chemical elements. Promotional requirements concern such things as the package's ability to attract attention, its comparison with competing packages, its adaptability to advertising and point-of-sale promotion, its reflection on product quality, and so on. Development of a package to serve these functions well is a more subjective process. Although technical problems of containment are very difficult ones for some products, for most products the promotional aspects of packaging pose the most difficult decision requirements.

The role played by the package in the marketing mix, and hence the importance of the package development function, depends on many things. Packaging is usually a more critical element for convenience goods than for shopping or specialty goods. Within the convenience goods category, its importance varies with differences in buying behavior of consumers; for example, fresh vegetables, which consumers wish to see and touch, and detergents, which they will buy sight unseen. Self-service enhances the role of the package. Product use requirements of consumers (for example, frequent reseal and reuse) may make the package a major sales influencing factor. For some products (for example, cosmetics, table salt) package differences among brands may be more important than anything else. In some cases promotional requirements (use of television, for example) may strongly influence package decisions.

Diverse effects of package decisions. Package decisions are complicated by the fact that they may have many indirect, and often unanticipated, effects on both the production and marketing functions. Such "side effects" are often difficult to foresee and even more difficult to evaluate. Take, for example, the decision of many soft-drink manufacturers to package their products in cans as well as in returnable bottles.[3]

In the 1950s, soft-drink companies began experimenting with the sale of soft drinks in cans. Cans were thought to have several distinct advantages: (1) They did not need to be returned and thus relieved consumers of an inconvenience and removed a major problem for supermarkets, who objected to handling bottle returns. (2) They substantially reduced product weight. A case of 24, 6-ounce bottles weighs 50 pounds, while a case of 48, 6-ounce cans weighs about 25 pounds and takes one third less space. (3) Bottles are hard to stack and take a great deal of room in storage. Cans could be stacked in displays and on shelves just as any other canned goods.

Among the side effects associated with this product change are the following: (1) Taste. It was feared consumers might object to the slight metallic flavor picked up by carbonated beverages in cans. (2) Price. Although cans cost less per unit than bottles, the average returnable bottle made about 25 round trips. Thus, canned drinks would have to sell for $3\frac{1}{2}$ to $4\frac{1}{2}$ cents more per unit. (3) Channels of distribution. Present distribution was through bottlers who purchased syrup from soft-drink firms. These bottlers were not equipped for canning of soft drinks. (4) In-store promotion. Present promotion strategy relied heavily on bottlers, who made frequent deliveries to retail stores, set up displays,

---

[3] The following illustration is based on *Orange Crush Company* (Michigan Business Cases, Marketing Series, No. 21).

and so on. The soft-drink manufacturer was not equipped to do this. (5) Present distribution through bottlers. If canned soft-drink distribution bypassed bottlers, yet cut into their sale of bottled beverages, their profit position might be endangered. This might lead them to dilute their sales efforts by adding other soft drinks or, in extreme cases, to relinquish their franchise. As bottled soft drinks were expected to continue to account for at least 90 percent of sales, this would seriously hurt the soft-drink firms.

In the 1960s, canned soft drinks grew from 2 percent to 10 percent of total soft-drink sales. This, along with other package changes in the industry, has changed the entire distribution structure. Only high-volume bottling plants can justify the expense of installing canning lines. This has probably had no small part to play in the reduction in the number of bottling plants in the United States for 4,300 in 1962 to 3,600 in 1968.[4] Parent companies have taken on the job of supplying smaller bottlers with canned soft drinks. What started as a "simple" package change has revolutionized the whole industry.

Package development *is* product development; hence, the steps in package development are the same as those already discussed but with some change in emphasis. There is the same need to elicit ideas and for screening these ideas, for pretesting, and for test marketing.

Legal constraints on packaging. The principal legal constraints upon packaging decisions are those contained in the Food, Drug, and Cosmetic Act of 1938. The provisions of this act relating to packaging have two basic purposes: (1) to protect health, and (2) to prevent deception. Health protection is the purpose of provisions prohibiting packaging under unsanitary conditions, the use of packaging materials which may cause the contents to be injurious to health, or enclosing such potentially dangerous items as children's favors in the package along with its contents. Prevention of deception is the objective of provisions outlawing any food, drug, or cosmetic container which is "so made, formed, or filled as to be misleading." For food containers, minimum standards of fill are prescribed.

Information to appear on or within the package is controlled by the Food, Drug, and Cosmetic Act as well as by the Wool Products Labeling Act of 1939, the Fur Products Labeling Act of 1951, and the Textile Fibers Products Identification Act of 1958. For foods, Section 401 of the Food, Drug, and Cosmetic Act requires the establishment of definitions and standards for foods whenever such action will "promote honesty and fair dealing in the interest of consumers." The provisions for the labeling of drug products have long been very exacting and in 1964 were further strengthened by an amendment to the act. The

---

[4] *Marketing Insights,* March 4, 1968, p. 15.

other three acts mentioned above are primarily designed to prevent deception by requiring on the label an accurate and clear description of the product's composition.

Government imposed standards of packaging and labeling have long been a subject of controversy. Some consumer groups and government agencies recommend more rigid controls. Extensive hearings were held by the antitrust subcommittee of the U.S. Senate, chaired by Senator Phillip A. Hart, in 1961. Witnesses contended that the use of odd weights and sizes by competing brands made price comparison difficult, that net contents were often obscurely stated in small print, that illustrations, descriptions, and terms such as "giant half-pound" and "jumbo quart" were misleading. Many other charges of consumer abuse through packaging were also strongly pressed.

The outgrowth of these and subsequent hearings and congressional debate, spread over five years, was the passage in 1966 of the so-called Truth-in-Packaging law.[5] When finally passed, the act was a substantially watered-down version of the one originally introduced. The only mandatory provisions remaining concerned certain information to be included on the label; all other provisions are discretionary. A brief summary of the act follows:

Mandatory labeling provisions. A primary objective of the act is to promote uniformity and simplification of labeling. The bill provides that:

1. The identity of the commodity shall be specified on the label.
2. The net quantity of contents shall be stated in a uniform and prominent location on the package.
3. The net quantity of contents shall be clearly expressed in ounces (only) and, if applicable, pounds (only) or in the case of liquid measures in the largest whole unit of quarts or pints.
4. The net quantity of a "serving" must be stated if the package bears a representation concerning servings.

Discretionary labeling provisions. The act authorizes the administering agencies to promulgate regulations when necessary to prevent consumer deception or to facilitate value comparisons:

1. To determine what size packages may be represented by such descriptions as small, medium, and large.
2. To regulate the use of such promotions as "cents off" or "economy size" on any package.
3. To require the listing of ingredients in the order of decreasing predominance.
4. To prevent nonfunctional slack fill.

---

[5] Public Law 89–755, 89th Cong., S 985 (November, 1966).

Packaging provisions. The act provides for the *voluntary* adoption of packaging standards. It authorizes the secretary of commerce to call upon manufacturers, packers, and distributors to develop voluntary standards whenever he finds that undue proliferation of weights, measures, or quantities impairs the ability of consumers to make value comparisons. If voluntary standards are not adopted, the secretary of commerce shall report this fact to Congress together with his legislative recommendation.

Enforcement. Responsibility for enforcing the provisions of the act is divided between the Food and Drug Administration (FDA), which has jurisdiction over food and cosmetics, and the Federal Trade Commission (FTC), which is supposed to regulate the labeling of all other consumer commodities. The Truth-in-Packaging law does not provide for criminal penalties.

Branding

Another integral part of almost every product is a brand. Products which traditionally have been sold unbranded (such as fresh fruits and vegetables) are increasingly making use of product branding. For some products (such as cosmetics, some watches) the brand and its implicit connotations may be the most important value received by the consumer when he makes a purchase. Selection of an appropriate product brand, one which produces maximum acceptability of a product, is an important part of the product development process.

A brand is any letter, word, name, symbol, or device or any combination thereof which is adopted and used by a manufacturer or merchant to identify his goods and services, and to distinguish them from those manufactured, sold, or, in the case of services, performed, by others.[6] The term "brand" is a business term; the term "trademark" is its legal counterpart. A brand name is that part of the brand that can be vocalized. It should be remembered, however, that "brand" refers to *anything* which serves to distinguish one product from another.

There are many types of brands. In addition to those which identify products, there are "service marks" (for example, name of motel, laundry, or car-rental agency), "certification marks" (for example, the Good Housekeeping Seal of Approval), and "collective marks" (for example, seals of labor unions and trade associations). Brands owned by manufacturers are known either as "manufacturers' brands" or as "national brands," regardless of the scope of the area served. Brands controlled by wholesalers or retailers are known either as "distributors' brands" or as "private brands."

Basic objective of branding. The basic objective of branding is market control. A brand is essential to promotional activities of the firm. Through promotion, acceptance or preference for a product can be estab-

---

[6] For definitions of brands and trademarks and other terms related to them, see the Lanham Act, Public Law 489, Title 10, "Constructions and Definitions."

lished among consumers. If the product bears a manufacturer's brand and is available through many retail outlets, the goodwill of consumers is directed toward the manufacturer. Retailers will find it difficult to substitute other products for the branded one consumers prefer. On the other hand, if the wholesaler or retailer places his brand on a product, the goodwill of consumers attaches to the wholesaler or retailer, and the manufacturer loses much of his control over the market for his product.

The degree of market control which can be established through branding varies greatly. It depends very much on the distinctiveness of the product in the eyes of consumers, on whether this distinctiveness is based on hidden or apparent product qualities, and on the extent of consumer knowledge about a product. The industrial buyer who is a trained engineer, for example, will rely on his own judgment of a product's quality rather than on the reputation of a brand. In addition, the effectiveness of a company's brand strategy affects the degree of market control which is achieved.

Brand selection. Selection of a brand for a new product is an extremely important, and often treacherous, operation. New product names such as Chrysler's Valiant, Du Pont's Corfam, and Cities Service's Citgo grow out of meticulously planned campaigns involving computers, psychological tests, opinion surveys, and other scientific procedures. Too much is at stake to leave the choice to flashes of inspiration.

A good brand must meet two important requirements: (1) maximum promotability, and (2) minimum risk of loss of ownership rights. Promotability is a result of a combination of factors, and no absolute criteria can safely be established. Normally, however, those brands are considered best which are short; easily pronounced, spelled, and remembered; distinctive; appealing; and adaptable to various promotional media. A hidden nuance in a name can do a lot of damage, undermining the consumer's image of the product. For this reason, some companies insist on "nonsense" words for brand names, and rely on computers to find them. Among these is Du Pont, who reasons that a nonsense word is likely to have fewer connotations than a word familiar to consumers.[7]

Ownership rights to a brand can be lost in many ways, the two most common being infringement of another brand and by becoming a generic term. The danger of inadvertent infringement is great. There are more than 300,000 brands registered with the U.S. Patent Office and at least that many more registered with state bureaus; and according to the U.S. Trademark Association, there are probably a million more that aren't registered but could lead to lawsuits if copied.

---

[7] Max Gunther, "We've Got to Call It Something," *The Saturday Evening Post,* September 11, 1965, pp. 60–61.

A brand name becomes generic when the public adopts it as a word to describe a general class of products. The courts may then rule that it is a part of the American language and cannot be appropriated for the exclusive use of one firm. Until 1921, "Aspirin" was a brand name of the Bayer Company. Then it became a generic name. In the same way, Du Pont lost "Cellophane," the Haughton Elevator Company lost "Escalator," and American Thermos Product Company lost "Thermos."[8]

Unfortunately, there is a conflict between the twin objectives of promotability and protection for brands. The factors which make a brand promotable are also the ones which might tend to cause it to be infringed by others or to become generic. There is need in brand administration to reconcile these two objectives, to achieve the optimum level of each without jeopardizing the other. Registration of a brand under the Lanham Act (Trade Mark Law of 1946) is a partial aid in accomplishing this goal.

Registration of brands. Under common law, ownership rights in a brand are based on priority of use; whoever first used a particular brand in commerce is the "owner" of that brand. Registration of a brand is not essential to the protection of fundamental rights in that brand, but registration under the Lanham Act modifies and extends basic ownership rights.

The Lanham Act is administered by the U.S. Patent Office. It provides for registration of brands on either the Principal or Supplemental Register. Full benefits of registration are accorded only to marks placed upon the Principal Register; the Supplemental Register provides more limited protection to marks which, for one reason or another, do not qualify for the Principal Register. The major purpose served by registration on the Supplemental Register is protection of a brand used in sales to foreign countries. In many countries, rights to a brand derive from registration rather than from priority of use. Registration in these countries often can be made only for marks already registered in the seller's own country. Hence, the Supplemental Register was created to provide U.S. firms selling abroad the sort of protection for their brands they have at home under the common law.

Among the more important benefits which are gained by registering a brand on the Principal Register under the Lanham Act are the following:

1. *Registration is prima facie evidence of ownership.* This means that in case of conflict over ownership rights in a brand, the burden of proof is on the owner of the unregistered brand. Because use of a particular brand by both parties may have begun many years ago, and evidence of the exact date of use is often skimpy, this can be a very important advantage.

---

[8] Ibid., p. 61.

2. *Registration is constructive notice of registrant's ownership claim.* Under the common law an infringer can often gain ownership rights to a brand if the infringement was innocent, made without knowledge of the existence of the infringed brand. If a brand is registered, all parties are *presumed* to know of its existence, whether they do in fact or not, and cannot claim innocent infringement.

3. *Registration permits cases of infringement to be tried in federal courts.* This is important to protection of a brand because federal courts will interpret cases in light of provisions of the Lanham Act, with its relatively clear provisions, rather than under the common law, which is far from clear, as will the state courts.

4. *Possible collection of triple damages.* In cases of brand infringement, courts normally award damages to the owner of the infringed brand. Under the Lanham Act, federal courts are authorized to assess up to three times the actual damages. This serves as an obvious deterent to infringement.

5. *Protection against imports which infringe registered brands.* Brands recorded on the Principal Register are filed in the U.S. Treasury Department and are checked against brands on imported goods to discover and halt cases of possible infringement.

6. *Achievement of incontestability.* After five years of registration on the Principal Register, a brand becomes "incontestable." As defined in the Lanham Act, this means that ownership rights cannot be lost to someone else on the grounds of priority of use. This limits to five years a risk which under common law is eternal.

Other lesser benefits are also derived from registration. Of those listed above, although all of them are important, incontestability is probably the most significant. Before passage of the Lanham Act, registration was no more than a claim to priority of use, which could be set aside if someone else could prove he was the first user of a particular brand. Now, after five years of continuous use, even though someone else proves prior use, the owner of the registered mark is assured he can continue to use the brand in which he may have invested large sums. It is possible that the first user may gain the right of concurrent use, either on a different product or in a different market area.

Warranty policy

Decisions on warranty policies are also a part of the product development process. The assurance provided by a warranty to the consumer that he will actually receive the utility he anticipated is a part of the value of his purchase. A warranty is an obligation to the buyer assumed by a seller. It provides that the seller shall be answerable to the buyer for various matters relating to the product.

Warranties may be either express or implied. An *express* warranty is one that is stated by the seller in either written or spoken words.

A warranty is *implied* if, from the nature of the sale and the circumstances of the parties, the law believes it reasonable that a warranty was intended, although none was actually mentioned. Implied warranties have been codified and incorporated in the Uniform Commercial Code, which has been adopted by the legislatures of most states. Among the principal implied warranties are: (1) warranty of title, (2) warranty that goods sold by description are as described, (3) warranty that goods sold by sample conform to the sample, and (4) warranty that goods intended for consumption are fit for consumption. With regard to product quality, (5) there is no implied warranty as to quality or fitness for any particular purpose, except where the buyer makes known to the seller the particular purpose for which the goods are required and relies on the seller's skill or judgment. Also, an implied warranty as to quality or fitness for a particular purpose may be annexed by the usage of trade.

Objectives of warranty policy. Specific objectives of warranty policy might be any in a long list of possibilities. Most of these can be classified as part of one of two general objectives: promotional advantage or protection of the seller. When a product is offered on a "satisfaction or your money back" basis, the purpose is usually to induce trial of a product by removing risk to the purchaser. On the other hand, an express warranty which restricts the buyer's redress to claims approved by the seller, and at the same time disclaims all other liabilities, expressed or implied, has as a major purpose protection of the seller against buyer claims.[9] The situations noted here represent the two extremes in warranty terms. If these are thought of as the extrema of a continuum, the terms of any particular warranty can fall at any point in between.

These two general purposes of warranties are not necessarily mutually exclusive. Surprisingly, perhaps, it is possible to serve both of these objectives at the same time. This is a result of the role of warranties in consumer purchase behavior. Consumers rarely subject written warranties to careful scrutiny and are thus uninformed of the extent to which their rights are assured or restricted. They seem primarily concerned with whether or not a written warranty accompanies the product, not in its terms. Any written warranty, no matter how restrictive, is assumed to be better than no written warranty. Actually, a highly restrictive warranty may offer less protection than no warranty at all because it disclaims liability under implied warranties.

The ability of manufacturers to limit their liability by use of disclaim-

---

[9] For example, Chrysler Corporation's warranty for new 1972 model passenger cars states: "This warranty is in lieu of any other warranties or conditions, including merchantability or fitness for a particular purpose. The remedies under this warranty are exclusive and neither Chrysler Corporation nor Chrysler Motors Corporation assumes nor authorizes anyone to assume for them any other obligation."

ers is increasingly being restricted by the courts. It has long been held that a manufacturer cannot disclaim responsibility for his own negligence. Increasingly, court decisions have held manufacturers strictly accountable for damages suffered by consumers, even though negligence cannot be proved.[10] Courts are moving away from the principle that warranties do not "run with the product." For example, automobile warranties have long been held to be part of the contractual relation between manufacturer and dealer. The dealer, in turn, warrants the product to the car purchaser. The consumer's only claim is against the dealer. The only exceptions to this principle recognized were for products taken internally (foods, drugs, beverages, etc.) or where negligence on the part of the manufacturer could be proved. Increasingly courts are taking the view that restriction of warranties to privity of contract is unrealistic in these days of mass distribution and are extending the responsibility of manufacturers to consumers even though no contractual relationship between these parties exists.

Warranty terms versus warranty administration. A warranty may be administered either strictly or liberally with respect to the terms it contains. For many years, the standard automobile warranty specified terms of 90 days or 4,000 miles, whichever came first. During this same period, however, it was customary for dealers, backed up by the manufacturer, to provide free service under the warranty for one full year. The change (in 1961) to a 12-month, 12,000-mile warranty did not necessarily represent a change in the service the consumer actually received, but merely modified the written warranty to bring it into conformance with what was already practiced. In 1963, vehicle manufacturers adopted a 24-month, 24,000-mile warranty as standard for the industry. At the same time, Chrysler adopted a five-year, 50,000-mile warranty on power-train components. In 1967, the rest of the industry followed suit. Just how much this liberalized the granting of redress under warranty is uncertain. However, high costs of warranty administration presumably account for reducing warranty terms for automobiles to 12 months with the introduction of the 1969 models. With the introduction of 1971 models all manufacturers discontinued the 50,000 mile power-train warranty.

Whether a restrictive warranty, liberally administered, or a more generous warranty, restrictively administered, is the better strategy depends on the objectives to be attained. Liberal administration of a restrictive warranty probably has a favorable psychological effect on a firm's customers; they are receiving more by way of service than they have a right to expect. If a company's objective is to build loyalty among its present customers, this might well be a good policy to follow. On the other hand, a warranty with more generous terms can be very useful

---

[10] Arthur Southwick, "Mass Marketing and Warranty Liability," *Journal of Marketing,* April 1963, pp. 6 ff.

as a promotional weapon, underscoring a company's confidence in the quality of its products. Ford Motor Company was the first to adopt the 12-month, 12,000-mile warranty for automobiles. It promoted this more generous warranty heavily at that time in conjunction with its promotional theme of "The Car that Cares for Itself." This is probably a better approach for a company whose primary goal is to expand its market share than it is for the company that wants to hold its present customers. A more liberal warranty also may serve as a means of promoting service business for dealers—it tends to tie consumers to the dealers for service for a longer period of time.

Product service

The term "service" is used loosely in marketing; it is employed in reference to promptness of delivery, returned goods privileges, treatment of customers by retail salesclerks, and so on. By "product service" we have reference to service work intimately associated with the physical product itself—its adjustment, maintenance, and repair so as to assure the consumer the utility he can reasonably expect as a consequence of his purchase. Such service is sometimes referred to as "technical service," although the amount of technical expertise involved varies widely. In the industrial market the adaptation of products to the individualized needs of the buyers may call for a high order of engineering knowledge, whereas repair of some consumer durables may be essentially a task of exchanging a new part for one which has proven defective.

Product service is today a major problem area for manufacturers of many products.[11] The increased complexity of products and the rapid growth of markets have outstripped the development of service facilities. As a consequence there is widespread dissatisfaction among consumers with the general quality of product service, and widespread concern among manufacturers because of their inability to cope satisfactorily with the situation.

Manufacturers are uncertain of the role product service should play in marketing strategy. For example, should a manufacturer stress his service program in his promotion, or will this have a negative effect on the consumer's purchase decision because it brings to mind service problems he has previously experienced? Evidence exists that consumers pay little attention to future service requirements when making a purchase. One study shows future service needs to have been overtly considered by only 2 percent of buyers.[12] Product service, to the consumer,

---

[11] See "The American Repairman: A Vanishing Breed?" *U.S. News and World Report,* September 13, 1965, pp. 88–90.

[12] George Katona and Eva Mueller, "A Study of Purchase Decisions," Lincoln H. Clark, ed., *Consumer Behavior* (New York: New York University Press, 1955), p. 49.

is something like a toothache; he does not look forward to it, wants immediate attention when his need arises, and wishes to forget about the matter as quickly as possible. Perhaps the greatest need for a manufacturer concerning service is to develop a rationale concerning the role of service in his total operation—what should be its objectives and how should it "fit in" with other elements in his marketing program.

Product service strategies. Manufacturers follow many different strategies with regard to product service. Their strategies are, in part, an outgrowth of the ways in which they view product service—the philosophies and attitudes concerning it which shape their thinking about its role in marketing strategy. Among the more common approaches to product service among companies are the following.[13]

The negative view. This view holds that product failures are clearly mistakes, and that product service is a kind of fire-fighting operation; the cost of performing it is a penalty paid for shortcomings in engineering and manufacturing performance. Product service is not seen as an activity providing added value to a product, but as an unfortunate expense which should be kept at an absolute minimum until the deficiencies which causes it can be removed. Automobile manufacturers have been accused of adhering to this view in servicing automobiles which have been involved in recall campaigns.[14]

The quality policeman view. This view of product service is an extension of the negative view and places primary emphasis upon the information gathering role. Product defects are clues to needed product improvements. Careful records must be kept of the nature and incidence of defects so that the extent of the problem, as well as the need for corrective action, can be assessed. Primary allocation of product service resources should be to such information gathering, and only secondary consideration should be given to correction of defects in products now in the hands of consumers. Product service is basically an adjunct of technical research rather than a means of building consumer goodwill in the short run.

The service-is-a-business view. Service can be looked at as a business in itself, as a profit-making opportunity which should be exploited. When service is inevitable and the out-of-warranty product population is large, the opportunity profitably to employ this approach is present. Automobile manufacturers, among others, cultivate service business at a profit through the manufacture and sale of replacement parts and the provision, through their dealers, of service facilities. A basic problem associated with this approach is the possibility of conflict between the service end and the manufacturing end of the business; product improvement

---

[13] The views of product service presented here are not necessarily mutually exclusive. Approaches to product service often reflect a combination of these views.

[14] *Time,* May 8, 1972, p. 79.

can cut directly into service profits by reducing the incidence of repair. An attempt to compromise these two profit goals may lead to confusion of purpose.

The natural agent view. This view holds that the dealer, rather than the manufacturer, has primary responsibility for product service. Because he is nearest to the customer, he has a higher capacity to act quickly and economically. Also, he is the one to whom the customer will naturally turn when he has a service problem. Acceptance of this view by the manufacturer limits his obligation to seeing that the dealer is properly supplied with the parts, service manuals, and so on, that he needs to perform his service function. The dealer becomes the prime service factor, with the manufacturer assuming a facilitating role.

The factory service view. Diametrically opposed to the natural agent view is the factory service view. It is argued that the manufacturer has most at stake, that his brand appears on the product, and hence that it is he the consumer will blame if the product is faulty. It is also pointed out that dealers have defaulted on the service function, that the manufacturer is more competent, and that consumers have more confidence in service provided by the manufacturer. In recent years automobile manufacturers have experimented with factory service centers in metropolitan areas. Appliance manufacturers have moved heavily in this direction.

The limited obligation view. This view holds that the manufacturer's product service responsibility is limited to the length of the warranty, that this is all he promised when the consumer made his purchase. After expiration of the warranty, service is the function of independent repair shops, which can and do provide such service at a profit on a wide array of products. It can be argued that the reduction in the manufacturer's service cost which might be associated with this approach may lead to reduced product prices, thereby compensating the consumer for any increase in the cost of out-of-warranty service.

The competitive weapon view. Product service is, of course, an effective marketing tool which can be used to influence product value, acceptance, and brand reputation to a significant degree. To achieve this objective, the service organization and its policies and functions should be designed around a concept of customer needs and wants in relation to produce service. The promotion of Zippo lighters is a good case in point. This company has long advertised that "no one has ever had to pay for repairs on a Zippo lighter." The effect of such promotion on sales is, of course, difficult to measure.

The competitive weapon approach is not limited to small and inexpensive products, although the risks inherent in such a policy are least for such products. In the case of automobiles, some foreign makes have had disappointing sales in the United States because of consumers' concern about adequacy of service. Volkswagon has placed heavy stress on the quality and availability of its service, perhaps thus gaining a competitive advantage over other imports.

The optimum quality view. This view of product service holds that service can be useful in permitting an optimum level of quality to be attained. Product failure patterns are studied carefully and continuously to discover areas where too much money is spent on quality as well as those where quality improvement is needed. Cost dollars can then be shifted away from areas which indicate little complaint activity to areas having high complaint ratios and service costs, thus achieving the optimum relationship between product quality and service requirements.

The socioeconomic view. Product service presents excellent opportunities to influence a firm's public image. Service provides opportunity for the "personal touch," the chance to demonstrate that the large, impersonal corporation is concerned about the individual consumer and his personal problems. Conversely, the failure to provide competent and responsible service may be considered the manifestation of a "public be damned" attitude. Some public utilities seem to have learned this lesson well. Through extensive services reflected in their rate structures, they have gained widespread support among consumers. Others, often with lower rates but fewer services, have very unenviable reputations. Organizations whose activities are extensively controlled by public boards, who in turn are responsive to public opinion, can ill afford such adverse public reactions.

Quality–service interrelationships. The complementarity of product quality and product service, and the trade-offs possible between the two, are not always clearly recognized. Critics of business are fond of pointing out that the quality of many products is below the quality level possible. Vance Packard, in *The Wastemakers*, makes much of this charge. What such critics often fail to recognize is that the highest quality is not necessarily the "right" quality in terms of demand and cost considerations. Sellers must offer consumers what they want, and they often prefer lower quality to higher prices.

This suggests that there is an optimum relationship between product quality and product service, although that point might be hard to locate. The optimum relationship depends on many things, among them such factors as: (1) consumer attitudes toward the inconveniences associated with product service; (2) consumer purchase behavior—for example, do consumers weigh service requirements heavily or lightly in purchase decisions? (3) the capabilities of a company's service organization; and (4) a company's ability to control quality.

Some of the criticism of business that is embodied in charges of "planned obsolescence" seems to involve a lack of recognition of the relationship between product quality and service cost. In a competitive economy, it is unlikely that business does not build products of as good quality as they are able to build, given the price at which these products must be offered. They do, however, control quality, and accept certain product service costs, in order to provide consumers something that best meets their needs and buying patterns.

Service versus exchange. A basic trend affecting the service task has recently emerged and already seems rather well established. Increasingly, exchange of products and parts is replacing field service. General Electric Company was the first to begin a policy of exchange rather than repair of electric blankets during the warranty period.[15] This practice has now spread to many other small appliances. Automotive repair increasingly consists of installing new or rebuilt parts rather than attempting field repair of defective units.

There are several reasons for this trend. Foremost among them is rapidly rising field repair costs because of increasing wage rates. The cost of repairing is rising much faster than the per unit manufacturing costs of new or rebuilt parts, the production of which can benefit from economies of scale. Compounding this problem is the growing technical complexity of many products, which complicates the repair function. In addition, there is the failure of service personnel and facilities to grow apace with the expanding economy. Increasingly, young people shun such employment.

Special service problems for industrial goods. Service often plays an even larger role for industrial goods than for consumer goods because of the specialized nature of the products and the need for continuous operations of the industrial user. It is not unknown for the cost of service to exceed the cost of the physical product itself.

One simple classification of industrial service is based on the time at which the service is performed: presale, time-of-sale, or postsale. In each of these cases the amount of service rendered may greatly exceed what is normal for consumer goods. For time-of-sale and postsale service the problems differ from those associated with consumer goods primarily in degree, not in kind; presale service causes the greatest perplexities.

Presale service may consist of extensive and expensive engineering studies necessary to adapt a seller's offering to the specific requirements of the potential buyer. It may be composed of detailed cost studies essential to the buyer's purchase decision. These studies, or others like them, may utilize high-priced talent and consume much time.

The purpose of such presale service is, in large part, to convince the buyer he should purchase. It is a particularly expensive form of promotion. If the service is rendered and no sale is made, a substantial

---

[15] Harry R. Tosdal, "General Electric Company (A)" case in *Introduction to Sales Management* (4th ed.; New York: McGraw-Hill Book Co., 1957), p. 93.

loss may be suffered. If an attempt is made to charge separately for presale service, its promotional value is reduced. If the seller attempts to recoup his loss in higher prices to those who do purchase, his competitive position is threatened. The seller faces a real dilemma from which there is no easy escape.

Approaches to the solution of this problem vary widely. In most cases they involve an uncomfortable effort to reconcile these various considerations to arrive at a viable approach to the market. Firm policies are hard to establish, and a normal result is to "play it by ear," compromising as necessary with regard to each potential sale.

Organization for product development

Effective organization for product development poses many problems, and companies have adopted various approaches to their solution. Most basically, there is the problem of overcoming the still too widespread belief that formal organization for new product development is unnecessary. Often, this function is thought to be a part of everyone's job, and therefore it is the responsibility of no one. Because product development is a complex function, involving nearly all aspects of a business operation, there is a difficult problem of coordination. The skills of many people in many departments (technical research, engineering, production, market research, finance, etc.) must be brought together to compose an effective overall effort. In addition, top management must be intimately involved in the product development process because often the very future of the business enterprise is at stake. In less extreme cases, profits may still be greatly influenced, now and in the future, by product development decisions.

The organization for new product development presented in Figure 7–2 is that of a large, widely diversified company with a strong success record in product innovation. Obviously, this particular organizational approach is not suitable for all companies, but it contains many specific ideas and procedures which have wide applicability.

In this company, each product (operating) division is responsible for research and development of new products associated with its present activities. The New Products Division is responsible for research and development of products not associated with present product divisions. The product divisions, however, may call on the New Products Division for advice and assistance and may "employ" them to carry out certain functions. The New Products Division is charged with coordinating product development activities throughout the company.

The New Products Screening Committee reports directly to top management. Ideas for new products which are received by top management

FIGURE 7–2

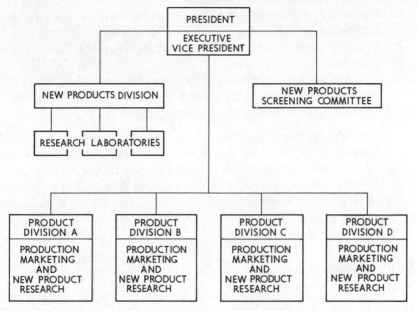

are referred to the committee for evaluation. Members of the committee come from major functional areas which are affected by the product decision. This group may reject a proposal on the basis of initial review or, very rarely, give immediate approval to proceed. Most commonly the proposal is referred to the New Products Division for careful analysis of technical, market, financial, and legal matters, and a report is returned to the Screening Committee. If it approves, the New Products Division is then authorized to proceed further with development.

Within the New Products Division each "unrelated" new product is organized as a small business unit with personnel responsible for market research, advanced product development, experimental manufacturing, and test marketing. Each such new business unit is headed by a project manager who is fully responsible for all phases of the new business development program. Its basic goal is to put itself out of business as soon as possible. It achieves this goal when it completes the following tasks to the satisfaction of the top management. The "new business" is then turned over to an operating group, either one already in existence or a new one formed for this purpose. The tasks are:

1. Determine market potential for the new product.
2. Establish goals for research and development people.
3. Supervise technical and market research.
4. Design and develop the package.

5. Investigate competitive products.
6. Determine if present productive capacity can be used or if new facilities are needed.
7. Evaluate extent to which the new product is patentable.
8. "Test sell" the new product.
9. Evaluate market acceptance of the new product.
10. Work out a profit target for the new product.
11. Obtain a "go" decision from top management.

Not evident in this description of one company's approach to product development is the normally heavy use of the committee system in organizing for new product development. The fact that successful product development involves all parts of the business firm and that successful integration of their efforts is a major key to success makes the committee system appropriate.

Conclusion

The approach of many companies to new product development has, in the past, been casual. It has often been thought of as a one-shot activity to be engaged in when necessary and then forgotten until the need for additional new products can no longer be ignored. Such an approach is not adequate to today's dynamic market. One of the strongest assets a company can have in a world of rapidly changing consumer wants is an effective product development capability.

Questions

1. The introduction of a new product into the market is a treacherous business, with the chance of failure greater than the chance of success. In the light of this situation is it ever desirable for a firm to undertake the sale of a new product without extensive market testing?
2. The Tosca Company, manufacturers of automotive electrical equipment, recently introduced a new automotive battery into the market. Sales have been very disappointing to date. This puzzles the company's executives because they are convinced this is a very superior battery. It is carefully made, and its quality has been carefully checked in the laboratory. Although it is higher priced than other batteries on the market, it carries a five-year warranty in contrast to the typical two- or three-year warranty. Thus, its cost per year of use to the consumer is less.

    The president of the company believes that the fault may lie in the standards used in the laboratory to check quality. He has, therefore, called on you, a management consultant, to advise him on: (1) how laboratory standards should be determined, and (2) once determined, how much reliance can be placed on conformance to these standards as an indicator of market success. What do you advise?

3. P. Lorillard Company originally offered its king-size and filter Old Gold cigarettes in packages virtually identical with the package containing its regular-size Old Gold cigarettes. Both the king-size and filter cigarettes failed to sell in the volume anticipated. In order to improve their sales performance, the company undertook to differentiate the packages of both its king-size and filter cigarettes.
   1. How might this package similarity be at least in part responsible for the unsatisfactory sales of the king-size and filter cigarettes?
   2. What steps should P. Lorillard have taken in developing new packages for its Old Gold King Size and Old Gold Filter cigarettes?

4. In an article entitled "Packagers Rap Hart Bill" (*Business Week*, May 8, 1965), Lee S. Bickmore, president of National Biscuit Company, was quoted as calling the proposed packaging bill "stupid." Albert N. Halverstadt, a Procter & Gamble vice president, reportedly said it would "grant federal officials extraordinary powers to impose their preferences on the marketplace." On the other hand, the Department of Commerce saw the bill as a boon to consumers.

   Evaluate the gains and losses to consumers and to business likely to result from passage of the Hart bill.

5. A brand, to be of value to its owner, must have some meaning and significance to consumers. Under what circumstances is a brand most likely to possess such meaning and significance?

6. How might it be argued that there is a basic conflict between the promotional requirements of a brand name and the protection of ownership rights in a brand name?

7. Contrast the warranty policies you consider appropriate to (1) a manufacturer of cigarette lighters and (2) a manufacturer of air conditioners.

8. Discuss the role of warranties in marketing strategy for small appliances. What are the implications of this role for a decision on whether or not to liberalize warranties on small appliances?

9. Some manufacturers of consumer durables argue that the retail dealer is the "natural agent" to provide product service to consumers; others endorse the view that the manufacturer has prime responsibility for service. (1) What is the rationale behind each of these positions? (2) To what extent are the views in conflict? (3) What major problems would you expect to be associated with each of these two policies?

10. Many service problems now faced by consumer goods manufacturers would partially disappear if manufacturers built into their products the higher quality of which they are capable. Are they shortsighted not to do so?

cases for part three

CASE 3–1

Holmes Manufacturing Company*

Decision to offer a new product

In December of a recent year, the sales executives of the Holmes Manufacturing Company were faced with the problem of devising a comprehensive marketing program for the Wheel-Burner, a combination wastepaper and leaf incinerator, outdoor grill, and garden wheelbarrow which had recently been added to the company's line of products.

The Wheel-Burner had been conceived by Mr. Carter, the company's sales manager, as a result of his personal experience with the problem of household wastepaper disposal. Mr. Carter had observed that modern automatic home heating systems had one rather significant drawback—they could not be used as incinerators for wastepaper and other combustible material which families formerly could dispose of in coal-fired furnaces. This meant that many households which had gas or oil heating systems had to acquire outdoor paper burners.

The ordinary burner, however, was deficient in several respects. Many of them were unsafe. They were frequently made of steel wire in an open mesh construction, through which hot ashes and sparks could be blown about. This constituted a significant fire hazard which could be overcome satisfactorily only by having most of the incinerator enclosed. Added to the danger of the conventional burner was its unattractiveness and the damage that it usually caused by scorching the lawn area where it was used. Moreover, ash disposal was generally a dusty and unpleasant chore when the ordinary burner had to be emptied.

In recognizing these limitations of existing incinerators, Mr. Carter realized that the utility of a burner designed to be safer and cleaner than those then on the market would be enhanced considerably if it could be used for purposes other than burning household wastepaper and leaves. He had noticed that many families were purchasing outdoor picnic grills. He also felt that, in line with a general trend to more

---

* Written by William J. Watkins, Research Associate, Bureau of Business Research, Graduate School of Business Administration, The University of Michigan.

informal, outdoor activities, they were spending more time gardening than formerly.

These observations suggested to him that in designing a superior wastepaper burner, he might with slight additional effort devise a product that could also be used as an outdoor grill and as a wheelbarrow for gardening tasks. His reasoning was that to overcome the problem of burning the lawn area where the conventional trash burner was placed, it would be desirable to have the burner on a *raised* platform. To overcome the problem of ash removal, it would be desirable to have the burner on a *portable* platform. A low, flat wheelbarrow onto which

EXHIBIT 1
Wheel-Burner for use as leaf burner

the burner might be fastened seemed to be the answer to these requirements. Moreover, if the incinerator were designed properly, this portability would enable it to be stored in a garage or shed, out of sight. As a leaf burner, portability was a desirable characteristic because the burner could easily be wheeled to piles of leaves and loaded. These leaves could then be burned as the user raked other piles together. (See Exhibit 1.)

An additional requirement had to be met if Mr. Carter's burner was to be superior to the type then on the market. The burning chamber had to be enclosed within a box or cylinder made of some nonflammable material such as sheet metal. This would prevent sparks or embers from being blown about when paper or other waste was being burned. When this was accomplished, Mr. Carter observed that the box constituted a rigid enclosure which would easily support an insert which, in turn, could be used to hold a charcoal fire (Exhibit 2). Since the top of the Wheel-Burner was about waist-high for adults when the insert was in place, the owner had a portable outdoor grill at a convenient level for outdoor cooking (Exhibit 3).

The Holmes Manufacturing Company was a producer of gas-fired water heaters and of burners for installation in conventional furnaces to convert them to the use of natural or artificial gas. The company normally employed about 130 workers and had specialized in the production of gas appliances since its organization in 1936. All of its manufac-

EXHIBIT 2
Charcoal grill insert

turing operations were conducted in the company's home city of Oakdale, Michigan.

The sales organization of the company consisted of Mr. Carter and his two assistants. The company's field selling activities for its established products were in the hands of 20 manufacturers' representatives throughout the nation. They sold to wholesale distributors in the heating and plumbing industry who, in turn, sold to local dealers. The Holmes Company had several accounts with public utilities; these were handled by direct sale. Sales promotion of water heaters and conversion burners was limited to trade paper advertising directed toward dealers and distributors.

Fabrication of the Wheel-Burner was essentially a metalworking task. The component parts were either stamped to shape or cut to the proper length and then assembled. The company's labor force was well

EXHIBIT 3
Wheel-Burner Grill

acquainted with the necessary processes as a result of the firm's long experience in the production of its major lines.

Although the company's engineers had never developed a product similar to the Wheel-Burner, they were able to embody most of Mr. Carter's ideas in a light, compact, and well-made piece of outdoor household equipment. The finished product had many construction features that added to its serviceability. Several concealed expansion joints, for example, had been provided to avoid the warping that might develop in the sides of the burner without them. The grill insert was so designed that it provided complete temperature control by allowing the user to elevate or lower the fire to any desired position. A partition was included with the grill insert so that if only a small charcoal fire was desired, it could be built in one end of the grill. Consideration had even been given to the width of the tread of the semipneumatic tire used on the wheelbarrow. It had been decided to use one relatively broad wheel rather than two of a narrower tread to avoid the formation of ruts or lines on the owner's lawn. In addition, one-wheel construction allowed lower production costs and permitted easier handling and dumping of ashes.

Although no quantitative estimates of the market for the Wheel-Burner had been made by Mr. Carter or his staff, it was felt that the product met the needs of a sufficiently large number of homeowners to warrant its introduction to several furniture, hardware, and appliance dealers within a radius of about 80 miles from the company's home city. This resulted in arrangements with 29 dealers in 11 cities, all of which were within broadcasting range of the television station in the city of Harperville, 40 miles to the north of Oakdale.

In selling these retailers, Holmes did not follow the practice of giving exclusive agencies. Instead, two or three outlets were usually sold in each of the communities where initial distribution had been achieved.

This pattern of distribution had been selected as an initial measure because the company had undertaken a limited amount of television advertising of the Wheel-Burner. Oakdale had no television station; the nearest was at Harperville. The program, which carried announcements of the product, dealt primarily with new cooking and homemaking topics. The only promotion of the Wheel-Burner directly to dealers consisted of a small brochure which outlined the product's uses and construction features. No trade paper advertising had been attempted, although the Wheel-Burner had been exhibited at garden merchandise shows in New York and Chicago.

The television program which the company had sponsored appeared on Monday, Wednesday, and Friday for one-half hour during the early afternoon of each day. The Holmes Manufacturing Company sponsored the program for a six-week period during October and November of the introductory year. During this time, there were two sales messages devoted to the Wheel-Burner on each program. In addition to the television program, the company offered to share with any dealers who would participate the cost of one one-quarter-page newspaper advertisement announcing the television program and describing the Wheel-Burner. The total cost for the program and the cooperative newspaper advertising during this period was approximately $2,500.

The results of this preliminary promotional activity were not discouraging (55 units were sold by the 29 dealers), but Mr. Carter felt that there was a strong seasonal factor involved in the purchase of outdoor household equipment, even though it might be designed to be used on a year-round basis. He felt that the grill and the garden wheelbarrow aspects of the Wheel-Burner would heighten its salability in the coming spring season and provide much more customer appeal than the leaf and paper burner improvements alone had during the period of recent promotion.

Despite the Wheel-Burner's novel combination of several basic products and its distinct improvement over them in many respects, the sales executives realized that the device faced substantial competition. For example, there were other *portable* incinerators making their appearances on the market. They consisted, usually, of wire basketlike containers which were mounted on a pair of wheels. There were other *enclosed* burners on the market, but they were typically designed to be used in one part of the owner's yard as a permanent installation, and thus lacked the portability of the Wheel-Burner.

The executives were well aware of the fact that outdoor cooking grills had been available for many years. In this area, there was a much broader range of product types than in the case of incinerators. There were modest picnic grills that could be quickly disassembled and stored in the luggage compartment of the family automobile. There were elaborate and expensive grills that had motor-driven spits and ceramic condiment containers. Between these two extremes, there were grills at many different price levels which provided varying degrees of outdoor cooking convenience and luxury.

In the case of wheelbarrows, there was much less diversity in product types than was true of outdoor grills. Even here, however, there had

EXHIBIT 4
Terms and prices

Model	Suggested list price	Dealer's net price	Distributor's net price
Wheel-Burner............	$36.95	$24.76	$18.47
Wheel-Burner grill......	11.95	8.01	5.97
Terms: Net 30 days from date of invoice, f.o.b. Oakdale, Michigan.			

been developments which had made them more useful to householders. The use of light metals and the design of two-wheeled "garden carts" were some of the improvements that had recently been embodied in products intended to serve the function for which conventional wheelbarrows had been used.

The strength of this kind of competition was not underestimated by Mr. Carter and his staff. At the same time, they felt that the Wheel-Burner's combination of products, together with the actual improvements which it contained in the component elements (burner, grill, and wheelbarrow), gave it a sales appeal not matched by any of the three product types individually.

The sales executives had devised a price schedule for the Wheel-Burner and for the grill which was sold as an attachment available at extra cost. The prices were based upon cost and profit estimates for production volumes of between 5,000 and 10,000 units per month. Terms and prices decided upon are shown in Exhibit 4.

In early discussions with representatives of one of the large mail-order chains, it was pointed out to the executives of the Holmes Manufacturing

Company that the Wheel-Burner was considered to be too expensive for the market which that retail organization attempted to serve. Mr. Carter and his staff were inclined to agree with this observation, but felt that in view of the materials, workmanship, and design of the Wheel-Burner, it was actually not overpriced. They were of the opinion that the product provided a great deal of utility and could fill a real need for a large number of families in the middle and upper-middle income levels. In support of this view, they had the experience of several reorders by some of the merchants to whom Wheel-Burners had originally been sold. One of these retailers, a hardware store owner, had canceled his account, but the others had continued to handle the product and looked forward to a greater rate of sales in the spring.

The field saleswork for the Wheel-Burner had been entirely in the hands of one of the assistant sales managers, a Mr. Webster. Mr. Webster had handled the exhibits of the product at the garden merchandise shows and had obtained all the accounts which the company had with

EXHIBIT 5

Model	Suggested list price	Dealer's net price
Wheel-Burner...............	$29.95	$20.07
Wheel-Burner grill..........	9.95	6.67

retail outlets. So far, no wholesale distributor had indicated any significant interest in the Wheel-Burner. Mr. Webster was assigned to the sales development of the Wheel-Burner on a full-time basis and had been traveling extensively about the state to solicit new retail accounts. He also felt that consumer acceptance for the product would increase with the warmer weather and was attempting to place the Wheel-Burner with as many retail outlets as possible before the advent of the spring merchandising season.

Mr. Webster and Mr. Carter had discussed the possibility of attempting direct distribution of the Wheel-Burner to dealers and of changing the price structure for the Wheel-Burner to the levels shown in Exhibit 5.

At this time, however, no decision had been reached concerning the contemplated price adjustment and change in distribution from the use of distributors.

CASE QUESTION

Should the Holmes Manufacturing Company have added the Wheel-Burner and grill to its line of products?

CASE 3–2
Yard-Man, Inc. (A)*

Adding new products to line as means of utilizing excess capacity

Yard-Man, Inc., of Jackson, Michigan, was one of the nation's largest manufacturers of hand- and power-operated lawn mowers. For over a decade, the firm had sold its entire output to Sears, Roebuck and Company for distribution under the Sears "Craftsman" label. Early in 1957, the management of Yard-Man, Inc., was considering the problem of how to utilize excess plant capacity. When this problem had first arisen in 1953, the advisability of marketing power mowers under the Yard-Man brand, outside the Sears channel, had been considered and rejected. In 1957, the firm was investigating the possibility of adding new products to the line as a means of utilizing excess plant facilities.

Historical background

The Yard-Man Company had been incorporated in 1933 to produce a new type of lawn mower. Its unusual design was based on the use of hardened steel blades which did not touch the cutter bar. This new concept resulted in a mower that was efficient, long-lasting, and almost silent in operation.

In the years that followed, the company grew slowly, building up distribution through hardware jobbers, who in turn sold to hardware retailers. In 1938, Sears, Roebuck, having been impressed by Yard-Man's evident skill in low-cost production of quality merchandise, requested that the company design and produce a power-operated lawn mower for exclusive distribution under the Sears Craftsman brand. Yard-Man agreed to do so, and 1938 marked the production and distribution of 5,000 such mowers.

The year following, Sears requested that Yard-Man develop a hand-mower line for similar distribution. This also was done, but not until after a pricing agreement had been reached in which Sears was to give price protection to Yard-Man's dealers by selling the Craftsman mower at a retail price $1 higher than the comparative model that Yard-Man distributed through orthodox jobber-retailer channels.

This policy of dual distribution continued until World War II curtailed civilian production, but as early as 1943, Sears was negotiating

---

* Written by Martin R. Warshaw, Professor of Marketing, Graduate School of Business Administration, The University of Michigan.

with Yard-Man to become an exclusive supplier of Sears in the postwar era. The management decision to produce solely for distribution through the Sears organization was made that year. However, Yard-Man did reserve the right to maintain its brand name and to use it in conjunction with the Sears Craftsman label. It was felt that this arrangement would prevent the trade name from becoming void through nonuse, and would provide brand identification in case Yard-Man wanted to return to its former type of distribution in the future. Accordingly, all jobbers were

EXHIBIT 1
Ten years summary of sales and earnings

Year ended June 30	Net sales (*)	Profit before federal income taxes	Percent of net sales (pretax)	Net profit	Earnings per share (†)	Cash dividends per share (†)
1947......	$ 2,509,223	$ 319,502	12.7	$198,225	$0.41	$0.09
1948......	3,444,064	729,619	21.1	452,364	0.94	.375
1949......	4,250,015	848,090	19.9	523,090	1.09	.375
1950......	4,826,863	931,851	19.3	576,569	1.20	.375
1951......	6,433,711	1,339,785	20.8	538,085	1.12	.375
1952......	5,820,798	936,936	16.0	419,936	0.87	.375
1953......	6,816,574	1,000,112	14.6	440,112	0.92	.375
1954......	9,404,942	1,211,278	12.8	531,278	1.11	.375
1955......	10,991,454	1,547,696	14.0	729,498	1.52	.375
1956......	12,256,601	1,424,185	11.6	722,476	1.50	.50

* Practically all sales have been to Sears, Roebuck and Company.
† In terms of the 480,000 shares of common stock outstanding June 30, 1956.

informed that their relationships with the company were being terminated well in advance of the resumption of peacetime business.

Some measure of the results of this decision may be seen in Exhibit 1, which dramatically shows the increasing success of the Sears Yard-Man team in the postwar decade. During the period between 1947 and 1956, sales increased from approximately $2,509,000 to $12,257,000 (532 percent), while net profit increased from $198,225 to $722,476 (365 percent).

Composition of product line

Yard-Man had concentrated on the top-quality mowers in the Sears line. Other sources furnished mowers for Sears selection of over 30 different models available to the Sears stores. The only deviation from this policy of producing high-priced units occurred in 1956, when Sears requested that a stripped-down mower be produced that could compete on a price basis with the many off-brand mowers that were appearing on the market and being sold by many nontraditional outlets such as low-price variety stores, furniture stores, and department stores. The result was the production of a model that was marketed under the Sears economy brand "Dunlap."

Cost estimation

At the beginning of each fiscal year, Sears would estimate their needs for mowers during the coming period. Yard-Man formulated cost estimates based on the Sears volume forecasts. To these would be added an increment that would provide a flat rate of return to Yard-Man. This total would be the price that Sears would pay for the volume specified. A Yard-Man executive emphasized the fact that Sears' concept of merchandising was to allow their suppliers to realize a fair profit on sales. He further noted that this arrangement was not entered into lightly, but rather after the two companies realized the partnership nature of their relationships. The president of Sears commented on this situation when he stated:

. . . The buyer must be certain that the manufacturer believes in good engineering and product development; that he is a capable, low-cost producer. The manufacturer must be certain that Sears will assure continuous production over a long period of time, and buy at a fair and equitable price.[1]

Engineering and design

Product design was carried on in Yard-Man's own engineering department. The firm owned all patent rights on unique patentable features. The designs originated in the company, but conferences held with Sears representatives resulted in an integration of both Sears' specifications and Yard-Man's design developments to produce the best results from both performance and cost standpoints.

The chief engineer of Yard-Man stated that the pressure for product improvement was constantly coming from management, who emphasized the fact that competition was always pressing from two sources: from other manufacturers distributing through outlets other than Sears and from the other models in the Sears line itself.

It was further noted that only through good design and efficient production and management could Yard-Man hope to compete in the marketplace.

Nature of the selling task

The vice president in charge of sales explained that rather than selling to one large buyer, Yard-Man was in actuality supplying the needs of over 700 independently managed Sears stores in addition to the Sears mail-order division. He further explained that the Sears setup gave each

---

[1] F. B. McConnell, president of Sears, Roebuck and Company, in an address before the New York Security Analysts on February 2, 1956.

manager considerable autonomy in choosing the items to be carried in his store. Sears was made up of five regional divisions, and each divisional headquarters sent a list of suitable products to store managers. Each manager could choose from the wide assortment offered and could price the merchandise to suit local competitive conditions.

Yard-Man's vice president in charge of sales and his staff of three men performed continuous missionary saleswork by personal visits to the Sears retail outlets. Yard-Man was one of the few companies which had Sears' permission to make retail contacts with their stores. The purpose of these visits was to inform sales personnel of product features and selling points; the men were also trained to help with service, display, and other technical problems, and to assist in setting up service facilities in the Sears stores.

The continuing nature of the task was made necessary by the high rate of turnover of Sears retail sales forces due to shifts within or from the Sears organization. The task of making these contacts had been eased by an innovation developed jointly by Sears and Yard-Man, in which mower demonstration clinics were held in each of the Sears districts in the spring. The clinics were generally held at a golf course or other grassy spot, and representatives from all the Sears stores and from all Sears mower and engine sources were present for product demonstration and general discussion of new features and service procedures. It was felt that by means of these clinics a great part of the retail selling force of Sears could be contacted, either directly or indirectly, just prior to the beginning of the major selling season.

Until 1956, Yard-Man had printed and distributed full-line folders to Sears. In 1957, Sears was introducing a complete garden equipment catalog, and Yard-Man was charged pro rata for space devoted to their products.

The service function

Until 1954, Yard-Man had provided the major part of the service required by Sears through its own repair shop facilities. Warranty service was done free of charge, while other service was charged to the Sears' store at current rates. In 1954, Sears' policy of servicing what they sold, plus the rising cost of freight, caused the shifting of the service function from Yard-Man to the Sears organization. The factory service shop was still kept open for special jobs and for training. Yard-Man still maintained an extensive parts inventory and sent out periodic service and operational bulletins to the Sears service shops.

Financing inventory

Although Yard-Man sales showed a very strong seasonal bias in favor of the second six months of the fiscal year, January through June, production was scheduled to take place throughout the calendar year. July through December was primarily devoted to building up a balanced inventory.

Inasmuch as the annual requirements of Sears were fairly well estimated in advance of production, this task was performed with greater assurance of accuracy, although changes in demand due to market or weather variables could cause serious problems. Leveled-out production permitted more even use of plant and labor. This made possible savings which more than compensated for the risk of carrying excess inventory. It was not unusual in recent years for inventory buildups in anticipation of the selling season to reach as much as $3 million.

The financial pressure of assuming the inventory storage function was somewhat relieved by arrangements with banking sources in Jackson, Detroit, and Chicago which accepted either commitments from Sears or inventory produced for Sears at 100 percent collateral for loans up to $4 million.

Production

The Yard-Man plant was modern and well equipped. It covered an area of over 5½ acres and had five production lines. In the annual cycle of manufacturing operations, hand mowers were produced first. They had fewer components and required less storage space when completed. After estimated inventory levels for hand mowers had been reached, production shifted to the lines producing power-operated machines. The work force was stabilized at about 200 people in 1957 and was noted for its low turnover and high morale. Labor flexibility was very great in that workers could be shifted from place to place depending upon the need at the time. This flexibility gave Yard-Man a high degree of labor productivity and made the workers proficient in many areas of mower production.

Shipments to Sears stores were made directly from the Yard-Man factory either by rail or motor freight depending on time and cost variables. All shipments were f.o.b. Jackson, Michigan.

Development of the problem of excess capacity

The first president of Yard-Man, Inc., one of the company's original founders, retired early in 1952. He was replaced by a man who had had considerable experience in the production of lawn mowers for sale through orthodox jobber-retailer channels. In attempting to orient himself, the new president reviewed the situation which had developed since civilian production had been resumed in 1946. In this postwar period, demand had been so great that deliveries were made to Sears as soon as the mowers came off the production line. There was no seasonal fluctuation, no inventory problem, and no need for storage and warehousing facilities other than had existed before the war. In 1947 and 1948, the demand continued in excess of ability to produce, although assuming a more normal seasonal pattern.

However, the new president was concerned with the estimated 30 percent excess of plant capacity which appeared to have been caused in prior years by the inability of motor suppliers to furnish sufficient numbers of components to allow Yard-Man to produce all the units it could have produced and sold. In the early 1950s, he found the excess capacity problem further complicated by a slackening off in sales volume caused by the changing of consumer preference in favor of the rotary type mower over the reel type, in which Yard-Man had specialized.

By 1952, this preference for rotary power mowers had had a serious effect on Yard-Man's sales figures, and management realized that this could be overcome only if Yard-Man produced rotary mowers of its own design. Such mowers were in late stages of planning and were scheduled to be introduced in 1953.

The president's proposal

As of 1952, the president felt that sales could be increased in the future if Yard-Man would return to its prewar policy of dual distribution. In its agreement with Sears in 1943 which heralded the beginning of a period of exclusive production for distribution through the Sears organization, Yard-Man had retained the right to keep its brand name and to have it incorporated with that of Sears' Craftsman brand. The president felt that by utilizing the prestige of the Yard-Man brand, a line of mowers entirely different in appearance could be produced and distributed to independent retailers. He envisioned a gradual policy of covering the market with an eventual goal of doubling the company's sales volume.

The task of evaluating the president's proposal was given to the management committee, which consisted of the senior executives of the firm. In discussing the proposal, the committee gave careful consideration to the following factors:

a) Costs of tooling and design necessary to develop a new line sufficiently different from that being sold to Sears.
b) The time and expense necessary to build and train a sales force.
c) The promotional costs necessary to achieve distribution and to gain brand recognition.
d) The financial ability of the company to undertake such a venture.
e) The length of time necessary to reach breakeven.

Committee recommendations

After considerable study, the committee discovered, first, that to obtain the degree of product difference required, tooling and design costs would be extremely high. They estimated that a minimum volume of 40,000 units would be needed to break even on these costs alone.

Second, time and financial limitations would allow only a small selling and promotional program to be developed the first year, and an orderly penetration of the market would probably result in the sale of 5,000 units.

Third, on the basis of sales projections and consideration of variable as well as fixed costs, it was felt that a minimum of five years would be needed before the new venture would assume profitable proportions.

Thus, on the basis of the difficulties involved, the long period to break even, and the risk of disturbing what had hitherto been an excellent relationship with Sears, the management committee suggested to the president that he table his proposal. These deliberations continued until fiscal 1954, and although the management committee had pointed out the difficulties involved in dual distribution, Sears was asked to

EXHIBIT 2
Recent changes in relative demand for different classes of product (by percent)

Fiscal year	1952	1953	1954	1955	1956
Hand mowers.............	34	31	20	11	9
Power mowers					
Reel type...............	63	50	33	22	14
Rotary type.............	0	15	44	63	74
Parts and attachments......	3	4	3	4	3

release Yard-Man from its agreement to produce solely for distribution through Sears' outlets. This release was granted by Sears in the fall of 1954.

Early in 1955, however, a vigorous resurgence of sales took place (see Exhibit 2). As in the past, the supply of engines for power mowers became the only factor limiting output. Under these circumstances, there was no longer any problem as to the utilization of excess plant capacity. This fact, plus a change in the top management of Yard-Man, led company officials to abandon the idea of developing a new line of power mowers and of distributing them under the Yard-Man brand through independent wholesale-retail channels.

Recurrence of the excess capacity problem

During the remainder of 1955, production continued at a rate limited only by the availability of power-mower engines. As long as this condition continued, Yard-Man operated on only a one-shift basis. Yet management felt that the best utilization of plant would require the operation of two 40-hour shifts per week. By 1956, accordingly, when an adequate supply of engines became available, Yard-Man was in the position to be able to double its output without requiring additional capital expenditures.

In an effort to reduce unit costs, moreover, certain improvements in plant and equipment had been made which served greatly to increase productivity. Thus, the number of production lines had been increased from two to five as a means of gaining flexibility in production scheduling. An elaborate overhead conveyor system had also been installed. Automatic electrostatic paint booths had likewise been added.

Then, too, the greater emphasis on rotary power mowers in the product mix resulted in a striking increase in ability to produce. The simplified work processes required in the production of rotary mowers as compared with reel mowers had reduced direct labor requirements by two thirds. With the same labor force, therefore, Yard-Man production lines were able to produce rotary mowers almost three times as fast as when reel-type models were being made.

As a result of these developments, Yard-Man entered 1956 with the ability to make a substantial increase in output of power mowers over and beyond 1955 accomplishments. However, while Sears' requirements served to increase total sales from about $11 million in 1955 to $12 million in 1956, an unseasonably cool spring and summer limited Sears' sales to an amount considerably less than Yard-Man facilities could have produced. Indeed, Yard-Man officials felt that unused productive capacity was exceeding tolerable limits by the end of 1956. Early in 1957, accordingly, top management again faced the problem of finding ways to increase sales to the point where the firm's substantially greater capacity to produce could be fully utilized.

A review of possible lines of action indicated that there were two major alternatives open to the firm. One possibility would be to reconsider the proposal of 1952 that the company produce power mowers under the Yard-Man brand for distribution outside of Sears channels. This alternative was not given serious consideration, however. Since 1952, the relationship with Sears had developed so well and had been so profitable that Yard-Man officials did not wish to reopen the question.

A second alternative was to seek new products to add to the Yard-Man line. If suitable new products could be developed and marketed, such action would serve not only to utilize excess production capacity but also to diversify the firm's manufacturing activities. Careful consideration of all aspects of the problem led Yard-Man executives to decide upon the second line of action. The steps taken to implement this decision are outlined in a report dated February 1957, as follows:

Yard-Man is widening its search for appropriate products to help diversify its manufacturing activities. Particular consideration is being given to product lines which offer the possibility of fitting into the seasonal pattern of its mower business, of using present plant facilities, and of being consistent with Yard-Man's long-established relationship with Sears, Roebuck and Company, as distributor of its lawnmowing equipment. . . . Emphasis is being placed on expanding the corporation's engineering staff to develop such products and to examine such lines for their sales and earnings potential.[2]

CASE QUESTIONS

1. Would Yard-Man have been wise to follow the president's proposal of 1952 to return to its prewar policy of dual distribution?

2. As of 1957, should Yard-Man reconsider dual distribution or should it seek new products to add to its product line?

CASE 3–3

Maslin Oil Company*

Decision to retain or sell a business

Maslin Oil Company, with headquarters in New York City, was a large, integrated producer of petroleum and petroleum-based products. In 1961 its researchers discovered that novahexalene, when certain stabilizers were added, made an excellent industrial fuel. Novahexalene, a by-product of petroleum cracking, was until then a product of limited value, with few important uses. Maslin applied for and received a patent for composition and use of its process for stabilizing novahexalene.

Industrial fuels were fuels used in the metal working industry for welding, flame cutting, brazing, and flame hardening of metals. The major industrial fuels used were acetylene (with about 50 percent of the market), propane gas, and natural gas. Stabilized novahexalene possessed several advantages over these other gases. It was safer because it was more stable. It produced a higher temperature flame than propane gas or natural gas. As a petroleum by-product, it had the potential

---

[2] S. D. Loring Co., *Yard-Man Report*, February 1957.

* Written by Stewart H. Rewoldt, Professor of Marketing, Graduate School of Business Administration, The University of Michigan. Identifying names have been changed. All sales figures and prices have been multiplied by a constant.

to be a lower cost fuel. Because it could be contained in smaller and lighter cylinders than acetylene, it offered the convenience of more fuel per unit of weight. When properly used, it performed equal to or better than other industrial fuels in two thirds to three fourths of all metal-working jobs.

Maslin had no distribution to the metal-working industry. The major suppliers of industrial fuels to this market were Shane Corporation and Reeves-Martin, Inc. Together these two firms accounted for well over one half of industrial fuel sales. They not only produced and marketed broad lines of fuel gases, but also produced and marketed broad lines of equipment and supplies. They had large and well-established distributor networks. Shane, for example, had a network of over 500 distributors. Because of the strong position of these two companies in the marketing of industrial fuels, Maslin approached them with an offer to provide them with stabilized novahexalene. After careful consideration, both Shane and Reeves-Martin decided that they did not want to add nova-hexalene to their lines of industrial fuels at that time. Their reasons for this decision were not fully known. There had been previous attempts to market other new industrial fuels in the past which had not been successful. Also, novahexalene could be expected to gain sales only at the expense of their already established gases.

Decision to market novahexalene

The decision of Shane and Reeves-Martin not to add to their lines of fuel gases was a disappointment. Maslin had an excellent product with high profit potential, but no ready way to get it to market. Total sales of fuel gases were in the neighborhood of 500 million pounds per year. With its inherent advantages, stabilized novahexalene should be able to capture a significant share of that market.

Maslin began to explore the feasibility of marketing novahexalene itself. Investigation of the industrial fuels market revealed several important demand characteristics which would have to be taken into consideration if Maslin decided to take this important step:

1. The user of industrial fuels needed immediate delivery from a nearby source. Users possessed limited capacity for storage of fuel gases and therefore needed prompt delivery to assure continuity of production.
2. Industrial fuels were normally a minor part of a user's total purchases of industrial equipment and supplies; therefore, he wished to buy them in a convenient fashion along with other industrial supply items.
3. Because of the above considerations, the adequacy of local service and delivery might very well be the single most important factor in a potential customer's buying decision.

4. Most users of industrial fuels were not highly skilled in the selection, handling, and use of gases.

These market factors suggested to Maslin executives that to market novahexalene themselves would be a major undertaking. The need for ready availability in the market ruled out direct distribution to users and required obtaining a large number of distributors. Many distributors already represented Shane and Reeves-Martin, who would be strong competitors and could be expected to discourage distributors from pushing Maslin's industrial fuel. Distributors were also needed because novahexalene was Maslin's only product entry in the metal-working industry, and users wanted to purchase gases along with other industrial supplies. The fact that users of industrial fuels had limited skill in using industrial gases would require a strong educational and technical assistance effort. Otherwise, users could not be expected to recognize or realize the advantages of novahexalene over other industrial fuels.

In spite of the difficulty of the task of marketing novahexalene, Maslin decided to go ahead. The long-range profit potential of this new industrial fuel practically dictated this decision. The task of marketing novahexalene was assigned to Maslin's Special Products Division. The trade name "Novex" was selected and registered. Maslin contracted with other petroleum producers to purchase all their novahexalene. Hence, they controlled most of the domestic supply of this new industrial fuel.

Maslin decided to introduce Novex only in the Southeast rather than to try for national distribution at this time. Immediately they began to recruit and hire salesmen and technical servicemen (known as R & D men). Large trucks were outfitted as demonstration vans that went from city to city, demonstrating the uses and advantages of Novex for both potential users and potential distributors. While the salesmen attempted to line up distributors, the R & D men called on potential users and demonstrated how they could improve their operations with the use of Novex.

Slowly Maslin began to sign up distributors. These were distributors of welding and cutting equipment and supplies, including industrial fuels. At first, Maslin signed only distributors who did not represent either Shane or Reeves-Martin. This policy was soon changed because Shane and Reeves-Martin distributors tended to be among the better distributors available.

Distributors required a readily available source of Novex because of the rather limited quantities they were equipped to carry on hand. Maslin set up what was known as a "service company system" to supply Novex to distributors. These were, in essence, bulk tank stations for the storage and distribution of Novex. Each service company was an independent operator, who invested his own capital. He did not purchase Novex from Maslin, but was paid a "go through" fee for all Novex delivered to distributors. The service company installed tanks in distributors' and users' facilities and retained title to them. No real sale of Novex occurred until it was actually used in some production process. The fact that Maslin kept title to Novex until the time of actual use gave Maslin the control of distribution it desired in order to assure high-quality service. For example, if distributors or users used the same tanks alternately for Novex and other fuels, the efficacy and safety of Novex would be affected.

Novex sales in the Southeast region were 573,000 pounds in 1963. In 1964 sales reached 1,005,000 pounds. The Maslin sales force had grown to ten salesmen plus five R & D men.

Maslin's experience in marketing Novex in the Southeast convinced them that it would be very difficult to market Novex by itself, without associated equipment and supplies. The most essential associated items were tips and cylinders. The tip controlled the mixture of fuel and oxygen and determined the length and type of flame. Hundreds of tip styles would have to be provided because of the great variety of torches in use. Cylinders would have to be provided in only limited variety. It would be uneconomical for Maslin to produce these items because of the limited volume requirements. Hence, Maslin arranged to purchase these items from outside suppliers.

National distribution of Novex

Sales of Novex in the Southeast region were less than Maslin had hoped to achieve, but the experience was sufficiently encouraging to make Maslin executives optimistic about the longer range future for Novex. Maslin executives began to wonder whether they should now move toward national distribution. One of the problems of selling only in the Southeast was that it was difficult to switch one plant of a multiplant firm to Novex. A company was likely to switch all of its plants, or none, to this new industrial fuel. Many of the best potential customers in the Southeast were production facilities operated by multiplant companies. Another way of looking at this situation is that once one plant in a multiplant firm was converted to Novex, it was relatively easier to sell Novex to other plants of the same firm. Regional marketing made it difficult to capitalize on this advantage. After careful consideration, the decision was made to expand to nationwide distribution.

The decision to establish national distribution was made in early 1965. Immediately, Maslin began expansion of its sales and R & D forces. The sales force was eventually expanded from 10 to 31 men, and the R & D force from 5 to 14. The signing of distributors was undertaken in the same manner as had been previously used in the Southeast. A sufficient number of service companies was established to support national distribution.

Having decided to go national, Maslin executives wondered whether the available supply of novahexalene would be adequate to support anticipated future sales of Novex. The entire estimated supply available as a by-product of petroleum cracking was 22 million pounds. By 1973 the supply of novahexalene was expected to be vastly augmented, as several new petroleum cracking plants came into operation. In the interim period, however, the supply would be inadequate to support the demand that Maslin hoped to generate for Novex. In order to assure an adequate supply of novahexalene, Maslin decided to construct a new plant to produce novahexalene.

The new plant would be ready in 1969. Its capacity would be 70 million pounds per year. It would, however, be necessary to use a direct

EXHIBIT 1
Sales results after national distribution

Year	Sales in pounds
1965	3,809,000
1966	7,359,000
1967	11,703,000
1968	17,566,000

process to produce novahexalene rather than to obtain it as a by-product of petroleum cracking. This direct process involved a much higher cost per pound produced. However, if a sufficient volume of sales were generated, reasonably profitable results could be anticipated.

After having decided to establish national distribution, sales results for the next few years are shown in Exhibit 1.

Offer to purchase Novex business

Late in 1968, Shane Corporation executives approached Maslin with a proposal that negotations be undertaken with a view toward the purchase of the Novex business from Maslin by Shane. After preliminary discussions, Maslin executives decided not to pursue these negotiations further. Although sales of Novex to date had been somewhat disappointing, they continued to be optimistic about Maslin's ability to develop a profitable market for Novex. They were fearful that if, on the other hand, they sold exclusive rights to market Novex to Shane, Shane might "sit on" Novex in order to protect its market for its present industrial fuels. This would deny Maslin a market for its bulk supplies of novahexalene.

Reevaluation of Novex program

In June 1969, Claude Taylor was appointed sales manager for process chemicals within the Special Products Division. In this position he was directly responsible for Novex sales, in addition to sales of other products. After reviewing the sales history of Novex, he was concerned that Novex sales had been consistently below Maslin's objectives. Although sales were expected to be over 22 million pounds in 1969, this would still represent only 4 to 5 percent of the industrial fuels market.

Mr. Taylor noted that Maslin was heavily dependent on distributors who also represented Shane and Reeves-Martin. Such distributors made up two thirds of Maslin's distributor network. If Shane and Reeves-Martin should develop a substitute gas with properties similar to Novex, Maslin's present distribution would be very vulnerable. Shane and Reeves-Martin were far more important suppliers of these distributors than was Maslin, and they would probably be able to push Maslin out.

Marketing expenses for Novex had turned out to be much higher than originally expected. Physical distribution costs were particularly high. Novex had to be delivered not only to a specific plant, but to all work stations throughout the plant where it was used. Maslin also was often forced to establish distribution in unprofitable market areas to service customers who had plants in both high-demand and low-demand areas. The narrowness of the Maslin line prevented spreading of marketing costs over a greater dollar volume. Because Novex was a new product, market development costs had been high. As a consequence, marketing expenses for Novex ran close to 50 percent of sales, while Shane and Reeves-Martin had marketing expenses of only 5 or 6 percent.

These higher-than-expected marketing expenses had forced Maslin to announce a series of price increases for Novex. From an average price per pound of $.1733 in 1962, the average price per pound rose to $.2873 in 1968. In spite of this substantial increase in price, Maslin's net return per pound had not risen. Although still less costly than acetylene, the difference in price between the two fuels had narrowed.

Alternative courses of action

After reviewing the Novex situation, Mr. Taylor concluded that there were three alternatives open to Maslin:

1. Develop and manufacture metal-working equipment and other industrial fuels in order to broaden the Maslin line.
2. Buy out a firm already manufacturing and selling metal-working equipment and other industrial fuels.

3. Sell all or part of the Novex business to another firm, such as Shane or Reeves-Martin.

The second alternative—to buy a firm already established in this industry—was ruled out quickly by Maslin's legal department because of antitrust implications. The first alternative—manufacturing and selling metal-working equipment and other industrial fuels—posed certain problems. In the manufacture and sale of equipment, Maslin would be entering an entirely different business, one in which it had no experience. In starting from scratch, Maslin would experience high costs until volume could be built. To build satisfactory volume in competition with well-entrenched competitors would be a difficult task. If Maslin should choose not to manufacture these additional items, but rather to purchase them from outside suppliers, available margins would be very low.

The third alternative—to sell all or part of the Novex business to another company—had to be explored more fully before the desirability of following this course could be known. Therefore, Mr. Taylor requested permission from Maslin's top management to reopen negotiations with Shane, who had previously shown an interest in acquiring the Novex trademark and business. This permission was granted, and these negotiations were reopened.

After extensive negotiations between Maslin and Shane, the latter offered to purchase, at a price satisfactory to Maslin, the following:

1. All rights to the Novex trademark in the domestic market.
2. The existing customer list for Novex.
3. Maslin's distributor contracts.
4. Maslin's rail cars used in distribution of Novex.
5. Maslin's tip and cylinder inventories.
6. Safety information and handling procedures manuals.
7. All literature and promotional supplies.

If Maslin should accept Shane's offer, it would retain its basic patent for stabilized novahexalene, its manufacturing plant, and all rights to the Novex trademark outside the United States. Instead of marketing Novex through its own organization, it would become a bulk supplier of novahexalene to Shane. Also, the Shane offer stipulated that Maslin would not sell novahexalene to anyone else for resale in the domestic fuel gas market for a period of two years. Shane also agreed to interview all of Maslin's Novex salesmen and R & D men to determine if it wished to make job offers to some or all of them. These personnel could be absorbed elsewhere in the Maslin organization, if necessary.

CASE QUESTIONS

1. Should Maslin have undertaken to market Novex in the manner it did?
2. Should Maslin accept the Shane offer?

CASE 3–4

Dutch Food Industries Company (A)*

Marketing strategy for the introduction of a new product

In September 1967, Jan de Vries, product manager for Dutch Food Industries' new salad dressing product was wondering what strategy to follow with respect to this new product. His assistant had prepared information concerning alternative promotional methods to use to introduce the new product, and he was concerned with exactly which of these alternative promotion methods he should recommend for the product's introduction. He also wondered what price the new product should retail for and when the company should introduce the new product. Mr. de Vries had to decide these issues in the next couple of days, as his report containing his recommendations on the introduction of the new salad dressing was due on the desk of the director of marketing the following Monday.

COMPANY BACKGROUND

The Netherlands Oil Factory of Delft, The Netherlands, was founded in 1884. This firm, which supplied edible oils to the growing margarine industry, merged in 1900 with a French milling company. The new firm then operated under the name Dutch Food Industries Company (DFI).

From this origin, the brand name DFI became increasingly strong and was eventually given to all of the company's branded products. More recently, the name was registered for use internationally.

In the course of the 1920s, DFI became an important factor in the margarine market. The company was a troublesome competitor for the Margarine Union, the company formed by the merger in 1927 of the two margarine giants, Van den Bergh and Jurgens. In 1928, an agreement was reached by which DFI joined the Margarine Union.

In 1930, the interests of the Margarine Union were merged with those of International Industries Corporation—a large, diversified, and international organization. It was in this way that DFI became a part of the International Industries complex of companies.

---

* Written by Kenneth L. Bernhardt, Assistant Professor of Marketing, Georgia State University, Atlanta. Assisted by Joseph H. Viehoff, Research Assistant, Netherlands School of Economics, Rotterdam.

International Industries Corporation (IIC) is a worldwide organization with major interests in the production of margarine, other edible fats and oils, soups, ice cream, frozen foods, meats, cheeses, soaps, and detergents.

The total sales of IIC in 1967 were more than four billion guilders (over $1 billion).[1] Profits before taxes were 700 million guilders ($56 million).

Within IIC, DFI proceeded with its original activities after its margarine factory was closed, namely developing its exports of oils and fats, its trade in bakery products, as well as a number of branded food products. The following list indicates the range of consumer products which the company marketed: table oil, household fats, mayonnaise, salad dressing (several varieties), tomato ketchup, peanut butter, and peanuts.

DFI's total sales in 1967 were between 50 and 100 million guilders ($14–28 million). Profits before taxes were between 5 and 10 million guilders ($1.4–2.8 million).

BACKGROUND ON THE DRESSING MARKET

A large and growing percentage of Holland's population eats lettuce, usually with salad dressing, with their meals. In 1965, 82 percent of the people ate lettuce with salad dressing regularly (see Exhibit 1).

EXHIBIT 1
Household habits study ("How often do you eat lettuce with salad dressing?")

Housewives' responses (by percent)	*1959*	*1961*	*1963*	*1965*
At least once per week (heavy users)...........................	60	63	68	69
At least once in two months, but not at least once per week...............	10	10	10	13
Total users......................	70	73	78	82
Less than once every two months.......	3	5	3	2
Never.............................	27	22	18	16
	100	100	100	100
Number of housewives..............	(1816)	(1203)	(904)	(812)

The salad dressing market has extreme seasonal demand as shown in Exhibit 2. This seasonal pattern coincides with the periods of greatest production of lettuce in Holland. Thus, 50 percent of the total year's volume for the salad dressing market occurs in the four months beginning in April. During this period, lettuce is plentiful and sells for approximately 20 Dutch cents[2] per head.

---

[1] One guilder (florin) is equal to U.S. 28¢ or $1.00 U.S. equals f 3.60.

[2] There are 100 cents to a guilder. Thus 20 cents = $.056 U.S.

EXHIBIT 2
Seasonal analysis of salad dressing market (percentage of annual total market sales—bimonthly periods)

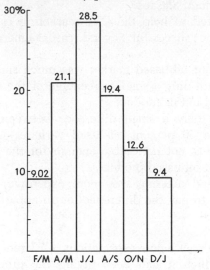

EXHIBIT 3
Total salad dressing market and DFI market share

Year	Index of total market (1960 = 100)	Growth (in percent)	DFI market share (in percent)
1960...............	100	—	20.7
1961...............	104	4.2	19.7
1962...............	108	4.0	19.0
1963...............	117	7.7	17.8
1964...............	126	8.3	17.0
1965...............	135	7.1	16.6

The total market for salad dressings at manufacturer's level in 1967 was between 25 and 30 million guilders ($7 million and $8.4 million).

As shown in Exhibit 3, the total market was growing at approximately 7 percent per year. At the same time, DFI's market share had been declining, and the company was looking for ways to halt this decline and, in fact, increase DFI's share of this growing market.

In 1966, the salad dressing market was composed of two segments. The first was a 25 percent oil-based salad dressing, which comprised 90 percent of the total market. The other 10 percent of the market consisted of 50 percent oil-based salad dressing, a slightly creamier product. Previously, DFI, in an effort to increase its market share, had introduced a new product which was 50 percent oil based. Up to that time,

DFI sold only 25 percent oil-based salad dressing. The product, called Delfine, was not successful in obtaining the desired volume and profit. While DFI still marketed Delfine, almost all of DFI's volume came from its 25 percent oil-based product, Slasaus.[3]

A research study was conducted to help the DFI marketing executives determine why Delfine was not successful. Several reasons emerged:

1. The potential of the 50 percent oil-based market was much smaller than originally anticipated, and only a small percentage of the total population was even interested in this product.
2. The consumers could detect only a small difference between the 25 percent oil-based and the 50 percent oil-based varieties when blind-tested. The difference was not noticeable enough for the consumers to prefer the 50 percent oil-based product.
3. The 50 percent oil-based salad dressing was more expensive, and the consumer was not willing to pay the difference for an apparently almost imperceptible difference.

Because the Delfine sales were well below expectations, DFI removed the heavy promotion support which it had been giving the product. The executives decided to wait for a significant breakthrough of a product with unique advantages. The Delfine experience indicated to them that it would take a totally new type of product for DFI to increase its market share significantly.

BACKGROUND AND DEVELOPMENT OF SLAMIX

Every two years, the company conducted a housewives' habits study in which a panel of 700 consumers was asked about their household and their food preparation habits. In August 1965, the company received the most recent study, called PMC-11. The housewives were asked how they prepared their lettuce and what ingredients they used. The results showed that an extremely large percentage of the housewives added not only salad dressing to lettuce, but also added other ingredients such as salt, pepper, eggs, onion, gherkins, etc. Thus DFI executives got the idea that putting some of these ingredients in the salad dressing would result in a real convenience for the housewife, and DFI would have the significant new product for which they had been searching. The laboratory, in August 1965, began developing a "dressed" salad dressing which included some of the ingredients which many housewives were accustomed to adding.

In early 1966, a committee called the Slamix Committee,[4] was formed to make sure that every part of the company was involved in the devel-

---

[3] Literally translated, Slasaus means "lettuce sauce."

[4] Slamix is literally "lettuce mix."

opment of this new product. The committee, which was headed up by the product manager, had representatives from various parts of the company, including development, production, and marketing. The committee studied production problems, laboratory findings, and in general, was charged with the responsibility of seeing that the development progressed as scheduled. The committee did not have decision-making powers but either invited decision makers to important meetings or wrote reports to the people who were in a position to make the required decisions.

After several product tests concerned with taste and keeping properties were conducted at the factory, the company, in August 1966, undertook its first consumer test of the new "dressed" salad dressing. A panel of housewives was shown a bottle of the new product which was a salad dressing containing pieces of gherkins, onions, and paprika. Several conclusions emerged from this study:

1. The "dressed" salad dressing was seen by the housewives as more than a salad dressing with ingredients. It was seen as a completely new product.
2. There were two sides to this newness:
   a. By looking at the product, they thought that it had a new taste.
   b. The convenience aspect was strongly stressed by the housewives.
3. The housewives thought that the new product would be good for decorating the lettuce. With its new color (light red with colorful ingredients), they thought that they could decorate the lettuce much better than with present salad dressings which were creme-colored and very similar to mayonnaise.
4. When asked about the ingredients, one half of the housewives were favorable towards paprika, and half were against it. This apparently was a troublesome ingredient. However, because of the convenience aspect, gherkins and onions were favored by the housewife.

In November 1966, a second consumer study was conducted by the Institute of Household Research in Rotterdam. A sample of 140 housewives who actually used salad dressing on lettuce was given a bottle of the new product to take home. Then, they were visited in their homes. Much useful information emerged from this study. After looking at the product, but before trying it, the housewives said that it looked like a fun product, it made them happy, and they thought that it would taste good. When asked what they thought the product contained, they said tomatoes, red paprika, celery, gherkins, and green paprika.

However, the company was disappointed with the housewives' overall evaluation of the product. Only 20 percent of the housewives said that they thought the product was very good, 11 percent did not like the product, and 69 percent of the housewives said that there were some favorable and some unfavorable aspects of the product. The main reason for the 80 percent unfavorable reaction was the consistency of the new salad dressing. It was too thin. The housewives could pour it too easily and it rapidly went to the bottom of the bowl. Because it fell to the bottom, the housewives said that it was much harder to decorate their salad. It was also uneconomical because they felt that they would put too much on if the product was that thin. There were also problems with taste. Many of the housewives thought it was too sour or too sharp. The paprika was the main reason for the dissatisfaction.

In spite of the above problems, there were several aspects of the study which encouraged the company to proceed with the development of this new product. When asked how they would change the ingredients in the "dressed" salad dressing, only 47 percent of the housewives suggested changes. Most recommended that more onions be added. The

EXHIBIT 4
Preference test: Slasaus versus "Dressed" salad dressing (figures shown indicate percent)

Prefer	Taste	Appear-ance	Decoration aspects	Con-sistency	Con-venience
"Dressed" salad dressing........	59	73	46	18	50
Slasaus......................	38	20	44	65	20
No preference/no difference.....	3	7	10	17	30
	100	100	100	100	100

housewives were asked for their preference between DFI's Slasaus and the new "dressed" salad dressing. As shown in Exhibit 4, the housewives preferred the new product, except for its consistency. Sixty percent of the housewives said that they would buy the product if it were possible to buy it in the store. Since this was a very high positive response, the company was very encouraged.

The marketing, production, and development groups, coordinated by the Slamix Committee, began work on incorporating the required changes made evident by this consumer study. DFI's development group experimented with changes in the consistency, taste, and ingredients. The production group experimented with a new production process. DFI had intended to introduce the new "dressed" salad dressing in the early part of 1967. However, the top corporate executives decided that, before the new product could be introduced, an extensive test of its keeping properties (vulnerability to deterioration) would have to be conducted.

The keeping-properties test showed that after several months the light red-colored product changed to a pink color. The difference in color was only slight, but DFI executives thought that the consumer reaction to this change should be tested. They decided that at the same time they would conduct a consumer test to find a name for this new product. A sample of 180 housewives from the Institute of Household Research was used to get at these questions. Only 2 out of the 180 housewives saw that there was a difference in color between the two bottles of the new product. When they were told that there was a slight difference and were shown the two bottles together, most of the housewives could not see the color change, and those that could were not unhappy about it.

The housewives were then asked what the name for this product should be. The phrase "mixed salad dressing" kept coming up. The housewives were then asked what they thought of two names which the company had screened, "Slamix" (lettuce mix) and "Spikkeltjessaus" (sauce with little spots). Eighty-one percent thought that Slamix was a very good name. Only 26 percent thought that Spikkeltjessaus was a good name. The name Slamix was chosen for the new product. Interestingly, that was the name that the company had used internally for the new product when it was first being developed.

By August 1967, DFI had solved the color-change problem. The company now thought that it had a product ready to be marketed, so a final consumer test was undertaken to test the effect of all of the changes that had been made during the previous year.

Two versions of Slamix, a white one and a pink one, were tested at the Institute for Household Research. One hundred eighty housewives were asked what they thought of the product and whether they would buy it or not. The negative reactions to the product were minimal. Almost no negative comments were voiced. The problems of consistency, color, taste, and ingredients had apparently been solved. When asked if they would buy the product, 76 percent of those shown the pink product and 70 percent of those shown the white product responded in a positive manner. After tasting the two versions of Slamix, the housewives revealed a strong preference for the pink Slamix. The DFI executives felt that the product was now ready to be marketed.

DFI executives next reviewed the financial projections prepared by Mr. de Vries, the product manager. Almost no capital investment would be required as the Slamix would be produced by using present production facilities. Only a few machines, at a total cost of 40,000 guilders ($11,000), would be required.

At an early stage in the development of the product, Slamix sales had been forecasted at 3.7 percent of the total market at the end of the first year. Encouraged by the results of the consumer tests, DFI executives revised their estimate of sales. The August 1967, forecast was for approximately 6.7 percent of the market. (See Exhibit 5.)

EXHIBIT 5
Forecasted sales of Slamix

Year	Share of market (by percent)
Original estimates	
1968	3.7
1969	3.9
1970	4.4
Revised estimates (August 1967)	
1968	6.7
1969	11.7

The directors of the company thought that they finally had the product for which they had been waiting. The consumer tests were complete, and the product had found very high favor with the consumers. There was significant technological development involved in the product, and DFI executives thought that it would take considerable time for the competition to duplicate the product. The product manager's projected sales seemed reasonable. Mr. de Vries was asked to prepare a comprehensive report concerning the introductory marketing strategy to be used to introduce the new product.

MARKETING STRATEGY

The first problem that the product manager had to resolve concerned the suggested retail price that the company should charge for Slamix. To help Mr. de Vries make his recommendation, the assistant product manager had made a list of the following considerations:

1. The company's total cost for a .30-liter sized bottle of Slamix was 70 cents (approximately $.20 U.S.). This was 20 percent higher than DFI's regular salad dressing, Slasaus.
2. The gross margin for Slasaus was 22 percent. Because of the unique qualities of Slamix, large development costs, and possible substitution with Slasaus, a higher gross margin for Slamix might be considered.
3. DFI gave the wholesalers a 7.9 percent margin and retailers a 14.6 percent margin for Slasaus. Possibly these should be increased for Slamix to encourage greater acceptance and promotion by the trade channels of distribution.
4. The two leading salad dressings in 1967, Salata by Duyvis and Slasaus, both had a retail price of f 0.99 (28¢ U.S.) for the .30-liter bottle. The retail price for the .60-liter bottle was f 1.72.[5] Private label salad dressings were f .79 (22¢) for a .30-liter bottle. The

---
[5] f 1.72 is one guilder and 72 cents (or approximately 48¢ U.S.)

average price for all salad dressings was approximately f 0.92 ($.26 U.S.).

5. In November 1966, DFI had conducted some research on the optimal price of Slamix. After using a sample of the product, 140 housewives were asked what price they would be willing to pay for Slamix. Their responses, by percent, were:

f 1.10 ($.31) or less	45
between f 1.11 ($.31) and f 1.44 ($.40)	41
f 1.44 ($.40) or more	14
Total	100

The average price mentioned was f 1.20 ($.34)

The assistant product manager also prepared the table shown in Exhibit 6. The first column shows the retail price, trade margins, and gross

EXHIBIT 6
Alternative prices for Slamix*

	Slasaus	Slamix 1	Slamix 2	Slamix 3	Slamix 4	Slamix 5	Slamix 6
Retail price............	f 0.99	f 1.16	f 1.22	f 1.23	f 1.28	f 1.32	f 1.37
Retail margin.........	(14.6)	(14.6)	(17.5)	(14.6)	(17.5)	(14.6)	(17.5)
Price to retailer........	f 0.845	f 0.995	f 1.01	f 1.04	f 1.055	f 1.115	f 1.13
Wholesale margin......	(7.9)	(7.9)	(9.0)	(7.9)	(9.0)	(7.9)	(9.0)
Payment discount......	(2.5)	(2.5)	(2.5)	(2.5)	(2.5)	(2.5)	(2.5)
Price to wholesaler.....	f 0.76	f 0.895	f 0.895	f 0.935	f 0.935	f 1.00	f 1.00
Gross margin..........	(22.0)	(22.0)	(22.0)	(25.0)	(25.0)	(30.0)	(30.0)
Cost.................	f 0.59	f 0.70	f 0.70	f 0.70	f 0.70	f 0.70	f 0.70
				In dollars			
Retail price............	$ .28	$ .32	$ .34	$ .34	$ .36	$ .37	$ .38
Price to retailer........	.24	.28	.28	.29	.295	.31	.316
Price to wholesaler.....	.21	.25	.25	.26	.26	.28	.28
Cost.................	.165	.20	.20	.20	.20	.20	.20

* Selected figures in this table have been disguised.
Numbers in parentheses indicate percent.

margin for Slasaus. The remaining six columns show alternative retail prices for Slamix, resulting from different trade margins and gross margins. Mr. de Vries wondered which of these prices he should recommend to the Board of Directors.

PROMOTION ALTERNATIVES

The Board of Directors told the product manager that he had 725,000 guilders ($203,000) for his promotion budget. Of this, 25,000 guilders ($7,000) was to be allocated as Slamix's share of the general corporate advertising which aided all DFI products. The 725,000 guilders was determined by using a percentage of the "expected gross profit of the first year" for Slamix.[6] DFI's policy was to break even in the third year of the new product, attaining a total payback within five years. The company is generally willing to spend the gross profit for the first year as part of the total investment.

The company had already given considerable thought to the sales message and the brand image desired for Slamix. The information below was sent to the advertising agency to help in planning the promotional program of the company:

Sales message: It is now possible, in a completely new way, to make delicious salad. Sla + Slamix = Sla Klaar. (Lettuce + Slamix = Lettuce Ready)

Supporting message: Slamix is a salad dressing with pieces of onion, gherkins, and paprika.

Desired brand image: With Slamix you can make, very easily and very quickly, a delicious salad that also looks nice. Slamix is a complete, good, handy product. DFI is a modern firm with up-to-date ideas.

Thus, the company wanted to get across three principal points. They are: (1) that Slamix is a completely new product, (2) that it is convenient, and (3) that it is a salad dressing with ingredients making it a complete salad dressing.

The product manager was undecided as to how to divide the 700,000 guilders ($196,000) among the following alternatives:

1. television
2. radio
3. newspaper advertising
4. magazines
5. sampling
6. coupons
7. price-off promotion
8. key-chain premiums
9. trade allowances

Television

The product manager thought that television would be advantageous because of the ability to show the product in actual use—a housewife pouring Slamix onto the lettuce. The cost of using the television medium is shown in Exhibit 7. The company did not have a choice among the seven blocks of time, but had to take whatever was available. For planning, however, they figured an average cost of a 30-second ad would be

---

[6] It was possible that the percentage could be greater than 100 percent. This would mean that the company was willing to spend more than the first year's gross profit for initial promotion.

EXHIBIT 7
Data on Dutch television media

Station	Block number	Time	Cost of 30-second ad Guilders	Dollars
Nederland 1........... 1		Before early news	f 8,250	$2,300
Nederland 1........... 2		After early news	f 8,250	$2,300
Nederland 1........... 3		Before late news	f10,500	$2,950
Nederland 1........... 4		After late news	f10,500	$2,950
Nederland 2........... 5		After early news	f 1,800	$ 500
Nederland 2........... 6		Before late news	f 3,000	$ 840
Nederland 2........... 7		After late news	f 3,000	$ 840
Average cost per 30-second television ad...................			f 6,500	$1,800
Production cost for a TV ad.............................			f25,000	$7,000

TV coverage per 1,000 households = 850 or 85 percent.
Only about one half of the homes can receive Nederland 2.

f 6,500 ($1,800). Mr. de Vries felt that at least 25 advertisements were necessary before the TV advertising would have maximum impact.

Radio

The chief attraction of radio was its extremely low price. Each 30-second radio ad cost 450 guilders ($126) on Radio Veronica, a popular station during the daytime. Production costs for a radio ad are approximately 3,000 guilders ($840). Only 60 percent of the households could receive Radio Veronica, mainly in the western part of the country. Mr. de Vries felt that if radio were used, a minimum of 100 spots should be purchased.

Newspapers

Mr. de Vries thought the main advantages of newspapers would be the announcement effect and its influence with the local trade. Nationally, the cost of each half-page insertion would be 50,000 guilders ($14,000).

Magazines

Magazines would be a desirable addition to the promotional program for several reasons. Due to the ability to use color, the company could show the product as it actually looks on the shelf. By using several women's magazines, the company could reach a select audience of people reading the magazine at its leisure. Data on selected Dutch magazines are shown in Exhibit 8. Mr. de Vries thought that, if they were to use a magazine campaign, at least ten insertions would be necessary before the advertising would be very effective. Of the possibilities in Exhibit 7, the agency thought that the combination of *Eva, Margriet,* and *AVRO-Televizier* would be most effective for DFI, since the combination would reach a large number of people at a relatively low cost.

EXHIBIT 8
Data on selected Dutch magazines

Magazines	Type	Circulation	fre-quency	Price for full-page ad Black and white	Color	Cost per 1,000 Circulation*
Eva.................	woman's	375,000	weekly	f 2,752	f 5,027	f13.40
				$ 770	$ 1,400	$ 3.75
Margriet.............	woman's	825,000	weekly	f 7,250	f12,290	f14.90
				$ 2,100	$ 3,440	$ 4.15
Libelle..............	woman's	570,000	weekly	f 5,056	f 8,356	f14.60
				$ 1,416	$ 2,340	$ 4.10
Prinses.............	woman's	213,000	weekly	f 2,360	f 4,200	f19.75
				$ 660	$ 1,175	$ 5.55
Panorama..........	general	403,000	weekly	f 4,640	f 7,705	f19.20
				$ 1,300	$ 2,150	$ 5.40
Nieuwe Revu........	general	261,000	weekly	f 3,292	f 5,497	f21.00
				$ 920	$ 1,540	$ 5.90
Spiegel.............	general	175,000	weekly	f 2,536	f 4,741	f27.00
				$ 710	$ 1,325	$ 7.55
Het Beste...........	digest	325,000	monthly	f 3,450	f 5,770	f17.50
				$ 965	$ 1,615	$ 4.90
Studio..............	TV guide	575,000	weekly	f 5,448	f 8,648	f15.00
				f 1,525	$ 2,420	$ 4.20
NCRV-gids..........	TV guide	482,000	weekly	f 5,080	f 8,180	f17.00
				$ 1,420	$ 2,290	$ 4.75
Vara-gids...........	TV guide	504,000	weekly	f 5,360	f 8,460	f16.80
				$ 1,500	$ 2,370	$ 4.70
AVRO-Televizier.....	TV guide	950,000	weekly	f 9,312	f13,812	f14.50
				$ 2,600	$ 3,870	$ 4.05
Combination of *Eva, Margriet* and *AVRO-Televizier*.......				f17,600	f27,800	f13.00
				$ 4,900	$ 7,785	$ 3.65

* Cost of one-page color ad, in guilders, divided by circulation in thousands. Using *Eva* as an example, cost per 1,000 circulation = $\dfrac{f5,027}{375}$ = f13.40 or $\dfrac{\$1,408}{375}$ = \$3.75.

Sampling

Although he realized that it was very expensive, Mr. de Vries considered the use of direct-mail sampling. A small 12 cm. by 18 cm. (approximately 5″ × 7″) folder could be mailed to Holland's 3.7 million households for 70,800 guilders ($20,000). The cost, however, would increase substantially if a small bottle of the product were to be included in the direct mailing. This cost would be 20 cents for handling, plus 75 cents for the actual sample. Thus, it would cost 3.5 million guilders ($980,000) to sample the whole country.

Coupon

Mr. de Vries was considering whether or not to include a coupon good for 13 cents ($.04 U.S.) off the purchase of Slamix with one of the other DFI products—mayonnaise, for example. He estimated that 900,000 coupons would be distributed. At a redemption rate of 5 percent, the cost would, thus, be approximately 6,000 guilders ($1,700).

Price-off

DFI made use of a reduced retail price for most of its new product introductions. Thus, the product manager thought it quite normal to consider the use of reducing the retail price by 25 cents ($.07 U.S.) per bottle and identifying this price reduction on the label of the product. It was felt that this reduced price would encourage the housewives to try Slamix. It was also quite normal to follow up this sales promotion with a similar price reduction approximately five months after the product was introduced. This would encourage those who had still not tried the product to purchase a bottle and would encourage those who had already bought one bottle to continue purchasing the new product. The cost of this price-off promotion is shown in Exhibit 9.

Key-chain premium

It was very unusual to use a free premium to introduce a new product, but Mr. de Vries was considering this alternative for several reasons. Many products in Holland during 1967 were using key chains as a premium. As shown in Exhibit 10, an extremely large percentage of the people in Holland was collecting key chains.

EXHIBIT 9

	Guilders	Dollars
Introduction:		
720,000 bottles at 25 cents ($.07 U.S.) off each......	f 180,000	$50,400
Handling and display materials..................	10,000	2,800
Total.....................................	f 190,000	$53,200
Follow-up five months later:		
600,000 bottles at 25 cents ($.07 U.S.) off each......	f 150,000	$42,000
Handling and display materials..................	10,000	2,800
Total.....................................	f 160,000	$44,800

EXHIBIT 10
Percentage of households collecting key chains

	June 1967	July 1967	September 1967
Households with children...............	45	N.A.	N.A.
Households without children...........	5	N.A.	N.A.
Total (weighted average).............	34	37	41

The details of the research showed that mothers and daughters were more likely to collect key chains, especially if the children were between eight and eleven years of age. Mr. de Vries felt that if he used key chains as premiums for the introduction of Slamix he could have a follow-up promotion five months later using either key chains or price-off deals. Selected cost information on the key-chain promotion is shown in Exhibit 11.

EXHIBIT 11

	Guilders	Dollars
Introduction:		
720,000 bottles = about 220 metric tons		
750,000 key chains at 20¢ ($.056 U.S.).....	f 150,000	$42,000
Handling costs and display materials........	60,000	16,800
Total................................	f 210,000	$58,800
Follow-up five months later:		
600,000 bottles = about 180 tons		
625,000 key chains at 20¢ ($.056 U.S.).....	f 125,000	$35,000
Handling costs and display materials........	50,000	14,000
Total................................	f 175,000	$49,000

Trade allowances

The product manager also considered the use of trade allowances to encourage the retailers to accept and promote the new product. The company traditionally offered one guilder ($.28) per case of 12 bottles. Thus, if it was decided that trade allowances were desirable, the cost would be 60,000 guilders ($16,800) for the initial introduction and an additional 50,000 guilders ($14,000) used during the follow-up promotion five months later. Trade allowances could be used together with either the price-off promotion or the key-chain promotion. The product manager felt that trade allowances would not be very effective without one of the two consumer sales promotions.

Distribution

Outside of the question of what trade margins to use and whether or not to use trade allowances during the consumer sales promotions discussed above, Mr. de Vries did not see any problems with distribution. DFI had a sales force of approximately 50 men who regularly called on 10,000 outlets in Holland. It was felt that the sales force could handle the introduction of the new product with no problem.

The last problem the product manager faced concerned the timing of the introduction of Slamix. The product would be ready for introduction in October 1967. Mr. de Vries wondered whether the seasonal nature of the demand for the product would make it more desirable to hold off the introduction until March of 1968.

CASE QUESTION

Develop a marketing plan for the introduction of this new product.

CASE 3–5

Dutch Food Industries Company (B)*

A product policy decision

In January 1970, Dutch Food Industries (DFI) executives were reviewing the past marketing strategy and results for their salad dressing product, Slamix. While a relatively large percentage of the population was aware of Slamix, they were concerned how they could increase the usage of Slamix to improve their market share. As a means of accomplishing this objective, a new variety of Slamix had been developed which had significantly different taste characteristics. The marketing executives had to decide the question of what policy to follow with respect to the branding of the new product.

In March 1968, DFI introduced its new salad dressing product, Slamix.[1] The new product manager, Tom van der Lugt, had decided to wait until March for the introduction of Slamix, even though the product was ready to be marketed in October. Seventy percent of the salad dressing market sales are in the six months beginning with April, and Mr. van der Lugt thought that if the product were introduced in October, the advertising would be wasted because people weren't buying and trade resistance would be high because the product would be in the lowest point of its seasonal pattern.

The introductory price was f 1.28 ($.36). Mr. van der Lugt recommended this price because he thought that it was within the realistic

---

* Written by Kenneth L. Bernhardt, Assistant Professor of Marketing, Georgia State University, Atlanta. Assisted by Joseph H. Viehoff, Research Assistant, Netherlands School of Economics, Rotterdam.

[1] See "Dutch Food Industries (A)" case for information concerning the background on the company and on the introduction of Slamix.

price range of housewife acceptance and would allow higher margins for both the company and the channels of distribution.

The main promotional emphasis was placed on the key-chain premium promotion. By March 1968, 50 percent of Dutch households were collecting key chains which were by this time available on a number of products. Mr. van der Lugt thought that the key-chain premium would be a strong inducement for people to try the new product, particularly those families with children. In an earlier test on one of DFI's other products, sales of the product increased 11 times previous average monthly sales without the key chain. Trade allowances were not used, as it was felt that a strong consumer promotional program and higher

EXHIBIT 1
Slamix television commercial

Comm.: Here are the Tastemakers.

They are proud of their newest product Slamix.

Prepare your salad with this.

Slamix: That means onions, paprica, and pickles

in a mild sauce.

With Slamix you make everything much tastier,

especially salad.

An idea from the Tastemakers.

trade margins than the average for the category would result in very high distribution for Slamix.

Mr. van der Lugt decided that television was the best medium available to promote the product. He felt that television would allow demonstration of the product in actual use and also would effectively communicate the story about the new added ingredients. The actual advertising used is shown in Exhibit 1. Although Mr. van der Lugt wanted to place all of the media advertising in television, this was not possible, as only 15 advertisements were available. The remainder of the media budget was spent in magazines. Four advertisements were placed in *Eva* and *Margriet*, women's magazines, and in *Avro-Televizier*, a TV guide. The actual promotional budget is shown in Exhibit 2.

INITIAL RESULTS

By June 1968, Slamix had obtained distribution in 86 percent of the grocery outlets in Holland. Market share for Slamix was slightly over

5 percent of the total market, and very little substitution with DFI's other salad dressing, Slasaus, was evidenced, as that product's market share remained steady. In late August 1968, five months after the introduction, DFI had the Institute for Household Research study the awareness and trial levels for Slamix. A test was conducted using a panel of 1200 housewives. Seventy-eight percent of the housewives were aware of DFI Slamix and 27 percent had already tried the new product. Of the 27 percent who had tried Slamix, 20 percent were still using it (see Exhibit 3).

EXHIBIT 2
Slamix promotional budget—introductory year

	Guilders	Dollars
Media:		
Magazine advertising (Four pages each in *Eva*,		
Margriet, and *AVRO-Televizier*)................	f108,000	$30,240
Television (15 30-second ads).....................	93,000	26,040
Production costs...............................	24,000	6,720
Total.......................................	f225,000	$63,000
Consumer promotion:		
Key chains....................................	f312,000	$87,360
Handling of key chain promotion.................	103,000	28,840
General display materials.......................	25,000	7,000
Miscellaneous (samples, etc.)....................	10,000	2,800
Total consumer promotion....................	f450,000	$126,000
Corporate advertising share......................	f 50,000	$ 14,000
Total promotion budget...........................	f725,000	$203,000

EXHIBIT 3
Test panel of 1200 housewives

	Percent
Awareness of Slamix:	
Unaided awareness............................	36
Awareness after mentioning name................	33
Awareness after showing bottle..................	9
Total swareness.............................	78
Don't know the product.......................	22
	100
Usage of Slamix:	
Use it regularly...............................	9
Use it now and then...........................	11
Used it once..................................	7
Total who have tried Slamix...................	27
Have heard of it, but not tried it..................	51
Have never heard of it........................	22
	100

At the same time DFI introduced Slamix, a small competitor introduced a somewhat similar product called Snekke. This product was a salad dressing similar to the other dressings on the market at that time, but had pieces of onions and herbs added. The product sold for f 1.13 for a .30-liter bottle[2] and was similar in appearance to the other dressings on the market. DFI conducted some taste tests of Snekke versus Slamix. They found that even though the taste was not very much different, Slamix was preferred over Snekke by most of the respondents, mainly due to its superior appearance. Snekke's market share reached approximately 1 percent of the market and then began to decline.

NEW DEVELOPMENTS

After the successful introduction of Slamix, Mr. van der Lugt directed his attention to the problem of how to maximize the profitability of the new product. The first step taken was to introduce Slamix in a second, larger size. In January 1968, a .50-liter size bottle was introduced and by June the large size Slamix had achieved distribution in 68 percent of the grocery outlets.

DFI next developed a product, slightly different from Slamix, to be marketed under large retail grocery chains' private labels at a price approximately 20 percent below the retail price of Slamix. This was a large and growing portion of the salad dressing market (about 50 percent of the market) and DFI wanted to participate in this growth. Plans were to begin marketing the private label Slamix in a .50-liter bottle size in March 1970.

The most important new development, and the one causing Mr. van der Lugt the most difficulty, concerned the marketing of new varieties of Slamix. A market research study conducted five months after the introduction of Slamix showed that the most important reason people gave for not using Slamix, after being given a sample, was their dislike of the taste of the product. DFI marketing executives thought that there was a great opportunity to increase Slamix's share of the market by introducing new varieties of salad dressings and attracting users with different taste preferences. The success of Slamix had convinced DFI that the idea of a convenience salad dressing product with special ingredients was a good one, and they now wanted to capitalize on this idea.

Mrs. Holthousen, a famous creator of recipes in Holland, was hired to develop several possible new salad dressings based on the Slamix concept. Working with the DFI development laboratories, Mrs. Holthousen created ten new recipes. Of these, Mr van der Lugt decided to have

---

[2] One guilder (f 1.00) = approx. $.28 U.S. Therefore f 1.13 = approximately $.32 U.S.

five tested at the Institute for Household Research. From the five tested, Mr. van der Lugt recommended that the best one, which had received very favorable ratings from the housewives in the research panel, be introduced at the beginning of 1970. He next began developing a marketing strategy for the new version of Slamix.

Mr. van der Lugt thought that price and distribution would not be problems. The cost of producing the new version of Slamix was almost the same as for the original Slamix. There was very little investment cost to recover, so Mr. van der Lugt planned to recommend to the Board of Directors that the same price as for the original version, f 1.28 ($.36), be used. Because of the success of Slamix, they expected little trouble in gaining distribution for the new product.

The main problem concerned what to name the new product. The new recipe of Slamix had several herbs in it that the original Slamix did not have, and had a special aroma, but was similar to the original version, except for the color. The new variety was orange, while the original version was pink. With the exception of the above, the two products were quite similar.

In naming the original mixed salad dressing Slamix, DFI executives had been aware of possible problems later if they decided to expand the product line of salad dressings. They named the original product Slamix because they had a whole new concept in dressings to promote, and they thought that it would be most effective if the new product were called by a name which described exactly what the product was.

Mr. van der Lugt thought there were two alternatives open to him in choosing a name for the new variety. First, the orange product could have a completely new name unrelated to the original Slamix. Secondly, DFI could change the name of the original pink variety, maintaining the overall name of Slamix as an umbrella name for whatever new varieties were to be introduced.

The advantage of the first alternative was that confusion for the consumer would be minimized. DFI could promote the features of the new product without jeopardizing the brand image of the original product. The disadvantages include the additional cost involved in marketing two separate products with two different stories to promote and the inability to take advantage of the well-known Slamix name.

Using the above reasoning, DFI's advertising agency urged the company to use the Slamix name as an umbrella, recommending that the names Slamix 1, Slamix 2, Slamix 3 be used for the various varieties.

The DFI executives thought that they should consider using nationalities, similar to the way Kraft and other competitors in other countries used them. They decided to test this approach, which would use names such as French, Italian, Dutch, etc. together with the Slamix name.

The Institute for Household Research tested several of these names using a consumer sample of 134 housewives. After seeing the new, orange product, the housewives mentioned a preference for some names (see Exhibit 4).

Fifty percent of the housewives could not describe what taste they thought should be in a product called Swedish Slamix or Danish Slamix. They were sure, however, of what should be included in Dutch Slamix (onion, gherkins, herbs, vegetables, and pickles), Italian Slamix (paprika, tomatoes, and garlic), and French Slamix (garlic and paprika).

Mr. van der Lugt had originally thought the name Danish Slamix would be best because he thought the ingredients were most typically Danish. He was quite surprised by the name preferences showing that the housewives though it should be called Italian Slamix (after seeing the product). He was even more surprised by the preferences listed in Exhibit 5 which shows that the housewives still thought it should be called Italian Slamix after tasting it.

The last questions in the test concerned the possibility of renaming the original Slamix. It was explained to the housewives, and they were asked what they thought of the idea of calling it Dutch Slamix. The responses were favorable (Exhibit 6).

EXHIBIT 4
Name preferences after seeing new product

Product name	Percent
Italian Slamix	31
Dutch Slamix	21
French Slamix	21
Danish Slamix	16
Swedish Slamix	11
Total	100

EXHIBIT 5
Name preferences after tasting new product

Name originally selected (from seeing the product)	After tasting the product (by percent)
Italian Slamix	79 still best name
	21 not such a good name
Dutch Slamix	47 still best name
	53 not such a good name
French Slamix	59 still best name
	41 not such a good name
Danish Slamix	31 still best name
	69 not such a good name
Swedish Slamix	78 still best name
	22 not such a good name

EXHIBIT 6
Responses to Dutch Slamix name

	Percent
Outstanding	20
Very good	31
Good	30
Fairly good	7
Not so good	7
Don't know	4
	100

Mr. van der Lugt wondered what he should recommend concerning the names of the two varieties of Slamix.

CASE QUESTIONS

1. In light of your analysis of "Dutch Food Industries Company (A)," did DFI follow sound procedures in introduction of Slamix?
2. Should DFI have sold to private branders?
3. Should new varieties of Slamix be introduced?
4. What branding policy should be followed?

part four

DISTRIBUTION STRATEGY

DISTRIBUTION strategy is concerned with making goods available to potential customers. It involves the selection of paths or channels through the maze of marketing middlemen which composes the distribution structure. In this first phase of distribution strategy, the producer attempts to identify those channels of distribution which will most effectively reach the markets he wishes to serve. He then tries to gain the support of those intermediaries in the desired channels so that they will take on the line and move it to market.

Another distribution strategy decision area deals with the number of middlemen to use at each level in the channel. Here the producer must weigh the benefits of intensive coverage of the market gained by using large numbers of middlemen versus the benefits derived from using fewer middlemen each of whom can give the line more concentrated promotional support.

Finally, decisions have to be made as to how the goods are to be distributed physically once the channel or ownership paths have been decided. A level of customer service must be specified which is consistent with the overall marketing strategy of the firm. Then different physical distribution systems can be analyzed to find the one which meets the required service level most efficiently.

8

The distribution
structure

FEW PRODUCTS are sold by producers directly to consumers. More commonly, products pass through one, several, or many market intermediaries—institutions which exist for the distribution, rather than the manufacture, of goods. In contrast to manufacturers, who provide products with form utility, these institutions create time, place, and possession utility. It is not sufficient that products capable of satisfying human wants exist. They do not truly serve a purpose unless consumers are able to obtain them when and where they are needed. Marketing institutions help in the storage of goods from time of production until time of consumption, and they see to it that these goods are available at the particular place the consumer needs them. Performance of these activities is as essential to consumer well-being as is the creation of form utility at the factory. It is the sum total of the marketing institutions which perform these functions—agent middlemen, wholesalers, and retailers—which constitutes the *distribution structure* through which manufacturers must work in marketing their products.

The course through this structure which a manufacturer chooses for his product to follow on its way to the consumer is referred to as a "channel of distribution." Any manufacturer, in selecting a channel of distribution, would usually choose to sell through only a very small percentage of the institutions which make up the distribution structure. If he chooses his channel of distribution wisely, he will be in a position to obtain adequate market coverage and sales volume for his product. If he chooses unwisely, he will deal a crushing blow to his chances for marketing success.

This structure of market intermediaries can be thought of as the "anatomy" of distribution. It is the framework within which and around which the marketing man must work in formulating his entire marketing program. And, just as the surgeon must have a sound knowledge of human anatomy to proceed with confidence and skill when performing an operation, so the marketing manager requires a thorough knowledge of the anatomy of distribution in order to bring his product to market successfully. He must understand the function, the strengths, and the weaknesses of each of the institutions available to serve as links in his distribution channel. Otherwise, he cannot make effective use of them.

Exchange and market intermediaries

The existence of the complex of marketing institutions which form our distribution structure, and which results in products often passing through many hands on the way to consumers, causes much criticism of marketing and distribution costs. One of the suggestions commonly made for reducing the cost of distribution is to "cut out the middleman." It is a popular belief that costs are least when producers sell directly to consumers as, for example, in the case of door-to-door sales of vacuum cleaners and cosmetics. Quite the contrary is true. This is a very high-cost channel of distribution. Sometimes manufacturers who use such a direct channel attempt to capitalize on this misunderstanding by claiming an ability to charge lower prices because they have circumvented the middlemen who make up the distribution structure. This helps to perpetuate this misunderstanding. To overcome this misconception, a better understanding of the nature of the exchange process and the role played therein by marketing institutions is necessary.

Exchange without intermediaries

Why have so many market intermediaries arisen to carry out the exchange process? Why do producers and consumers not deal directly with each other to a greater extent than they do? To illustrate the basic, and perhaps obvious, but still ignored, principle underlying the existence of market intermediaries, let us assume a primitive society consisting, for the sake of simplicity, of but five families. Initially these families were self-sufficient, each producing all things needed for its own existence. Soon it was discovered, however, that each family produced some things better than others. It would be to the advantage of all if a family concentrated on producing the product it could produce best, and then the families exchanged products with each other. Because of the commonly recognized advantages of division of labor, this would give a larger total product. As illustrated in Figure 8–1, one family concentrated

FIGURE 8–1
Exchange without market intermediary

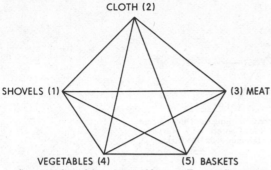

Source: Adapted from Wroe Alderson, "Factors Governing the Development of Marketing Channels," in Richard M. Clewett, ed., *Marketing Channels for Manufactured Products* (Homewood, Ill.: Richard D. Irwin, Inc., 1954), p. 7.

on the production of shovels, one on cloth, one on meat, one on vegetables, and one on baskets. By trading among themselves, each then acquired a supply of the other items.

Let us now focus on the exchange process involved in Figure 8–1. In order for each family to acquire all five products requires that ten exchanges take place. The number of exchanges required can be expressed by the formula $\dfrac{n(n-1)}{2}$, where n is the number of consuming units involved.[1] The number of exchanges (10) in relation to the number of products (5) is high. Each exchange, of course, involves a cost in time and effort. If the families are located close together, this cost may be low. If the distances involved are great, the cost will be high.

In Figure 8–2 we assume that some sort of market intermediary, say a trading post, is established to facilitate the exchange process. Each family now brings the amount of the product it has produced in excess of its own needs to the trading post and there exchanges it for the other four items that it requires. In this case only five transactions are necessary in contrast to the ten required when no market intermediary was present. The time and effort (cost) involved in the exchange process has been greatly reduced. If our trading post is just an unmanned meeting place, no cost may attach to its existence. When a structure and manpower become necessary to carry out the market intermediary functions, there will be a cost. However, if the resultant saving in time and effort is great, this cost may be small by comparison.

The ratio of advantage from use of a market intermediary in our

---

[1] Each family (n) must contact all other families ($n-1$) and, when such contact is made, two (2) products change hands.

FIGURE 8-2
Exchange with market intermediary

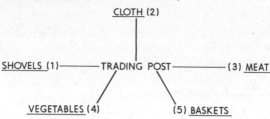

Source: Wroe Alderson, "Factors Governing the Development of Marketing Channels," in Richard M. Clewett (ed.), *Marketing Channels for Manufactured Products* (Homewood, Ill.: Richard D. Irwin, Inc., 1954), p. 7.

illustration is small (2:1) because the number of consuming units is small.[2] In the real world, the number of producing and/or consuming units would be far larger. If there were 25 such units, the ratio of advantage would be 12 to 1. If there were 100, it would be 49.5 to 1; if 500, the ratio would be 249.5 to 1; and if 1,000, the ratio of advantage would be 499.5 to 1. These are not large numbers in the real world of exchange. It is apparent, therefore, that use of market intermediaries greatly expedites the exchange process.

The wholesaler and exchange

To make more realistic the role played by middlemen in our real-world distribution structure, let us apply the above reasoning to the presence of a wholesaler who distributes the products of several manufacturers to a number of retailers. Figure 8–3, which is grossly oversimplified, contains five manufacturers and five retailers. Each manufacturer produces one of many products carried by each of the five retailers. If each manufacturer sold directly to each of the five retailers, a total of 25 transactions would be involved.[3] However, if each manufacturer sold only to the wholesaler, and then the wholesaler combined these five products and sold them to the retailers, a total of only ten transactions would be required. In even this simple illustration, involving a mere handful of manufacturers and retailers, the use of a wholesaler reduces the number of transactions by 60 percent. If our illustration

---

[2] The ratio of advantage is $\dfrac{n(n-1)}{2}/n$.

[3] Because we are now assuming that the manufacturers in our illustration sell only to retailers, and not to each other, the formula for calculating the number of transactions used in our previous illustrations must be modified to:

$$\frac{n(n-1)}{2} - \frac{n}{2}\left(\frac{n}{2} - 1\right).$$

FIGURE 8–3
Role of the wholesaler

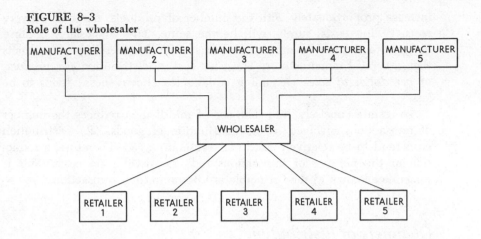

were more realistic, containing hundreds of manufacturers and perhaps thousands of retailers, the ratio of advantage from use of a wholesaler would be far greater. The ability of the wholesaler to reduce transactions in this manner is the fundamental explanation for his existence.

Number of transactions and marketing costs

By now it should be clear that the existence of a distribution structure made up of various types of middlemen serves to reduce the number of transactions involved in getting goods from producer to consumer. It has been implied that this increases the efficiency of distribution and thus reduces marketing costs. But we have really not explained why this is so. The answer lies in the fact that distribution costs tend to be *relatively fixed per transaction.*

Consider some of the activities involved in the sale of goods to a retailer, regardless of whether this sale is made by a manufacturer or a wholesaler. Some sort of contact must be made with the retailer, probably by a salesman. This involves travel and the costs associated therewith, plus the time spent in talking with the retailer. If this is a new account, a credit investigation should be made. Assuming an order is received, it must be processed. The goods must be delivered, and, finally, the retailer must be billed for the price of the order.

The cost of a sales call on a retailer will be approximately the same whether the salesman is selling one product or many products. The many costs of getting the salesman to the account do not vary on this basis. The time spent on the sales call itself may vary somewhat with the number of products, but not proportionately. The cost of a credit check will be the same in either case. Order-processing costs will not increase proportionately with the number of products, nor will delivery costs. Billing costs, surely, will be the same. The wholesaler, because he represents many manufacturers, has a far broader line of products than a typical manufacturer. Thus, his cost of distribution *per product, or per dollar of sales* (assuming equal sales effectiveness) tends to be less.

To restate concisely: (1) The use of middlemen reduces the number of transactions involved in the distribution of goods. (2) Distribution costs tend to be relatively fixed per transaction. (3) Therefore, a reduction in the number of transactions reduces distribution costs. This is sometimes known as the "principle of minimum total transactions."

Channels of distribution

The number of specific channels of distribution utilized by manufacturers is so large that all channel alternatives cannot possibly be described. It is possible, however, to point out certain basic types of channels and compare them with each other. In doing so, we shall speak in general terms and not distinguish between types of institutions at either the wholesale or retail level. (That will be done later in this chapter.) Rather, emphasis here is placed on whether a particular *institutional level* in the available distribution structure is or is not included in the channel appropriate to certain types of goods.

Major channels—Consumer goods

The major basic types of channels used for manufactured consumer goods are the following:

Manufacturer....Consumer
Manufacturer....Retailer......Consumer
Manufacturer....Wholesaler...Retailer......Consumer
Manufacturer....Agent........Wholesaler...Retailer...Consumer

Although there are many examples of the sale of consumer goods by manufacturers directly to consumers, this is a relatively unimportant channel from the standpoint of both number of products and sales volume. It is most significant for perishables and specialty products. Eggs, fresh fruits and vegetables, and other perishables are sometimes sold in this manner. The appeal of freshness is strong and will compensate for other inefficiencies attached to the use of this channel. Such specialty products as encyclopedias, cooking ware, and high-priced vacuum cleaners employ this channel because it permits use of highly aggressive selling. Usually these are products for which consumers do not feel a great need until they are demonstrated. Under such circumstances, aggressive and high-cost selling can have a substantial "payout." The greater sales volume realized may well offset the high costs that use of this channel involves. Because this is true for relatively few products, this channel is quite unimportant.

Sales by manufacturers directly to retailers is a more important channel of distribution. Its use is, however, almost always associated with restricted retail distribution. Products which need to be sold through only a limited number of retail outlets can be distributed directly to retailers at reasonable cost if retail outlets buy in sufficiently large quantities. Although the number of transactions is larger than if a wholesaler were employed, the ratio of advantage from use of a wholesaler is limited because of the restricted number of retail accounts. One of the major products sold through this type of channel is clothing, for which style considerations are important. This places a premium on close contact with the consumer market, in order to keep abreast of style trends, as well as on speed of delivery so the product will be available at the particular time it is in demand. The fact that a direct channel is more effective on these two counts is a significant offset to the higher costs stemming from the larger number of transactions.

Sales by manufacturers to wholesalers, who in turn sell the retail trade, is the channel commonly employed for products requiring widespread distribution, such as groceries, drugs, hardware, and automotive parts. Because of the large number of retailers involved, each accounting for but a very small fraction of total sales, direct contact between manufacturer and retailer would be prohibitively expensive. The number of transactions would be very high in relation to sales, and there would be insufficient offsetting benefits derived from the direct contact. Of course, where sales are to large retail units, such as grocery chains and large department stores, this same reasoning does not apply, and a direct channel is normally employed.

When the manufacturer is very small, has a narrow product line, and sells to a widely dispersed or sparse market, it is common to interpose an agent middleman between the manufacturer and wholesaler. This reduces the number of transactions that would otherwise be involved in sales to a large number of wholesalers. Canned vegetables are a good case in point. The typical food canner is small and has a narrow line because he usually processes only those products native to the region in which he is located. Yet the market served is widespread and reached by a very large number of wholesale and retail accounts. Another complicating factor is the seasonality of his production. For all these reasons, canned foods are normally sold through food brokers. This is more economical than if the canner dealt directly with the wholesalers.

Major channels—Industrial goods

The major channels of distribution employed for manufactured industrial goods are:

Manufacturer.......Industrial user
Manufacturer.......Manufacturer's agent.....Industrial user
Manufacturer.......Industrial supply house...Industrial user

In contrast to the situation for consumer goods, the most important channel of distribution for industrial goods is a direct one, involving no middlemen between manufacturer and the industrial user. In light of our previous discussion of exchange and the role of middlemen in the exchange process, this should not be surprising. Unlike the consumer market, the industrial market is made up of a smaller number of relatively large buyers. In addition, these buyers often are concentrated geographically. Thus, the ratio of advantage stemming from the use of middlemen tends to be far lower than for consumer goods. Also, industrial goods are often technically complex and require skilled selling. The gain in sales from more skillful selling can more than offset the higher costs brought about by the larger number of transactions because of not using middlemen. Where conditions such as those mentioned are not present, and the industrial market is more like the consumer market, indirect channels again tend to predominate.

Manufacturer's agents are used in the marketing of some industrial goods for the same reasons that agent middlemen are used for consumer goods—the manufacturer is small, has a narrow line, and sells in a dispersed market. The use of a manufacturer's agent reduces transactions and provides for a reasonable cost level, but not to the same degree as would the use of a wholesaler. This limitation is offset, however, by the more aggressive selling effort the agent provides compared to the wholesaler. The employment of a manufacturer's agent is sort of an "in-between" choice between direct sale and going through wholesalers. He provides some of the advantages of direct sale to a greater degree than does the wholesaler, while at the same time providing some reduction in the number of transactions.

The industrial supply house—the wholesaler of industrial goods—is used primarily for supply and maintenance items and for low-cost, fairly standardized industrial equipment. These are products which have highly dispersed markets, yet the products must be readily available when needed. Also, such products require no high degree of selling ability. They could be described as the "convenience goods" of the industrial market. Like convenience goods in the consumer goods category, the reduction in number of transactions, and therefore distribution costs, by use of a wholesaler is very great.

Use of higher cost channels

Two seemingly contradictory facts have now been established: (1) Indirect channels tend to be lower in cost, as a percentage of sales, than are direct channels. This is due, of course, to the reduction in the required number of transactions that the use of market intermediaries makes possible. (2) In spite of the fact that more direct channels tend to be higher cost channels, they are extensively used in the distribution of goods. This situation suggests an obvious question: *Why does a manufacturer choose to use a higher cost channel when lower cost ones are available?*

The answer to this seeming paradox is, in general terms, quite simple. Low distribution cost as a percentage of sales is not necessarily a reasonable objective for a manufacturer to pursue. His objective, rather, is to maximize profit on investment. Frequently this goal can be better achieved by the use of higher cost channels rather than lower. This is true because these higher cost channels may produce sales that would not otherwise be realized. If sales are increased more than costs, profits will be greater. A 10 percent return on sales of $1 million, for example, may provide a far better return on investment than a 20 percent return on sales of $100,000. It is the favorable effect on sales that explains the use of shorter channels.

Use of multiple channels

Some manufacturers choose to follow but one path through the distribution structure, while others elect to use multiple channels of distribution. There is a basic difference on this score between manufacturers of different types of products, and frequently different manufacturers of the same product choose to follow different policies. Higher priced consumer specialty products often move to market through a single channel, while most convenience goods, such as food products, move through several channels. For a given product, such as appliances, one manufacturer will choose to sell only to franchised retail outlets, while another will sell to any retailer wishing to buy—including discount houses.

For certain products a single channel of distribution may be capable of reaching a substantial part of the available market. This tends to be true of specialty products for which there exists a strong brand preference. Automobiles are a case in point. Although a given make of automobile can normally be acquired by the consumer through one channel only, sales are not unduly handicapped because the consumer will make substantial effort to acquire this particular product. The market for many other products, however, is such that restricting distribution to any one channel means a severe reduction in market coverage. A grocery manufacturer, for example, who elects to sell only through independent wholesalers is cutting himself off from the market represented by retail grocery chains. If he elects to sell only directly to chains, he loses the market made up of independent grocery retailers who normally buy from independent wholesalers. In the case of products for which, because of consumer buying patterns, broad availability is important, use of only one channel can restrict sales unduly. Because most products are in this category, the use of multiple distribution channels is common.

One product for which broad availability is extremely important is oil filter cartridges for automobiles. Every car owner must change oil filter cartridges at intervals, and he wishes to have this done along with other normal maintenance services. He has little brand preference and will normally accept any cartridge the serviceman chooses to install. Under these circumstances, broad market availability is essential to maximizing sales and profits. Figure 8–4 illustrates how this broad availability is achieved through the use of multiple channels of distribution. The filter manufacturer sells his product through vehicle manufacturers to car dealers. Car dealers, however, account for a very small part of the filter cartridge replacement business, so the manufacturer also sells to mail-order houses and chains in order to reach the self-repair market, through direct jobbers and warehouse distributors to reach the general repair trade, and through the parts programs of oil and rubber companies in order to gain access to the retail trade they control. The net result of use of these several channels is achievement of a higher probability that the car owner will find a particular brand of oil filter cartridge in whatever type of outlet he chooses for maintenance services.

The use of multiple channels of distribution helps to create many marketing problems. Those involving promotional strategy and pricing we shall ignore until later chapters. The most basic and important problem is the creation of interchannel rivalry. Note in Figure 8–4 that four different types of middlemen compete for the oil filter cartridge business of the vehicle dealer, three compete in sales to the repair shop, and five sell to service stations. All of these retail service shops, in turn, compete with mail-order houses and chains in sales to consumers. Such overlap in the markets served by different distribution channels is commonplace, but it can cause ill will and difficulties for the manufacturer. Middlemen tend to resent the competition that such a channel policy creates. As a result, they are less willing to push the manufacturer's product, and sales effort is low in aggressiveness. This pushes back onto

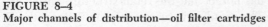

FIGURE 8–4
Major channels of distribution—oil filter cartridges

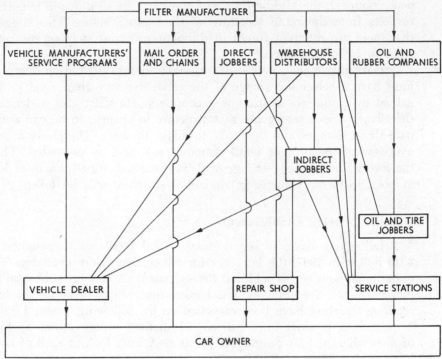

Source: C. N. Davisson, *The Marketing of Automotive Parts* (Michigan Business Studies, vol. 12, no. 1 [Ann Arbor: Bureau of Business Research, The University of Michigan]), p. 652.

the manufacturer the job of doing whatever demand creation is necessary.

When a manufacturer elects to use multiple channels of distribution, he is usually sacrificing "sales push" in order to gain availability. For many products this choice must necessarily be made, because sales push cannot possibly compensate for not having the product readily available in the market. The problems, therefore, which go with use of multiple channels are very often unavoidable.

The retail structure

Everyone is a consumer and makes purchases in many types of retail stores. Therefore, everyone has some knowledge of the general retail structure and of the types of institutions that make it up. What is less well known and understood, even by marketing managers, is why the retail structure is as it is, and what forces cause it to change. Everyone who has traveled abroad has noted that the retail structure varies greatly from country to country. The retail structures of Great Britain, the European continent, the Middle East, and the Far East all differ in important respects from the retail structure of the United States. This suggests that there are different forces in different countries shaping the retail structure in different ways.

A marketing manager, in order to make sound distribution decisions, must have a better knowledge of the retail structure than what he has gained by casual observation as a consumer. He must also understand the change agents that cause that structure to change, so he can anticipate those changes and be ready to adapt to them. Therefore, a brief overview of the present retail structure will first be presented. Then, the forces that produce change will be discussed. Finally, a brief look at possible future changes in the retail structure will be taken.

Classification of retail establishments

Retailing en masse is big business. Total retail sales amounted to $310 billion in 1967, the last year for which figures are available. This grand total, however, is achieved through many diverse types of retailing establishments. Traditionally, retail institutions which make up the total retailing structure have been classified on the following bases: 1) size, 2) extent of product lines carried, 3) method of operation, 4) form of ownership, and 5) geographic location. A brief look at each of these bases of classification follows.

Size of retail establishment. Figure 8–5 classifies retail establishments by size, on the basis of annual sales. Even a cursory examination of the data reveals that, although retailing in the aggregate is a large vol-

FIGURE 8–5
Retail trade, 1967—United States, sales by size of establishment

Sales size of establishments	Establishments			Sales volume		
	Number (000)	Percent	Cumulative percent	Sales ($000,000)	Percent	Cumulative percent
Total, all establishments.....	1,763			$310,214		
Establishments operated entire year, total........	1,671	100.0		299,430	100.0	
With annual sales of:						
$1,000,000 or more........	50	3.0	3.0	132,876	44.4	44.4
$500,000–999,999.........	55	3.3	6.3	38,464	12.9	57.3
$300,000–499,999.........	74	4.4	10.7	28,110	9.4	66.7
$100,000–299,999.........	359	21.5	32.2	60,290	20.1	86.8
$50,000–99,999..........	323	19.3	51.5	22,888	7.6	94.4
$30,000–49,999..........	227	13.6	65.1	8,769	2.9	97.3
$29,999 or less............	583	34.9	100.0	8,033	2.7	100.0

Source: *U.S. Census of Business, 1967,* vol. I.

ume operation, most retail establishments are relatively small. Nearly 70 percent of them do an annual volume of less than $100,000. Those with an annual volume under $30,000 make up an astonishing 35 percent of the total, but account for only 2.7 percent of total retail sales. Assuming these small stores have an average gross margin of 25 percent, even those at the upper end of the category have only $7,500 per year to cover all expenses, including salaries, and to provide a profit. Many stores in this category, perhaps most of them, operate at a loss. On the other hand, stores with an annual volume of over $1 million account for only 3 percent of all establishments, but do over 44 percent of total volume. On the basis of size alone, retail establishments are clearly a highly varied lot.

Extent of product lines carried. On the basis of the product lines they carry, retail establishments are usually classified as: 1) general merchandise stores, 2) single-line stores, and 3) specialty stores. Each of these general classifications can, in turn, be broken down into categories with designations very familiar to all consumers—drugstores, hardware stores, bakeries, etc. Figure 8–6 provides information on the relative importance of different types of stores and reveals the changes in relative importance over, roughly, a 20-year period.

General merchandise stores offer a wide variety of products. Included are such stores as department stores and variety stores. An examination of Figure 8–6 reveals that department stores have significantly increased their share of total retail sales. This is explained not so much by growth

FIGURE 8–6
Total retail sales and percentage of total sales, by kind of business, in millions of dollars

	1967 sales ($000,000)	Percentage of total sales		
Kind of business		*1967*	*1958*	*1948*
Retail trade, total.....................	$310,214	100.0	100.0	100.0
Building materials, hardware, farm equipment dealers..................	17,200	5.5	7.2	8.6
General merchandise group............	43,537	14.0	10.9	12.3
Department stores...................	32,344	10.4	6.7	7.3
Variety stores.......................	5,407	1.7	1.8	1.9
Food stores...........................	70,251	22.7	24.5	22.7
Eating-drinking places.................	23,843	7.7	7.6	8.3
Automotive dealers....................	55,631	18.0	15.9	15.6
Gasoline service stations..............	22,709	7.3	7.1	5.0
Apparel and accessory stores...........	16,672	5.4	6.3	7.5
Furniture, home furnishings, equipment stores......................	14,452	4.7	5.0	5.4
Drugstores, proprietary stores.........	10,930	3.5	3.4	3.1
Other retailers.......................	27,274	8.8	9.2	9.7
Nonstore retailers....................	7,623	2.4	2.7	1.8

Source: *U.S. Census of Business: 1967, 1954, Retail Trade, United States Summary.*

of the long-established, full-line department store, but by the rise of a new type of department store, an illustration of which might be K-Mart stores operated by S. S. Kresge. The growth of this type of store is due not only to changes in the method of operation they brought to retailing, but to the increasing appeal to consumers of one-stop shopping.

Single-line stores stick essentially to one basic line of products. Typical examples are clothing stores, hardware stores, gift shops, and jewelry stores. The definition of what is a single line, however, is gradually being broadened. Drugstores and supermarkets are still considered single-line stores, but they have added to their lines many products that, historically, they did not carry. The whole concept of "single line" in classifying stores may soon have to be abandoned.

Specialty stores are those stores that specialize in carrying only part of a total line of products. Examples are bakeries, furriers, and shoe stores. Such stores typically carry a fuller assortment of the products in which they specialize than do single-line and general-line stores.

Form of ownership. In terms of ownership, retail establishments can be broadly classified as independent stores, corporate chains, and voluntary associations of independents, which includes franchise operations. Independent stores make up the vast majority of all stores, constituting 88 percent of the total, according to the 1967 *Census of Business.* They are to be found in every field of retailing, but their relative importance varies greatly by field. Usually they are small and serve limited markets. They have several advantages. They have a better opportunity to provide a personal touch. Perhaps this is why they are so important in clothing retailing. They often offer location convenience, which explains why neighborhood grocery stores continue to exist, in spite of their substantially higher prices. They are more flexible than chains in adjusting to changed conditions.

Corporate chains are those organizations consisting of two or more stores which are centrally owned and managed. They are far fewer in number than independents, but tend to have much larger sales. Their importance varies tremendously among different types of stores. Chains of four or more stores account for 82 percent of sales of variety stores, 91 percent of sales of department stores, but only 34 percent of drugstore sales and 17 percent of the sales of furniture, appliance, and home furnishing's stores.[4]

Corporate chains have many advantages. Because of their much larger volume, they offer many economies of scale. Because division of labor is possible, they gain in efficiency of operation. They usually have much better, more professional management. They are able to spread risks and also to spread promotional costs over many outlets.

---

[4] *U.S. Census of Business,* 1967.

Voluntary associations of independents are of several types. In the grocery field, for example, there are so-called voluntary chains and re- tailer cooperative chains. The difference is that the voluntary chain is sponsored by a wholesaler who enters into contractual relations with a number of retailers. Each party agrees to do certain things. The whole- saler may agree to deal with all sources of supply, provide certain man- agement services, make private brands available to retail members, ad- vertise jointly for all stores, etc. The retailer may agree to identify his store in a prescribed manner, carry the private brands, participate in all sales events, etc. The retailer cooperative chain is similar, as far as operations are concerned, but there is no wholesaler sponsor. Fran- chise operations, such as Kentucky Fried Chicken, McDonalds, General Motors' dealer network, etc., are essentially voluntary chains and provide for a similar sharing of functions between the franchisor and the franchisee.

Geographic location. This classification of retail stores is simple and obvious and will not be discussed, only mentioned. Stores can be classi- fied as downtown stores, suburban stores, or rural. They can also be classified on the basis of whether they are located in shopping centers or are freestanding. A basic trend in recent years, of course, has been for the decline of downtown stores and the rise of suburban stores, often located in shopping centers.

Forces influencing the retail structure

The retail structure is highly dynamic and constantly changing in form. The retail structure of today is substantially different, for example, than the one that existed just ten years ago. Existing institutions change their nature, new institutions become part of the structure, and some institutions drop out of the structure. Because the marketing manager must adapt his marketing strategy to reflect these changes, he must understand the forces that produce change and how they do so. He must be able to anticipate change if he is to be ready for the changes when they occur.

In a general sense, all factors present in our environment have some impact on the retail structure. The retail structure is a reflection of the total environment in which we live. Because it is patently impossible to discuss all of them, emphasis will here be placed on a few of the most basic social and environmental factors, with special attention paid to the effect of competition on the retail structure.

Social and environmental factors. Some of the more basic factors shaping the retail structure are: 1) population density, 2) population mobility, 3) standards of living, and 4) social custom. Each of these will be briefly discussed before the effects of competition are considered.

Everyone is familiar with the general store of yesteryear, as a result of watching western movies on television, although few people today have come in direct contact with such an institution. It was a store that sold a highly varied line including foods, hardware, clothing, farm supplies, and many more types of items. The reason this type of store existed is very obvious. Population density was so low that a store handling only a single line of products could not achieve a sufficient sales volume to be economically viable. As population density gradually increased through the years, the trend in retailing was toward more specialization. Single-line stores became the most common type and the general store became a rarity. The trend toward single-line stores, however, did not continue indefinitely. In recent years the trend has been in the opposite direction, toward again carrying a multiplicity of lines. When population density reaches a certain point, with the accompanying traffic congestion and shortage of parking spaces, one-stop shopping offers great appeal. Today, we call this "scrambled merchandising," but, in terms of breadth of lines carried, many of today's stores resemble, in basic form, the general store of yore. Of course, there are many differences too, in types of products, depth of stock, merchandising methods, etc. However, in terms of basic structure we have come full-circle.

An increase in population mobility has effects similar to an increase in population density. It enables stores to serve a much larger trading area and thus permits more specialization. There are other effects on the retail structure. In the past, when consumers were heavily dependent on public transportation, stores in central business districts flourished because they were readily accessible by rail or bus. The rise in automobile ownership has changed that. Today, stores in outlying areas are more easily reached than those downtown, and parking is far easier. Outlying stores are increasing rapidly in number, and the share of the market served by downtown stores has declined sharply. At one time, mail-order houses served primarily a rural market where they had great popularity because of the isolation of rural residents and the difficulty of traveling to cities to shop. Today, most mail-order sales are made in urban areas. Because of the automobile, rural residents no longer find it difficult to shop in stores. On the other hand urban residents, because of traffic congestion and parking problems, find buying by mail relatively more attractive.

The living standard a people possesses has many effects on the retail structure. A low living standard reduces mobility, because it limits car ownership. It also restricts the number of in-home appliances. Where refrigerators are few in number and/or small, food buying must be done frequently and in small quantities. This favors smaller, conveniently located stores. Freezer compartments in refrigerators are common only in the United States. This, too, affects the way consumers buy and where they buy. In Europe, where refrigerators are small and usually do not have freezer compartments, mobile vendors who come to the home to sell groceries, baked goods, and even beer are commonplace. In the United States, they are rare. Living standards also affect the relative demand for different types of products. This, in turn, affects the assortment of goods retailers offer, the size of retail establishments, etc.

Social custom affects the retail structure in subtle ways. In many countries, shopping is a major social event for housewives. It is a way to meet one's friends, exchange gossip, and to find out what is going on in the neighborhood. People are very much creatures of habit, and changes in the retail structure are often impeded by this.

Competition. Although very much an environmental factor in the same category as those discussed above, competition is treated separately here because of its very special, and often unrecognized, effect on the retail structure. Two kinds of competition act as change agents. One is competition between retail institutions of different kinds, for example between supermarkets and single-line independent grocery stores. Another form of competition that affects the retail structure is that between institutions of the same kind, such as competition of supermarkets with one another. The effect of competition between different types of retail institutions on the retail structure is readily understood. Some, for any of many reasons, are more successful in attracting patronage than are others. Therefore, they grow in numbers and importance while the less successful decline. The effect of competition between retail institutions of like kind on the retail structure are not as clearly perceived. The nature of this effect can best be explained by an illustration.

Let us choose supermarkets for illustrative purposes and trace their history and the way intrasupermarket competition has changed them. Assume a city of about 50,000 population back in the early thirties when supermarkets first came into being. One supermarket opened its doors in X City and operated in a way typical of that day. This meant that it emphasized low prices, provided a limited choice of brands, had simple, if any, store fixtures, and offered no auxiliary services. This merchandising approach appealed, say, to one fourth of X City's population and made a high-volume, high-turnover operation possible and profitable. Soon, however, a second supermarket opened. Assuming it operated in a manner identical with the first and appealed to the same market segment, the market available to the first supermarket was reduced by one half. This second supermarket was followed by a third, a fourth, and a fifth. If all were equally successful, the market share available to the first supermarket had been reduced by 80 percent. It must take some sort of action in order to continue to operate.

The most obvious action it could take would be to attempt to broaden its appeal so as to attract patronage from among the 75 percent of the market not now being served. This would require changing its merchandising methods. More brand choice must be provided, more elaborate fixtures installed, services added (check cashing, carry-out boys, etc.). This would increase costs and require larger margins. Prices would have to be increased. The basic reliance on a price appeal would be diluted, at least.

The above is just what happened to supermarkets between the early 1930s and today. Supermarket margins rose during this period from 6 to 17 percent. This left an opening for lower cost retailers, and today discount food retailing is rapidly gaining ground. The same sort of history can be traced for department stores, whose margins climbed from 15 percent in 1850 to 38 percent in 1968, and to limited price variety stores, where margins went from 24 percent in 1890 to 38 percent today.[5] This tendency for retail institutions to begin as low-cost, low-price outlets and to gradually become higher price outlets, opening the door for new, lower cost types of retail institutions has come to be known as "the wheel of retailing."[6] All retail institutions don't evolve in this way, but a significant number do. Others start as high-cost, high-price institutions and continue as such, or even change to become lower cost, lower priced outlets.

Retailing in the future

The only thing that can be said, for certain, about retailing in the future is that it will be different from what it is today. However, change is becoming more rapid than it has ever been. Conventional department stores achieved a mature stage in about three quarters of a century. Variety stores, which came later, reached maturity in about 50 years. Supermarkets required only about 25 years. Fast-food chains and franchising organizations achieved maturity in about 10 years.[7]

E. B. Weiss, a well-known authority on changes in retailing, foresees for the future such retailing innovations as the following:[8] 1) underground pipelines to deliver food to the home, as is currently done for gas and oil, 2) completely automated and unattended stores, 3) shopping via closed circuit television, 4) shopping directly from warehouses by

[5] A. C. R. Dreesman, "Patterns of Evolution in Retailing," *Journal of Retailing*, vol. 44, no. 1 (Spring 1968), pp. 64–81.

[6] See M. P. McNair, "Significant Trends and Developments in the Postwar Period," in A. B. Smith, ed., *Competitive Distribution in a Free, High-Level Economy and Its Implications for the University*, (Pittsburgh, Pa.: University of Pittsburgh Press, 1958), pp. 1–25. Also, Stanley C. Hollander, "The Wheel of Retailing," *Journal of Marketing*, vol. 24, no. 3 (July 1960), pp. 37–42.

[7] William R. Davidson, "Changes in Distributive Institutions," *Journal of Marketing*, vol. 34, no. 1 (January 1970), pp. 7–10.

[8] E. B. Weiss, "What Will Retailing Be Like in 1975?" *Advertising Age*, vol. 37 (March 7, 1966), pp. 119–22.

Touch-Tone telephone, and 5) drive-through stores so the consumer can shop without leaving his car. Perhaps some, if not all, of these things will come to pass. Other changes in the retail structure also will surely occur.

The wholesale structure

Basic types of wholesale middlemen

Wholesale middlemen can be divided into two broad categories: agent middlemen, who do not take legal title to the goods they buy or sell, but rather perform these functions on behalf of others, and merchant wholesalers, who do take title and sell primarily to retailers and industrial buyers. Within each of these general classes there are many variations, each variation reflecting some specialization of function. Also, some wholesaling institutions cut across the boundary lines of these classes. Combination wholesaler-retailers, for example, are common in the marketing of some products.

Agent middlemen. Agent middlemen are paid commissions for their services. They can be roughly divided into five classes: brokers, commission merchants, resident buyers, manufacturer's agents, and sales agents. The *broker* may represent either buyer or seller, and his basic function is to bring the party he represents into contact with the other. He seeks out potential buyers for sellers, and potential sources of supply for buyers. He then negotiates the transfer of title. The broker cannot bind his principal, which means that each transaction must be approved by the broker's client before it is binding. He does not physically handle the goods he buys or sells. He usually represents many clients, and not necessarily on a continuing basis. Brokers offer a low-cost method of distribution because they represent many parties, provide minimum services, may be used only when and as needed, and are compensated only if they produce results.

A *commission merchant* is in many ways similar to a broker, but differs in two essential respects. He can bind his principal and usually takes physical possession of the goods. For these reasons sale through a commission merchant is less time consuming than sale through a broker. Commission merchants are common in the marketing of fresh fruits and vegetables because of the high degree of perishability of these products. They are also used in the marketing of many other products.

Resident buyers are of importance primarily in the marketing of style goods. They are located in various style and production centers and represent retailers throughout the country. They provide their clients with information on style and sales trends and buy merchandise for the account of their principals. They are particularly significant in the purchase of "fill-in" orders.

The *manufacturer's agent* (or manufacturer's representative) is one of the more ubiquitous of agent middlemen. He serves, in effect, as the salesman for several manufacturers who, for a variety of reasons, do not find it desirable to have their own salesmen in the market. The manufacturer's agent handles complementary rather than competing products. He usually is limited by the manufacturer to a certain geographical area and is quite carefully controlled in other ways as well. Narrow-line manufacturers may use manufacturer's agents in all markets in which they sell. Broader line manufacturers may use them in sparse markets, and employ their own salesmen in more concentrated areas.

The *sales agent* performs many more functions than does the manufacturer's agent. He offers the manufacturer, in effect, a marketing department—often providing design services, marketing research, advertising and sales promotion, and so on, as well as field representation. He may take a manufacturer's entire output and handle its distribution in all markets. Because he represents a number of manufacturers, he can perform the marketing operation more cheaply than manufacturers can provide it for themselves. This is particularly true in the case of manufacturers who have limited sales in a widely dispersed market.

Merchant wholesalers. In contrast to agent middlemen, merchant wholesalers take title to the goods they sell and, therefore, assume the risks associated with product ownership. There are many types of wholesalers and a complete classification of them at this point will not be attempted. One of the more basic distinctions is between *full-service* and *limited-function* wholesalers. Full-service wholesalers provide a wide range of traditional wholesaling services, such as carrying stocks, making delivery, extending credit, maintaining a sales force, and so on. Limited-function wholesalers, in contrast, restrict in one way or another the functions they perform. Cash-and-carry wholesalers, as their name suggests, neither grant credit nor make delivery. Drop shippers do not physically handle the products they own and sell; hence they perform none of the functions associated with physical handling. Wagon (or truck) jobbers limit the inventory-carrying function. Other limited-function wholesalers restrict functions in other ways.

The typical wholesaler, whether full-service or limited-function, restricts himself to all or a portion of the product line carried by a particular type of retailer. Thus, we have grocery wholesalers, drug wholesalers, auto parts wholesalers, and so on. A special terminology applies to wholesalers in some fields. Petroleum wholesalers are known as "bulk tank stations" because of the type of facilities required by the products they handle. Wholesalers of consumer durables are generally known as "distributors." In the industrial goods field, wholesalers are referred to as "industrial supply houses." If they sell to the mining industry, they are "mine supply houses"; if they serve machine shops, they are "mill supply houses."

Some wholesalers are more important in the assembly than in the distribution of goods. Agricultural products must be brought together from many relatively small producers into lots sufficiently large for economic handling. Local grain elevators, for example, buy the grain of local area farmers. They ship this in carload lots to terminal elevators, which bring together the grain of many local elevators. At this point begins the job of distributing the grain to the many and varied users.

Oftentimes wholesaling functions are integrated into the operations of manufacturers and retailers. Manufacturers may operate wholesale establishments, known as *manufacturer's branches*. Large retailers, such as grocery chains, operate district and regional warehouses which perform for their retail units many of the same functions independent wholesalers perform for independent retailers.

Size and importance of wholesale trade

The total volume of wholesale trade usually comes as a surprise to most people. Although there has long been talk of the decline of the wholesaler, as manufacturers more and more choose to sell directly to retailers, the dollar volume of wholesale trade has continued to increase, as can be seen in Figure 8–7. It is true that the percentage of wholesalers' sales that go to retailers fell from 59 percent in 1939 to 39 percent in 1967, but this decline has been offset by an increase in sales to industrial and institutional buyers. It is also interesting to note that wholesale trade is substantially larger than retail trade. The explanation for this, again, is the large volume of sales in the industrial and institutional markets.

In another way the importance of the wholesaler has declined through

FIGURE 8–7
Total wholesale trade in United States compared with total retail stores

Year	Number of wholesaling establishments	Wholesale sales (billions)	Retail sales (billions)
1967	311,000	$459.5	$310.2
1963	308,000	358.4	244.2
1958	287,000	285.7	200.4
1948	216,000	180.6	130.5

Sources: *U.S. Census of Business: 1967; Wholesale Trade, United States Summary; Retail Trade, United States Summary;* and *U.S. Census of Business, 1954.*

time. Before 1920 the wholesaler was the dominant link in distribution channels. Until then, manufacturers were usually small and short on capital. They were heavily dependent on wholesalers to get their products to market. Retailers likewise were usually small and undercapitalized. They could not afford to buy directly from manufacturers and carry substantial inventories. They were also dependent on the wholesaler for credit. Now the situation has changed. Manufacturers today tend to be large. They have become aggressive marketers and have adopted branding, mass advertising, etc. Many have broadened their product lines, which reduces their dependence on wholesalers. Mass retailers, too, are less dependent on wholesalers. They can often afford to buy directly from manufacturers in carload lots at lower prices. As a result of these changes, wholesalers are no longer the dominant link in the distribution channel and cannot dictate to manufacturers and retailers, as in days past.

Conclusion

If consumers are to have readily available the vast variety of products required in order for them to complete their demand assortments with reasonable effort and at reasonable cost, a complex distribution structure is a necessity, not a sign of waste in distribution. But it cannot be denied that this situation complicates the problem of channel choice for the manufacturer, who must choose the right path through this intricate maze of marketing institutions. In making this choice, many variables must be considered. We have mentioned in this chapter only the most basic of these. The following chapter, which considers at greater length the problem of channel selection, will focus attention on other things.

The most fundamental consideration, however, in making decisions about the channel of distribution to be used is the one stressed in this discussion of the distribution structure—the relative importance of sales effort on one hand and market availability on the other. If aggressive sales effort is required within the channel, then shorter, higher cost channels may be the correct choice. To gain better selling effort, one must usually expect to pay the price of restricted distribution, because such channels can provide widespread market coverage only at prohibitive cost. If market availability is more important than sales push, then a longer, more indirect channel is better because it can provide such availability at reasonable cost. The greater the need for widespread availability, the more likely also is the decision to use multiple channels. Other considerations will always be present to modify and becloud this basic choice, but they will not remove the necessity for making it.

Questions

1. What is the basic difference between agent middlemen and merchant middlemen?

2. Compare and contrast (1) a manufacturer's agent with (2) a sales agent.

3. In general, the costs of distribution (as a percent of sales) are less when an indirect channel rather than a direct channel is used. Why is this so?

4. If indirect channels are less costly than direct channels, why do so many sellers choose to sell (at a higher cost as a percentage of sales) through a direct channel?

5. A few years ago a major publisher of encyclopedias failed in an attempt to sell encyclopedias through department stores. An attempt by Sears, Roebuck to sell encyclopedias by mail also failed. What do you think caused these failures?

6. The X Company produces baking powder, baking soda, and other staple grocery products, with total sales of roughly $100 million per year. The company has long been dissatisfied with the lack of aggressive selling of its products by wholesalers and is considering distribution directly to retail stores. Would you recommend that this change be made? Justify your answer in terms of (1) the relative costs of the two channels, and (2) the difference in attainable sales volumes for the two channels.

7. A reduction in transactions that is a result of using indirect channels of distribution is a function of the discrepancy in the assortment of goods at various levels of distribution. Explain.

8. How might it be argued that the choice of a channel of distribution depends largely on the nature of buyer behavior?

9. Refer to Figure 8–4. Explain why manufacturers of oil filter cartridges use multiple channels of distribution. Discuss the problems this causes.

10. How might a manufacturer adjust his marketing strategy so as to minimize the problems inherent in the use of multiple distribution channels?

11. Explain the effect of competition among stores of like kind on the evolution of the retail structure.

12. Why do wholesalers' sales continue to rise, although an increasingly large percentage of manufacturers elect to sell directly to retailers?

9

Distribution policy decisions

The distribution structure described in Chapter 8 is the sum total of all channels of distribution used by all sellers. An overview of this distribution structure has been presented, and some of the major channels of distribution have been described. With this background we now turn to a consideration of the kinds of distribution policy problems which confront the marketing managers of individual manufacturing firms in developing and executing a plan which will achieve a profitable flow of their products to the ultimate consumer or industrial user. The problems faced by the firm introducing a new product are especially complex and challenging. Among the more important distribution policy decisions which must be made are the following:

1. Should the manufacturer sell direct to the final buyer or should middlemen be used?
2. If middlemen are to be utilized, what specific types (both wholesale and retail) are most appropriate?
3. What degree of selectivity is desirable at the several levels of the distribution structure?
4. How much control should be sought over the institutions in the channel and how does this affect the channel problem?

The executive's task is complicated by the fact that these several decisions are not mutually exclusive. For example, a decision concerning the appropriate degree of selectivity bears on the decision concerning the degree of directness in the channel which should be employed. A policy of restricted retail distribution tends to reduce the costs of direct sale. If other factors are favorable, therefore, restricted distribution might make it profitable for the manufacturer to eliminate wholesalers from his channel and sell directly to selected retail outlets. In contrast, a decision to seek widespread distribution would tend to make it costly for the manufacturer to sell directly to the retailer and thus would favor a policy of using wholesalers instead.

A decision as to the amount of control a manufacturer wishes to exercise over his middlemen also has a bearing on the choice of a channel. The less direct the channel of distribution, the more difficult it is to exercise control over channel institutions. The manufacturer might willingly give up some of the cost savings typically associated with an indirect channel in order to gain a larger measure of control over retailers.

Space is not available to discuss all decisions concerning distribution policy which the marketing manager might be called upon to make. Instead, we shall concentrate attention on the more basic channel policy decisions. Specifically, we shall discuss the issues of directness and selectivity as outlined above. We shall also bring in issues of selection of specific types of middlemen and determination of the appropriate degree of control. These various issues are interrelated, but for clarity of presentation they will be treated separately.

Degree of directness

The degree of directness which can appropriately be used in a channel of distribution is influenced by many specific factors. For purposes of simplicity we shall organize these specific considerations under the major headings of (1) nature of the product or product line, (2) characteristics of the market, (3) nature and availability of middlemen, and (4) characteristics of the manufacturer. Where possible the relationship of these major considerations to sales volume, costs of distribution, and profit contribution will be traced. Obviously, the aim of the executive is to select the degree of directness of distribution which will produce the maximum contribution to profits for the firm. In our thinking we should also avoid the temptation to identify the "ideal" channel for a particular product. Instead, we should focus our attention upon the realities of the environment in which the manufacturer operates and recognize the importance of working out a decision which it will be feasible for the firm to execute.

Nature of the product

The selling effort required to maximize sales volume depends upon the nature of the product and the needs of the prospective buyer. Technical complexity in a product, for example, increases the amount of skill and knowledge necessary on the part of the salesman as compared to what would be required in the sale of a simple, standardized item. Likewise, prospects are likely to devote more time and attention to the purchase of an item of high unit value than would be true where the product is not regarded as an important purchase. Executives considering the purchase of an electronic computer, for example, might be expected to devote considerable attention to this matter. Considerable knowledge and skill would also be required on the part of the salesman to explain the benefits of owning such equipment and to point out the merits of his own particular brand as compared with alternative makes. Both the importance of the purchase and the technical complexity of the computer would require a considerable amount of high-caliber selling effort on the part of the salesman.

In resolving the issue of directness under such circumstances, it is pertinent for the executive to inquire whether the available middlemen have the requisite order of skill and knowledge to sell the product effectively. If it appears that available middlemen would not be likely to furnish the desired selling effort, this factor would then favor direct sale by the manufacturer's own sales force.

The average industrial distributor handles a large number of items and represents a considerable number of manufacturers. His salesmen, accordingly, are not in a position to devote much selling time to the product of an individual firm. Instead, their approach is to take orders for whatever products the industrial user needs. For the same reason, it is likely to be difficult to get industrial distributors to undertake promotional work for a firm's product on their own initiative. If the manufacturer's product needs aggressive sales support to achieve satisfactory sales volume, industrial distributors are not likely to provide it. These considerations help to account for the fact that most complex products tend to be sold directly to industrial users by the manufacturer's own sales force.

The service requirements associated with the product should also be considered in deciding whether to sell directly to the final buyer or distribute through middlemen. Where the buyer requires highly technical service, this requirement tends to favor the use of direct distribution. Middlemen are not likely to have the interest, the training, and the equipment to provide such high-quality service. Such would tend to be the case, for example, for electronic data processing systems. On the other hand, the need for relatively simple but readily available service may favor the use of middlemen. Where ready availability of service close to the user is important, and available middlemen are able and willing to maintain service facilities of the desired quality, then there is an advantage in distributing through them. An example of these conditions is found in the case of manufacturers of relatively simple, standardized, industrial machine tools. One of the factors which might lead such a firm to favor distribution through industrial supply houses is that these middlemen maintain service departments which are available to provide repair service when needed.

Another product characteristic which should be considered in analyzing the issue of directness is the bulk of the item. Handling, transportation, and storage costs tend to be relatively high for bulky products as compared with nonbulky items. The distribution costs which must be covered by the price paid by the ultimate user tends, therefore, to be less if the product is sold directly to the final buyer as compared to the expenses which have to be covered when middlemen are used. Producers of sand and gravel, for example, would find the loading and unloading costs associated with the indirect channel prohibitively high. Consequently, sand and gravel are typically sold by the producer directly to the ultimate buyer. The same reasoning would apply to bulky manufactured products where high storage costs are involved. There is a tendency to use a direct channel to minimize such costs, even though there may be some sacrifice in product availability in the market.

Still other products are perishable in either a style or a physical sense. Style perishability, growing out of fashion changes, places a premium upon the producer maintaining close contact with the ever changing market. Speed in distribution is also essential. Both of these factors tend to favor direct sale by the manufacturer to the retail middleman, as opposed to the use of wholesalers. Products which are physically perishable, such as milk, eggs, and bakery products, require speed in distribution, although refrigeration and cold storage facilities may lengthen the time which may elapse before freshness is lost and spoilage takes place. As a consequence, such products tend to be either distributed directly to the consumer or through specialized middlemen who are geared to the tasks of providing the necessary refrigeration, storage, and rapid transportation facilities.

In analyzing the issue of whether to use middlemen or sell directly to the buyer, it is helpful to consider the unit value and/or the unit sale of the product. Contrast, for example, how this factor might influence the analysis in deciding upon the degree of directness desirable in the distribution of $100 watches and table salt priced at 10 cents per package. In either case it may be assumed that direct sale to retailers would be more costly than distribution through wholesalers. Let us also assume that the sale of fine watches directly to retailers would add $1 to the distribution costs of each watch. This would have a relatively minor effect on the demand for such watches, since an increase of $1 in costs of distribution would add only 1 percent to the final retail price paid by consumers. In contrast, if $1 were added to the distribution costs of each package of table salt, thus raising the price from 10 cents to $1.10, the effect upon demand would be catastrophic.

In addition to unit value of the product, it is necessary to consider the average size of order which may be expected. If the typical order were for ten-case lots of table salt, then the dollar value of the order (price times quantity) might be large enough to absorb the higher costs of direct sale. For some low-unit-value products this is the case. The significance of the unit value of the product in the analysis, therefore, is to provide a floor below which the dollar value of the order cannot fall.

Products have other characteristics which affect the channel selection problem. Those mentioned, however, are sufficient to suggest the importance of product characteristics in resolving the issue of directness in distribution channels. They are the more important characteristics which need to be taken into account in the analysis.

Characteristics of the market

In analyzing the wisdom of direct sale versus the use of middlemen, it is logical to move from a consideration of the product to questions dealing with the influence upon our decision of the size and characteristics of the market. Helpful orientation is achieved by asking what types of prospects might purchase the product, where they are located, how many good prospects exist, and what their buying habits arè. If possible, market research should be used to provide answers to these questions. Research may help determine the size of the potential demand and serve to define market characteristics which will tend to influence the cost of alternative distribution approaches.

Extent of demand. The size of the market for the product is a key factor in determining whether or not it is feasible to sell directly either to retailers or final buyers. If the total demand for the product in each market area is large enough, it may be more profitable to use a direct channel and gain the benefits of more aggressive representation and better control. Since the distribution costs involved in a direct channel tend to be relatively fixed in total, there is a minimum sales volume below which sales should not fall if direct sale is to be advantageous.

Assume, for example, that a manufacturer of complex technical equipment is currently selling to industrial distributors, who receive a discount of 16 percent of the final price to compensate them for their services, and that their total sales amount to $48,125,000. Since the manufacturer believes that his product would benefit from the increased aggressiveness of direct sale, he has worked out some cost estimates for setting up a sales force which would give him approximately equal market coverage, together with cost estimates for establishing the necessary branch warehouses and sales offices required by the new arrangement. Let us also assume that he plans to pay his salesmen on a salary basis and that the total additional costs of the necessary sales force, supervisors, warehouse and office space, order-handling clerks, warehousemen, and shippers would amount to $7,700,000. A large portion of these costs would tend to be fixed in total, regardless of sales volume.

Under these circumstances, the elimination of the industrial distributors would provide the manufacturer with additional income equal to the 16 percent gross margin on the combined sales, or $7,700,000, which these firms now receive. If the proposed plan of selling direct to users is to add to the firm's profits, the market for the product must be large enough so that the sales can be increased to substantially more than the distributors' current sales volume of $48,125,000. At this figure, the industrial distributors' margin of 16 percent, or $7,700,000, is just equal to the additional costs involved in performing the distributors' functions as estimated above. If the market is large enough so that direct sale will increase sales volume to $75 million, the new plan will clearly increase profits. Now the distributors' margins saved would amount to $12 million while the additional costs of direct sale would only be $7,700,000—a gain of $4,300,000. If there is no possibility of expanding sales above their current level, there would be no profit advantage of switching to the more direct method of distribution. Once the costs of direct sale have been estimated, then, analysis of the size of the demand which may be created for the product is an important consideration influencing the line of action to be taken.

Anticipated fluctuations in the demand for the product in the future also have a bearing on the wisdom of direct distribution. In the above case, assume that a recession sets in after three years and that sales of only $25 million are achieved. Since the costs of direct distribution tend to be fixed, they would remain at approximately $7,700,000. Had industrial distributors been handling the product, their discounts would have only amounted to 16 percent of $25 million or $4 million. Accordingly, the firm's profits would suffer to the extent of $3,700,000 as a result of the decision to adopt direct distribution (additional costs $7,700,000 — margin saved of $4,000,000 = deficit of $3,700,000).

Concentration or dispersion of demand. An important factor influencing the cost of distribution is the extent of geographic concentration or dispersion of demand. In the sale of industrial goods, localization of industry tends to produce geographic concentration of prospective buyers for many products. This favors direct sale to the user, since the cost of maintaining a sales force tends to be low in relation to realized sales. If prospects are dispersed widely throughout the entire United States, salesmen will have to travel more extensively to reach them and achieve a similar sales volume. Fewer calls per working day and higher travel expenses would tend to make direct sale less attractive than the use of middlemen even if the size of the average order were the same.

If there is only a limited number of prospects and they may be expected to place large orders, as may be the case with certain industrial goods, this type of concentration of demand would also tend to favor direct sale. Tire manufacturers selling to automobile firms for original installation provide an example of such a situation. In contrast, the demand for replacement tires by ultimate consumers generally involves relatively small purchases (one to four tires) by buyers located throughout the entire United States. Where the average purchase is small and there are large numbers of prospects scattered throughout a large area, direct sale to consumers is clearly out of the question, and the use of retail middlemen is commonplace. In selling to retailers, the concentration or dispersion of demand is still an important consideration. Because tires should be available in each community where motorists live, sale through a relatively large number of retail outlets is desirable. Costs of direct sale to independent retailers tend to be high under these conditions, and if the average size of order is small, circumstances favor the use of wholesalers. Petroleum companies maintaining their own service station outlets, however, are in a position to place relatively large orders. The possibility of securing large orders from the operators of service station chains, together with the limited number of sales calls involved in securing such business, tends to favor direct sale to such customers.

Buying patterns. Not only are the total yearly requirements of the final buyer or the retailer middleman important in determining directness, but also the frequency of purchase, the regularity with which orders are placed, and thus the average size of order which may be anticipated. If buyers anticipate their needs for a product, buy in substantial quantities, and carry an inventory from which their recurring needs can be met, such behavior may result in an average size of order large enough to favor direct distribution. (In effect, demand is concentrated.) On the other hand if they prefer to follow a hand-to-mouth buying policy, maintain small inventories, and expect quick deliveries, then the average size of order will be substantially smaller and the costs of distribution higher, thus making direct distribution less feasible.

To take an extreme illustration, if consumers anticipated their requirements for cigarettes for ten years in advance and, being heavy smokers, purchased a carload quantity of cigarettes at one time, it would be economically feasible for the manufacturer to sell directly to consumers. If, instead, consumers wished to purchase one package of cigarettes per day throughout the ten-year period, the costs of selling directly to them would be prohibitive as compared to the small average size of purchase. When consumers purchase in this latter manner, market availability of the product becomes of prime importance. It is then necessary to have small stocks of the product available in many retail outlets scattered widely over the market so that consumers can follow their established purchase patterns with the minimum of inconvenience and effort.

The extent to which purchase of a product can be postponed determines the need for stocks located near to consumers and thus has an important bearing on the costs of direct distribution. Consumers can postpone the purchase of a new automobile for a period of time, but they cannot defer the purchase of gasoline if they use their car to commute back and forth to work each day. Automobiles would thus require a lower degree of availability in each market area than gasoline, and fewer retail outlets would be required to serve consumer needs for cars than for motor fuel. A smaller number of automobile dealers per market area than service stations tends to make it less costly to reach them through direct sale than to distribute to gasoline dealers in this way. The need for availability, therefore, is an important consideration in determining the number of retail outlets required to service a market adequately and thus influences the cost of direct distribution as opposed to the use of middlemen.

Other aspects of consumer buying behavior may also influence the directness which is appropriate in distributing a particular product. In the sale of industrial goods, for example, prospective buyers may prefer to purchase directly from the manufacturer rather than through middlemen. If the costs of serving them are reasonable when compared with the size of orders they may be expected to place, their preferences might well be controlling. Again, if consumers place heavy emphasis on price and are willing to accept less service in order to achieve such savings, an indirect channel tends to have an advantage. Consider, for example, the distribution of milk. Household delivery is convenient, involves a minimum of effort on the part of the housewife, and offers the advantage of weekly or monthly payment of bills. Distribution of milk through supermarkets tends to be lower in cost, however, because it is sold under conditions of self-service, cash and carry. If the housewife's family consumes enough milk each week so that she is anxious to buy as economically as possible, she may tend to buy her dairy supplies in the supermarket. Where a milk producer believes that a substantial segment of his potential market is price conscious, therefore, he may wish to reach these prospects through retail supermarket channels.

Characteristics of the manufacturer

Two companies with similar products appealing to the same market may reach different decisions as to the use of a direct versus an indirect channel of distribution. This does not mean that if one firm is correct in its decision, the other must necessarily be wrong. Instead, manufacturers themselves may differ in important respects which have a bearing on the channel selection problem.

Size and resources. One of these differences is the size and financial resources of the manufacturer. Assume, for example, that a firm has developed an improved food product which requires widespread availability in grocery outlets throughout the United States if sales are to be maximized. While the product is superior, it needs to be promoted aggressively to consumers through advertising and to grocery stores through personal selling in order to get them to add it to their stocks. Under these circumstances, direct sale to chain stores, supermarkets, and independent stores would achieve the desired exposure to purchase. A new firm, with limited financial resources, however, would find it prohibitive to organize and train the necessary sales force for direct sale to retailers, set up branch warehouses, purchase a fleet of trucks for delivery of merchandise, undertake necessary advertising and promotion to create consumer demand, and do the other things required to achieve a profitable level of sales. Instead, such an organization might find it necessary to rely primarily upon wholesalers to sell its new product to retailers because of the smaller financial resources required in using this channel. It might restrict its introductory effort to one market initially because of its limited budget, utilize local advertising to stimulate consumer demand for the product, and offer free-deal inducements to wholesalers and retailers to get them to stock the product. Later the same method might be applied in other areas, opening up only as many markets at any one time as resources permit. Such an approach might well require several years before national distribution could be secured.

In contrast, a large, well-financed manufacturer distributing an established line through wholesalers would have been in a position to provide the sales force necessary to sell the product directly to retail stores throughout the entire market area during the introductory period, undertake extensive consumer advertising, and perform other tasks essential to securing national distribution of the new product within the desired time period. Even though two or three years of effort might be required before a breakeven volume was achieved, the large firm could afford to make the necessary investment, but the limited finances of the small firm would probably make it impossible for it to wait that long for the ultimate payoff.

Width of product line. The choice between a direct and indirect channel is influenced by the width of the product line which the manufacturer is already marketing to the target market. The broader the line of products a manufacturer is selling to a given market, the higher the average order which salesmen can secure, and therefore, the more feasible the use of a direct distribution channel. As the manufacturer broadens his line of products, he takes on more and more the characteristics of a wholesaler in that he can spread distribution costs over a greater array of products and thus lower distribution costs per unit. In contrast, manufacturers of narrow product lines may find it difficult to secure an average size of order which will cover the costs of direct sale. For them, indirect distribution channels may be more feasible.

Stage of development. It is also clear that the stage of a company's development is a factor which has a bearing on the issue of directness. An unknown company introducing a new product may have to be very aggressive in order to establish a foothold in the market. Direct sale to final buyers in the industrial field, or to retail middlemen in the consumer market, offers greater aggressiveness in the introduction of the new product than the use of less direct channels. Whether the firm can utilize the direct channel depends, of course, upon the anticipated sales volume which might be achieved in relation to the estimated costs of the more direct approach. The character of the product, whether the market is concentrated or dispersed, and the size of the potential average order, among other factors mentioned above, must be weighed along with the need for aggressiveness. A firm with a line of well-established products is in a position to accept the lower level of aggressiveness of indirect channels in the sale of its line. In this case, the new product will benefit from the reputation of the remainder of the line, especially if a family brand is used.

Experience of executives. A direct channel is, in a sense, a "do-it-yourself" project. Successful use of this approach requires that company executives have the know-how and experience to deal with the various problems that may be encountered. Executives lacking such background may regard this as a good reason for selling through middlemen. In this manner they may be able to take advantage of the marketing experience and customer contacts which the middlemen possess.

Nature and availability of middlemen

In analyzing the issue of directness, it is clear from earlier discussion that an important consideration is the nature of the middlemen who are available to perform the necessary distribution functions. In this analysis, one side of the coin is the definition of the distribution tasks which must be performed, and this we approached through an analysis of the characteristics of the product, the market, and the manufacturer. The opposite side of the coin is to ask what types of middlemen might the firm seek to perform these tasks and whether these types of organizations are likely to function as effectively as the manufacturer's own direct-selling organization might be able to do. How aggressively is the selling function likely to be performed by the middleman and would this degree of support make a substantial amount of difference in the sales volume which might result? Where do prospective buyers customarily purchase the product, and are middlemen likely to conform better to these buying habits than our own direct-sales organization? How important is widespread availability of our product and can we achieve the desired coverage more economically through middlemen than through direct sale? Is the contribution to profits likely to be larger if the firm distributes through middlemen than through its own marketing organization? Answers to such questions involve a thorough understanding of the nature of the middlemen who serve the industry.[1]

Although the foregoing analysis may indicate that indirect channels including certain types of middlemen should ideally be used, it may not be possible to get these firms to order the product. This difficulty is commonly faced by the manufacturers of new products and may force a more direct channel than theoretically desirable. The producer of a new type of deodorant, for example, did not attempt to get distribution through drug wholesalers and retailers originally, although this would have been a desirable channel. Instead, the sales manager of this company decided to try to get initial distribution by selling directly to Chicago department stores. Although he offered to pay for advertisements over the retailers' names if they would place an initial order for a specific quantity, he was rebuffed by several cosmetic buyers before he finally secured initial orders from three department stores. When advertising produced an unusual sales response, the sales manager was able to use this experience to help him get distribution through department stores in other cities. Only after the product had proved to be profitable in department stores was the firm able to get distribution through drug wholesalers and retailers.[2]

Another situation is illustrated by a small manufacturer of industrial casters located in Michigan who had built up a sales volume of about $300,000 through direct sale to automobile companies. As a means of trying to increase sales throughout all industrial areas in the United States, the president of the company explored the possibility of distributing through materials-handling equipment distributors. He found, however, that most of the good distributors in the areas he wished to reach

---

[1] Brief mention of the characteristics of different types of middlemen has been made in the previous chapter. Further background may be secured in references such as C. F. Phillips and D. J. Duncan, *Marketing: Principles and Methods* (6th ed.; Homewood, Ill.: Richard D. Irwin, Inc., 1968), Parts III and IV; R. S. Alexander, J. S. Cross, and R. M. Hill, *Industrial Marketing* (3d ed.; Homewood, Ill.: Richard D. Irwin, Inc., 1967), chap. 7.

[2] Adapted from N. H. Borden and M. V. Marshall, *Advertising Management*, rev. ed. (Homewood, Ill.: Richard D. Irwin, Inc., 1959), pp. 498–519.

had long since been retained by the firm's older competitors. He was of the opinion that it would be difficult to get distributors through advertising, and his firm lacked the resources to finance the hiring of a sales force adequate to do the job. The possibility of developing a channel through distributors was therefore limited.[3]

These examples indicate that the new company, or the firm considering new channels, will generally find that preferred types of outlets are already handling competing products. Such middlemen tend to be reluctant to add another brand to the variety they now offer unless the prospective dollar gross margin is sufficient to outweigh increased inventory and other costs of adding the line. The problem of overcoming the reluctance of middlemen to stock new brands may be solved if the firm has developed an attractive product and has the resources to work out an effective strategy for getting distribution. The difficulty of getting middlemen to accept a new brand should not be underestimated, however, in the process of arriving at a decision on whether to use direct or indirect channels.

Selectivity in channel selection

A basic policy decision concerns the number of outlets at each of the several levels in the distribution structure that the manufacturer will strive to obtain in the marketing of his product. A sound decision on this issue is important, since both cost and effectiveness in distribution can be vitally affected by the action taken. A policy of attempting to gain distribution through any and all outlets of good credit risk willing to carry a product is referred to as intensive distribution. When a firm follows the policy of limiting the sale of the product to chosen middlemen who meet certain criteria, it is using selective distribution. If this policy of restricting distribution is carried to the extreme of selling the product through only one reseller in a given geographic area, the policy is commonly referred to as exclusive agency distribution. This section is concerned with the number of resellers through which the firm distributes: wholesale distributors, if they are used, and retail dealers.

Illustrations of the above policies

Intensive distribution. While the goal of intensive distribution is sale through all of the chosen types of middlemen with good credit

---

[3] Adapted from *Midwest Precision Co.*, Michigan Business Case No. 32, written by L. B. Milliken and Peter Repenning, Research Assistants, Bureau of Business Research, The University of Michigan.

standing who will stock and sell the product, actually the density of distribution attained will vary among companies and products. One study indicated, for example, that 12 firms producing toothpaste secured retail coverage of from 71 to 98 percent of the drugstores, while 7 firms producing tooth powder had retail coverage of from 51 to 97 percent of the stores surveyed.[4] While these firms aimed at intensive distribution, they had achieved varying degrees of success in executing their policy.

Selective distribution. At the point where a firm decides that it is advisable to restrict distribution to chosen retailers according to specified criteria, then a selective distribution policy is being followed. The degree of restriction will tend to be a compromise between the desire to have the product on sale wherever prospective buyers might expect to look for it and the desirability of limiting the number of middlemen in each market area as a means of encouraging desired reseller sales support, adequate inventories, and suitable service facilities (if needed), among others. The number of outlets per market area resulting from a policy of selective distribution commonly varies depending upon the size of the area, the total number of outlets serving it, and the share of market the firm has in mind as a goal. One manufacturer of automobile tires, for example, reported that on the average the firm had 5 retailers in cities of 100,000; 12 retailers in cities of 1 million; 25 in Chicago; and 35 in New York City. Likewise, on the average a manufacturer of shoes had 2 retailers in cities of 10,000; 25 retailers in cities of 100,000; 150 retailers in cities of 1 million; 300 in Chicago; and 700 in New York City. The extent to which representative firms restricted distribution is indicated by dividing the number of dealers used in New York City by the number commonly selling the product as reported in the census. The percentage of possible outlets used by companies varied as follows: automobile tires 0.7 percent, mechanical refrigerators 3.9 percent, men's suits 5.5 percent, shoes 6.4 percent, radios 10.4 percent, and ladies' silk hosiery 14.2 percent.[5]

Theoretically, the percentage of outlets used could be much larger, and still constitute selective distribution, as long as the firm selects less than the total potential number which might be available. Competition among sellers for distribution, together with the desire of resellers to limit the number of competing brands carried, tends to reduce the percentage of outlets which will sell a given brand in a particular market to a figure considerably less than the total number of outlets in that area stocking the type of product under consideration. It is conceivable, however, that a policy involving only a limited degree of restriction

[4] J. D. Scott, *Advertising Programs for Products with Selected Distribution* (Business Research Studies No. 26 [Boston, Bureau of Business Research, Graduate School of Business Administration, Harvard University]), p. 5.

[5] Ibid., p. 13.

on the part of one manufacturer might approximate the degree of coverage secured by another who aims at intensive distribution but experiences difficulty in getting retailers to stock his product.

Exclusive agency. Although exclusive agency distribution might be regarded as simply an extreme policy of selectivity, common practice is to distinguish between them. An exclusive agency restricts the sale of the manufacturer's brand to one reseller within a specified market area. When more than one reseller is used per market area, but the number of outlets is restricted as a matter of policy, then selective distribution is being practiced.

Even under an exclusive agency policy there is some opportunity for variations in the extent to which distribution is restricted. One source of difference is the size of the geographic area within which the reseller has exclusive sales rights. The area may be relatively small, such as a community of 5,000 population, or it may include a market as large as the metropolitan New York City trading area. An illustration of a highly restrictive policy of exclusive agency distribution is a manufacturer of high-grade pianos which appointed only one retail outlet within a community and its trading area. Even in markets the size of Chicago and New York City, the brand was sold through only one retailer. In international trade, also, the exclusive territory of a reseller sometimes consists of an entire country, or possibly even a group of countries.

An important feature of the exclusive agency agreement is the designation of the brand to which exclusive selling rights apply. Some manufacturers may find that an exclusive agency policy tends to limit sales unduly in large-city markets but may be reluctant to modify the arrangement because of the strong preference of dealers for it. One way of achieving a more satisfactory share of market in a large city is to add a second or a third brand to the line and appoint a different exclusive outlet for each new brand.

Although the policies of selective and exclusive agency distribution have been discussed separately, they are commonly combined in actual practice as a means of adjusting the degree of product exposure to potential market areas of different sizes. A manufacturer of women's shoes, for example, had only one outlet, on the average, in communities of 10,000 population—an exclusive agency. In cities of 100,000 population, two dealers were usually selected, while in cities of one million population the number of outlets averaged four or five. In Chicago the firm had 20 dealers, and in New York City 30 sold the brand.[6] Thus, the policies of exclusive agency and selected distribution were combined as a means of achieving desired coverage of markets of different sizes.

---

[6] Ibid., p. 11.

Wisdom of restricting distribution

Obviously, policies which restrict distribution limit the market availability of a product. For some products such a limitation may be offset by benefits which justify the policy in terms of contribution to profits. For other items the opposite may be true. Clearly, policies of selected and exclusive agency distribution should, therefore, be adopted only after discriminating analysis. Let us turn, therefore, to a consideration of the merits and limitations of restricted distribution with the goal of coming to a better understanding of the considerations which should be taken into account in making policy decisions.[7]

Benefits of restricted distribution. The more restricted the distribution of a particular product, the more the interest of the middleman comes to parallel the interest of the manufacturer. Restriction of distribution makes the product more valuable to retail and wholesale outlets which sell it. They must share the market with fewer competitors; hence they have greater market opportunity. A policy of restricted distribution, therefore, tends to stimulate resellers to be more aggressive in their selling and promotional efforts than they would be under a policy of intensive distribution. To a varying degree, depending upon the extent to which distribution is restricted, the individual reseller is in a position to reap the benefits of his own aggressive selling effort without benefiting his competitors. In consequence, he is willing to put forth more aggressive efforts than otherwise would be the case.

For what types of products is aggressive selling and promotion by resellers important? Clearly, aggressive sales effort is especially beneficial for mechanical or technical products which require explanation and demonstration. New-model automobiles and household appliances would certainly fall in this category. Where sales resistance must be overcome because the product is an important purchase (high unit price) and is purchased infrequently, aggressiveness by the reseller is required to offset the natural tendency of prospects to procrastinate in making a purchase decision. The task of getting retail dealers to stock and push a new product also requires aggressiveness on the part of the middlemen charged with such an assignment. A beverage wholesaler secured aggressive sales support for a new chocolate drink, for example, by granting exclusive agencies to retail milk distributors.

Then, too, for products such as shoes and paint, retailers are required to make a large investment in order to provide an adequate stock of the manufacturer's product. If the retailer's competitors are selling the

---

[7] Portions of the discussion which follows are adapted from ibid., pp. 14–15.

same brand, the available sales volume may be too small to justify the investment necessary to provide an adequate inventory of the item. The retailer may then carry an inadequate stock with the result that sales will suffer. On the other hand, even though a large investment is required, he will tend to carry an adequate stock of the brand provided distribution is restricted sufficiently to give an adequate return on investment.

For products such as household appliances, where manufacturers often produce a complete line of items, the market protection they receive through restricted distribution would also tend to encourage resellers to carry the full line of products, including the less desirable along with the more desirable items.

There are other products, usually mechanical in nature, that require repair and maintenance service if they are to operate satisfactorily. Color television sets, automatic washers and dryers, and automobiles are good examples. To maintain a properly equipped service department with adequately trained personnel, however, involves the reseller in considerable expense. If the manufacturer sells his products through as many dealers in a given community as will stock the item, and still expects them to provide the necessary service facilities, the result is almost certain to be an inferior grade of service or no service at all. By restricting distribution, the manufacturer makes it worthwhile for the dealer to provide the desired quality of service.

Consideration must be given to the size of the market area required to provide resellers with a profitable sales volume. The characteristics of expensiveness, high unit price, incidence of the need (or desire) for the product among consumers, and infrequent purchase tend to limit the potential sales volume for certain products to a relatively small amount per 1,000 population. Such products as high-grade silk hosiery and pianos are good examples. Where the potential market is thin per 1,000 population, the policy of intensive distribution tends to make the line unprofitable for the dealer. In contrast, properly administered policies of selected or exclusive agency distribution tend to make the line profitable and serve to develop a more enthusiastic, successful and cooperative dealer organization than would otherwise be possible.

For this reason, retailers selling high-grade men's suits and high-grade men's hats prefer exclusive agencies if they are to handle a given manufacturer's line. Because of this a policy of restricted distribution helps a firm build up a strong dealer organization.

A number of the products cited above might be classified as either specialty goods or shopping goods. The benefits of restricted distribution are not necessarily limited to these classes of merchandise, however. This is illustrated by the example of a manufacturer who was following a policy of intensive distribution and was selling to about 90 percent of all the retail stores in the country handling his type of merchandise.[8] Many of the customers were small stores, and many of the orders were ridiculously small. Yet the firm's salesmen called upon these stores on an average of once a week. A study was made of the cost of serving customers in two of the firm's branches. It was found that two thirds of the company's orders and almost half of its accounts were costing more in marketing expense than they were worth in terms of gross profit. As a result the firm increased the size of the minimum order sixfold and drastically reduced the number of contacts the salesmen had to make. Unprofitable customers were dropped. Sales increased 82 percent, marketing expenses were reduced from 31.8 to 18.2 percent, and operating profit rose from 4.7 to 14.8 percent. Wherever the potential volume of business to be secured from resellers during a given time period varies widely, it is desirable to analyze the contribution to profits made by customers of different sizes and then ask whether a policy of selective selling (restricted distribution) might not be desirable.

A policy of restricted distribution may help a manufacturer deal with the problem of predatory price cutting at the retail level. When the aim is intensive distribution, competition between a number of retailers in the same community may tend to result in price cutting which makes the brand unprofitable for the retailers who handle it, with the result that desirable types of retailers refuse to stock the item. The manufacturer may also feel that price cutting damages the reputation of his brand. The policy of exclusive agency distribution eliminates competition between retailers in the same community and tends to prevent price cutting. A manufacturer of textiles, for example, reported that it was not uncommon for several retailers in a single shopping area to carry the same brand of sheets. In several instances this fact had caused price cutting; a few mills therefore adopted an exclusive agency plan of distribution in order to overcome price cutting.

The above discussion serves to call attention to the fact that the control which a manufacturer exercises over the members of his channel of distribution is based primarily upon achieving cooperation through policies which recognize the reseller's point of view and which appeal to his self-interest. The degree of "control" (or cooperation) which can be exercised by the manufacturer depends upon the value of the franchise to sell his product. If it is a valuable right highly regarded by resellers, the manufacturer is in a favorable position to gain cooperation from them (or exert control over them). Automobile manufacturers, for example, exert a large measure of control over the marketing policies of their retail dealers. This they are able to do because the right to

---

[8] C. H. Sevin, *How Manufacturers Reduce Their Distribution Costs* (Washington, D.C.: U.S. Government Printing Office, 1948), p. 17.

sell a particular brand of automobile can be a very valuable right to the dealer. In contrast, the manufacturer of chewing gum or cigarettes is able to exercise virtually no control over retail outlets handling his product. The policies of intensive distribution which such firms follow mean that the right (or the franchise) to sell an individual brand of such products tends to be of very limited value to the individual retailer. Restricted distribution, if it is consistent with consumer buying habits, is a means of increasing the value to middlemen of the right to sell a given product. The manufacturer provides this benefit to resellers in his channel of distribution as a means of gaining for himself some or all of the advantages mentioned in the preceding paragraphs.

Limitations of restricted distribution. In considering the wisdom of restricting the distribution of his product, the manufacturer should count not only the potential benefits he may receive but also the limitations (or "costs") which may result. A key question is: In the light of consumer buying habits, what will be the effect of restricted distribution upon sales? If the firm produces convenience goods, the sacrifices involved in gaining the benefits of restricted distribution will be too great. Consumers insist on buying these items with a minimum amount of effort. Consequently, ready availability throughout the market is the single most important factor influencing sales volume. Examples of products in this category are cigarettes, razor blades, staple food products, and candy bars. They tend to be purchased frequently and usually have relatively low unit value. To the extent that restricted distribution reduces market availability, it would make serious inroads on sales. While such products may benefit from favorable point-of-purchase promotion, they generally do not require explanation or demonstration. (An exception might be a distinctive, new product being introduced to consumers for the first time.) Usually the inventory investment required to support satisfactory sales volume is small as compared, say, with women's shoes or men's clothing. Service is generally not required. Except for reducing the distribution costs of reaching dealers, restricted distribution of such products has only limited benefits to offer as a counterbalance to the serious sacrifice involved in limiting exposure to sale.

By way of contrast, the manufacturer of specialty goods is likely to find the benefits of restricted distribution substantial indeed. Such products characteristically have achieved brand preference among consumers, who are willing to make considerable effort to seek out the retail outlet (or outlets) which stock them. Accordingly, the limitation in exposure to sale involved in restricted distribution is of little consequence when compared with the benefits which such a policy can bring in terms of dealer cooperation and support.

Where a substantial proportion of the prospective buyers shop around in the purchase of a product, restricted distribution may likewise offer benefits which considerably outweigh limitations on exposure to sale resulting from the policy. Consumers are willing to make considerable effort to inspect and compare different brands of high-grade women's dresses and furniture, for example, in making their selection. Adequate inventories and aggressive sales promotion encouraged by restricted distribution would be important advantages to be gained.

In addition to buying habits, the preferences of resellers also should be taken into account in reaching a decision on the wisdom of a restricted distribution policy. A strong preference for the exclusive agency arrangement among retailers is an important reason why certain manufacturers of high-grade men's clothing have adopted this policy. Yet some of these firms find that this policy limits product availability so much that large-city markets are not adequately developed.

A policy of restricted distribution creates another difficulty which is not encountered under intensive distribution arrangements. Because the number of outlets appointed per community is limited under a policy of restricted distribution, it is necessary for the manufacturer to make certain that the local source of supply is identified through signs, window displays, and advertising over the retailer's name. Unless this identification is made, the demand created by the manufacturer's general advertising may be dissipated because of the consumers' lack of knowledge of where to go in order to buy the product. Failure to recognize the importance of this problem may result in ineffective advertising. If the difficulty is recognized, of course, appropriate promotional policies and procedures may be developed to correct the deficiency.

Finally, restricted distribution may tend to promote substitution. Dealers who cannot get the agency for a given brand may double their efforts to take business away from that brand by offering substitutes. The seriousness of this problem will depend upon the strength of the brand preference which the manufacturer can create. If information is secured through market research on the degree of brand discrimination which has been created for the product, this knowledge can be taken into account in deciding whether restricted distribution is desirable, and if so, the extent to which the firm should go in limiting the number of outlets per market.

Both the benefits and sacrifices involved in a policy of restricted distribution are illustrated by the experience of the Consumer Products Division of the Magnavox Corporation.[9] This firm markets through a franchised dealer network of 3,000 outlets, which facilitates the maintenance of list prices, service, and advertising standards. An executive of the company, however, admitted that Magnavox is losing "tens of millions of dollars" by making it too difficult for consumers to buy the

---

[9] *Advertising Age*, May 6, 1963, p. 26.

product. "We've got to find other ways of getting product exposure," he said. One way, he said, was the company's current agreement with Singer retail centers to sell Magnavox products. This move secures the patronage of people who don't normally go into the firm's franchised stores. So far, Magnavox dealers are not "up in arms" about this development, he reported.

Still another way to reduce the "cost" of gaining the benefits of restricted distribution is illustrated by an example from the paint business. In order to provide consumers with an adequate range of choice among different types and colors of paint, it is essential that retailers carry a large inventory of the brands they sell. Yet they are reluctant to make the necessary investment unless they are granted the protection from sharing their markets with competitors which restricted distribution provides. Accordingly, exclusive agency distribution is typically used in marketing paints, except in large metropolitan markets, in order to encourage the maintenance of adequate stocks. The buying patterns for paint are such, however, that restricted distribution often involves a substantial sacrifice of sales volume. Although the prospective buyer will make considerable effort in the purchase of paint when he is buying large quantities for a special purpose, he will not do this when he is picking up a very small amount for use in routine household maintenance. Consequently, restricted distribution means reduced availability and lost sales in this segment of the market. In recognition of this problem, certain paint manufacturers sell paint under a number of different brand names and grant "exclusive" distribution rights on each of these brands. In this way each of the retailers is provided with protection from direct competition on the particular brand for which he has a franchise. At the same time, the manufacturer is assured of an adequate number of outlets for his paints and thus is more likely to achieve a desired share of market. While this practice probably limits the value of the franchise on a particular brand to the retailer, some benefits still remain, since consumers may not be aware of the fact that the same firm produces competing brands. Undoubtedly the manufacturer is able to achieve greater dealer cooperation in marketing each of the brands (and thus greater "control") than if he followed a policy of intensive retail distribution.

Legal aspects of restricted distribution

At the present time, there are no legal restraints on the practice of restricted distribution *as such*. The courts have long upheld the right of a seller to choose his customers even when this extends to the practice of choosing to sell to only one customer in a certain market. From time to time, so-called "right-to-buy" laws have been proposed, but they have not been enacted, and there is at present no great prospect that they will be. The intent of these laws is to force a seller to make his product available to any one who wishes to purchase. This would, of course, make impossible the practice of effective restricted distribution.

Certain practices often associated with restricted distribution, particularly with exclusive distribution, are of doubtful legality. The most important and most controversial of these are: (1) exclusive dealing, and (2) territorial protection. Exclusive dealing is the practice of not allowing the dealer to carry competing products. Not all exclusive agency contracts involve exclusive dealing. The manufacturer may agree to sell through no competing dealers in a particular market but still allow the dealer to carry competing products. On the other hand, many manufacturers have sought to restrict the dealers to their own products under exclusive agency contracts.

The major reason why a manufacturer might wish to practice exclusive dealing is to encourage more aggressive selling and promotion on the part of his dealers. The retailer who handles only one brand of a particular type of product has no alternative items to push in competition with it. He must succeed in the sale of this one brand, or he will find his sales of the generic product unsatisfactory. For this reason he is likely to be a more aggressive dealer than if he carried competing brands. He is also likely to be more cooperative in maintaining necessary inventories of the line, in providing repair service of satisfactory quality where necessary, and in maintaining resale prices if the manufacturer requests such action.

Territorial protection clauses in exclusive agency agreements were common practice prior to the late 1940s. The essence of such agreements is that the manufacturer will attempt to prevent the sale of his product by any other party in a territory assigned to an exclusive outlet. The request for such clauses in exclusive agency agreements is likely to come from the dealer rather than from the manufacturer. The dealer wishes to protect himself against direct competition from other retailers who are handling the same brand. Various ways of enforcing such clauses have been utilized. These may involve penalty payments from the dealer who has made a forbidden sale to the dealer whose territory has been invaded. If such violations are continued, they may, of course, lead to cancellation of the franchise of the invading dealer.

Legal status of exclusive dealing

Section 3 of the Clayton Act prohibits exclusive dealing contracts where the effect of such agreement "may be to substantially lessen competition or tend to create a monopoly in any line of commerce." Note that exclusive dealing contracts are not illegal as such, but rather their legality depends upon the effect that they have upon competition.

The bench mark court case involving exclusive dealing was that involving the Standard Oil Company of California, decided in 1949. In this case the Department of Justice had charged that the company, in its exclusive agency contracts, had violated both Section 1 of the Sherman Act and Section 3 of the Clayton Act. The specific complaint was that the company's practice of entering into agreements with its 6,000 plus dealers for exclusive handling of its petroleum products and automotive accessories substantially lessened competition and tended to create a monopoly. At that time, this kind of contract was common in the petroleum industry as well as in many other industries. The Standard Oil Company of California then accounted for 23 percent of gasoline sales in the Pacific area; its products were sold through 10 percent of the available independent retail outlets. The stations with which it had exclusive dealing contracts pumped only 6.7 percent of the gasoline in this area. An additional 6.8 percent of gasoline sales in this area was made through stations owned and operated by Standard. The firm attempted to demonstrate that its exclusive dealing contracts did not substantially lessen competition. It cited its small share of the total market, the still smaller share of gasoline sales through outlets with which such contracts had been arranged, and the fact that its share of the market had not increased during the time these contracts were in force.

In spite of this defense, the district court ruled against the Standard Oil Company of California, and its decision was upheld by the U.S. Supreme Court in 1949.[10] The Court made two main points. First, it held that these exclusive dealing contracts violated Section 3 of the Clayton Act because they covered a substantial number of outlets and a substantial volume of sales. When this is true, said the Court, a substantial lessening of competition is a natural result and an actual reduction in competition need not be proved. This is the per se or "quantitative substantiality" doctrine. Second, the Court called attention to the fact that there had been widespread adoption of exclusive dealing contracts by other major competitors in the area with the result that independent producers were foreclosed from distributing through the outlets serving a substantial share of the market in the area. When the exclusive dealing contracts of a particular firm involve a substantial volume of trade and when there is widespread use of such contracts by the firm's competitors, therefore, there is serious danger that such arrangements will be regarded by the courts as a violation of Section 3 of the Clayton Act.

Under different conditions, however, a manufacturer may make use of exclusive dealing contracts without violating Section 3 of the Clayton

---

[10] *Standard Oil Co. of California* v. *U.S.*, 337 U.S. 293 (1949).

Act. The J. I. Case Company, for example, followed a policy of exclusive dealing in the distribution of its farm implements. The firm made a serious effort to get dealers who would carry the full line and devote the major part of their activity to Case implements where the market in the area justified it. The handling of two full lines (Case plus a competing brand) was consistently discouraged. Dealers handling competitive lines to the detriment of Case were dropped. These practices led the firm to be charged with a violation of section 3 of the Clayton Act. In a 1951 ruling, however, the district court found the evidence insufficient to establish an adverse effect upon competition.[11] During the trial no evidence was presented from any farm implement manufacturer that his outlets had been restricted by Case's policy and, further, there was no indication that available outlets had been narrowed in any way thereby. Because of the nature of the market, strategic location for dealers in farm machinery was not essential. Apparently, competitors had found no difficulty in obtaining dealers. There was an adequate number of full-line and short-line manufacturers represented in most markets in agricultural areas.

As pointed out in a 1961 Supreme Court decision Section 3 of the Clayton Act was not intended to reach every remote lessening of competition—only those that were substantial—but earlier Court decisions had not drawn a line to indicate where "remote" ends and "substantial" begins. The case involved was that of the Tampa Electric Company, where the district court had ruled that an exclusive contract violated Section 3 of the Clayton Act, but where the Supreme Court reversed the judgment.[12] In reviewing this case, the Court indicated that an exclusive dealing arrangement does not violate Section 3 unless the Court believes it probable that execution of the policy will foreclose competition to a substantial extent. In determining the probable effect upon competition, the Court outlined the following considerations which must be taken into account: (1) the line of commerce—i.e. type of goods; (2) the geographic area of affected competition; and (3) whether the competition foreclosed constitutes a substantial share of the affected market (relative strength of the competing firms and the percentage of the total volume of business involved). Applying these guidelines, the Court reasoned that the exclusive dealing contract in this instance did not foreclose competitors from a substantial share of the business in the relevant market area. In effect this approach applies the "rule of reason" in evaluating the effects of exclusive dealing contracts. The central issue is the ease with which rival suppliers can secure access to customers in alternative ways.

---

[11] *U.S.* v. *J. I. Case Company*, 101 F. Supp. 856 (1951).

[12] *Tampa Electric Co.* v. *Nashville Coal Co.*, 365 U.S. 320, 327–29 (1961).

It should be borne in mind, however, that Section 5 of the Federal Trade Commission Act has also been used by the Commission in attacking exclusive dealing contracts. Here the approach has been to charge that such contracts may constitute an unfair method of competition which may substantially lessen competition. In the *Brown Shoe Company* case, for example, retailers who promised not to sell shoes made by competitors received a combination of benefits ranging from architectural plans and display materials to sales training and group rate insurance. The FTC issued a complaint against this exclusive dealing arrangement on the grounds that it denied Brown's competitors the opportunity of selling to a substantial number of dealers. Brown argued that dealers were not coerced to join the plan, the FTC hadn't shown any harmful effect upon competition, only 650 out of 6,000 dealers participated, and these outlets bought only 75 percent of their shoe stocks from Brown. The Appeals Court set aside the FTC decision on the grounds that the Commission had failed to prove the system an "unfair method of competition."

In 1966, however, the Supreme Court reversed this ruling in an opinion written by Justice Black.[13] If the attack had been brought under the Sherman or Clayton Acts, Justice Black said, such injury to competitors would have had to be proved. But, he added, the purpose of the FTC Act was to stop unfair competitive practices before they become monopolistic. This case shows beyond doubt, he wrote, that Brown, the country's second largest manufacturer of shoes, has a program which requires shoe retailers substantially to limit their trade with Brown's competitors. This obviously conflicts with the central policy of both the Sherman Act and the Clayton Act. In rejecting the argument that the Commission need prove injury to competition, Justice Black said that the Commission has power under the FTC Act to arrest trade restraints "in their incipiency" without proof they amount to an outright violation of the other provisions of the antitrust laws.

While the decision does not mean that all exclusive dealing systems are illegal, it does suggest that large companies are especially susceptible to attack if the plan is used to help the firm gain a more dominant position in the industry. The ability to challenge potential restraints of trade in their incipiency tends to make such plans more vulnerable to attack than in the past.

Legal status of territorial protection

In addition to the questions raised concerning exclusive dealing, the legality of other aspects of exclusive agency arrangements are very much

---

[13] *Wall Street Journal*, June 7, 1966.

in doubt. In granting an exclusive agency to a dealer, the manufacturer agrees to limit his distribution in a specified geographic area to this outlet. In effect, this protects the dealer against neighboring retailers who might otherwise be competitors. In return for this protection, the manufacturer hopes to gain better cooperation from the dealer in maintaining inventories, giving service, and providing aggressive promotional support for his brand. The granting of exclusive distributorships in a specified territory is not covered by Section 3 of the Clayton Act as long as there is absence of restrictions on the sale of competitive products. Indeed, certain consent decrees have permitted such firms as the Wurlitzer Company and Philco to designate geographic areas as areas of primary responsibility for specific distributors.[14]

The manufacturer may, however, go one step further and require his dealers to confine their sales activities to a described geographic territory—that is, prohibit them from invading the territories of other exclusive agents handling the firm's brand. While such territorial security clauses have never specifically been ruled illegal in a higher court of law, much has occurred to raise serious doubt as to their legality. In 1949, for example, General Motors consented to the entry of a judgment which restrained the firm from incorporating in any contract a provision excluding dealers from any designated territory.[15] Later, all automobile manufacturers dropped the so called "territorial security and antibootlegging" clauses from their dealer contracts. Philco Corporation also signed a cease and desist order of the FTC which prohibited such clauses in dealer contracts.[16]

Even though the territorial security provisions tend to be suspect, in a 1963 decision on the *White Motor Company* case the Supreme Court refused to support a district court decision declaring vertical territorial limitations illegal per se.[17] The White Motor Company allocated exclusive territories to distributors but reserved government, fleet, and large national accounts to itself—a vertical territorial limitation. In presenting the case in the district court, the Justice Department had merely presented evidence establishing the company's use of exclusive territories and the accompanying vertical territorial limitations, without attempting to prove that these practices unlawfully restrict competition. Accordingly, the district court handed down a summary judgment without full trial. The Supreme Court held that whether vertical territorial limitations violated antitrust laws could not be determined on motion by summary judgment in the absence of evidence which would enable

---

[14] *U.S.* v. *Wurlitzer Co.*, D.C., New York (1958); *U.S.* v. *Philco*, D.C., Penn. (1956).

[15] "G.M. Precaution," *Business Week*, Oct. 1, 1949, p. 52.

[16] *U.S.* v. *Philco Corp.*, D.C., Penn. (1956).

[17] *The White Motor Co.* v. *U.S.*, 83 Sup. Ct. 696 (1963).

the Court to determine whether the arrangement had the effect of stifling competition or had some redeeming virtue. The Court explained it was reluctant to declare vertical territorial arrangements illegal per se because this was the first case involving such a restriction in vertical arrangements and too little was known about the "economic and business stuff" out of which such an arrangement emerged.

The Justice Department is reported to have interpreted this decision as a mandate to bring up more cases and to try them more exhaustively. Federal judges, on the other hand, have accepted the companies' argument that competition is sometimes best served by letting companies contain the struggle for business among their own distributors in order to concentrate on "the real enemy"—i.e. their competitors.[18]

One of these cases involved a charge by the Justice Department that the General Motors Corporation and three associations of automobile dealers violated the Sherman Act by participating in an alleged conspiracy to discourage dealers from selling to auto discounters. This case grew out of the action of some Los Angeles Chevrolet dealers who, in the late 1950s, began to sell cars through discount houses and "referral services" at bargain prices.[19] Of the 100,000 Chevrolets sold in the Los Angeles area in 1960, about 2,000 were sold through discounters. About a dozen of the 85 dealers in Los Angeles were furnishing cars to discounters in that year. As the volume of discount sales grew, nonparticipating dealers began to feel the pinch. The problem was discussed at a meeting of one of the dealer associations; then General Motors took action to deal with the matter. GM notified the offending dealers that sales to discounters violated the provision in their franchise contracts fixing dealership's locations and got them to promise not to do business with discounters in the future. Later, a private investigator was hired to police this agreement. By the spring of 1961, the campaign to eliminate discounters from the sale of Chevrolets was a success. In mid-1962, the Justice Department brought a civil antitrust suit in the U.S. District Court for the Southern District of California to enjoin GM and its dealers from conspiring to prevent discount selling of Chevrolets. The district court ruled in favor of General Motors, but the case was appealed directly to the Supreme Court, where the decision was reversed on April 28, 1966.

The defendants had argued that dealers who sold through discounters were violating the "location clause" in their franchise agreements which prohibits them from moving to, or establishing a new or different location, branch sales office, branch service station, or place of business without the prior written approval of Chevrolet. The defendants con-

---

[18] "Is the Franchise System Legal?" *Business Week*, April 3, 1965, p. 66.

[19] *U.S. v. General Motors Corp. et al.*, no. 46, *Supreme Court Reporter*, vol. 86, no. 14 (May 15, 1966), pp. 1321–32 (St. Paul, Minn.: West Publishing Co.).

tended that the described arrangements with discounters constituted the establishment of additional sales outlets in violation of the clause. They also claimed that the location clause was lawful and that GM acted lawfully to prevent its dealers from violating this clause.

In the Supreme Court decision, Mr. Justice Fortas said that it was not necessary to rule on the meaning, effect, or validity of the "location clause." He said:

We have here a classic conspiracy in restraint of trade: joint, collaborative action by dealers, the defendant associations, and General Motors to eliminate a class of competitors by terminating business dealings between them and a minority of Chevrolet dealers and to deprive franchised dealers of their freedom to deal through discounters if they so choose. Against this fact of unlawful combination, the "location clause" is of no avail.

There can be no doubt that the effect of the combination or conspiracy here was to restrain trade and commerce within the meaning of the Sherman Act. Elimination, by joint collaborative action, of discounters from access to the market is a *per se* violation of the Act. . . . Where businessmen concert their actions in order to deprive others of access to merchandise which the latter wish to sell to the public, we need not inquire into the economic motivation underlying their conduct.

He also pointed out that the effect of this combination was a substantial restraint upon price competition—a goal unlawful per se when sought to be effected by combination or conspiracy. He explained that there was evidence that one of the purposes behind the concerted effort to eliminate sales of new Chevrolet cars by discounters was to protect franchised dealers from real or apparent price competition. On the basis of these findings, therefore, the Supreme Court reversed the decision of the district court and remanded the case to this court for the fashioning of appropriate equitable relief.

This case illustrates the importance of the choice of methods used by a manufacturer in attempting to prevent his dealers from selling through discount houses. The Court did not rule on the validity of the "location clause" or whether it may be used to prohibit a dealer from selling through discount houses. Nor did the Court express an opinion as to whether GM could, by unilateral action, enforce the clause without violating the antitrust laws. Had GM acted alone in this matter without involving either dealer associations or individual dealers in its approach, then the decision might possibly have been different. It was the evidence of the existence of a "classic conspiracy" which led directly to the Supreme Court's decision.

It is noteworthy, also, that discount selling of automobiles has thrived only when regular retail car sales were sagging. The impact of the Supreme Court ruling in the GM case may be nominal, therefore, as long as new auto sales through franchised dealers hold at a prosperous level. If sales slack off, however, and inventories begin to pile up, the problem may become acute. Better sales forecasting in periods of changing demand coupled with quick intelligence identifying areas where inventories are beginning to pile up, might enable an alert management to take steps to minimize the problem out of which sales to discount houses tend to grow.

Justification of legal restraints

Any restraints on distribution policies imposed either by legislation or by court interpretation are likely to cause substantial controversy among those parties who have a stake in the distribution of goods. The legislation and court rulings concerning territorial security, the franchise system, and exclusive dealing are no exception. Are such restraints in distribution policies warranted?

Business is, in a sense, like an athletic contest. Various parties compete with each other and vie for attainment of a specified goal. Everyone would agree that ground rules are necessary in an athletic contest. The same is true of business. Rules are necessary and desirable in order to channel the competitive efforts of business along lines which best serve the interest of the entire economy. The real question is not whether rules and regulations are necessary, but rather whether these rules are sound and also whether they are properly administered.

It would seem that the prohibition of territorial security clauses in exclusive franchise agreements is sound and serves a major social purpose, namely, the enhancing of competition. To permit such clauses would give dealers a degree of monopoly in territories in which they are located. This, by serving to remove them from various competitive pressures, might reduce the quality of service which they render to consumers and conceivably could be a factor causing higher prices for consumers. Manufacturers, however, must be realistic if they hope to gain the benefit of aggressive selling by their dealers. To accomplish this objective they must offer the dealer a franchise which has value to him. Appointing too many "exclusive dealers" would be tantamount to a policy of nonexclusive distribution, would give minimum benefits to dealers, and would deny to the manufacturer the benefits he sought when he initially embarked on a policy of exclusive distribution. Recognition of this point should prevent harm to dealers by the absence of territorial security clauses.

Whether it is socially desirable to limit the action a manufacturer may take to prevent his dealers from selling through unauthorized discount outlets is a debatable question. An automobile manufacturer may claim that his dealers are already in vigorous competition with each other in view of the limitations on territorial protection which now exist.

Also, they are certainly competing aggressively with dealers handling other makes of automobiles in the same territory. In addition, legal limitations on action which may be taken to prevent dealers from selling through discount outlets may serve to erode the franchise system, which depends upon the strategic location of dealerships to make sales and service facilities and parts conveniently available to consumers. To permit dealers to sell through discount outlets might negate the manufacturer's attempts to build strong dealers through the use of the exclusive agency system. Moreover, the manufacturer would have no control over the amount and quality of service offered by discounters, who in practice provide little or no service.

On the other hand, we should bear in mind that the prevention of sales through discounters may serve to protect dealers from the keen price competition of outlets capable of operating on a low markup. The spur of meeting such competition might stimulate innovation in the character and methods of operation of automobile dealers which would tend to benefit consumers in the long run. Also, prohibition on sales through discount outlets prevents dealers from exercising their freedom to dispose of surplus inventory at a low markup when they find themselves overstocked because of sudden changes in the rate of consumer buying, miscalculation, or the establishment of unrealistic sales quotas. Finally, choking off automobile sales through discount outlets denies consumers the benefits of low markup discount selling which have been available in the purchase of household appliances, jewelry, and many other types of goods.

On balance, it is probably not wise to impose such strict legal restrictions as to prevent a manufacturer from taking any action to limit sales by his dealers through discount outlets. Both consumers and dealers benefit from the maintenance of a franchise system which makes sales, parts, and service readily available through reputable firms. It might be wise, however, for automobile manufacturers to encourage certain of their dealers to experiment with types of operations which permit low costs of distribution and hence low markups and prices. It may be that certain dealers in large metropolitan areas could specialize on low-cost sales operations at the same time that others in the same area provide necessary parts and service facilities. It is also evident, however, that better market intelligence, sales forecasting by dealer areas, and closer control over physical distribution need to be practiced as a means of preventing the accumulation of excess inventories which tend to encourage dealers to turn to discount outlets for relief.

The legislative and court rulings concerning exclusive dealing have the same laudable objective as those applying to territorial security, i.e. the maintenance of competition. However, a good case can be made for the fact that they have not served this objective very well. The per se doctrine does not clearly recognize the effect upon competition of exclusive dealing practices. The mere fact that a substantial volume of trade is involved is not the equivalent of a substantial lessening of competition by any stretch of the imagination. Indeed, exclusive dealing contracts could serve to enhance the degree of rivalry practiced by the dealer who must devote all his effort to the sale of one brand of a particular product because he has no others to distract his attention. This gives him the same stake in the sale of the manufacturer's product within his territory as the manufacturer himself has.

Yet when the firm practicing exclusive dealing is a large manufacturer, and other leading competitors also follow the same policy, the result may be to foreclose a substantial segment of the retail outlets from use by smaller firms seeking distribution for their products in that market. Under these circumstances, such potential competitors might be injured by the exclusive dealing policies of dominant firms in the industry. Whether competition within the industry suffers, however, depends upon how vigorous the established firms are in vying with each other for market position and whether smaller firms can develop a strategy which will enable them to develop a profitable business in spite of the limitations imposed by exclusive dealing practices of leading companies.

If conditions prevail which are similar to the situation in the farm implement industry, where competing manufacturers were not foreclosed from reasonable access to retail outlets in markets where they wished to distribute, then it would seem that exclusive dealing might be as likely to increase competition as to reduce it. The difficulty faced by the courts, of course, is to draw the line between situations where exclusive dealing may tend to produce a substantial lessening of competition and those where a reduction in competition is relatively remote. Certainly, it is socially desirable that the Justice Department and the courts exercise discrimination in analyzing the exclusive dealing arrangements as practiced by different companies in different industries. It is to be hoped that the "rule of reason" will be applied to the end that the policy may be used where it is likely to bring about a favorable effect upon competition and discouraged where it may tend to have a substantially unfavorable influence upon competitive activity.

Conclusion

Distribution policy decisions are among the most basic and important decisions the marketing executive must make in planning his marketing strategy. He must decide whether to sell direct to the final buyer or through middlemen. If an indirect channel is decided upon, he must select the types of middlemen to use, determine the desirable degree of selectivity to employ, and establish methods of control over channel institutions. These decisions in turn, will profoundly affect physical distribution requirements, promotional strategy, and pricing strategy. The influence of distribution policy decisions on other aspects of marketing strategy will be seen in subsequent chapters.

Questions

1. Under some circumstances, after-sale service requirements cause a manufacturer to employ a direct channel of distribution; under other circumstances, service requirements cause an indirect channel to be employed. What circumstances surrounding service push a manufacturer in each of these directions?

2. Approximately 37 percent of machine tools are sold directly to industrial users, while 45 percent are sold to the industrial market through manufacturer's agents. The remainder is sold through industrial supply houses. *Why* are some machine tools sold directly to users, while others go through manufacturer's agents and industrial supply houses?

3. The H. J. Heinz Company and Standard Brands, Inc., both broad-line manufacturers of grocery products, previously sold direct to small independent grocery stores. In the past ten years both have switched to selling through grocery wholesalers. What sort of changes in the situation surrounding the sale of grocery products probably explain this change in distribution channels?

4. Some manufacturers in an industry may utilize an indirect channel of distribution, whereas other companies in the same industry may elect to sell through a direct channel. What might explain this difference in choice?

5. Distinguish between intensive, selective, and exclusive agency distribution.

6. Manufacturers of major brands of household appliances usually follow a policy of selected retail distribution. What is the explanation for this choice?

7. As products move through their life cycles from the innovation stage to maturity, their distribution often becomes less selective. What explains this?

8. The Ahso Radio Corporation of Japan has made a decision to export its line of transistor-operated portable color television sets to the United States. The company enjoys an excellent reputation in Japan but is largely unknown elsewhere. The product line includes three models, and each contains the basic feature of remarkably clear reception on an 8-inch screen, with power coming solely from a rechargeable battery. Under most conditions a built-in "rabbit ears" antenna is sufficient for effective operation. Model A, featuring the basic set in a simple metal

case, will sell at $199.95. Models B and C contain certain additional features, such as deluxe cases, with more convenient controls and will sell for $229.95 and $269.95 respectively. Each set weighs 23 pounds and can be carried easily. Competition is confined to the newly introduced Fuji portable set, also a Japanese import, and several models made by American firms. The American products were judged by management to be less convenient to use and poorer in reception, with the result that sales success has been disappointing.

The firm is undecided concerning the distribution scheme to be used in the American market; but management feels that exclusive retailers should be employed. Evaluate the tentative plan for exclusive distribution. What recommendation would you make to management?

9. A large manufacturer of low-priced ($9.95–$29.95) transistorized radios secured his distribution through approximately 100 wholesalers and 20,000 nonexclusive retail outlets. Most retail dealers sold radio lines of a number of well-known competitors whose radios were in the same price range. The question arose as to whether the company should continue the present distribution policy or adopt a selected-dealer distribution in which a limited number of dealers in each community would be given franchises and special consideration and help. For example, in the city of Chicago the company proposed to reduce the number of retail outlets from 450 to 100 selective, semiexclusive accounts. It was asserted that franchises would thus become more valuable immediately and cause dealers to exert greater willingness to promote the line through an extensive use of displays and campaigns. The distribution would be placed in the hands of larger, well-known dealers and removed from the weaker, smaller outlets. Some executives contended that the proposed reduction in number of outlets might seriously jeopardize the company's competitive position, since it was difficult to forecast the probable effect on sales volume.

What should be done? Why?

10. Distinguish between exclusive agency distribution and the practice of exclusive dealing. Is one ever found without the other?

11. Discuss the effect of exclusive dealing on competition. Under what circumstances might it reduce competition? Might it sometimes serve to increase competition?

12. Do territorial protection clauses in franchise agreements tend to reduce competition? Explain.

10

Physical distribution

THE PRECEDING chapters have discussed the structure of distribution as well as those policy decisions made by management in developing paths through the structure to reach the market. These decisions dealt with the type and number of resellers to be used, the extent of promotional effort to be expended by these intermediaries, and whether or not some portion of the output of the firm was to be sold directly to end users.

After channel-of-distribution strategy has been determined and policies established for its implementation, management must consider a closely related set of questions dealing with the physical distribution of goods. Such questions include, among others, the location of fixed facilities, the size of inventories to be held in these facilities, and the modes of transportation to be used to move stock from factories to warehouses and thence to resellers or to direct-buying customers.

Answers to the above and similar questions must be found and incorporated into policies which govern the performance of the physical distribution function. Effective management here is doubly important because not only does physical distribution account for a considerable portion of a firm's outlay for marketing, but it also provides a level of service for customers which increasingly is becoming a prime weapon in the firm's struggle for competitive advantage.

The purpose of this chapter will be, therefore, to provide a brief overview of the physical distribution function in terms of what it encompasses, how it is related to the other functions of the firm (both marketing and nonmarketing), and why effective management of the physical distribution function is so important, given the nature of the present business environment.

Reasons for renewed interest

Physical distribution has been called "the other half of marketing" because it accounts for approximately one half of the total outlay for marketing effort by American business firms.[1] While the promotional processes of seeking out buyers and persuading them to buy are relatively well known by businessmen and consumers alike, that portion of the marketing task which is responsible for the distribution of goods after they have been produced has been shrouded in mystery. Indeed, only during the past decade or so has a real effort been made to re-examine that portion of the marketing task which provides time and place utilities in goods by moving them and storing them. The reasons for this revived interest in physical distribution (or PD as we shall sometimes refer to it) are varied. Three basic reasons are noted below.

Rising costs

The costs of performing the functions of physical distribution have been rising steadily since the close of World War II. These costs have been incurred for labor, equipment, storage facilities, inventory holding, and transportation. Although cost behavior in this area has not been appreciably different from that in other sectors of business activity, the increased outlays needed for physical distribution have attracted the attention of management. Costs of physical distribution have also increased rapidly because of changes in overall product line strategy. Lines have been expanded in both depth and breadth, and this activity has resulted in a sizable increase in the costs of handling and holding inventory. Figure 10–1 illustrates how inventories increase 60 percent when three items are used to gain the same volume that had previously been brought in by one item. If volume with three items increases 50 percent, inventory must be at a level 25 percent greater than held previously.

Cost-saving potential

A second reason for the increased attention being paid to the area of physical distribution is that although costs have been rising throughout all segments of business, there appears to be a greater opportunity to achieve cost reductions in the logistics area than elsewhere. For example, physical distribution activities offer opportunities for organization and systematization which are not available in the promotional area.

---

[1] Paul D. Converse, "The Other Half of Marketing," in *Twenty-Sixth Boston Conference on Distribution* (Boston: Boston Trade Board, 1954), pp. 22–25.

FIGURE 10–1
Inventory behavior as the product line is broadened
and sales volume increases

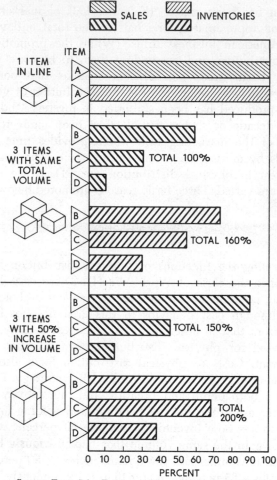

Source: From John F. Magee, "The Logistics of Distribution,"
Harvard Business Review, vol. 38, no. 4 (July-August 1960), pp.
89–101.

Further, these opportunities have not been fully exploited over the years, as has been the case with similar opportunities in the area of production.

Promotional potential

Last, but far from least, management has discovered that effective physical distribution is a potent promotional weapon. Prompt deliveries, a minimum of back orders, infrequent customer need to file damage claims, etc., can provide the seller a considerable advantage over rivals who do not provide equivalent levels of service. Of special interest to management is the fact that the cost of providing a given level of service to customers can be calculated and compared with the costs of other promotional alternatives of both a price and nonprice variety.

Implications

Because of the reasons stated above, many firms have ceased to view physical distribution as a peripheral area supporting their production and promotional activities. Instead, managers in these firms are treating physical distribution as a major functional area responsible for the movement of goods to customers and for the coordination of supply with demand as stimulated by the firm's promotional activities. By bringing the two halves of marketing—promotion and physical distribution— closer together, by coordinating efforts in both areas, and by giving physical distribution more attention than it has received in the past, these managers hope to achieve a synergistic effect. Their goal is a more desirable combination of cost savings and competitive advantage than would be achieved if promotion and physical distribution were treated as separate and unrelated functions.

Increasing costs are the prime motivating force behind a managerial review of how the firm is performing its physical distribution job. These costs may be the outlays required to sustain a given level of functional performance or they may be profits foregone because of lost sales due to ineffective logistics. Regardless of specific causation, management action is usually aimed at reducing both outlay and opportunity costs from present levels. After such reductions have been achieved, then attention can be given to increasing the extent of customer service provided by a given expenditure.

Firms vary widely in how far they go in attempting to tackle their physical distribution problems. A recent analysis of 26 companies indicated that their efforts fall into three categories:

1. The narrowest of these can appropriately be labeled the *traffic department* concept. Here, the principal role of the distribution function is to secure the most advantageous rates and routes, usually with a strong bias toward a single mode of transportation.
2. Less narrow is the *transportation* concept, which concentrates on minimizing total transportation and warehousing costs. Companies which are governed by this distribution philosophy often show considerable skill and imagination in ferreting out the lowest cost ways to transport their products.

3. The most sophisticated of the three approaches can be termed the *total logistics* concept. Companies committed to this approach, by thoughtfully balancing the economics of transportation against other key factors such as customer service, manufacturing, and warehousing, are able to get markedly more from their distribution dollars than the other companies in the sample.[2]

Of the 26 companies surveyed, 5 appeared to be doing an outstanding job of managing the distribution function. These companies applied the total logistics concept, with consistent regard for the total economics of getting the product to the customer being manifested in three ways: (1) by dealing with distribution activities on a corporate, rather than a functional, basis, (2) by having transportation personnel free from functional parochialism, and (3) by stressing adequate and timely cost information to enable them to identify and price out alternatives as a basis for making trade-offs.[3]

The "total logistics" concept is, essentially, a systems approach to the management of the physical distribution function. Our attention in this chapter will, therefore, be oriented to a brief discussion of systems analysis in general. This will be followed by a more detailed coverage of a physical distribution system in terms of its design and operation.

In conclusion, some attention will be paid to the management organization problems of systems implementation in the firm.

Systems analysis[4]

During World War II, scientists and engineers who were faced with the problem of developing advanced weapon systems often found that although parts of the system worked within acceptable tolerances, the system as a whole would not perform well. Adjustment of the interactions or linkages among components was necessary before the master system would operate as required. This focusing of attention on system performance rather than on component performance, and the subsequent experimentation with alternate system designs to improve efficiency, marked the birth of modern systems analysis.

In the years following the close of the war, systems analysis came into prominence in many fields of human endeavor. Our interest here is, of course, in the application of systems analysis to the area of physical

---

[2] Robert P. Neuschel, "Physical Distribution—Forgotten Frontier," *Harvard Business Review,* vol. 45, no. 2 (March-April 1967), pp. 125–34.

[3] Ibid. p. 133.

[4] See Donald J. Bowersox, "Research Procedure in Distribution System Design," in Edward W. Smykay, ed., *Essays on Physical Distribution Management* (Washington, D.C.: The Traffic Service Corporation, 1961), pp. 17–26.

distribution. A brief review of some systems terminology and logic will be helpful before we move to a discussion of the physical distribution system.

Systems terminology and logic

A system is composed of three basic elements: input, components, and output. It is designed to operate in a given environment, which is usually constraining, and to achieve certain goals or levels of output.

A system is stimulated into action by the receipt of an input signal. The exact nature of this signal depends upon the system, but among other things it may be a specific type of data or condition. The components accept the input and perform a single or series of functions as directed. The output of a system consists of some result or variable which, hopefully, is measurable.

Systems may be classified as open or closed. In an open system there is no connection between input and output. When output controls the extent of input by means of a feedback channel, then the system is said to be closed. A common example of a closed system is a home heating system. The fuel is the input, and heat measurable in British thermal units is the output. The thermostat is the feedback mechanism that regulates the input to the system by measuring the output of the system. If the home heating system had no thermostat, it would be an open system, and fuel would not be provided automatically to the furnace when needed in order to maintain a desired temperature.

Systems may be structured or semistructured. In a structured system, outputs are statistically predictable, given standard inputs. For example, a furnace will provide so many BTU's per cubic foot of natural gas input. A semistructured system is one in which outputs vary widely, given standard inputs, and prediction of results with any degree of accuracy is most difficult.

A function in systems terminology refers to an activity of a component. It is important to recognize that a component itself is a system of functions. When a component is part of a larger system it is said to be a subsystem. Thus, a furnace is a subsystem of the heating system.

Trade-off is the process by which subsystems (components) are integrated into the master system. The trade-off concept is vital to systems analysis. It is by "managing trade-offs" that system designers and operators balance benefits against costs and thus improve system performance and efficiency.

The performance of a system may be measured in terms of how well the system output measures up to what the system was designed to do. The term "figure of merit" is sometimes used as the basis against which actual or simulated output is measured when system configuration or input is changed. System efficiency is quite another measure and, quite simply, is the ratio of system output to system input.

A physical distribution system

Now that we have some terminology, let us look at a simple distribution system. In the Figure 10–2 we see a system in which the order is the input, transport is the component providing for the delivery function, and an actual delivery of an order is the output. It is a closed system in that delivery of the order in a satisfactory manner or an unsatisfactory manner might provide feedback that, in turn, would trigger either a new or replacement order, as the case might be. Because people are involved in most physical distribution systems, these systems are semistructured. Thus, output per given input is not as predictable as would be the case if the system were structured.

FIGURE 10–2
A simple distribution system

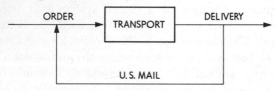

As additional components are added to a simple physical distribution system, the interaction among these components becomes more complex. The more complicated the system, the more difficult system analysis, operation, or alteration becomes. Before we discuss the nature of the components, however, it is necessary to make a few generalized statements about the inputs and outputs associated with a physical distribution system.

System output. The level of service provided to customers is generally the measurement variable for the output of a PD system. Called CSL (customer service level) in the trade, this variable is a complex combination of several factors. The length of the order cycle (time between submission of an order and receipt of goods), the percentage of orders received in which some goods are back ordered because the supplier was out of stock, and the physical condition of goods when received are three of the more important factors which go to make up a CSL.

System input. The most widely used input variable for a PD system is the cost, measured in dollars, of men and materials utilized in the operation of the system. The determination of costs associated with the performance of the physical distribution function is very difficult because traditional accounting practices do not usually identify the cost elements of a firm in terms of whether or not they have been expended to create time and place utilities.[5] In fact, the commonly used methods of accounting may distort the cost consequences of a PD decision. Figures 10–3 and 10–4 illustrate such a situation.

Figure 10–3 compares the costs per hundred pounds (cwt.) of shipping goods rail-direct with shipping by a rail-barge combination. By reducing the costs of preparing and storing goods for shipment within the plant, by reducing transportation costs, and by assuming increased

FIGURE 10–3
Comparison of direct-rail and barge-rail

	Cost per cwt.	
	Rail-direct	*Barge-rail*
Production plant cost		
Packaging...........................	$1.00	$0.00
Storage and handling................	.30	.10
Financial costs inventory..............	.10	.25
Administrative.......................	.15	.05
Subtotal........................	$1.55	$0.40
Transportation cost		
To customer........................	1.60	.20
To terminal.........................	—	.30
Subtotal........................	$1.60	$0.50
Terminal expense		
Packaging...........................	.00	1.00
Storage and handling................	.00	.30
Financial costs inventory..............	.00	.15
Administrative.......................	.00	.15
Subtotal........................	$0.00	$1.60
Total cost per cwt.	$3.15	$2.50
Total cost 20,000,000 lbs. per year	$630,000	$500,000

Source: H. G. Miller, "Accounting for Physical Distribution," *Transportation and Distribution Management*, December 1961, p. 10.

terminal expense, total costs are lowered from $3.15 to $2.50 per cwt. Annual savings accrue to $130,000, on a volume of 20 million pounds.

Figure 10–4 illustrates the change in accounts resulting from the change in distribution methods. In-plant physical distribution cost reductions show up as lowered production costs, while decreases in transportation costs appear as increases in net sales. The terminal expenses which are assumed to make the other cost savings possible resulted in an accounting effect which indicates a substantial increase in field warehousing costs.

[5] George G. Smith, "Know Your P.D. Costs," *Distribution Age*, January 1966, pp. 21–27.

FIGURE 10–4
Change in accounts resulting from change in distribution method

	Cost per cwt.	
	Rail-direct	*Barge-rail*
Production costs (plant)		
All costs except PD............................	$10.00	$10.00
Physical distribution............................	1.55	0.40
Total production cost..........................	$11.55	$10.40
Accounting effect—apparent reduction in plant production cost		
Transportation cost		
Gross sales price................................	$15.00	$15.00
Net freight cost..................................	1.60	0.50
Net sales......................................	$13.40	$14.50
Accounting effect—net sales dollars increase		
Warehousing and storage..........................	$ 0.00	$ 1.60
Accounting effect—field warehousing cost substantially increased		

Source: H. G. Miller, "Accounting for Physical Distribution," *Transportation and Distribution Management*, December 1961, p. 10.

Unless care is taken to dig behind the traditional accounts or, preferably, until accounting procedures are changed to reflect better the true costs of physical distribution, the calculation of input cost to a PD system will be a difficult undertaking.[6]

System linkages. We will touch upon the problem illustrated above in greater detail when the total cost approach to PD systems management is discussed. But even at this point, when the PD system is being viewed in terms of its elements, it becomes apparent that decisions in the area of physical distribution impinge upon production as well as the non-PD portion of the marketing function. Thus, PD, itself a system, must be viewed as a subsystem of the master system which is the firm. As such the PD system is linked to the other subsystems within the firm. In addition, the PD system is linked to other systems which are external to the firm.

Figure 10–5 illustrates a PD system which has been defined to include the storage and handling of raw materials and parts prior to assembly. Our definition of PD in this chapter is a narrower one in which PD is concerned with the distribution of finished goods. Nevertheless, the figure illustrates the connections which exist among subsystems within the firm prior to its shipment of finished goods. In addition, the figure

---

[6] An attempt to improve accounting procedures for PD management has been sponsored by an industry trade association. See Michael Schiff, *Accounting and Control in Physical Distribution Management* (Chicago: The National Council of Physical Distribution Management, Inc., 1972).

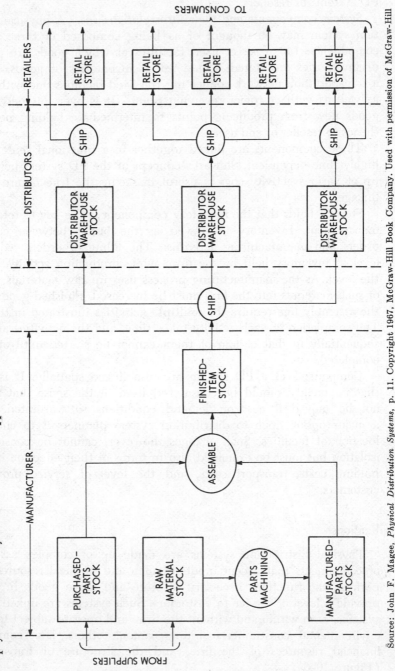

FIGURE 10–5
A physical distribution system for a consumer appliance manufacturer

Source: John F. Magee, *Physical Distribution Systems*, p. 11. Copyright 1967, McGraw-Hill Book Company. Used with permission of McGraw-Hill Book Company.

shows how the PD system of the firm must be interlinked with those PD systems of resellers.

System components and their interrelationships. A physical distribution system may be thought of as being composed of three principal components: (1) a set of fixed facilities at which goods are produced or inventories are stored; (2) a set of inventories of goods; and (3) a transportation network connecting the fixed facilities one with another as well as with customer receiving points. It is over this network that goods flow from producing points to intermediate holding points and thence to reseller or end users.

These components are linked together in a functional sense and are highly time dependent. Stewart's concept of the PD system being made up of various activity cogs is useful in seeing the true nature of these linkages.

Stewart holds that the inventory component is the key to total system management. Inventory is viewed as the buffer between customers' orders and manufacturing activities. The filling of orders reduces the level of inventory held by the firm, while production activity increases the level. As the manufacturing process uses up raw materials, the flow of such materials into the firm must be increased. Finished goods leaving the assembly line require the multiple activities illustrated in the figure. The completion of each activity takes time, and the activities are linked sequentially in that certain of them cannot be started until others are completed.

Components of a PD system are also linked spatially. It is evident that no facility should be considered fixed in the sense that it would not be moved if cost or demand conditions so warranted. Indeed, a major option open to distribution system planners is to change the location of facilities. Such changes, however, cannot be considered in isolation but must be examined also in terms of their effect on inventory holding costs, transport costs, and the level of service provided to customers.

Implications

Physical distribution systems are made up of complex assortments of components that accept inputs of men and physical resources. They perform the functions necessary to store and move goods in order to provide a level of service to customers. Such systems are linked to other systems, both within and without the firm, and operate subject to various environmental constraints including, among others, law, competition, financial resources of the firm, and the structure of transportation (Figure 10–6).

Our purpose in the following section is to discuss the design of a

FIGURE 10–6
Activity cogs in a physical distribution system

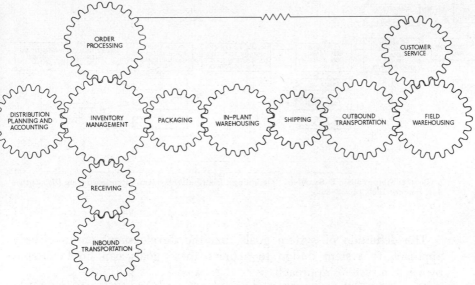

Source: Wendell M. Stewart, "Physical Distribution: Key to Improved Volume and Profits." Reprinted from *Journal of Marketing*, vol. 29 (January 1965), p. 66. Published by the American Marketing Association.

PD system and the testing of system alternatives. Because of the nature of a PD system, it is quite clear that decisions pertaining to components must be made in the context of the effect on the total system.

Each unique system has its own associated total costs and customer service level. The objectives of PD system design may be to (1) improve CSL at the present level of expenditure, (2) reduce cost while maintaining the present CSL, or (3) to provide a higher or lower level of service with concomitant increases or decreases in total system costs.

Designing a physical distribution system

The design of a physical distribution system must begin with a clear statement of system objectives. Certainly, management wants a system which provides a given level of service at least cost, but not everyone has the same definition of what CSL really means. For example, how important is the prevention of stock-outs? How great is the need to improve market coverage or to avoid loss to competitors of customers located on the market periphery? How much freedom must be allowed the marketing people in their efforts to create demand? These and many other similar questions must be considered before system design can begin.

FIGURE 10–7
A systems approach to designing a physical distribution system

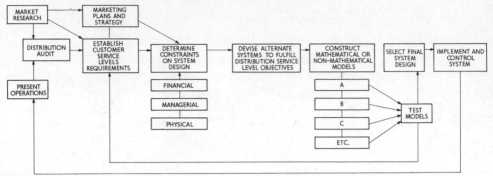

Source: From William B. Saunders, "Designing a Distribution System." Reprinted from *Distribution Age*, January 1965, pp. 32–36.

The definition of system goals and the development of an orderly approach to system design to achieve these goals can be facilitated by use of a systems approach.

Figure 10–7 illustrates that a key part of system design is the establishment of CSL requirements. These requirements are a function of the present and future marketing plans and strategies of the firm as well as of the competitive environment which presently exists and is predicted for the future. Meeting these requirements as efficiently as possible is, of course, the immediate purpose of the analysis of the system. A subsequent, and perhaps more important, objective is the design and testing of alternate systems to find a new system which will provide higher levels of service at cost levels which make these service improvements economic.

How does one go about reaching these objectives? One authority states that "the first principle to bear in mind is that you have to start where you are."[7] Finding out where you are, however, is not an easy task and requires an approach which is called a distribution audit. After the audit has defined the present cost/service relationship then attention may be directed at improving this relationship or in developing a new system which will have a cost/service relationship superior to any that can be obtained by changing the present system.

The distribution audit

A traffic analysis is the first component of a distribution audit. Determination should be made of what shipments are made from where to

---

[7] William B. Saunders, "Designing a Distribution System," *Distribution Age*, January 1965, pp. 32–36.

where, in what frequency, under what conditions, by what modes, and with what degree of reliability. Obviously, the cooperation of people in traffic, warehousing, order processing, and marketing will be required here.

The second part of the distribution audit is concerned with a buildup of the costs associated with the present performance of the PD function. This is a time-consuming task because PD costs are dispersed throughout the firm and are often difficult to identify or to quantify. The step is vital to the analysis, however, because determining the cost of providing the present CSL is a prerequisite to justifying investments of time and money in system improvement or alteration.

The utilization of a graphic representation of the distribution organization in terms of its cost components, as illustrated in Figure 10–8, is most helpful in performing the cost analysis. Bowersox notes with reference to system costing that:

During the audit stage of systems analysis, it is desirable to obtain management agreement concerning standards to be used in system costing. Since very few firms carry on detailed distribution cost accounting, establishing standards can be an essential first step. While developing standards at this point may appear to be putting the cart before the horse, it may also take considerable time to arrive at final agreement on appropriate distribution costing. A typical problem concerns interest on capital invested in inventory. Interest rates currently in use vary from 5 to 35 per cent of inventory capital value. To a large extent, the final rate selected will depend on top management's evaluation of a great many factors. A highly liquid firm's attitude is normally very different from that of one involved in a capitalization program.[8]

Regardless of the methods used and the assumptions made, the essential requirement of an audit is that it provide dependable background information to facilitate the development of the system study.

Marketing requirements and the distribution audit.[9] The final portion of the distribution audit is aimed at finding out what level of customer service is realistically required in light of the firm's current marketing programs and longer run marketing strategies. Because marketing activities impose loads on the PD system which materially affect its costs of operation and because many marketing requirements are system constraints, a substantial responsibility for system design and operation must be assumed by marketing management. Product line policy, channel policy, and promotional policy are all intimately related to PD system design in that they determine to a large extent what the system has to do. Conversely, PD system performance can influence the effectiveness of the marketing mix.

---

[8] Bowersox, "Research Procedure in Distribution System Design," p. 23.

[9] See John F. Magee, *Physical Distribution Systems* (New York: McGraw-Hill Book Co., 1967), pp. 25–26, 96–97.

FIGURE 10-8
Cost components of a physical distribution system

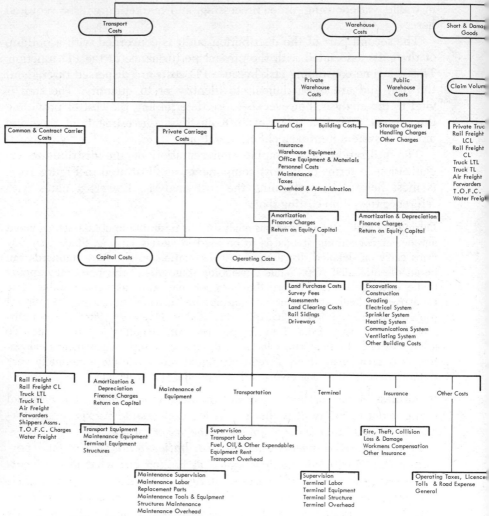

Source: William B. Saunders, "Designing a Distribution System." Reprinted from *Distribution Age*, January 1965, pp. 32-36.

In discussing the relationship of marketing and PD in the context of a distribution audit, Magee suggests that the following steps be taken:

1. Data on the company's markets and customers should be gathered, organized, and analyzed. The system study starts with study of customers, not so much by field interview as by organizing market data that are available. Occasionally a moderate amount of skilled—not routine—interview work may

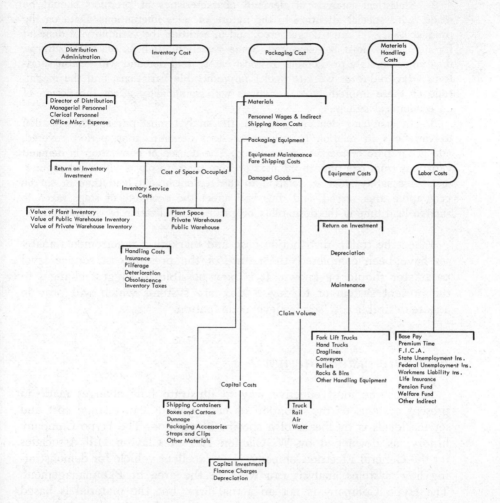

help obtain customers' estimates of service requirements and their comparisons of the company's distribution skills and policies with those of competitors.

Analysis of sales data should be directed at such questions as these: Are there several different markets, served by different channels? Are these located differently? Do they buy in different patterns, in different quantities, and with different service and stock availability requirements? How are sales distributed among customers? Do they follow [recognizable] patterns . . . ?

Do the same customers tend to buy high-volume items as buy low-volume items? The answer to this question has an important bearing on how slow-moving items, for which distribution costs are often relatively high, should be handled. While opinions on this question usually can be readily found, few companies seem to have really analyzed the question.

2. Statistical analysis of demand characteristics of products should be made, with special attention to the nature of sales fluctuations. Data on the product line . . . must be gathered, and in addition the variability of demand for item sales must be measured. Some variation, such as seasonal patterns, may be reasonably predictable. In most cases, item demand will exhibit short-term (day-to-day or week-to-week) unpredictable variations, and the magnitude of these unpredictable variations will significantly affect the design of an economical system.

3. In analyzing demand variation, the analyst must pay special attention to variations in relation to volume of item demand, time period covered, and geographic or market area covered. The degree of correlation in demand variations from one time to the next or from place to place will affect requirements for safety stock in relation to the replenishment lead time or to the geographic area served, and thus will affect the economy of steps taken to shorten lead time or the desirability of greater centralization of warehousing.[10]

When the traffic, distribution cost, and marketing requirements analyses have been completed, the nature of the present cost/service level parameter should be known. It is now possible to suggest changes in the present system or to devise alternate systems which will provide a more desirable cost/service level combination.

Alternate systems design

Perhaps the most effective way to illustrate how changes made in present systems or the adoption of new systems can change cost and service levels is by means of a specific illustration. The Hypo Company history, as developed by W. Clayton Hill of Clayton Hill Associates for the General Electric Company, is an excellent vehicle for demonstrating how systems analysis can work in the area of PD management. The Hypo Company is not an actual firm, but the material is based on data collected from 65 real distribution points handling a wide variety of products.[11]

Hypo Company

The Hypo Company, with headquarters in Indianapolis, Indiana, has an annual sales volume of $50 million dollars. It ships 500,000 units of merchandise a year at an average price of $100 per unit and at an average value of $1 per pound. The Hypo product line consists of

---

[10] Magee, *Physical Distribution Systems,* pp. 96–97.

[11] W. Clayton Hill, "Distribution Systems Management: Key to Profits in the Sixties." Reprinted from Charles H. Hindersman, ed., *Marketing Precision and Executive Action,* pp. 121–28. Published by American Marketing Association, 1962.

1,000 stock items and is distributed to 10,000 dealers by means of a 100-point distribution system.

The company operates with a warehouse replenishment time of 25 days, and it attempts to provide a CSL of 90 percent, defined by the company as having 90 percent of products on hand for shipment the day that the order is received from a customer.

The company undertook a systems analysis to determine the effects of making changes in the present system or of selecting a new system from among several alternates. The first decision faced by Hypo was whether or not to reduce the number of distribution points from the present level of 100.

Decision I: Number of distribution points

To make a decision as to the optimal number of distribution points to employ, it was necessary for Hypo to analyze the impact of such

FIGURE 10–9
Distribution cost/delivery service comparison of five
alternate distribution systems

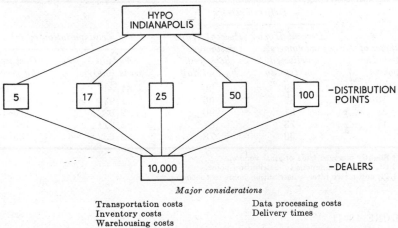

Major considerations

Transportation costs   Data processing costs
Inventory costs   Delivery times
Warehousing costs

a decision on system distribution costs and delivery times. The major considerations are illustrated in Figure 10–9.

Delivery service/transportation costs. Figure 10–10 indicates that the ability of Hypo to provide first-day delivery service to its customers is markedly reduced as distribution points are decreased in number. The ability to provide second-day delivery is also impaired but not as much as with first-day service.

Transportation costs increase as the number of distribution points is decreased. This is because with fewer distribution points more tonnage travels longer distances at less-than-carload (LCL) or metropolitan rates which are often 50 percent higher than are carload (CL) rates.

It is clear that if a decision were to be made only on the basis of delivery service and transportation cost criteria, it would be in favor of maintaining the present 100-point system. There is, however, more evidence to be considered.

Warehouse handling costs. Figure 10–11 indicates that as the number of distribution points decreases, there is a rather marked decline in the costs of receiving, retrieving, locating, and loading stock. This is due to the smaller total inventory required to sustain a system of fewer distribution points. This smaller inventory, in turn, reduces total handling costs.

The analysis of warehouse handling costs indicates that a reduction in the number of distribution points would reduce costs. This conclusion is in opposition to that which would be reached if delivery service and

FIGURE 10–10
Behavior of delivery service and transportation costs as number of distribution points is decreased

	Delivery service		Transportation costs†	
Number of distribution points	*Percent Hypo customers* delivered on 1st day*	*Percent Hypo customers* delivered by 2nd day*	*Annual costs (000)*	*Cost index (by percent)*
100............	89	90	$1,847	100
50............	87	90	1,934	105–110
25............	81	90	2,082	110–120
17............	73	87	2,211	120–130
5............	30	78	2,632	135–145

* Slightly changed from original version.
† CL rate—Indianapolis to distribution point.
LTL and metro rates—distribution point to customer.

FIGURE 10–11
Hypo Company warehouse handling costs (present methods)

Number of distribution points	*Hypo cost (in thousands)*	*Warehousing cost index (by percent)*
100...............	$514	100
50...............	368	65–75
25...............	265	45–55
17...............	235	40–50
5...............	190	35–45

Receiving—Retrieving
Locating—Loading

transportation costs were the only items under consideration. The next step is to look at an analysis of data processing costs.

Data processing costs. These costs associated with the provision of order service, inventory control, and billing are illustrated in Figure 10–12.

In this example it can be seen that data processing costs behave in much the same way as did warehouse handling costs. As the number of distribution points decrease, the various transactions which require data processing decrease in number and increase in size. Thus, once more costs go down as the number of points in the system decreases.

Inventory investment and maintenance costs. The final area to be considered before arriving at a decision with respect to the number of points to include in the PD system deals with the investment and maintenance costs of inventory. As can be seen in Figure 10–13, the investment in inventory needed to sustain sales of $50 million annually for this company is very great and varies widely as a function of the number of distribution points in the system. An estimated annual maintenance cost of 22 percent of average investment in inventory has been used. Because the need to duplicate inventory assortments in diverse

FIGURE 10–12
Hypo data processing costs under present methods

Number of distribution points	Hypo cost (in thousands)	Data processing cost index (by percent)
100	$777	100
50	585	70–80
25	496	60–70
17	486	60–70
5	448	55–65

FIGURE 10–13
Investment in inventory and inventory maintenance costs *

	Investment		Maintenance costs	
Number of distribution points	Hypo inventory (in thousands)	Inventory investment index (by percent)	Hypo cost @ 22 percent†	Inventory maintenance cost index (by percent)
100	$14,418	100	$3,172	100
50	11,423	75–85	2,513	75–85
25	9,079	60–70	1,997	60–70
17	8,004	50–60	1,761	50–60
5	5,475	35–45	1,205	35–45

* 25-day replenishment time, 90 percent customer service level.
† Capital charge, insurance, taxes, depreciation and obsolescence, storage space.

locations is diminished with fewer distribution points, the amount of inventory needed to sustain a system and to provide a given level of service goes down drastically with a reduction in the number of points at which stock is held. Figure 10–13 illustrates the behavior of investment in inventory and maintenance costs with a 90 percent CSL and a 25-day replenishment time.

Optimizing number of distribution points

Now that the various elements of the decision have been examined individually, it is time to put them together in order to arrive at an optimum solution to the problem of how many distribution points to utilize. Figure 10–14 is an attempt to portray, graphically, the total cost/service characteristics of each of the five proposals for system design. The 100-point system gives maximum service but at maximum cost. The 5-point system is very economical, but the service level is extremely low. On the basis of this analysis, it appears that a change to a 25-point system is merited.

Moving from a 100-point system to a 25-point system will allow a 35 to 40 percent reduction in inventory, a total cost reduction of between 20 and 25 percent, and a 9 percent reduction in first-day service. Hypo executives felt that the small reduction in first-day service would not have harmful competitive consequences and that the $1.4 million in cost savings made the move to 25 points a desirable one.

Decision II: Customer service level (CSL)

After finding that a substantial cost saving could be realized by changing from a 100-point system to a 25-point system with very little deterioration in *delivery* service levels, the attention of Hypo executives shifted to the problem of *customer* service level. They felt that CSL was extremely important because of its impact on customer patronage motives and thus upon the success of Hypo's marketing efforts.

As noted earlier, Hypo defined CSL as the percentage of products available for shipment to customers on the day an order was received. Hypo's CSL goal was 90 percent and this applied to each of the 1,000 items in the line. An analysis of selected warehouses in the system indicated that CSL's offered by many of them fell short of the level that Hypo considered necessary in the face of competitive levels. In Boston, for example, the CSL was 75 percent. An analysis of the Boston warehouse indicated that to achieve a 90 percent CSL would require that investment in inventory be almost doubled from $211,000 to $402,000 (see Figure 10–15).

Using the estimate of 22 percent per year of average inventory invest-

FIGURE 10–14
Total distribution costs and delivery service levels associated with five system alternatives: 5, 17, 25, 50, and 100 distribution points

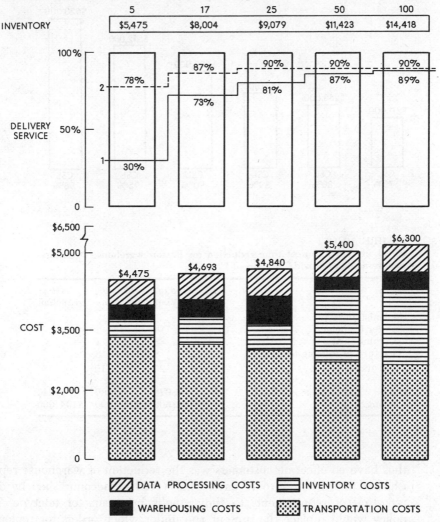

ment for inventory maintenance costs, it can be shown that costs would increase $42,600 per year in this one area alone if the CSL were raised 20 percent from its current level of 75 percent.

Decision III: Warehouse replenishment time

Faced with this problem, Hypo executives considered other changes in the system. One such alteration which would be purely internal and

FIGURE 10–15
Inventory investment required to provide various levels of customer service at the Boston warehouse (25-day replenishment time)

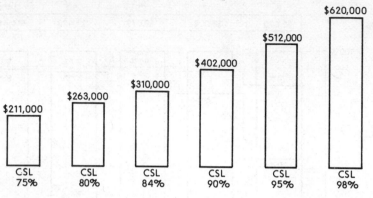

FIGURE 10–16
Effect of replenishment time reduction on Boston warehouse inventory requirements to provide 90 percent CSL

	25-day lead time	10-day lead time	Net reduction
Replenishment time			
Order frequency...................	14	1	
Communications...................	3	1	
Factory processing transit.........	8	8	
Total time....................	25	10	
Units...........................	4,020	2,080	1,940
Amount.........................	$402,000	$208,000	$194,000

thus have no effect on customers was the reduction of warehouse replenishment time from 25 to 10 days. This would be accomplished by daily reporting of requirements to Indianapolis by means of teletype. This policy would replace the present one under which orders for replenishment were made up each two weeks and mailed to Indianapolis.

If such a change could be accomplished, a smaller inventory would be needed in each warehouse to sustain a given volume of sales and a given CSL. Figure 10–16 shows that with a 10-day lead time the Boston warehouse could provide a 90 percent CSL with about the same amount of inventory ($208,000) as was needed currently to provide a 75 percent CSL. Of course, associated with the reduction in lead time are increased costs of daily ordering and of using more expensive communication methods.

Once the analysis of Boston was completed, an attempt was made to see what the impact of lead-time reduction would be on the operations of the 25-point system.

Lead-time reduction for 25-point system. The analysis of the 25-point system indicated to Hypo executives that the levels of customer service provided by the various warehouses in the system varied between 70 and 90 percent with an average of 80 percent. To move from this level to an average level of 90 percent with a minimum of variability would require a 50 percent increase in inventory investment under current policy. A systemwide change from a 25-day to a 10-day replenishment lead time, however, would allow the provision of a systemwide 90 percent CSL with a *reduction* in inventory investment of $773,500. Applying the 0.22 factor to this amount gives an inventory maintenance cost saving of $170,000. Hypo management felt that the changes needed to reduce

FIGURE 10–17
Investment in inventory needed to sustain different CSL's with 25- and 10-day replenishment times (25 point system)

	Customer service level		
	80 percent	*90 percent*	*95 percent*
25-day replenishment time			
Total...................	$6,165,800	$9,079,000	$11,318,000
10-day replenishment time			
Total...................	$3,790,050	$5,392,300	$ 6,623,750
Difference..............	$2,375,750	$3,686,700	$ 4,694,250

lead time from 25 to 10 days could be made without expenditures exceeding the inventory maintenance cost savings. They also felt that a 95 percent CSL was not required to maintain a competitive advantage and, therefore, did not warrant the investment in inventories which would have been required. Figure 10–17 gives some idea of inventory investment required in a 25-point system as lead times and service levels change.

Decision IV: Selective stocking

To see if further improvements in system operation were possible, Hypo executives returned to the analysis of the Boston warehouse, which they considered as being fairly representative of other distribution points. A breakdown of sales at Boston indicated that the 1,000 items in the Hypo line fell into four distinct categories. Fifty items accounted for almost three quarters of the sales volume and almost half of the inventory. The other 950 items were slower movers and could be categorized as B, C, or D items depending upon their sales-to-inventory ratio. Figure 10–18 shows the relationship among the four classes of items in the line.

The next step in the analysis was to propose that groups of items be handled differently and to estimate the cost consequences of these alternatives. It was decided that A and B items would have to be kept at Boston, but the really slow movers in groups C and D could be

FIGURE 10–18
Breakdown of sales by item at Boston warehouse

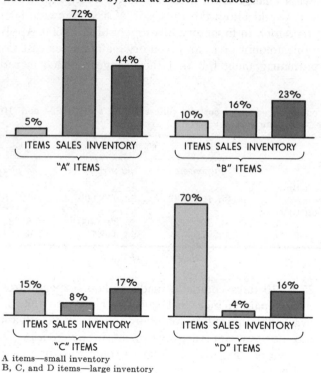

A items—small inventory
B, C, and D items—large inventory

held in reserve at the factory or at the distribution point located in New York. The cost/service consequences of stocking C and D items at the factory and using either LTL truck shipments or airfreight to supply them to Boston, as well as stocking C and D items at New York and using LTL truck shipments to supply Boston, are illustrated in Figure 10–19. It is clear that alternative (1) offers the lowest cost while alternative (3) provides the best service.

An extension of the selective stocking proposals to the full 25-point system was analyzed. Three alternative proposals were evaluated on the basis of cost and service criteria. The first was to keep the present

FIGURE 10–19
Selective stocking alternatives (A and B items at Boston; C and D stocking alternatives)

	(1) At factory using LTL	(2) At factory using air-freight	(3) At New York using LTL
Inventory at Boston			
Reduction in inventory........	$112,540	$112,540	$112,540
Cost			
Net cost reduction.............	$ 19,071	$ 2,311	$ 15,116
Delivery service (days)			
A and B Items (88 percent total sales) 90 percent CSL........	Same	Same	Same
C and D items (12 percent total sales) 90 percent CSL........	6–7	4–5	3–4

FIGURE 10–20
Cost/service parameters of three alternatives for selective stocking in a 25-point system (90 percent CSL, 10-day replenishment time)

	Inventory investment	Inventory maintenance costs @ 22 percent	Delivery service, (by percent)	
			1–3 day	4–10 day
A. Stocking 1,000 items each point............	$9,079,000	$1,997,000	90	100
B. A and B items local; C and D items 5 dual warehouses, New York, Indianapolis San Francisco, Atlanta, Dallas.......	$8,182,000	$1,851,000	88	100
C. A and B items local, C and D items factory..............	$5,118,000	$1,323,000	79	100

policy of stocking each of the 1,000 items at each distribution point. The second was to keep A and B items on hand locally while C and D items were held at five dual warehouses located across the country. The third alternative was to stock A and B items locally while C and D items were held at the factory. All transportation would be by LTL truck shipments. Figure 10–20 illustrates the cost/service parameters of the three alternatives.

Alternative A, keeping current policy and stocking 1,000 items at each point, provides the highest level of delivery service but also requires the largest investment in inventory. Alternative C is the lowest cost, but as C and D items are kept at the factory the service level for one-to three-day delivery falls to 79 percent from a former level of 90 percent.

Alternative B, in which five dual warehouses are used for stocking C and D items, offers a $146,000 cost saving over alternative A while only dropping 2 percentage points in one- to three-day delivery service. Hypo executives felt that this saving was sufficient to override the minor decline in delivery service and suggested that alternative B be adopted.

Total system optimization

The results of the analysis of the Hypo system indicated that the following might be achieved by system redesign and optimization: (1) a net saving of $1,460,000 from reducing the number of distribution points from 100 to 25; (2) a net saving of $801,000 from shortening the warehouse replenishment time from 25 to 10 days; and (3) a net saving of $146,000 by selective stocking using five dual warehouses.

The total savings possible, through system redesign and optimization, total $2,417,000 or 4.8 percent of current annual sales. These savings can be obtained, however, with a concomitant increase of customer service level from a range of 75–80 percent to 90 percent. There will be only a slight (2 percent) decrease in 1- to 3-day delivery service and no change in 4- to 10-day delivery service.

Although the results of system redesign have been calculated on the assumption that sales volume will remain stable, it is very likely that the increase in CSL will markedly improve Hypo's competitive position and thus increase its sales.

Inventory management

In the Hypo example, various cost components were examined as a distribution system was subjected to both design and operating policy changes. It soon became quite clear that the largest cost was that associated with maintaining inventories. Although marketing management is not solely responsible for inventory policy, the demands which its members make on the distribution system are sufficiently large so that marketing executives must be in on major inventory decisions and share responsibility for them.

Before managers can make meaningful decisions with respect to inventory policy, it is necessary for them to have some understanding of the basic function of inventory as well as of the various specific types of inventories which serve to fill special needs. With respect to basic function Magee notes:

Fundamentally, inventories serve to uncouple successive operations in the process of making a product and getting it to consumers. For example, inventories make it possible to process a product at a distance from customers or from raw material supplies, or to do two operations at a distance from one another (perhaps only across the plant). Inventories make it unnecessary to gear production directly to consumption or, alternatively, to force consumption to adapt to the necessities of production. In these and similar ways, inventories free one stage in the production-distribution process from the next, permitting each to operate more economically.[12]

There is no denying the fact that inventories provide economic benefits, but they also incur costs. The big question facing managers with respect to inventory decisions is at what point do the benefits of holding inventory cease to justify the costs involved. Before tackling that question, however, it would be useful to be able to specify the type of inventory being considered.

Some inventories are needed because goods are in transit for a period of time and are thus unavailable for consumption. These are called "movement" or "process" inventories, and the size of such inventories is a function of the average sales rate and transit time. Thus, the size of the movement stock required to sustain a given volume of sales may be reduced by changes in the distribution system which shorten transit times. Of course, the inventory maintenance savings must be balanced against the costs of using the more expensive modes of transport which are usually required to move goods more quickly.

Movement inventories may be contrasted with what have been called organization inventories. These inventories allow different parts of a production-distribution system to operate with a minimum of coordination. If inventories of this type are already being used efficiently, they can only be reduced by assuming the expense of greater organization effort, including scheduling and expediting.[13]

There are three major kinds of organization inventories: (1) replenishment or lot-size inventories, (2) fluctuation or "safety stock" inventories, and (3) seasonal or anticipation inventories.

The replenishment or lot-size inventory is the most common type used in business. Such inventories are maintained whenever it is advantageous to produce or to purchase in quantities larger than are currently needed. The benefits gained by holding lot-size inventories may accrue from purchase discounts based on quantity, ability to provide quick delivery to customers, and so on.

Fluctuation or safety stocks cushion the shocks arising from unpredictable fluctuations in demand or in replenishment lead time. The cost of maintaining such stocks must be balanced against the costs of sales lost due to stock-outs.

---

[12] John F. Magee, "Guides to Inventory Policy I. Functions and Lot Size," *Harvard Business Review,* vol. 31, no. 1 (January–February 1956), p. 51.

[13] Ibid., p. 52.

Anticipation or seasonal inventories are held when the demand for goods, although predictable, is highly seasonal. The buildup of inventory allows a stabilization of production and employment over the year. The savings so realized must be compared with the added costs of holding stock. Such stocks may also be built up in anticipation of special selling events or some other contingencies.

Because lot-size or replenishment inventories are so important, a great deal of attention has been devoted to them. Of special interest has been the answering of the questions of when to order (order point) and how much to order (order quantity). The first of these variables, the order point (R), is a function of the lead time required between order placement and receipt of goods. It is also a function of the rate of usage or depletion (D) of inventory, as well as the CSL requirements. The higher the degree of variability of lead time or usage rate, the higher must be the order point (R) to sustain a given CSL.

FIGURE 10–21
Characteristic pattern of lot-size stocks

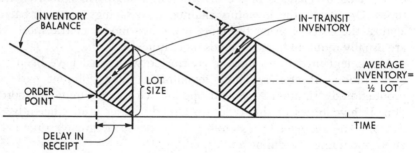

Source: John F. Magee, *Physical Distribution Systems*, p. 51. Copyright 1967, McGraw-Hill Book Company. Used with permission of McGraw-Hill Book Company.

Given the sawtooth pattern which typifies the behavior of lot-size inventories, the problem of when to order is quite clearly defined. Assuming constant rates of usage and a stable lead time, the reorder point is easily found, once the optimal order quantity has been determined.

The optimal-size lot to purchase is known as the economic order quantity (EOQ) or simply Q^*. It is determined by balancing the costs of placing an order against the cost of holding inventory. Figure 10–22 illustrates a graphic method of finding Q^*.

By summing the two cost functions to obtain a total cost function and by dropping a line from the low point on the total cost curve to the horizontal axis, Q^* can be determined. The quantity can also

FIGURE 10–22
Costs of holding and ordering stock as function of order size

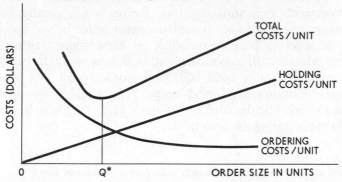

be derived mathematically. Let:

Q = Order quantity in units.
C = Unit cost per item.
I = Annual carrying cost as percent of unit cost.
S = Cost to place one order.
D = Number of units demanded per year.

The total cost function T is as follows:

$$T = CD + \frac{D}{Q}S + IC\frac{Q}{2}.$$

Finding the first derivative of T with respect to Q:

$$\frac{dT}{dQ} = -DS/Q^2 + IC/2.$$

Setting the first derivative $= 0$, and solving for Q,

$$Q^* = \sqrt{\frac{2DS}{IC}}.$$

Let us look at a simple example of formula application. Demand estimates show that about 400 items per year will be needed on a fairly steady basis. Each item has a cost of $100. Annual inventory maintenance costs will run about 0.25 of average inventory investment and the cost to place one order has been estimated at $5. The problem is to determine Q^*:

$$Q^* = \sqrt{\frac{2(400)(5)}{0.25(100)}} = \sqrt{160} \text{ or } 12.8.$$

Thus Q^* can be considered as 13 units, and an order could be placed in that amount each time the last item in stock was sold, assuming instant replenishment. Unfortunately, such service is not usually available, and it is necessary to place a replenishment order before the last item is sold in order to have some stock on hand while waiting for the new order to arrive. If replenishment lead time were three days and daily demand $1\frac{1}{9}$ units (400/360), the reorder point (R) would be when current inventory fell to 4 units. This would keep enough stock on hand to cover the demand of $3\frac{1}{3}$ units ($3 \times 1\frac{1}{9}$) which would be expected to occur during the lead time.

FIGURE 10–23
Safety stock used as a buffer against stock-outs caused by variations in usage

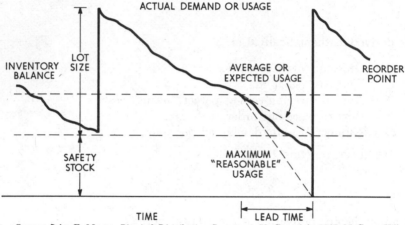

Source: John F. Magee, *Physical Distribution Systems*, p. 53. Copyright 1967, McGraw-Hill Book Company. Used with permission of McGraw-Hill Book Company.

In this simple example the two questions have been answered. An order is placed whenever the inventory is down to 4 units and the size of the order is 13 units. Unfortunately, many of the assumptions underlying the above example do not hold in reality. Usage rates are rarely constant, and lead times are not always dependable. What is required is a "safety stock" or additional inventory to serve as a buffer against stock-outs. The larger the safety stock, the less will be the costs incurred by lost sales. However, the larger the safety stock, the greater will be the costs of inventory maintenance.

Figure 10–23 illustrates the use of a safety stock to cushion against stock-outs caused by variations in usage. The safety stock could be used also to protect against the effects of variations in the lead time.

There is an approach to finding a Q^* and R^* (optimal reorder point) combination which will balance the costs of holding stock against the costs of ordering and of being out of stock. The user of this approach must estimate the dollar cost to him of being out of stock and must also determine the probability of expected usage during the lead time period exceeding the reorder point (R). Using the same notation as in the previous example and adding (π) as the stock-out penalty, u for usage rate during lead time, $E(u > R)$ as expected usage in excess of the reorder point during lead time, and $\bar{u}$ as average usage during the lead time, the following total cost function may be constructed:

$$T = CD + \frac{D}{Q}[S + \pi E(u > R)] + IC\left[\frac{Q}{2} + (R - \bar{u})\right].$$

Finding the first derivative of the above function with respect to Q and setting same equal to zero:

$$Q^* = \sqrt{\frac{2D[S + \pi E(u > R)]}{IC}}.$$

Once Q^* is found, R^* can be calculated. It is not our purpose to go more deeply into this approach here, but several excellent references are noted below.[14] Regardless of the complexity of the formulation and the introduction of probability into the problem, the issues are still the same: the balancing of costs and benefits.

It is also clear that effective inventory management is dependent on accurate forecasts of demand. With the advent of the computer it has been possible to develop tracking models which follow demand patterns for individual items and trigger lot-size reorders when the appropriate levels of stock on hand have been reached. Perhaps the computer will allow management to apply more widely the techniques which have been available technically but which have not until recently been economically feasible.

Location decisions

Just as the decisions pertaining to the amount of inventory which is to be held in a physical distribution system are vital to efficient system performance, so are the decisions which determine *where* goods are to be produced, processed, stored, and delivered. The distribution system manager is, therefore, concerned about the location of producing points, storage and transit warehouses, transportation facilities, and customer receiving points. Because most of these locations must be assumed

---

[14] Robert B. Fetter and Winston C. Dalleck, *Decision Models for Inventory Management* (Homewood, Ill.: Richard D. Irwin, Inc., 1961); J. L. Heskett, Robert M. Ivie, and Nicholas A. Glaskowsky, Jr., *Business Logistics* (New York: Ronald Press Co., 1961), chap. 11; John F. Magee, *Production Planning and Inventory Control* (New York: McGraw-Hill Book Co. 1958).

to be fixed, at least over the short run, they are constraints on system design and operation. In the longer run, however, fixed facilities may be relocated or new facilities can be planned. In such circumstances the logistics considerations may play an important role in the location decision.

The term logistics, rather than physical distribution, is used to indicate that location decisions are a function of the total flow of materials through a fixed facility, rather than of the flow of goods leaving a facility. For the producing plant this means that the costs associated with receiving, storing, and handling raw materials and purchased parts must be considered along with the costs of physical distribution of finished or semifinished goods. In similar manner the costs associated with the inflow of goods as well as with the outflow has an impact on the location of warehouses, transport terminals, and customer receiving points.

The impact of logistics costs on the location decision differs with respect to the firm's product line and the type of facility involved. If a company produces a line of scientific instruments which is composed of assembled items which are light in weight for their value, the costs of logistics is not an important factor in plant location. As the transportation costs of inbound raw materials and outbound finished goods increase, these costs, which are known as transfer costs, assume greater importance in the firm's locational decisions. Studies of plant location checklists have indicated that transfer costs are only one of six major cost categories to be considered and that "Of nineteen major factor categories listed, only two deal directly with matters of logistics."[15] In contrast, logistics factors can be of crucial importance in warehouse location. Decisions here can influence system service levels as well as related costs.

Unless the firm wields considerable economic power, it cannot usually influence the location of fixed transport or receiving facilities owned by others. This does not mean that a firm may not get a rail spur built to its plant or may not offer suggestions for the location of a customer's warehouse. What is implied is that such changes are not under the direct control of the management of the firm and thus cannot be considered as changes which can be accomplished in a relatively short period of time. We shall, therefore, concentrate our attention here on the locational decisions involving the relocation of a single producing plant as well as the location or relocation of storage warehouses. Although of necessity brief, this coverage will give some idea of the approaches possible in resolving some of the firm's locational problems. We shall consider single-plant relocation by the ton-mile-center approach first.

---

[15] Heskett, Ivie, and Glaskowsky, Jr., *Business Logistics*, p. 181.

Single-plant relocation

A relatively unsophisticated but useful method in considering the relocation of a producing plant is to calculate the ton-mile center of the geographic market area. This approach, suggested by several of the early locational economists, has been formalized and described in detail in recent literature.[16] The basic idea underlying this approach is to identify that point in the geographic area under consideration where the producing plant might be located to minimize the number of ton-miles traveled by raw materials moving from their sources to the factory and by finished goods moving from the factory to the various customer receiving points.

This process requires that a grid overlay be placed on a map of the geographic area under consideration. Then the location of raw material supply points and customer finished goods receiving points can be identified and assigned grid coordinates. The next step is to calculate the weights of materials moving between points, the distances traveled by these materials, and the costs of transport. The object of the analysis is to find a location for the producing plant that will minimize the total cost of inbound raw material transport plus outbound finished goods transport. Several assumptions must be made. One of these is that freight rates are linear with distance. This is not a valid assumption in terms of the actual tapered behavior of rates, but it can simplify the calculations and indicate a location which then can be rechecked on the basis of actual freight rates.

The Comclean Company example developed by Heskett *et al.* is useful in illustrating the ton-mile-center approach (sometimes called the least-cost transportation center approach). The Comclean Company, a manufacturer of industrial cleaning compounds located in Easthampton, Massachusetts, received its raw materials and served a group of customers located in that portion of the eastern United States shown in Figure 10–24. A grid overlay divided the geographic area into boxes approximately 80 miles square.

The Comclean Company recognized that its markets were moving westward. In considering a new location for its manufacturing facility, management came across a very attractive site near Pittsburgh, Pennsylvania. A logistics least-cost analysis was made to see where the optimal location for the company might be and also to compare the present location and the Pittsburgh location with the optimal location.

The results indicated that the logistics least-cost location was situated in the box marking the intersection of row 5 and column 5.

---

[16] Edward W. Smykay, Donald J. Bowersox, and Frank H. Mossman, *Physical Distribution Management* (New York: Macmillan Co., 1961), pp. 176–201.

FIGURE 10–24
Comclean Corporation: Raw material sources, manufacturing plant, and customer locations

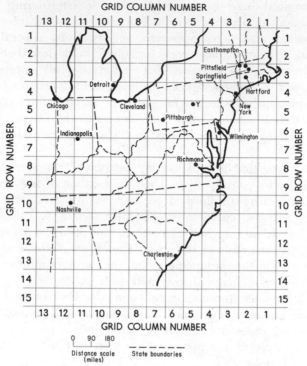

Source: J. L. Heskett, Robert M. Ivie, and Nicholas A. Glaskowsky, Jr., *Business Logistics—Management of Physical Supply and Distribution* (New York: Ronald Press Co., 1964), p. 188.

It is marked by a Y in Figure 10–24 and is in central Pennsylvania, a considerable distance northeast of Pittsburgh. Location of a manufacturing plant somewhere near point Y would offer total logistics cost savings of over $316,000 per year as compared with Easthampton. A move to Pittsburgh, however, would incur additional costs of $407,000 over those expended for logistics at Easthampton.

Although the grid size used on the map is large and does not pinpoint a specific location, the analysis can indicate the approximate magnitude of the increase or decrease in logistics costs over current levels associated with plant relocation to different parts of the geographic area. Such information is most useful in evaluating a site in terms of logistics costs in relation to other cost factors, such as production costs, building and land costs, and power costs. Logistics cost data are also important in evaluating a site in relation to its intangible costs or benefits, such as climate, quality of surrounding territory, educational facilities, and potential for growth. Given a possible site for a new factory which offers many intangible advantages as well as nonlogistics cost savings, the logistics least-cost-center approach can indicate the size of the transportation cost penalty which must be paid to gain the other benefits offered by the site.

The location of the least-cost center is only the first step in the locational decision process. Other steps to be taken include: (1) the investigation of the actual behavior of transport rates with special attention being given to obvious nonlinearities; (2) the consideration of whether or not a shift of a few miles would place the plant in another transport rate territory which would offer rate advantages; (3) the investigation of possible alternate sources of supply for raw materials; (4) the desirability of rate negotiation with present carriers under implied threat of relocation; (5) the extent and variety of transport service to and from the proposed location; and (6) the trend of directional growth of the company's markets.[17]

Multiple-facility location

The decision where to locate an additional producing plant when one or more plants are already in existence can be quite a difficult one. This is because it is based on a series of other decisions, many of which are made for nonlogistics reasons. For example, if a decision is made that the new plant will produce the same product mix as is being currently produced by the one existing plant, the problem becomes one of two single-plant locations. If, on the other hand, the new plant will not produce the same array of products as the existing plant and if it has different production costs as well as logistics costs, the problem becomes so complex as to defy solution except on a trial-and-error basis. It is not our purpose here to delve into this area. What this chapter is concerned with is physical distribution, and the best way to see how locational decisions, with respect to fixed facilities, affect physical distribution costs and customer service levels is to reorient the multiple-facility location problem from producing plants and toward warehousing facilities.

Warehouse location and relocation

The decision where to locate warehouses is more of a logistics problem than is the decision where to locate producing plants. The location of warehouses in the PD system determines to a large extent the ability to provide a given level of service to customers and also has an important

---

[17] Heskett, Ivie, and Glaskowsky, Jr., *Business Logistics*, pp. 191–92.

influence on overall system operating costs. The warehouse location (or relocation) decision is essentially a cost-balancing one. We have seen in the Hypo example that the greater the number of distribution points (warehouses) in a PD system, the higher are some components of cost and the lower are other components of cost.

Single-warehouse decisions can be handled very much like single-plant location decisions. The least-cost-center analysis can indicate that geographic location which will minimize the costs of inflow of goods and outflow of goods. The approach has been modified by Bowersox to enable the use of time rather than transport costs in location determination when time is the key factor in a firm's marketing strategy.[18]

In addition, consideration must be given to the size of the warehouse, as scale of operation will affect unit costs of handling throughout. With scale comes the associated problem of the service area of the warehouse. This decision will affect the level of operation of the warehouse and thus, once more, the unit costs of handling goods.

One very useful approach to determine the service area of a warehouse is the Bowman-Stewart formulation.[19] This mathematical approach can be used to determine the service area of a single warehouse in relation to that of the producing plant (which may have warehousing facilities) as well as to other proposed warehouses in the system. The approach is based upon the cost behavior illustrated in Figure 10–25.

FIGURE 10–25
Factors influencing the total costs of supplying an area from a given location

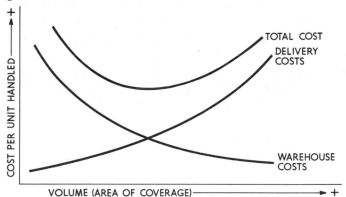

Source: Edward H. Bowman and John B. Stewart, "A Model for Scale of Operations," *Journal of Marketing*, vol. 20 (January 1956), pp. 242–47.

---

[18] Donald J. Bowersox, "An Analytical Approach to Warehouse Location," *Handling and Shipping* (February 1962), pp. 17–20.

[19] Edward H. Bowman and John B. Stewart, "A Model for Scale of Operations," *Journal of Marketing*, vol. 20 (January 1956), pp. 242–47.

The model assumes that as coverage area increases, and if volume of business per unit of area (concentration of demand) is constant, the unit warehousing cost will decrease and the unit delivery cost will increase. Although all other costs associated with warehouse operations were assumed to be equal regardless of location, the model can accommodate cost differences arising from intrafacility shipments such as from plant warehouse to field warehouse. The model further assumes that costs associated with warehousing and materials handling vary inversely with volume, and that costs associated with delivery vary directly with the square root of the area served (relation of radius of a circle to its area), and the other categories of costs would not change with changes in volume handled or area served.

The following is the Bowman-Stewart expression of total costs to serve an area through a distribution warehouse:

$$C = a + \frac{b}{V} + c \sqrt{A},$$

when

C = Cost (within warehouse district) per dollar's worth of goods distributed, the measure of effectiveness.

V = Volume of goods, in dollars, handled by the warehouse per unit of time.

A = Area in square miles served by the warehouse.

a = Cost per dollar's worth of goods distributed independent of either the warehouse's volume handled or area served.

b = "Fixed" costs for the warehouse per unit of time, which when divided by the volume will yield the appropriate cost per dollar's worth distributed.

c = The cost of the distribution, which varies with the square root of the area; that is, costs associated with miles covered within the warehouse district, such as gasoline, truck repairs, and driver hours.

To apply the formula it is necessary to find the values of C, V, and A for each warehouse currently in the system. By using multiple regression techniques it is possible to use past experience to determine values for the parameters a, b, and c which when used in conjunction with the actual values of V, and A for each existing warehouse, will be the closest predictors of the actual C or cost per dollar's worth of goods distributed through each warehouse.

To use this approach for warehouse location or relocation, it is necessary to find a value for A which will result in a minimum cost. This step requires that density of sales per area be determined. This expression is called K with $K = V/A$ and $V = KA$. Substituting into the original formula gives:

$$C = a + b/KA + c\sqrt{A},$$

and differentiating C with respect to A and setting the derivative equal to zero,

$$dC/dA = -b/KA^2 + c/2\sqrt{A} = 0,$$

and solving for A,

$$A = (2b/cK)^{\frac{2}{3}}.$$

Once A is calculated for any site based on appropriate values for variable K and parameters b and c, then the radius (r) of the service area which will minimize cost C can be found (radius of a circle as a function of area, $r = \sqrt{A/\pi}$).

If the value of r equaled 10 miles, then a circle could be drawn on a map to scale with its center at a proposed warehouse location. The entire market area could then be viewed as being covered by circles of varying diameters, each circle representing the most economic service area for a given size warehouse. Individual warehouses either currently in operation or proposed might then be evaluated in terms of optimal combination of location and scale of operation.

The above approach is but one of several which have been suggested to improve the quality of the location decision. Another approach, for example, which shows considerable promise is computer simulation. Consultants who designed a system simulation for the H. J. Heinz Company to test costs and service levels associated with different numbers and locations of warehouses reported that the company was able to redeploy its warehouses, improve service levels, and reduce costs.[20] Other writers have described the use of heuristic programs based on certain rules of thumb for warehouse location[21] and the uses of modified linear programming techniques.[22]

Regardless of the method used, the location problem must be attacked in a logical manner. The system itself must be clearly defined as well as the environmental constraints which limit its operation. Although service and cost oriented, locational decisions must provide for flexibility

---

[20] Harvey N. Shycon and Richard B. Maffei, "Simulation—Tool for Better Distribution," *Harvard Business Review*, vol. 38, no. 6 (November–December 1960), pp. 65–75.

[21] Alfred A. Kuehn and Michael J. Hamburger, "A Heuristic Program for Locating Warehouses," *Management Science*, July 1963, pp. 643–66.

[22] William J. Baumol and Philip Wolfe, "A Warehouse Location Problem," *Operations Research*, March–April 1958, pp. 252–63.

in system design. Fixed facilities are not easy to move once they are located, yet sources, markets, and competitors rarely stay fixed over time. It is a poor system which is designed for optimal performance today but is so inflexible that it cannot be readily and economically changed to accommodate future contingencies.

Managing the physical distribution function

The discussion which has preceded this concluding section of the chapter should by now have clearly indicated that effective management of the PD function requires coordination among the diverse activities of the business enterprise. A PD system must be tuned to receive inputs from the production process as well as to furnish output as required by the marketing department. Even within the heart of the system the problems of managing the functions of transport, warehousing, and inventory holding must be considered as interrelated issues.

Unfortunately, the typical firm is not organized to facilitate fully such coordination. Traffic seeks to route goods as economically as possible. Sales promises prompt delivery of goods. Warehouse managers try to run their show as efficiently as they can. But, in all too many instances, there is no one person or group of persons to manage the cost trade-offs available among diverse functional areas and thus to optimize the performance of the total distribution system.

Some of the nation's more progressive firms have sensed that great opportunities for gains in performance and reduction in costs could be exploited if the systems approach could be applied to PD and if the components of the PD system could be viewed as pieces of the whole. These companies have attempted to provide the management structure needed to implement the systems approach.

In certain companies, for example, committees have been formed to set service-level goals and to coordinate the activities necessary for the attainment of these goals. The authority of these committees cuts across traditional functional lines and is exercised to prevent what is called suboptimization or the seeking of higher levels of performance by components at the expense of total system performance. Other companies have gone still further by establishing a separate department for physical distribution. The status of this department may be equivalent to that granted to production and marketing. The more usual procedure, however, is to recognize the PD function and to place it under the control of an established function such as production, control, or marketing. Those firms which are cost conscious and do not have service level problems generally choose to place PD under production or control. Those firms which are concerned with the levels of customer service provided for a given input of resources generally place the function within the marketing area.

The exact location of responsibility for PD management within the firm is not the major issue. Rather, what is vitally important is the recognition by top management that wherever management responsibility is located the people involved must have the authority to effect the coordination of activities both within and without the firm which is essential if distribution efficiency is to be fully achieved.

Conclusion

This chapter has provided a brief overview of the physical distribution function. Marketing managers must be familiar with the scope of the PD function as well as how it is related to the other functional areas of the firm. Of special importance is the concept of the customer service level (CSL) as an important means of nonprice competition. Effective management of the PD function, wherever located in the hierarchy of the firm, requires the coordination of those activities both within the firm and without which are necessary if the required PD services are to be provided as efficiently as possible.

Questions

1. What are some of the reasons for renewed interest in the area of physical distribution?
2. Explain how the implementation of the "marketing concept" by many firms has had an impact on their performance of the functions of physical distribution.
3. Why do firms vary with respect to how far they go in attempting to implement the "total logistics" concept?
4. What is systems analysis and why is it so useful an approach for managing the functions of physical distribution?
5. What is the output of a physical distribution system? How is system input measured? How would one determine the efficiency of a physical distribution system?
6. What difficulties might you expect to encounter if you attempted to implement the systems approach in a situation where traditional accounting methods were used?
7. "A physical distribution system encompasses elements beyond the boundaries of the firm." What is meant by the statement? What are the implications for management?
8. Why is a statement of system objectives so crucial to the design of a physical distribution system?

9. What is a distribution audit? How is it related to the firm's marketing requirements?
10. What criteria should management consider in choosing from an array of distribution system designs?
11. Why is inventory management so important a component of a physical distribution system? What is the basic compromise involved in the design of an optimal inventory policy?
12. Of what value is the "logistics least-cost" approach to facility location? What are its limitations?
13. What is the economic purpose of a warehouse?
14. The physical distribution manager has been called, "a manager of trade-offs." Explain what this means. Also, discuss where in the organizational structure of the firm the physical distribution function should be located.

cases for part four

The Upjohn Company*

Decision on channels of distribution for new veterinary product

The research and development division of The Upjohn Company had discovered a new product for the treatment of mastitis in dairy cattle. If established distribution and sales policies were followed in the marketing of this discovery, it was anticipated that sales would be limited to a fraction of the potential market. As a means of capitalizing to the maximum possible extent on research findings, therefore, company officials were considering the possibility of opening new distribution channels and of deviating from customary promotional policy. They did not want to act without giving the matter careful consideration, however, because of the likelihood that such innovations would meet with disfavor by veterinarians who provided the traditional outlet for such products. There was also concern over the possible reaction of physicians and laymen, either users or potential users of the company's main product line of human-use pharmaceuticals.

History

The Upjohn Company, producers of ethical drugs and pharmaceuticals was established in 1886 in Kalamazoo, Michigan, and its headquarters and manufacturing plants are still located there today. The company was founded by Dr. W. E. Upjohn, at the time a practicing physician, for the purpose of manufacturing better pills, which were the most common form of medication at that time. After pills declined in popularity, the company began to move toward its present line of ethical drugs and pharmaceuticals. A reputation for outstanding research, high-quality products, and aggressive merchandising have all contributed to making The Upjohn Company one of the largest ethical drug firms in the industry.

---

* Written by Donald Mattison, Marketing Research Department, The Upjohn Company.

Distribution and sales policies

Ethical pharmaceutical houses are distinguished from proprietary drug firms by the fact that their promotional efforts are aimed at the profession (physician, druggist, hospital buyers) rather than at the ultimate consumer. Over the years, The Upjohn Company has followed the basic distribution policy of selling directly to retail druggists. In accordance with the "ethical" formula, the Upjohn sales force has been responsible for "creating" a demand for the firm's prescription drugs by "detailing" the physician (i.e., by missionary saleswork with doctors) and by selling the retail druggist on stocking Upjohn products. Heavy sales of nonprescription items such as vitamins, however, have resulted from direct sales and promotional efforts of the retail druggists.

Physical distribution of Upjohn products was handled through 18 company-owned sales branches and warehouses located throughout the country. No account was farther than two days' delivery service from any branch warehouse. Most major trading centers received either same-day or following-day service.

While the company's main line of products was human pharmaceuticals, over the years ambitious salesmen had started calling on veterinarians to obtain additional sales on certain items of their line which also had applications in the DVM's practice. Examples of such products were antibiotics, sulfa drugs, cortisone, vitamins, antidiarrheal preparations, and cough products. The basic policy of selling direct to retail professional outlets (druggists, hospitals, etc.) made it possible to open new accounts in allied fields such as the animal health market.

Company officials had recognized this segment of business by establishing a separate research unit and sales force to give specific attention to its development. Ten salesmen had been added recently to call upon DVMs at an estimated annual cost of $150,000 for salaries and travel expenses. These men did not call upon druggists, farm supply stores, cooperatives, or hatcheries. The regular Upjohn sales force did call upon druggists, however, and took orders for pharmaceuticals which the druggist dispensed for the treatment both of humans and animals.

In addition to the establishment of the separate sales force, a special line of products was being developed for veterinarians. In the year prior to the discovery of the new product, the sales of products in the animal health market amounted to approximately $250,000.

Background for problem

In the animal health goods market, according to an Upjohn official, the veterinarian's role is somewhat different from that of the physician in the human health goods market. In the human field, the physician and druggist act as a team with the physician "creating" the demand by writing a prescription to be filled by the druggist. In the animal health field, prescription writing is at a minimum with the exception of a few small animal hospitals. The DVM, for the greater part, considers the druggist as a competitor. Different types of outlets, accordingly, serve the animal health goods market. These are: (1) the veterinarians, (2) drugstores, (3) farm supply stores and cooperatives, (4) hatcheries, (5) all other types (door-to-door, mail order, etc.).

EXHIBIT 1
Estimated annual sales by type of outlet, all animal health pharmaceuticals (at manufacturer's level)

Type of outlet	Estimated sales (add 000)	Percent of total sales
Veterinarian	$ 28,000	25
Drugstore	31,000	28
Farm supply and cooperatives	35,000	32
Hatcheries	9,000	8
All other	8,000	7
	$111,000	100

Source: Company studies.

EXHIBIT 2

Pharma-ceutical	Types of outlets listed in order of importance
Antibiotics	1st—DVMs; 2d—Farm supply; 3d—Drugstores
Sulfa drugs	1st—Drugstores; 2d—DVMs; 3d—Farm supply
Anthelmintics	1st—Farm supply; 2d—Drugstores; 3d—DVMs

As of the year of the new product discovery, the relative importance of each type of outlet in the sale of pharmaceuticals was as shown in Exhibit 1.

Among the more important pharmaceuticals included in the sales figures shown in Exhibit 1 are antibiotics, sulfa drugs, and anthelmintics.[1] The most important types of outlets for these three kinds of pharmaceuticals vary considerably, as indicated in Exhibit 2.

According to a company official, the proportion of pharmaceuticals administered to animals without diagnosis by a DVM varies widely

---

[1] Anthelmintic—an agent to expel or destroy intestinal worms, thereby improving growth.

by class of livestock and poultry and by disease being treated. The farmer can administer any and all to his animals if he so desires. If he believes he knows what the nature of the illness is, he may secure and administer what he thinks is the proper drug himself. His choice of what drug to give may be based on previous treatment of the same illness by a DVM, upon his own background in veterinary medicine, upon the advice of his neighbors, or information from literature, advertising, and so on. If the animal does not readily respond, a DVM is normally called. Also, if the farmer does not have confidence in his own ability to diagnose a particular illness, he would usually call in the DVM to examine the animal and supervise the treatment. Since only 25 percent of the sales of animal health pharmaceuticals are made through veterinarians there is a strong implication that a large proportion of the drugs are administered by the farmer without the benefit of professional help.

Unless the advice of a DVM is required in the treatment of an animal, the buying habits of farmers do *not* differ in purchasing remedies for specific illnesses like mastitis, as opposed to vitamins, food supplements, and similar items.

Statement of problem

The research and development division of The Upjohn Company developed a new product called "Corbiot" for the treatment of mastitis in dairy cattle. Mastitis is a disease of milk cattle which renders the milk useless until the disease is cured. This results in a serious economic loss to the farmer. In most cases the farmer diagnoses mastitis without the services of a DVM. If he knows of a suitable remedy, he can also administer it without the aid of a DVM. Where a case does not respond, however, a DVM is normally called.

Corbiot was proven to have definite advantages over any product on the market at that time. However, it was suspected that competitors would, in a relatively short time, have a similar product on the market. It was believed that six months to a year would be the maximum time in which Upjohn could hope to maintain this competitive advantage.

The estimated market for mastitis products at that time was in the neighborhood of $5 million at manufacturers' level or close to $10 million at retail level. While good estimates of the breakdown of this market, by types of outlet, were not available, it was assumed that it approximated the breakdown of all pharmaceuticals for animal health as shown in Exhibit 1.

Under the company's basic sales and distribution policies, the product, if announced, would be placed with and actively promoted to veterinarians, who accounted for 25 percent of the market. However, without active promotion to farmers it was doubtful whether Upjohn could expect active introductory sales support from druggists. If Upjohn actively promoted the new product to farmers, it was feared that serious objection would be raised by the veterinarians, possibly to the point where they would not only refuse to accept the new product but also would discontinue using other Upjohn products.

The key question facing Upjohn management, therefore, was that of determining what marketing strategy would maximize the returns from the new product discovery. The effect of such decisions upon the existing sales of other products to veterinarians, as well as its effect upon sales of human products, was also a major part of this problem.

The importance of establishing sound distribution and sales policies for this new product was underscored by the fact that two other products were nearing the end of the development period and would soon be ready for marketing. It was also anticipated that other products would be forthcoming in the future as the research and developmental work gathered impetus.

Alternatives

In evaluating the problem, Upjohn management listed and considered the following alternatives:

1. Announce this product only to the veterinarian. It was realized that under this alternative the company would be competing in only 25 percent of the potential market for the product.
2. Follow the basic company policy of announcing the product both to the DVM and the drugstore with no direct consumer advertising (i.e., advertising to the farmer). Without promotion to the farmer, the druggist could be expected to provide little active support for the product, even though he accounts for 28 percent of the animal health products market.
3. Announce the new product both to the DVM and the drugstore, but also back the druggist with heavy consumer advertising (i.e., advertising directed to farmers). Here the company would be actively competing in 53 percent of the market (25 percent for DVM + 28 percent for drugstore). However, Upjohn would be taking the risk of the veterinarian's disfavor, a reaction which might possibly affect the entire line. In the past, other pharmaceutical companies had tried to promote their products to farmers and sell DVMs simultaneously. In these cases the reaction of the DVMs had been negative, but the degree of buying resistance resulting had not been

measured. It was the observation of this experience that led Upjohn officials to anticipate unfavorable reactions from DVMs if Corbiot were heavily promoted to farmers. Some of the drugs distributed by competitors through channels other than DVMs were advertised to farmers, others were not.

4. Follow alternative No. 3 above, reaching DVMs and drugstores by direct sale, but also add jobbers to obtain distribution in other farm outlets (i.e., farm supply stores, co-ops, hatcheries, and so on). It was thought that jobbers would have to be allowed a 20 percent margin to get them to handle the line. From the standpoint of the farmer, purchase of Corbiot through outlets other than the DVM would offer advantages of (1) convenience, (2) availability of credit, and (3) possibly a lower price. This plan would provide active competition in 100 percent of the market, but might possibly result in a stronger DVM reaction than anticipated in reaction to No. 3 above.

5. Sell under one trade name for the veterinarian market and select a second trade name for sales to all other outlets. The product having the second name would then be advertised to farmers. It was not known what the DVM's reaction would be to such a plan, but it was suspected that there would be at least some degree of objection.

6. Announce the new product to the veterinarian under the Upjohn label and, also, either sell the product to another company for distribution to other outlets under its label or have Upjohn produce for marketing under private labels for feed companies and/or distributors. By giving up the marketing of the new product to all outlets except the veterinarians, it was recognized that profits from the research discovery would be shared with others.

7. Form a subsidiary company or acquire another company with established distribution in outlets other than the DVMs. This alternative would give distribution under a different brand name in the missing types of outlets and might possibly overcome the DVM's objections to alternatives No. 3 and No. 4. However, it brought up the serious question of whether one or two products plus future expectations which could not be fairly evaluated at the time, were enough to warrant such a drastic step.

CASE QUESTIONS

1. Assuming no change in brand policy, which of the first four alternatives should the company choose? Why? (Disregard alternatives No. 5 through 7 in this phase of the analysis.)

2. Next, broaden your analysis to take into consideration possible changes in brand policy outlined in alternatives Nos. 5, 6, and 7. Which line of action would you now recommend? Why?

CASE 4–2

Yard-Man, Inc. (B) (1958–62) *

Gaining independent distribution to offset loss of major private brand account

Immediately after the end of World War II, Yard-Man, Inc. of Jackson, Michigan, accepted a proposal from Sears, Roebuck and Company to manufacture lawn mowers for sale exclusively under the Sears Craftsman brand name. By the end of 1946, Yard-Man sales to Sears exceeded $1 million. During the next 10-year period, sales volume rose to $12 million, and Yard-Man profits on these sales were more than $700,000. The product line at this time consisted of silent hand mowers as well as powered reel and rotary mowers. In 1958, Sears decided to manufacture their own mowers. They announced that Yard-Man would be phased out over a three-year period as their principal supplier.

The decision of Sears to sever relations with Yard-Man prompted an immediate reorganization of the latter's operating personnel. An executive with an outstanding record as sales manager at Sears, Roebuck was appointed vice president in charge of sales for Yard-Man. A short time later, a sales manager experienced in independent distribution was brought in and given responsibility for the sales program. At the same time, the vice president in charge of sales moved to the position of executive vice president. In August 1958, these two men sat down to figure out a strategy that would create a new marketing program for the Yard-Man corporation.

The problems facing the company were numerous. They included: (1) the task of winning support from the independent wholesale distributors, who had been alienated by the selling practices of the company during its relationship with Sears; (2) the necessity to regain the public acceptance that the Yard-Man brand name had lost during the time that it was subordinated to the Sears' Craftsman label; (3) the intense competition faced by Yard-Man from manufacturers of low-priced, medium-quality mowers as well as from five manufacturers of quality products, who were firmly established in the existing trade channels; and (4) the fact that there was very little money available for retooling. In addition, plant overhead was costly, since it was based on the capacity

---

* Written by Martin R. Warshaw, Professor of Marketing, and Tom Buck, a student in the Graduate School of Business Administration, The University of Michigan.

needed to produce from $10 to $12 million worth of lawn mowers, most of which had formerly been sold to Sears. There was little surprise, therefore, at the industry's attitude that Yard-Man was in serious trouble.

The two men came to the following conclusions after considering these problems: First, they felt that the product line, although needing improvement, was of a caliber that could compete against the products of other manufacturers. Second, the jobbers' antagonism seemed sufficiently strong to preclude Yard-Man from getting their support in distributing to retailers. In addition, these jobbers (especially the hardware jobbers) were apparently not doing a good job with those products that they did carry. The two executives decided that if Yard-Man were to penetrate the market, they would have to go directly to retail dealers, although this would be a most costly method of distribution. The long-range strategy was to do such an effective job of selling directly to key dealers that jobbers would before long recognize the importance and the profitability of the Yard-Man line and welcome the chance to sell it to many smaller retail outfits.

If direct selling were decided upon, the planners for Yard-Man had two alternative courses of action: to use manufacturer's representatives or to develop their own company sales force. They calculated that although company men handling only the Yard-Man line would provide greater concentration of selling effort, the cost of maintaining a nationwide sales force would be about $160,000 per year. During the initial stages of the selling program, this cost could be spread over only a limited number of units (sales for the first year were estimated to run about $1 million). The cost of this alternative was deemed to be prohibitive, and the decision was therefore made to use manufacturer's representatives working on a commission basis. Under this plan sales costs would be variable, depending on sales volume. The comparison was as follows: 10 company salesmen averaging $16,000 a year in salary and travel expense per man would cost $160,000. These costs were contrasted with the alternative cost of paying a 5 percent commission on $1 million worth of sales to manufacturer's representatives, which would amount to $50,000.

Having decided to use manufacturer's representatives, and having estimated the cost of this type of distribution to be $50,000, the planners discussed whether distribution would be on a selective or intensive basis. Because the Yard-Man line was high in quality and priced accordingly, it was decided to use selective distribution to obtain dealers with an equally high reputation. The Yard-Man product had to be sold by retailers having good service facilities and able to engage in skillful and energetic merchandising. The executives of Yard-Man felt that circumstances might warrant offering exclusive dealerships to the better retailers handling hardware and lawn, garden, and farm implements.

In order to reestablish the Yard-Man name, to build up sales volume quickly, and to locate selected dealers, advertising was given an important role. Yard-Man decided to enter into a cooperative advertising program with dealers, covering media such as newspapers, radio, and television. In addition, $80,000 was budgeted for national consumer and trade advertising. In respect to personal selling, three company fieldmen were to be appointed to supplement the efforts of the manufacturer's representatives.

The first year's program

Within 30 days after the initial planning session of August 1958, a nationwide organization of manufacturer's representatives was formed. In October, the Yard-Man line was formally introduced at the National Hardware Show in New York City. By the following June, sales through independent channels had risen from zero to $920,000. Yard-Man executives regarded this as a good start, considering the many problems which the company faced. The product line in addition to mowers consisted of go-carts, motor scooters, and school furniture. It is interesting to note that none of these additions to the line proved profitable, and they were therefore dropped within a year or two after their introduction.

Because of the phasing-out program of Sears, Roebuck, sales to that corporation amounted to $7.5 million.

The second year

Somewhat encouraged by the first year's results, the company decided to tailor its program to the larger dealers and to feel out the effect which the initial direct-to-dealer program had had on jobbers. Therefore, a program of sliding discounts based on volume purchases was emphasized during the second year. This movement in the direction of jobber distribution had to be accomplished diplomatically so as not to disturb relations with those dealers who were buying directly. To this end, purchasing classifications were established on a "dealer" and "key-dealer" basis. The margins to "dealers" were reduced slightly, and the margins to "key-dealers" were increased to a point where they were sufficient to compensate jobbers. During the second year, independent sales reached $2,649,428. Once again Sears contributed about $7.5 million. In addition to setting up "key-dealers," Yard-Man made its first sale to a large chain organization—the retail affiliates of the Firestone Rubber and Tire Company.

The third year

After appraising the results of the second year of operations, Yard-Man executives were convinced that they should make a more definite move in the direction of jobber distribution. Feedback from the field indicated that jobbers were beginning to have more respect for the Yard-Man line. The terms "key-dealer" and "dealer" in the discount schedule were replaced with "AA" and "A" classifications. The "AA distributor" was now receiving a full jobbing discount. The idea here was that only a jobber could obtain the stipulated volume that would make the buyer eligible for this higher margin—a margin which was adequate to allow redistribution to retailers. Margin adjustment in anticipation of full jobber distribution was thus undertaken. The increasing prestige of the Yard-Man brand would, of course, make it easier to secure the proper acceptance of this program.

The "AA" classification brought in between 40 and 50 jobbers. In addition, Yard-Man started producing a special silent hand mower for the O. M. Scott and Sons Company under the Scott name. Additional sales were made to Firestone as well as to two hardware-buying co-operatives. Sales to these customers were $3,254,436. In their last year as a Yard-Man customer, Sears' purchases were $3.7 million.

The two cooperatives which purchased from Yard-Man represented a combination of 800 retail stores which engaged in a very aggressive selling program. Buying cooperatives were a new development for the hardware industry but were gaining strength so rapidly that hardware jobbers who did not keep up with modern distribution methods and promotional programs were losing out. Many of the hardware jobbing companies were old organizations that had lost their aggressiveness and had neglected to adapt to the changing needs of their retailer customers. Regular jobbers disliked cooperatives because retailers who were members of a cooperative received broader margins and could therefore charge lower prices or realize greater profits than the customers of the traditional jobber organizations. Yard-Man accepted the risk that they might alienate the newly formed jobber organization by selling to the two cooperatives. It was thought, however, that cooperatives represented the distribution methods of the future and would continue to affect sales of the hardware jobber. In any event, dual distribution was initiated, and Yard-Man attempted to adjust the program so that the two types of wholesalers could live with each other. No immediate problems occurred with respect to the jobber organization at this time.

During this year, the inefficient manufacturer's representatives were weeded out of the distribution program and replaced by company salesmen. This measure was feasible because Yard-Man sales volume had reached the point where it could economically support the salary and travel expenses of the company salesmen. Each of the salesmen was given a defined territory that may or may not have been covered by manufacturer's representatives. Each of these company salesmen was held responsible for attaining monthly quotas set by the sales manager after he had conferred with the salesman.

The fourth year

By this time Yard-Man executives felt that the way had been sufficiently prepared, by gradual reductions in dealer margins and the building of brand recognition and product reputation, to achieve full jobber distribution. Therefore, it was decided to eliminate the "A" and "AA" classifications and to use one margin to sell only to jobbers.

Yard-Man also made the decision to sell through some of the larger department stores and to accept offers from some of the trading-stamp people. Not only did this latter group represent another type of outlet, but their high standards were a complement to the excellent reputation of the Yard-Man line. The success of the sales to cooperative buyers in the previous year, achieved without greatly irritating established jobbers and dealers, indicated to Yard-Man that it would be advantageous to sell to more of these cooperative buying organizations.

During the fourth year, full jobber distribution was attained without much objection from retailers who had formerly bought directly. The Yard-Man product line was selling well, and dealers and jobbers alike readily accepted the terms of distribution set up by the company. The shock of these innovations was not severe for the retailers, because the change in margins was made gradually, and jobbers were chosen who offered the retailers a great deal of support.

During this fourth year, Montgomery Ward, Sears' traditional competitor, purchased Yard-Man reel mowers for sale under private label and indicated that there might be a possibility of full-line purchases in the future. Another large cooperative gave Yard-Man its business which had formerly gone to Yard-Man's top competitor, who had withdrawn from distribution through cooperatives. Dealings with this new customer proved even more lucrative later in the year when the cooperative added 300 additional highly successful stores. Yard-Man, Inc. also sold in considerable volume to one of the larger trading-stamp companies. The last great stride in extending distribution during the fourth year was taken when sales of the Yard-Man line were made to the J. L. Hudson Company of Detroit and other large department stores.

All of these additional accounts, although still in the initial stages of development, combined to give Yard-Man a total sales volume of $5,664,029. As mentioned previously, Sears, Roebuck made no purchases from Yard-Man during this year.

CASE QUESTIONS

1. Comment on the company's channel policy. What problems are especially pressing for a firm changing from private brand supply to distribution through independent channels?

2. What do you think of company policy with respect to sales to buying cooperatives, stamp companies, department stores, Firestone, and Montgomery Ward?

3. Do you approve of the company's willingness to manufacture for sale under reseller brands after its experience with Sears, Roebuck?

CASE 4–3

Yard-Man, Inc. (C) (1962–70)*

Decisions on product line and distribution

Yard-Man, Inc. of Jackson, Michigan, was organized in 1933 to produce what was then a new type of hand lawnmower. It utilized hardened steel blades which did not touch the cutter bar. This concept resulted in a mower that was efficient, long-lasting, and almost silent. Distribution was developed through hardware jobbers and hardware retailers. In 1938, Yard-Man began to produce lawnmowers for Sears, Roebuck for sale under Sear's Craftsman label. After World War II, Yard-Man terminated its relationships with hardware jobbers and hardware retailers and became exclusively a supplier of Sears, Roebuck.

Yard-Man sales to Sears grew gradually to an annual volume of over $12 million. In 1958, Sears decided to manufacture its own lawn mowers and announced that purchases from Yard-Man would be phased out over a three-year period. During this phase-out period Yard-Man fought an uphill battle to reestablish distribution through independent distributors and retailers. At first, sales had to be made directly to retailers because distributors were unwilling to carry the Yard-Man line. As Yard-Man sales grew at the retail level, distributors became increasingly willing to carry the Yard-Man line, and distribution through distributors was gradually developed.[1]

The situation in 1962

In 1962 the Yard-Man line consisted of handmowers and reel and rotary power mowers. Between 40 and 50 distributors had been signed

---

* Written by Stewart H. Rewoldt, Professor of Marketing, Graduate School of Business Administration, The University of Michigan.

[1] See "Yard-Man, Inc. (A)" and "Yard-Man, Inc. (B)" for more background information on Yard-Man during the pre-1962 period.

up. Yard-Man also sold, under the Yard-Man name, to Firestone Stores, to two hardware cooperatives, and to two trading stamp firms. Under private labels, Yard-Man supplied mowers to Montgomery Ward and to O. M. Scott and Sons Company. Sales were $5,664,029 and profits, after taxes, were $76,464. Although Yard-Man had been badly shaken by the termination of its role as a supplier to Sears, it had survived and was again a viable operation.

Period of consolidation: 1962–65

Yard-Man lawnmowers were of high quality and able to compete on a quality basis with other well-known brands. The Yard-Man line, however, contained a limited number of products, all of which were in demand during only one season of the year. Additional products would improve Yard-Man's position in the market. However, new products were out of the question at this time. The resources required for product development, tooling, and market introduction were not available. Yard-Man would have to do the best it could with the product line it had.

Distributors. Improvement of distribution offered a more feasible opportunity to improve Yard-Man's sales and profit picture. Distribution was still somewhat spotty, and some distributors were less effective than might be desired. Yard-Man executives decided that the major effort for the next several years should be directed at improvement of distribution.

Experience showed that the most effective distributors of Yard-Man products were lawn and garden specialists. The second most effective distributors, as a group, were farm equipment distributors who specialized in smaller farm equipment and supplies. The third most effective type of distributor was the hardware distributor who gave special emphasis to lawn and garden products. The typical hardware distributor did not have this orientation and was of limited effectiveness.

Yard-Man undertook a program for upgrading its distributors. Wherever possible, stronger distributors were substituted for those who were weak and ineffective. Several smaller distributors were often replaced with one larger distributor. Distributors were signed in areas where Yard-Man had not previously had distribution, or where it was underrepresented. Gradually the quality of distributors improved. Yard-Man conducted training programs for distributors and their salesmen. Missionary salesmen periodically called on retail accounts with the salesmen of distributors in an attempt to improve their effectiveness.

Yard-Man distributors had exclusive territories in the sense that only one distributor was appointed in a given area. Distributors usually carried other brands of lawn and garden equipment. Yard-Man products were of high quality, selling at relatively high prices. Distributors found

EXHIBIT 1
Yard-Man, Inc., financial summary, 1962–69 (years ended June 30)

	1969	1968	1967	1966	1965	1964	1963	1962
Net sales..............	$26,165,909	$21,823,155	$15,884,067	$12,486,197	$8,346,033	$8,539,708	$6,651,879	$5,664,029
Earnings before income taxes.............	880,161	1,313,624	924,151	715,265	168,767	305,936	217,411	146,464
Federal and state income taxes.............	450,000	650,000	440,000	340,000	75,000	145,000	106,000	70,000
Net earnings..........	430,161	663,624	484,151	375,265	93,767	160,936	111,411	76,464
Net earnings per share..	.94	1.45	1.06	0.80	0.20	0.33	0.23	0.16
Current assets........	4,793,390	6,224,869	4,610,664	4,517,921	3,032,641	3,434,855	3,122,670	2,938,807
Current liabilities......	1,365,169	2,728,162	1,678,119	1,289,950	341,020	568,375	357,237	292,652
Current ratio..........	3.51 to 1	2.28 to 1	2.75 to 1	3.50 to 1	8.89 to 1	6.04 to 1	8.74 to 1	10 to 1
Working capital........	3,428,221	3,496,707	2,932,545	3,227,971	2,691,621	2,866,480	2,765,433	2,646,155
Stockholders' equity.....	5,389,958	5,076,509	4,517,480	4,317,951	3,998,856	4,005,367	3,892,551	3,781,140
Book value per share....	11.67	11.10	9.99	9.15	8.48	8.32	8.09	7.86
Shares outstanding......	461,741	457,891	452,141	471,772	471,272	481,200	481,200	481,200

it necessary to cover a wide price range and added other brands at the lower price levels. Distributors usually did not carry other brands of lawn and garden equipment that were directly competitive in quality and price with the Yard-Man line.

Dealers. Retail dealers for Yard-Man products were chosen by the distributors. Yard-Man exercised no direct control over their selection. Experience indicated that the best dealers for Yard-Man products were lawn and garden specialists, but the Yard-Man line was also sold through department stores, hardware stores, appliance stores, automotive outlets, and an assortment of other types of retail outlets. Dealers were not granted exclusive territories, but the number appointed in a market was restricted to the number demand would support. Dealers usually carried other brands of lawn and garden equipment at lower price levels.

Results of these efforts. The campaign to improve distribution was viewed by Yard-Man executives as successful. By 1965, nationwide distribution had been achieved through 88 distributors and some 6,000 dealers. The general quality of both distributors and dealers was relatively high. Sales had risen from $5,664,029 in 1962 to $8,539,708 in 1964. After-tax profits rose during these two years from $76,464 to $160,936. In 1965, both sales and profits fell slightly, but this was due to a special circumstance. A supplier to Yard-Man had provided a faulty part which had to be replaced in almost all units of one riding mower model which had been sold that year. This caused a fall in net profits and was probably responsible for a 2.5 percent drop in sales.

Yard-Man continued to sell throughout this period to Montgomery Ward and to O. M. Scott and Sons under private labels, as well as to two hardware cooperatives, Firestone stores, and two stamp companies, under the Yard-Man name. Sales to these accounts continued to increase, while distribution through independent distributors and dealers was expanded.

Period of change: 1966–69

Now that sales and profits had reached more satisfactory levels and a strengthened distribution structure had been established, Yard-Man was in a position to consider broadening its product line. There were strong incentives to do so. Demand for present Yard-Man products was highly seasonal, yet production had to be at a reasonably steady pace in order to achieve economical costs of production. This meant that substantial working capital had to be tied up in the carrying of large inventories. Distributors, independent retail dealers, and private brand accounts were all interested in achieving product assortments that offered year-round sales opportunities and favored suppliers that could provide them. Consumer preferences for lawn and garden equipment were changing, producing an increasing demand for self-propelled and riding equipment. Responding to these forces, Yard-Man executives agreed upon a program for broadening the product line.

New products. Because of the evidence that a strong trend toward purchase of riding equipment existed and could be expected to become more pronounced, the first addition to the product line was the Mustang series of riding mowers. The Mustang was offered in three models: standard, deluxe, and supreme. A snowplow attachment was available. The Mustang was an improved riding mower that was efficient, safe, and easily operated. Introduced in 1966, it was well-accepted both by the trade and by consumers.

In January 1967, Yard-Man purchased, for cash, the George Garden Tools Division of Community Industries, Ltd., located at Sullivan, Illinois. George Garden Tools Division manufactured the highly regarded Earthbird garden tiller and the Snowbird snowthrower. Yard-Man marketed these products as the Yard-Man Earthbird garden tiller and the Yard-Man Snowbird snowthrower. Along with these two new products, Yard-Man acquired a 50,000-square-foot manufacturing facility.

Later in 1967, the Yard-Man Jet Sweep was introduced in both 3- and 5-horsepower sizes. The Jet Sweep produced a high-velocity air stream for blowing leaves, grass clippings, and lawn debris into a pile for easy removal. The Jet Sweep was produced at the newly acquired George Garden Tools Plant.

A garden tractor, complete with accessories, was introduced in January 1968. Later in 1968, Yard-Man introduced the Vac Sweep. The Vac Sweep was a large, outdoor vacuum sweeper with a 3-horsepower motor and a 9-cubic-foot grass bag, for cleaning lawns, walks, driveways, patios, garages, etc.

In 1969, Yard-Man introduced two new garden tractor models and new, lighter weight, self-propelled, and push-type rotary mowers. Past sales of Yard-Man rotary mowers had been disappointing. They were heavy and possessed many special features, whereas the trend in consumer preference was toward lighter weight, simple-to-operate models.

Also in 1969, Yard-Man introduced its first product that was not clearly within the lawn and garden category—the "SnoCub" snowmobile. Snowmobiles had enjoyed rapid sales growth in recent years, and these sales occurred at a time of year when Yard-Man sales were below those of other seasons. The SnoCub was smaller and lighter than other snowmobiles, with a maximum speed of 20 miles per hour. It would fit in a standard car trunk, and two SnoCubs could be carried in the standard station wagon. The suggested retail list price was $399.95, plus freight.

Traditionally, snowmobiles were sold through marine distributors and dealers. Yard-Man decided to limit distribution to its present outlets. This would give these outlets additional opportunities for sales during the winter season and would maintain good relations. Some Yard-Man distributors did sell the SnoCub, however, to marine dealers.

Changes in distribution. Since the early 1960s, Yard-Man had sold to two hardware cooperatives, each of which had many hundreds of affiliated stores. Sales through hardware cooperatives had never been proportional to the number of outlets represented. Affiliated retail outlets typically were self-service and concentrated on low-ticket items. They did not provide the type of atmosphere, sales effort, or after-sale service required for high-ticket, mechanical products. However, Yard-Man considered them to be desirable outlets because of the exposure they provided for Yard-Man products.

Yard-Man's independent distributors and dealers often complained about hardware cooperatives being allowed to carry Yard-Man products. Such outlets were strongly price-oriented and offered Yard-Man products at prices substantially below the prevailing prices quoted by independent dealers. These dealers felt they could not compete with these prices and also offer the higher quality sales effort and after-sale service expected of them. Because of the attitude of independent distributors and dealers, Yard-Man decided to discontinue sales to hardware cooperatives under the Yard-Man label. Such sales to one hardware cooperative were discontinued in 1967 and to the other in 1968.

Past Yard-Man efforts at marketing its products outside the United States had met with little success. In 1969, Yard-Man signed an agreement with Wolf-Gerate GmbH of West Germany to market Yard-Man products abroad. Wolf-Gerate had distribution in some six countries. Early results indicated that this arrangement would result in substantial future sales of Yard-Man products.

Planning for the future: the 1970s

By the end of 1969, Yard-Man had increased its product line more than three-fold since 1962 and now offered products for all seasons of the year. All products were of high quality, up-to-date design, and compared very favorably with the products of competitors. Sales volume had increased from $5,664,029 in 1962 to $26,165,909 in 1969, and after-tax profits had grown from $76,464 to $430,161. Company executives viewed the product line as complete for the time being, and planned only modifications of existing products for the next several years.

A rough breakdown of Yard-Man sales by products in 1969 is shown in Exhibit 2. This distribution of sales does not, of course, reflect the full impact of new products added in 1968 and 1969. These products were new in the market and still in the process of establishing themselves. The SnoCub, for example, had not yet reached its first selling season. As

EXHIBIT 2
Product sales for 1969

Product	Percent of sales
Riding mowers and tractors..................	50
Rotary mowers...........................	20
Handmowers and reel power mowers..........	10
Snowthrowers...........................	15
Tillers....................................	5

these new products became established, this distribution of sales, by products, could be expected to change.

Yard-Man's market position varied substantially, by products. For handmowers (with over 16" cut) it held over 50 percent of the total market. For reel power mowers, it held approximately a 15 percent market share. In the case of riding mowers and tractors, it had approximately 10 percent of the market. In the snowthrower market, its share was close to 10 percent. For garden tillers, Yard-Man's share of the market was only around 2 percent and for quality rotary mowers, about 3 percent. It was hoped that market acceptance of the new lighter weight rotary mowers introduced in 1969 would substantially improve Yard-Man's position in this field.

Yard-Man had, for many years, been following a policy of multiple distribution, but was uncertain about the ideal mix of distribution channels for Yard-Man products. Since discontinuing sales under the Yard-Man name to hardware cooperatives, Yard-Man had as major accounts its independent distributors and dealers for the Yard-Man brand, and Montgomery Ward and O. M. Scott and Sons for private-label business. As minor accounts, it had two trading stamp companies, who sold under the Yard-Man brand, and two hardware cooperatives who did a small volume under private labels. Yard-Man's private-label business represented a substantial share, but less than one half, of total sales volume. Montgomery Ward was by far Yard-Man's largest private-brand account.

Yard-Man executives believed that multiple distribution offered many advantages. It allowed Yard-Man to reach a variety of market segments, each best served by a different distribution channel. Wards and Scott each had many loyal customers who could not be reached without selling under their private labels. If Yard-Man did not sell to these accounts, other suppliers undoubtedly would. Different segments of the market reacted to different appeals. Independent distributors offered effective personal selling and good service, Wards placed greater emphasis on price, and Scott offered the appeal of quality lawn care that was associated with their name.

By selling through multiple channels Yard-Man reached a greater portion of the total market, achieved greater sales volume, and thus had lower per unit costs of production. This, Yard-Man executives believed, allowed Yard-Man products to be more competitive in all market segments. Yard-Man had the protection, too, of "not having all its eggs in one basket." As market trends changed to favor one distribution channel in relation to another, Yard-Man was in a strong position to capitalize on these market changes.

Although Yard-Man executives believed that multiple distribution provided these advantages, they were concerned about what was the proper "mix" of channels. Should Yard-Man have discontinued sales under the Yard-Man brand to hardware cooperatives? Should Yard-Man sell through additional distribution channels, if the opportunity arose? What sort of balance should be sought between sales under the Yard-Man brand and sales under private labels?

Various retail outlets inevitably compete with each other, and they compete on different bases—on price, service, etc. Yard-Man's experience has been that price differences between different outlets sometimes became very substantial, and this led to strong complaints from those outlets who competed more on a nonprice basis. This problem was not entirely eliminated if price competition came mainly from those retailers who sold Yard-Man products under private labels. Ward's salesmen, for example, commonly told consumers that their private-label lawn and garden care products were made by Yard-Man, and this fact was commonly known in the trade.

Yard-Man was one of the top four producers of better quality lawn and garden care products. Until recently it was the only one with multiple distribution. One major competitor recently began to move toward multiple distribution. The other two major competitors continued to rely, exclusively, on sales through independent distributors and dealers.

CASE QUESTIONS

1. Evaluate Yard-Man's product and distribution policy for the 1962–69 period.

2. What is the proper "mix" of distribution channels for Yard-Man? Why?

CASE 4–4

Ross-Evans, Inc.*

Marketing strategy for specialty advertising company

In mid-1969, Mr. Robert Williams was named president of Ross-Evans, Inc., a family-held and long-established specialty advertising company. He was the first nonfamily person to hold this post. As his first major task, he undertook a review of Ross-Evans marketing strategy to determine what, if any, changes should be made to assure future growth and profitability.

The company

Ross-Evans, Inc., was founded in Des Moines, Iowa in 1904 to produce and market calendars. The company was successful from the start and produced a profit in every year of its history. In 1969, with sales of approximately $5 million, it ranked fourth or fifth in size in the specialty advertising industry. However, the largest specialty advertising firm in the industry was ten times as large, with sales of over $50 million.

EXHIBIT 1
Sales by product line, 1969

Product line	Percent of sales
Calendars	50
Specialties	20
Gifts	30

From the time of its founding until 1962, Ross-Evans produced and sold only calendars. In 1962, it added a gift line and an advertising specialties line, with the result that sales volume doubled between 1962 and 1969. The breakdown of company sales by product lines in 1969 was approximately as shown in Exhibit 1.

Ross-Evans specialized in "utility" calendars in contrast to "art" calendars. A utility calendar provides something useful in addition to the recording and dividing of time, such as space for recording memoranda, notes, appointments, or pockets for holding bills and receipts. Many

---

* Written by Stewart H. Rewoldt, Professor of Marketing, Graduate School of Business Administration, The University of Michigan.

of these calendars were patented. This served to provide Ross-Evans representatives with unique products not available from other sources. The price range for Ross-Evans calendars, imprinted with the customer's advertising message, was 17 cents to $2, while the average price received per calendar was between 40 and 50 cents. Ross-Evans manufactured most of the calendars in its line. However, since it was impractical to manufacture all styles of calendars, the line was augmented with a few of the better lines of what are known as "job line" calendars (i.e., calendars purchased from outside sources).

While calendars may be considered as being within the broad spectrum of advertising specialties, the term "specialties" is used within the industry to refer more specifically to the literally thousands of other products—pens, pencils, billfolds, key chains, ashtrays, etc.—which are imprinted with the customer's advertising message and distributed by him to his present or potential customers. Ross-Evans did not manufacture specialties, but purchased them from outside sources. Although an "exclusive" was occasionally obtained, the same specialties were usually available to all specialty advertising firms. Prices of specialties varied widely, but most were in the low-priced category.

Gifts are distinguished from specialties in that they are not imprinted with an advertising message. Also, the price range is broader and generally much higher. Most items in the Ross-Evans gift line were priced between one dollar and fifty dollars. These were sold to business firms and, in turn, presented to valued customers—usually at Christmas or on other special occasions. Ross-Evans acquired all the gifts in its line from outside suppliers. Generally, the same gift items were available to their competitors.

The market

The total size of the specialty advertising market was not precisely known, but had been estimated to be close to one billion dollars per year. Almost any business firm, from the large, nationwide corporation to the neighborhood grocery, bank, or service station, was a potential customer. Anyone with a need to establish name identity, build customer loyalty, or direct attention to his products or services might be turned into a customer. However, large businesses often dealt directly with printers in the purchase of calendars, and directly with manufacturers of gifts and advertising specialties in acquiring those items, in order to lower their costs. The specialty advertising firms such as Ross-Evans sold to some large firms on the basis of quality service, but small and medium size firms constituted the bulk of their market.

Ross-Evans, Inc. had historically been strongly oriented toward the rural market. Its first calendars, just after the turn of the century, were designed to appeal primarily to farmers. These were highly successful and the company built on this base. The company has continued to be strongest in rural and small-town markets.

In the opinion of William Morris, vice president and sales manager of Ross-Evans, the purchase situation for the several product lines of Ross-Evans creates some special marketing problems. Rarely does the average prospective customer clearly perceive the need for creating name identity or holding loyal customers, and he usually is unaware of how a specialty advertising firm can be of service to him.

A situation such as this requires creative selling—sales representatives with the ability to discover a potential buyer's needs and demonstrate how advertising specialties could meet those needs. In the case of calendars, the sales situation was made more difficult by the fact that calendars had to be ordered a year or more before the scheduled delivery date. This required customers to project their planning substantially into the future, which many resisted doing. The average order received by Ross-Evans was in the neighborhood of $100.

Distribution

Ross-Evans products were sold by approximately 150 salesmen. These salesmen were not employees of Ross-Evans, but rather were "independent contractors" who were granted exclusive rights to sell the company's products in a specified territory. They were paid a commission—about 20 to 25 percent on most products—on all orders submitted. This sales force concentrated its efforts on the sale of Ross-Evans products, but some sales representatives also sold a limited volume of products which they acquired from other sources. A few outstanding salesmen achieved incomes of $20,000 to $30,000 per year, but most had incomes far below this level.

Ross-Evans distribution was concentrated in the western half of the United States, with only spotty distribution east of the Mississippi River. It was strongest in rural areas and small towns, and weak in metropolitan areas. For example, it had no distribution whatsoever in such major metropolitan areas as New York, Chicago, or Detroit.

Throughout the specialty advertising industry, salesman turnover was relatively high. One of Ross-Evans larger competitors, for example, had to hire 1,200 new sales representatives per year to keep an average of 850 salesmen in the field. Ross-Evans' turnover rate for sales representatives was well below the industry average, but still higher than they would like. This situation made the recruitment, selection, and training of sales representatives a major and continuous activity.

Ross-Evans had three regional selling managers—one located in Los Angeles, one in Portland, Oregon, and one in Denver. These regional selling managers recruited, trained, and supervised sales representatives in the southwestern, northwestern, and Mountain States regions. The

Los Angeles manager had nineteen men reporting to him, the Portland manager had seven, and the Denver manager had ten. All other sales representatives reported directly to William Morris, vice president and general sales manager. The regional selling managers served as sales representatives as well as being managers. On their own sales they were paid the same commissions as other sales representatives. In addition, they were paid an override on sales of the men they hired, trained, and supervised.

Home office marketing organization

Marketing responsibility was shared by three Ross-Evans vice presidents, each of whom reported directly to Robert Williams. William Morris, vice president and general sales manager, supervised the three regional selling managers and the over 100 sales representatives who reported directly to the home office. In addition, recruitment, selection, and training of new sales representatives required a major portion of his time. He was aided by an administrative assistant.

David Scott had the title of vice president, product planning. He was reponsible for product line development. He continually searched for new items and ideas for each of the company's three lines and brought these to the attention of a product selection committee made up of top executives. He kept a close watch on items already in the line and recommended appropriate action, such as dropping or restyling an item, when such action seemed appropriate. New products were chosen on a more-or-less intuitive basis. If the selection committee thought an item would be successful it was added to the line and its sales closely watched. It was announced to the sales representatives in the company's house organ and by special flyers. Care was taken not to burden the sales representatives with too many new items at one time so that the new additions would receive the attention and push they required.

Walter Hensley was vice president and treasurer of Ross-Evans, but he also had some marketing responsibilities. He was responsible for sales service, promotion, and development of the company's line of booklets.

The competitive situation

Ross-Evans is what is known in the specialty advertising trade as a "direct house," of which there were about a dozen in the industry in 1969. A "direct house" sells its wares directly to business firms through its own salesmen or sales representatives, rather than selling through jobbers. All direct houses manufacture at least some of the products they sell. The largest direct house in the specialty advertising field, Brown and Bigelow of St. Paul, Minnesota, sold over $50 million per year. In the next size category, with sales ranging from $5 million to $10 million, were three or four other direct houses. The remaining direct houses, about a half-dozen, had sales of less than $5 million per year. All direct houses sold calendars and gifts as well as specialties.

The major share of the market for specialty advertising was served by jobbers, of which there were about 2,700 in 1969. The average jobber employed three or four outside salesmen. Specialty advertising jobbers manufactured none of the products they sold, but rather purchased all of them from outside sources. Because most sources for advertising specialties sold to anyone who wished to purchase, jobbers generally had no exclusive products in their lines, as did the direct houses.

The total sales of specialty advertising jobbers have been growing more rapidly than total sales of direct houses. This has been due primarily to two factors. First, jobbers have been increasing rapidly in total number, with each additional jobber getting at least some share of the total market. Second, many sales representatives of the direct houses decided to go into business for themselves as jobbers. When they did so, they often took some of their previous customers with them. The attrition of men has slowed somewhat in recent years (since 1962 for Ross-Evans) as the direct houses have added "jobbed lines" to supplement their own manufactured lines, and thus made their men competitive with the broader lines of jobbers. However, jobbers possessed more flexibility in their operations. In contrast to the direct houses, which generally maintained a firm price structure, jobbers often negotiated on price.

Mr. Williams was most concerned about the competitive situation as it related to calendars. Calendars accounted for one half of Ross-Evans sales and, because they were the only line the company manufactured, they accounted for a larger share of profits. The Ross-Evans manufacturing plant had substantial excess capacity. The volume produced could easily be doubled if this increased output could be sold. Because of the specialized nature of the plant's machinery and equipment, it could be utilized only in the manufacture of calendars.

While an increase in calendar sales would be of great benefit to Ross-Evans, such an increase would be very difficult to achieve. The calendar industry is a mature industry. There has been some overall growth in calendar sales with increases in population and business activity, but the specialty advertising industry has not shared in this growth. Rather, the growth has been primarily in retail sales of entirely different styles of calendars, without an advertising imprint, by stationers, bookstores, department stores, and other types of retailers. Ross-Evans executives viewed the retail calendar market as an entirely different business than the one they were in. It could not be reached effectively through their present sales organization.

The rural market, to which Ross-Evans has long been oriented, had declined greatly in relative importance and this decline was expected to continue. Hence it offered little opportunity to increase calendar sales. Sales growth would have to be achieved in metropolitan and industrial areas.

Ross-Evans has been attempting to expand its distribution in areas where it has been unrepresented or underrepresented, but the task proved difficult for a number of reasons. In a tight labor market, such as existed throughout the 1960s, sales representatives were difficult to recruit. The task required sales personnel with particular qualifications, who were hard to find. A new representative had to be willing to accept a low income for an extended period while he became established.

The development of new markets, particularly for calendars, was not an easy task. When a business firm had selected a calendar to bear its advertising imprint, it tended to select the same calendar in subsequent years to maintain image continuity. For this reason, most calendar sales were repeat sales. This benefited Ross-Evans in its established markets, but it benefited other specialty advertising firms in markets where Ross-Evans had not previously established distribution.

William Morris, vice president and general sales manager, has recommended that the number of regional selling managers be increased from three to eight in order to expedite the expansion of distribution. The five additional selling managers would have the same responsibilities as the present three and would be compensated on the same basis.

CASE QUESTION

What actions should Mr. Williams take?

CASE 4–5

The Dow Chemical Company *

Distribution of drycleaning chemicals

Located in Midland, Michigan, The Dow Chemical Company was a large, diversified producer of chemicals, metals, plastics, packaging, agri-

---

* Written by Stewart H. Rewoldt, Professor of Marketing, Graduate School of Business Administration, The University of Michigan.

cultural, pharmaceutical, and consumer products. The Drycleaning Chemicals Sales Group was responsible for sales of Dow Chemicals to the drycleaning industry. In 1934, Dow pioneered the use of perchloroethylene as a drycleaning solvent. Since then Dow has been one of the largest sellers of synthetic drycleaning solvents in the United States.

Products

The Dow Chemical Company manufactured "Dow-Per," "Dow-Clor 811," and "Dow-Per C-S," for sale to the drycleaning industry. Dow-Per was Dow's registered trade name for synthetic perchloroethylene. This was the basic product in Dow's line of drycleaning solvents. Since introduced in 1934, perchloroethylene gradually replaced naphtha and similar petroleum based products to become the most widely used drycleaning solvent. Dow-Per was by far the leading selling product in Dow's line of drycleaning solvents.

Dow-Clor 811 was first introduced in the market in 1964 under the name "Norge-Clor 811." It had been developed specifically for use in Norge coin-operated drycleaning machines which Norge had introduced into the market in 1960. In contrast to perchloroethylene, which required the addition of detergents and sweeteners in the drycleaning plant, Norge-Clor 811 already included these additives, thus making it a safe and simple product for use in coin-operated machines. In 1969, Dow changed the name of this product to Dow-Clor 811 in order to more closely identify it with the Dow Chemical Company and with the Dow distributor and service network. It was not changed physically and was still intended only for use in Norge equipment. At about this same time another chemical producer introduced a competing product for this same market. Previously, Dow had had no direct competition on Dow-Clor 811.

Dow-Per C-S was introduced in 1967. Like Dow-Clor 811, it was a combination product that already included detergents and sweeteners. Unlike Dow-Clor 811, it was aimed at a much broader market. It was intended for use in both professional and coin-operated machines (except Norge). It offered several advantages to conventional drycleaners. Because detergents and sweeteners were preadded the drycleaner did not have to perform this function. It also eliminated the need to periodically test the detergent concentration in the solvent system. It reduced the transfer of lint between garments. Like Dow-Clor 811, it was simple and easy for amateurs to use in coin-operated machines.

Distribution

Within the drycleaning industry there were over 30,000 drycleaners using perchloroethylene. Some of these drycleaners were large, but the vast majority were quite small. To reach this dispersed market of many small drycleaners, Dow sold through 140 distributors. Again, some of these were relatively large with multiple locations, but most distributors were smaller, single-location operators. Some were broad-line chemical products distributors, but most specialized in selling drycleaning equipment and supplies to the drycleaning industry.

Distributors of Dow drycleaning solvents had been carefully chosen and were, as a group, the best in the industry. Distributors did not have exclusive territories, but the number of distributors authorized to sell Dow drycleaning solvents was limited to the number the available market would support. Dow wanted a sufficient number of distributors to assure access to 100 percent of the drycleaning market.

Dow salesmen called only on distributors who had been authorized to sell Dow products and did not attempt to sell Dow drycleaning solvents to distributors who represented competing suppliers of perchloroethylene. It wanted to retain the loyalty of its distributors and did not feel it could do so if it sold to every distributor who was willing to purchase Dow products. In return for this protection against unlimited competition in the sale of Dow solvents, Dow expected its authorized distributors to concentrate their purchases of drycleaning solvents with Dow.

Delivery of Dow-Per to drycleaners was usually by tank truck, much as fuel oil is delivered to consumers. Thus there was no brand identification of the product when received by drycleaners. The drycleaner knew he was receiving Dow-Per, rather than a competitive brand of perchloroethylene, only because he had placed his order with an authorized Dow distributor.

Dow provided extensive technical services to its distributors, helping them solve drycleaning problems of their customers. It provided more extensive services than any other supplier of perchloroethylene.

The competitive situation

Dow was the largest of nine domestic suppliers of perchloroethylene to the drycleaning industry, with over 25 percent of the available market. The next two largest producers each had sales about one half those of Dow. The other suppliers had smaller market shares, some of them with only 2 to 4 percent of the market.

In the 1930s there were only two producers of perchloroethylene. As time passed, other firms entered the market and fought to establish distribution. The latest company entered the market only in recent years. As a consequence of the increased number of competitors, Dow's market share gradually fell to less than 30 percent, from a high of over 50 percent. Because of the growing use of perchloroethylene, however, absolute sales continued to gradually increase.

Because of the nature of the drycleaning market, all suppliers of perchloroethylene sold through distributors. Because the number of distributors, particularly the better ones, was limited, this created strong competition among suppliers for distributor representation. As the number of suppliers increased, this competition became intense.

Price competition on perchloroethylene was severe. No supplier could command a price premium without risking serious loss of market share. The price of perchloroethylene varied by geographical regions depending on the competitive situation. On the East Coast, for example, the price was substantially lower than elsewhere in the United States because of the competition that existed from lower priced imports of perchloroethylene. This, and other competitive forces, caused price differences among other regions as well. Within a given region, Dow attempted to maintain a uniform price structure. However, when a distributor representing another supplier offered a price concession to a drycleaner who had previously purchased from a Dow distributor, Dow might, depending on the situation, make a price concession to its distributor to enable him to hold that account.

Encroachment by competitors on Dow distributors

As noted above, Dow had the strongest distributor organization in the drycleaning industry. Because drycleaners tended to choose, and then stay with, a particular distributor, this was a source of marketing strength for Dow. To preserve this advantage, Dow tried to build distributor loyalty by: 1) not selling to any distributors other than authorized Dow distributors; 2) providing extensive services to distributors and their customers.

Other suppliers of perchloroethylene did not follow the same policy. Salesmen from other suppliers continued to call on Dow distributors, attempting to sell them at least a portion of their needs for perchloroethylene. Such efforts were particularly strong by those suppliers who were relatively new to the marketing of drycleaning solvents and were trying to build distribution. With most of the better distributors already taken by Dow and others, this appeared to them to be a sound course to follow. To the extent competitive suppliers were successful in selling other brands of perchloroethylene to Dow distributors, Dow could expect to lose sales and market share. Unfortunately, many Dow distributors did begin to buy a portion of their drycleaning solvents from these other suppliers.

Dow distributors offered a number of reasons for buying a portion of their needs from other sources. They said that they "wanted to know if Dow's price was right," or that "they wanted to keep Dow honest." Purchase from other sources gave them a basis for price comparison. In some cases, competitors would offer a special price on "just one truckload" in order to get a portion of the Dow distributor's business. Competitors' salesmen would call on drycleaners, obtain orders for their brand of perchloroethylene, and then turn these over to distributors to be filled. Some suppliers threatened a distributor that they were determined to sell in his market. If he wouldn't give them a portion of his business, they would establish a competing distributor who would probably take away some share of his sales. Some distributors explained their purchases from other suppliers by saying that they wanted an alternative source of supply in case their supply from Dow was cut off by a labor strike.

In addition to the obvious threat to Dow's market position posed by these distributor purchases from competing suppliers, certain other problems were also created. When a drycleaner purchased perchloroethylene from an authorized Dow distributor, he automatically assumed he was getting Dow-Per. Because his order was delivered by tank truck there was no brand identification, and he did not know he was receiving the product of another supplier. If he had any trouble with the product, he blamed Dow. Also, because he thought he was buying Dow-Per, he continued to expect Dow to provide him with technical and business service. Distributors likewise expected Dow to continue to provide them with full services, even though they bought a portion of their needs from other suppliers.

This situation posed a serious problem for Louis Brown, manager of drycleaning chemicals sales for Dow. He wanted to find a way to halt this invasion of Dow distributors by other producers of perchloroethylene but was uncertain about what course of action to take. He wondered whether Dow's policy of having its salesmen call only on authorized Dow distributors should be changed. Dow could call on distributors representing other suppliers and probably obtain some portion of their business. This would compensate for the loss of Dow distributor volume to competitors. On the other hand, this would probably further threaten the loyalty of Dow distributors and cause them to increase their purchases from other sources. Dow might lose some of its distributors entirely to its competitors. With the strongest distributor network in the industry, this would be a great risk to take. To do nothing, however, would invite further erosion of Dow's market share.

CASE QUESTION

Should the Dow Chemical Company change its distribution policy for drycleaning chemicals? If so, how?

CASE 4–6

*Ford Motor Company**

Air freight distribution of automotive parts

In March 1965, the Transportation and Traffic Office of the Ford Motor Company, under the direction of R. Haupt made a presentation to several air carriers entitled, "Ford's Planned Use of Air Freight." The purpose of the presentation was to indicate Ford's interest in expanded use of air freight and to solicit carrier response and ideas on the use of air freight to ship automobile parts on a normal basis. The carriers' response to the presentation indicated they were not ready at that time, in terms of equipment or costs, to meet the needs of the automotive industry for regular, planned air shipment of automobile parts.

The Transportation and Traffic Office continued to pursue different methods of using air freight to reduce Ford's distribution costs. Early in 1967, the Traffic Department at Ford's Automotive Assembly Division submitted a proposal calling for consolidation of several million pounds of freight annually from the Detroit area to eight assembly plants and requested the Transportation and Traffic Office to solicit competitive bids from contractors for the consolidation.

Historical background

Several factors have played important parts in the development of air freight. Aircraft types have evolved from the single engine bi-wing planes, which were the first cargo aircraft (they carried the mail), through the C-47/DC-3 (the first good cargo plane), to the present day jet freighters, which regularly carry more than 100,000 pounds of freight coast-to-coast. Air cargo services have also developed from the one-man mail carrier to the present myriad of operations. The small one- or two-man operations still exist, but the majority of freight is carried by the large, commercial airlines. Other factors, such as four major wars, the growth of the economy, and the race for space have entered into the development of air freight.

Physical distribution for the automobile industry is a complex, ever-changing job. The change in the character of the product from Henry

---

* Written by George W. Bechthold while an MBA student in the Graduate School of Business Administration, The University of Michigan.

Ford's Model T to many models and options have placed a strain on the distribution system used to transport the parts from manufacturing plants to assembly plants nationwide. The volume of parts being moved dictates that a high-volume, low-cost transportation method be used. Air freight provides neither high volume or low cost. However, breakdowns in the normal distribution pipeline, such as supplier production failure, delay or failure of the normal transportation mode, or changes in consumer demand, force auto builders to put millions of pounds of production parts into the air each year.

In order to fulfill their need for rapid distribution of vitally needed production parts, the automotive industry has called upon a wide range of air freight carriers and forwarders. Specialized carriers have been formed to haul automobile parts. The uncoordinated growth of the carrier industry, coupled with the rapid increase in automobile parts air freight tonnage, presents a great number of opportunities to design lower cost air distribution systems without sacrificing speed or reliability of delivery.

Current situation

During the period 1955 to 1965, Ford Motor Company's use of air freight increased five times. This increase was due to a number of reasons, and the growth was expected to continue over the next several years.

In 1955, Ford offered four basic car lines (Ford, Mercury, Lincoln, and the newly introduced Thunderbird). By 1967, the company offered nine different car lines to the consumer (Falcon, Fairlane, Ford, Thunderbird, Mustang, Cougar, Comet, Mercury, and Lincoln). In addition, a much wider range of models and options was offered in 1967. The growth in the number of car lines, models and option choices was expected to continue for several years.

In addition to the proliferation of choices offered to the consumer,

EXHIBIT 1
Top ten air freight commodity classes, by weight (1955 versus 1965)

1955	*1965*
1. Machinery parts and equipment	1. Machinery parts and equipment
2. Cut flowers	2. Auto parts and accessories
3. Electrical products	3. Wearing apparel
4. Wearing apparel	4. Printed matter
5. Printed matter	5. Electrical products
6. Auto parts and accessories	6. Fresh fruits, vegetables, and berries
7. Aircraft parts	7. Cut flowers
8. General hardware	8. Magazines and books
9. Advertising display matter	9. General hardware
10. Photographic film	10. Metal products

the automobile industry had grown, in number of units produced, from just under eight million in 1960 to well over ten million in 1966. (1965 production was over eleven million units.) Production was expected to continue at this level, and Ford expected to maintain or increase its share of this market.

The air freight industry had also grown considerably since 1955. Domestic ton-miles had increased over five times between 1955 and 1967 (see Exhibit 1). A large part of this increase was due to the introduction of the jet freighter in the early sixties. The jet freighter has enabled the air freight industry to take maximum advantage of the natural attributes of the air mode: speed and service reliability, and high capacity available at ton-mile costs well below those of the piston type aircraft. By 1967, several air lines were providing scheduled air freighter service from Detroit to a number of major cities. A schedule, as of mid-1967, is found in Exhibit 2.

EXHIBIT 2
Airline flight schedules from Detroit, Michigan—1967

From Detroit to:	Airline	Flight	Dep.	Arr.	Equip-ment	Detroit lift capacity
Atlanta	Eastern	9041	12:20a	3:25a	727	2 containers
	Air Lift	451	3:00a	7:25a	DC7	1 container
	United	2751	11:05p	2:02a	727	2 containers
Chicago	United	2779	12:40a	12:43a	727	1 container
	American	825	1:55a	1:53a	707	1 container
	United	2701	7:00a	6:45a	727	1 container
	TWA	609	1:33p	1:36p	707	1 container
Dallas	American	855	5:50a	8:49a	707	4 containers
Kansas City	TWA	649	3:40a	6:30a	727	4 containers
Los Angeles	American	825	1:55a	5:14a	707	3 containers
	United	2893	2:45a	4:20a	DC8	2 containers
	American	829	4:40a	6:12a	707	2 containers
	F. Tiger	143	8:30a	10:05a	CL44	2 containers
	TWA	609	1:33p	4:40p	707	1 container
	F. Tiger	243	3:00p	4:35p	CL44	1 container
Mpls.-St. Paul	United	2753	5:00a	5:27a	727	3 containers
	NW	931	6:20a	7:02a	727	2 containers
N.Y. (Newark)	NW	912	1:10a	2:28a	727	4 containers
	United	2752	2:55a	4:11a	727	4 containers
	American	846	7:30a	8:56a	707	3 containers
	TWA	668	8:53a	10:17a	707	3 containers
	United	2704	9:15a	10:31a	727	2 containers
St. Louis	TWA	649	3:40a	4:58a	727	6 containers
San Francisco	United	2779	12:40a	6:03a	727	1 container
	TWA	667	2:20a	5:57a	707	2 containers
	American	847	3:15a	4:57a	707	2 containers
	F. Tiger	241	8:30a	12:35p	CL44	2 containers
	American	839	11:30a	4:38p	707	1 container
	United	2899	4:10p	10:17p	DC8	1 container

Since the late 1950s, the firm Zantop Air Lines has played a significant part in the movement of automobile parts. Zantop, operating as a supplemental air carrier, offered a unique service to the automobile industry which was specifically designed to meet the emergency needs of the assembly plants. This service offered a large number of aircraft dedicated to automobile parts shipments and flying on a regularly scheduled basis. In addition, Zantop offered a large number of aircraft for charter by the automotive companies. In short, Zantop flew when and where the automotive companies dictated. In return for this service, Zantop charged rates considerably above common carrier rates.

As Ford and the other automotive companies became accustomed to the premium service offered by Zantop and came to rely on this type of service, they realized that air freight, properly utilized, could protect continuous assembly line production. Service, not price, was the prime reason for the use of Zantop.

In late 1966, Zantop was sold to other interests and renamed Universal Air Lines. The new management began to actively solicit the military contract business arising from the Viet Nam conflict. Also, the old Zantop fleet had outlived its useful life and the new Universal management planned to replace the old planes with a smaller number of larger capacity aircraft. Both of these efforts contributed to a decline in the level of service offered by Universal. However, a substantial volume of automotive tonnage continued to flow through Universal.

Commercial air line rates in early 1967 were based on an incentive system where volume users received a lower rate than small-package shippers. In addition to the incentive rate scale, a special tariff provided added incentives to shippers who loaded freight into air containers. (The largest is the "igloo" or "A-type" container shaped to fit the contour of a jet freighter.) These rate provisions and rates to several destinations are summarized in Exhibit 3.

The proposal submitted by the Automotive Assembly Division Traffic Department was based on the premise that by consolidating a large number of air freight shipments moving from the southeastern Michigan area to Ford assembly plants, Ford could take better advantage of the incentive rates offered by the commercial air carriers. The Automotive Assembly Traffic Department estimated that shipments on commercial airlines averaged 1,000 pounds each without consolidation.

Pooling of freight is not a new concept, nor is it foreign to the automotive industry. Several factors are generally present before a freight pool can be effective. There is usually a geographical concentration of shipping locations, a large number of relatively small shipments made on a regular basis, a carrier rate structure that provides lower rates for volume shipments, and destination locations that receive a large volume of the small shipments.

EXHIBIT 3
Air freight rate provisions

A. *Incentive rates:* An incentive rate scale provided lower rates for higher weight shipments. Example:

Weight (pounds)	100	1000	2000	3000	5000	10,000
Rate ($/100 pounds)	8.10	7.30	6.75	6.35	6.10	6.00

B. *Container tariff provisions:* Additional incentives were available to shippers who loaded their own airfreight containers. These incentives are summarized as follows for the A-size (igloo) containers:
   1. *Minimum weight:* 7 pounds/cubic foot
      Example: A-size igloo 464 cubic feet, minimum weight 3250 pounds.
   2. *Loading incentive:* the basic rate for 3000 pounds (see A above) less $1.00 per hundred pounds. This rate would apply to the minimum weight, and all weight above the minimum until the shipment density reached the density incentive point.
   3. *Density incentive:* When the density reaches 10 pounds/cubic foot, an additional 33 percent may be subtracted from the loading incentive rate.
      Example: a) Basic rate: $6.35
               b) Loading incentive: $5.35 (applies on weight from 3250–4640 pounds)
               c) Density incentive: $3.58 (67 percent of $5.35)
   4. Container sizes and rental (1 trip):
      a) A1-400 cuft, $8.00 rental, used on 727-DC7 equipment
      b) A2-450 cuft, $9.00 rental, used on CL-44, DC8 equipment
      c) A3-464 cuft, $10.00 rental, used on 707 equipment
C. *Rates:* (in cents per hundred pounds)

| | Weight | | | | Rates via Universal |
City	100	1000	2000	3000	(all weights)
Atlanta............	880	800	745	705	900
Chicago...........	645	645	610	570	No Service
Dallas.............	1145	1065	1015	975	1200
Kansas City.......	880	800	745	705	900
L.A...............	245	2085	0975	1895	No Service
St. Paul...........	745	665	610	570	No Service
Newark...........	745	665	610	570	750
St. Louis..........	745	665	610	570	800
San Francisco......	2300	2135	2030	1950	No Service

The freight forwarders such as REA Express and Emery Air Freight are excellent examples of freight pooling or consolidation operations. However, few individual firms have sufficient volume or the type of distribution system to allow use of freight pools.

The automotive industry does have a large volume of freight, a concentration of shippers in the Great Lakes Region, and a production parts distribution system that allows volume shipments to single locations. Therefore, they have thoroughly utilized pooling and consolidation of surface freight.

Shipments via Zantop/Universal were consolidated for movement simply because a great volume of air freight moved through their terminal at Willow Run Airport, near Detroit. However, since Zantop/Universal charges the same per hundred weight rate, regardless of volume, there could be no cost advantage in consolidating the shipments. In fact, there is a cost penalty since Zantop/Universal rates are above commercial carrier rate levels.

The Transportation and Traffic Office, acting on the basis of the information supplied by the Automotive Assembly Division Traffic Department, requested bids for a consolidation service from several contractors including truck lines, air freight forwarders, and airlines. The specified service included receiving freight from a variety of carriers, handling and loading the freight into airline containers, handling all paperwork necessary to tender the shipment to the airline, and tracing/flight-following services. All service was to be on a 24 hour per day, seven day per week basis.

Of those contractors who responded, only two quoted what was considered to be a reasonable rate and appeared to have the capability of providing adequate service. Contractor A, with facilities located at Detroit Metropolitan Airport, quoted a rate of $1.35 per hundred pounds, minimum $3000 per month. Contractor A might not be able to provide service until July of 1969 when construction of a new freight handling facility would be completed. Service could be started on a limited basis using their existing facility.

Contractor B, located at Willow Run Airport, quoted a rate of $1.50 per hundred pounds, minimum $3000 per month. Contractor B would be able to begin service on sixty days' notice. Cartage service was available from Willow Run to Metropolitan Airport at $.50 per hundred pounds.

From this point, the Transportation and Traffic Office set out to analyze the savings potential of the proposal. Expected annual tonnage figures are shown in Exhibit 4. It was expected that tonnage would

EXHIBIT 4
Revised tonnage data (estimated annual air freight poundage from the southeastern Michigan area to various Ford assembly plants)

Assembly plant location	Pounds (000)
Atlanta	1,800
Chicago	1,900
Dallas	2,300
Kansas City	2,100
Los Angeles	3,800
St. Paul	2,000
Mahwah, N.J.	3,100
Metuchen, N.J.	2,900
St. Louis	2,400
San Francisco	4,200
	26,500

EXHIBIT 5
Monthly and weekly tonnage variations

Monthly variations		*Weekly variations*	
Month	*Percent of total weight*	*Day*	*Percent of total weight*
January	8	Sunday	10
February	6	Monday	30
March	5	Tuesday	20
April	5	Wednesday	12
May	4	Thursday	8
June	7	Friday	06
July	12	Saturday	4
August	8		100
September	11		
October	15		
November	10		
December	9		
	100		

EXHIBIT 6
Summary of freight density information

1. A survey of air freight container loads in 1966 by the Air Transport Association indicated an average density of 8.6 pounds per cubic foot for all container freight.
2. A one-month survey by Flying Tiger Lines of automotive freight indicated that container loads varied from 6.8 to 13.5 pounds per cubic foot density.
3. An estimate by Universal Air Lines stated that automotive freight (loose loaded) would have an average density of 7 to 8 pounds per cubic foot.
4. An average density of 9.5 pounds per cubic foot was experienced in 20 container shipments of Ford Service parts in 1967.

vary from month to month and within the week. An air freight bill analysis was made and the results of this analysis are shown in Exhibit 5.

Since freight density plays an important role in the analysis, the Transportation and Traffic Office surveyed a number of information sources on freight density. A summary of this survey is shown in Exhibit 6.

CASE QUESTIONS

1. Should the proposal submitted by the Automotive Assembly Division, Traffic Department be accepted by the company?
2. Estimate the cost savings, if any, which might accrue to Ford Motor Company under terms specified by Contractors A and B.

part five

PROMOTIONAL
STRATEGY

THIS SECTION deals with the fundamental issue of how best to sell the firm's product. Decisions on other elements of the marketing mix (product, brand policy, distribution policy, and price) influence promotional strategy. The fundamental task is to determine what message to communicate to prospective buyers and then to decide through what channels to transmit this message. What to say will depend upon an understanding of consumer behavior gained both through research and experience. Once the message has been determined, the problem is to choose appropriate methods of communication from among available alternatives (advertising, personal selling, consumer promotions, and reseller stimulation) and to combine them into an effective promotional mix. These are the issues with which we shall be concerned in Chapter 11.

Closely intertwined with the decision on the character of the promotional mix is the question of how much to appropriate for such activity. In Chapter 12, a theoretical solution to this problem is first developed and then methods used by business firms are examined to see how closely they approximate this ideal. Problems to be resolved in reaching a sound decision include (1) how to separate long-run and short-run results of promotional effort, and (2) how to measure the contribution to gross margin which may be expected from various sized expenditures upon advertising, consumer promotions, personal selling, and reseller stimulation. Suggested research approaches for dealing with these questions will be evaluated.

Finally, Chapter 13 explores the promotional implications of brand strategy decisions. It is concerned with issues relating to family versus individual brands, brand-price-quality relationships, and the wisdom of manufacturing products to be sold under distributors' brands as opposed to the firm's own brand.

11

Promotional
strategy decisions

Business success depends upon the firm being able to sell, at a profit, the merchandise it produces. Earlier discussions have demonstrated that the ability to sell a product depends upon sound action by executives on questions of product policy, branding, pricing, and the selection of effective channels of distribution. Yet these activities are wasted unless consumers or users are led to buy as the result of effective selling efforts.

What is the most effective way of selling a given product? This is the central issue with which we shall be concerned in the present chapter. Later we shall deal with the important related question of how much to appropriate to support the promotional program. We shall then turn to a consideration of the promotional aspects of brand strategy. In this discussion our point of view will be that of the marketing manager of a manufacturer or producer.

The development of an effective program of sales promotion involves both effective planning and skillful execution of plans. Because of the fundamental importance of sound sales planning activities, we shall give emphasis to this phase of the problem in our discussions here. Questions of execution can best be considered in the specialized courses which customarily follow the basic marketing course.

Determination of basic promotional strategy

Promotion involves communication

The cutting edge of the marketing instrument is the message which is communicated to prospective buyers through the various elements in the promotional program. But the messages communicated by advertising, personal selling, and point-of-purchase promotion constitute only a portion of what the firm's marketing program tells prospective buyers. When the prospect perceives the firm's product, certain impressions are communicated—either positive or negative—and thus the product serves as a symbol of communication. Indeed, the product comes to have a "personality" or image in the prospect's mind as a result of its design, appearance, and who uses it, among other influences. So, too, the trademark and brand name are symbols which communicate messages to the prospective buyer. The package also communicates ideas which may enhance or detract from the product's image. The price communicates ideas as to quality, and the images which consumers have of the middlemen who display and sell the brand may add to or detract from the brand's image. Realization of the ways in which these aspects of the marketing program assist or detract from the image of the brand underscores the importance of recognizing the communication value of these factors and of shaping them to provide the desired impressions.

Even so, it is the promotional program which serves as the primary channel of communication to prospective buyers. It will help us in the planning of effective promotional programs if we review communication theory briefly and show its application to the development of promotional strategy.

How communication works[1]

The term *communication* comes from the Latin *communis,* common. When we communicate, therefore, we are trying to establish a "commonness" with someone. The marketer, for example, is attempting to share information about the features of a brand, the benefits it will provide users, and the desires its consumption will satisfy.

The basic elements of a communication system are the *source,* the *message,* and the *destination.* A source may be an individual (such as a salesman) or a communication organization (such as a television broadcasting system, a newspaper, or a magazine). The *message* may be in the form of printed words (as in a direct-mail letter), a spoken radio commercial, a picture, a symbol (such as the Chrysler Pentastar), or any other "signal" capable of being interpreted meaningfully. The *destination* may be an individual consumer listening, watching, or reading; the members of a group (such as housewives invited to the home of Mrs. Consumer to watch a demonstration of Tupperware), a football crowd (seeing a helicopter towing a sign promoting frankfurters), or

---

[1] This section is adapted by permission from Wilbur Schram, "How Communication Works," in Wilbur Schram, ed., *The Process and Effects of Mass Communication* (Urbana, Ill.: University of Illinois Press, 1955), pp. 3–26.

an individual member of a mass television audience watching Johnny Carson on the "Tonight" show.

What happens when a source, say, a manufacturer of Buick automobiles, tries to build up a "commonness" with intended receivers (prospective buyers)? First, the Buick advertising manager has his advertising agency encode his message (prepare a television commercial involving words and pictures). Next, the signal (television commercial) must be transmitted via a television network. If this message is to have effect, owners of television sets must tune in the channel upon which the commercial is broadcast, remain in the room while the commercial is being presented, pay attention to the message transmitted, and decode it. That is, the meaning of the words and pictures must be interpreted by the consumer. If the full meaning of the message is to be understood, the fields of experience of the creative men who prepare the commercial

FIGURE 11–1
Diagram of a communication system

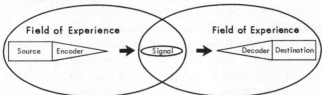

Source: Wilbur Schram, "How Communication Works," in Wilbur Schram, ed., *The Process and Effects of Mass Communication* (Urbana, Ill.: University of Illinois Press, 1955), p. 6. Reprinted by permission.

and the consumers who view it must have a large area in common. (Figure 11–1 is a diagram of this communication process that illustrates what has been said.)

If the consumer who receives the message understands its meaning, he may respond in various ways. That is, he may become a sender and encode some kind of message in return. If the commercial offers an attractive premium for a box top and 25 cents, the housewife who receives the message may buy the product and send the box top plus the money to the manufacturer. If the message urges the consumer to visit the Buick dealer and see the most recent model, just put on display, he and his wife may decide to make such a visit within the next few days. If the commercial is designed to get the consumer to consider the brand the next time she is in the market, then no immediate action may result, but a favorable attitude may be created which will lead to examining the brand when the need for it arises. Of course, the consumer may also simply do nothing at all.

If communication is between a salesman and a prospective buyer, we need to add the element of *feedback* in our conceptual scheme. As the prospect hears the sales message of the salesman, he will decode it, interpret its meaning, and encode a response. The element of feedback enables the salesman to determine whether his message is being understood and whether it is having the desired effect. He can then adjust subsequent messages accordingly. In mass communication such as a television broadcast, this direct type of feedback is impossible, and indirect responses must be substituted. Of course, interviews with television viewers may provide important feedback which will indicate whether the message is understood, believed, and has influenced attitudes toward the brand.

In summary, if communication is to have effect it must (1) gain attention, (2) employ signs which refer to experience common to both sender and destination to get the meaning across, (3) arouse personality needs in the destination and suggest some way to meet those needs, (4) suggest a way to satisfy needs which is appropriate to the group situation in which the destination finds himself at the time when he is moved to make the response desired by the source.

Let us now return to the point that the promotional program is the primary channel through which messages are communicated to prospective buyers. If this is to be done effectively, obviously the marketing executive must have a good understanding of who the prospective buyers of his product are, what desires may be satisfied through its use, what prospects know about his brand, what attitudes they hold toward it, and what image it holds in their minds. Research is needed to gain this information, and the planning of this research is helped by an understanding of consumer behavior and appropriate models of the buying process presented earlier in this book. Research to get feedback from prospective buyers on the impact of the messages communicated is also essential if weak links in the process are to be identified and communication improved in the next campaign.

The above discussion underscores the importance of the selling program in providing the methods by which appropriate information and persuasive messages are communicated to prospective buyers. Unless this job is done effectively, the entire marketing program fails. Let us turn now to a consideration of the determination of basic promotional strategy.

Determining the promotional mix

In determining how best to sell a given product, the basic decision which has to be made deals with the character of the promotional mix which is likely to be most effective. Specifically, how should advertising, personal selling, consumer promotions (contests, premiums, and combination offers), and dealer promotional activities be combined into an effective selling mix? The solution of this basic problem involves two subissues: (1) What promotional methods should be selected for use from among the alternatives available? (2) In what proportions should they be combined in order to get the best results?

In the solution of this problem, the business executive may be compared with a skilled cook who is going about the task of baking a cake. Depending upon the kind of cake to be made, the cook begins by selecting the various ingredients which will produce the desired product. These ingredients must be mixed together in proper proportions if the cake is to come up to expectations. In the same way, the development of an effective selling program involves selection of the right ingredients and mixing these ingredients together in the proper proportions in order to get the desired result. Let us now turn to a consideration of the various promotional methods from which the executive may choose the ingredients of his program.

Promotional methods

Listed below are the more important promotional tools (order-getting ingredients) which may be used in building an effective selling program.

1. Advertising
2. Personal selling
3. Consumer promotions ("forcing methods")
   a) Premiums
   b) Contests
   c) Combination offers
4. Methods designed to stimulate dealer advertising and promotion
   a) Cooperative advertising
   b) "Merchandising the advertising"
   c) In-store promotions
   d) Display and advertising aids
5. Shows and exhibitions
6. Reciprocity
7. Warranty and service
8. Competitive bidding

Choice of promotional methods

In view of the wide variety of promotional methods from which to choose, the question naturally arises, "How does the business executive approach the task of selecting those ingredients which will work most effectively for his particular product?" Unfortunately, there is no generally accepted mix of promotional methods which will fit the wide variation of circumstances which surround the marketing of the many different products produced and sold in our country today. Experience has demonstrated that different types of products require different mixtures of selling ingredients. This may be illustrated by contrasting the promotional strategies which might normally be used for an industrial product as opposed to a consumer good.

In the sale of diesel locomotives to railroads, for example, the Acme Corporation relies primarily upon personal selling because of the size of the investment, the technical nature of the product, the fact that the order will be placed by railroad executives, and the further fact that the number of prospective buyers is relatively limited (in number) while the size of the individual order is likely to be large. Along with personal selling, a supplementary campaign of advertising in trade journals read by railroad executives is also used.

In the sale of a patent medicine, however, the Mandell Company places the sole emphasis upon consumer advertising. This method is used because it offers the most economical way of reaching the large number of prospects who are scattered throughout the United States. The company has found that the demand stimulated through such advertising is strong enough to pull the product through wholesale and retail channels of distribution. Since the company has no sales force, orders from wholesalers and large retailers are received by mail. Thus, it is apparent that the patent medicine, a consumer good, requires an entirely different selling strategy from that needed for the diesel engine, an industrial product.

Even within the same industry, however, it may not be wise for all firms to use the same mix of promotional methods in the sale of their various brands. Experience has shown that variations in the characteristics of competing brands, as well as differences in brand policy, distribution channels, and pricing policy, tend to require differences in the promotional mix if profitable results are to be achieved. The influence of these factors upon basic promotional strategy will be illustrated in the following paragraphs.

1. *Influence of brand policy.* A manufacturer may elect to sell under his own brand, under the private brands of middlemen, or without brand identification. The decision reached on this question will exert an important influence upon the character of the promotional mix. In considering alternative branding policies, for example, a coffee roaster may decide to supply a chain of supermarkets with coffee for sale under the chain's private brand. If this is done, then the chain will be responsible for all selling and promotional effort directed to the ultimate consumer. Personal contact between an executive of the coffee roaster and the buying offices of the chain may be the only selling effort required on the part of the firm furnishing the coffee to the supermarkets. In contrast, if the coffee roaster were to decide to market under his own brand, then the executives of this firm might well decide to make use of (1) personal selling to get middlemen to stock and promote the product at the point of sale, and (2) consumer advertising in order to create a brand preference for the item.

2. *Influence of channels of distribution.* Basic decisions on distribution policy will also influence selling strategy. One manufacturer of ladies' hosiery may distribute his brand to the ultimate consumer through house-to-house canvassing. A second firm may sell the same type of product to ultimate consumers by a mail-order plan. Where house-to-house canvassing is used, the main emphasis is placed upon personal selling. If consumer advertising is used at all, it would probably be for the supplementary purpose of paving the¹ way for the company's sales organization. In contrast, where ladies' hosiery is distributed through the mail-order method, personal selling is omitted and reliance is placed upon consumer advertising to get mail orders.

A third manufacturer of ladies hosiery may follow the practice of distributing his high-grade brand direct to selected department stores and specialty shops. In this situation, the firm might well decide that the best way to sell the brand would be to get the selected dealers to push the brand aggressively at the point of sale. As a means of encouraging retailers to undertake aggressive selling efforts on behalf of the brand, the manufacturer might offer to share the cost of each retailer's advertising of the product on a 50–50 basis and to furnish advertising aids and display materials without charge. Salesmen might also be hired whose job it would be to take orders for the brand from the retailers and to assist them in the planning of point of sale display and promotion. Note the wide differences in promotional strategy followed by the firm distributing through retailers, the manufacturer distributing by mail-order methods, and the company relying upon house-to-house canvassing.

3. *Influence of pricing and price policy.* In the pricing of a given product, wide variations in practice may be observed. On the one hand, a manufacturer may decide to compete largely on a price basis, with the result that only a narrow margin is available for selling activities. A sugar refiner might well follow such a policy. As a result, this refiner might make use of no consumer advertising and might rely entirely upon the personal relations between his sales force and both chain supermarkets and grocery wholesalers to sell his brand.

On the other hand, a different firm may set prices which allow wide margins and at the same time make plans to compete through emphasis on "nonprice" factors such as product quality, service, or advertising. A manufacturer of patent medicine might well illustrate such an approach. This firm might price its brand so as to permit a margin of

50 percent of its price to be devoted to selling expenses. The entire promotional burden might then be placed upon an aggressive campaign of consumer advertising with no provision for sales contacts with the wholesalers and retailers who stock the brand. Here the pull of consumer advertising is relied upon to force retailers and wholesalers to handle the product. Clearly, there is a definite interrelationship between the promotional methods which a firm may use and the size of the margin available to cover the costs of these methods.

4. *Suggested approach to the determination of promotional strategy.* Since it has been demonstrated that no single mixture of promotional methods is suitable for all products, or even for different brands of the same product, how then should the business executive proceed in the selection and combination of selling ingredients? The most promising approach involves three steps. First, it is helpful to appraise the opportunity of making profitable use of advertising, personal selling, and other order-getting ingredients, in the light of certain basic considerations which have been found, by experience, to influence the success of their application. Some of the more important of these factors are:

1. The characteristics of the product and its stage in the life cycle.
2. Buying habits and buying motives of consumers or industrial users.
3. Point of view of middlemen.
4. The promotional strategy of competitors.
5. Probable size of promotional funds.

The significance of these considerations will be explained and illustrated at appropriate points in the following discussion of individual selling methods.

The preceding analysis will indicate in broad terms the relative emphasis which should be placed upon advertising, personal selling, and other order-getting ingredients in order to achieve desired promotional objectives. The second step then involves the use of this background in determining the total promotional appropriation and in working out its optimum allocation among the promotional methods to be used. In theoretical terms, the task is to set the total promotional appropriation at the point where the marginal revenue produced (output) equals or just exceeds the marginal cost of the last unit of input. Likewise, the amounts devoted to each promotional method (advertising, personal selling, dealer stimulation) should be set at levels where the marginal gain per dollar cost among all promotional methods is equal. The practical adaptation of the marginal approach to the allocation of promotional dollars among alternative methods will receive consideration later in this discussion.

Third, wherever possible, it is desirable to check the decisions reached by this analytical process, through the use of research designed to measure the effectiveness of the promotional methods chosen, as well as alternative combinations of promotional ingredients. Thus, if analysis indicates that there appears to be a good opportunity to make effective use of advertising, it is wise to check this decision by utilizing suitable research techniques to measure the results of using the advertising method. If possible, research should also be used to verify decisions to include other methods in the promotional mix. Also, various combinations of advertising, personal selling, and dealer promotion should be tried out on an experimental basis as a means of identifying the most effective mix of these elements. Such research will serve to narrow the margin of error and will provide the facts needed to improve the quality of executive judgment.

At the same time, it should be recognized that the problem of measuring the results of using any given promotional method or combination of methods will often be a difficult one. Where the product has high unit value and is purchased at infrequent intervals, it may well be impossible to devise any small-scale test which will measure within a three to six-month period the sales results of using advertising, personal selling, or other available promotional methods. Since many factors exert an influence upon sales in the marketplace, it may also prove to be very difficult for the manufacturer of such a product to isolate the influence of a single method, such as personal selling, where a given mix is subjected to appraisal by actual trial throughout the entire market. The point to keep in mind is that while under certain conditions, research may provide helpful checks on management decisions on the choice of selling methods, there are other circumstances where research has little to contribute because of the complexities of the problem. Where this is true, success depends upon the artistry and judgment of the executive as he attacks the problem of choosing the ingredients of his promotional plan. We may still conclude, however, that wherever possible it is wise to check decisions on the choice of promotional ingredients through the use of appropriate research methods.

Let us now turn to a discussion of some of the more important promotional methods available and the considerations which may guide the executive in the task of selecting the proper ingredients for the selling mix.

Advertising

Advertising includes any paid form of nonpersonal presentation and promotion of ideas, goods, or services by an identified sponsor.[2] It is

---

[2] *Marketing Definitions: A Glossary of Marketing Terms*, compiled by the Committee on Definitions of the American Marketing Association, Ralph S. Alexander, Chairman (Chicago: American Marketing Association, 1960), p. 9.

evident that advertising may be classified into two main types: (1) product advertising, and (2) institutional advertising. Institutional advertising is designed to create favorable attitudes toward an institution or an idea. Since our primary concern is with the use of advertising as a selling tool, the following discussion will deal with product advertising.

Product advertising may be used by manufacturers or producers to perform a variety of tasks as the following outline indicates:

1. Promote the sale of a manufacturer's or producer's brand through present retail dealers
   a) by getting new customers to buy, and
   b) by getting present customers to buy more of the product than in the past.
2. To assist in the sale of a branded product by giving consumers the names and addresses of the selected retailers who carry the item.
3. Where products are sold house-to-house, to help sell the brand
   a) by paving the way for the salesmen, and
   b) by getting leads for salesmen to follow up.
4. To help get distribution for a new product, or extend the distribution of an old product
   a) by stimulating a demand at retail stores through consumer advertising, and
   b) by arousing interest of retailers in the product through advertising directed to them.
5. To encourage retailers to display, advertise, and sell the product actively
   a) by telling them through advertising of the opportunity for increasing profit through such activity, and
   b) by informing them of the manufacturer's promotional plans and encouraging them to capitalize on such effort through tie-in promotion.
6. To expand the sales of an industry, or to counteract an adverse sales trend
   a) by advertising sponsored by a group of competing manufacturers or producers.

In the performance of the foregoing tasks, you will note that advertising may be directed to (1) the ultimate consumer or industrial user and (2) the middlemen involved in the distribution of the product. In the discussion which follows, we shall be concerned with an appraisal of the opportunity of making profitable use of advertising addressed to ultimate consumers or industrial users for the purpose of promoting the sale of the manufacturer's or producer's brand.

If advertising campaigns were analyzed to determine their objectives, we would find that they could be classified into two basic types, depending upon the nature of the appeals used. On the one hand is advertising designed to stimulate a *primary demand,* which is a demand for a generic type of product. In order to accomplish this aim, primary appeals are used in the advertisements—appeals which may be expected to arouse a desire for a certain type of product rather than for an individual brand. Another kind of advertising is that which aims to stimulate a *selective demand,* which is a demand for the brand of an individual manufacturer. Where such advertising is used, no attempt is made to increase the demand for the type of product. Instead, the purpose is to secure for the brand which the manufacturer sells as large a percentage as possible of this volume. The method which is generally followed is to show that the advertiser's brand will satisfy a given desire more effectively than other brands. This is done by dwelling on the superior qualities or individualizing features of this brand which make it a better solution to the desire than other brands would be. Appeals of this sort are called selective appeals, since they aim to get the consumer to purchase only the advertiser's brand.

By far the greater proportion of the advertising of individual manufacturers and producers is designed to increase the share of the market secured by the seller's individual brand—i.e., it is intended to stimulate a selective demand. The discussion which follows, accordingly, will deal with the problem of appraising the opportunity to make profitable use of consumer advertising to stimulate a selective demand.[3]

In deciding whether to choose advertising as a sales-making ingredient, the executive must do more than arrive at a judgment on whether the use of advertising will increase sales. He must estimate the cost of an adequate campaign of consumer advertising, and then determine whether that advertising will stimulate enough additional sales—at profitable prices—to cover advertising costs and leave a margin sufficient to increase profits.

Appraising the opportunity to make profitable use of consumer advertising

In estimating the opportunity profitably to stimulate selective demand through advertising to consumers or users, accordingly, the following leading considerations stand out:

First, advertising is likely to be more effective if a company is operating with a favorable *primary demand trend* than if it is operating with an adverse trend.

The second condition governing a concern's opportunity to influence its

---

[3] For a discussion of appraising the opportunity to stimulate primary demand, see N. H. Borden and M. V. Marshall, *Advertising Management: Text and Cases,* rev. ed. (Homewood, Ill.: Richard D. Irwin, Inc., 1959), chap. 4.

demand is the presence of a *large chance for product differentiation*. When products can be significantly differentiated, advertising is likely to be effective. Conversely, advertising is of smaller help when there is a marked tendency for the products of various producers to become closely similar.

A third condition is the relative importance to the consumer of the *hidden qualities of the product* as contrasted with the external qualities which can be seen and appreciated. When these hidden qualities are present, consumers tend to rely upon the brand, and advertising can be used to associate the presence of the qualities with the brand. Conversely, when the characteristics of a product which are significant to a consumer can be judged at time of purchase, brand tends to lose some of its significance, and advertising is not needful in building mental associations regarding these characteristics.

A fourth condition is the *presence of powerful emotional buying motives* which can be employed in advertising appeals to consumers. Conversely, if such strong appeals cannot be used effectively, then the advertising opportunity is not so great.

A fifth condition of importance is whether the concern's operations provide *substantial sums with which to advertise and promote* its products in the markets it seeks to reach. Advertising must be done on a scale large enough to make an effective impression upon its market. Consequently, the size of the advertising fund is an important consideration in an appraisal of advertising's opportunity. The matter of an advertising fund for any period depends upon the number of units of the product which can be sold in the period and upon the margin available for advertising. The size of the margin depends very largely upon the effectiveness of advertising in influencing consumer valuations for a product. This influence of advertising, in turn, is dependent upon the extent and significance of product differentiation and upon the strength of appeals which may be employed to present the differentiated qualities. The amount of margin available for aggressive selling work depends also upon conditions of competition within an industry, that is, whether competition is carried on in price or in nonprice forms.

Other conditions which may bear upon the opportunity of individual concerns to make effective use of advertising in influencing the demand for their brands need not be enumerated, for the five conditions mentioned above are most universal and are of first importance. It should be stressed, however, that the opportunity to use advertising effectively generally depends not so much on the presence of one of these conditions alone, but upon the combination of conditions which exists.[4]

When should advertising receive main emphasis in the promotional mix?

After having appraised the opportunity to make profitable use of consumer advertising, the executive is then in a position to determine its relative importance in the selling mix. While consumer advertising

---

[4] Adapted from ibid., pp. 162–65.

may be the only promotional method used in certain exceptional cases, more commonly other selling ingredients, such as personal solicitation and dealer promotional efforts, are likely to be included in the mix. The combination of several promotional methods is often likely to be more effective in producing desired sales results than the exclusive reliance upon one.

The process of determining whether the main burden of selling should be placed upon advertising, with other promotional ingredients occupying supplementary positions in the mix, begins with a careful estimate of the opportunity to make profitable use of each method which appears likely to make a useful contribution to the achievement of desired objectives. Consumer advertising is likely to receive main emphasis under the following conditions: (1) When appraisal indicates that conditions are especially favorable for affecting consumer valuations and for the creation of quick buying action through the use of consumer advertising. (2) When analysis leads to the conclusion that retail personal selling is not important in the profitable marketing of the product. (3) When dealer promotional efforts and other selling methods, if used alone, appear to offer less promise in consummating sales than consumer advertising.

Examples of situations where a firm might be wise to rely primarily upon the pull of consumer advertising to sell its products would include the following: (1) promotion of citrus fruits by the California Fruit Growers Exchange; (2) sale of proprietary medicines such as Geritol; (3) sale of highly individualized grocery specialties such as Maxim freeze dried coffee; (4) promotion of cosmetics and beauty preparations such as Miss Clairol Shampoo Formula; (5) sale of individualized dentifrices such as Mint Crest.

Other problems of advertising management

If a careful appraisal indicates that there is a profitable opportunity to make effective use of advertising, the executive responsible for the management of the advertising force faces additional problems. (1) A decision must be reached on how much to spend on advertising. (2) Media to carry the advertising message must be selected. (3) Arrangements must be made for the preparation of effective advertisements. (4) Steps should be taken to measure the effectiveness of advertising, through pretesting and posttesting, where appropriate, as a means of maximizing returns from the money spent. The task of preparing and placing effective advertisements is usually turned over to an advertising agency. The agency also assists in the selection of media, in recommending how much to spend, and in devising means of measuring the results of advertising.

Space does not permit detailed discussion of these problems of advertising management. They constitute the subject matter of courses in promotional strategy and advertising management.[5]

Personal selling

Personal selling is a second important order-getting ingredient available to the executive responsible for determining the promotional mix. It involves face-to-face contact between the seller or his representative and the prospective buyer. Among others, the purpose of such personal contacts may be: (1) to get an order for the product; (2) to get retailers actively to promote and display the product at the point of purchase; (3) to get wholesalers to cooperate with the manufacturer by selling the products actively or by encouraging retailers to tie-in at the point of purchase with the seller's advertising and promotional efforts; and (4) to educate those who may influence purchase to favor the company and its product.

Personal solicitation differs from advertising in that the selling message is delivered by personal contact as opposed to presentation through nonpersonal media such as newspapers, magazines, television, or industrial papers. For this reason, the salesman may adapt his message to the needs, interests, and reactions of the prospect. The same advertising message, however, is delivered to all who see or hear the particular medium carrying the advertisement. Herein lies an important difference between advertising and personal selling.

Several different kinds of personal selling may be distinguished. Most familiar, perhaps, is retail selling as illustrated by the activities of the clothing salesman in a men's shop. While the activities of the automobile salesman also illustrate retail selling, they often involve contacts with prospects in their homes rather than in the dealer's place of business. House-to-house selling by the representatives of a manufacturer, such as the Fuller Brush Company, illustrate a third type of approach. A fourth would be personal contacts with industrial users by the salesmen of a firm manufacturing producers goods. The sale of electronic computers to manufacturers by the representatives of International Business Machines would illustrate this type of sales job. A fifth type would be the manufacturer's salesmen calling upon wholesalers, as is illustrated by the representatives of the R. J. Reynolds Tobacco Company who take orders for Winston filter cigarettes from tobacco, drug, and grocery wholesalers. The manufacturer who has his salesmen call directly upon

---

[5] For a discussion of these topics, see J. F. Engel, H. G. Wales, and M. R. Warshaw, *Promotional Strategy*, rev. ed. (Homewood, Ill.: Richard D. Irwin, Inc., 1971), parts III and IV.

retailers would illustrate a sixth kind of selling. Here an example would be the salesmen of Standard Brands, Inc., selling coffee, tea, and yeast to grocery retailers. A seventh kind of selling job is that of the salesman for a wholesaler whose function is to take orders from retailers. The salesmen of wholesale distributors representing the General Electric Company in calling upon dealers who retail color television sets would illustrate this type of selling.

In each of the above examples, the main function of the salesman is to secure an order. Manufacturers distributing through wholesalers, who in turn sell to retailers, also may use missionary salesmen in carrying out their marketing plans. Missionary salesmen are sometimes used to extend distribution by getting orders from retailers and turning them over to wholesalers to be filled. Missionary salesmen may also call upon retailers for the purpose of encouraging them to promote and display the manufacturer's brand more actively. On such calls, the salesman may help the dealer plan advertising and display activities featuring the company's brand, may set up window or floor displays, may train retail salesclerks to sell more effectively, or may simply encourage the dealer to tie in more aggressively with the manufacturer's promotional program.

In the sale of prescription drugs, manufacturers customarily use "detail men" who perform missionary selling functions. In this field, however, they are generally assigned the task of calling upon physicians and pharmacists in order to inform them about new drugs being introduced or promoted. If appropriate, samples may be provided. The task of the detail man is, thus, basically educational; generally he is not expected to seek orders. If the pharmacist does place an order, however, it is usually turned over to a drug wholesaler for handling, provided such a middleman is the customary source of supply.

The introduction of Pablum baby cereal, by Mead Johnson & Company illustrates a situation where the main burden of selling was placed upon detail men. In keeping with Mead Johnson's status as a pharmaceutical house strongly identified with ethical drug specialties, Pablum was distributed through the drug trade. The product was promoted entirely through physicians by Mead Johnson sales representatives.[6]

Factors influencing the use of personal selling

Whether the manufacturer sets up a sales force to call upon ultimate consumers or industrial users is influenced by decisions on distribution policy of a type which have been previously discussed. Thus, if a deci-

---

[6] L. L. Duke, *Packaging Problems in Redesigning a Product Line* (*American Management Association Packaging Series No. 42* [New York: American Management Association, Inc.]), pp. 31–32.

sion is reached to distribute through middlemen instead of selling directly to the consumer or industrial user, then the manufacturer relies upon the dealers to furnish the kinds and amounts of personal sales contact with prospects that appears to be essential. If personal contact is essential, he may then seek types of dealers who have the necessary sales organizations to perform the desired task. To make sure that his brand is supported by effective personal selling by middlemen, he may also assist dealers to do a better job of selecting and training salesmen.

Whether a manufacturer organizes a sales force to call upon retailers is likewise determined largely by decisions on distribution policy. The seller has the alternative of selling directly to retailers or of relying upon wholesalers to provide the necessary retail sales contacts. If a decision is reached to use wholesalers, the task of maintaining sales contact with dealers rests upon their shoulders. Under some conditions, however, the manufacturer may decide to set up a missionary sales force to supplement the work of the wholesalers' sales representatives. Whether a missionary sales organization is necessary will depend, in part, upon the kind of support which may be expected from the salesmen of the wholesaler. If the wholesalers' lines are wide, and salesmen are little more than order takers, occasions may arise when the manufacturer feels that missionary salesmen would be desirable to provide more aggressive contact with retailers. If the company plans to introduce a new product, special effort will be needed in order to gain distribution through retail outlets. Missionary salesmen are often used temporarily to help build distribution for the new line. Where active dealer promotion and display is desired as a tie-in with the manufacturer's advertising effort, missionary salesmen may be used to encourage the necessary retail cooperation. Of course, the use of missionary salesmen is justified only where enough additional sales result from such effort to justify the additional expense incurred.

Where wholesalers are used, most manufacturers will set up a sales organization to maintain sales contracts with them. Except where advertising is strong enough to pull the brand through channels of distribution, the manufacturer is likely to rely upon personal selling to make sure that his brand is stocked and given the customary sales support by the wholesalers' sales organizations. Where consumer advertising is especially effective, as may be the case with individual brands of patent medicines, for example, firms have been known to operate without a sales organization and to rely upon securing orders from wholesalers by mail. Such cases are rare, however.

Even where distribution is achieved through middlemen, the manufacturer is still faced with the problem of determining whether personal selling to consumers or industrial users should be included in the marketing mix. If best results appear to come through emphasis on personal contact with consumers at the point of purchase, the manufacturer will want to take active steps to influence dealers to provide the necessary personal sales effort to reap maximum returns. Experience indicates that the following considerations tend to determine the wisdom of including personal solicitation of ultimate consumers or industrial users in the selling mix.

Personal salesmanship appears to be an effective method when the size of the purchase is relatively large, when the product has features which require explanation and demonstration, when the item is purchased at infrequent intervals, and when prospects already own old models of the product upon which they will want a trade-in allowance.

When a consumer has to sacrifice a considerable amount of his surplus for discretionary spending in order to buy a television set, a mechanical refrigerator, an automobile, or a home, it takes persuasion on the part of a salesman to overcome the natural resistance to purchase which is likely to be felt. Likewise, when the installation of a textile machine involves an expenditure of $30,000, those responsible for the buying decision may need a certain amount of urging to bring themselves to the point of signing an order. Aggressive personal selling tends to be an essential method of marketing such items.

Again, there are a number of products like an automobile, a television set, a private airplane, and a broaching machine, with features which need to be explained and demonstrated in order to facilitate purchase. Catalog descriptions, direct mail, or other types of printed or oral advertisements, cannot explain a complicated product nearly so well as a salesman who, at the same time, can also show how the product operates. For this reason, personal selling to consumers or users tends to occupy a key part in the sale of such products.

If a product has a relatively long life and thus need not be repurchased for some time, the owner may tend to postpone buying a new model until absolute necessity forces the issue. Automobiles and household appliances would fall in this class. As a means of increasing sales by speeding obsolescence, many of the manufacturers of such products make it a practice to redesign their products periodically. Such action opens up the possibility of encouraging earlier replacement than might normally occur. The normal consumer tendency to procrastinate in making such a purchase still must be dealt with, however. The salesman is especially effective in helping to make the owner of an old model car realize fully how out-of-date his automobile really is. Where the life of the product is long and replacement may be delayed, therefore, personal selling coupled with the introduction of significantly improved new models may be used to stimulate replacement earlier than would normally occur.

There are a number of products like automobiles, trucks, sewing machines, vacuum cleaners, and even television sets, where it is common practice for the owner of an old model to seek a trade-in allowance on the purchase of the new product. Such allowances are generally the result of bargaining;

face-to-face negotiations between prospect and salesman are required to deal most effectively with such a transaction. Personal selling tends to be common practice in the handling of such products.[7]

In the marketing of certain industrial goods a survey of the prospect's needs is an essential preliminary to the making of a sale. Heavy installation equipment may sometimes need special adaptations in order to fit into the prospect's production line. Installation service may also need to be planned. In such cases, personal contact between the manufacturer's sales force and the industrial user is an essential element in the selling plan.

When should personal selling receive main emphasis?

Consideration of the factors outlined above enables the executive to make an estimate of the opportunity to make profitable use of personal solicitation in the selling program.[8] The question next arises as to when it is likely to be desirable to place the main burden upon personal solicitation in the selling mix. If the product is distributed through middlemen, such an approach involves getting the retailer or the industrial distributor to organize and maintain an effective personal selling organization. From what already has been said, it is clear that the policy of placing the main burden upon personal selling would tend to be desirable when two sets of conditions are present. (1) Circumstances would have to be unfavorable to the profitable use of consumer advertising to stimulate either primary or selective demand. Otherwise, a balanced program including both advertising and personal selling would seem to be indicated. (2) Conditions would have to be favorable to the profitable use of personal selling.

An example of a situation where the main burden should be placed upon personal selling would be in the marketing of electronic computers. Advertising to users would tend to occupy a relatively minor role because of the high price of such equipment and the infrequency with which such installations are made. These same factors, along with the need for explaining how the computer can be used in different situations and the necessity for adaptation of the installation to individual circumstances, would indicate the necessity for heavy reliance on personal solicitation.

---

[7] Adapted from J. D. Scott, *Advertising Principles and Problems*, © 1953, pp. 321–22. Reprinted by permission of Prentice-Hall, Inc., Englewood Cliffs, N.J.

[8] For the results of a landmark study of the personal selling function, see P. J. Robinson and Bent Stidsen, Marketing Science Institute, *Personal Selling in a Modern Perspective* (Boston: Allyn & Bacon, Inc., 1967).

Other problems of sales force management

Once the decision has been made to include personal selling in the marketing mix, then a number of important problems arise for consideration by the manager of the sales force. Among the more significant are: (1) how to recruit and select salesmen of the desired caliber; (2) how to train new salesmen so that they will perform their functions effectively; (3) what methods of compensation to use; (4) how to stimulate the men to exert maximum effort on the job; (5) how to supervise the men so that they will make the most of the opportunities existing in their territories; (6) how to determine the territories in which the men are to operate; and (7) how to evaluate the salesmen's performance. Space does not permit the discussion of these problems of sales force management. Those interested will find these topics discussed in specialized sales management texts and in advanced courses in this field.[9]

Dealer promotion

Dealer promotion is a third order-getting ingredient which many manufacturers may want to include in the selling mix. Dealer promotion efforts may include various kinds of advertising, window and interior displays, demonstrations of the product, use of consumer contests, use of premiums, use of combination offers, distribution of free samples, and other activities designed to promote the sale of a given brand.[10] Regardless of how limited or how extensive the promotional efforts desired of the retail dealer in the promotion of a manufacturer's brand, it should be noted that the retailer's voluntary cooperation must be enlisted if the project is to succeed. Before the dealer can be led to promote a manufacturer's brand, he must be convinced that it is to his advantage to do so. Securing retail cooperation in promotional work, therefore, requires careful planning and execution on the part of the manufacturer. In considering whether to include dealer promotion in the selling mix, accordingly, the problems involved in getting the desired cooperation should be kept in mind.

At the outset, it is obvious that only those manufacturers or producers who distribute through retail dealers or industrial distributors will be concerned with whether to include dealer promotion in the selling mix. Among those who would not use this selling method would be: (1) manufacturers selling by mail order to consumers or users; (2) firms

[9] See K. R. Davis and F. E. Webster, Jr., *Sales Force Management* (New York: Ronald Press Co., 1968).

[10] This discussion adapted by permission from Scott, *Advertising Principles and Problems,* chap. 7.

whose salesmen call directly upon the consumer or user; and (3) producers who sell their products to chains or department stores to be marketed under the distributor's private brand.

It is also noteworthy that the need for identifying the retail middleman with the manufacturer's brand is related to the firm's distribution policy. Thus, where the policy of selected retail distribution is followed, it becomes essential for the manufacturer to take active steps to see to it that the local source of supply is identified with his brand.

Under the policy of selected distribution, a relatively small percentage of the available retail outlets will stock the manufacturer's brand; where exclusive agency representation is followed, it will be only a single retailer in the community. Unless the local source of supply identifies himself with the manufacturer's brand through signs, window displays, and advertising over his own name, the demand created by the manufacturer's general advertising may be dissipated because of the consumer's lack of knowledge of where to go in order to buy the product. Failure to recognize the importance of this matter may result in ineffective general advertising.

Among those manufacturers who distribute through retail middlemen, two contrasting types of promotional strategy may be distinguished. One approach involves pulling the product through channels of distribution by placing main emphasis on a strong program of consumer advertising. Where this is the approach, dealer promotion is used in a supplementary role. A contrasting method is to rely upon dealer push to consummate sales. Here the manufacturer relies upon his dealers to promote his brand locally through retail advertising, window and interior displays, or other promotional devices. Accordingly, the manufacturer's efforts are primarily directed at the dealer in order to encourage him to promote the brand aggressively. Dealer's sales and advertising helps may also be provided as a means of facilitating the dealer's promotional work. The manufacturer, however, undertakes little or no consumer advertising on behalf of his brand.

When should dealer promotion carry the main burden?

Under what conditions would it appear to be wise to place the main burden of selling upon dealer promotion? The first condition which would encourage an executive to consider this strategy would be the lack of an opportunity to stimulate a profitable demand through consumer advertising. Since a poor consumer advertising opportunity may stem from several conditions, let us comment briefly upon some of the more important possibilities. At the same time, let us consider whether these conditions would tend to interfere with the possibility of getting effective dealer push.

Where the product is relatively standardized, the opportunity to make profitable use of consumer advertising tends to be limited. A standardized item such as cheesecloth, however, may be sold profitably by retailers provided it is displayed on aisle tables where there is considerable consumer traffic. Thus, the Claybon Company persuaded a department store to carry a special display of cheesecloth in handy-sized packages for one week. During this test period, the store sold 25,000 yards, which was 50 percent of its previous yearly sales. Dealer displays would therefore appear to offer a promising method of promoting the sales of a standardized item of this sort.

Again, when the important qualities of the product may easily be judged at the point of purchase, the possibility of stimulating brand discrimination through consumer advertising is very limited. This tends to be the situation in the sale of inexpensive children's toys, where prospects tend to select the product on the basis of personal observation of the qualities of design, color, and motion represented in the individual items. Nevertheless, these surface qualities lend themselves particularly well to effective retail advertising and to attention-getting window and interior displays. Dealer push would thus be an especially fruitful method of promoting the sale of children's toys.

Likewise, products likely to be purchased on impulse lend themselves especially well to sale through displays at points where a large number of consumers pass by. Items such as candy, neckties, inexpensive costume jewelry, and perfume fall in this category. Even though such products may not provide an opportunity for profitable use of consumer advertising, they may be sold effectively by getting retailers to display them in busy locations.

In contrast to the foregoing products, there are items with few important hidden qualities, in the purchase of which consumers are willing to exert more effort. Women's dresses are a good example. Qualities such as style, color, and type of material are surface characteristics which may be appraised by the consumer in the retail store. Yet women are willing to make a special trip into town and visit several stores in the process of buying a new dress. Products in this class may also be sold very effectively not only through window and store displays but also through retail advertising. Getting retailers actively to advertise and display such products is therefore sound strategy.

There are some products in the sale of which the retailer's name is likely to be more important than the manufacturer's brand. Rayon cloth manufactured by Burlington Mills is a good example of such an item. Bedspreads, curtains, tablecloths, shower curtains, bath mats, fiber rugs, and window blinds, among others, are other examples of such products. Although the influence of fashion, the lack of hidden qualities, and the absence of individualizing features may tend to make the producer's brand unimportant, such items may be sold effectively through display. Manufacturers of such products might well aim at getting adequate dealer promotion as the key point in their selling strategy.

Finally, there are situations where the product is distinctive and has hidden qualities but will not support an adequate expenditure for consumer advertising. A limited market, price resistance, or infrequency of purchase may prevent the early response needed to cover advertising costs. Or the firm may be handicapped by limited financial resources. Under these conditions, there is much to be said in favor of adopting the inexpensive strategy of encouraging active dealer display and promotion of the firm's brand.

When advertising is emphasized, how necessary is dealer promotion?

In the preceding section, conditions were outlined under which a manufacturer would be wise to follow the strategy of placing primary emphasis upon getting retailers actively to advertise, display, and sell his brand. When the main selling burden should be placed upon consumer advertising, however, how necessary is dealer promotion? Carefully conducted sales tests demonstrate that window displays of nationally advertised brands tend to stimulate substantial sales increases in the store where the displays are located.

Similar tests of the use of interior displays appear to show conclusively that an advertised product would benefit considerably by being promoted in an appropriate manner within the retail store.

There are a number of conditions which tend to explain why window and interior displays increase the retail sales of even those brands which are most responsive to the pull of consumer advertising.

1.   The effectiveness of advertising designed to stimulate a brand discrimination is enhanced by window and store displays which reinforce the advertising message, serve as a reminder of a need, and encourage an immediate purchase.

2.   Where a product is purchased infrequently, brand advertising is especially dependent upon window and store displays to recreate buying urges which have become dormant, to remind of a need, and to encourage immediate action.

3.   Where a substantial portion of customers shop for the generic product in a self-service store, prominent display at the point of purchase tends to stimulate sales.

4.   Since a substantial portion of those who trade in self-service stores do not arrive with a shopping list, point-of-purchase displays serve to remind them of what they need.

5.   Any brand which is purchased on impulse by a portion of the buyers will tend to benefit from point-of-purchase display.

Retail advertisements tend to enhance the effectiveness of a manufacturer's brand advertising. They provide the additional stimulus which may be needed to convert a brand preference into a buying urge. They add to the penetration of the advertising message within a local market. They serve as reminders of a need.

Of course, there are some highly individualized patent remedies of a personal nature which are sold entirely on the basis of consumer advertising without the support of either display or retail personal selling. Lydia Pinkham's Vegetable Compound is such a product. In such instances very powerful buying motives, together with a lack of substitutes as far as the consumer is concerned, result in the buyer asking for the product by brand name. Because the brand satisfies a strong need on the part of the consumer, its purchase tends to be planned and not made on impulse. Under these circumstances, display at the point of purchase assumes a position of relatively small importance. Such examples are in the minority, however.

It is apparent from the foregoing discussion that with some exceptions, even where the main selling burden is placed upon consumer advertising, the addition of retail advertising, display, and promotional efforts tend to enhance the effectiveness of the promotional program. Although dealer promotion would thus appear to be an essential part of the selling mix in the majority of these instances, we should not lose sight of the fact that its position is strictly supplementary to consumer advertising.

When retail personal selling is emphasized, how necessary is dealer promotion?

In an earlier discussion, it was pointed out that retail personal selling tends to be effective when the size of purchase is large, when the items need explanation and demonstration, when purchase is infrequent, and where trade-in allowances are offered on old models. When the main emphasis is placed upon retail personal selling, how necessary is dealer advertising, display, and promotional effort?

If the manufacturer follows the policy of selected retail distribution, it is important for him to take active steps to make certain that his dealers identify themselves as the local source of supply. Otherwise, the desire to examine the brand before making a buying decision may be frustrated by lack of knowledge of where to go for a demonstration. Although a diligent search might uncover the name of a dealer, the manufacturer would be well advised to make it as easy as possible for the prospect to acquire the necessary information. Advertising over the dealer's name, store identification signs, and window displays thus serve a useful purpose in helping to bring prospects into contact with retail salespeople.

Where the price is relatively high, as in the case of a color TV set, the prospect has to sacrifice a substantial portion of the family's surplus for discretionary spending in order to make the purchase. If the product also has a relatively long life and thus is replaced infrequently, the natural resistance to the price may lead the prospect to postpone the purchase. Under these conditions, the manufacturer's brand advertising needs to be supplemented by strong direct-action stimuli designed to get prospects to visit the dealer's store and examine the new model. Since dealers tend to favor advertising designed to bring an immediate response, the manufacturer may find it wise to encourage active dealer advertising and promotion.

If a product requires aggressive personal salesmanship by the dealer's organization, this effort may be made most effective if it is supported by an active program of dealer promotion. The retail salesmen need to be assisted in making contact with likely prospects. Retail advertising, display, and promotion will tend to bring such prospects into the store or stimulate them to inquire by telephone or mail. With such assistance the salesman can make the most effective use of his time and his persuasive talents.

Method of encouraging dealer promotion

After determining the role of dealer promotion in the selling mix, the manufacturer then faces the problem of selecting suitable methods for encouraging the desired degree of dealer support. A common method is to provide retailers with dealer helps which will aid them in their display, promotional, and advertising work. Some firms offer dealer cooperative advertising allowances as a means of encouraging local advertising. Others rely upon the persuasive efforts of their salesmen to encourage dealers to tie in with the manufacturer's general advertising by using retail advertisements, window displays, counter displays, and other promotional methods. Factors to be considered in selecting proper methods include: (1) how important active dealer promotion is believed to be; (2) whether distribution is selected or nonselected; (3) competitive practice; and (4) relative cost of alternative methods.

Consumer promotions

A fourth classification of order-getting ingredients includes various types of short-run consumer promotions designed to stimulate a quick buying response—contests, premiums, combination offers, coupons, and consumer price-offs, among others. Since these devices employ strong direct-action stimuli to force immediate purchasing action, they may also be termed "forcing methods." The basic appeal is to the desire for a bargain or to get something for nothing. Closely related are various types of trade promotions such as free goods, allowances, and special discounts which are designed to influence reseller cooperation. Such methods relate to the task of stimulating dealer promotion, previously discussed.

Consumer promotions are designed to achieve quick impact at the point of purchase, possibly along with òne or more underlying goals. Specific objectives commonly identified include the following:[11]

1. Getting prospects to try a new product (through "forced sampling").
2. Calling attention to improvements in established products.
3. Stopping the loss of old customers resulting from vigorous competition.
4. Encouraging active point-of-purchase display and promotion.
5. Helping and stimulating the firm's sales force.

The use of consumer promotions is highly controversial. Some argue that their use is harmful, since it diverts advertising and promotional effort away from the merits of the product and toward the contest, the premium, or the bargain which is being offered. Others say consumer promotions are a useful way to stimulate "forced sampling" of a new product or to inject interest in an advertising campaign through the "change of pace" provided by a creative consumer promotion. Others adopt their use as a defensive measure in an attempt to nullify the effect of competitors' consumer promotions.

Obviously, the need for strong stimuli in the promotional program depends upon whether or not an early buying response may be expected to result from the combined impact of consumer advertising, personal selling, and dealer promotion. Quick buying action may be expected (1) where strong, dynamic appeals may be made to consumer buying motives; (2) when the price of the product is small and the potential market is relatively large; (3) if promotion appears at a time when consumers' needs for the generic product are greatest; and (4) where the product is bought frequently. If these conditions are met, there is little need for using consumer promotions to force an early response. Where such conditions do not exist, however, the use of consumer promotions may properly be considered.

Even where a strong stimulus appears to be necessary to achieve a desired degree of early buying response, the wisdom of including a consumer promotion in the mix tends to depend upon the following considerations.[12]

---

[11] From the Marketing Science Institute, *Promotional Decisions Using Mathematical Models*, p. 10. © Copyright 1967 by Allyn & Bacon, Inc., Boston.

[12] Adapted by permission from Scott, *Advertising Principles and Problems*, chap. 6.

1. In addition to a quick buying response, what underlying objectives does management wish to achieve through the use of the proposed consumer promotion? (See common objectives listed above.) Are these goals in harmony with, or antagonistic to, the objectives established for other elements in the promotional mix?

2. In planning the introduction of new products, would a properly designed consumer promotion plus consumer advertising be likely to stimulate more prospects to sample the product than the use of consumer advertising alone? Considerable buyer resistance must usually be overcome to get prospects to switch brands and try a new product. Properly designed consumer promotions may stimulate forced sampling at a lower cost than distribution of free samples door to door, through the mail, or via space advertising. If the new brand is superior to competing products and its qualities may be appraised through usage, a properly chosen promotion would appear to be wise. This is especially true where frequent repurchase of the brand may be anticipated if it meets with consumer favor. If the product cannot be evaluated through usage and purchase is infrequent, the advantage of using a promotion may be limited, and its cost may not be justified by the incremental revenue produced.

3. Does a relatively large percentage of the prospective buyers of the generic product lack brand loyalty? That is, would they be willing to accept any one of several leading brands (including the firm's brand), or do they have no brand discrimination at all? This may be the case where the generic product has reached the stage of maturity in its life cycle and the leading brands have all been improved until they are equally satisfactory to the consumer. If the firm's brand is equally as good as competition, then a portion of the prospects who buy it under the stimulus of a consumer promotion will tend to make repeat purchases after the promotion is withdrawn.

4. Are competitors likely to retaliate with similar strong inducements to win back lost customers and to maintain their shares of industry? If so, then gains from consumer promotions may tend to be temporary. Ultimate winners in such a tug-of-war would tend to be the firms offering the most imaginative and creative types of promotions against the background of effective promotional and marketing mixes.

5. Are prospective buyers partially sold by advertising? Some firms use consumer promotions periodically to make customers out of prospects who have been previously influenced by advertising but who may still be in the "twilight zone of indecision." Such action would appear to be helpful where primary and selective appeals used in advertising are not strong enough to lead a substantial portion of prospects to take quick buying action. The habit of buying at infrequent intervals would also tend to increase the number of partially sold prospects over what

might be expected where users make repeat purchases frequently. Carefully spaced use of consumer promotions would tend to provide partially sold prospects with a reason for choosing the firm's brand.

6. Will the promotion tend to build up the audience for the firm's TV or radio programs? If so, this will tend to make its advertising more effective.

7. Will the forcing method help get valuable free publicity for the brand? If so, and this publicity is of the proper type, it may add significantly to the effectiveness of the promotional effort.

8. Will the consumer promotion assist and stimulate the company's sales force? Wisely planned promotions used at properly spaced intervals may make retailers more receptive to sales effort and may serve as a device to stimulate the sales organization.

9. Will forcing methods tend to encourage active dealer promotion? If properly planned and tested, promotions tend to bring quick action at the point of purchase. Anticipation of such results may tend to stimulate dealers to tie in with appropriate display and promotion in support of the brand.

Consumer promotions are short-run, tactical devices aimed at stimulating an early response at the point of purchase. Applied under proper circumstances, along with other elements in the promotional mix, short-run gains may result from their use. Long-run benefits of using promotions are more problematical, however. Where they are used to promote forced sampling of a new product, long-run benefits may indeed result. When they are utilized in the promotion of well-known, established brands, increases in share of market are usually temporary.

Under what circumstances might we expect the use of a promotion to prove an exception to the common experience and achieve long-run gains? The following questions are suggestive: (1) Will consumers like the brand when they try it? (2) Are price, distribution methods, and advertising policies favorable to the improvement of the brand's competitive position? (3) Have successive and frequent use been made of forcing methods so that smaller and smaller incremental gains may be expected?

While such considerations may help to identify circumstances where both short-run and long-run gains may be anticipated, a recent Marketing Science Institute study summarizes the limitations of our knowledge on this topic as follows:

It is plain that promotion plays an important role in marketing, but our knowledge of its effectiveness is lacking. The unfortunate facts that many promotional efforts seem to be prosaic, that no distinct goals are set, that postaudits are unimaginative, and that brand profits are jeopardized by intrinsic risks or wrong decisions may be attributed primarily from our inability to effectively tailor promotional endeavors to particular products, markets and circumstances. This problem of promotional selection is essentially the executive's responsibility, although effective research can assist in narrowing the areas for unaided judgment.[13]

As a means of improving decision making in this area, this MSI study emphasizes the following points: (1) the desirability of establishing explicit goals for consumer promotions; (2) the need of writing down such objectives so that all participants in the company's marketing effort will see what they are expected to do to achieve the desired objectives; (3) the wisdom of evaluating past performance to develop guidelines for the present and future; (4) the need of conducting scientifically designed tests or experiments to guide in decision making; and (5) the necessity of making carefully planned postaudits of both short-run and long-run results of consumer promotions used.

The primary purpose of the MSI study was to explain and demonstrate some applications of quantitative techniques, using real data, to measure and evaluate market response to promotions. While space does not permit a discussion of the quantitative methods used, those interested will find it rewarding to examine the study itself for further information.

Determining the promotional mix

As you think back over the preceding discussion, it is apparent that the task of determining the promotional mix includes the following steps. (1) Decide which of the various available promotional methods to include in the mix. Factors to consider in appraising the opportunity to make effective use of consumer advertising, consumer promotions, personal selling, and dealer promotion have been outlined in the previous pages. (2) Determine whether it is likely to be most profitable to place the main burden of selling upon consumer advertising, personal selling, dealer promotion, or other selling methods chosen for use. Estimates of the relative suitability of these several methods will guide this decision. (3) Reach a decision on how supplementary promotional methods may be combined with the method to be emphasized in order to perform necessary selling tasks and to achieve maximum effectiveness from the total mix. Most promotional programs are a combination of several methods. This fact highlights the need for careful integration of methods chosen to comprise a well-coordinated, total program. This desired coordination may be achieved through a careful definition of sales and promotional tasks and the intelligent choice of the various methods to be used in performing these necessary tasks. The use of checklists showing tasks to be performed and methods selected to achieve desired goals may be helpful in achieving proper integration of effort. Timing sched-

---

[13] Marketing Science Institute, *Promotional Decisions Using Mathematical Models,* p. 17. Reprinted by permission of the publisher.

ules listing jobs to be done and those responsible for their performance may also assist in bringing about the necessary coordination.

While the generalizations outlined above may be of assistance in the determination of an effective promotional mix, preliminary decisions based upon desk analyses should be checked by local area test campaigns wherever suitable and possible. Procedures should also be set up for measuring the results of the various promotional methods utilized. Such information will provide the basis for modification and improvement in subsequent campaigns in the light of previous experience.

Adaptive Planning and Control Sequence (APACS)

The foregoing discussion of the determination of the promotional mix focuses on the decision-making process and discusses the considerations to be taken into account in analyzing the various subissues involved in working out a solution to the problem of how best to sell a given product. Let us now turn briefly to a Marketing Science Institute study of the process of promotional decision making based upon procedures followed in 12 companies and involving interviews with 100 key personnel within these organizations and their advertising agencies.[14] This will serve to position our discussion within the total planning and control sequence involved in the allocation of funds among the elements of the promotional mix and will also introduce the topic of determination of the promotional budget which follows.

The MSI study was concerned with how funds for the promotional mix of advertising, personal selling, and sales promotion are allocated in the marketing of new products. It covers the process of promotional decision making from the time work is begun on planning the program to the allocation of funds for specific activities. Out of the analysis of the practices of the 12 companies, a conceptual model of the decision-making process was developed. It is called the "Adaptive Planning and Control Sequence," or "APACS." According to this conceptual model, the promotional decision-making process is a series of eight steps, each of which is listed and described briefly below.

1. *Define problem and set objectives.* Define problem associated with promotional actions to be planned, and set objectives conforming with overall corporate goals.

2. *Appraise overall situation.* Determine market potentials, manufacturing costs, pricing policies, competitive activities, channels of distribution, buying habits and motivations, and practical constraints; and review past experience.

[14] From P. J. Robinson and D. J. Luck, *Promotional Decision Making* (New York: McGraw-Hill Book Co., 1964), chap. 3, and Exhibit 1 opposite p. 244. Copyright 1964 by Marketing Science Institute. Used with permission of McGraw-Hill Co.

3. *Determine tasks and identify means.* Define subgoals to be accomplished and identify appropriate means to achieve these aims.

4. *Identify alternative plans and mixes.* Delineate feasible alternative marketing strategies and promotional mixes, and identify additional information required.

5. *Estimate expected results.* Employ judgment and analogous experience, field tests, and any suitable management science techniques to forecast results in terms of accepted performance criteria (for example, market share, sales quota, profit).

6. *Review and decision by management.* Submit line and staff advice to supplement management's judgment in adopting plans and budgets and delegating authority to conduct approved program.

7. *Feedback of results and postaudit.* Provide for communication of field data and market intelligence and for monitoring performance of pilot or full-scale operation.

8. *Adapt program if required.* Revise or reaffirm goals, subgoals, and expenditures as necessary.

    a) If at this stage (or any other stage in the sequence) agreement cannot be obtained, or the program appears infeasible, return to previous stages and recycle as necessary.

    b) Proceed with other problems if satisfactory promotional allocation plan is achieved.

It will be noted that the discussion earlier in this chapter relates especially to steps 3, 4, 5, and 7 in the APACS model.

In summing up their findings, the authors state that their study offers effective evidence that a systematic approach such as the one provided by APACS would benefit promotional decision making. The following deterrents to systematic decision making were identified, among others: failure to maintain records of performance of previous promotional programs, lack of sufficient information about overall corporate goals and objectives, and failure to define specific objectives for promotional activities. It was noted that the tasks of forecasting performance and evaluating risks were two of the decision maker's most perplexing problems. It was also pointed out that there was a need for carefully designed experiments and proper field testing, if promotional decision making were to be improved. A better understanding of current techniques for measuring marketing performance was likewise identified as essential.

Conclusion

We have turned, in this chapter, from the basic questions of product policy and development, branding, pricing, and selecting channels of distribution to the all-important area of selling the product. To sell one must communicate, so we have described the nature of communication. The special theme of the chapter is the importance of sound promotional strategy and of effective selection of appropriate methods of communication, from those available, in order to achieve the best promotional mix. The decisions the marketing manager of a manufacturer or producer makes as to emphasis on advertising, personal selling, dealer promotion, or consumer promotion will be crucial to the success of the entire marketing program and of the business. It becomes clear that different products and different marketing situations call for different mixes of selling ingredients.

We now move on, in Chapter 12, to the decisions involved in determining the promotional appropriation.

Questions

1. Define "communication." Explain and illustrate the basic elements in a communication system using the following situations:
   a) A Ford Mustang salesman talking with a lower-middle-class prospective buyer who has a three-year-old Ford Torino to trade in.
   b) RCA-Victor advertising color television sets in The Netherlands.
   How do these two situations differ? What implications do these differences have for marketing management?
2. What conditions must be present if communication is to be effective?
3. Give examples which illustrate how prior decisions on product, brand policy, distribution policy, and price influence the promotional mix.
4. Using the following as examples, illustrate how the position of a product in its life cycle would tend to influence the character of the promotional mix:
   a) Diet Cola.
   b) Xerox photocopying equipment.
   c) Crest toothpaste.
5. How might the buying habits of consumers influence the promotional mix for the following products?
   a) Hickey Freeman suits.
   b) Wrigley's chewing gum.
   c) Aluminum siding for houses.
6. Explain how the character of middlemen used and their point of view might tend to affect the nature of the promotional mix for the following products:
   a) A new brand of mentholated shaving cream in an aerosol can being introduced by Alberto-Culver.
   b) Cessna aircraft for pleasure and personal use.
   c) Volkswagen automobile.
   d) An imported Japanese camera offered exclusively by a large mail-order house at a special bargain price.

7. Illustrate how the possible size of promotional funds available would tend to influence the character of the promotional mix in the following situations:

   a) Introduction of a new spray deodorant by a firm which had only $50,000 of working capital at the time the marketing program began.

   b) Introduction of antiperspirant in an aerosol can by a firm capable of investing $1 million in the first year's promotional effort.

8. Distinguish between (a) product advertising and institutional advertising; (b) dealer promotion and consumer promotions; (c) missionary salesmen and detail men.

9. Using Borden's criteria, appraise the advertisability of the following products (assuming adequate funds available to perform necessary promotional tasks):

   a) Sugar.

   b) Patent remedy offering a sure cure for athlete's foot.

   c) Toys for three- to five-year-old children (colorful, offering movement and sound).

   d) Fine furniture in colonial styles sold nationally through 40 department stores, each with an exclusive agency for its market.

10. Other things being equal, what influence would the presence or absence of "hidden qualities" have upon the opportunity for making effective use of consumer advertising for the following products?

    a) Pillsbury Cake Mix.

    b) Velvet sport jackets for men.

    c) A cold remedy containing antihistamine, decongestant, and aspirin.

11. a) What considerations tend to determine the wisdom of using personal selling in the promotional mix?

    b) Would you place the main burden of promotion upon personal selling in the following situations?

       (1) A line of cosmetics.

       (2) A central home air-conditioning system.

       (3) A new brand of freeze-dried coffee.

       (4) A line of apparel offering 200 different styles, including knit suits, dresses, slacks, sweaters, and blouses in casual designs aimed at the homemaker market and sold at modest prices.

12. a) Under what circumstances should dealer promotion carry the main burden of selling?

    b) Would you place the main emphasis upon dealer promotion in the sale of the following products?

       (1) Neckties.

       (2) Drapes for the living room.

       (3) A new soft drink with unusual thirst quenching qualities.

       (4) Women's high-grade nylon hosiery.

       (5) Necklaces for men.

13. When advertising is emphasized in the promotional mix, is dealer promotion necessary? In answering, apply your analysis to the following products:

 a) Marlboro cigarettes.
 b) Toni hair coloring.
 c) Maxim freeze-dried coffee.

14. When retail personal selling is emphasized, is dealer promotional activity necessary? Answer by applying your analysis to the following products:
 a) Hickey Freeman high-grade men's suits.
 b) Singer sewing machines.
 c) Hi-fi sound systems.
 d) Vacuum cleaners sold through department stores.

15. In the following cases, where dealer promotion is essential, would you favor the use of dealer cooperative advertising allowances to encourage the desired effort, or would you emphasize "merchandising" the advertising to retail dealers to get their support?
 a) High-grade men's shoes with selective retail distribution.
 b) Medium-grade upholstered furniture.

12

Determining the promotional appropriation

CLOSELY RELATED to the decision on the character of the promotional mix is the task of determining the size of the promotional appropriation. If analysis indicates that the main burden should be placed upon consumer advertising, the size of the promotional appropriation is likely to be larger than if the strategy should place primary emphasis on dealer push. Conversely, the size of the expenditure which the product will support and which the company can finance is an important consideration in determining what promotional strategy is likely to be most effective for a given product and in deciding the appropriate combination of promotional methods to include in the selling mix.

The task of determining the promotional appropriation is of key importance, since the ultimate decision will have a significant influence upon the effectiveness of the promotional program and, hence, upon profits. Therefore, we have singled this problem out for special consideration at this point. Our primary purpose is to provide essential background on the approaches commonly used by executives in determining the appropriation for the total promotional effort in a given year, or, in the case of new products, for a period of several years. A secondary goal is to suggest some of the more important considerations to be taken into account in reaching a decision on this important problem.

Theoretical analysis of the problem

The marginal approach to the determination of the promotional appropriation provides a useful theoretical framework against which we can later compare actual business practice. This approach is illustrated in Figure 12–1, which is a short-run analysis developed by Joel Dean based upon the following assumptions:[1] (1) Advertising cost is assumed to include all pure selling costs and is identified by the curve SC. Incremental advertising costs are the additional expenditures required to produce one additional unit of sales. (2) Incremental production costs are assumed to be constant at 20 cents per unit over the range of output covered in this example. In the short run, this tends to be true for firms whose production is mechanized. (3) Unit price is assumed to be constant at 70 cents over the range of volume under consideration and does not change as a result of changes in selling costs. (4) The relationship between incremental advertising costs (SC) and sales vol-

FIGURE 12–1
Short-run determination of advertising outlay by marginal analysis

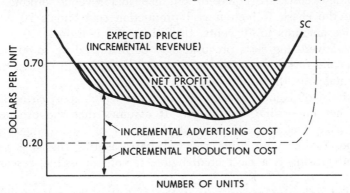

ume is assumed to approximate a "**U**-shaped" curve which first declines as volume increases, then is constant, and then rises at an accelerating rate. Incremental advertising costs (SC) may be determined from Figure 12–1 by identifying a given volume of sales and by running a vertical line to intersect curve SC. Then run a horizontal line from the point of intersection with SC to the vertical axis to read off the corresponding dollars per unit figure shown there—for example, 50 cents. From this figure subtract incremental production costs of 20 cents per unit to get selling costs of 30 cents (50 cents — 20 cents = 30 cents). In this way it may be determined that incremental advertising costs amount to $1 per unit at low volume, decline progressively as sales increase until a low point of 15 cents is reached, and then increase rapidly, as volume increases still more, until a figure of $1 is reached once again.

What is the rationale behind the **U**-shaped incremental advertising

[1] Adapted from Joel Dean, *Managerial Economics*, pp. 356–61, © 1951. Reprinted by permission of Prentice-Hall, Inc., Englewood Cliffs, N.J.

cost curve? The declining phase is explained in part by the economies of specialization: (1) As the appropriation increases in size, it becomes possible to make use of expert services. (2) Larger expenditures tend to make it possible to use more economical media. Even more important, however, are the economies that come from repetition of the advertising message and the learning that results. The increasing phase of the advertising cost curve results primarily because successively poorer prospects tend to be reached as the advertising expenditures are increased. Then, too, increasing advertising expenditures may progressively exhaust the most vulnerable geographic areas or the most efficient advertising media.

Based on these assumptions, then, how should the advertising appropriation be determined? Clearly it would be profitable to increase advertising expenditures step by step until the incremental costs of advertising and production (as measured by the SC line) intersect the price line (i.e. until these costs are equal to the marginal revenue produced). In terms of the chart, if incremental production cost equals 20 cents and the price amounts to 70 cents, then the gross margin is 50 cents. Accordingly, advertising costs per unit may be increased up to 50 cents per unit. Beyond this amount, the incremental revenue will be less than the incremental costs, the total profits will be reduced.

This analysis, of course, represents an ideal which most firms find difficult, if not impossible, to achieve. It assumes that the executive is able to make accurate estimates of the effect of advertising upon sales volume. Yet for most firms, the task of measuring the sales generated by advertising is a most challenging, if not impossible, research problem.

Part of the difficulty grows out of the fact that the sales volume achieved in any given year is the effect of both external environmental forces—such as general economic trends, changes in primary demand, competitive activity—and internal influences, such as the marketing program. Within the marketing program itself, changes in sales volume may result not only from changes in the level of promotional expenditures but also from changes in the impact of other elements in the marketing mix, such as product improvements, increased effectiveness of the distribution organization, and changes in prices. Finally, there is the problem of tracing any residual changes in sales volume which might result from the total promotional program to the individual elements of which it is comprised—i.e., changes in advertising, in personal selling, or in sales promotional activities. Truly, the task of measuring the sales influence of a single factor, such as advertising, is a complex, challenging, and often impossible task. While a few firms have been able to devise research approaches which they claim have enabled them to measure the sales results of promotional investments of different size, such organizations are the exception rather than the rule.

Again, this theoretical analysis does not recognize the cumulative effect of past advertising upon current or future sales. Many firms find that only a portion of the results of this year's advertising occur in the form of present sales, while the remainder will tend to carry over into future years. This problem is especially acute in the promotion of products of high unit value and infrequent purchase, such as automobiles. For such firms a sizable proportion of this year's advertising expenditure is likely to pay off in terms of creating awareness, preference, or intent to búy which will tend to influence sales—one, two, or more years into the future. At the same time, past advertising will have created attitudes which will lead to current purchases. Since the advertising of many firms has such carry-over effects, the short-run marginal analysis outlined above tends to have only limited value.

In spite of these limitations, this theoretical analysis makes some conceptual contributions of practical importance. If the major part of the firm's advertising is designed to stimulate an immediate response, and if conditions are favorable to such results, then the marginal approach provides a simple test of how much to spend and when to stop. It is also useful in providing management with guidelines as to the kind of information needed in making a decision on how much to spend on advertising. By the same token, it serves as a guide in designing research to evaluate the results of advertising and in gathering information which will help improve the quality of the appropriation decision.

Common approaches to determining the appropriation

Now that we have outlined the theoretical approach to the determination of promotional expenditures, let us turn to a consideration of some of the more common approaches followed by business firms in actual practice. Four of the more important alternative methods will be discussed: (1) percentage of sales; (2) all available funds; (3) competitive parity; (4) research objective. While our discussion will be in terms of determining the advertising appropriation, the analysis may be applied equally well to the determination of budgets for personal selling and sales promotional activities.

In making a survey of approaches to the determination of the advertising appropriation for the Association of National Advertisers some years ago, Richard Webster recommended that advertisers use a two-way classification originally suggested by C. M. Edwards and W. H. Howard: (1) breakdown, and (2) buildup methods.[2] The breakdown method

---

[2] Adapted by permission from Richard Webster, *Setting Advertising Appropriations* (New York: Assoc. of National Advertisers, Inc., 1949), pp. 3–19.

is described as providing a lump sum to be disbursed by the advertising department as it sees fit, and the buildup method is characterized as an appropriation that tells in detail exactly how the funds are to be expended. Since this classification will aid us in our analysis, let us take a moment to explain the principle upon which it is based.

In the breakdown method, the lump sum granted by management is the control. After the lump sum has been determined, advertising executives work out what they believe to be the most effective division of this amount by different kinds of promotional effort and by types of advertising media. Under this approach, the primary emphasis is placed upon what the firm can afford. In the buildup method, the task to be accomplished by advertising is the control. Once the task has been defined, the budget is built up by determining the kinds and amounts of advertising and promotional efforts needed to achieve the desired goal and by estimating the cost of the necessary program.

Percentage of sales[3]

A common approach falling under the breakdown classification is where a lump sum for advertising is determined by multiplying dollar sales by a more or less arbitrarily chosen percentage. In making this computation, either past sales or estimated future sales may be used. The percentage applied may be either fixed—remaining the same over a period of years—or variable—changing from year to year. A variation of this plan is to substitute a specified number of dollars per unit for a percentage figure and multiply this figure by unit sales instead of dollar sales.

Fixed versus variable percentage. In evaluating this approach, let us begin by considering the use of a fixed percentage in determining the lump sum available for advertising. This approach is quick and easy. It has the further advantage of keeping the advertising appropriation within what the firm can afford—since expenditures are tied to revenue. Indeed, this is the key consideration in such an approach. Then, too, it may lead to competitive stabilization. If all or most of the competitors in an industry used this method and applied the same percentage of sales, competitors' advertising expenditures would be roughly proportional to their market shares. This would tend to have a restraining effect upon advertising competition.

If a fixed percentage is used over a period of several years, however,

[3] For a more complete discussion of all methods commonly used in determining the advertising appropriation, see A. W. Frey, *How Many Dollars for Advertising* (New York: Ronald Press Co., 1955), pp. 48–82. See also David L. Hurwood, "How Companies Set Advertising Budgets," *The Conference Board Record*, March 1968, pp. 34–41.

it is evident that no allowance is being made for the differences in the promotional needs of a new product, as compared with the requirements of the same item after it has become established. It also fails to take into account changes in the competitive situation and changes in the responsiveness of prospective buyers as they react to actual or anticipated changes in their incomes, as well as differences in the ability of a firm to finance advertising in periods of prosperity as compared with times of recession.

Of prime significance, however, is the fact that the fixed percentage-of-sales method assumes that the advertising appropriation should be a *result* of sales achieved rather than a *cause* of sales increases. It overlooks the fact that advertising, when appropriately used, has the power of *creating* the income out of which its expenditures may be covered—and that in so doing, it may add to profits.

Some of the objections to the percentage-of-sales method may be removed if the percentage allowed for advertising is changed from year to year. Within the limits of the operating budget, a larger percentage of sales may be set aside to help introduce a new product than would be provided when the new brand has achieved an established place for itself in the market. Subject to the limitations of the budget, the percentage may also be changed to reflect changes in competition, responsiveness of buyers, and business conditions. Since the size of the percentage is still controlled by what the firm can afford in a given year, however, the amount appropriated for advertising will tend to fall far short of what might be made available if management were primarily guided by the size and the nature of the promotional tasks to be accomplished. Where the advertising appropriation is governed primarily by the size of the job to be done in a given year, executives may provide a sum for promotion which results in a substantial current period loss if it is anticipated that revenue in the next year or two will counterbalance this figure and result in long-run profits.

Past sales versus future sales as a base. In the earlier years, the percentage figure was often applied to past sales to arrive at the advertising appropriation. Where this is done, the appropriation is actually made out of "money in the bank," since management has the chance to study actual sales in the previous year, as well as the resulting profits, before deciding on the percentage of past sales to set aside for advertising for the year ahead. This approach may result in appropriations which are either too small or too large, depending on how the sales prospects for the coming year compare with the year just past. This would be especially undesirable in periods which are turning points in the business cycle and where industry sales may, therefore, change more than usual. Looking backward may also lose a firm its best opportunities for maintaining or expanding its position in the industry. Clearly this approach is entirely unsuited to the task of setting the appropriation for a new product. It is apparent from these comments that the major weakness of the use of past sales as a base is the assumption implicit in the approach that advertising follows sales instead of creating them. This limitation is most serious when a fixed percentage of past sales is used. Even though the use of a varying percentage may make partial allowance for changes in the job to be done, the fact that this percentage is applied to past sales may still result in lost opportunities.

Because of these limitations, the percentage-of-past-sales approach has been generally abandoned. Instead, estimated future sales tend to be used as the base by those favoring the percentage of sales (or break-down) approach. If estimated future sales are taken as the base, then the advertising appropriation will be better adjusted to anticipated market conditions than when past sales are used. There will be less danger of overspending or underspending than when a percentage of past sales is applied.

Of course, the case in favor of using estimated future sales as a base depends upon the ability of executives to estimate future sales results. If experience indicates that their estimates vary widely from actual sales, then it may be unwise to base the advertising appropriation upon a percentage of estimated future sales. If sales forecasts have been reasonably accurate, however, then the practice of using a percentage of estimated future sales is to be preferred over that of applying this percentage to past sales.

We should remember, however, that the percentage-of-future-sales approach still gives primary emphasis to keeping advertising expenditures within the limits of what the firm can afford, taking into account the constraints of the operating budget for the coming year. Giving primary emphasis to what the firm can afford, instead of to the income-producing potentialities of advertising, is still a serious limitation.

Indeed, it is clear that the percentage-of-future-sales approach involves a logical inconsistency. If we agree that the size of the advertising expenditure affects the sales volume achieved, as is certainly the case where a favorable advertising opportunity exists, then how can future sales be estimated without knowing how much is to be spent upon advertising during the coming year?

It is clear from these comments that the variable percentage of estimated future sales is the most defensible variation of this breakdown method. The following conditions make the best possible case for using this approach: (1) if the product is well established and has achieved a satisfactory share of market; (2) if the external environment is relatively static during the period, so that the job to be done by advertising varies little from year to year; (3) if management believes that a substantial change in advertising expenditures would be likely to stimulate strong, competitive retaliation; (4) if there is considerable uncertainty as to the effectiveness of advertising and thus some merit in giving considerable emphasis to what the firm can afford in determining the appropriation.

Since this approach treats advertising as an effect rather than a cause, however, it is still, in most instances, a questionable approach for management to use. Instead we might argue that it would be preferable to use an approach which makes the job to be done the guiding principle, and then check the firm's ability to finance the resulting appropriation by expressing it as a percentage of estimated sales.

All available funds

An extreme example of the breakdown approach is where a firm allocates a share of all available liquid resources and borrowable funds to support the advertising program. This approach was followed by Brooks-Ledford Company in determining the initial advertising appropriation for Galaxy hairdressing and conditioner. Taking into account what portion of the sales dollar was needed to pay for direct production expenses, overhead, and amortization of bank loans, the firm allocated the remainder for selling and advertising expenditures. Salesmen were used in getting distribution and point-of purchase promotion for Galaxy, while $75,000 was made available for cooperative advertising. This promotional program started Galaxy on its way to becoming a market leader in its field.

Note, however, that the limit of the appropriation following this method is the immediate availability of funds rather than estimated future profits.

The "all-available-funds" approach is likely to come closer to supporting the performance of necessary promotional tasks than when the appropriation is limited to an agreed-upon percentage of sales which fits within the operating budget of a given year. If the advertising opportunity is good, but sales results are likely to be delayed for one or two years, then the allocation of all available funds to promotion may result in more rapid progress toward desired share of industry than when the effort is limited to a percentage of sales which is adjusted to permit current profits on the product.

Even where advertising may be expected to bring highly profitable results ultimately, financial embarrassment may occur if short-run cash and credit limits are ignored in deciding upon advertising expenditures. From the viewpoint of financial management, therefore, there is merit in limiting promotional outlays to what the firm can afford, in terms of immediately available funds. If what the firm can afford is interpreted without recognizing the long-run income-producing possibilities of effective advertising, however, opportunities for increasing profits through aggressive promotion may be foregone. This is a serious danger, since the controlling principle in appropriating "all available funds" is what the firm can afford to allocate to the promotion of a particular product.

This leads us to the most serious limitation of the all-available-funds approach. It is that there is no logical connection between the availability of funds and the advertising opportunity. This approach may lead a firm to limit the advertising appropriation for a new product to an amount far below the point where marginal revenue produced by advertising is just equal to the marginal cost of the promotional effort. At the other extreme, the advertising budget for a successful, established product may conceivably be pushed beyond the point where the marginal revenue produced is equal to or less than the marginal cost of the effort.

Under what circumstances, then, might this approach be defensible? (1) This method might be justified where there is an excellent opportunity to make use of consumer advertising in the introduction of a new product and where such promotional effort may be expected to produce an early, measurable sales response. Here, current profits may well be sacrificed in favor of attaining a sizable market share for the brand and, accordingly, a favorable rate of long-run profits. (2) Where the firm can estimate the marginal effectiveness of advertising, it may result in reasonably satisfactory appropriations, as long as the product is operating short of the point where incremental advertising costs and incremental revenue are equal. Note that the use of such knowledge involves a combination of the marginal approach with the all-available-funds method.

At best, then, the all-available-funds approach is only a temporary expedient which may appear to meet the requirements of a new, inadequately financed firm, or a company which is short of working capital because of rapid growth. Circumstances may force the firm to give primary emphasis in setting the advertising appropriation to what the firm can afford. If this is the case, management should be impatient to shift to a more defensible approach, as soon as circumstances will permit. We might argue, however, that it would be preferable to approach the determination of the appropriation by estimating the advertising opportunity, by defining desired promotional tasks, and then by considering whether management can find some way to finance the necessary expenditures to implement the desired program.

Competitive parity

The guiding principle of the competitive-parity approach is to base the advertising appropriation in some systematic way upon what competitors are doing. One variation is to match competitors' advertising dollars. Another is to use the same percentage of sales for advertising as key competitors use, or the same ratio as is representative of the industry. A more sophisticated variation is to make the product's share of industry advertising dollars equal to its share of market.

Is it wise to use the average percentage of sales spent on advertising by the industry as the ratio to be used in setting the advertising appropriation for the firm's own product? Such an approach might be advocated on the grounds that the industry ratio represents the combined wisdom of competitors. It might appeal especially to a firm entering a new market in which it lacks experience. A medium-sized manufacturer of industrial timers, wishing to introduce a new automatic timer to consumers to control lights and appliances automatically, would be a good example. Lacking experience in consumer marketing, the executives of such a firm might be attracted by the idea of basing the advertising appropriation for the new automatic timer upon competitive parity.

Such an approach would, however, be highly questionable. The advertising ratios of individual firms in the industry might be expected to vary considerably from the industry average. In a study of the percentage invested in advertising by 22 manufacturers of small appliances, some years ago, for example, it was reported that the median was 5.12 percent, but the range was from 0.83 to 45.0 percent.[4] Clearly the industry average is of little value as a guide, since the ratios of individual firms may be expected to vary depending upon their size, objectives, share of market, promotional strategy, and marketing mix.

Moreover, where industry ratios are available, the data will reflect the advertising decisions of the past year and *not* the ratios planned for the coming year. Yet it is future advertising ratios of individual competitors which would be most useful in working out promotional strategy and the appropriation required to implement such plans. Such data are generally regarded as highly confidential and are closely guarded from competitors.

In spite of these limitations, it might be argued that the competitive-parity approach will tend to safeguard against advertising wars which might result if other methods of setting the appropriation were followed. Here a parallel is being drawn between the retaliation which may result, under conditions of oligopoly, when one firm makes a drastic price cut. An increase in the amount spent on advertising by one firm, however, is less likely to stimulate quick retaliation from competitors than would

---

[4] S. H. Sandage and S. R. Bernstein, *Advertising Expenditures per Dollar of Sales.* Copyright, 1956, University of Illinois and Advertising Publications, Inc. For a comprehensive report based on Internal Revenue Service sources, see "Percentage of Sales Invested in Advertising in 1968–69," *Advertising Age,* April 10, 1972, p. 48.

a price cut. An increase in advertising effort is harder for competitors to identify. Information on planned appropriations is not customarily made public by the decision maker and estimates of advertising expenditures secured by research organizations through counting advertisements and applying published media rates are generally available only after considerable time lag. Moreover, the results of increased advertising by one firm are difficult for a competitor to measure. These problems tend to slow down competitive retaliation to increased advertising effort.

Even if retaliation is to be expected ultimately, this should not necessarily stop a firm from increasing its advertising of a brand in an effort to expand its share of market. How else can the manufacturer of a new brand with a demonstrable individualizing feature expand sales until a profitable target share of market is achieved? Even though some of the ground gained through increased advertising may be lost later on as a result of competitive retaliation, the net result may still be an increased scale of output, together with lower unit production costs which will produce higher long-run profits.

Although competitive parity does not make sense in setting the advertising appropriation for the new brand, this approach may be more defensible for the firm with an established brand which ranks in second or third place in an oligopolistic industry. If the firm is making reasonable profits on its brand, executives may hesitate to provoke retaliation from larger firms in the industry by increasing the advertising ratio substantially—especially if conditions are such that this action is likely to be noticed by competitors.

Even so, the competitive-parity approach provides no guides as to the appropriation strategy which will result in the most favorable long-run profits. The advertising outlays of competitors will, of course, influence the size of the expenditures required to achieve a desired increase in share of market. But the responsiveness of the market to the firm's brand is influenced by other factors, such as the advertising opportunity and the effectiveness of the marketing mix. Accordingly, the industry advertising ratio will be of no value in helping the executive to determine how much advertising expenditures may be increased before the point is reached where the last $1,000 spent on advertising produces just enough additional revenue to cover its cost.

A more sophisticated variation of the competitive-parity approach is to make the product's share of total industry advertising expenditures equal to the brand's desired share of market. That is, if a 35 percent share of market is desired, then the advertising appropriation would be set at a figure which would represent 35 percent of total estimated advertising expenditures for the industry. The idea for this approach grew out of studies of the relationship between percent of industry advertising by a single advertiser and that firm's market position. Preliminary studies of this sort, for example, led one researcher to state the hypothesis that to maintain or increase share of market, the percent of industry advertising for the product involved should be equal to, or exceed, the market position desired. Conversely, if advertising volume, as a percent of total industry volume, is less than the brand's share of market, it can be forecast that market position will decrease.[5]

This approach is an improvement over using the industry advertising ratio as the base, since consideration of the desired share of market for the brand involves an attempt to define the size of the job which must be performed by advertising during the coming year. It assumes, however, that the desired share of market, say 25 percent, may be achieved by investing 25 percent of estimated industry advertising expenditures in the promotion of the company's brand. This may or may not be true. The market position achieved by a brand tends to be influenced by how it compares with competing brands in terms of product innovation, quality of distribution organization, price-quality relationships, and effectiveness of promotional strategy, as well as the size of the expenditures allocated to personal selling, sales promotion, and finally advertising.

Significant light is thrown on this matter by General Electric's extensive analysis designed to test the hypothesis that there is a direct and measurable relationship between share-of-industry advertising and share-of-industry sales.[6] The study extended over a period of 4 years and covered 16 different products: 6 major appliance product lines, 5 traffic appliance lines, 1 consumer supply line, and 4 industrial component or supply lines. G. A. Bradford summarized results of this research:

> An objective summary of the study would have to state that the analysis did *not* prove the theory "that there is a direct relationship between share-of-industry advertising and share-of-industry sales." At the same time, it did not *disprove* the theory, but rather underlined the importance of other factors and influences in the selling situations.

He also commented that the tests did provide some hints as to other factors which appeared to influence the relationship under study. (1) High-saturation industries did not show the same sensitiveness to changes in share-of-industry advertising as did low-saturation industries. (2) Significant differences were noted in the advertising payoff enjoyed by the leaders of the industry versus the followers. (3) Evidence would

---

[5] C. J. Coward, "A Definitive Approach to Determining the Advertising Budget," *Marketing Times* (Marketing Services, General Electric), July 1958, p. 3.

[6] Adapted by permission from G. A. Bradford, "What General Electric Is Doing to Evaluate the Effect on Sales of Its Industrial and Consumer Advertising," a paper presented at the Association of National Advertisers, *Advertisers Evaluation Workshop,* January 27, 1960.

suggest that there is a ceiling on the share of advertising any company should attempt to run. (4) Influences other than advertising can swing the anticipated share of market completely out of the ball park. (5) Predicting the direct influence on sales of any single element in the marketing mix is an unlikely possibility. The only way correlation studies will make an ultimate contribution in the future, he concluded, is to measure and correlate the effect of several key influences on market share at one and the same time.

The approach of making the brand's share-of-industry advertising equal the brand's market share also involves the problem mentioned earlier of being forced to work with past data rather than with information on competitors' planned future advertising outlays. This version of the competitive-parity approach likewise fails to consider whether the required share-of-industry advertising expenditure will be profitable or not. While anticipated advertising activity by competitors should obviously be considered by a firm in determining the appropriation for its product, strict adherence to the competitive-parity approach would, therefore, be unwise. Instead, it may be preferable to undertake experiments in an attempt to determine what share of industry advertising expenditure is required in order to achieve a desired brand market share. The findings which result might then be considered, along with other data, in working out the decision on next year's advertising appropriation.

Research objective

The research-objective approach (sometimes called the objective-and-task approach) is in direct contrast to the methods discussed up to this point.[7] It is a buildup method where the job to be done receives primary emphasis, whereas the all-available-funds, percentage-of-sales, and competitive-parity approaches emphasize the appropriation of a lump sum for advertising which is then broken down by specific types of promotional methods and media, as advertising executives see fit.

Under the research-objective method, the firm first undertakes research to serve as a guide in setting reasonable objectives for the coming year's advertising. Guided by additional research, the firm then determines how much and what kind of advertising is necessary to achieve the stated objectives. The estimated cost of such advertising is the size of the appropriation to be recommended to top management. At this

---

[7] In his landmark study of advertising appropriation methods, A. W. Frey substitutes the label "research-objective method" for the traditional title, "objective-and-task approach." This change in nomenclature appears desirable, since it emphasizes the reliance upon research which would characterize the approach. See Frey, *How Many Dollars for Advertising*, p. 51.

point, consideration is given to the question of whether the budget will permit the appropriation of the sum believed to be necessary to achieve desired goals. If the initial sum appears to be excessive, then the firm will have to proceed more slowly and scale down the objectives until the estimated cost of their achievement comes within what the advertiser can afford.

The research-objective approach, if properly applied, is clearly superior to the methods previously discussed. It encourages management to think in terms of realistic objectives for its promotional effort, to seek the most effective methods of achieving these goals, and then to recognize the necessary relationship between the costs of the resulting advertising program and the size of the job specified in the planning effort. While ability to finance the recommended advertising effort is taken into account, management is encouraged to think of advertising not as just a cost but also as an income-producing method. Imaginative and aggressive use of advertising is thus encouraged.

This approach also implies reliance upon research to provide management with facts upon which to base decisions as to appropriate goals, proper methods, and necessary amounts of promotional effort to achieve desired objectives. Intuition and guesswork in setting the appropriation should therefore be reduced and, hopefully, the quality of decision making improved.

The chief limitation of the research-objective approach, as commonly defined, is that it does not require the decision maker to determine whether his stated objectives are likely to contribute enough incremental revenue to justify the costs involved in achieving them. Instead, it assumes that agreed-upon goals are always worth the cost of achieving them. This criticism has two parts. (1) While the research-objective approach requires the identification of reasonable objectives, it does not specify that these goals should be related to desired sales increases. Indeed, because of the difficulty which many firms face in measuring the sales results of advertising, they tend to identify their promotional goals in terms of changes in awareness, preference, and intent to buy. While such goals are helpful in guiding the planning of promotional programs, they contribute little to the development of advertising appropriations. If objectives are to be helpful in this respect, they must be stated so that they are measurable in terms of incremental sales results. To relate communication goals to sales results requires ingenuity in research, which is not identified as a requirement under the common definition of the research-objective method. (2) The research-objective method does not specify that the value of achieving stated objectives be measured in terms of the incremental revenue which will result. Only when this is done is it possible to determine whether the additional costs of achieving desired goals are justified by the incremental revenue produced. Such information is required, of course, if alternative objectives are to be properly evaluated and the most appropriate goals identified.

If the research-objective approach is modified to eliminate the deficiencies noted above, it approximates the marginal approach which was identified as the theoretical ideal earlier in this discussion. Even then, executives who attempt to use this modified method face challenging research problems in (1) determining how much and what kind of advertising is required to achieve stated objectives; (2) estimating the incremental sales which may result from the achievement of specified communication goals. While the difficulties involved are challenging, the modified research-objective approach tends to direct analysis and research efforts into promising channels. While we are still a long way from solving the problems involved in developing an ideal approach to the determination of the advertising appropriation, several significant attacks have been made on various aspects of the problem. In the following section we shall review certain key developments.

Advertising as an investment

In previous discussion it has been noted that advertising has two effects: (1) it stimulates sales during the current year; (2) it builds awareness, preference, and favorable attitudes toward the firm which tend to produce sales in the future. Advertising which has an immediate effect may properly be treated as a current expense, but that which brings results in the future takes on the character of an investment and may justifiably be treated as such.

Consider, for example, the situation faced by Brooks-Ledford in planning to introduce a new aerosol shaving lather to the market under the brand name, Jupiter. Jupiter shaving lather was a protein-based cream and thus was less irritating to the skin than the customary soap-based product. Because of this competitive edge, it was believed that the new brand could secure 7 percent of the market the first year, 10 percent the second, and 15 percent the third. To reach these objectives, the advertising agency believed that it would be necessary to outspend the market leader the first year. Advertising pressure might then be reduced somewhat during the second and third years as the new brand became established. Nevertheless, it was anticipated that it would take three years for the full effects of the introductory effort to be felt and for the brand to achieve break-even status.

Accordingly, the payout and spending plan for the first three years, shown in Figure 12–2, was worked out to guide decision making on the advertising appropriation. These estimates were based on a $1 retail price, a 40 percent discount for wholesalers and direct-buying chains,

FIGURE 12–2
Payout and spending plan

	Year 1	Year 2	Year 3
Share objective (by percent)...............	7	10	15
Estimated dollar sales (000)...............	3,200	4,700	7,400
Contribution available (000)...............	1,600	2,350	3,700
Advertising expense (000).................	3,200	2,350	1,850
Profit/loss (000).........................	−1,600	—	+1,850
Cumulative P/L (000)....................	−1,600	−1,600	+250
Advertising/sales ratio (by percent)........	100	50	25

and a contribution to advertising and profits of 80 percent of the unit price the firm collected.

Note that the expenditure necessary to launch the product was expected to result in a loss of $1,600,000 the first year, no profit the second year, and a profit of $1,850,000 the third. On a cumulative basis, therefore, it was anticipated that it would take three years for Jupiter shaving lather to reach the desired market share objective of 15 percent and to achieve a break-even status on the investment made to introduce the new brand. In a situation such as this, management would clearly have to regard advertising as an investment in order to justify the heavy expenditures of the first year and the resulting substantial loss. Only if management were willing to treat advertising as an investment and wait three years or longer for the payoff, would the proposed advertising appropriation strategy be approved and steps be taken to develop the full potential of the new brand.

In recognition of the fact that advertising often produces benefits which provide a payoff in the future, Joel Dean has suggested that such advertising be treated as a capital investment.[8] He argues that determination of the advertising appropriation then becomes a problem of capital expenditure budgeting. Profitability of capital invested in advertising would then be determined by the estimated amount and timing of added investment in comparison with added earnings, the duration of advertising effects, and the risks involved. Productivity of capital invested in this way should be measured by the discounted cash flow method in preference to the payback period approach. In short, advertising which is expected to have long-run effects should be placed in the capital budget. Promotional investments should then compete for funds on the basis of profitability, that is, discounted cash flow rate of return.

---

[8] The material in the two following paragraphs is based upon Joel Dean, *Managerial Economics*, pp. 368–69; and Joel Dean, "Does Advertising Belong in the Capital Budget?" *Journal of Marketing*, vol. 30, no. 4 (October 1966), p. 21. Published by the American Marketing Association.

The chief deficiency of the return-on-investment approach is the difficulty of estimating the rate of return to be secured on advertising investments. Problems encountered involve (1) distinguishing investment advertising from that expected to have short-run effects; (2) estimating the evaporation of the cumulative effects of advertising; and (3) measuring the effect of advertising accumulation upon long-run sales volume and eventual price premiums. These measurement difficulties tend to rule out this approach as the sole criterion for decisions on investment-type advertising appropriations. Thinking about appropriations for institutional and cumulative advertising in this manner, however, would encourage research oriented toward providing the kind of estimates that are relevant to the decision. Experimentation along these lines is, therefore, encouraged.[9]

Research to determine expenditure levels

A key problem in setting the advertising appropriation is to determine how much advertising is required to achieve a specified goal. Experimentation with different levels of advertising expenditures in different test markets is one way to attack this problem. The approach used by Du Pont in deciding how much to appropriate for advertising "Teflon" coated cookware is an interesting example.[10]

Test marketing cookware coated with Du Pont Teflon. The research design used was to undertake television advertising in 13 carefully chosen test and control cities. Three levels of advertising effort were tested in two 11-week periods—from October to December 1962, and from January to March 1963. By means of an experimental crossover design, it was possible to test at national levels of $1 million (10 one-minute commercials in the fall and 7 one-minute commercials in the winter), $500,000 (5 and 3), and $250,000 or a promotional campaign (5 and none).[11]

Originally it was planned to conduct an extensive audit of retail stores to measure the impact of the varying levels of expenditures in television advertising on the sales of Teflon-coated utensils. This proved to be impractical, however, because certain retailers refused to cooperate in the research venture. Thus, the research measurement of sales was based

---

[9] For an explanation of capital budgeting theory, see Harold Bierman, Jr., and Seymour Smith, *The Capital Budgeting Decision* (New York: Macmillan Co., 1960).

[10] J. E. Moyer, "Teflon, an Advertising Case History" (mimeographed case published by Advertising Department, E. I. Du Pont de Nemours & Co., Wilmington, Del., 1964), pp. 28–30. Reprinted by permission.

[11] For a detailed discussion of the experimental crossover design, see J. C. Becknell, Jr., and R. W. McIsaac, "Test Marketing Cookware Coated with 'TEFLON,'" *Journal of Advertising Research,* vol. 3, no. 3 (September 1963), pp. 2–8.

on telephone interviews with 1,000 female heads of households, randomly selected, in each of the test markets and during each of the test periods in the fall and winter.

The results of this research effort indicated:

1. Sales of cookware finished with Teflon could be increased with a proper level of advertising.
2. Test markets where advertising on TV was carried on at the lower levels showed no discernible effect on sales.
3. Promotional effort in test markets at the $1 million level resulted in the doubling of purchases of Teflon-coated cookware, as compared with the lower level or no-advertising test markets.
4. There was strong evidence of a "carry-over" effect of advertising in test cities where promotion was carried on at the $1 million level of expenditures.

These and other data provided Du Pont with a solid basis for planning a national advertising effort. The advertising agency prepared a media schedule which included network television advertising to consumers at a level which cost $1,035,000 for time and $110,000 for production, or a total of $1,145,000 in 1964. Based on the evidence secured from the research in test markets, Du Pont management approved this appropriation.

In the Teflon case, research in test markets was an essential step in determining the advertising appropriation. Although it seemed advisable for Du Pont to undertake advertising on behalf of Teflon, top management originally was reluctant to make the huge budgetary commitments anticipated without having facts upon which to base judgments. They wanted assurance that such advertising would in fact produce results. Also they wanted data on what level of advertising would be required to move Teflon-finished cookware. They also wondered whether the funds required to do an adequate promotional job in the consumer market would be prohibitive from Du Pont's point of view. The test-market research provided the necessary data on the level of advertising support required to accomplish the desired objectives. This research also indicated the sales results which might be expected and thus provided management with a basis upon which to decide whether the anticipated sales would justify the estimated cost.

It is noteworthy that the researchers were not able to get retail cooperation to permit the measurement of sales results through the retail-audit approach. Instead the less satisfactory approach of determining purchases through telephone interviews had to be substituted. While this change resulted in some sacrifice in accuracy in the sales estimates, the data were apparently accepted by Du Pont management as providing a rough indication of the results that widely different levels of advertising expenditure would tend to produce. This provides a good illustration of the problems researchers encounter in attempting to plan experiments which will measure the sales results of advertising. Nevertheless, it is still desirable to make the effort in a situation such as that which Du Pont management faced.

Relation of advertising outlays to market-share objectives. Firms marketing nondurable goods in food stores and drugstores can make use of syndicated research services, such as those offered by A. C. Nielsen Company, to measure the relationship between advertising expenditures and retail sales of their brands expressed in share-of-market terms. Here sales are determined by the retail inventory method based on audits of the operations of a scientifically selected sample of food and drug outlets. Through analysis of the actual results secured in the marketing of both new and established products, the firm may discover useful guidelines as to the amount of advertising required to achieve market-share objectives. The possibilities of this type of research are illustrated by a study of 34 new brands of consumer nondurable goods made by James O. Peckham, executive vice president of the A. C. Nielsen Company.[12]

The purpose of this study was to determine whether useful guidelines could be developed from the analysis of past experience concerning the relationship between advertising outlays and share-of-market objectives. With this in mind, Peckham selected 34 new brands that had achieved a "respectable market position" within the first two years from the decision to launch and actively market the brand nationally. Of this number, 5 were food products, 11 were household products, 6 were proprietary drug brands, and 12 were toiletries. The criteria used in choosing these products were as follows: (1) The brand selected actually had to be new—not merely an added flavor, package, form, size, or formula change of an existing brand. (2) It had to be a brand generally considered to have a demonstrable consumer-plus, both recognizable by and merchandisable to the consumer—not merely a "me too" brand. (3) The new brand had to sustain a share of market position at least reasonably close to its attained two-year introductory market share in subsequent years. Almost without exception these brands were developed with the benefit of adequate consumer product studies, thoroughly market tested in the crucible of actual sales conditions at the retail store level, introduced to the trade by a skilled sales force (either manufacturer or broker), and finally subjected to whatever introductory

---

[12] Adapted by permission from James O. Peckham, executive vice president, A. C. Nielsen Company, "Can We Relate Advertising Dollars to Market Share Objectives?" *Proceedings, 12th Annual Conference, Advertising Research Foundation,* October 5, 1966, pp. 53–57. © Advertising Research Foundation, Inc., 1966.

inducements were necessary to secure adequate distribution, trade support, and consumer trial.

Once these 34 brands were selected, their performance was examined over a 24 month period to determine whether there was any meaningful relationship between advertising dollars and market-share objectives. Share-of-industry sales figures for each brand were taken directly from *Nielsen Retail Index* reports. Share-of-industry advertising expenditures were based upon estimates of newspaper, magazine, newspaper supplement, network TV, and spot TV advertising expenditures derived from published sources. These two sets of data were plotted for each brand on a chart such as that presented in Figure 12–3 for new Food Brand 102.

FIGURE 12–3
New Food Brand 102—ratio of share of advertising to share of sales

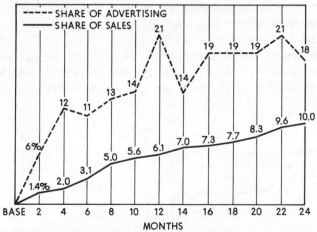

As Figure 12–3 indicates, over the entire two-year period Brand 102's share of advertising averaged about 16 percent. Since the brand attained a 10 percent share of market by the 24th month, we see that the share of advertising devoted to the brand was about 1.6 times the share of market secured.

In the same manner, the average share of advertising for the 34 brands during the 24 month introductory period was compared with the attained share of sales at the end of the period. Dividing the share of advertising percentage by the share of attained sales percentage, ratios were secured for each of the product groups studied, Figure 12–4.

When all of these 34 new brands were considered as a whole, the relationship between average share of advertising and attained share of sales over the initial two-year period was so consistent that it was possible to derive a "marketing experience curve" showing the approxi-

FIGURE 12–4

	Ratio of share of advertising to share of sales	
Product group	Average	Median
5 brands of food products.............	1.7	1.5
11 brands of household products........	1.9	1.7
6 proprietary drug brands.............	1.8	1.8
12 toiletry brands....................	1.5	1.5

mate relationship between these two variables. This experience curve, shown in Figure 12–5, was secured by plotting a given brand's share of sales to scale, horizontally from left to right, against the same brand's share of advertising to the same scale, vertically from bottom to top. The slope of the curve or the relationship between the vertical distance, representing a share of advertising, and the horizontal distance, representing share of sales, is approximately 1.5 to 1.6.

Of course, this share-of-advertising—share-of-sales experience—curve is only an approximation of the situation for the average brand. Note that Brand 301 attained a 29.8 percent share of market after two years,

FIGURE 12–5
Attained share of sales—average share of advertising experience curve—first two years, 34 brands of consumer nondurable goods

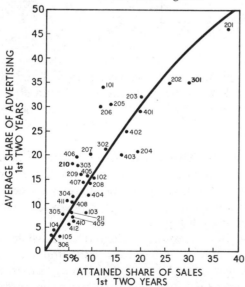

with a share of advertising expenditure of only 35 percent, while the experience curve derived from studying all 34 brands indicates that a firm should normally expect to advertise at a 45 percent rate to obtain a 29.8 percent share. In contrast, Brand 210 spent an 18 percent share of advertising and only secured a 6 percent share of sales, instead of the 10 percent share called for by the experience curve.

In commenting on how these findings might be used as a guide in determining the advertising appropriation for a new brand, Peckham made the following suggestions: (1) Set the share-of-market goal within the practical range that marketing judgment and experience indicate can be attained—preferably aided by the result of a sales campaign in test markets conducted over a long enough period of time to establish consumer buying and repeat patterns under actual competitive conditions. (2) With this share of market as a goal for the new brand, use the experience curve to provide a basis for estimating the share of advertising ·that should be maintained over the brand's normal growth period—normally two years on the average. (3) Estimate *total* advertising expenditures for all brands combined over the two-year period— including the firm's own brand. (4) Multiply total advertising expenditures by the required share of advertising to get an estimate of the dollar advertising investment required to realize the share of industry established as the objective. (5) If the new brand is really unique with a strong consumer-plus, it may be possible to reduce the advertising expenditure below what would be indicated by the average share of advertising to a share-of-sales ratio of 1.5 or 1.6 to 1. Just how much of a reduction may be possible is a matter of judgment and experimentation. If the new brand is the second or third brand to exploit a particular consumer-plus characteristic, or if the product advantages are minor or difficult to develop into an effective copy story, it may be necessary to increase the advertising outlay by 50 percent or more above the average shown by the experience curve (a share of advertising— share-of-sales ratio of 2.2 plus). Here again judgment and experimentation would have to be used in reaching the final decision.

Now that we have Peckham's formula before us, it is desirable to ask whether the approach he suggests is a satisfactory way to deal with the problem of determining what level of advertising expenditure is required to achieve desired goals.

1. At the outset, it is wise to remind ourselves that the share of sales which may be achieved by a new brand will be influenced by the entire marketing mix and not just by the amount spent on advertising. In selecting his 34 case histories, Peckham implicitly recognized that market share would be influenced by uniqueness of product, introduction by a skilled sales force, and use of introductory inducements to get distribution, trade support, and consumer trial. Accordingly, he

picked brands where these various mix elements had been handled wisely so that their impact on share of sales might be expected to be roughly the same. While no mention was made of the important variable of price, this sales influence might also have had approximately equal weight among the 34 brands if each were priced at approximately the competitive level. As Peckham suggests, then, the individual firm would have to utilize each of these marketing-mix elements effectively if the experience curve were to be of any value.

2. Then, too, most of the new brands chosen for study by Peckham were unique food, drug, and toiletry products with a demonstrable consumer-plus. As such they would meet the criteria for advertisability, and consumer advertising was, therefore, probably the dominant sales-producing element in the promotional mix. Influence of point-of-purchase promotion and retail personal selling probably had a much smaller impact than consumer advertising. Accordingly, application of the findings of the experience curve would have to be limited to new products of equal superiority and where primary reliance might likewise be placed upon consumer advertising. As Peckham explains, adjustments would have to be made in the share of advertising investment to make allowance for deviations from the average quality of the 34 brands and hence the average level of the effectiveness of the advertising done on their behalf.

3. It should also be recognized that the share of sales results would be influenced not only by the amount of advertising but also by the effectiveness of the media mix and the creative approach used. Presumably, deviations of individual brands from the experience curve are explained, in part, by differences in the effectiveness of media and message. Research is recommended, therefore, to identify the most effective media mix and the best creative approach. Once this is accomplished, then these factors may be held constant and attention directed to the amount of advertising required to achieve the desired market share.

4. These comments underscore the problems involved in separating the impact of advertising dollars from other marketing-mix influences upon the brands' share of sales. They also serve as a reminder of the difficulty of using past results in making future plans. We can see that planning and executing research to measure the sales results of advertising is a difficult and challenging task. It becomes clear that Peckham's formula does not remove the need for well-planned research in determining the level of advertising needed to achieve desired market position for a new brand. It does suggest, however, the kind of research which may be useful in providing information needed by management in arriving at a judgment on how much to spend on advertising.

5. While Peckham was able to develop an experience curve by relat-

ing share of advertising and share of sales for nondurable products, it is significant to recall that General Electric failed to establish such a relationship in analyzing data covering experience with 16 product lines—in the durable goods classification—major appliances, traffic appliances, consumer electrical supplies, and industrial components and supplies. Among other factors, this may be due to the smaller influence of advertising in the selling mix for such items as well as the infrequency of purchase which characterizes them. As General Electric suggests, the only way correlation studies will make a useful contribution for such products is to measure and correlate the effects of *several* key influences on share of market at one and the same time. Clearly the research approach must be determined in the light of the nature of the product, the frequency with which it is purchased, and the role of advertising in the promotional mix.

Relation of communication objectives to sales results

As mentioned previously, manufacturers of durable goods purchased infrequently find it difficult, if not impossible, to measure advertising results in terms of sales. This leads them to adopt communication goals for their advertising instead of sales or share-of-industry goals. A problem then arises in deciding whether the desired objectives are worth the costs involved in their achievement. Recognition of this problem has led to research designed to study the relationship between communication objectives (such as awareness, preference, intent to buy) and actual sales results. This experimentation has led to the development of the "media-schedule" approach to setting the advertising appropriation, a method which falls within the research-objective category and involves practical applications of the ideal-incremental approach previously discussed.[13]

Of particular interest to us is the manner in which objectives are identified in following this approach. The basic idea involved is to recognize that advertising creates sales by making conscious impressions upon the minds of prospective buyers. Thus, the goal of the advertiser is to purchase an optimum number of conscious impressions with his dollars. It is recognized that the effectiveness of an advertisement scheduled a given number of times in any medium—a magazine, for example—results from a screening sequence somewhat as follows: (1) The magazine has a total circulation among people who are potential buyers or "influencers." (2) A larger number than this actually reads the magazine.

[13] Reprinted by permission from A. W. Frey, "Approaches to Determining the Advertising Appropriation," in George L. Baker, Jr., ed., *Effective Marketing Coordination,* pp. 326–39. Published by the American Marketing Association, 1961.

(3) A smaller number of individuals than readers of the magazine is "exposed" to the page on which the advertisement appears. (4) A still smaller number actually pays attention to the advertisement. (5) A still smaller number receives a conscious impression. (6) The conscious impressions (*a*) make some readers *aware* of the product for the first time, (*b*) strengthen already present awareness in others, (*c*) move some people from mere awareness to a favorable *attitude,* and (*d*) move some people all the way to a *purchase.*

In recognition of this screening sequence, research is then undertaken to establish the relationship among (1) conscious impressions, (2) awareness and favorable attitudes, and (3) purchases of the product. If such a relationship is established, then the next step is to determine the number of conscious impressions which may be secured through various combinations of media schedules. The advertiser is then in a position to determine the optimum advertising appropriation.

This approach is illustrated by C. Maxwell Ule's solution of a media problem at a 4A's convention some years ago.[14] The problem, which was assigned to three advertising experts, involved the preparation of a media schedule for a brand-new revolutionary kind of filter-tip king-size cigarette, produced by a major U.S. cigarette manufacturer. It was assumed that the product had been test marketed for 26 weeks under various conditions in various sizes of markets in different regions of the country. The test-marketing results were very satisfactory; the manufacturer planned to move the brand into national distribution as quickly as possible. Distribution was to be accomplished almost automatically, since the new brand would be sold by the company's nationwide sales force handling other tobacco products manufactured by the company.

The marketing objectives for Sputnik cigarettes, as defined by Ule, may be stated as follows: (1) The goal was to capture 8 percent of the total cigarette market, or 20 percent of the filter-tip market. (2) To achieve this sales goal, the aim was to get 10 million of the nation's 50 million smokers to try Sputnik cigarettes—from which 4 million would become regular Sputnik smokers. This was based on past general experience of the relationship between experimental buyers and regular customers. (3) To achieve this sales goal, a level of product awareness of 80 percent would have to be attained by the advertising input, figured accumulatively by the end of the fiscal year. That is, 80 percent of the prospects would have to become well enough aware of the brand by the end of the year to recall the brand, unaided, in a consumer survey. Based upon experience in other fields, it was estimated that this cumulative awareness by the end of the year would produce enough

---

[14] Reprinted by permission from G. Maxwell Ule, "A Media Plan for 'Sputnik' Cigarettes," *How to Plan Media Strategy,* papers from the 1957 Regional Conventions, pp. 41–52. Copyright, American Association of Advertising Agencies, 1958.

experimental buyers to deliver a market share equal to 8 percent of the total market, or 20 percent of the filter-tip market.

With this background, the following communication goals were then established:

1. To achieve these marketing sales objectives, it would be necessary to reach 80 percent of the U.S. households with an average of 40 conscious advertising impressions per household reached during the introductory year. Multiplying the coverage objective (80 percent) by the number of conscious advertising impressions to be delivered (40), the communications objective for the year became 3,200 rating points of conscious advertising impressions.

2. Each conscious advertising impression had the estimated net effect of creating an unaided brand awareness of 2 percent among the households reached. Forty impressions would create 80 percent awareness among the 80 percent of U.S. households reached (40×2 percent).

The next step was to work out the optimum media schedule to deliver the desired number of conscious impressions (3,200 rating points). Ule's proposed media schedule for the first 13 weeks of the year would deliver 1,280 conscious advertising rating points by using 39 commercial minutes on network TV, 35 class-A Spot TV announcements, six full-page color insertions in Sunday supplements, four 1,500-line color insertions in newspapers, and 50 radio spot announcements weekly for eight weeks. A more limited schedule on network TV, spot TV, and Sunday Supplements would also deliver another 1,920 conscious rating points during the remaining 39 weeks of the year, thus providing the total of 3,200 conscious advertising impressions.

Finally, the cost of this optimum schedule was estimated at $10,488,000 for the introductory year. This amount was then recommended as the advertising appropriation.

While this media-schedule approach has conceptual value, the critical question is whether the individual advertiser will be able, through research, to establish a useful relationship between conscious impressions, awareness, favorable attitudes, and purchases. It is reported, however, that some advertisers have been able to establish this relationship to their own satisfaction.[15] Certainly an attempt should be made to do so, if at all possible. If no satisfactory relationship can be found for certain types of products, however, the obvious answer is to disregard the goal of purchases and select a certain goal of awareness and favorable attitude as a guide. This is a better goal than is used by some advertisers in their decision making.

---

[15] For a helpful discussion of the use of marketing experiments in determining the relationship between communication and sales, see Charles K. Ramond, "Must Advertising Communicate to Sell?" *Harvard Business Review,* September–October 1965, pp. 148–59.

Conclusion

The task of determining the size of the promotional appropriation is an important, but difficult problem. The character of promotional strategy influences the size of the appropriation; simultaneously, the size of the funds available is an important consideration in deciding what type of promotional approach will be most effective. Ways of dealing with this problem which break this circularity are suggested in this chapter.

We have evaluated commonly used approaches such as basing the appropriation decision on a percentage of sales, using "all available funds," considering competitive parity, and applying the research-objective (or task) approach. It is concluded that a modified research-objective approach, if properly applied, is clearly superior to the approaches previously mentioned. We shall now proceed to a discussion of brand strategy decisions.

Questions

1. *a)* Explain the basic essentials of the marginal approach of determining the advertising appropriation.
   b) What practical difficulties are encountered in applying this approach in actual practice?
2. What are the basic principles behind (*a*) the breakdown and (*b*) the buildup methods of determining the promotional appropriation? Which approaches discussed in this chapter fall into each classification?
3. *a)* Under what conditions may a case be made for the use of a variable percentage of estimated future sales in determining the promotional appropriation?
   b) Even under the best of circumstances, what criticisms may be made of this approach?
4. Under what conditions can you defend the use of the all-available-funds approach to determining the appropriation? What limitations does this method have?
5. *a)* Evaluate the plan of setting the advertising appropriation by making the product's share of total industry advertising expenditures equal to the brand's desired share of market.
   b) Would this be an appropriate plan to follow in determining the appropriation for a new brand just being introduced? An established brand which rates number 3 in share of market? Number 1 in share of market?
6. *a)* What are the basic essentials of the research-objective approach to setting the promotional appropriation? What are its chief limitations?
   b) How might the plan be modified to eliminate these criticisms?

7. *a)* Under what circumstances might it be desirable to treat advertising as an investment?

   b) What difficulties are involved in following this approach? Does it appear likely that these problems may be overcome?

8. Does Peckham's study of the relation between advertising outlays and market-share objectives provide a helpful guide for setting the advertising appropriation:

   a) For a new product like Simba, which is promoted as a means of quenching the "African thirst"?

   b) For a new portable color TV set?

   c) For Cessna aircraft marketed for pleasure and personal use?

9. *a)* Under what circumstances would it appear to be desirable to base the advertising appropriation upon communication objectives rather than upon sales goals?

   b) What difficulties are encountered in following this approach (as illustrated in the media-schedule method)?

   c) What attitude should management take toward the use of this method?

13

Brand strategy decisions

IN AN EARLIER DISCUSSION, consideration was given to issues of brand policy related to product development decisions. We turn now to certain major questions concerning branding which arise in the process of working out the basic promotional strategy of a manufacturer. Of particular significance are the following issues: (1) What policies should be followed regarding the number and coverage of brands to be marketed by the firm? Specifically, should the manufacturer use one brand to identify many different products, as opposed to marketing each product under its own individual brand name? Where different qualities of the same product are produced, should all be sold under a single brand name or should high-, medium-, and low-quality products be identified by separate trademarks? (2) Should the firm manufacture products to be sold under distributors' brands or concentrate exclusively upon marketing products under its own brands? Each of these topics has important promotional strategy implications and will be analyzed on the pages which follow.

Family brands versus individual brands

A producer following a manufacturers' brand policy faces the important question of whether to market his line under a family brand or under individual brand names. A family-brand policy is where two or more products are sold under the same brand name. Avon Products, Inc., is an example of a firm which follows this approach. In a recent year, the firm sold approximately 300 items under the "Avon" brand name including fragrances, makeup articles, bath products, skin care items, hair preparations, dental care accessories, deodorants, and shaving products, among others. Although products appealing to women were emphasized, items were also marketed for children and men.[1]

What advantages might Avon gain from this family-brand policy? Since Avon products were sold house-to-house by company salesmen, a key advantage of family branding would be the possibility of gaining ready acceptance by regular customers of new products added to the company's line. The favorable brand image held by users of existing Avon products would tend to influence them to accept new items carrying the same brand more readily than if new individual brand names were used. This, in turn, would tend to reduce the amount of introductory advertising required to create a demand for the new products and would also cut down the time and effort required on the part of the salesman to get orders for these new items.

While Avon management obviously believe that family branding is desirable, Lever Brothers Company made the opposite decision when introducing a new beauty soap in test markets early in 1968. This new product, which was being tested in Albany, New York, and Columbus, Ohio, was identified by the brand name, "Caress." Rather than attempting to associate Caress with the firm's established brand, Lux Toilet Soap, Lever Brothers apparently intends to promote Caress separately as a means of more effectively exploiting this new entry into the competitive beauty soap market. While this approach may require a larger appropriation for advertising and promotion, such an investment is customarily made in the expectation that it will produce larger sales and profits than the decision to market under a family brand would yield. The contrast in brand policy illustrated by the Avon and Lever Brothers examples lead naturally to the question as to what guidelines to use in making a decision concerning family versus individual branding when a new product is being added to an established product line. In considering this issue it is helpful to approach the problem from the consumers' viewpoint. What is the psychological explanation of the tendency to develop generalized preferences for different types of products identified by a common family brand? What product characteristics tend to foster such generalization? What tend to discourage it? These questions will be considered in the following section.

Generalized preferences for family brands[2]

The policy of family branding is based on the assumption that this practice leads to a "connection in consumers' minds" which generalizes

---

[1] Seymour Freedgood, "Avon: The Sweet Smell of Success," *Fortune,* vol. 70, no. 6, December 1964, pp. 111, 113.

[2] Reprinted by permission from Joseph N. Fry, "Family Branding and Consumer Brand Choice," *Journal of Marketing Research,* vol. 4 (August 1967), pp. 237–47. Published by the American Marketing Association.

consumer preferences to all product categories under a brand. A brand name linkage acts as a medium through which consumers spread or generalize preferences and loyalties from one category of products to another. The psychological theory which underlies this assumption deals with the effect of cognitive set on perception. The cognitive set influence important in this analysis is the "assimilation effect," the tendency of people to assimilate, or to shift classification of set-related stimuli in the direction of their existing set. According to Fry:

Extension of assimilation effects to family branding seems quite reasonable. A consumer's attitudes toward a family brand (his brand image) can act as a set-inducing cognitive variable. Through assimilation the consumer's perception of characteristics of individual products under the brand will be drawn in the direction of this set. In other words, his judgments of products under a family brand will tend to be consistent with his overall brand image. He will tend, for example, to ascribe to any individual product the quality he thinks is generally represented by the brand. This assimilation effect applies only to attributes which the products under consideration have in common, such as taste appeal in the case of foods or cleaning power for soaps and detergents. Except as they support (or detract from) such basic attributes, characteristics unique to particular products are of no concern.[3]

Generalized preferences for family brands are intervening variables that influence consumer brand choice. Since they are not directly observable, they are inferred from consumer buying behavior. Fry tested the hypothesis that consumers have generalized preferences by analyzing consumer purchasing behavior as reported by the *Chicago Tribune* consumer panel. Analyses were limited to frequently purchased packaged goods and covered about 600 households resident in metropolitan Chicago. Purchases of the following family brands of packaged goods were analyzed among others:

1. Canned goods—Del Monte, Libby's, Hunt's, Heinz.
2. Frozen foods—Birds Eye.
3. Paper products—Scott, Kleenex.
4. Baking products—Pillsbury.

The degree of generalized preference for a given family brand was measured by analyzing the behavior of consumers in purchasing two different product categories (for example, canned peaches and canned corn) under a single family brand (for example, Del Monte). What percentage of the consumers who purchased Del Monte canned peaches also purchased Del Monte canned corn? How does this compare with the percentage of the consumers who purchased *only* Del Monte canned peaches or *only* Del Monte canned corn? More precisely, this comparison

---
[3] Ibid., p. 238.

was made by using a probability model, as follows: Assume a family brand is available in two product categories, A and B, and that a population of consumers who have made purchases in both product categories has been identified. Denote by $P(A_1, B_1)$ the joint probability that a consumer selected at random from the population will have purchased the family brand in *both* product categories. For comparison, denote by $P(A_1)$ and $P(B_1)$ the marginal probabilities that a randomly selected consumer will have purchased the family brand in product category A *only* or B *only*. A generalized preference for the family brand is said to exist if:

$$P(A_1, B_1) > P(A_1) \cdot P(B_1).$$

The degree to which the joint probability $P(A_1, B_1)$ exceeds the product of multiplying the marginal probabilities $P(A_1) \times P(B_1)$ is used as the index of the degree of generalized preference for the family brand under analysis. The results of this analysis as applied to the Del Monte family brand are illustrative. Thus, 39 comparisons were made of the behavior of consumers in purchasing two different products (such as peaches and corn) marketed under the Del Monte family brand. In 36 out of 39 comparisons the index of generalized preference was positive—i.e., a generalized preference for the family brand was demonstrated. In only 3 of the 39 comparisons were the estimates negative, indicating no generalized preference for the family brand in the purchase of these particular pairs of products. According to Fry, statistically significant indexes of generalized preference for the Del Monte family brand were found in over half of the product pairings analyzed.[4]

Analysis of the data for all of the family brands of frequently purchased packaged goods listed above led Fry to conclude that consumers do have generalized preferences for family brands.[5] The results were consistent with the hypothesis for a variety of brands, product categories, and purchase classifications indicating degree of brand loyalty.

Fry also inquired as to what factors contribute to the degree of gen-

---

[4] Technical note: In more complete terms, it can be said that if there are two events, A_1 and B_1, and the two events are independent of each other, then the joint probability, $P(A_1, B_1)$, that is, the chance of both events occurring together, is the multiple of the individual, or marginal, probabilities.

1. For independent events: $P(A_1, B_1) = P(A_1) \cdot P(B_1)$.

If the two events are not independent, then the actual occurrence of one event increases the probability of the other's occurrence. This is the conditional probability, or the probability of the second event, given that the first has already occurred. Using the same notation as above, the joint probability for the two nonindependent events is the product of the conditional probability of the second event given that the first has occurred, $P(B_1/A_1)$, and the marginal probability of the occurrence of the first.

2. For nonindependent events: $P(A_1 B_1) = P(B_1/A_1) \cdot P(A_1)$.

[5] See ibid., pp. 241–47, for a more complete discussion of the evidence resulting from this analysis.

eralized preference. He hypothesized that the degree of generalized preference for a family brand varies directly with (1) the degree of similarity in the competitive brand sets of two product categories identified by a family brand, and (2) the degree of price similarity of the brand in two product categories.

Analysis of the data gave tentative confirmation to these secondary hypotheses. Accordingly, the findings of this study provide support for the common and important assumption that for frequently purchased package goods the promotion of one product under a family brand has beneficial effects for other products under that brand. The study does not, however, throw any light on the relative efficacy of family and individual branding.

Semantic generalization and family branding[6]

In contrast, a study of semantic generalization as applied to family brands of household appliances raises some doubt as to the use of a common brand name as a means of transferring attitudes between dissimilar products of high unit value. As in Fry's study, the starting point is the principle of generalization which holds that people have a tendency to view individual items as being similar, disregarding points of character that would differentiate them. Generalization may occur on either the physical or semantic level. Kerby is concerned about semantic generalization where a person views two or more objects as similar because they carry a *common meaning*, even though the objects themselves may have different physical characteristics. Specifically, he tested the hypothesis that meaning should be transferred between two or more products that are physically dissimilar, if they share a common brand name.

Kerby had a group of 99 female homemakers in Maplewood, New Jersey, evaluate eight branded products. Four of these products had different physical characteristics but shared a common brand—i.e., vacuum cleaners, automatic washers, portable TV sets, and refrigerators made by General Electric and Westinghouse. The other four products corresponded with the first four in terms of physical characteristics, but each had an individual brand name—i.e., Sunbeam and Eureka vacuum cleaners, Philco and Maytag automatic washers, Motorola and Admiral portable TV, and Norge and RCA refrigerators.

Respondents were asked to evaluate the eight branded products listed above in terms of 47 semantic differential scales using carefully selected adjectives such as: safe-hazardous, superior-inferior, follower-pioneer,

⁶ Reprinted by permission from J. K. Kerby, "Semantic Generalization in the Formation of Consumer Attitudes," *Journal of Marketing Research*, vol. 4 (August 1967), pp. 314–17. Published by the American Marketing Association.

exorbitant-reasonable, adequate-inadequate, dull-colorful, unsanitary-sanitary, simple-intricate, satisfactory-disappointing.

The completed questionnaires were subjected to factor analysis to determine how similar the respondent's rating of one product (GE vauum cleaner) was to that for another product (GE automatic washer). If a housewife saw a similar meaning between two or more products marketed under a family brand, she would mark the semantic differential scales for the two items similarly. The resulting intercorrelations between these products would then be relatively high and the resulting factor loads relatively large.

The factor matrix in Figure 13–1 is one of the 99 matrixes from the study and illustrates the nature of the results of the analysis. Note that the factor loadings on the second factor are uniformly high for the GE group of products and relatively low for products in the hetero-

FIGURE 13–1

Variable	1	2	3	4
GE vacuum cleaner..............	0.216	0.762	0.032	−0.108
GE automatic washer.............	−0.017	0.785	0.149	0.033
GE portable TV.................	0.107	0.910	0.016	0.076
GE refrigerator.................	0.070	0.706	−0.240	0.002
Sunbeam vacuum cleaner........	0.925	0.030	−0.129	−0.156
Maytag automatic washer........	0.868	0.165	0.187	0.033
Admiral portable TV............	0.931	0.156	−0.025	0.072
RCA refrigerator................	0.973	0.061	−0.038	0.016

geneous-brand group. Such an arrangement indicates that this particular respondent saw a similar meaning between the four GE products and is evidence of a strong tendency toward generalization.

The above matrix illustrates the criteria used in evaluating the study's results. In general, if all four factor loadings associated with the family-branded group of products were large relative to the remaining factor loadings (a spread of about 20 or so percentage points), a respondent was classed as giving "very strong indication" of semantic generalization. If all four factor loadings were larger than the others by a spread of about 5 to 20 percentage points; if three of the four were larger than the others by about 20 or more points; or if two of the four were larger than the others by about 50 or more points, the respondent was classed as giving a "good indication."

If three of the four were larger than the others by about 5 to 20 percentage points, or if two of the four were larger by about 20 to 50 points, the respondent was classed as giving a "weak indication." If none of the patterns described above appeared in the factor matrix, the respondent was classed as giving "no indication" of semantic generalization.

Applying these criteria to each of the 99 factor matrixes produced the results listed in Figure 13–2. Of the 99 respondents in the study, therefore, only one exhibited a very strong tendency toward semantic generalization. An additional 5 respondents showed a reasonably strong tendency in that direction, but the remaining 93 had either a weak tendency or no tendency toward semantic generalization.

Why did such a large proportion of the respondents show little or no tendency toward semantic generalization in rating family brands as opposed to individual brands? Kerby suggests two possible explanations. (1) Perhaps the physical characteristics of major appliances varied too greatly to permit the occurrence of effective generalization. (2) Or perhaps semantic generalization comes in only when the products involved

FIGURE 13–2

Very strong indication	1
Good indication	5
Weak indication	11
No indication	82

are relatively unimportant, requiring a minimum of intellectual and emotional effort.

Factors influencing choice of family versus individual brands

The empirical evidence just cited points up the importance of careful analysis in reaching a decision on whether a new product should be marketed under a family brand or an individual brand. In making such an analysis, it is helpful to begin with considerations which may tend to foster or retard the consumers' tendency to develop generalized preferences through the process of assimilation.

1. Is the new product of the same type as the existing line? The Del Monte family brand, for example, is applied to canned fruits and vegetables. Also, the Kleenex label covers facial tissues, paper napkins, and paper towels among others. In both cases the products covered by the family brand are of the same general type, although they are still individual items. In contrast, let us consider an illustration involving the Avon Company. As explained earlier, this firm applied its family brand to cosmetics and toiletries. As a matter of policy, the firm refused to add nonrelated items, such as floor polishes, to its line under the family brand.

2. Is the new product similar in quality-price relationship to the existing line? Where this is true, the quality image which consumers associate with the established brand may be extended through assimilation to the new product. This may make them more willing to try the new product than if the innovation were introduced under a new and unfamiliar brand name. One of the highly successful products initially marketed by Brooks-Ledford Company for example, was Galaxy—a superior hair dressing for women—which achieved a position of market leadership and for which women had a substantial feeling of brand loyalty. When company research developed a superior new hair fixative six years later, it was introduced nationally under the family brand as Galaxy Hair Spray. Undoubtedly, the sale of the new product under the highly regarded Galaxy label was one factor which helped Galaxy Hair Spray to gain initial acceptance and become a top-selling brand in the hair fixative field within 11 months.

3. Is the new product similar to the established brand in terms of uses to which it is put, basic consumer desires which it may satisfy, and appeals to buying motives which may be used in its promotion? For some time, Standard Brands, Inc., has packed peanuts under its Planters label. Early in 1968, the firm introduced five snack products packaged in corrugated cans with tear-open lids. The five varieties are Cheese Curls, Cheese Balls, Corn Chips, Corn Stix, and Potato Stix. Since peanuts are also used as snacks along with various types of refreshments and satisfy the sense of taste, it was appropriate to market the five new snack products under the Planters brand.[7]

In contrast, Brooks-Ledford developed a new product which was described as "the first all-clear floor wax" and in a recent year, was testing it in Minneapolis and other markets. This new floor wax was not marketed under a family brand but instead was identified as "Saturn Floor Wax." Such action appeared wise since the product was a floor wax and not a hair preparation and accordingly differed as to uses, basic desires satisfied, and appeals to buying motives which might be used to sell it to the ultimate consumer.

4. Is the market for the new product likely to be found among the same segments of the population when classified by sex, race, age, income, and social status as currently constitute the prospective buyers of the established brand? Obviously, we are not thinking about a new product which might be a substitute for an established brand but instead a new item which is complementary or which might also be purchased by a substantial proportion of the same prospective buyers, thus increasing the total sales of the company. If the same consumers purchase

---

[7] "DFS New Product News," mimeographed publication of Dancer-Fitzgerald-Sample, Inc., New York, April 1968, p. 12.

both the old and the new product, then there is maximum opportunity for generalization to take place. If none of the firm's current customers is a prospect, then there is no opportunity for associating the two products in the consumers' minds. Consider, for example, Ivory toilet soap and Ivory liquid detergent—products showing a considerable degree of generalization in Fry's study of family brands. Since Ivory toilet soap is used in the bath while Ivory liquid detergent is used in the wash, these products are not substitutes. Yet they might be expected to find their potential markets among approximately the same prospective buyers and thus would offer a good opportunity for generalization to take place through family branding.

In contrast, prior to 1959 Brooks-Ledford marketed all its products to women. In that year the firm developed a new hair dressing for men which was available either in tube or aerosol can. Although the new product was a hair preparation, the firm decided against introducing this item under the Galaxy brand name. Since its potential market was among men and not among women, the firm identified the new item as "Jupiter Hair Dressing" thus avoiding an association with a brand which had a feminine image. The firm's marketing strategy was effective, and by 1962 Jupiter Hair Dressing was among the six best selling hair preparations for men in the country.

In addition to factors that tend to influence generalization through family brands, there are considerations which relate to the efficiency with which a new product may be introduced to the market. Let us consider these briefly.

1. Can the new product be distributed through the same types of retail outlets as the existing line? If this is possible, then the existing sales force and distribution organization may be utilized in the introductory process. If retailers are familiar with the established brand, they may be more willing to stock the new product when offered under this label than if the product were sold under an entirely new brand name. They will be influenced, of course, by their estimate of the reputation which the established brand has among consumers and consequently by whether they believe use of the family brand will help to get consumers to try the new product. If the new product must be sold through entirely new types of retail outlets, however, there will be no opportunity to use the reputation of the established brand to help sell the new item. An individual brand would then be equally acceptable as far as getting retail distribution is concerned.

2. Can the new product be promoted jointly with other established products being sold under the family brand? If joint promotion is possible, this will tend to reduce the cost of introducing the new product. Joint promotion would be favored if the products appeal to similar market segments, are similar in nature, are associated in use, are alike

in quality-price relationships, and appeal to similar buying motives. If these criteria are not met, however, joint promotion under a family brand may not be as effective as a separate campaign for the new product under its own individual brand name. Against the higher costs of such effort may be balanced the increased aggressiveness and effectiveness of the special introductory campaign. The introduction of new cosmetic products under the Avon family brand is a good example of a situation where the new items may be sold effectively along with existing items. While Avon's line included approximately 300 items of cosmetics and toiletries which had an established market, the firm was active in product development and added a number of new items each year— all under the Avon family brand. As a new product was added, advertising would serve to announce the availability of the new item under the Avon name and to stimulate a desire for it. Salesmen calling in the prospects' homes could also introduce the new product and attempt to take orders for it, but they would also be able to sell other items in the line during the same visit. This possibility would tend to reduce the cost of introducing the new product. Such economies would appeal to small firms with limited financial resources and lead them to favor family branding.

The foregoing discussion emphasizes the cost efficiencies which may result from family branding under certain circumstances. Even more important, however, is the question of whether introduction of a new product under a family brand will produce a larger sales volume, profit, and return on investment than the alternative of marketing the new item under its own individual brand. It will facilitate our consideration of this question if we shift our point of view and focus attention on the considerations which may tend to favor the use of an individual brand as opposed to a family brand.

This leads us to ask, is the new product individualized in ways important to the consumer? The opportunity of making effective use of consumer advertising depends in part upon the extent to which the new product is distinctive when compared to competing brands. (Other considerations influencing advertising opportunity include a favorable primary demand trend, presence of hidden qualities, ability to use strong emotional buying motives, and ability to support an adequate advertising program.) If the new product is highly individualized in ways important to the consumer, then this factor favors the strategy of giving it its own brand name and of introducing it to the market through an aggressive campaign of advertising and promotion. Although this would probably require a larger advertising appropriation than if the new product carried a family brand, the sales results would probably be substantially greater. By associating the distinctive features of the product with its own individual brand name, a stronger and sharper brand image could be created in consumers' minds than if the new item was identified by a family brand which it shared with other products. The family brand becomes associated only with the common characteristics of the various products it identifies—such as uniform high quality—and not with all of the special features of the product which set it apart from competing brands. The process of generalization involved in creating a family brand image, therefore, involves a loss as well as a gain. For the highly distinctive product, the loss far overshadows the gain.

In our opinion, the results which may be achieved by giving a product an individual brand name and promoting it aggressively are illustrated by the experience of Bristol-Myers in the introduction of Ban deodorant.[8] Prior to the introduction of Ban, Bristol-Myers marketed Mum—a cream deodorant which they rated as one of the two leading deodorants on the market. Stopette, a competing spray deodorant had recently been introduced to the market and had quickly achieved a market share which placed it among the top five brands then available. Undoubtedly this event spurred product research at Bristol-Myers as a means of developing an improved product which would counter the competitive threat of Stopette as well as other brands. Recognizing that both the cream and spray types of deodorants were messy to use, Bristol-Myers undertook research work which resulted in an effective liquid deodorant to be applied by a large plastic marble mounted in the end of a bottle—a "roll-on deodorant." Although the new product was tested in six leading markets as "Mum Rolette," the firm finally decided to market the new product as "Ban" lotion deodorant. The method of application made Ban highly distinctive, and introductory advertising claimed that Ban was "more effective than creams; easier to apply than sprays!" Ban was introduced to the market through a national advertising campaign, including newspapers, magazines, television, and radio, which cost $1 million during the first eight months. By the end of this period, Ban had achieved number 3 position in the industry and in 17 months had become the top-selling deodorant in dollar volume in drug and food outlets combined. In this case the effectiveness of the deodorant lotion and the convenience of the roll-on applicator individualized the product in ways important to the consumer. Not only was Ban individualized as compared with competing brands, it was also significantly different from Bristol-Myers' own brand—Mum. By assigning the new product its own brand name—Ban—and by supporting it with an aggressive introductory advertising campaign, the firm was able to push Ban into market leadership within a relatively short time. This strategy was prob-

---

[8] This case is reported in more detail in N. H. Borden and M. V. Marshall, *Advertising Management: Text and Cases*, rev. ed. (Homewood, Ill.: Richard D. Irwin, Inc., 1959), pp. 519–33.

ably much more effective than that of calling the new item "Mum Rolette" and of relying on the reputation of Mum plus a joint advertising campaign to help it gain acceptance among consumers.

It is clear that a policy of individual branding is favored where a product is highly individualized as compared with the competition, a condition which suggests an aggressive pull type of promotional strategy. If these distinctive features also make the new product different from the remainder of the company's line, as we might expect, then the case favoring an individual brand is strengthened. In contrast, a new product which is not distinctive but which is as good as, but no better than, competing brands, would offer only a mediocre opportunity for individual promotion through consumer advertising. If this new product does have characteristics in common with the existing line, then it would benefit by being promoted as a new addition to a reputable family brand. Here the process of generalization might well offer a substantial net gain. What the brand strategy should be when the new product falls in between these extremes—i.e., when it has minor points of difference as compared with competition and with other items in the firm's own line—would appear to be a matter which would have to be decided through executive judgment supplemented by appropriate market testing of alternatives.

In this connection, the decision of Procter & Gamble brand managers to introduce their new mint-flavored stannous fluoride toothpaste under the established name "Crest" is interesting. The original Crest (with stannous fluoride) was flavored with wintergreen and had developed a significant market share. It faced direct competition from other fluoridated toothpastes, which were also available only in wintergreen flavor. There was no major stannous fluoride mint-flavored product. Research indicated that a segment of the market which wished the protection against tooth decay provided by a fluoridated brand, did not like the wintergreen flavor of Crest but did like mint flavor in toothpaste. In recognition of this preference, P&G undertook the difficult task of developing an acceptable mint-flavored stannous fluoride toothpaste. After considerable time and effort, the research team came up with a new product which received favorable responses in consumer taste tests. The new product, accordingly, differed from the original Crest primarily in flavor (mint instead of wintergreen). While its stannous fluoride formula may have differed from competing fluoridated brands in some respects, its chief distinction was its mint flavor. The new product might have been given an individual brand name as is generally the policy when new products are added to the P&G line. The brand group, however, recommended marketing the new mint-flavored fluoridated toothpaste under the name "Mint Crest." From this action it may be inferred that P&G decision makers believed that the new product would gain substantial benefit from the reputation achieved by the original Crest brand. Here the benefits from generalization were apparently believed to be greater than any promotional advantages which might result from using an individual brand name. By calling the new product "Mint Crest," however, the brand group obviously hoped to attract a new segment of consumers who may have tried wintergreen-flavored Crest but who turned away from it to buy a less effective mint-flavored competing brand. It is noteworthy, however, that P&G introduced new Mint Crest with a heavy campaign of advertising and promotion. While new Mint Crest was featured, it was associated with, but distinguished from, the original Crest (wintergreen).

Summary and conclusions

In summary, the following factors would tend to favor marketing a new product under its own individual brand: (1) If it is highly individualized, as compared with competing brands, and also meets other criteria which indicate a profitable opportunity to make use of consumer advertising. (2) If it differs in product features, benefits, and hence selective appeals from the firm's own established brand and thus requires individual promotion. (3) If it is either higher or lower in quality than other products sold under the existing brand. (4) If it offers an opportunity to expand the company's market coverage by appealing to new segments of consumers. (5) If it should be distributed through retail outlets different from those handling the existing brand.

In contrast, the following considerations would tend to favor selling the new product under an established family brand: (1) If the new product is of the same type as the existing line. (2) If it is similar in uses, wants satisfied, and in appeals to buying motives. (3) If it is of the same quality-price relation as the existing brand. (4) If its market is likely to be found in the same segments of the population as the present line. (5) If it can be distributed through the same types of retail outlets as now used. (6) If it can be promoted jointly with established products sold under the family brand.

In the final analysis, what must be done is to estimate the sales volume, profit, and return on investment which may be achieved if the new product is introduced under the family brand, as compared to what might be expected if it is sold under its own individual brand, and choose the alternative which offers significantly greater returns. Since the results of such analysis may not be clear cut, judgment may be improved if market tests involving an introductory strategy based on an individual brand may be compared with that making use of the family-brand approach.

Company name combined with individual brand

Some firms have found it desirable to establish an association between individual brands by tying them together with the company name. One example is the Kellogg Company, which consistently uses the company name along with individual brand names such as Corn Flakes, Rice Crispies, Sugar Corn Pops, and Pop-Tarts. Here the new products may be given individual promotional support and may develop individual brand images, yet they all gain from the association with the well-established Kellogg name. Another example is the Ford Motor Company, which gives strong emphasis to individual brands of automobiles such as Lincoln, Mercury, Thunderbird, Cougar, Torino, Mustang, and Pinto. Yet the entire line is tied together under the Ford name through such corporate advertising themes as: "The Ford Family of Fine Cars (1955–59); "Ford Built Means Better Built" (1959–64); "Ford Has a Better Idea" (1965 to 1969); and "Ford Listens Better" (1970 to date).

This strategy enables a firm to gain family recognition for its products at the same time that the benefits of individual branding are also achieved.

Promotional implications of brand-quality-price relationships

In the foregoing discussion, quality-price relationships were identified as an important consideration in deciding whether to seek generalization by using a family brand or aim at distinctiveness by using an individual brand. In those instances where the new product being introduced is of the same identical type as the existing line, for example, cameras, but is of either higher quality or lower quality than the present product, the question of whether to sell both products under the same brand assumes special importance. If the firm markets a high-quality line of men's shoes under a highly regarded brand name such as "Status," for example, adds a medium grade line under the same brand, and promotes the new line aggressively, the sales of the medium-priced line will tend to increase at the expense of the higher priced product. Consumers may tend to impute the high quality associated with the brand name, Status, to the medium-priced line and thus buy it in the belief that they are getting a bargain. This phenomenon is commonly identified as "trading down." Management should recognize the possibility of getting the trading-down effect when considering the wisdom of selling a lower quality version of the product under the brand name already associated with a higher quality level. Whether such action is wise depends upon a number of considerations.

A key factor is whether consumers are able to discriminate between the higher and lower quality versions of the same product. If the characteristics of importance to the consumer are "hidden qualities," then the prospective buyer is likely to assume that the quality of the lower priced item is the same as the higher priced item and buy it thinking she is getting a bargain. If she can appraise these qualities through usage, however, then she will be disappointed in the lower priced item, and this will damage the reputation of the firm's higher quality product. If these hidden qualities cannot be evaluated through usage, the consumer will probably be satisfied with her purchase and will continue to buy the lower priced item. Under these circumstances, the firm will be trading sales of the lower priced item for the higher priced product. If this result is being sought in the belief that it will bring greater long-run profits than to produce only the higher quality item, then addition of the lower quality item under the established brand name may be justifiable. If this shift in volume from high- to low-quality product is not desired and results in lower long-run profits, the action would be unfortunate.

If the characteristics important to the consumer are features of design, style, or appearance which can be evaluated through inspection, then the consumer will probably be able to distinguish the low-quality item from the high, and will not be confused as to what she is buying. If she really values the features which are associated with the high-quality item, she will pay the higher price for it. Those who buy the lower quality item will probably constitute a different market segment not reached by the high-quality version of the brand. By reaching a new market segment, management may expand the total market for its brand.

Another consideration is whether the new, low-quality item will be sold through different retail channels from the high-quality product. High-quality men's watches, for example, might be sold through jewelry stores. The manufacturer might then add a lower quality version under the same brand name and distribute it through discount houses and mail-order firms in the hope of expanding the market for his brand to include price-conscious lower income prospective buyers. If the prospective buyers of the higher quality watch shop only the jewelry stores in making their purchase then the addition of the lower quality line in discount stores will not tend to erode the original market. If these prospective buyers do shop the discount houses, however, they may confuse the quality of the two lines and purchase the lower priced version. Research on buying habits would be necessary to resolve this question.

Still another factor to be considered is whether salesmen are present in the retail store to aid the consumer in making a selection. If the same retail store carries both the higher and lower quality versions of the brand, salesmen could justify the higher price by pointing out its higher quality. In this case there would be no confusion as to quality, and prospective buyers of both the higher and lower quality items would be reached. If salesmen are not properly trained and supervised, however, they might have a tendency to give up too easily when they run into sales resistance in trying to sell the higher quality product. Instead of pointing out the benefits of buying the higher priced item, they might switch to pushing the lower priced version on the grounds that it is almost as good, but substantially lower in price. If this danger were recognized, the firm could take steps to minimize it by giving dealers larger margins on the high-priced item than on the low, and by taking steps to make sure that salesclerks are properly trained to push the higher priced item adequately before bringing out the lower priced product. In considering whether trading down is likely to occur, therefore, management should make a careful assessment of the kind of behavior which may be expected from the retail clerks selling the line.

What has been said above relates to consumer goods. If the firm is selling industrial goods, however, there is little danger that the addition of a lower priced line under the established brand will result in a shift of volume from the higher quality to the lower quality product. Industrial buyers are likely to specify the quality of product desired and inspect the items delivered to make sure that they conform to specifications. Several persons are likely to influence the purchase. Buying is likely to be more rational. Purchasers are not likely to buy the wrong quality because the price is lower.

In summary, when a manufacturer wishes to add a lower or higher quality version of an existing product to his line and wishes to maintain sales of the original item, he would be well advised to give it a separate brand name in those cases where consumers are not likely to be able to discriminate between the two products at the point of purchase, where quality can be evaluated through usage, where consumers are likely to shop the different types of retailers who handle the different quality levels, and if salesmen are likely to switch too readily to the sale of the lower quality item when sales resistance appears. If the market for the higher quality version is shrinking to unprofitable levels, however, the firm may wish to take advantage of the trading-down effect to help build up sales volume of a lower quality line which will tap a new market segment. While we might question the ethics involved in deliberately setting out to confuse consumers, the above discussion indicates how the firm might proceed to achieve the desired result.

The reverse of the above situation occurs when a firm originally sells a low-quality product and adds a higher quality version of the same item to the line. If management wishes to reach a higher income segment of the market through this action, the brand policy to follow will depend upon the same factors mentioned above. If consumers cannot distinguish the two quality levels, are unable to judge quality through usage, and find both the higher and lower quality items in the same retail outlets, then management would be well advised to sell the higher quality line under a separate brand name. If the objective of management is to get a trading-up effect, however, then the higher quality version should be given the same brand name and should be promoted aggressively. The prestige associated with the higher quality version will tend to rub off on the lower quality item, and the sales of the lower quality product will increase. Under this strategy the potential of the higher quality item will not be fully achieved, since it is being used as a means of stimulating the sales of the original lower quality line. Again we might question the ethics of a firm which relies upon confusion of the consumer to gain its objectives. Nevertheless, it is important to understand this phenomenon so that management will make its brand policy decision with a full realization of the probable consequences.

Finally, if consumers can discriminate between the two quality levels through inspection, and the two lines are distributed through different channels not customarily shopped by the same prospective buyers, then both higher and lower quality lines may be sold under the same brand name with little risk.

Another way to distinguish between quality levels, while still identifying the different items with the family name, is to follow the practice used by automobile manufacturers. Oldsmobile, for example, combines the family name with a model designation to distinguish between products with different price-quality levels within its line as follows: Delta 88, Ninety-Eight, and Toronado. Here there is little danger of confusion between quality levels, but the different lines all benefit from association with the Oldsmobile family name.

Whether to manufacture under distributors' brands[9]

This issue is of fundamental importance to manufacturers, since the decision made has an important bearing not only upon the promotional strategy followed by the firm but also upon product development, distribution policy, pricing, production, and finance. Reaching a wise decision may influence market share and profit performance for years to come. Recognition of this fact has led some of our largest corporations to set up special task forces to make a thorough study of the risks

---

[9] Summarized from Victor J. Cook and Thomas F. Schutte, Marketing Science Institute, *Brand Policy Determination*, pp. 66–97. © 1967 by Allyn and Bacon, Inc., Boston. By permission of the publisher and the Marketing Science Institute.

and opportunities of supplying large-scale distributors with products to be sold under their private brands.

While there has been a substantial resurgence of distributors' brands during the years since World War II, the impact of private brands upon different industries varies considerably. In a recent study of brand policy by the Marketing Science Institute, it was found that the share of industry achieved by distributors' brands varied as follows: shoes, 52 percent; replacement tires, 36 percent; major appliances, 33 percent; gasoline, 16 percent; grocery products, 13 percent; and portable appliances, 7 percent. It is apparent that the opportunities of profiting from distributors' brand production, as well as the risk involved in following such a policy, vary widely in different product classifications.

There are three basic brand policy options available to the manufacturer. A company can elect to produce only its own brands, and follow a "manufacturers' brand policy." Or a firm can follow a "distributors' brand policy" where it produces exclusively for sale under private labels and manufactures nothing under its own brand. In between these two extremes falls the "mixed-brand policy," where both private and national brands are produced. Analysis indicates that each of these policy options may be appropriate under certain conditions. Reaching a wise decision therefore calls for careful analysis and discriminating judgment.

The executive faced with such a decision may get helpful guidance from the findings of the MSI study mentioned above.[10] This study was based upon intensive interviews with 112 different manufacturing organizations. Of this number, 33 companies had a manufacturers' brand policy, 65 were committed to a mixed-brand policy, while 14 produced only private brands. Factors influencing management in following each of the alternative policies are outlined below.

Distributors' brand policy

Companies following a distributors' brand policy are essentially experts in the production of a given product line. The major marketing function is shifted to distributors. They tend to have a limited sales force and capability in market research, restricted product development and consumer research activities, limited warehousing and distribution facilities, and undertake little promotion and advertising. Such firms tend to have low sales volume, often less than $50 million. Most of these companies share a common characteristic. At a crucial point in their histories, usually prior to World War II, they lacked the management resources or the financial backing to strengthen a dwindling market position and began producing distributors' brands as a means of increas-

---

[10] Ibid.

ing sales and profits. The distributors' brand policy was probably the best alternative open to these companies. Although the management of some of these companies hope eventually to go into the production, distribution, and promotion of their own brands, most of them do not have the management capabilities or financial strength necessary to compete effectively as producers of their own nationally advertised brands.

Manufacturers' brand policy

In contrast are the companies which are fully committed to the manufacturing and marketing of their own brands—to a manufacturers' brand policy. These firms are often giants in their industries with broad product lines, large brand shares, and established distribution systems. Such companies consider themselves to be specialists, not just in production, but in marketing and distribution as well. Often they have the required management and capital resources to keep their complex operations going at a highly profitable level. Management of some of these firms does not view private brands as a serious threat, and in other companies, management does not even view private brands as serious competition. Accordingly, these firms do not produce distributors' brands because they feel that to do so would mean giving up more than they would gain.

Mixed-brand policy

There are other manufacturers, however, with marketing capabilities and sales volumes comparable with the top manufacturers' brand concerns, who choose to enter private-brand production under a mixed-brand policy. These firms are often large, well established, experienced in marketing, and with sufficient financial resources to stay near the top of their industry with their own brands, yet they still turn to the production of private brands. Indeed, in all the industries studied, MSI found that an increasing number of manufacturers were turning to a mixed-brand policy. Moreover, a mixed-brand policy is probably the most common brand policy in existence today in most consumer product industries, both in terms of the number of companies involved and in the proportion of industry volume they represent. What rationale explains the adoption of a mixed-brand policy? Among the more important considerations are the following.

1. *Recognition of profit opportunities in the production of private brands.* The vice president for marketing of one firm, for example, stated: "We were advised that the percent of private-label merchandise was

growing—it's now between 11 and 23 percent of total chain-store sales in most markets. We're losing millions in sales by refusing to produce chain brands."[11] Especially where earnings per share have been declining for a number of years, competing for substantial private-brand volume may appear to offer the quickest way to improve the picture.

2. *An interest in reducing the average collection period, and improving the working capital position.* Adoption of a mixed-brand policy enabled some firms to channel more sales into a few large-volume, quick-paying accounts (private-brand distributors) and proportionately less into many small-volume, slower paying accounts.

3. *Gains in production efficiency.* Many of the firms studied were led into private-brand business by production considerations. From a short-run viewpoint, a mixed-brand policy may be used as a stopgap measure to deal with sudden declines in sales volume, temporary excess capacity, or overproduction. The petroleum industry, for example, is characterized by continuous production and high shutdown-startup costs. As a result, refiners frequently sell excess output to independents for distribution under private brands. While the production of private brands as a stopgap maneuver may appeal to certain nondurable goods manufacturers, this approach is not as applicable to companies producing consumer durables. Here, too much long-term planning is needed before entering into private-brand production, and withdrawal from such business is equally difficult.

Certain manufacturers may also enter into private-brand production as a means of achieving stability in normal production scheduling operations with attendant gains in production efficiency. Neither this consideration, nor the stopgap tactic, however, proved to be crucial elements in the large, long-term, private-brand programs studied by the MSI. Instead, two other production advantages were found to be extremely important in certain situations. First, long-term contracts with large distributors may provide a basis for plant expansion resulting in a general reduction of unit costs on both national and private-brand volume through economies of scale. Second, even where private-brand volume does not justify large building programs, manufacturers may still experience a significant reduction in unit costs as a direct result of the distributors' brand business.

4. *Marketing considerations.* Gains in the marketing area are often important considerations leading to the decision to adopt a mixed-brand policy. Among the more important are the following:

a) Private-brand production provides a way of achieving rapid market information feedback. In the process of controlling their operations, the operators of large chain-store organizations collect valuable informa-

---

[11] Ibid., p. 89.

tion upon changes in consumer demand as they relate to product features, price lines, and new products, among others. Regardless of whether this information is freely shared with the manufacturer, or must be inferred from the character of private-brand orders, it is valuable feedback which could not be gained cheaply or quickly in any other way.

b) A mixed-brand policy enables a firm to get detailed knowledge of the merchandising operations of a distributor (who is a major competitor) by supplying him with private-brand products.

c) The close working relationship between the manufacturer and his private-brand account may allow him to exert some influence upon the product line and merchandising programs of this distributor (who is also a competitor). One manufacturer, for example, was asked by a private-brand account to provide assistance in merchandise planning. As a result, the producer and the distributor agreed that they would both be better off if the appeal of the private brand were to be based upon value rather than price, and that traditional price lines would not be departed from significantly by the private label.

d) A mixed-brand policy may also provide a manufacturer with the opportunity of spreading marketing overhead to the added output generated by the private-brand contracts. Indeed, many companies interviewed in the MSI study found this advantage to be more important than the ability to spread manufacturing overhead.

e) Some manufacturers with broad product lines may adopt a mixed-brand policy as a way to escape defensive, costly promotional competition encountered on certain of their products. Although the national brands of such firms may be market leaders in product categories accounting for most of their sales volume, they may be unable to maintain leadership in others where large advertising and sales promotion expenditures are made by competition. By manufacturing these products for private-brand distributors, they may recoup their volume at the same time that the burden of promotional competition is passed on to distributors.

f) One of the important reasons for adopting a mixed-brand policy is the high degree of pricing flexibility which may be achieved. Under the Robinson-Patman Act, a seller is prohibited from discriminating in price between different purchasers of commodities of *like grade and quality* where the effect of such discrimination may be substantially to lessen competition or tend to create a monopoly. The difficulties of justifying price differences in the sale of the manufacturer's own brand tend to discourage the quoting of special discounts to large chain distributors. If a firm decides to adopt a mixed-brand policy, however, it may produce variations of its product to meet the specifications of large-scale distributors, who will then sell these items under their own private brands. Indeed, if these private brands differ enough from the manufacturer's own brand so that he may justifiably claim that they are not of "like grade and quality," this will take them out from under the restrictions of Section 2(a) of the Robinson-Patman Act and enable the firm to charge such buyers lower prices than his own national brand customarily brings. In this manner greater pricing flexibility may indeed be gained, since the limitations imposed by the Robinson-Patman Act may be avoided.

The feasibility of following such an approach depends upon the nature of the products which a firm produces. The critical question, of course, is how much of a change must be made in the product produced under the manufacturer's brand to remove the private brand from the jurisdiction of the Robinson-Patman Act and how much these modifications are likely to cost. Unless the costs of such variations can be held to a limited amount, the ability of the manufacturer to quote an attractive price to the large distributor may be wiped out. With these points in mind, then, it is apparent that the ability of firms to make minor variations of limited cost in their private-brand products will differ considerably as between items such as household appliances and packaged food products. Minor modifications in appearance and design of a household refrigerator may be enough to meet the specifications of a chain distributor and thus permit the manufacturer to justify a special discount on the private-brand item. A packaged-food processor, in contrast, may find it difficult, if not impossible, to make obvious physical differences between its private-label merchandise and its national brand without incurring costs which would eliminate the profits of private-brand business. Failure to make the private brands different would open the producer to the risk of an FTC charge of violating the Robinson-Patman Act.

While it is difficult to assess the degree of risk of an FTC charge in the latter case, the court decisions in the *Borden Company* v. *Federal Trade Commission* case may provide producers with some helpful guidelines.[12] In this case the Borden Company sold physically identical evaporated milk at a lower price to distributors under private labels than it charged for the Borden brand. While the Supreme Court ruled that the products sold under both brands were of "like grade and quality," it remanded the case to the Fifth Circuit Court of Appeals for a finding on whether the sale of the private brands at a lower price injured competition. The circuit court found that the difference in price between the Borden brand and the private brands was roughly equivalent to the consumer appeal of the Borden label and that, accordingly, competi-

---

[12] *Federal Trade Commission* v. *Borden Company*, No. 106, decided March 23, 1966, 86 *Supreme Court Reporter*, 383 U.S. 685, pp. 1092–1106.

tion was not injured.[13] Although these decisions might encourage pack-aged-goods producers to consider turning to a mixed-brand position by merely changing the label on the product, there would still appear to be considerable risk in such an action. Unanswered in the circuit court decision is the question of how much of a price differential an established manufacturer of a national brand might quote in selling a private brand for the first time. How could he measure, initially, the value of the consumer preference for his own brand at the retail level as compared with the new private brand? The lack of some objective guideline might make it difficult to justify the differential should he be charged with illegal price discrimination by the FTC.

Then, too, it is apparent that the circuit court decision ran directly counter to the guidelines previously followed by the FTC in determining whether to charge violations where the issue of "like grade and quality" is involved. Since Borden won its case in circuit court of appeals, it is entirely possible that the FTC might wish to institute another test case to attempt to get a Supreme Court ruling on the question of how much of a price differential may be permissible as a measure of the "commercial value" of the manufacturer's national brand. In short, it would still appear to be risky for a packaged-goods manufacturer to offer his product without change, under private brands, as a means of achieving greater price flexibility than he now has in selling his national brand. As pointed out earlier, however, producers of other types of products which lend themselves more easily to distinctive minor variations tend to regard the increased flexibility in pricing achieved by moving to a mixed-brand policy as an important advantage of this approach.

5. *Risks of a mixed-brand policy.*[14] It is recognized that certain risks are involved in the adoption of a mixed-brand policy. Accordingly, it is helpful to identify the risks anticipated by firms considering production under distributors' brands and to discover how serious these problems turned out to be in actual practice. Findings of the MSI study relating to these points are reviewed below.

a) Loss of trade support for the national brand. Manufacturers relying on franchise outlets for distribution of their national brand were concerned that the production of private-brand merchandise might result in a reduction of sales efforts by their dealers and even a loss in franchise outlets. For a few manufacturers these fears were realized. Others found dealers less critical than they expected, however. Still others found it possible to minimize adverse dealer reactions by offering wider margins made possible by accepting private-brand business, or by handling the

---

[13] *Federal Trade Commission v. Borden Company,* U.S. Court of Appeals for the Fifth Circuit, 381 F. 2d 175, No. 20463, July 14, 1967. Commerce Clearing House, *Trade Cases,* 1967, p. 84, 171–84, 176.

[14] Summarized from Cook and Schutte, *Brand Policy Determination,* pp. 93–96.

private-brand business through subsidiary companies not identified directly with the parent concern.

b) Recognition by consumers that products of the same manufacturer are available under both national and private brands. This risk is especially serious where personal selling is used at the point of purchase, since the source of the private brand may be mentioned by the clerk in attempting to make a sale. Even where products are sold on a self-service basis, such identification may also take place if package designs and container shapes are the same for both national and private brands, since they are often stocked side by side on retail shelves by distributors. Manufacturers adopting a mixed-brand policy usually did all they could to minimize recognition by consumers that their products were available under both national and private labels. Some took steps to make the appearance of the private brand different from that of the national brand. Others put provisions in contracts with distributors to prevent mention of the supplier's name in promotion. Yet for some companies, the problems of consumer recognition were well known in advance and were accepted philosophically as a part of the private brand business.

c) Loss of exclusive rights to new product developments through adoption by private-brand customers. Where distributors work closely with manufacturers on research and development work, and contribute significant amounts to R.&D. activities, they may be expected to want equal access to new product developments which may result. Before entering into such an arrangement, of course, the gains and losses may be evaluated and cooperative R.&D. activities undertaken only if the net result is beneficial. One firm saw the advantage of fast, widespread distribution and consumer acceptance in simultaneous introduction of a major innovation under both national and private labels. A disadvantage of this approach, however, was the risk of consumer recognition that the same company manufactured both the national and private label and the possibility that the manufacturer's brand might, therefore, achieve a lower share of market than otherwise possible.

d) Disclosure of costs and operating data to a major competitor (the private-brand distributor) through known cost contracts—this was recognized as an unavoidable problem of a mixed-brand policy, although few executives believed that this information would be used to their disadvantage by their private-brand customers.

e) Certain risks long associated with private-brand business were recognized by firms adopting a mixed-brand policy, but were discounted as being of less concern than the problems discussed above. One was the risk that a mixed-brand policy might result in trading volume and dollars under the manufacturers' brand for volume and fewer dollars under the private label. Only a few firms following a mixed-brand policy actually experienced a drop in sale of their own brands with private-brand production. On the contrary, the result was most often a substantial increase in total volume and at least maintenance of previous sales levels under the manufacturers' brand.

Another commonly recognized risk is that of becoming unduly dependent upon giant private-brand distributors through gradual increases over time in the proportion of output going into distributors' brands. While firms moving from complete reliance on national brands to a mixed-brand policy recognized this potential danger, many expressed a keen interest in increasing their private-brand sales—some even by 100 percent or 200 percent. Apparently they regarded this potential risk as one not of immediate concern in view of the magnitude of their current national brand volume.

6. *Relative profitability of different brand policies.* According to the MSI study, firms following a mixed-brand policy were more profitable than firms committed entirely to private-brand production, but were less profitable than producers following a manufacturers' brand policy. Even so, examples of highly profitable mixed-brand organizations were found during the course of the study. According to MSI, "It cannot be concluded that a manufacturers' brand firm is likely to suffer a loss in profits by adopting a mixed-brand policy."[15] This finding led the researchers to examine the characteristics of the more profitable mixed-brand policy manufacturers in an attempt to discover why they had been unusually successful in their approach. The results of this analysis are outlined below.

a)   Such firms have formal policies which provide for the production of private brands on a continuing basis as an integral part of each company's operation, rather than for short-run, in-and-out tactics.

b)   They have a full-time, private-brand administrator reporting most often to the vice president of marketing.

c)   Most of these firms have specific criteria used in making a careful selection of private label customers.

d)   Corporate resources—such as research and development staffs, marketing research data, and merchandising and promotional planning experience—are made available to the private-brand administrator.

e)   The use of "known-cost" contracts—the type of contract which provides details on the manufacturers' cost structure—is one of the characteristics shared by the more profitable mixed-brand policy companies. The known-cost contract often appeared responsible for a close management contact between supplier and customer, another distinguishing characteristic of the more profitable firms.

7. *Summary.* As indicated in the foregoing discussion, many well-

---

[15] Ibid., p. 83.

established firms view private-brand production under a mixed-brand policy as a normal, profitable market opportunity. Often they see production under private labels as a means of reaching a market segment not covered by their national brand business. In considering adopting a mixed-brand policy, it is recognized that there may be serious risks involved. Such recognition indicates the wisdom of careful analysis of corporate, financial, production, and marketing considerations in evaluating the desirability of adopting a mixed-brand position. Judging from the MSI study, many firms believe that the advantages of a mixed-brand policy outweigh the risks associated with the production of private brands. Then, too, the mixed-brand policy is viewed as the most flexible of the three policy options. It offers the opportunity to adapt quickly to basic changes in the market structure as large-scale distributors grow and capture an increasing share of industry for their private brands. It also opens up large amounts of volume that would remain unavailable under a policy of producing only manufacturers' brands. Companies included in the MSI study that integrated private-brand production into the mainstream of corporate activity by developing well-planned, long-term policies, apparently found that this approach resulted in higher volume, greater overall market strength, and improved profits.

Decision-theory approach to mixed-brand policy choice

The foregoing discussion of the problem of whether a national brand producer should seek private-brand business makes it abundantly clear that the consequences of such action are not known with certainty. This suggests that management might well consider the possibility of applying the "decision-theory" approach to the analysis of this problem— i.e., the method of *individual decision making under risk.*

The decision-theory approach may be illustrated in terms of a hypothetical problem fashioned by Buzzell and Slater to approximate actual conditions in the wholesale bakery market, which one of the authors had studied for a number of years.[16] In this model bakery market let us assume that there are three wholesale bakeries designated as A, B, and C; and two chain bakeries, those of the Blue Chain and the Red Chain. Wholesale baker Z, located in a nearby city, is a potential "outside" competitor. The customers served by these bakeries are designated as follows: Blue, Red, and Green corporate chains; retailer cooperatives I and II; voluntary chain I; independent supermarkets; small independent stores. Let us assume that the Blue Chain asks baker B, the second

---

[16] The following discussion is reprinted by permission from Robert D. Buzzell and Charles C. Slater, "Decision Theory and Marketing Management," *Journal of Marketing,* vol. 26, no. 3 (July 1962), pp. 7–16. Published by the American Marketing Association.

largest wholesale baker in the market, to produce a private brand of bread for sale in the Blue Stores. The problem is, how should baker B respond to such a request?

The decision-theory approach to the solution of this problem may be summarized briefly as follows:

1. *Identification of alternative possibilities.* The decision maker, B, must choose among several possible "acts" or "strategies" denoted as $A_1, A_2 \ldots A_n$. The different possibilities open to baker B are as follows:

> A_1 Ignore the request.
> A_2 Make a counteroffer to produce a "secondary brand" bread to be sold at a lower price than the regular "B brand" bread.
> A_3 Reduce the price of the regular brand.
> A_4 Accede to the request of the Blue Chain.
> A_5 Institute a system of price differentials based on quantity and service rendered by baker B.

2. *Identification of possible states of nature.* Choice among the above "acts" depends upon certain *conditions* which cannot be predicted with certainty. The conditions may be termed "states of nature" and designated as $S_1, S_2 \ldots S_m$. These states of nature include all factors which determine the effects of a decision—for example, the responses of customers, and competitors' reactions. If baker B follows possibility A_1 and ignores the Blue Chain's request, there are six possible outcomes:

> S_{11} Blue is supplied by outside baker Z. Having achieved a foothold in the market, Z also supplies private-label bread to the Yellow Chain and to Coop I.
> S_{12} Blue is supplied by Z, but Z fails to get any other business.
> S_{13} Blue is supplied by local bakery A or bakery C.
> S_{14} Blue acquires its own bakery plant and decreases its purchases from B.
> S_{15} Blue decides to wait; but resentful of B's refusal, adopts minor countermeasures, including reduced display space and less careful maintenance of B's display stocks.
> S_{16} Blue decides to wait and does *not* adopt any countermeasures.

In similar fashion, the outcomes of other decision possibilities should be enumerated.

3. *Exploration of further possibilities and outcomes.* The analysis cannot stop realistically with a single "round" of actions and their outcomes. Instead it is necessary to explore the whole chain of effects and reactions that would follow a given decision by baker B. To illustrate, let us return to decision A_1 and the possible outcomes outlined above. Suppose baker B refuses (A_1) and baker Z supplies the Blue Chain as well as the Yellow Chain and Coop I (S_{11}). Baker B is then confronted by a new set of possibilities: he can retaliate by supplying retailers

in Z's own market, hoping to drive Z out of the local market; or he can meet Z's competition locally. If he retaliates in Z's market, the outcome will again depend on the "state of nature." The possible outcome, for instance, is that legal action will be taken against B for geographic price discrimination. An illustrative series of moves and outcomes is shown in a tree diagram in Figure 13–3.

4. *Estimation of payoffs.* For each alternative decision and each outcome, the "payoff" to the decision maker should be estimated through tracing the effects upon the firm's sales, costs, and profits. Baker B's

FIGURE 13–3
Illustrative analysis of decision possibilities and outcomes—A_1: B refuses Blue's request (payoffs in thousands of dollars)

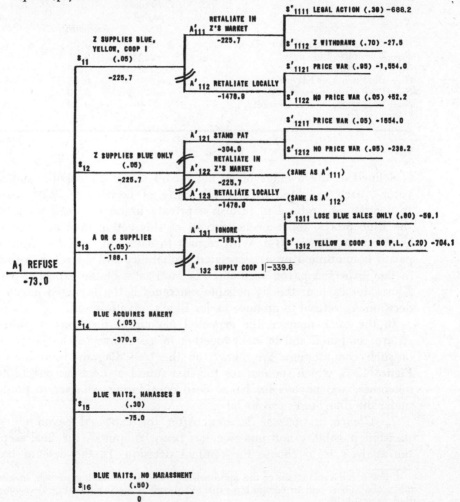

computations cover profits for a five-year period, discounted to present values.

5. *Assessment of probabilities.* Since the outcome of a given decision is uncertain, a key element in the analysis is to assign probabilities to the various possible "states of nature." These probabilities represent the decision maker's "betting odds" as to the probable responses of customers, competition, and so forth. This is a difficult step, but it is an essential element in decision theory. The probabilities associated with the six possible outcomes of decision. A_1 are shown in Figure 13–3.

6. *Computation of expected payoff.*[17] The expected payoff of an act

FIGURE 13–4

Outcome	Estimated payoff (000)	Probabilities	Expected payoff (000)
S_{11}—Z supplies Blue, Yellow, Coop I.......	$-225.7	0.05	$-11.285
S_{12}—Z supplies Blue only................	-225.7	0.05	-11.285
S_{13}—A or C supplies.....................	-188.1	0.05	-9.405
S_{14}—Blue acquires bakery.................	-370.5	0.05	-18.525
S_{15}—Blue waits, harasses B...............	-75.0	0.30	-22.500
S_{16}—Blue waits, no harassment...........	0	0.50	0
Total expected payoff.............			$-73.000

is defined as the average of its net payoff under all possible states of nature, each weighted by its probability of occurrence. With respect to decision A_1, refusal to furnish a private brand of bread for sale in the Blue Stores, the expected payoff of this action may be computed as shown in Figure 13–4. With respect to each outcome, the estimated payoff is multiplied by its associated probability and the result is shown in the "expected payoff" column. The sum total of the expected payoff figures for each of the six possible outcomes is the expected payoff for decision A_1, refusal to produce under Blue's private brand.

In the same manner, the expected payoffs of decisions A_2 through A_6 are computed and brought together in a summary table. The results of such computations are shown on the tree diagram reproduced in Figure 13–5, which summarizes the first round of decision possibilities, outcomes, and payoffs for baker B in considering whether to produce under the Blue Stores private label.

7. *Choice of optimal decision.* After the expected payoff of each decision possibility and outcome has been computed, the final step in the analysis is to choose the optimal decision. In the case of baker

---

[17] For a full explanation of the approach followed in estimating payoffs, in assessing probabilities, and in computing expected payoff of each alternative decision, see Ibid., pp. 14–15.

FIGURE 13–5
Summary of first round of decision possibilities, outcomes, and payoffs for wholesale bakery private-label decision (payoffs in thousands)

A₁ IGNORE OR REFUSE −73.0

S₁₁ Z SUPPLIES BLUE AND OTHERS (.05)	− 225.7
S₁₂ Z SUPPLIES BLUE ONLY (.05)	− 225.7
S₁₃ A OR C SUPPLIES BLUE (.05)	− 188.1
S₁₄ BLUE ACQUIRES BAKERY (.05)	− 370.5
S₁₅ BLUE WAITS, HARASSES B (.30)	− 75.0
S₁₆ BLUE WAITS, (.50)	0

A₂ COUNTER OFFER −265.2

S₂₁ Z SUPPLIES BLUE AND OTHERS (.02)	−225.7
S₂₂ Z SUPPLIES BLUE ONLY (.03)	−225.7
S₂₃ A OR C SUPPLIES BLUE (.01)	−188.1
S₂₄ BLUE ACQUIRES BAKERY (.01)	−370.5
S₂₅ BLUE WAITS, HARASSES B (.01)	− 75.0
S₂₆ BLUE WAITS (.02)	0
S₂₇ BLUE ACCEPTS A AND C FOLLOW SUIT (.90)	−275.1

A₃ REDUCE PRICE BY .02 −1337.0

S₃₁ Z SUPPLIES BLUE AND OTHERS (.03)	− 225.7
S₃₂ Z SUPPLIES BLUE ONLY (.04)	− 225.7
S₃₃ A OR C SUPPLIES BLUE (.02)	− 188.1
S₃₄ BLUE ACQUIRES BAKERY (.01)	− 370.5
S₃₅ BLUE ACCEPTS, A AND C DO NOT MEET (.05)	− 450.8
S₃₆ BLUE ACCEPTS, A AND C MEET, B RETAINS ADVAN. (.10)	−1249.2
S₃₇ BLUE ACCEPTS, A AND C MEET, RETURN TO ORIGINAL SHARE (.75)	−1554

A₄ ACCEDE −260.7

S₄₁ BLUE ACCEPTS, A AND C OFFER SECONDARY (.70)	− 22.2
S₄₂ BLUE ACCEPTS, A AND C REDUCE PRICES (.10)	−1442.7
S₄₃ BLUE ACCEPTS, A AND C SUPPLY COOP I AND YELLOW (.20)	− 504.3

A₅ PRICE DIFFERENTIAL SYSTEM +125.2

S₅₁ Z SUPPLIES BLUE AND OTHERS (.05)	− 225.7
S₅₂ Z SUPPLIES BLUE ONLY (.05)	− 225.7
S₅₃ A OR C SUPPLIES BLUE (.05)	− 188.1
S₅₄ BLUE ACCEPTS, A AND C FOLLOW SUIT (.80)	0
S₅₅ BLUE ACCEPTS, A AND C REDUCE PRICES (.25)	+ 828.5

FIGURE 13–6

Acts		Expected payoff (000)
A_1	Ignore the request......................	$- 73.0
A_2	Counteroffer............................	- 265.2
A_3	Reduce price...........................	-1,337.0
A_4	Accede................................	- 260.7
A_5	Adopt price differential system...........	+ 125.2

B, the expected payoffs for all possible acts or decisions are summarized in Figure 13–6. Examination of the expected payoff figures above indicates that A_5—adoption of a price differential system—would be the optimal decision for baker B since the firm would be likely to achieve an increase in net profit of $125,200 while the remaining four alternatives would all result in losses ranging from −$73,000 ($A_1$) to −$1,337,000 (A_3).

Evaluation of decision-theory approach

Decision theory provides an approach for analyzing problems where the outcomes of possible alternative decisions involve considerable uncertainty (or risk). The problem of whether to adopt a mixed-brand policy certainly falls into this category. Such an approach encourages the identification and analysis of *all* the possible decisions which might be made (including doing nothing). Of particular significance is the emphasis on thinking through the possible consequences of the whole chain of events which may result from each possible action. Note that the process does not stop with a single "round" of actions and their outcomes. If possible, it should be carried through a second round and—if estimates of payoffs and probabilities can be made with satisfactory confidence—through a third and possibly even a fourth round. This aspect of the approach focuses attention on the critical issues involved in the various possible ways of dealing with the problem.

In most cases of this sort, determination of the probabilities for the relevant "states of nature" (reactions of consumers, competitors, and so on) is difficult. A firm does not make a mixed-brand policy decision often enough to gain experience which may guide future estimates. Nevertheless, even very crude approximations of probabilities for various states affecting outcomes of a decision are better than none at all. Decision theory forces executives to recognize the subjective "betting odds" that lie behind their judgments and put them into quantitative form as probability estimates.

Likewise, the task of estimating profit payoffs for each possible line of action several years into the future tends to encourage executives to be more careful in their analyses. Estimating payoffs and determining probabilities, accordingly, tends to encourage management to examine the mixed-brand problem in concrete terms and provides a stimulus to more systematic thinking on the part of those involved. Equally important, structuring the problem in formal terms helps to indicate the direction which future research should take if such analyses are to be improved.

It should be recognized, of course, that application of decision theory to the mixed-brand policy problem will encourage estimates which may be based upon inadequate data and thus may represent only crude approximations of the information desired. It is necessary, therefore, to avoid imputing greater accuracy than they merit to the figures on estimated payoff which represent the end results of the analysis. If the limitations of the data are kept in mind, however, the decision-theory approach may aid management in the difficult task of making choices among alternative lines of action under conditions of uncertainty.

Perhaps the chief advantage of decision theory grows out of the fact that this approach requires the executive to *formalize* his thinking about a problem—to structure his judgment and write it down in black and white. It is self-evident that this is likely to improve the quality of executive judgment. Experimentation with this approach, therefore, would appear to be desirable.

Conclusion

Decisions on brand strategy have important promotional implications. In this chapter, we have focused on issues relating to family versus individual brands, brand-quality-price relationships, and the wisdom of manufacturing products to be sold under distributors' brands as opposed to the firm's own brand. Evidence has been cited that for frequently purchased package goods, the promotion of one product under a family brand has beneficial effects for other products under that brand through the principle of generalization. In contrast, a study of semantic generalization, as applied to family brands of household appliances, raises some doubt as to the use of a common brand name as a means of transferring attitudes between dissimilar products of high unit value.

On the question of distributors' brands versus manufacturers' brands, each of the three policy options open may be appropriate under certain conditions, but a Marketing Science Institute study indicates that a mixed-brand policy is probably the most common posture in existence today in most consumer product industries. In our discussion we also noted that the outcomes of adopting any one of the three alternative policies involved considerable risk or uncertainty. Accordingly, the possibility of applying the "decision-theory" approach was examined and its merits and limitations discussed.

Questions

1. Explain how the "assimilation effect" from psychological theory may be applied to family branding.

2. *a)* Did Fry's research verify the hypothesis that consumers have generalized preferences for family brands? To what product categories do his findings apply?

   b) What factors appear to contribute to the degree of generalized preference likely to exist in a given situation?

3. *a)* In studying semantic generalization, what hypothesis did Kerby test and for what types of products?

   b) Why do you suppose Kerby had consumers evaluate branded products in terms of "semantic differential scales" instead of in terms of percent of consumers purchasing one brand as compared with another?

4. Did the results of Kerby's research verify the hypothesis that "meaning should be transferred between two or more products that are physically dissimilar, if they share a common brand name"? How does Kerby explain his results?

5. The text suggests several factors which tend to foster or retard the development of generalized preference for family brands through the process of assimilation. In the light of these criteria, in which of the following situations would you recommend a policy of family branding?

   a) A new hair lightener for men to be introduced by Clairol, Inc., formerly marketing hair preparations exclusively for women.

   b) A double-edged razor designed for teen-agers by Gillette.

   c) A new snow blower added to its line by Yard-Man, Inc., a manufacturer of power lawn mowers.

   d) A stereo-phonograph added to its line of sewing machines by Singer Company.

   e) A diaper pail spray in an aerosol can introduced by the owners of the firm producing Lustur-Seal, an automobile paint conditioner.

6. Under what conditions might it be desirable to combine an individual brand name with the corporate name in identifying a product? When might it be undesirable?

7. Until 1965, Polaroid Land Cameras capable of producing color pictures in 60 seconds were priced at about $135 and $165. In 1965, Polaroid announced the addition of Model 103 to sell at about $90 and Model 104 priced at $60. Later that same year, an economy model producing only black-and-white pictures was introduced at about $20. All of these models were sold under the Polaroid name. What is your analysis of the

probability that these actions would result in trading down? If you believe that trading down would be likely to occur, would you regard this result as desirable or undesirable? Why?

8. In which of the following hypothetical situations would trading down be likely to occur?

   a) If Cadillac introduced a medium-priced car under the Cadillac name.

   b) If a manufacturer of high-grade women's dresses identified by the Smartset brand added a medium-grade line under the same brand name.

   c) If the manufacturer of the Hamilton high-grade watches were to offer a low-priced watch available only through mail-order houses.

   d) If a materials-handling company making industrial fork trucks selling at $7,000 introduced an economy line priced at $1,500 under the same brand name.

   e) If the Kroehler Co., emphasizing medium- and low-priced upholstered furniture, were to add a high-grade line under the Kroehler brand name and sell it through retail outlets handling the original line.

9. Under what conditions are firms likely to concentrate their production on the manufacture and sale of products under distributors' brands? What are the risks of such a policy? How may these risks be minimized (if at all)?

10. Under what circumstances are firms likely to limit themselves entirely to the manufacture and sale of their own brands? What limitations, if any, does this policy have?

11. List briefly the considerations which tend to lead a firm to adopt a mixed-brand policy.

12. Identify briefly the risks of following a mixed-brand policy.

13. In view of the risks which such a policy involves, why have many well-established firms adopted this approach in the marketing of their products?

14. *a)* What are the merits of applying the decision-theory approach to the solution of the question of whether to manufacture for sale under distributors' brands (assuming the firm now concentrates on its own brands)?

   b) What conditions should exist if the decision-theory approach is to be applied successfully?

cases for part five

Rector Pharmaceuticals, Inc.*

Review of marketing strategy

Rector Pharmaceuticals, Inc. was the first to develop and market an oral antidiabetic product which relieved many diabetics of the necessity of taking daily insulin shots. Under the brand name, "Resitone," the new product was first marketed in 1959. Although sales were somewhat below expectations the first year, Resitone soon caught on in the market and sales grew rapidly. By 1969, sales of Resitone exceeded $40 million and Rector Pharmaceuticals held over 80 percent of the oral antidiabetic market. At this time it became evident that Jos. Oldman and Company, a major competitor, would soon enter the oral antidiabetic market. In the light of this impending increased competition, Donald Sylvester, director of market development for Rector Pharmaceuticals, undertook a review of the marketing strategy being used for Resitone to determine what changes, if any, should be made.

The company

Rector Pharmaceuticals, Inc., producers of ethical pharmaceuticals, was established in 1906 in Chicago, Illinois. The company was founded by Dr. Howard Rector, at the time a practicing physician, for the purpose of manufacturing better drugs, which were often unreliable and unsafe at that time. The company grew rapidly and gradually developed its present line of ethical pharmaceuticals. A reputation for outstanding research, high-quality products, and aggressive merchandising have all contributed to making Rector Pharmaceuticals one of the largest ethical drug firms in the industry.

Ethical pharmaceutical houses are distinguished from proprietary drug firms by the fact that their promotional efforts are aimed at the profession (physician, druggist, hospital buyers) rather than at the ultimate consumer. Over the years, Rector Pharmaceuticals has followed

---

* Prepared by Stewart H. Rewoldt, Professor of Marketing, Graduate School of Business Administration, The University of Michigan.

Identifying names have been changed. All sales figures have been multiplied by a constant.

the basic distribution policy of selling directly to retail druggists. In accordance with the "ethical" formula, the Rector sales force was responsible for creating a demand for the firm's prescription drugs by "detailing" the physician (i.e., by missionary sales work with doctors) and by selling the retail druggist on stocking Rector products. Heavy sales of nonprescription items such as vitamins, however, have resulted from direct sales and promotional efforts of the retail druggists.

Physical distribution of Rector products was handled through 20 company-owned sales branches and warehouses located throughout the country. No account was farther than two days' delivery service from any branch warehouse, with most major trading centers receiving either same-day or following-day service.

The competitive situation

The development of Resitone represented a real breakthrough in the treatment of diabetes, a disease characterized by failure of the body to release sufficient insulin to control blood-sugar levels. Until this development, the standard treatments for diabetes were diet control and daily injection of insulin. Only the mild cases could be controlled by diet alone. Insulin injection represented a great inconvenience to the patient. Resitone worked by causing the patient's blood-sugar levels to return to normal ranges.

It was estimated by the American Diabetic Association that there were 2.5 million diabetics in the United States at the time Resitone was introduced, of which number only 1,330,000 had been diagnosed. Each year many more people developed diabetes and many more existing diabetics became known. Resitone was most successful in achieving sales relating to treatment of adult, newly discovered diabetics. Physicians appeared reluctant to switch to Resitone patients whose conditions were already stabilized by insulin injections. Known diabetics on insulin were estimated at 890,000.

Two smaller drug firms had followed Rector's entry into the antidiabetic market with oral antidiabetic products. Brown & Smith introduced "Methylor," and Martin Pharmaceuticals marketed "Panadiene." Methylor was of greater potency than Resitone and Panadiene. However, larger doses of Resitone could safely be given when higher potency was required. In 1968 and 1969 the dollar sales and market shares of all products used in the treatment of diabetes were as shown in Exhibit 1.

Because of its greater potency, Methylor was taken by most patients only once per day, whereas the most common prescribed dosage for Resitone was two tablets per day. The price, per tablet, for Methylor was only slightly higher than the per-tablet price of Resitone, so the net cost to the patient was lower. The per-tablet cost of Panadiene was lower than for Resitone. As a result, the typical annual cost to

EXHIBIT 1
Domestic antidiabetic market (dollars in millions)

Product	1968		1969		Increase/Decrease 1968–69	
	Dollars	*Percent*	*Dollars*	*Percent*	*Dollars*	*Percent*
Resitone............	$35.9	48.4	$42.8	51.4	$ 6.9	19
Methylor............	5.3	7.2	6.9	8.3	1.6	29
Panadiene...........	1.7	2.2	2.6	3.0	0.9	53
Total oral.........	$42.9	57.8	$52.3	62.7	$ 9.4	22
Insulin—Oldman.....	$25.2	34.0	$26.7	32.0	$ 1.5	5
Martin.....	3.5	4.7	2.1	2.6	−1.4	−39
S.I.H.......	2.1	2.7	1.7	2.0	−0.4	−18
Read.......	0.5	0.8	0.5	0.7	—	− 2
Total insulin.......	$31.3	42.2	$31.0	37.3	$−0.3	− 1
Total antidiabetic market............	$74.2	100.0	$83.3	100.0	$ 9.1	+12

the diabetic for each of the three drugs was: Resitone, $89; Methylor, $47; Panadiene, $52.

The price that Jos. Oldman and Company would establish for its new oral antidiabetic when it was introduced into the domestic market was, of course, unknown at this time. However, it had already introduced an oral antidiabetic, named "Dianase," in England and Australia at the same price, per tablet, as the domestic price of Resitone. Oldman claimed potency for Dianase similar to that of Methylor. Therefore, if the same price were established domestically as abroad, Jos. Oldman would have a substantial price advantage in terms of potency.

Reports from the field indicated that many physicians were switching patients from Resitone to Methylor when "secondary failure" occurred, rather than increasing the Resitone dosage. A "secondary failure" occurred when a patient who had been controlled by Resitone again lost control of his blood-sugar level. The extent of this switching, and the reason for it, was not known.

Market research study

Because so much was unknown about the market for antidiabetic drugs and the decision-making process involved in prescribing these drugs, Mr. Sylvester requested that a survey be conducted of a representative sample of physicians. He subsequently received the following report from the Marketing Research Department.

INTEROFFICE MEMORANDUM

TO: Donald B. Sylvester   SUBJECT: Resitone physician survey
FROM: J. D. French   DATE: May 29, 1969

Introduction

This memo reports on the major findings of an April 1969, survey of the antidiabetic market comprising 106 G.P.'s and 79 internists. These 185 physicians have a patient load of almost 5,000 diabetics, averaging 17 patients per G.P. and 40 per internist.

Summary of major findings

1. Resitone is currently prescribed by 91 percent of the physicians surveyed.
2. Resitone is clearly the drug of choice for newly diagnosed maturity-onset diabetics; 79 percent of physicians state they would prescribe Resitone for such a patient versus 10 percent for Methylor and 3 percent for Panadiene.
3. Physicians consider relatively few of their patients presently on insulin alone as probable candidates for oral therapy.
4. A majority of the physicians believe that few of the diabetics now controlled by diet alone will ever need drug therapy.
5. More than half the physicians currently using Resitone had previously discontinued use of Resitone for at least one patient.
6. "Failure to control" is by far the most frequent reason given for termination of Resitone therapy.
7. When a patient on a daily dose of two Resitone tablets loses control, only 42 percent of all physicians are willing to increase the Resitone dosage in an effort to regain control.
8. Approximately 9 percent of the patients on Resitone therapy are switched to Methylor in a one year period, and 38 percent of Methylor users were previously on Resitone therapy.
9. If we were to introduce a drug similar to Methylor for cases of "secondary failure," its maximum potential for the first year would be $3.2 million (9 percent of Resitone's 1968 sales). This figure unrealistically assumes that we would capture every patient now being switched from Resitone to Methylor, and that the cost to the patient for the new drug would be the same as for Resitone.
10. The cost to the patient of Resitone (and the other oral drugs) is not a major factor in physicians' decisions to switch from insulin or to change from one oral to another.

Conclusions and recommendations

Results of this survey confirm once more the outstanding acceptance of Resitone by the medical profession. Not only is it used by more than 90 percent of all physicians, but, despite new competition, it remains overwhelmingly the drug of choice for newly diagnosed maturity onset diabetes. Its cost has not been a restraining factor in its growth.

Survey findings also suggest that Resitone's future growth possibilities rest primarily in two areas: (1) continuing to acquire newly diagnosed diabetics; and (2) reducing the number of so-called "secondary failures" who are taken off the drug. Little opportunity for growth remains available among patients currently controlled with insulin or diet.

We have been somewhat less than successful in persuading the practicing physician to increase the Resitone dosage when his patient loses control. These so-called secondary failures represent our greatest current loss in sales and, with the exception of newly diagnosed patients, our greatest unrealized sales potential. In 1968, we estimate we lost $3.2 million to Methylor alone through such failures. Because of this situation, it is recommended that future Resitone detailing and advertising emphasize and reemphasize the advisability of increasing the Resitone dose when necessary.

Obviously, increasing the Resitone dose will not always prove successful. For those instances (and only those instances) where larger amounts of Resitone fail to yield adequate control, a new antidiabetic compound should be made available and recommended. It should be promoted for use only after a maximum Resitone dose has been tried.

We estimate that if all patients switched to Methylor because of secondary failure could be diverted to such a new Rector drug, this would yield a maximum sales target of $3 to $3.5 million—depending on whether the product is priced at the Resitone or Methylor level. Obviously, we could not hope to capture all these patients . . . some we hope would be maintained on higher Resitone doses . . . so that a realistic forecast of first year volume for such a product would be between $1.5 and $2.0 million.

Major findings

I. Physicians' use of oral drugs

Resitone and, to a lesser extent, the other oral products have achieved wide physician acceptance—95 percent of G.P.'s and internists are currently using one or more of the oral products.

Percent of physicians by single and multiple use of oral drugs

	Percent of physicians
Resitone only.....................................	42
Resitone and Methylor...........................	19
Resitone and Panadiene...........................	17
Resitone, Methylor, and Panadiene................	13
Total Resitone users...........................	91
Methylor only...................................	3
Panadiene only..................................	1
Methylor and Panadiene only.... *..............	0
Total Panadiene and Methylor *only* users.........	4
Total Methylor users............................	35
Total Panadiene users...........................	31
Total using orals...............................	95
Not using orals.................................	5
Total..	100

II. Current insulin patients as candidates for oral therapy

There is relatively little potential for the oral products to make further inroads on patients currently being treated by insulin.

Number of insulin patients who might

be controlled on oral therapy

Number of patients who might be switched	Percent of physicians having such patients
None	78
1–5	13
Over 5	4
Don't know	5
Total	100

When asked why they did not switch eligible patients to oral drugs, the most frequent answer was "high cost" or "added expense." However, the majority of physicians making this response indicated that the additional expense was for frequent lab tests and office visits required to maintain or establish proper control with oral drugs, rather than the drug cost itself.

III. Physicians' reluctance to increase Resitone dosage

Probably the most significant findings of the survey was the apparent unwillingness of physicians—particularly G.P.'s—to increase the dosage of Resitone when a patient loses control of his diabetes. The physicians were asked the following questions:

"Suppose you have a diabetic patient who, after six months successful therapy of diet and 2 Resitone tablets daily, loses control of his diabetes. Assume that this patient has followed the prescribed drug and diet regimen faithfully. What action would you take first in an effort to reestablish satisfactory control of the diabetes?"

Their responses were:

Action taken first	Percent of G.P. mentions	Percent of internist mentions
"Increase Resitone"	39	45
"Switch to insulin"	27	31
"Hospitalize patient"	10	8
"Switch to Methylor"	5	8
"Add insulin"	7	2
"Switch to Panadiene"	2	1
"Go to another oral"	1	1
Miscellaneous responses	9	4
Total	100	100

The above table explains why previous surveys have reported such a high percentage of secondary Resitone failures by practicing physicians in the face of considerably lower rates of failure experienced by clinicians. When a patient loses control, clinicians are willing to increase the dosage up to the recommended six tablets per day, while the majority of practicing physicians surveyed choose some other course of action.

IV. Average daily dose of Resitone prescribed by physicians

Past surveys have shown that the most frequent dose of Resitone is two tablets per day. The present survey confirms this estimate, with more than half of the physicians surveyed stating their average dose is two tablets per day.

Average daily dose of Resitone
prescribed by physicians

Average daily dose	Percent of physicians prescribing
½ tablet.............	2
1 tablet..............	13
2 tablets.............	56
3 tablets.............	21
4 tablets.............	7
5 tablets.............	1
Total..............	100

V. The market potential for a Rector drug for "secondary failures" of Resitone

One of the purposes of this survey was to help evaluate the potential market for a drug for secondary failure of Resitone. The drug currently under consideration for this purpose is almost identical to Methylor. It is therefore reasonable to assume that its potential market would be secondary failures (both genuine cases and others) of Resitone currently being switched to Methylor.

Half of the G.P.'s and a third of the internists who have patients on Methylor had switched one or more of these patients from Resitone to Methylor in the previous six months. During this period, 19 percent of current Methylor patients had been previously on Resitone therapy. Theoretically, almost all these patients would be candidates for a Rector drug promoted for secondary failures of Resitone.

Assuming the annual rate of switching to be twice that reported for the six-month period, this would represent $2.0 million of Methylor's $5.3 million 1968 sales. This switching also suggests an annual loss of 9 percent of Resitone patients, representing $3.2 million of Resitone's $35.9 million 1968 sales.

The difference between the Methylor dollar gains and the Resitone dollar losses is accounted for by the lower cost of Methylor to the patient. It does not follow that this amount could be obtained by our new product, since it is unrealistic to presume that no further patients would be switched from Resitone to Methylor once our new product was introduced. A more realistic forecast suggests first-year volume of $1.5 million–$2.0 million.

VI.   The Cost Factor

Previous surveys indicated that the cost of Resitone was not a major factor in causing physicians to avoid using the drug or in switching patients to other drugs. The present survey thoroughly confirms this belief. The physicians were asked to compare the oral drugs by six criteria, one of which was economy. The results were:

The oral drug most economical for the patient

Drug	Percent of physicians mentioning
Resitone.............	19
Methylor.............	11
Panadiene............	6
No difference.........	11
Don't know..........	53
Total..............	100

The cost of Resitone was also one of the least important factors causing physicians to switch to another drug or as a reason for remaining on insulin therapy.

The alternatives

After studying the marketing research report, Mr. Sylvester concluded that there were two major problems which threatened the future profitability of Resitone: (1) the tendency of physicians to switch to another oral diabetic in the event of secondary failure rather than to increase the Resitone dosage; (2) the impending entry of Jos. Oldman's Dianase into the antidiabetic market. To counter these threats, the following alternative courses of action appeared to be possibilities:

1.   Undertake a massive promotional campaign to encourage physicians to increase the Resitone dosage, in the case of secondary failure, before switching to another drug. This campaign would also serve to counter Jos. Oldman's promotional efforts.

2. Introduce a new, higher potency antidiabetic to which doctors could switch in the case of secondary failure without leaving the Rector family of drugs.
3. Do both of these things.

Planning for promotion

Before proposing to the vice president for marketing that a promotional campaign be undertaken, Mr. Sylvester worked out the following plan (Exhibit 2) to serve as a basis for deciding whether this alternative should be chosen.

Product policy

If a promotional campaign for Resitone were undertaken, would this be sufficient to stop the loss of Resitone sales due to secondary failure? Would a new higher dosage antidiabetic still be needed for those physicians who could not be induced to increase the dosage? Would a new product by itself be sufficient, making the promotional campaign for Resitone unnecessary? Rector had been developing a higher dosage antidiabetic for some time, and it could be introduced into the market in the near future.

If the alternative of introducing a new product were chosen, many other important decisions would have to be made. For example, should it be sold only as a product for use in the event of secondary failure, or as a drug for initial treatment? How should it be priced in relation to Resitone?

Pricing policy

It was expected that Jos. Oldman would introduce Dianase in the domestic market at a price that, if potency is taken into account, would be about one half the price of Resitone. From an economic standpoint, under these circumstances, should Rector reduce the price of Resitone?

This same situation has existed between Resitone and Methylor since the latter drug was introduced, yet Resitone continues to hold over 80 percent of the market. As could be noted in the market research report, when physicians were asked which antidiabetic was most economical for the patient, 19 percent answered Resitone and 53 percent did not know. Only 11 percent answered Methylor and 6 percent Panadiene. None mentioned switching from Resitone to Methylor after secondary failure because increasing the dosage for Resitone would be more expensive. This seemed to indicate that the oral antidiabetic drug cost to patient was reasonable enough not to be a major deterrent in selecting therapy.

The average difference between Resitone and other antidiabetics was between $25 and $50 per year to the patient. Rector executives thought

Tentative promotional program for Resitone (market research)

Customer data (patient and M.D.) on the oral antidiabetic market	Why is this clue important?	What could we do about this "promotionwise?"	What promotional group could best take major advantage of this point?	Specific program assignments (from a standpoint of greatest efficiency, work up some alternate proposals covering these points)			
				Copy or detail story	Media or special sales group	Target	Cost
Promotional clue No. 1 9 percent of the Resitone patients a year are switched to Methylor because of claimed "Secondary Failures" (as against 3 percent during our own clinical trials).	70,000 patients a year lost to Methylor through secondary failures		1. Regular field selling 2. Hospital selling 3. Samples 4. Advertising* 5. Trade and guest 6. Public relations, etc.			What group or groups of doctors should be the *major target* at which to beam this message —G.P.'s only —Internists —Hosp. doctors —Others	How much each of these alternatives cost
58 percent of these patients were switched immediately to Methylor without attempting to regain control with larger doses of Resitone.	App. 46,000 of these *might* be retained if we could educate the practicing M.D. to *first* up dosage of Resitone before he considered switching.	Have a stepped up educational program to try to get the message to the practicing M.D. to raise Resitone dosage to as high as 6 tablets a day *before* considering a new drug.	Since the regular field salesmen have so many other things to do, in a major sense it could be assigned to *advertising***	From a standpoint of *copy, design,* or *detail story* what would be the best way to get this message across	From a standpoint of media, what specific media (and further, the *actual magazines, programs,* etc.) should be used through which to *communicate* this *message?*		
Promotional clue No. 2 27 percent of the total diabetic patients are treated by 10 percent (16,000) of the doctors. These 16,000 are the specialists in internal medicine.	This points up the fact that whatever product or company controls this group, controls, to a large extent, the treatment of the diabetic and the oral antidiabetic market.	Have a continuous "barrage" of highly ethical promotion on the treatment and total care of the diabetic patient so that they always think of Rector as the diabetic treatment company, aimed at this highly influential, but small, group of M.D.'s.	Ditto above statement for advertising*—this includes many tools such as: *Journal ads, direct mail, national and state convention exhibits, special displays, etc.	Ditto above	Ditto above	Ditto above—only this time it's pretty well spelled out for us as the 16,000 specialists in internal medicine. However, in addition there are two ancillary groups of M.D.'s that should be reached with similar programs— 1) the interns and residents at the *medical* wards in teaching and other major hospitals. 2) All special influential groups such as	Ditto above

Promotional clue No. 3			
Present information would lead us to expect new major competition in the form of Oldman's Dianase (acetohexamide) —just when this product will be announced in the United States we do not know. Our best guess would be the middle of 1970. This product has been announced in England and Australia with claims of about one-third more potency (or stated differently with about 33-1/3 percent price advantage).	Because Resitone has approximately 80 percent of the current oral antidiabetic market. In general terms, this means that Oldman's Dianase can only become a major product in this field by enlarging the market (which does not have too much elasticity in it) or by taking business from Resitone. The Resitone business they probably would get first would be: —our new patient Rx's —our large hospital bid business —our teaching institution business —our government business	Have a well thought-out promotional plan ready to announce that would "neutralize" as much of Oldmans' promotion as possible in the four areas we expect to bear their major attack, namely: —new Rx business —large hospital bid business —influence on teaching institutions —government business (show example of each)	This could be primarily a job for our *field selling force*—both the *regular* and *hospital* salesmen.
			Ditto above
		Ditto above	
	Ditto above		
			Ditto above
the American Diabetic Assn. and the instructors in pharmacology and physiology, at all the medical schools. Also consideration should be given to additional new products that might enhance our image as *the Diabetic House*.	Ditto above	Ditto above

that the higher price of Resitone was justified because it had the longest record of efficacy and safety of all antidiabetics. If the price of Resitone were reduced, it would be difficult to make up the profit loss through increased sales. A 5 percent reduction would require a 40,000 increase in patient load to maintain current gross profit. A 15 percent reduction would require a 141,000 increase in patient load. Approximately 750,000 diabetics were currently on Resitone. Such a high percentage increase would be difficult to achieve.

CASE QUESTION

What changes in the marketing strategy for Resitone should Rector Pharmaceuticals make?

CASE 5–2

Michigan State Apple Commission*

Decision on how best to utilize increased promotional budget

In January, 1968, Mr. F. G. Hasler, secretary-manager of the Michigan State Apple Commission, was reviewing his promotional budget for the 1968–69 fiscal year, which would begin July 1, 1968. This work was particularly important for the Michigan State Apple Commission and its secretary-manager, because the Michigan apple producers and processors, at the request of the Michigan State Apple Commission, were to vote in March on an increase in assessments to enable the Commission to expand its advertising and promotional program. Mr. Hasler was faced with the problem of how best to utilize the increase in his promotional budget which might occur if the increased assessment passed.

History of the Apple Commission

The Michigan State Apple Commission was created by the Baldwin Apple Act in 1939 as one of many similar commissions in all apple-producing areas in the United States. Its sole purpose, like the other commissions and the national trade association, The National Apple Institute,

---

* Written by Bradley D. Lockeman, Assistant Professor, Idaho State University.

was to promote the use of apples. Although it was a state government agency, the Commission was financially supported through assessment of Michigan apple producers. Initially the apple growers were assessed 1 cent per bushel sold, but this levy was raised to 2 cents in 1955. In 1958 it was changed to 6 cents per hundred pounds of apples sold for fresh market use and processing. Producers who sold apples for juice, cider, or vinegar (by far the least lucrative use of apples) were exempt from payment. Any other producers who did not wish to participate could claim exemption and receive a rebate of their contribution to the Commission during the fiscal year.

Trends in apple consumption

Although the meaning and usefulness of statistics on per capita consumption of apples were much disputed, particularly by Mr. Hasler, it appeared evident that the apple industry had for some time been faced with a steadily declining primary demand. From 61.3 pounds per year in 1909, national per capita consumption had declined to 19.3 pounds per year in 1954 and 15.9 pounds by 1966. Michigan consumption was slightly, but not significantly, above the national average. With the increased use of refrigerated railroad cars and other modern methods of handling produce, the more perishable fruits, mainly citrus, had become available in all markets throughout the year. Fresh Michigan apples competed not only with these increasingly available citrus fruits, bananas, and pears but also with apples produced in such other regions of the United States as New York State, Appalachia, and Washington State, which had its own apple commission to advertise "Washington, the world's finest apples." Michigan apple products, which consisted primarily of applesauce, frozen slices, and various forms of juice, had become increasingly important in the market, but so had competing items: new frozen and dehydrated citrus products, as well as frozen slices and juice produced outside of Michigan.

Mr. Hasler was not particularly worried about the apparent long-range decline in consumption of apples. In the first place, he doubted the validity of the high per capita consumption figures recorded earlier in the century. Second, by the end of World War II the effect of competition from citrus fruits had been felt in all markets, and he believed that the rate of decline in apple consumption was decreasing so rapidly that per capita consumption would soon level off and stabilize. This belief seemed to be supported by a study which showed that processed apple products in 1966 were gaining in acceptance, while fresh use was remaining about the same. Since 1957, there had been only a 5 percent drop in the number of fresh apples eaten in the entire country. And although only one family in five, or 20 percent, was believed to use apples regularly, about 95 percent had purchased some fresh apples within the preceding 12 months, according to a nationwide survey of homemakers.

The market

The Michigan apple market covered the United States from eastern Ohio to the western Dakotas and from the Gulf of Mexico all the way up to and including parts of Canada. The heart of this mid-American market was the territory north of Nashville, Tennessee, west of Cleveland, Ohio, and east of Fargo, North Dakota. This market had generally absorbed nearly 100 percent of the fresh apples produced in Michigan, although apples from other apple-producing regions of the United States competed with Michigan apples in this same market. This was the territory where Michigan enjoyed the greatest transportation advantage over other apple-producing regions of the United States. East of Cleveland, the Michigan apple growers faced a transportation disadvantage compared to the situation of competing growers in the Appalachia area and New York State. As a result, Michigan apples had not usually been able to compete effectively in the eastern states.

The size and composition of the crop in each U.S. apple-producing region determined to a large degree the boundaries of the market which each producing region carved out and attempted to serve each year. If one apple-producing region had a bad crop in one year, another region was almost certain to exploit the situation and extend its own sales efforts into the other's market.

Whenever the Michigan Apple Commission's market expanded because of an abundant supply of apples, the expansion was usually into the southern states of Georgia, Alabama, and Florida—rather than westward—because there were more people immediately to the south than to the west and because any expansion to the west encountered increasingly stiff competition from the powerful Washington State Apple Commission which enjoyed almost national distribution. In years when the Michigan growers did not exploit this tri-state southern market, it was usually served by apple producers in the Appalachia region or New York State. These three southern states were thus supplied as a rule by apple producers in Washington, Michigan, Appalachia, and New York.

The state of Michigan ranked third among the states in commercial apple production in 1965, and the value of apple production in that year was nearly $25 million. Approximately 75–80 percent of this apple production was sold outside the state. About half the fresh apples sold in the Detroit metropolitan market originated in Michigan, this proportion increasing during the fall harvest season and decreasing in late winter and early spring. In remote parts of the Michigan growers' market or places closer to other apple-producing regions of the country, the proportion of Michigan apples to those originating from other regions was apt to be somewhat less than half, dropping to one sixth or one seventh at times in a few of the markets in the South. About 60 percent on the average of all apple products sold in the heartland market were processed from Michigan apples.

Fifteen years earlier each Michigan grower had sold his apples independently to jobbers and wholesalers in the area, but by 1960 a change had occurred in the marketing structure. The producers had formed sales organizations. These were private corporations made up of perhaps ten principal producers, with some growers as associate members who had merged their selling efforts to effect economies in operations and to obtain better quality control through centralized packaging, sorting, and handling. It was estimated that in 1968, five sales organizations made more than 50 percent of the sales of fresh Michigan apples; a large part of these sales went to chain store buyers.

Consolidation had also taken place in the buying practices of most chain food stores. For example, at one time each of 20 Kroger divisions had bought Michigan apples directly from the growers. In 1965, a centralized purchasing department bought all of Krogers' requirements for all of their divisions, a change that eliminated most of the contact between the food chain divisions and the Michigan Apple Commission's members. Similar consolidations in the market had taken place with most of the Commission's other large chain customers, such as A&P and Safeway. Mr. Hasler felt that as a result the sales organizations had lost some rapport with consumers and some of their ability to tailor offerings to the needs of a particular supermarket division or locality, where different types of fresh apples might be desired or where some uses might be more prominent than others.

The Michigan State Apple Commission had achieved some success in developing Michigan apples into a standardized product through its efforts to establish standard grading and to reduce the number of varieties produced. In 1945, ten major varieties were grown in Michigan, but by 1955 the number of major varieties had been reduced to four— Jonathan, McIntosh, Delicious, and Northern Spy. Since about 85 to 90 percent of the Northern Spy apples were used for cooking or for processing, these apples were not generally sold for fresh consumption as were the other three varieties.

Price

The prices that a producer obtained for one hundred pounds of apples were largely determined by the demand for a particular variety and the supply available at any given time, although prices did not invariably increase to reflect a rising demand, especially in the short run. Consequently, even if demand increased as a result of the Commission's promotional effort, the price to grower would not necessarily increase, since pricing was beyond the control of the Commission. While the Commission had suggested from time to time that the number of apples available and the rate at which they were selling would justify higher prices, the processors and growers were under no compulsion to follow the Commission's suggestions; and there were times when the quantity demanded in the market increased without any attempt by the growers to exploit the situation by charging more for their apples.

The marketing of fresh apples had been characterized in the past by an excessive supply and a concentration of sales in the months of October, November, and December, when most of the apple crop was harvested. This problem had been alleviated by controlled-atmosphere storage. By means of this modern innovation in inventory methods, fresh apples could be sold throughout the year. Apples can now be stored perfectly well for one full season—until the following November or December if necessary. Under laboratory conditions the storage period can extend to three years. Prices for apples from storage have generally been higher. While in the fall of 1967 producers received an average of approximately $3.50 per 40 pounds of fresh apples, in the spring of 1968 the apples sold from controlled-atmosphere storage brought an average of about $4.25 per 40 pounds.

The National Apple Institute

Promotion by the Michigan State Apple Commission complemented the primary promotion done by the National Apple Institute and paid for by the contributions from the members of the regional apple commissions belonging to the Institute. Beyond its political activities in representing the interests of apple growers in Congress and acting as a political watchdog for the industry, the National Apple Institute sponsored two distinctly promotional activities. It maintained the Apple Kitchen, essentially a public relations program, which for the last 15 years had produced a continual series of recipes, photos, and story material for public release through food editors across the country. A second promotional project engaging the interest of the National Apple Institute had been to teach schoolchildren to value apples for their taste, the part they can play in the care of teeth, and their importance to nutrition. Teaching aids, film strips, and other audio-visual aids had been circulated to school systems, health organizations, and other interested groups. Teaching guides on the same subject were made available to teachers, and advertisements were placed in national journals of education. Additional advertising space had also been purchased from time to time in medical and dental journals with national distribution.

The fact that the National Apple Institute performed these functions freed the Michigan Apple Commission's funds for additional promotion in the several remaining areas.

Promotional strategy

Back in 1955, H. F. Patterson, a former secretary-manager of the Michigan State Apple Commission, had expressed a definite opinion about the organization's promotional efforts, and these have obtained in a general way until the present time. He felt that the Commission's function was to ensure that apple merchandising by retailers at least keep up with efforts made for other fruits, or even surpass them if possible. He believed that the dealers must be continually convinced of the profits in good apple merchandising. In the attempt to stimulate consumption of Michigan apples, the Commission had therefore emphasized point-of-purchase promotion and had developed a point-of-purchase kit from which the average store could assemble an attractive display to be set up in the produce section to stimulate the purchase of apples. This kit could be easily used even by untrained employees, and it had been well accepted in previous years. Retailers received the kits free of charge at their direct request.

In its annual promotional campaigns, the Commission had extensively promoted these kits to retailers. An added push was given by two full-time merchandising representatives which the Commission maintained in the field, as discussed later. Experience had demonstrated that grocery retailers would sell more apples if they gave them a larger-than-usual display. According to a 1966 USDA national survey of homemakers, two thirds of the respondents said that high quality and attractive displays would have the most effect in encouraging purchases of fresh fruit.

Therefore, the Commission concentrated much of its effort on persuading retailers to give Michigan apples more display space during the season, and the promotion kit was used to further this objective. In the past the kits had succeeded in gaining adequate display space and point-of-purchase promotion for Michigan apples. Many retailers had also participated actively in building displays for contests sponsored by the Commission. During periods of greatest use of displays, grocers had reported that their sales of Michigan apples rose from 25 percent to 300 percent, with an average sales increase of around 75–100 percent. The greater sales were usually maintained to some extent for about three weeks after the promotion ended.

Relationship of budget to crop

Because the size of the assessment had not been increased since 1958, the funds available to the Commission to support all of its promotional activities depended on the size and composition of the apple crop each year. In general, the size of the crop had been increasing; and therefore the Commission's budget had been growing in total, even though the assessment rate in cents per hundred pounds of apples had not changed since 1958. Two notable exceptions to the consistent increase in production and in the contributions to the Commission's promotional budget occurred in 1966–67 and 1967–68. During 1966–67, many of the apples harvested were so small that they had to be used up in cider, vinegar, and juice. As a result, the Commission did not collect any revenue from the many small apples which were marketed for these uses. Although the apples harvested in 1967–68 were of normal size, they were fewer. For the second successive year the Commission's anticipated revenue did not fully materialize, and economies had to be effected, the principal source being cancellation of nearly all of the Commission's planned consumer advertising for the 1967–68 fiscal year.

Merchandising representatives

To assist in its promotional activities, the Michigan State Apple Commission had hired two full-time fieldmen or merchandising representatives in the early 1960s to work with wholesalers and large retailers. These representatives were to keep customers appraised of the number and variety of apples available in the market and provide point-of-purchase materials for retail apple displays. One of their key objectives was to get the cooperation of retail stores in setting up displays and utilizing the point-of-purchase materials which the Commission supplied. Each man covered half of the Michigan apple growers and processors' market, one handling the territory to the east and the other the territory to the west of the Mississippi River. These merchandising representatives mainly promoted fresh apples, although from May through August, that is, in the four months before the new crop of apples would become available, they promoted processed frozen apple slices, apple sauce, juice, and so on. The activities of these merchandising representatives reached only as far down as the divisional level of the Commission's large retail chain customers. Consequently, one of the Commission's two representatives might have called at the divisional headquarters of a retail chain to encourage the produce manager to push fresh apples and the grocery manager to push applesauce, but he would not call on individual retail store managers.

Marketing of processed apples

Over the past 10 years or more, there had been striking innovations in food processing and storage; and consumers had become more pressing in their demands for more convenient forms of food. As a result, Michigan apple growers and processors had witnessed a shift from fresh to processed apple products. Sharp increases had occurred in the quantity of apples that were being canned, frozen, used for vinegar, or processed in other ways. In the 1967–68 season, for example, 53 percent of the production was processed and 47 percent was sold fresh, whereas the percentages had been reversed only a few years before, and in the late 1950s, two thirds of the apples marketed by the Commission had been fresh. In line with this trend toward relatively greater sales of processed fruit, the Commission's point-of-purchase materials and other promotional efforts were being directed somewhat more at processed apple products rather than fresh apples, although since the processors tried to imitate the fresh product, it was felt that the promotional emphasis should still remain on the fresh fruit.

A survey conducted by Mr. Hasler in 1964 had indicated that the bulk of the Michigan's processed apples were sold either as applesauce or frozen slices. Of all the processed apples sold, 58 percent was marketed in consumer packs, usually under an A&P, Kroger, or other private label, and 42 percent in institutional packs.

More than 75 percent of the consumer-packed processed apples were in the form of applesauce. From time to time as funds permitted, the Commission had advertised at the consumer level to promote the sale of ready-to-serve applesauce. In addition to the spot radio or magazine ads which had been used in the past 10 years, the Commission also included displays about applesauce in some of the point-of-purchase materials it sent on request to retailers in its market area.

Of the 42 percent of all processed apples sold in institutional packs, 80 percent went to the wholesale market in the form of frozen slices. These could be shipped, stored, and put through many different final processes to appear in a large variety of consumer products, chiefly apple pies, TV dinners, frozen cakes, apple strudels, turnovers, and so on. The frozen slices were not promoted at the consumer level, since the consumer never saw the product in this form. They were, however, advertised to the food industry in the two leading monthly trade magazines, *Institutions* and *Cooking for Profit*.

Branding of fresh apples

Growers generally sold fresh apples, shipped in large wooden boxes, to packagers who sorted and graded the fruit before placing it in plastic bags, containing from 3 to 20 pounds. These were the packages that the consumers would ultimately find in their retail food stores. Because the Commission's marketing activities were less highly organized than many similar groups, fresh Michigan apples were not always marketed under a uniform brand name as are some other fruits, for example, California "Sunkist" citrus fruits. A few large Michigan growers attached their own trademark stickers to the crates of apples they sold; but the trademarks used by these growers were not the same from one grower to the next, and the practice was not widespread. The name "Michigan Flavorbest Apples" had been adopted by the Commission for promotion, and it was later registered as the Commission's trademark. But "Flavorbest" was not applied to all apples and apple products, nor was it used by as many growers and processors as the Commission desired. Information indicating what portion of the Commission's growers were actually using the Flavorbest trademark was not available.

While the Commission's registered trademark might be applied to the boxes of apples which were shipped from the producers to packagers, the trademark was primarily designed for use at the consumer level. Sometimes the packagers were permitted to use standard plastic bags printed with the trademark, "Michigan Flavorbest Apples." But many large purchasers demanded that apples be in their own bags displaying their own brand names. Both Jewel Tea and Kroger had specially designed bags, for example, and this precluded the use of the "Flavorbest" trademark on the package. Other retailers, however, allowed the phrase "Michigan Flavorbest Apples" to be used on the bag under their own brand name. In this way they could tie in with any point-of-purchase and consumer advertising promotions which might be sponsored by the Michigan State Apple Commission in their local area.

More and more frequently the Commission had been asked to drop the "Michigan" from the trademark in some of its promotions of processed apple products. This would mean that customers who bought fresh apples or frozen slices to reprocess would be free to obtain their apples from sources other than Michigan if necessary. In the interest of improving relationships with its members' large customers, the Commission had in some cases acceded to these demands.

1967–68 promotional program

By July 1, 1967, the promotional program and the budget for the 1967–68 fiscal year had been approved and put into effect, with the principal objectives of furthering the demand and sale of Michigan Flavorbest apples.

The Commission's fiscal 1967–68 budget totaled nearly $245,000. Funds were allocated roughly as shown in Exhibit 1.

The first three items listed in the 1967–68 budget were considered to be very nearly fixed from year to year, although if the new assessment proposal were to pass, it would eliminate the approximately $25,000 in rebates which the Commission would have to pay out in the next year. There was little change from one year to the next in the salaries paid to the Commission's headquarters personnel or in its operating expenditures.

The Commission's marketing information service, which was called "Michigan Apple Council," was established in 1960 to provide growers,

EXHIBIT I

Rebates to growers requesting exemption		$ 25,000
Salaries and operating expenditures		40,000
Marketing Information Services (Michigan Apple Council)		35,000
Merchandising, advertising and promotion:		
Fresh apple promotion	$49,000	
Processed-apple.programs	12,000	
Merchandising services:		
To National Apple Institute	$29,000	
Two merchandising representatives and P-O-P		
materials	45,000	
	74,000	
		135,000
Budget reserve		10,000
Total 1967–68 Michigan State Apple Commission Budget		$245,000

packagers, and processors with market information which would be useful as a guide to marketing decisions. Three biweekly reports were issued: (1) a storage report, showing the stocks of the various kinds of apples which were available at that time; (2) a bulletin telling of new promotions and marketing activities which might be of importance to the Commission members and their customers; and (3) a voluntary traffic association service for members, whereby sales people exchanged price and movement information for various grades of apples.

The really volatile portion of the Commission's budget, and the segment which was by far the largest, was the $135,000 allocated for merchandising, advertising, and promotion. By relying on these funds to absorb the fluctuations in income which were the result of basing assessments on annual sales, the Secretary-Manager could retain the personnel necessary to ensure continuity of operations at headquarters and the continuation of the marketing information services rendered by the Commission.

Of the $135,000 which had been allocated to merchandising, advertising, and promotion during the 1967–68 fiscal year, $49,000 went for trade advertising, display contests, sales incentives, point-of-purchase materials, and other special promotions for fresh apples. Nearly 70 percent of the $49,000, roughly $34,000, represented some form of point-of-purchase promotion, while the remaining $15,000 went for trade advertising. Three publications carried this trade advertising: *The Packer*, weekly trade newspaper; *Supermarket News*, a weekly tabloid; and *Produce Marketing*, a monthly magazine. Out of this $135,000, the Commission also continued its financial assistance to Michigan State University for the study of apple storage and maturity problems, co-sponsored the Michigan Apple Queen contest, participated in numerous national and state conventions, meetings, and seminars, and sponsored exhibits at trade shows and at the Michigan State Fair stressing Michigan Flavor-best apples.

Of the $12,000 allocated to programs promoting processed apples, $7,000, went for point-of-purchase material, while the remaining $5,000 was expended for trade advertising of frozen apple slices in *Institutions* and *Cooking for Profit*, the two leading monthly trade magazines distributed to the food industry. In prior years advertisements in these two magazines had produced many inquiries from buyers regarding institutional packed apples.

The final category in the promotional budget represented $74,000 worth of promotional expenditures labeled merchandising services. About $29,000 of this amount constituted the Michigan State Apple Commission's annual contribution to the National Apple Institute, of which the Michigan Commission was a member along with similar groups in New England, Virginia, New York, and another in western New York. The remainder of this $74,000 was used for point-of-purchase materials and to compensate the two merchandising representatives for their full-time work in the field to promote Michigan apples and reinforce the Commission's point-of-purchase efforts at the wholesale and retail levels.

The point-of-purchase kit, which was continued through the 1967–68 fiscal year, consisted of two display pieces. First was a large 14-inch by 18-inch die-cut display hanger in four colors, showing four big red apples and a bunch of green apple leaves, with "Michigan Flavorbest Apples" printed in white letters across the top. Any number of these die-cut pieces could be used together in the same display.

The second display piece was an 11-inch by 14-inch price card. The retailer could use this card to show the price of the apples in his display. Enough additional space was provided to accommodate the word "special" or some similar announcement. This display card came in eight different designs to allow a variety from which the retailer could select one suited to his individual needs. For example, one presented the idea of fresh apples as an "Instant Dessert—Just Polish 'n Serve!" Another might emphasize processed apples with a picture of applesauce and fresh sliced apples to make an attractive four-color display. All eight price cards suggested different uses for Michigan apples.

The 1968 display contest took place between January 15 and February 29 and was open to all retailers in the Commission's mid-American apple market. Entries consisted of a photograph taken in the contestant's retail store in which displays of Michigan apples were combined with the "Michigan Flavorbest Apple" point-of-purchase display material issued by the Commission. Contest photos were judged on sales appeal, originality, and appearance, and the first-place winner received a 1968 Chevrolet Camaro. Ten color-pack Polaroids were awarded to the runners-up. This program was aimed at getting produce managers to sell more apples in their stores; it was reasoned that most all the apples sold as a result of this regional contest would be Michigan apples.

Consumer advertising

As a result of budgetary restrictions, the Commission had found it impossible to do any consumer advertising during the past three fiscal years. In earlier years, when available funds permitted, the Commission had done some consumer advertising but only to promote fresh apples. Spot radio was the medium for most consumer advertising of fresh apples because of this medium's tremendous flexibility and the ease with which local retail stores could tie in with a tag line telling consumers where "Michigan Flavorbest Apples" were locally available. Spot radio had generally been used either to stress one variety of apple, such as Delicious—especially when the particular variety was in excess supply—or to give apples an extra push in some locality where sales had been sluggish or an oversupply had occurred. Blanket advertising had rarely been attempted by the Commission because it was much more economical to concentrate promotional effort in such larger cities within the market as St. Louis, Kansas City, Chicago, or Detroit. In addition, competition varied from region to region, and the Commission did not wish to advertise in regions where Michigan apples were particularly underrepresented and any benefits of the advertising might well accrue to producers and processors from apple-producing regions outside of Michigan.

Besides using its own taped radio jingle, the Commission had placed ads in regional editions of national magazines, including *Life, Ladies Home Journal, Women's Day,* and *Family Circle,* which were available in almost every market segment in the part of mid-America where Michigan apples were sold. Spot advertisements on color TV had also been considered for consumer advertising at one time, but they had never been used because of their high cost and the limited funds at the disposal of the Commission.

The planning for a consumer advertising campaign began with a meeting in March or April between the Commission and its advertising agency. After a consideration of alternatives and an estimate of the appropriation which would probably become available, a campaign would be in final shape about the end of June and completely locked in by the second week in July. The process of estimating the Commission's budget was made much easier by the U.S. Department of Agriculture's July 1 report on estimated production in September, October, and November. In February 1968, it was tentatively estimated that production in the 1968–69 fiscal year would surpass the previous year's 12 million bushels.

Promotional plans for the 1968–69 fiscal year

In laying plans for the 1968–69 fiscal year, which was to begin July 1, 1968, Mr. Hasler intended to continue putting major emphasis upon point-of-purchase materials and to assure that they would have a strong push from the Commission's two field merchandising representatives. The point-of-purchase materials were to be designed to attract attention in the retail stores. This appeal to retail customers appeared especially important in view of reports from recent surveys showing that most women did not use a shopping list but made their selections as they moved around the supermarket.

To complete the promotional picture in 1968–69, Mr. Hasler hoped the proposed assessment would pass so that the Commission could do as much consumer advertising as he felt was necessary to get the customer into the store to buy Michigan Flavorbest apples. The main emphasis would again be placed upon fresh apples; but each year processed apples had been getting a slightly larger share of the promotional budget, and for the first time in the Commission's 28-year history some consumer advertising would undoubtedly promote processed apple products.

The proposed revisions in the assessment would raise the rate to 8 cents per hundred pounds of apples sold for resale as fresh apples and 6 cents per hundred pounds of apples sold for processing. The apples which had been going for juice, cider, or vinegar—25 percent of the total tonnage—would bear an assessment of 2 cents per hundred pounds of apples sold for these uses. Finally, producers could no longer exempt themselves from paying the assessment; eliminating this provision would save rebating the payment of the $25,000 which had been refunded to growers who claimed this exemption in the preceding year.

The current assessment had provided the Commission with an average over the past five years of about $17,500 per million bushels of apples sold for all uses, or 1.75 cents per bushel. It was anticipated that the new proposal would yield $23,300 per million bushels of production, or 2.33 cents per bushel, if it were passed for the 1968–69 fiscal year. Mr. Hasler estimated that if the 1968–69 crop were the same as in the prior year, the new rate would bring in an extra $60,000. This could be devoted almost entirely to consumer advertising in the coming fiscal year if the increased assessment passed. It seemed probable, in fact, that the crop would be larger than the 12 million bushels produced during 1967 and that even more than $60,000 additional funds would become available for consumer advertising in 1968–69.

The following excerpt from the provisions and regulations of the proposal which was to be voted on in the March referendum provides the complete statement made by the Commission in its new assessment proposal regarding the objectives of its intended expenditures for advertising, promotion, and publicity:

The Committee will carry on or cause to be carried on such advertising, promotion and publicity programs as it may believe will create new markets for apples and for apple products or maintain present markets. Monies collected under this program shall be expended exclusively to advertise and promote and publicize the apple industry in fresh, processed and juice programs with a reasonable amount allotted to each.

One of the chief objectives of the Commission's consumer advertising, when it could afford to do any, had always been to get local retailers and chains to tie in with their own advertising and displays, and the Commission had merchandised its consumer advertising to the retailers throughout its market. Through such effort in the past, large chains had been persuaded to feature apples in their retail stores to coincide with consumer advertising placed by the Commission. If the assessment passed and additional funds became available for consumer advertising, Mr. Hasler hoped that the Commission's consumer advertising could be successfully merchandised to the retailers in its market area. In this way the benefit which might be realized from a very limited consumer advertising appropriation would be substantially increased.

In case the proposed assessment passed, Mr. Hasler was investigating the possibility of placing some four-color consumer advertisements in a large number of newspaper Sunday supplements to promote the increased use of fresh Michigan Flavorbest apples. As an alternative he was also thinking of using consumer advertising funds to purchase some spot radio time, as the Commission had done three or four years before. Flexibility would have to be the first consideration because of the impossibility of forecasting accurately in July the size and composition of the apple crop that would be harvested in September, October, and November.

Mr. Hasler hoped the assessment would pass. He felt that the Commission had fallen below the level of even its 1955 campaign because of inflation, a demand for more services by the growers, increased competition from organizations promoting other commodities as well as from others within the apple industry, and the increasingly large assessments levied against the Commission by the National Apple Institute. If the new assessment passed in March, the Commission planned to meet with its advertising agency to decide what might be done in newspapers or radio, or both, since each was capable of a different kind of promotion.

CASE QUESTIONS

1. *a)* Was there a profitable opportunity to stimulate the demand for Michigan apples through consumer advertising? Explain.

    b)   In the light of your analysis, had the Commission been wise in giving primary emphasis to the encouragement of point-of-purchase promotion in its past selling efforts? Why?

2.   If you were an important apple grower in Michigan would you vote to approve the proposed increase in assessment? Explain.

3.   If you were retained as a consultant by the Commission, what recommendations would you make as to an appropriate promotional strategy for Michigan apples?

4.   Did the Commission follow a sound approach in determining the promotional appropriation for Michigan apples? If your answer is negative, what approach would you recommend? Why?

CASE 5–3

Ford Motor Company (B) *

Planning promotional strategy for the 1972 Pinto

The Pinto economy subcompact was introduced by the Ford Motor Company in September 1970 to compete with the steadily growing influx of imported small cars. Early in 1971, at the end of the four-month introductory period, Ford Division executives and representatives of their advertising agency, J. Walter Thompson Company, were giving thought to the question of how to adjust the promotional mix for the Pinto in the 1972 model year. This group (identified here as the "Pinto team") was faced with a situation where their car was no longer "new" and with the realization that, to date, the marketing of new American subcompacts had produced no noticeable effect upon the growing share of the subcompact market achieved by the imports. New merchandising efforts were under perusal, along with a proposal to move away from the traditional "full line" selling patterns of American auto makers. Promotional budget levels for the Pinto were under consideration, as well as allocations of these funds among various types of demand stimulation effort.

---

   * Written by J. D. Lindquist, Research Assistant, Graduate School of Business Administration, The University of Michigan.

BACKGROUND

General

From 1967 to 1969 imported automobile sales in the United States surged upward from 7.3 percent of passenger vehicle sales to 11.0 percent. The overall compact, or economy, car segment of total car sales also had been growing throughout the period and, by the end of 1969, had reached 19.8 percent of total industry sales. The growth trend in both imports and compacts was detected prior to 1967 by Ford, and the Ford Division responded with two new vehicle developments. The major objectives of the Ford program were to attempt to stem the tide of the imports and to carve out a share of this expanding new market. In 1969 the Ford Division introduced its "simple machine," the Maverick. This vehicle was not intended to be a head-to-head match with the economy subcompacts, such as Volkswagen or Toyota, but was aimed toward the economy buyer who desired a little larger vehicle than was generally offered. Additionally, it was thought that some potential import buyers would be attracted to the car. Although a sales success, Maverick did not affect the continued surge of imported subcompact vehicles into the United States. In September 1971, Ford introduced Pinto, a true economy subcompact. The vehicle concept and design were products of extensive consumer research and were intended to meet the import challenge. A vehicle photo plus a list of major product features may be found in "Ford Motor Company (A)," page 191.

This new economy subcompact was targeted primarily at two competitors, the Vega and the Volkswagen. Additionally, consideration was given to efforts to win-over potential import buyers in general. Although not specifically supported with advertising copy, a push toward first-car buyers and multiple-car families was included in the firm's overall marketing strategy. A sales objective of 400,000 units was established for the 1971 model year along with a projection of 55 percent for incremental sales (i.e., 55 percent of Pinto sales to come from other sources than people who would have bought another Ford product).

Merchandising

The Ford Division sees merchandising as both a supplement and a complement to its advertising program. Merchandising is also used to presell dealers in a fashion similar to that of advertising presell of potential new car owners.

Merchandising is visualized by Ford as fulfilling three major functions. In a "Merchandising Strategy Presentation" made by Mr. M. S. Mc-Laughlin, president of Ford Marketing Corporation, and Mr. W. P. Benton, the general marketing manager of Lincoln Mercury Division, on November 12, 1970, merchandising philosophy was presented as follows:

Specifically, merchandising involves three major functions. The first is to maximize the effectiveness of the contact between the customer and our retail organization. We begin this activity each year with our new model introduction shows designed to presell our sales organization. Other activities, such as our salesmen training programs or our point-of-sale display materials, would also be examples of programs designed to accomplish this objective.

Another very important activity intended to improve the effectiveness of the contact between our dealers and customers is our contest and incentive activity. The specific nature of our contests or incentives, at any moment in time, is largely dictated by the sales situation. Sometimes we have a sales opportunity to exploit. Sometimes we have a problem which has to be solved. Sometimes competitive pressures make it necessary for us to respond . . . .

Our second function in merchandising is to communicate our national marketing strategy to our retail organization so as to encourage compatible and complementary dealer programs . . . . Our many dealer meetings throughout the year are designed to help accomplish our communication objectives.

Our third major function in the merchandising area is to provide an additional motivation for new car buyers to visit our showrooms. Special value vehicle promotions would be an example of the way in which merchandising attempts to build dealer traffic.

This, then, is a summary of the Ford Motor Company thinking, with regard to the merchandising side of the coin.

Advertising

The Ford Motor Division sees advertising as a device to communicate to prospective purchasers pertinent information about the product and as a means of placing specific products in line with the goals and needs of potential automobile buyers. Additionally, consumer advertising is seen as a tool to place properly the various vehicles of the Ford line with respect to their competition.

PROMOTIONAL MIX FOR 1971

Merchandising (customer-retailer contact)

To meet the first major merchandising function, maximizing the effectiveness of the contact between the customer and the retail organization, the Ford Team employed (1) introduction shows, (2) training, (3) recognition, (4) point-of-purchase materials, and (5) contests and incentives.

Introduction show. Work on the show for August 1970 began in October 1969. A single, combined effort for the dealers of the Ford Division, Lincoln–Mercury Division, and Ford of Canada was given in Las Vegas, Nevada. The show was built around the Pinto and the Lincoln–Mercury Comet and was held in the Convention Center. All the new cars were then put on display at the major hotels in town for further dealer perusal. Salesmen, this year, were shown an introduction film in the district headquarters' cities throughout the United States. An explanation of the 1971 marketing strategy was also given.

It should be noted that this show in Las Vegas was only the second time that a single effort has been employed by Ford. Most often in the past a travelling show had been used—generally, at the district or regional level.

Training. Training materials were prepared well in advance and were to be used by salesmen as an aid to selling the new product line. To boost salesmen's product knowledge, the company supplied (1) fact books used for training and reference, (2) records and sound-slide films that were to be coupled with reading materials, (3) news flashes offered on a periodic basis, and other printed matter. In addition to these actions, the Ford Division also held salesmen training sessions at district levels and, after the competitors had introduced their vehicles, additional training materials were provided in order for the dealer sales force to be informed of the relative position on product and price of the Ford line versus others. Competitive model comparison meetings were held in November 1970.

Although the training offered by Ford places major emphasis on product information, sales technique training has also been offered at dealer request.

Recognition. Commendable sales performance must be recognized in any sales organization, and this course was followed by the Ford Division. Programs were pursued which offer recognition to salesmen, sales managers, and dealers. Such awards as plaques, pins, and rings were offered. Such recognition served the twofold purpose of commendation for a job well done and fortification of the professionalism of recipients in the eyes of the prospective customer.

Point-of-purchase materials. Such items were used generally to tie in local actions with the national advertising theme at any given time during the sales campaign. These materials were also made available to dealers for individual promotional efforts. In the main, point-of-purchase materials are intended to be functional rather than decorative. Such items as color and trim books along with floor stand product-feature displays were provided as an aid to the prospective customer in his selection process.

With specific regard to Pinto, a do-it-yourself service manual was given to all buyers of this economy subcompact. Because of the potential buyer profile for this vehicle and in light of the general trends toward consciousness of cost of repair, this item served as an excellent promotional tool.

Contests and incentives. Generally, such efforts, though often costly, were used either to help in accomplishing specific marketing objectives and generating additional vehicle sales or to respond to the competition.

As an example, in a typical cash incentive program the dealers were assigned specific retail sales objectives, then the greater the fraction of the objective achieved, the greater the financial incentive earned. Exhibit 1 shows a typical dealer incentive program breakout. This might be employed to promote an individual car line and should have positive carry-over effects on other car lines.

Sometimes a retroactive payoff feature was incorporated, making the payoff considerably greater for the dealer.

Contests for sales managers, dealers, and salesmen were also significant tools in the merchandising plan at Ford. Dealer trip contests were used by Ford on a regular basis, typically sponsored for a two-month sales period. Winners were selected, based upon meeting sales objectives that were established especially for the contest duration. Generally, about 20 to 30 percent of all Ford dealers win such trips. Trip awards were based upon retail sales performance and not on wholesale purchases.

Of these merchandising actions cited, the dealers themselves picked up the cost of such things as (1) product training materials, (2) announcement showroom material and color and upholstery books, and (3) salesmen and dealer training costs. Also, the cost of some of the incentive programs had been shared by participating dealers, allowing corporation incentive dollars to go farther.

National marketing strategy communication

Actions to meet the goal of communication of marketing strategy to the retail organization included introductory business meetings, merchandising guides, periodic strategy meetings, monthly program summaries, and the new videotape system.

Business meetings. During new-model introduction, business meetings were held to provide the dealers with the market rationale for each of the new products. Additionally, the Ford team explained objec-

EXHIBIT 1
Typical dealer incentive program

Percent sales objective accomplished	Per unit incentive
0–50	$ 00
51–75	$ 25
76–99	$ 50
100+	$100

From November 12, 1970, Merchandising Strategy Presentation.

tives for the year and what the national marketing strategy would be. The objective of these meetings was to prepare the dealer to synthesize his own plans with the corporation objectives to provide the maximum of mutual effectiveness.

Merchandising guides. These merchandising guides provided the dealers with new-model marketing background information, an outline of the national strategy to be employed during introduction, and a series of action-plan sheets so that the dealers themselves could outline their own introductory plans. The dealer develops his action plan and then has the opportunity to have it reviewed by Ford's district sales organization.

With regard to Pinto, the dealers were asked to organize their show-room displays in order to take full advantage of the economy-oriented prospect traffic that was generated by this new subcompact. The Pinto plan also included information that was pertinent to ordering and stocking vehicles, training of salesmen, and some type of local advertising.

Strategy meetings. At periodic intervals throughout the year the district sales force management met with dealers to discuss the Ford Division marketing plans for the near future. Competitive comparison meetings were held in October and November to both review the price/product position of competitors and to review the program, to date, of Pinto and other Ford lines. This type of strategy session was held typically in January, the spring, and whenever a new major contest or incentive program was announced.

Monthly program summaries. These summaries were provided to dealers to indicate the programs then in effect, availability of marketing assistance, and suggestions as to what dealer action was appropriate in light of current national advertising efforts.

Videotape program. Videotape playback equipment was installed in all district sales offices. This system has been used to provide quick and consistent corporate guidelines and information to the field organization. The personal touch added by the videotape system was thought to have a strong advantage over the written word. Ford was considering the use of such a technique at the dealer level. Looking into the future, the Ford Team saw the possibility of live telecasts through the use of a closed-circuit television system.

Customer motivation

The final major merchandising function pursued was that associated with attempts to provide customers with additional motivation to visit dealer showrooms. Steps taken to meet this challenge included prospect lead-locator programs, joint or tie-in promotions, product displays, special value vehicle promotions, local market support, and other special activities.

Lead-locator programs. Market research indicated that one out of four introductory showroom visitors would purchase a new car within six months; therefore, tracking these people was essential. To acquire the names of such people, a visitor registration program was instituted. In the case of a Pinto, a Pinto key was offered to all who would register during the introductory period. The key included such things as a spark gap measuring device, a Phillips screwdriver, a regular screwdriver, and a small ruler. The Pinto registration form served as a recontact form for salesmen during the "follow-up" phase of the selling program.

Product displays. Ford participated in the major auto shows in Chicago, Dallas, Detroit, Los Angeles, and New York—and also in many other markets. As a matter of fact, Ford won the first-place award for its display in the Dallas show. The significance of these shows should not be underestimated in that millions of new-car prospects attend and often pay from $2 to $3 to do so.

As part of the guide entitled "Full Line Merchandising for 1971," the Ford Division provided showroom auto display suggestions as a function of showroom floor capacity. (See Exhibit 2 for an excerpt from this guide.)

Joint or tie-in promotions. This type of effort had been pursued by Ford in the past and generally consisted of joint ventures with com-

EXHIBIT 2

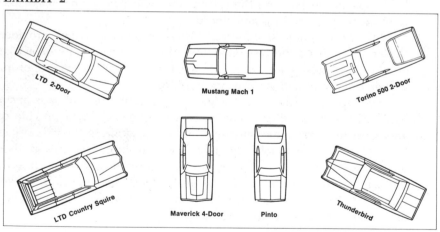

ADDITIONAL SUGGESTED SHOWROOM DISPLAYS

5-CAR	9-CAR	11-CAR
Pinto	Pinto	Pinto
Maverick 2-Door or 4-Door	Maverick 2-Door or 4-Door	Maverick 2-Door
Mustang SportsRoof or Hardtop	Mustang Mach 1 or Hardtop	Maverick 4-Door
Torino 500 2-Door	Torino GT	Mustang Mach 1 or Hardtop
LTD 2-Door	Torino 500 2-Door	Torino GT
	Galaxie 500 2-Door	Torino 500 2-Door
	LTD 2-Door	Galaxie 500 2-Door
	LTD Squire	LTD 2-Door
	Thunderbird	LTD 4-Door
		LTD Country Squire
		Thunderbird

plementary products to promote the respective offerings. During the month of September, Pintos were displayed in 200 large Sears stores throughout the United States, along with a Sears line of Pinto-styled women's sportswear. About 15 million people were exposed to the new Ford economy subcompact offering at Sears. Exposure to a higher income prospect group was achieved through "sneak peak" displays in 17 major airports for one month prior to introduction to the public in general. On the day of introduction, an actual vehicle was used to replace this teaser display. The airport effort was considered quite effective.

Special value vehicle promotions. Vehicles had been sold in the past with special trims, paints, or ornamentation—or, with option packages at a reduced price. Often direct-mail solicitation efforts by dealers were employed. These special values also offered the dealer's sales force an opportunity to talk about something new to prospects.

Local market support. Another method used to get more prospects into the showroom was to provide additional funds to support preapproved local programs. These programs were generally designed to handle unique problems and opportunities faced by a dealer.

Special activities. The Ford Division had sponsored the "Punt, Pass, and Kick" program for young boys, and over a million of these youths had participated each year. Another special program was a series of driver-education efforts supported by the company. Another effort of significance was the Cheerios' Pinto Toy Model Offer, whereby nearly 20 million Cheerios breakfast food boxes carried a special box-top offer for a free scale-model Pinto. The offer was promoted in supermarket chains and was seen as an excellent promotional device.

The Ford Division merchandising program, then, included such classic promotional tools as dealer promotion (reseller support promotion), personal selling, consumer promotions, point-of-purchase activity, joint or tie-in efforts, and sales force training. Note should be taken of the continued reference to support of national marketing strategy and national advertising.

Advertising

Advertising was used by the Ford Team to develop prospect awareness of the Pinto as a distinct entity, during the 1971 introductory campaign. This promotional tool was used to attempt to match this car with the prospect's needs for such vehicle qualities as economy, reliability, durability, safety, and comfort. The advertising actions taken were also used to attract prospects to Ford dealer showrooms and then to support subsequent personal selling efforts by salesmen. The major media vehicles used were television, radio, newspapers, outdoor, and magazines.

Promotional budget

The budget for the merchandising functions of the Pinto promotional mix was nearly $2.5 million[1] for the 1971 model year. To this figure may be added an additional amount as provided by the dealer organization which operates on an autonomous basis with funds collected from members. This dollar figure is unknown.

Approximately $10 million was allocated to the Pinto marketing group for advertising of the vehicle during the 1971 model year. During the introductory period about $4.5 million[1] was spent with an allocation among media as follows: 46 percent, television; 6 percent, radio; 15 percent, newspapers; 20 percent, outdoor; and 13 percent, magazines. Additional funds for cooperative-type local advertising were supplied by the dealer organization to its dealer members; no participation in this activity was undertaken by Ford.

The plans for the sustaining campaign from January through June of 1971 called for the breakdown in expenditures to be as follows: 50 percent, television; 23 percent, radio; 12 percent, newspapers; 2 percent, outdoor; and 13 percent, magazines. Funds for the entire January-to-August period were to be $5.5 million, with approximately $800,000 to be spent in July and August.

The dealer association planned to split its support of merchandising and advertising programs on a 90 to 10 basis.

Publicity

The Ford Motor Division was able to enjoy an unusual amount of publicity prior to, and during, the introduction of Pinto. The car was to be one of Detroit's answers to the import economy surge and, therefore, received more than its expected share of attention. As the campaign wore on, however, the amount of publicity offered the Pinto Team naturally diminished.

1971 INTRODUCTORY PERIOD RESULTS

The buyer—demographically

Exhibit 3 indicates comparative buyer demographics for Pinto versus its prime competitors for the four-month period after introduction.

A comparison of the demographic profile of the Pinto buyer with buyers of similar vehicles indicated the following:

1. The Pinto had been attracting buyers essentially the same as those who were initially attracted to Maverick.

---

[1] Author's estimate.

EXHIBIT 3
Buyer demographics

	1971 Pinto	1970 Maverick	1970 VW Beetle	1970 Toyota	1970 Datsun	1970 Average new car buyer
Age						
Median age............	33	34	28	32	31	42
Percent age 55 or older...............	7	9	5	7	11	21
Income						
Median income (×1,000)............	$12.5	10.5	10.5	12.0	10.8	12.1
Education						
Percent with some college or graduates.....	64	57	60	64	62	51
Sex and marital status						
Percent male..........	70	67	68	72	78	78
Percent married.......	68	67	71	79	75	74
Occupation						
Percent professional, technical, and managerial..........	42	42	40	38	44	38
Car ownership						
Percent multiple car....	73	65	66	70	74	62
Percent first new car....	31	36	NA	NA	NA	NA
Sample size.............	4,397	5,460	123	175	143	19,652

Ford Division Buyer Questionnaire, cumulative four months after introduction (Pinto and Maverick). *1970 National New Car Buyers' Study* (all other car lines).

2. Pinto buyers resemble import buyers in most aspects, with the exception of relative income.

Research also indicated that Pinto buyers were small-car oriented and that the most frequently mentioned makes seriously examined before purchase of Pinto were subcompact vehicles.

Sales results

The General Motors (GM) strike had an impact on the competitive situation in that it appeared to affect the sale of all automobiles, particularly American makes. As a direct result of the 10-week shutdown, Chevrolet sold only 22,363 Vega sedans, whereas Ford sold 76,038 Pintos. The positive effect of the GM strike on Pinto sales was not assessable. The other primary American competitor, the American Motors Gremlin, sold 39,701 units in 1970. Japanese imports continued their surge forward during 1970, as can be seen from Exhibit 4.

Import sales for 1970 totaled 1,230,961 units. This gave the imports a 14.7 percent share of all passenger car sales in the United States. The sales goal of 400,000 Pintos for the entire 1970 model year implied

EXHIBIT 4
Import new-car registrations in the United States in 1970

Manu- facturer	1970 registrations*
Volkswagen	569,182
Toyota	184,898
Datsun	100,541
Opel	83,189
Volvo	44,630
Fiat	36,642
Renault	19,584

* Data from *Automotive News Almanac* for 1970.

that sales of about 120,000 units[2] should have been sold during the introductory period. This figure was not met—probably due to general economic conditions, the GM strike, and the selling strategy employed by the Ford team. The incremental sales goal of 55 percent was ambitious considering past history, which indicated that 20 to 30 percent would have been more appropriate. As of December 31, 1970, however, the actual incremental sales level was 30 to 40 percent.

As an aside to the sales picture, the Ford executives noticed that within about one month after the Pinto was put on sale, the subcompact market seemed to be dividing itself into a luxury subcompact and an economy subcompact segment. The former class appeared to be emerging about the $2,000+ vehicles, with the latter in the $1,500–$1,600 cost range.

Merchandising results

In general, the merchandising efforts of the Ford Motor Division were successful. However, the Pinto Key Program was considered generally ineffective. This conclusion was reached as a result of poor dealer follow-up and the fact that the people attracted by the key were not seen as the same as those who would ultimately be interested in purchasing the car.

The sales strategy of switching customers to other Ford vehicles also resulted in lower sales of the Pinto.

Advertising results

From the standpoint of awareness of the Pinto as an entity and of placing it with respect to the remainder of the Ford line, the campaign was successful. The effects of the selling and advertising strategy combined on the sales of Pinto through December 31, 1970 was difficult, if not impossible, to assess.

[2] Author's estimate based upon historical seasonal trends.

PROMOTIONAL STRATEGY FOR THE 1972 MODEL YEAR

Early in 1971, Ford executives and their advertising agency representatives at J. Walter Thompson Company were faced with the problem of determining both the promotional mix for 1972 and the allocation of funds among the various promotional facets. Of particular interest were new merchandising alternatives in such areas as customer motivation and selling strategy, and budgetary size and allocation. The underlying assumption was that the target market for the 1972 model should remain relatively unchanged from 1971, with the exception of renewed interest in those people who might be Japanese-import prospects. Also, the promotional strategy was seen as being affected only in a minor way if the Pinto line were broadened somewhat and/or if the line were to include new option packages (i.e., rally options, etc.).

MERCHANDISING FOR 1972

In the fall of 1970, several merchandising methods were suggested for consideration by the Ford team. Although not all the following were implemented, ideas suggested included:

1. *"Rent-a-Pinto."* A possible plan for exposing more prospects to the vehicle through an actual test drive would be to offer an incentive to car rental agencies to offer and promote the renting of Pintos.
2. In order to get a picture of this economy subcompact in front of a wide audience, the suggestion was made that the small, single-serving sugar packages found in restaurants be embossed with a Pinto photo. A successful program, identical in nature, was used for Maverick.
3. A consumer promotion that would lead to an all-expense-paid vacation for two to somewhere such as Hawaii was also proposed. "Let Pinto, the little long-distance car, send you on a long-distance trip," or some other similar vignette, could be the key phrase in a sweepstakes contest tied to a test drive of the Pinto.
4. *"Pinto-to-the-people"* (PTTP) was another project under consideration by the Ford–J. W. Thompson team. The objective of this program would be to bring the car to the customer, rather than the usual reverse. Basically, demographics of the potential target market would be used to identify appropriate locations for the PTTP team to bring vehicles for test driving. Possibly, shopping centers or other similar locations could be used. Local salesmen would then offer short, test drives to anyone interested. Meanwhile, activities to keep the children occupied, such as pony rides or other attractions, would be available at no cost to the test drivers. A brief registration form would be filled out by the drivers for follow-up at a later date.

The program would bring the Pinto to the people instead of expecting them to come to dealer showrooms for test drives.

These, then, were a few of the possible merchandising activities that could be pursued by the Ford Division in support of the 1972 Pinto.

The Pinto selling strategy for the 1971 introductory period was summarized in these few lines from "Full Line Merchandising, 1971":[3]

If a Pinto shopper shows evidence of interest in another Ford car, don't miss the opportunity to sell him. The 2-door Maverick—either '70 or '71—is a natural switch unit. Quite possibly, he could buy a larger '70 model for less than he'd pay for a new Pinto. The '71 Maverick will be priced so that he can move up for about five dollars to seven dollars a month more . . . .

The 1971 strategy, then, was to push selling up from Pinto to other Ford lines.

Within the ranks of the Ford executives there were basically two opinions concerning how to sell Pinto. One, obviously victorious throughout the introductory period, took the position that "full line" selling is of paramount importance, and that this approach will lead to the greatest division profit levels. The opposing camp, which appeared to be gaining more support for the sustaining period (January–August 1971) felt that a hard sell of Pinto is appropriate in order to stem the import tide. Also, the group stated that sufficient sales of Pinto could be generated to offset the inevitable cannibalization effects that would result. This basic question, then, had to be decided with regard to the 1972 model year campaign.

PROMOTIONAL BUDGET

Allocation

The budgetary split between merchandising and advertising at the Ford Division level for Pinto in the 1971 model year was 20 to 25 percent for merchandising versus 75 to 80 percent for advertising. A measure of the relative dollar effectiveness of these two promotional categories, with respect to the sales goals of the company, was difficult, if not impossible, for the Pinto team to assess. They must, however, determine whether or not to continue this division of funds in planning the promotion of the 1972 Pinto. In light of the possible strategy switch (from "selling up" to "hard sell") under consideration, additional dealer stimulation would appear to be required. The costs of such a decision, coupled with the costs of some of the other suggested merchandising efforts, such as the "PTTP" program, could significantly affect fractional allocation of available funds.

---

[3] A Ford Division guide for dealers.

Size

It is interesting to note that the two major foreign competitors of the Pinto, namely Volkswagen and Toyota, spent $25,036,000 and $12,000,000 respectively on advertising in 1969; and it is estimated that 1970 spending for these brands was even higher. On the other hand, the Pinto allocation for the 1971 model year was somewhere near $10,000,000. At the $10,000,000/year level, with approximately $4,500,000 spent in the first four months, only 76,000 Pintos were sold toward a goal of 400,000 units for the year. (Granted, sales were affected by the General Motors strike, economic conditions, and the "sell up" policy.) Accordingly, a suggestion had been made that Ford double the Pinto advertising budget to $20,000,000 for the 1972 model year, and this proposal was being considered by the Pinto team in their preliminary planning sessions.

CASE QUESTIONS

1. It has been proposed that the Pinto team adopt the policy of selling the 1972 Pinto aggressively, as opposed to continuing the "full line" selling approach. Doubling the promotional appropriation would be an expression of this philosophy. Would you recommend such an approach? Why or why not?

2. Four proposals for merchandising the Pinto are outlined above. Which of these suggestions, if any, would you recommend that the Pinto team adopt? Why?

3. What should be the relative allocation of funds between merchandising and advertising for the 1972 Pinto? Explain.

CASE 5-4
Midwest Precision Corporation*
Relation of distribution policy to selling strategy

The Midwest Precision Corporation of Jackson, Michigan, was a small manufacturer of industrial casters and materials-handling trucks. The products were sold direct to users within 300 miles of Jackson and through materials-handling equipment distributors in other industrial areas in the United States. After reviewing the firm's progress during the previous five years, Mr. W. A. Bootes, president, was seeking ways of expanding his company's sales volume.

History

The company was founded by Mr. Bootes shortly after World War II. Its plant consisted of a large corrugated steel-sided building where from 12 to 24 men worked, and an attached two-room cinder block building where 3 men and a girl administered the business. The firm had sales of about $350,000.[1]

Midwest made a complete line of medium and heavy-duty casters for use on materials-handling equipment. The casters were precision made of high-quality bearings, bushings, wheels, and other parts, to withstand heavy loads. Practically all of the casters were a standard product, i.e., they were nearly the same in design and quality as those of competing brands. They were sold to industrial firms who made their own materials-handling equipment and to equipment manufacturers. The casters were used on platform trucks, dollies, bins, racks, and so on. Other applications of these casters were limited. Casters for furniture and light weight equipment were of different design, and conveyor manufacturers made their own casters. The 5,000 to 7,000 casters sold each year constituted about 40 percent of the company's dollar sales.

As time went by, many industrial firms that had formerly made their own materials-handling equipment and equipped it with Midwest casters began to buy their handling equipment complete with casters, and many equipment manufacturers began to make their own casters. Therefore, in order to become more competitive with the caster manufacturers

---

* Written by L. B. Milliken and Peter Repenning, Research Assistants, Bureau of Business Research, The University of Michigan.

[1] Sales figures have been multiplied by a constant.

who also made complete equipment, and in order to maintain volume production of casters, Midwest began making complete materials-handling trucks. It produced flat trucks, trucks with sides, and trucks for special racks or bins. Some were hand trucks and others were pulled in trains. About 50 percent of the cost of some trucks was in the casters. Although Midwest lost a few of its caster customers when it began competing with them in the sale of trucks, total dollar sales did not suffer. Trucks accounted for about 60 percent of the firm's sales.

The casters varied in price from $25 to $75 for a set of four, and trucks were sold for $60 to $300 including the casters.

Potential market

Mr. Bootes believed the potential market for Midwest casters and trucks covered all industrial areas in the United States. His casters could be used by any maker of medium-sized or heavy-duty materials-handling equipment. There was some variation in the quality of casters, but those produced by Midwest and its competitors were of uniformly high quality. There were some price cutters in the industry, but they were makers of lower quality casters and so were not really competitors. The leading manufacturers belonged to a trade association which had successfully promoted the idea of nonprice competition. Since the competitors had nearly uniform quality and prices, caster sales volume was dependent on sales ability and service. Practically all industries provided a potential market for Midwest trucks, but thus far all sales had been to auto manufacturers around Detroit. Midwest was small and a comparative newcomer in the market. It had about 1 percent of the industry sales. Among its larger competitors were the Rose Truck and Caster Company in Detroit; Albion Industries in Albion, Michigan; and the Bassick Company of Bridgeport, Connecticut.

Sales methods

Midwest casters and trucks were sold in two ways. Mr. Bootes and his assistant, Mr. Carpenter, sold direct to users within an area of about 300 miles from Jackson. The main customers in this area were the auto manufacturers around Detroit, including Ford, Chevrolet, Buick, Cadillac, and Fisher Body. The company supplied casters and trucks to all Ford plants in the United States, and the business was about 50 percent of all Midwest sales. About 75 percent of total sales were made by Mr. Bootes and Mr. Carpenter in the area.

The other 25 percent of sales were in casters sold by 20 materials-handling equipment distributors and 10 manufacturers' agents in major industrial centers. The distributors usually handled one or two lines of trucks, casters, conveyors, lift trucks, racks, and containers. They had warehousing facilities and did limited fabricating of special jobs for their customers. They delivered the equipment and often extended credit, which they refinanced at banks. Most of them had aggressive sales forces. Midwest often paid 50 percent of the cost of their advertising in telephone books, direct-mail pieces, and local trade papers. The manufacturers' agents usually handled the same line of products but performed none of the wholesale functions. They did no promotional work, but were considered quite aggressive salesmen. Midwest sold casters to both distributors and agents at 50 percent and 10 percent off list price. They in turn sold them at prices ranging from 30 percent to 50 percent off list, depending on the amount of business involved.

The main selling method used by Midwest and its distributors was personal contact with users of casters and trucks. In making a sale, usually the customer's industrial engineer or master mechanic was contacted first. He was shown the design features of the caster or truck. Then the purchasing agent was contacted and a price quoted or bid submitted. Since the quality of all brands of casters was about the same, the buying decision was usually made by the purchasing agent on the basis of price and service. In the Detroit area, Mr. Bootes and Mr. Carpenter worked with customers' engineers in designing casters or trucks for special applications. Mr. Bootes spent about 25 percent of his time selling and the remainder at the plant. Mr. Carpenter spent about 75 percent of his time selling.

Advertising and promotion

The company retained a small advertising agency, the Knickerbocker Press of Grand Rapids, to handle the promotion of its products. In regard to Midwest, the agency's objectives were to aid in:

1. Broadening and strengthening the dealer organization through advertising and personal selling by Midwest representatives.
2. Establishing brand-name recognition in industry through national trade journal and direct-mail advertising.
3. Increasing the sales volume through stimulation of inquiries which could be followed up by the distributors and agents.

Mr. Bootes and the agency agreed that advertising would not produce immediate sales increases. But since the company was a relative newcomer competing with well-established firms, they believed advertising to build recognition of the Midwest name was necessary.

To accomplish the objectives listed with the small appropriation available, the agency advocated the use of trade journal and direct-mail advertising. The theme of the space ads was that of inviting inquiries about Midwest casters. The ads contained pictures and factual information slanted toward industrial engineers. Many uses of the casters were listed. A direct-mail list was built from inquiries received and other lists purchased from trade journals. The mail pieces included a caster catalog, a card device which looked like a caster with windows cut in it so that the proper caster for any application could be "dialed" by turning the caster wheel, and several brochures describing specific casters and the trucks.

The company appropriated about $8,000 for promotion. About $3,500 was used for catalogs and direct-mail pieces. The remaining $4,500 was used for space advertising. Twelve 1/9-page ads were run in *New Equipment Digest* and also in *Equipment and Material Reporter.* The latter trade journal was circulated in 11 western states and had good circulation in the southern California industrial area. Mr. Bootes was very much interested in entering that market, but said that Midwest was not yet competitive there. The company was also listed in *Thomas' Register.*

Mr. Bootes was fairly well pleased with the results of Midwest advertising, although they were intangible. Sales had definitely increased over the past five-year period, but he did not believe much of the increase could be attributed directly to the promotion. The greatest sales increases had come from the Detroit area. The company usually received from one to five inquiries each day, and about 10 percent of the inquiries were converted to sales—some by the distributors and some directly by Midwest. Mr. Bootes was quite satisfied with the number of inquiries received but disappointed in the rate of conversion to sales. He did not have accurate information on whether these sales had covered the cost of advertising.

Efforts to increase sales volume

Although the firm had made progress during the previous five years, Mr. Bootes was concerned with the problem of how to stimulate an even greater rate of increase in sales volume. He and Mr. Carpenter were making 75 percent of the firm's sales direct to customers—mostly in the Detroit area. Sales by the distributors and agents in other markets were low in dollars and as a percentage of total sales. About one half of the sales were to the Ford Motor Company, so a more diversified customer list as well as increased sales was desired. There were two basic alternatives in the solution of the major problem. The firm could concentrate on the Detroit market and raise its sales direct to users. Or it could try to raise its sales through distributors and agents in other markets.

There were several advantages in selecting the first alternative. Through his contacts with other trade association members, Mr. Bootes knew many of them were making good profits on small sales in one industrial area. The company had done well in the Detroit market, and the fact that it had always been able to raise sales there by increased sales effort indicated that there was more potential for Midwest. Mr. Bootes and Mr. Carpenter knew the Detroit market well, were close enough to serve it well, and could control the sales effort there easily. One disadvantage of concentration there was the dependence on the auto industry, Ford in particular.

There were several ways of trying to raise sales in other industrial centers. The company could hire another salesman to sell direct in some of these areas. It could use space and direct-mail advertising to get more distributors and agents in other markets. Or it could try to stimulate the existing distributors and agents by having a Midwest representative call on them periodically and by sending advertising to them.

If another salesman were hired to sell direct in other areas, he would be paid a commission on his sales and given an expense allowance. Mr. Bootes did not know what the dollar cost of this compensation and allowance would be, or how much increase in sales would be necessary to cover the cost. He did know that the expense could not be met out of their current selling prices. He believed the cost of hiring a man could be covered if all advertising and promotion were eliminated. On the basis of the current promotion appropriation, there would have been about $8,000 with which to work.

Mr. Bootes believed it would be difficult to get more distributors through advertising. Most of the good distributors and agents in most industrial areas had long since been retained by Midwest's older competitors. Occasionally a distributor's salesman started his own business and sought sources of supply. Midwest had gained some good distributors and agents by retaining them. In general, Mr. Bootes believed top-quality distributors were not attracted by advertising.

Of course, the company desired to stimulate the sales efforts of the existing distributors and agents, but how to do it was not an easy problem to solve. The advertising agency believed Midwest should have a representative visit each distributor every six months. The representative would make calls with the salesmen to contact the users and advise the salesmen. It was believed such a visit would create goodwill and give the company opportunity to evaluate the distributors regularly. Although Mr. Bootes believed this was a good idea, he knew neither he nor Mr. Carpenter had time to do the traveling, and he thought it would cost $12,000 to $15,000 a year to hire the right man and pay his expenses. The company could not afford that expense.

Midwest had attempted to stimulate its dealers by using direct-mail pieces to merchandise its promotions. In the past two years, it had sent the distributors and agents pieces using such phrases as "We're on the ball," "Watch for ads . . . ," and "More volume and profits for you. . . ." These pieces had cost $150 for 500 copies, and Mr. Bootes believed that was too expensive for the effect created. In the future he planned to produce direct-mail pieces for the distributors to send to their customers.

After giving the matter considerable thought, Mr. Bootes decided to concentrate in the Detroit area first and build up sales in other industrial markets slowly. He believed about 10 of the 30 distributors and agents were doing a good job and decided not to worry about the others' performance until he had determined the success of the Detroit experiment. If it worked well, the poor distributors would be released. Mr. Carpenter's brother became a part-time salesman in the Detroit market. If sales rose enough, he would become a full-time salesman to sell in Detroit and other areas. He was paid a commission on his sales, and the expense was covered with funds formerly used in promotion. This required a reduction in the advertising appropriation for the coming year to $3,800. The firm's sales were still largely dependent on Ford, but increased sales to other auto manufacturers had added some stability.

CASE QUESTIONS

1. Appraise the distribution policy of Midwest. Would you recommend any changes? If so, why?

2. *a)* Would it appear to be profitable for Midwest to attempt to increase sales by concentrating on the Detroit market? Why?

   b) If this were to be done, what promotional strategy would you recommend? Why?

3. *a)* Does there appear to be a profitable opportunity to stimulate sales through giving emphasis to markets other than the Detroit area? Explain?

   b) If the firm were to follow this alternative, what promotional strategy would you propose? Why?

4. In the light of your analysis, do you agree with the president's decisions on promotional strategy to follow in order to achieve the desired sales increase? Explain.

5. How does the company's existing distribution policy influence decisions on appropriate promotional strategy?

CASE 5–5

The U.K. Monopolies Commission versus Procter & Gamble and Unilever*

Government recommendation to cut selling expenses

On Wednesday, August 10, 1966, the U.K. Monopolies Commission published a report recommending that Procter & Gamble and Unilever cut selling expenses, mainly advertising, by 40 percent on household detergents and pass the resultant saving on to the consumer in the form of a 20 percent cut in retail prices.

The major recommendations of the commission and the reaction of those involved were reported in the *Financial Times* and *The Times* on Thursday, August 11, 1966.

Producers to resist cuts in detergent prices[1]

Both Procter & Gamble and Unilever—together they hold 90 percent of Britain's £75 million-a-year household detergent market—intend to resist firmly any government request that they should cut their washing product prices by 20 percent.

This was made clear last night after Douglas Jay, president of the Board of Trade, had announced immediate discussions with the companies on ways to curb excessive advertising expenditure and bring down prices.

Mr. Jay told the Commons yesterday that he was in general agreement with a Monopolies Commission report, published earlier in the day, which declares that above-average profits are being made, prices are unnecessarily high, and too much is being spent on promotion.

Tough talks

The 20 percent reduction in wholesale selling prices for such products as Omo, Daz, Tide, and Persil is one of five main recommendations put by the commission before Mr. Jay, who has power to apply some form of price control.

---

* Excerpted from the *Financial Times* and *The Times*, both of London, England, by permission.
[1] By the Industrial Reporter of *Financial Times*, August 11, 1966.

E. Brough, chairman of Lever Brothers, the Unilever detergents enterprise, commented that he was aware that the two companies were about to be "strong-armed" by the government and that the forthcoming negotiations on implementing commission recommendations would be very tough.

Lever would enter the talks with a willingness to discuss matters, but it was its firm aim to convince the Board of Trade that there should be no reduction in prices.

A spokesman for Procter and Gamble stressed that it, too, had "major reservations," but naturally it would meet and discuss them with the Board of Trade at the appropriate time.

I understand that, even if the Board of Trade is able to frame a satisfactory formula to discourage excessive promotion, both companies will expect restrictions to apply to smaller and new competitors, such as Colgate-Palmolive and the Cooperative Wholesale Society.

Besides seeking price reductions, with the 20 percent figure as the basis for negotiations, the commission wants the Board of Trade to persuade the big producers to prune selling expenses by 40 percent. These expenses, including advertising, total over £16 million and are said to account for nearly a quarter of the final retail price paid by the housewife.

Yesterday, Mr. Jay was less forthcoming on this question. Guardedly, he stated: "While I shall continue to consider means of preventing excessive selling expenditure in the future, it will be open to the government to refer to the Prices and Incomes Board any increase in prices of household detergents which is thought to be unjustified."

At present, all household detergent prices are subject to a price freeze agreed on last autumn following a critical Prices Board report on costs, prices, and profits in the soap and washing-product industry.

Last night, both companies were strenuously defending their promotional policies. Unilever declared that research showed that housewives liked such things as premium offers and giveaway items, and it estimated that only about 10 percent of all housewives were conscious of price levels.

Procter & Gamble said modern advertising resulted in savings greater than their cost; and pointed out that the cost of Tide's TV advertising was only the equivalent of posting two postcards to every home in the United Kingdom each year.

At the same time both companies do not accept the view that they are making unduly high profits —53.2 percent on capital employed (historic cost basis), in the case of Procter & Gamble; and 23.4 percent for Unilever.

They intend to argue that a more realistic yardstick ought to be a calculation of profits earned according to sales. Lever declines to indicate its actual profit figure, but Procter & Gamble declared that it earned just over £5 million before taxes.

BIG CHANGES IN MAIN PRODUCERS' SELLING POLICIES CALLED FOR[2]

The Monopolies Commission yesterday recommended stringent changes in the selling policies of Britain's two major detergent producers—Procter & Gamble and Lever Brothers (Unilever group)—which, together, command 90 percent of the market.

In its 115-page report on the supply of household detergents, based on three years research and inquiries, the commission urges government intervention in reducing the scale of their promotional battle.

The policies pursued by both groups, on advertising and promotion and their price policies, are things done by them as a result of or to preserve their "monopoly" positions, which operate and may be expected to operate against the public interest.

But neither "monopoly" position, as such, operates against the public interest, nor may be expected to do so, the report states.

There are five main recommendations:

1. Substantial percentage reductions should be made in Unilever's and Procter & Gamble's wholesale selling prices for household detergents.
2. Appropriate reductions in these prices should be decided by the Board of Trade, in consultation with the two enterprises.
3. The Board of Trade should encourage the companies to agree that at least a 40 percent cut in selling expenses could accompany the price reduction.
4. In such event, consultations with the companies might well begin on the basis of an average 20 percent cut in prices.
5. For the longer term, the Board of Trade should consider the possibility of introducing some form of automatic sanction that would discourage excessive selling expenditure in the field of household detergents and should also continue to keep a watch on prices.

The largest suppliers

Setting out the background to its findings, the commission reports that the two principal manufacturers in 1964 accounted for about 90 percent of the total sales—96 percent of powders and flakes and 64 percent of liquids.

Sales in that year are shown in Exhibit 1.

The next largest suppliers are said to be Colgate-Palmolive, with

---

[2] *Financial Times*, August 11, 1966. Reproduced by permission.

EXHIBIT 1
Sales for 1964

	£ Million	Percent	Thousand tons	Percent
Unilever..................	30.4	44	195	45
Procter & Gamble..........	32.2	46	183	43
Others...................	7.1		50	
Total.................	69.7		428	

sales of £1.7 million, and the Cooperative Wholesale Society with just over £750,000.

Principal brands of the "big two" are named as:

Unilever. Persil and Rinso (soap powders), Omo and Surf (synthetic powders,) Lux (flakes), Lux Liquid, Quix and Sqezy (washing up liquid).

Procter & Gamble. Fairy Snow Soap and Oxydol (soap powders), Daz, Tide, Dreft (synthetic powders), Fairy Liquid (washing up liquid).

Post-war market

After tracing the history of the soap and detergent industry, including the acquisition of Thomas Hedley and Co. by the U.S.-controlled Procter & Gamble organization, the commission has concerned itself mainly with the postwar competition that developed when heavy advertising followed the introduction of synthetic washing powders in the early 1950s.

During the period 1954–56, both of the major suppliers adopted price cutting as a main means of competition, bringing about substantial changes in the market situation.

However, by June 1956, both companies are stated to have brought their prices into line for comparable products, and, since that time, the emphasis in competition has again been placed on advertising and sales promotion.

The commission finds that the central interest of its inquiry was in the methods by which the two companies competed with one another. Competition in advertising was not only one of the most striking features of the industry, from the public's point of view, but was also an extremely important element in their costs.

Balance of costs

Although some expenditure on promotion might result in cost saving elsewhere, the balance between promotion and cost saving achieved in the industry was not necessarily the ideal one.

While recognising that there had been improvements in the informative quality of labeling, the commission considers that promotional claims that might appeal to the more discriminating user usually gave way to those believed to be of more general appeal.

The two companies assumed that the housewife would be moved to prefer one brand over another, less by superior washing powers than by the competing attractions of the gifts which were part of many campaigns. These promotions distracted the customer's attention from the merits or demerits of the product and were "open to objection."

The commission reports that Unilever and Procter & Gamble in 1964 spent something over £8 million each on selling expenses (principally advertising, sales promotions, and market research) as shown in Exhibit 2.

EXHIBIT 2
Unilever and Procter & Gamble sales for 1964–65 (£ millions)

Unilever		
Factory cost		16.6
Selling expenses		8.3
Advertising	4.0	
Promotions	2.2	
Market research	0.5	
Sales expenses	1.6	
Distribution, research, and administration		2.8
Profit		2.7
Sales		30.4
Proctor & Gamble		
Factory cost		16.7
Selling expenses		8.7
Advertising	3.8	
Promotions	3.3	
Sales expeness and market research	1.6	
Distribution, research, and administration		2.7
Profit		4.1
Sales		32.2

Source: *Financial Times*—Thursday, August 11, 1966. Reproduced by permission.

Quarter of price

In terms of the final retail price, the commission points out that nearly one quarter of what the customer paid for the product was expended on manufacturers' selling expenses. This evidence forced the conclusion that there could be no doubt that the level of advertising and promotion expenditure in the household detergent industry was "exceptionally high."

The commission finds it a matter of concern that competition between the two leaders should be in the form of advertising and promotion competition, which was reflected in the level of their selling expenses and, ultimately, in their retail prices.

The manufacturers claimed that their expenditure in this field was not wasteful, since there were compensating economies in their production, other costs, and in retailers' margins. This was not disputed, and the commission does not doubt each company was able to make its products at a unit manufacturing cost which was lower than it would be if demand for the brands concerned had not been built-up by national advertising.

"It does not seem to us to follow that extra advertising and promotion undertaken by Unilever and Procter & Gamble to maintain their market shares against each other, result in extra economies elsewhere," states the report.

Price cutting by retailers

"So far as the retail margin is concerned, we think that there has been some effective reduction, on the average, in recent years because of an increase in price cutting by retailers," says the report. But the commission does not think that this, in itself, can be taken to justify the whole of the present advertising and promotional spending.

Dealing with the question of other producers, the report declares that it is difficult to see any reason, other than that the terms of entry are too onerous, why a profitable field should, with the exception of liquid detergents, have been left largely to the hands of two enterprises.

Deterrent

Some of the more obvious potential competitors, such as the large chemical manufacturers, were probably not deterred by the mere size of the initial investment required; but they might well feel reluctant to participate in, and perhaps intensify, the process of competition in promotional expenditure.

Several companies did participate in the washing up liquid field, but not in powder detergents. "We are indeed a little surprised that multiple stores which market their own brands of liquid detergents do not, as a rule, market their own brand of powders," declares the report. "It is certainly not impossible for them to buy powder detergents, either in bulk or made-up to their requirements, and when selling in their own stores they can avoid the kind of advertising and promotional costs that are incurred by Unilever and P&G. We think that the expenditures incurred are unnecessarily high, and that one effect is to keep new entrants out of market."

The commission accepts, in principle, that where two suppliers of comparable strength were competing for a similar market, neither could expect to retain, for long, any price advantage over the other—so prices tended to come together. This ought not to mean that neither party should ever seek to obtain such an advantage.

Quality differences apart, there were effective variations and differences in price from time to time. First, that was because there was no uniformity in the quantity of product offered at a given price, and second, because of temporary promotional price cuts.

Each company asserted that it earned its profits on household detergents by efficient production and distribution, which it was impelled to improve from year to year—not only because of the competition offered by the other, but also because if it were to relax efforts it would provide an opening for new competitors.

Rates of profit

Both companies said their prices had not increased as fast as the cost of living in recent years, but the downward trend in liquid detergents tended to disguise the trend for other products.

The commission estimates that Unilever's profit in 1965 on its household detergents business (5 percent of group business) was 23.4 percent on an historic cost basis and 16.4 percent on a replacement cost basis. For Procter & Gamble the figures were 53.2 and 37 percent respectively.

Figures resulting from calculations by the commission are said to demonstrate, without doubt, that Procter & Gamble earned rates of profit very much above the average from manufacturing industry on the basis of capital employed. Unilever achieved results which, though lower than its competitor, were substantially above the average for manufacturing.

Escalation of costs

The commission considers that selling costs play a more significant part than manufacturing costs in determining the pattern of prices. Its view is that competition between the two tends to result in the escalation of advertising and promotion costs—resulting in over-concentration on promotion to the detriment of effective, direct price competition and in unduly high profits—with the consequence that the public is charged unnecessarily high prices.

"If competition can be diverted from excessive advertising and promotion to prices, we believe that the result will not only be a saving in cost but also a more effective check upon profits than in the past," it adds.

"We believe that there are practicable remedies which can bring about these results, and we now find that the monopoly position of either company, as distinct from certain things that they do, operates or may be expected to operate against the public interest."

No regulation

After outlining the five main recommendations, the commission states that it does not think a permanent price regulation would be desirable. "The alternative would be to find some automatic sanction that would discourage any reversion to the practices which we have found to be against the public interest. One such, that has been recommended, is that selling expenses in excess of an approved percentage of net wholesale turnover should be disallowed as an expense for tax purposes (with an exemption for suppliers with a turnover in reference goods below a specified figure)."

The commission did not regard itself as qualified to judge the practicability of a proposal of this nature, but recommended that the Board of Trade should consider the possible introduction of some form of automatic sanction to discourage excessive selling expenditure in household detergents and should also continue to keep a watch on prices.

Lever Brothers Says Marketing Expenses Not Unduly High

Lever Brothers and Associates, in a statement on the Monopolies report, said it did not agree with the conclusions and recommendations, but would fully cooperate with the Board of Trade in discussions on the recommendations.

The commission has based its recommendation that we should reduce prices on an assessment that our selling expenses are too high. In fact, we believe that we compare well with other industries in total distribution cost, since others spend more on other components—for example, on direct selling. We do not accept, therefore, that our selling expenses are unduly high.

Samples? Premiums?

We also disagree with the commission on what advertising comprises. We believe that items such as samples, extra powder, and premiums, are of direct value to consumers and should not be treated as advertising. Moreover, in press and television advertising there is a considerable benefit to the consumer from the provision of a free television service and of newspapers and magazines which cost far less than they would without the subsidy of advertising. If adjustment is made for this subsidy, and promotions of direct value, we assess the cost of advertising to the consumer as follows:

Omo (typical retail price of large pack 2s. 3d.), → 1d.
Persil (typical retail price of large pack 2s. 3d.), → 1d.

Lever Brothers point out that the group has already recognized the importance of giving the consumer freedom of choice between different methods of marketing, and its "Square Deal" brands offer more weight every time, instead of periodic promotions.

Motivations

The role of advertising in modern society is a complex subject about which too little is yet understood," the statement continues. "Economic theory tends to over-simplify the facts about modern products and consumer preferences for them. It does not recognise adequately that modern man and his wife are motivated by psychological as well as material needs. Our experience and research invalidate a good deal of popular theory.

We should like to see initiated a serious, impartial study of advertising by social scientists and economists based on a careful survey of data available within a number of industries.

We think that the commission has seriously underestimated the role of advertising in the manufacturing and marketing of consumer goods and the great contribution which it makes to securing economies of scale in many fields of activity throughout the business.

Exercising her choice in competitive conditions in a free market, the British housewife has struck a good balance between the high cost of unlimited choice and the low cost of no choice at all.

Return on Capital

We understand the difficulty which faced the commission in judging profits, and we regret they still feel the need to make comparisons between industries solely by assessing the return on capital employed. We question the validity of this type of comparison, bearing in mind the structure of individual industries and the make-up of individual businesses within those industries, with their differing needs for capital, their differing rates of turnover, and, above all, the differing levels of risk.

Firm conclusions from costs of individual products and even of product categories need to be made with great care, in view of the many complicated and arbitrary cost allocations involved. This is especially so in our case since the investigation covered only one part of our business, while the costs involved cover other parts of the business also.

One way of gauging the present efficiency of the industry is by comparing domestic prices with overseas prices, and although international comparisons are complex and need careful interpretation, the British consumer gets very good value for money at our price levels. Value is what really matters because price is only one element of value. We believe our prices to be low in relation to value offered.

Consequences

It is difficult to assess, at this stage, the likely consequences of the commission's recommendation that our selling prices be substantially reduced. Much will depend on the details of the Board of Trade's proposals. These will be extremely difficult to formulate if the consumer is really to benefit in the longer term.

On the one hand, there will be the danger of proliferation of new brands with resultant higher costs and, on the other, a consolidation and intensification of the duopoly. We believe that the consumer is best served by competition in a free market.

Procter & Gamble Says
"Free and Vigorous" Competition

Procter & Gamble made these comments yesterday on the Monopolies Commission report:

We have major reservations about the basic approach underlying the commission's conclusions. We do not therefore agree with their recommendations, but naturally we will meet and discuss them with the Board of Trade at the appropriate time. We believe that the report should be viewed against the following facts:

1. The soap and detergent industry operates in conditions of free and vigorous competition. The disciplines of the highly competitive market effectively set a ceiling to the prices.
2. The price paid for household washing products by the housewife in this country is less than that paid in any other western European country.
3. Between mid-1958 and mid-1965 the retail price index rose by 18 percent. During the same period prices paid by the housewife for Procter and Gamble preferred products rose by only 8 percent.
4. Modern advertising and marketing techniques are selling tools. They result in savings greater than their cost because they generate economies of scale in our own operations and in those of our suppliers and distributors. This makes possible for the consumer lower prices than she would otherwise have to pay.
5. We spend our marketing money carefully. In fact the cost of Tide's TV advertising is only the equivalent of mailing two postcards to every home in the United Kingdom each year.
6. Household washing products are a basic and wholly beneficial element in the standard of living. Between 1955 and 1964 the population increased by about 6 percent, whereas the total market for household washing products increased by 52 percent. The soap and detergent market is not a static one, and competitive marketing is playing a valuable part in its expansion.

Welcomed by Grocers' Federation and Consumer Council

The National Grocers Federation said that it welcomed the recommendation that the wholesale selling price of household detergents should be reduced. "The Federation believes that this can best be done by a reduction in the promotional and advertising costs."

L. E. Rees-Smith, national secretary, said: "For over three years I have campaigned for the reduction in the amount of money spent on advertising and promotions, and consider that the Monopolies Commission's conclusions and recommendations are a vindication of the views expressed by the federation during the last few years."

The Consumer Council welcomed the report on detergents and its detailed discussion of many points raised by the Council in its evidence to the commission.

"In particular," said the statement, "the Consumer Council had drawn the commission's attention to the possibility that competition between manufacturers of powdered detergents had not always led to the lowest possible prices."

"The Consumer Council hopes that the suggested consultation with the Board of Trade will lead to a reduction in prices to consumers, and that any revision of marketing policies would also encourage developments in performance of detergent products and improvements in labelling which would benefit consumers."

MINISTER BACKS 20 PERCENT DETERGENT PRICES[3]

Study of steps to cut selling costs

The Monopolies Commission, in a report yesterday, recommended that Unilever Ltd. and Procter & Gamble Ltd. should reduce the wholesale selling prices of household detergents by 20 percent on average and suggested a 40 percent reduction in selling expenses. Both firms last night said they did not agree with the commission's conclusions and recommendations, but they would cooperate with the Board of Trade in discussions.

Mr. Jay, president of the Board of Trade, is entering into immediate discussions with Unilever and Procter & Gamble about measures to implement the recommendations by the Monopolies Commission.

In a written answer, Mr. Jay said he was in general agreement with the report. On the commission's longer term recommendations that the Board of Trade should consider the possibility of introducing some form of automatic sanction that would discourage excessive selling expenditure in the field of household detergents and should also continue to

---

[3] *The Times,* August 11, 1966. Reproduced from *The Times* by permission.

keep a watch on prices, Mr. Jay said: "While I shall continue to consider means of preventing excessive selling expenditure in the future, it would be open to the government to refer to the National Board for Prices and Incomes any increase in prices of household detergents which is thought to be unjustified."

The commission, in its report, says that in 1964 these two firms spent something over £8 million each on selling expenses—chiefly advertising, sales promotion, and market research. In terms of the final retail price, this meant that nearly a quarter of what the customer paid for the product went for these selling expenses.

The commission which has been investigating the detergents market for three years finds that monopoly conditions exist because Unilever and Procter & Gamble each supply more than one third of all household detergents in the United Kingdom. It says that neither monopoly position, as such, operates against the public interest, but the policies pursued by both companies on advertising, promotion, and prices do. It recommends that cuts in wholesale prices should be decided by the Board of Trade in consultation with the two companies.

The commission adds that competition between the two companies tended to result in the escalation of advertising and promotion costs, that this, in turn, deterred potential competitors from entering the industry and so removed the safeguard against excessive profits, and that, as a result, the public was charged unnecessarily high prices.

The commission states that in 1964 Unilever's share of the home market was £30,377,000—representing 44 percent. Procter & Gamble's was £32,240,000—(46 percent).

"Unprovable qualities"

The main criticism of the advertising and sales promotion policies of these two firms is that their advertising matter is concerned more with emphasizing unprovable qualities and building up a brand image than with informing the public about the practical attributes of the product and how the best use can be made of it.

According to the commission, this encourages the consumer to buy particular products for the benefit of gifts or prizes; and that the effect is uneconomic because it leads a manufacturer to market two very similar products under different brand names, and to launch new products or change the formula of existing products for the sake of "improvements" which are of little intrinsic value to the user.

"Not too high"

Discussing prices and profits, the commission find there is little genuine price competition between Unilever and Procter & Gamble, and that prices are unnecessarily high, due to the levels of advertising, promotion expenditure, and profits. In Unilever's case in particular, they say, the prices of soap products are kept at a higher level than would be necessary if its synthetic products were more profitable.

The report says the firms' replies to these criticisms are that each decides its prices independently, that the prices charged have not, according to their calculations, risen to the same extent as the cost of living, and that the prices charged have not attracted newcomers to the industry. In their view "this shows that the prices are not too high."

Unilever's detergents include Lux Liquid, Surf, Omo, Quix, Stergene and Sqezy. Procter and Gamble make Oxydol, Fairy Snow, Fairy Liquid, Tide, Daz, and Dreft.

CASE QUESTIONS

1. What is your appraisal of the rationality of the positions taken by
   a)   The Monopolies Commission?
   b)   P&G and Unilever?
2. On what evidence is each basing its conclusions? What line of reasoning and analysis is each using to interpret the evidence? To what extent are the conclusions of each logical or illogical?
3. What are the alternative courses of action open to those involved (i.e. the soap companies, the Board of Trade, the government, etc.)?
4. What are the objectives of those involved? Do you agree with these objectives?

part six

PRICING STRATEGY

THE SELECTION of a level of price for a product is but one of several pricing decisions which must be made by marketing management. In many cases freedom to price at levels different from the current competitive level is limited and, therefore, the marketing strategy of the firm emphasizes nonprice methods of attracting patronage. In other instances, however, the decision as to level of price is of special importance. These include, for example, when a price must be set for a new product, when an established price must be changed, and when a price must be chosen for a new addition to an existing line of products.

Once a level of price has been determined, the question becomes one of how to select and administer specific pricing policies. These policies may range from an immediate departure from the established level, by means of discounts and allowances, to an attempt to maintain a given level of price through resale price maintenance or geographic pricing systems.

The theme of this section is that pricing can be a potent promotional instrument. But successful pricing requires consideration of potential changes in competition, product development, and market acceptance. Thus, pricing decisions cannot be made without considering how these decisions are related to the other marketing strategy variables and to the overall marketing program of the firm.

629

14

Price determination

ALTHOUGH the concept of the marketing mix describes a blending process in which management combines various controllable elements in an attempt to develop an integrated program to achieve stated objectives, there is nothing in the concept which requires that all of the elements be added to the mix at the same time. In fact, quite the opposite is true. Once market targets are defined and environmental constraints considered, marketing management faces decisions in those areas of strategy dealing with the product, its distribution, and nonprice promotion. Only after decisions have been made here, which reflect the interrelationships among the variables concerned and which are consistent with the achievement of the specified marketing goals, can management attention be devoted to the remaining element of the mix: that of pricing.

Introduction

In the decision area of pricing, many different types of questions must be answered, ranging from the determination of a price for a new product to the redetermination of a price for an established product. In addition, strategies must be formulated to gain the promotional advantages of varying from an established level of price or, conversely, from preventing such variation by resellers.

Once the decisions have been made with respect to determining a level of price and whether or not to vary from that level, then, of course, these decisions must be integrated with those previously made in the areas of product, distribution, and (nonprice) promotional strategy. Adjustments in all areas are likely to be necessary in order to create a marketing mix which is consistent, integrated, and capable of achieving predetermined goals.

This chapter will consider the first part of the pricing decision, that is, the determination of a level of price for a new product, an established product, or an addition to a line of products. The following chapter will cover those pricing decisions of an essentially promotional nature which enable the seller to adapt better to diverse needs of customers or to competitive pressures. Although these chapters will illustrate the use of various tools borrowed from economics and accounting as aids to decision making, the point must be made at the outset that pricing is more of an art than a science. In the process of making pricing decisions, analytic tools are most helpful, but when the chips are down, the judgments of intelligent, experienced, and highly intuitive human beings are vital.

Price versus nonprice competition

Because most marketing managers would be well advised to work out the nonprice aspects of the mix before turning to the questions involving price determination and variation, some attention should be paid to the relative emphasis placed by business firms on price versus nonprice methods of promotion. Although it would be wrong for an individual firm to bias its strategy to conform with the norm of its industry, it is important for the managers of an individual firm to recognize the relative emphasis placed upon price versus nonprice promotion by their major competitors. This recognition would require an evaluation of the firm's position vis-à-vis competitors, in terms of products sold and markets served. Only after such an evaluation can the decision be made to follow industry patterns or to deviate from them.

Most firms making such an investigation will find that industry mixes are heavily biased in favor of nonprice methods of promotion. Product differentiation, broad market coverage to provide availability, and considerable personal selling and/or advertising effort to create selective demand seem to be the favored means of gaining patronage. Recourse to frequent or drastic price changes appears to be a less popular strategy in the present-day American economy.

This general emphasis on nonprice promotion, which is reflected in the assignment to price of a lesser role in the marketing mix, is the result of several factors. The increased numbers of consumers with disposable incomes has diversified demand. Consumers evaluate product design and quality, locational convenience of outlets, service, and the availability of credit as well as price. With increased consumer affluence, price, as a major determinant of the purchase decision, has lost ground to the other nonprice factors.

The techniques of influencing buyers have also improved greatly over the years, and sellers find that dollars allocated to nonprice promotion have a greater effect on stimulating sales than a like amount of dollars spent in granting a price reduction. Even if evidence is not available to support the contention that promotional elasticity of demand is greater than price elasticity of demand for their products, many businessmen act as if it were.

First, they habitually underestimate the sensitivity of demand for their output to changes in price.

Second, they are hesitant to risk making a mistake by changing a price, preferring, rather, to engage in nonprice promotion where mistakes are both less noticeable and more easily corrected.

Third, the reliance on nonprice modes of competition appeals to the individual seller because it promises a greater stability of patronage. Customers won on the basis of product design, availability, and service appear less vulnerable to competitive attack than customers gained on the basis of price.

Fourth, competing on a nonprice basis eliminates many of the headaches associated with short-run price adjustments. Nonprice competition does not require as frequent revaluation of reseller inventories, changes in price lists, or renegotiation of contractual arrangements as does competition involving frequent and fairly sizable price changes.

Fifth, and perhaps the most important of all reasons for the predominant bias toward nonprice methods of promotion, is the nature of competition faced by most large firms in the American economy. As will be discussed in more detail later, a few large sellers dominate our leading industries. Autos, rubber, cigarettes, soap, aluminum, and steel are just a few of the types of products produced and sold by a relatively small number of large firms. Essentially we have in these industries a competitive environment which is oligopolistic and in which price changes initiated by one member of the oligopoly result in a fairly predictable set of reactions on the part of the other members of the industry. Thus, in many situations a price move by one seller can result in a severe loss of business by him, a general industrywide price change which is advantageous to all, or an industrywide price change which is disadvantageous to all. Little wonder, then, that most firms in oligopolistic situations shy away from price changes unless there is considerable assurance that industry changes beneficial to all members of the industry are likely to result.

Special importance of pricing decisions

It is not too difficult to presume from the preceding discussion that price is not the major concern of the modern marketing manager. Perhaps, greater attention is paid to nonprice means of gaining patronage while prices are held at levels which reflect the product's relative value-in-use as compared with the prices of close substitutes. There are instances, however, when the pricing decision is of special importance. These are: (1) when a firm must set a price for a new product, (2) when the firm wishes to initiate a price change for an existing product, and (3) when a company producing several products with interrelated demands and/or costs is faced with the problem of pricing a new addition to the line. Before these areas are considered in more detail, however, some additional attention must be paid to the influence of the competitive environment upon the pricing decision-making process.

Pricing and the competitive environment

In order to understand better the environment in which pricing decisions are made by managers of individual firms, it is helpful to rely on economic theory. Although instances in which economics provides a ready-made answer to the pricing problem are rare, in an ever increasing number of applications economic theory has provided the insight necessary to improve the quality of the pricing decision.

If one would examine the nature of the pricing decision faced by the manager of a small wheat farm, one would find that it was very simple, indeed. All that this "manager" would have to do would be to check with the local grain elevator to see what the going prices were. These prices quoted by the elevator would, in turn, reflect the interaction of industry supply and demand in the grain market at Chicago. The economist would draw the diagram shown in Figure 14–1 to explain the derivation of industry price as well as the price as viewed by the individual firm. In the situation pictured, the farmer would sell quantity Q^* at industry price P^* if his goal were that of maximizing

FIGURE 14–1
Price determination in purely competitive markets

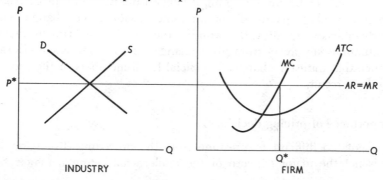

profits in the short run. This is because at quantity P^* the marginal cost of producing another unit is equal to the marginal revenue obtainable from its sale. At this output total profits are maximized.

It is not our purpose to delve into price theory to any great extent, but it is important to recognize that the wheat farmer producing a homogeneous product and unable to influence the industry price by dumping wheat or withholding it from the market has no opportunity to set a price for his output. Economists characterize this type of market situation as being "purely competitive." The choices open to the farmer include the decision to sell or not to sell wheat, the decision as to quantity to sell, the decision to effect changes in his farm's cost structure, or the decision to go out of business if the industry price drops below

FIGURE 14–2
Price determination by a monopolist

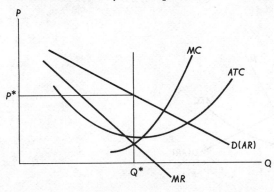

his level of costs. In no event does the farmer have the opportunity to make a true pricing decision.

The other extreme in terms of market environment is illustrated by the situation faced by the owner of an isolated water source in the midst of the Arizona desert country. As far as he is concerned, he is the only firm in the industry, and his picture appears as shown in Figure 14–2.

Because he does not have to face competition from others, he takes the aggregate or industry demand schedule as his own. This schedule is simply a curve relating the number of gallons of water that can be sold to the local inhabitants at varying levels of price. Inasmuch as he has no competition, he simply adjusts his output so that he will sell quantity Q^* at price P^*. Given the nature of his cost structure, he maximizes profits at the Q^*, P^* combination. This is the classic monopoly situation in which a single seller can set his price to sell whatever output he wishes to dispose of.

In the world of business we very rarely face either of the above types of market situations. Rather, most pricing decisions are made in market environments having characteristics of both pure competition and monopoly. Such market environments are described as being monopolistically or imperfectively competitive. In these types of markets we find that the firm does not view the industry demand schedule as its own. Depending on the degree of selective demand developed for its output, the firm may view its demand schedule as being somewhat independent of the industry schedule. Of course, the industry demand schedule is still the aggregate of all of the individual schedules of the member firms. The overall view, therefore, is of an industry schedule

FIGURE 14–3
Price determination in monopolistically competitive markets

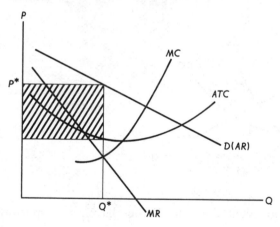

made up of many segments each of which may tilt or shift as competition or changes in buyer behavior causes changes in demand for the products of a given firm. Figure 14–3 illustrates some of these movements. Remember that this is a diagram of a firm and, as such, it resembles the picture of the monopoly situation. The difference here is that this firm is not alone in its industry but is one firm among many. There is, in addition, relative freedom of entry or exit of firms to or from the industry.

Figure 14–3 indicates the theoretical short-run profit maximization combination of price and quantity which would result if this firm were able to calculate its marginal cost and marginal revenue data at any given instance of time. Profit is indicated by the shaded area and at this combination of P^* and Q^* it is at a maximum.

Several important insights can be gleened from this theoretical model which are helpful in considering actual problems of price determination. These include:

1. Both the industry demand schedule and the segment of the industry schedule faced by a firm are downward sloping to the right. For the industry, of course, this means that if larger and larger quantities of output are to be sold, the price of this output must be reduced. Shifts in the curve's position come about as a result of changes in consumer tastes for the industry's product or as a result of interindustry competition. Such shifts in the industry demand schedule may, however, be accelerated by the combined effect of the promotional activities of the individual firms in the industry.

2. Although the individual firm usually faces a demand schedule which is downward sloping to the right, it is not without recourse to certain moves which can improve its profit position. Unlike the farmer, the manager of this type of firm can exercise some control over the prices he charges for his output. He can, for example, select some price other than the established industry price at which to sell his product. The extent to which he can exceed the competitive level of price is a function of the strength of the selective demand that he has been able to create for his output. This demand is, in turn, a function of his product's value-in-use, distinctive features, and general availability. In addition, the ability to price above the market level is related to the effectiveness of the firm's nonprice promotional efforts and the degree of competition faced from producers of substitute products or services.

3. The ability to price continually below the generally accepted industry level is dependent also upon the reaction of competitors. If pricing below the market level is a reflection of the firm's inferior position in terms of product features and/or market cultivation, then some price differential is probably sustainable. If the decision to price lower than competitors is the result of conscious strategy aimed at increasing market penetration, then competitive reactions of either a price or nonprice nature can be expected.

4. The alternative of nonprice promotion has as its objective the shifting of the demand schedule to the right so that a greater quantity can be sold at a given price. The seller would also like to get a greater slope ("tilt") in his schedule reflecting a lowered sensitivity of his demand to changes in price (especially upward changes).

In Figure 14–4 the firm is facing a demand schedule D. With price P, quantity of output Q can be sold. To sell output Q', three actions are possible:

1. Price P can be reduced to price P'.
2. Demand schedule D can be shifted to D' by vigorous nonprice promotion.

FIGURE 14–4
Price and nonprice moves in monopolistically competitive situations

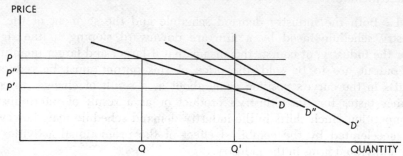

3. Some combination of lowered price and nonprice promotion can be selected, for example *P″* and *D″*.

Note that in cases 2 and 3, which involve some shifting of the demand schedule, the "tilt" or slope increases, thus reflecting what economists call greater price inelasticity of demand or less sensitivity of demand to changes in price. (For example, a percentage change in price will cause a smaller associated percentage change in quantity demanded along schedule *D′* than along schedule *D*.)

Implications

Without becoming too involved in price theory, it becomes evident that the pricing decision is closely interrelated with several other areas, both external to the firm and internal to it. Certainly the pricing manager must have a clear idea of the competitive environment in which he operates so that he can estimate the extent of pricing flexibility available to him. Although he will generally be operating under market conditions of monopolistic competition, in an ever increasing number of situations the number of sellers in the industry is few. Then the reactions of rivals become especially important, and the pricing decision area becomes more limited. These problems of oligopoly pricing (pricing when sellers are few) will be discussed in another section of this chapter.

In addition to knowing about the competitive environment, one needs to recognize the legal restraints which limit freedom of pricing action. This area will be covered in the next chapter.

Finally, pricing decisions must be related to the overall objectives of the firm and the marketing strategy designed to reach these objectives. Pricing decisions cannot be made in a vacuum, for they involve one of the firm's "action parameters" by which it seeks to reach its goals in a given market environment.

Pricing objectives

In addition to knowledge of the market environment in which prices are to be set, the marketing manager must define clearly those objectives of the firm whose attainment his pricing must further. As a result of a study by the Brookings Institution and an accompanying journal article by one of the principal investigators, some light has been shed on the major pricing objectives in selected large American business firms.[1]

The major pricing goals pursued by the 20 firms in the sample studied were: (1) pricing to achieve a target return on investment; (2) stabilization of price and margin; (3) pricing to realize a target market share; (4) pricing to meet or prevent competition; and (5) pricing to maximize profits.[2]

It is not the purpose of this text to discuss each of these objectives in detail. It is important, however, to recognize that the major pricing decision, that of setting a basic price for a product, is related not only to the external market environment but also to the goals of the firm. Price determination is a means to an end and not an end in itself. Recognition must also be given to the fact that rarely does a firm seek only a single objective. In most cases the goals sought are a combination. For example, a firm might seek maintenance or improvement of its market share while at the same time aiming for a target return on invested capital. Such a combination of goals may well describe the objectives of a large automobile manufacturing company such as General Motors or the Ford Motor Company.

The final goal of pricing, to maximize profits, does require some further discussion because it is rather ambiguous. Perhaps one might generalize by saying that all firms attempt to maximize profits in the long run. That is their basic objective, and all other goals, such as growth, control over markets, and freedom from excessive competition, are corollary objectives which are supportive of the goal of long-run profit maximization. In like manner, the goals of pricing are also supportive of the objective of long-run profit maximization. When, however, the pricing goal is that of short-run profit maximization, the situation is somewhat different. Here we have a goal which is consistent with one of the assumptions underlying the economic models discussed previously. In such a situation the economist's suggestion that short-run profits are maximized when marginal costs equal marginal revenues provides a good basic guide to price determination.

---

[1] A. D. H. Kaplan, Joel B. Dirlam, and Robert F. Lanzillotti, *Pricing in Big Business* (Washington, D.C.: Brookings Institution, 1958); Robert F. Lanzillotti, "Pricing Objectives in Large Companies," *American Economic Review*, vol. 48, no. 5 (December 1958), pp. 921–40.

[2] Ibid.

The first step in establishing a price system is, as Stanton notes, "consciously to formulate an objective and state it clearly in writing. Once the price objective is agreed upon, the executives can move to the heart of price management—the actual determination of the base price of the products or services."[3]

Setting the basic price for a new product

Assuming that those executives responsible for the pricing decision have a clear understanding of the competitive environment in which they must operate and that the pricing objectives of the firm have been specified, they can now begin to set the basic price for a new product.

FIGURE 14–5
The zone of demand resulting from a range of prices and a shifting of the demand schedule for a new product

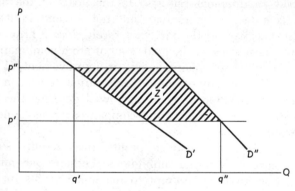

Their first task is to find out what the demand schedule for the new product might be like in terms of its location, its slope, and its degree of shiftability. It is not necessary, however, to be concerned with the entire schedule but only with that portion of the schedule which is meaningful in terms of the specific pricing decision under consideration. Figure 14–5 might be helpful.

Price p'' is the ceiling price or estimate of the highest price that might be charged for the new product. This estimate is based on an appraisal of the new product's superiority or inferiority as compared to close substitutes as well as on the need to sell a minimum quantity of output to cover associated costs. Price p' is the minimum price at which the firm would be willing to sell given the nature of its future

[3] William J. Stanton, *Fundamentals of Marketing*, 3d ed. (New York: McGraw-Hill Book Co., 1971), p. 420.

costs. Such a level is generally set by the price of the lowest priced substitute product, but quite often strategy considerations will result in a price considerably below that of close substitutes.

D' is the demand schedule which reflects the most pessimistic estimate of consumer acceptance and/or competitive retaliation assuming little or no nonprice promotion. D'', on the other hand, reflects the most optimistic view of consumer acceptance considering planned nonprice promotional efforts and anticipated competitive response. The zone of demand relevant to the decision is, of course Z, while the interval $p''-p'$ is the range of price under consideration, and the interval $q''-q'$ the range of quantity which might be sold under all combinations of price and demand within their respective ranges.

Demand estimation

Although the preceding discussion has conceptual value in terms of explaining the reason why an estimation of demand given a set of prices and assuming various combinations of promotional efforts (both by the firm and its competitors) is vital to the process of price determination, it does little in the way of producing usable data. What is needed is a more concrete evaluation of product utility.

Comparison with close substitutes. If the product is a new version of an established type of product, then, of course, some information is available as to the size of the present market for the generic product type. A careful evaluation of the relative ability of the new product to fill consumers' needs vis-à-vis available substitutes can give some idea of the share of total market the new product might capture over time if it were priced at the current level at which close substitutes were sold. Once this estimate has been made, consideration can be given to the effect upon sales and market share that prices slightly above or below market level (say 10 percent) would have. This type of analysis would, of course, be highly subjective, but it would force management to estimate the new product's superiority (or inferiority) with respect to available substitutes. In addition, estimates as to the sensitivity of demand to prices slightly above or below market levels would have to be made. By continuing to estimate possible sales at prices 15, 20, or even 25 percent over or under current levels at which close substitutes are sold, management can get some idea as to the location and slope of that portion of the demand schedule which is meaningful to the determination of basic price for the new product.

Asking customers. Estimation of demand by managers can often be improved by surveying the more astute members of the reseller organization. Wholesalers and retailers who are in closer contact with the market than are manufacturers develop an instinctive feel for what is a "right" price for a new product. They can evaluate its attributes from the buyer's point of view and reflect the buyer's appraisal of product utility. Such questioning of potential buyers need not stop at the reseller level but may well include questioning end users by means of consumer panels or personal interviews with selected individuals. It has been suggested that in those cases where the new product is so unique as to rule out the use of a similar type of product as a basis of comparison, the concept of the "barter equivalent" be applied.[4] In this approach the new product, surrounded by a diversity of other products whose uses and prices are well established, is placed in front of a consumer panel. The members of the panel are then requested to match up the new product with another product of roughly equivalent value. By such means insight can be gained as to how the consumer might value the new product without the opportunity of comparing it with close generic substitutes.

Test marketing. As the process of estimating demand at various prices proceeds, there comes a point where an actual market test is required. Only in this way can consumer response to a price level (or a variety of levels) be measured in a realistic manner. The market test allows demand response to be viewed under actual purchase conditions, with controlled nonprice promotional inputs, and in the face of real competition. The disadvantage of such testing is that the surprise effect of the new product introduction upon rivals is blunted. In many situations, however, where a wrong pricing decision could be most costly, market testing is desirable even if it alerts competitors to the introduction of a new product.

Capitalization of cost savings. The steps in the process of estimating demand which have been discussed briefly have a very strong consumer product orientation. This is not to say that a producer of a product for sale to the industrial market would not find the comparison of his product with close substitutes useful in terms of aiding him to set a basic price. Moreover, he would also find his distributors most helpful in appraising the salability of a new product at a given price or over a given range of prices. What is important to note, however, is that the value-in-use of industrial products is easier to measure than is product utility in the consumer market. This is because industrial buyers can measure cost savings which are likely to accrue from the use of a new product. These cost savings (which may differ by application) when capitalized over the life of the new product indicate the ceiling price which may be charged for a new product when used in a specific application. It is evident that if cost savings associated with the use of a new industrial product have a present value of $1,000, the purchase

---

[4] Joel Dean, "Pricing Policies for New Products," *Harvard Business Review*, vol. 28, no. 6 (November 1950), p. 30.

price must be somewhere below this figure unless some other technical factors are involved.

Derived demand. Because the demand for industrial goods as inputs to an industrial process is derived from the demand for the output of the process, it is less sensitive to price changes than is consumer demand. When demand for the end product is stable or falling off, sales of capital equipment are limited to the replacement market and prices must reflect the cost savings which the new machine can offer over continued use of the old. In viewing the economics of replacement, it is found that a rather large price reduction would be required to cause a replacement sale to be made in the absence of technologically induced cost savings. On the other hand, when end product sales are rising, prices of new machinery can be raised above the level of capitalized cost savings with little effect on quantity demanded.

Price sensitivity of demand for industrial goods varies with respect to the type of good being considered. Moving from capital equipment to accessory equipment, component parts, and operating supplies, one finds increasing price elasticity of demand. But in almost all cases such sensitivity is less in the industrial market than in the consumer market. Derived demand and its influence have been discussed in greater detail in Chapter 5.

The purpose of demand analysis is to provide some estimates of the market's evaluation of product utility or value-in-use. In addition to discovering the location of the demand schedule, some information as to its probable slope and shiftability is also needed. The end result of demand analysis, therefore, is the delineation of a range of prices acceptable to the market and the achievement of some idea of sensitivity of demand to various prices within this range. The top of this range is the demand "ceiling." The next step in the pricing process is to relate demand over the acceptable range of price to the cost of producing output. As demand sets the ceiling on price, costs set the floor.

The role of costs

Although costs may be viewed as setting a floor to price while demand constraints set the ceiling, those persons responsible for the pricing decision must recognize that there are several cost floors from which to choose. In any summation of costs for floor determination, the questions arise as to the type and amount of cost to be included in the buildup. Should overhead costs, for example, be allocated on the basis of standard volume? Over how long a period of time should research and development costs be amortized? Should estimates of future costs be used rather than past or present costs?

In attempting to wend their way through the maze of costs and the various methods by which costs can be allocated to products, the pricing executives must keep two points in mind. First, in most cases, over the long run an individual product should and must bring in revenues which cover fully allocated costs and provide a reasonable profit. The second point is that because there is little or no causal relationship between cost and price in the short run, for the individual firm a price that fails initially to cover "full costs" may be a good price.

Cost-plus pricing. Because of the confusion of short- and long-run goals, businessmen often engage in the cost buildup process and add to the cost floor thus obtained some amount of "plus" in order to arrive at a price. The plus is either described as providing a certain percentage return on invested capital associated with the introduction of the new product or, in a more general sense, as an attempt to guarantee that with each sale the firm will receive a predetermined margin of profit. In retrospect, however, such an approach is not as easy as it appears to be, nor is it a really safe one. The question arises as to what costs are to be used for the base. Should the price setter consider past costs, present costs, or future costs? How large should the "plus" be?

Regardless of how sophisticated the approach, one thing is evident: cost-plus pricing which ignores the demand aspect of the pricing problem involves circular reasoning. Because price influences volume to be sold and volume affects unit costs, it is obvious that costs are determined factors in the pricing process rather than determining factors. Although the "plus" is management determined, it is often set without a clear understanding of the consequences. Too large a "plus" can result in too high a price, too low volume, and too high unit costs. Thus, a hefty "plus" aimed at improving gross profit per unit may prove very disappointing if the resulting price fails to fit in with the market's evaluation of product utility or fails to consider alternatives offered potential customers by competitors.

The tier concept. A clearer understanding of what a cost floor actually is and how its definition is relevant to the pricing decision may be gained by examining the "tier" concept. This is merely a way of looking at the cost floor in terms of the layers of cost which make up its foundation. Visualize a cost floor consisting of three tiers. The first tier is composed of indirect costs or overhead items which are fully allocated to units of output. The second layer it made up of direct costs of a noncash nature, such as depreciation expense directly associated with producing a unit of the product. The third layer is composed of unit direct costs, commonly called out-of-pocket costs, which represent cash outlays for items such as labor and materials.

We see in Figure 14–6 that there are two subfloors in addition to the full-cost floor. If the demand ceiling were sufficiently high, the full-

FIGURE 14-6
Tiers or layers of cost with associated subfloors

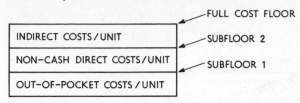

FIGURE 14-7
Demand ceiling above full-cost floor

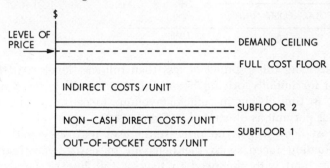

FIGURE 14-8
Demand ceiling below full-cost floor

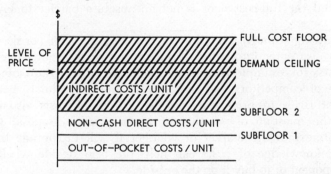

cost floor could be covered by price. This type of situation is illustrated by Figure 14–7.

If the demand ceiling were below the full-cost floor as illustrated in Figure 14–8, the price setter would have to consider whether or not he could set a price below the full-cost floor but above subfloor No. 2 representing the direct-cost floor.

Such a decision to price below the full-cost floor would be feasible only if the firm produced other products which could be sold at prices sufficiently high to make up for the lack of contribution to overhead

FIGURE 14–9
A dynamic view of the cost floor–demand ceiling relationship

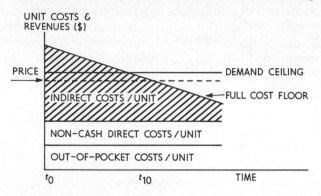

resulting from pricing this product at less than full-cost levels. Another possible reason for initially pricing below full cost would be that such a price would, in time, bring in sufficient volume to cause a reduction in full-cost levels per unit as illustrated in Figure 14–9.

Thus, the cost floor which the price setter uses may vary with the competitive situation faced, with the behavior of costs over time as volume changes, and with the need to have a full line or family of products. The revenues from all the products sold must, of course, cover full costs in the long run. In the short run, however, when single products are being priced the full-cost floor is not an absolute barrier to lower prices.

Costs and pricing strategy. In addition to setting the floor (or floors) to price, costs also enter into pricing strategy decisions. Knowledge of one's own costs, for example, provides insight into the nature of the cost structures of competitors and thus enables one to estimate better the reaction of rivals to pricing moves. Evaluation of costs also can help answer the question of whether or not a pricing proposal will invite competitors into the market or whether it will discourage their entry. Finally, knowledge of costs can help the firm decide whether to make a component or to buy it on the outside.

There will be a further discussion of pricing strategy a little later on. At this point, however, it is advisable to examine an approach in which demand and costs are considered together.

The interactive approach

It is far safer to view the pricing process as the interaction of cost and demand. If the firm starts with costs and tests various cost buildups against demand, the dangers associated with a purely cost-plus approach may be averted. In like manner, starting with demand and working back to costs is a more desirable approach than straight cost-plus pricing. Of course, in recommending the interactive approach, it is assumed that the pricing decision is concerned with manufactured goods which, although new, are not totally unknown (in a generic sense) to the market. In those cases where the product being sold is a highly specialized custom-built item purchased by a single buyer, cost-plus may be the only feasible way in which a price can be set.

Break-even analysis

In using the interactive approach to price determination, some method of visualizing the relationship among fixed costs, variable costs, volume, and price and the effects of these relationships on profit is almost a necessity. Break-even analysis is such a method. It calls attention to the various types of costs involved, such as those which are fixed over the range of output, those which vary with output, and those which vary with executive decisions. The analysis also allows management to visualize a series of preliminary prices which are then evaluated in terms of volume possibilities.

With known or estimated costs and a series of possible prices, the volume requirements to break even for any given price proposal are identified.

Break-even analysis also shows how rapidly profits can be increased if volume above the break-even level can be secured. In like manner, the analysis shows management the size of the loss at volumes below the break-even level.

In Figure 14–10 those costs which remain fixed over the range of output to be considered are estimated to be $10,000. Those costs which vary with output are zero at zero output and $10,000 at 500 units of output. They are $20 per unit in this illustration where variable costs are assumed to vary directly with output. This assumption is not necessary for the analysis, as costs which vary with output on a nonlinear basis could be portrayed by an appropriate curved line. In similar manner fixed costs which change abruptly at different levels of output could be illustrated by means of a step function.

The last element of the cost buildup is that which represents costs associated with specific executive policies relating, for example, to nonprice promotional efforts. In Figure 14–10 they are shown as being constant over the range of output and of the magnitude of $5,000. Thus, from zero to 750 units of output, total costs vary from $15,000 to $30,000.

Looking now at the revenue side of the picture, one sees three revenue lines each associated with a price proposal. The first price suggested is $100 per unit, the second $75 per unit, while the third proposal is

FIGURE 14–10
A break-even chart

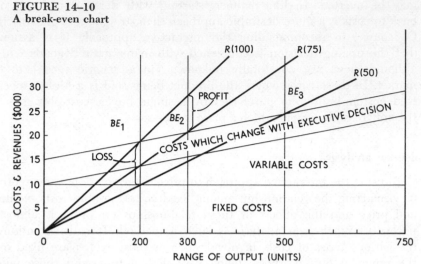

Source: Adapted from Wilfred J. Eiteman, *Price Determination* (Report No. 16 [Ann Arbor: Bureau of Business Research, Graduate School of Business Administration, The University of Michigan, 1949]).

$50 per unit. Each revenue line indicates the extent of gross income (price times volume) forthcoming from the associated price proposal over the range of output.

The volume requirements needed to cover costs (or to break even) for each price proposal are clearly seen to be 200 units at $100, 300 units at $75, and 500 units at $50. Profits are shown by the vertical distances between the total costs and the revenue line to the right of the break-even point. For example, at a price of $100 per unit, break even occurs when 200 units are sold. If 300 units are sold, profits would be about $8,000 as shown by the line segment labeled "profit." Losses are shown by vertical distances between total costs and revenues to the left of a given break-even point. For example, at a price of $50, break even occurs when 500 units are sold. If only 200 units are sold, the loss is approximately $8,000, as shown by the line segment labeled "loss."

The use of break-even analysis requires that levels of demand must be estimated for each price proposal. These estimates must take into account not only the impact of price but also the effects of the other elements of the associated marketing strategy mix and the likely reaction of competitors.

An approach to the problem of estimating the demand response to a given price proposal which has operational value has been suggested by Darden.[5] He recommends that a probability distribution of sales vol-

---

[5] Bill R. Darden, "An Operational Approach to Product Pricing," *Journal of Marketing*, vol. 32, no. 2 (April 1968), pp. 29–33.

FIGURE 14–11
Use of three volume estimates to fit a beta distribution at a given price
of $75

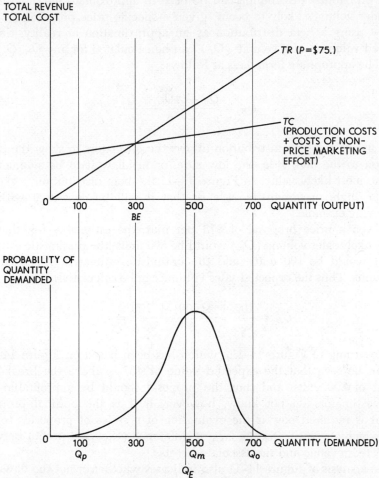

umes be developed for each price proposal and that the expected value of the distribution then be related to the volume needed to break even, given the cost consequences of the proposal. Figure 14–11 illustrates such a linkage.

As can be seen, three estimates of sales volume must be made for each proposal, with full consideration being given to the other strategy mix variables as well as to the environmental constraints. Thus, for any proposal (P_n) a most likely estimate of sales volume (Q_m) must be made as well as a pessimistic estimate (Q_p) and an optimistic estimate (Q_o).

By instructing the estimators to choose Q_m as the most likely value and Q_p and Q_o as values each with a probability of occurrence of .01, a beta probability distribution can be used to approximate the distribution of sales volumes likely to occur, given a specific price proposal.

By using a beta distribution as an approximation of reality, the expected value of sales volume (Q_E) can be calculated for any Q_m, Q_p, and Q_o. The appropriate formula is as follows:

$$Q_E = \frac{Q_p + 4Q_m + Q_o}{6}.$$

The use of the beta distribution allows the estimators to skew the distribution to the high side, the low side, or to allow it to be symmetrical to the most likely value. In Figure 14–11 the beta distribution is skewed to the high, or optimistic, side so that it will be consistent with the following example.

Given a price proposal of $75 per unit, the estimators felt that the most likely sales volume (Q_m) would be 500 units, the pessimistic estimate (Q_p) would be 100 units, and the optimistic estimate (Q_o) would be 700 units. Thus the expected sales volume can be calculated:

$$Q_E = \frac{100 + 4(500) + 700}{6} = 467.$$

Returning to Figure 14–11 (which has been based on Figure 14–10), it can be seen that the expected value of 467 is above the break-even point of 300 units, and thus the proposal should be a profitable one. The estimators do not know, however, if it is the optimal proposal. What is required now is the evaluation of a series of proposals to find out which one generates the largest difference (expected profit) between expected revenue and the associated costs.

An analysis of Figure 14–11 also indicates whether or not the downside risk for a given price proposal is large. In the example at hand, it can be seen that the bulk of the probability density lies above the 300-unit mark. Only if one of the more pessimistic estimates actually occurs will the sales volume be below break even; and if the demand estimates are correct, the probability of such an occurrence is quite small.

Value and limitations of break-even analysis. Break-even analysis is a useful technique in balancing demand and cost factors in the process of determining price. It requires of the pricing executive estimates of demand at different levels of price, and then it indicates the behavior of costs at various levels of output associated with different price proposals. Of course, the quality of the analysis can be no better than the quality of the cost data and demand data inputs, but the very nature of the approach forces a consideration of the interaction of demand and costs. As such, break-even analysis indicates well that neither cost nor volume is solely determinative of price.

Pricing strategy

Having a clear understanding of how the pricing decision is related to the achievement of the objectives of the enterprise and being familiar with a range of possible prices given the demand and cost constraints, the pricing executives can then consider those strategies which might be followed to attain the desired goals. In this area of decision, executives often share feelings held by military officers who are planning an assault on the enemy. In both the business and military environments, consideration must be given to the options available, the resources at one's disposal, the possible reaction of the enemy, and the consistency of one's moves with other elements of the overall program. Thus, pricing strategy like military strategy is uniquely associated with available opportunities and the means on hand for their exploitation.

It is senseless to talk of strategy unless some alternatives are available. Assume, for example, that the pricing executives face a situation in which the price they can set is limited on the high side by competition and on the low side by the full-cost floor. If the distance between the floor and the ceiling is fairly wide, the executives have some discretion as to whether to price near the ceiling or the floor or somewhere in-between the two extremes. If the floor and the ceiling are closer together, the discretionary range is smaller. It may even be nonexistent if the floor and ceiling coincide or if the floor is above the ceiling.

Let us look at examples A, B, and C in order to see what strategies might be available in each case. In situation A, where the range of discretion is fairly wide, the price might be set up near the demand ceiling. This would be called a "skim" type of strategy in which a high initial price for a new product would be set to "skim the cream" off of the market. Such a strategy could be expected to work over a period of time only if the product were protected from competition because of its technical or design uniqueness. If such were the case and the demand ceiling held at its original level over time, a skim pricing strategy accompanied by heavy nonprice promotion would offer considerable advantage.

Certain other attributes of a situation might suggest a skim strategy. Limited production facilities, need to recoup research and development expenses, and unclear nature of demand all would indicate that a high-price, limited-volume strategy would be best for the beginning. Such a strategy would be even more effective if the market could be divided into segments and promotion could be directed to those segments where demand was relatively insensitive to price.

The advantages of a skim strategy are great when product uniqueness provides protection from competition, thus allowing a high initial price to provide for new product introduction by means of generous trade margins and nonprice promotion. There are, however, situations in which a strategy of a low initial price might be called for. If, for example, the new product were of a type generally known to the consumer, if competition were a strong threat, if demand were estimated to be sensitive to price, and if sizable economies of production were associated with volume, then a low initial or "penetration" price might be superior to a higher one. It would allow the product to gain a mass market quickly, thus moving in ahead of competition. The low price would not allow for much nonprice promotion or for wide trade margins, but because of the sensitivity of demand to a low price, nonprice promotional

FIGURE 14–12
Illustration of three floor-ceiling combinations

DEMAND CEILING — D	DEMAND CEILING — D	FULL COST FLOOR — C_f
RANGE OF DISCRETION	RANGE OF DISCRETION	
	FULL COST FLOOR — C_f	DEMAND CEILING — D
FULL COST FLOOR — C_f		
		SUBFLOOR — C_s
A.	B.	C.

efforts could be kept to a minimum. Finally, although price were set at the full-cost floor, over time, as production economies took effect, the floor would be lowered thus producing greater profits.

Situation B in Figure 14–12 is a variant of situation A. In this second example the floor and the ceiling are much closer together and the range of discretion more limited. In situation C the demand ceiling (D) is actually below the full-cost floor (C_f). This means that the product's value-in-use is less than the producer's full costs of manufacturing and marketing or that competitors offer close substitutes at prices lower than the producer's costs. In this type of situation the manufacturer faces the alternative of either not introducing the product or of placing it on the market at a price under the present full-cost floor but above a cost subfloor such as the one representing direct costs. A strategy of pricing below full costs might be indicated when cost reductions are anticipated with volume or when the product is an essential part of a line and must be placed on the market even if its price will only cover part of its cost of production and marketing. If the price can cover direct costs, some contribution to overhead may be forthcoming.

Placing a new product on the market at a price below its present full costs may be a profitable move, especially when the new product is viewed as a member of a family of products each making different sized contributions to overhead and profit.

Strategy over time. The discussion of pricing strategy to this point has been essentially in static terms or at the very best has dealt with pricing in the short run. The concepts of demand ceiling or cost floors, although helpful in determining the range of discretion open to the price setter at the time of new product introduction, can be dangerously misleading if not viewed in a dynamic context. Demand ceilings change over time as do cost floors, and the price setter must be aware of these changes and anticipate them by changes in strategy.

We have already spoken of the case in which the price of a new product is set high to tap those segments of the market where demand is relatively inelastic and where the need is great to bring in revenues quickly. We have also looked at situations in which the initial price might be set close to the full-cost floor or even below it. There are strategies, however, where future product and/or market changes are considered. One such strategy has been called "sliding down the demand curve."[6] The firm following such a strategy starts with a high initial price emphasizing value more than cost in an attempt to skim the cream from successive market segments. However, the firm anticipates competition and reduces price faster than is required by the market. Thus, potential competition is forestalled, and the firm becomes an established volume producer over time with a price approaching the level that a penetration pricing strategy would have required initially.

Because new products age in that they lose their aura of uniqueness or face increasing competition from substitutes, pricing strategies suited to the introductory stage of the product's life cycle must be amended over time. As competition increases, prices are forced down, and price becomes the dominant element in the promotional mix. When brand preference weakens and private brands enter in force, there is little left to do but to reduce prices promptly to forestall private brand competition. This is merely the acceptance of the fact that in the mature stage of the product life cycle, competition is largely on a price basis.

Price redetermination

In addition to the problem of determining a price for a new product, marketing executives are often faced with the problem of changing the price of an established product. This process is called "price redetermina-

---

[6] D. Maynard Phelps and J. Howard Westing, *Marketing Management,* 3d ed. (Homewood, Ill.: Richard D. Irwin, Inc., 1968), p. 326.

tion," and the problems arising from it differ somewhat from those associated with the determination of initial price. Essentially, these differences are an outgrowth of the aging of the product. The problems of pricing in the competitive or mature stages of product life are less involved with uncertainty than are those dealing with setting the price for a product in the introductory stages of its development. In the competitive stage, for example, more is known about demand. The degree of sensitivity of demand to changes in the producer's promotional mix, to actions of competitors, and to variations in the overall economic environment is understood with greater clarity. In like manner, the producer has a clearer picture of his production and marketing costs with an established product than with a new one.

Motivation for redetermination

Management may decide to change a price for several reasons. It may be necessary to raise or lower a price to reflect a modification in the market's valuation of a product. On the other hand, the change may be the result of variations in costs of production, distribution, or promotion. Or the price move may come about to increase market share or to gain some other competitive advantage. Finally, a price change may be defensive to meet price or nonprice moves of rivals.

Change in market valuation. If demand for a given product slackens over time and if there have been no overt changes in the producer's promotional mix or the actions of competitors, then it is quite obvious that changes have taken place in the market. Perhaps the market segment composed of prospects who placed a high value-in-use on the product has been saturated. Or, perhaps, the novelty aspects of the product have worn off, and consumers have turned elsewhere to spend their money. Regardless of causation, the producer must readjust his promotional mix to conform to the realities of the marketplace. Usually, such a readjustment entails a reduction in price to enable the producer to tap segments of the market where demand is more sensitive to a price reduction than to additional nonprice promotion.

Changes in costs. Although demand is usually the controlling factor in the pricing of fabricated goods, cost changes can have a motivating or triggering effect on price redetermination. For example, cost reductions associated with volume production may allow price reductions which will either help maintain current volume levels or increase them. Price redetermination which is associated with a declining cost floor has several strategic implications which will be discussed shortly.

In contrast, product cost increases associated with (1) declining volume, (2) rising labor and/or material costs, or (3) both factors, may force consideration of higher product prices. The decision to raise price is, of course, influenced by the general sensitivity of demand to price and the possible reaction of competitors. Thus, it is quite evident that although cost changes might motivate price changes for established products, whether or not such changes are made depends on the demand factors, that is, on how consumers value the product and what substitutes are available to them.

Changes in strategy. Price redetermination, especially in the downward direction, may be used to implement a new marketing strategy. As was noted earlier, a desire to "slide down the demand curve" requires frequent evaluation of the competitive situation and correctly timed price reductions. Through these reductions the firm hopes to tap successive layers of demand which vary in price sensitivity. Timing is crucial, as the reductions must be made sufficiently early to dissuade competitive entry or to catch those rivals already in the market off guard.

Price increases as part of a process of redetermination also have strategic implications. For a firm with a highly differentiated product, a move to a higher level of price may reflect product superiority. The higher price may well bolster the quality image of the line. Such upward moves are, of course, easier to sustain when the nonprice promotional efforts have created a strong selective demand for the product. Price redetermination on the upside may reflect a decision to pursue a high-price, limited-volume strategy by reblending the marketing mix to give price a lesser role in relation to the other elements.

Changes in competition. Price changes, either upward or downward, after initial introduction of a product may be necessary to adjust to the actions of competitors. Such changes become especially necessary when the number of sellers in a given industry is few.

Let us start with a market situation in which there are many sellers in the industry and selective demand for the products of individual sellers varies from weak to strong. In this type of environment the firm which had developed the strongest demand for its product would have the greatest degree of flexibility in dealing with competitive change of a price or nonprice variety. The firms with weak selective demand would find that demand for their products would be very much affected by price or nonprice moves of rivals. Because of lack of product differentiation or other reasons which have denied them strong selective demand, the response of these "weak demand" firms is very much limited to changes in price. Thus, for a very large number of sellers in markets which are monopolistically competitive, price is the major vehicle by which they adjust to competitor-invoked change.

Price redetermination, when sellers are few. The problem of price redetermination becomes especially complex when the number of sellers in the industry is few and the degree of product differentiation is slight. The economist would call such a market situation an example of a nondifferentiated or pure oligopoly. In such an environment a firm would have to be very careful about redetermining its prices because such a redetermination could under certain conditions result in a redetermination of the *industry* price level and the industry marketing mix. As the degree of product differentiation increases when sellers are few, the extent of price differences among them may also increase. There still comes a point, however, when a price move by one firm will cause an industrywide reaction.

Perhaps some idea of the price behavior of firms in oligopolistic industries in the short run may be gained by viewing the "kinked" oligopoly demand curve.

In Figure 14–13, *p* is the industry price or the modal value of the

FIGURE 14–13
Kinked oligopoly demand curve

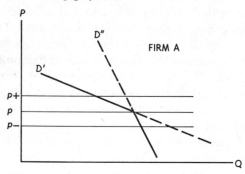

cluster of industry prices. If a firm in the industry raises its price to *p*+, one of two responses can be expected. If the rest of the firms in the industry feel that strength of demand or pressures of cost suggest an upward readjustment of industry price, they may follow the first firm up to price *p*+. In this case the operative demand schedule for the initiating firm would be the segment of *D"* above the intersection with *D'*. This segment is relatively inelastic because all suppliers of close substitutes also have raised their prices.

On the other hand, if the other firms do not follow the initiating firm, a great deal of the initiator's patronage will shift to other firms in the industry who offer lower prices. Thus, in this situation the demand curve which is operative for the initiating firm is the segment of *D'* above the intersection with *D"*. It is highly elastic, for demand falls off rapidly for the firm which raises its price above the industry level but does not have the degree of selective demand to support the differential in price.

Looking at the downside we see a similar pattern of behavior. If the initiating firm drops its price to $p-$ and the rest of industry is forced to follow, schedule D'' from the intersection with D' becomes operative. It is relatively inelastic for the initiating firm because all firms in the industry have matched the move. An important question to raise here, however, is, What effect will a lower industry price level have on industry demand?

If the initiating firm lowers its price and is not followed, then, of course, it will gain a great deal of patronage at the expense of its rivals. In this case the demand schedule D' from the intersection with D'' downward would be operative. Because rivals would react quickly, this highly elastic segment would not be operative for long, if at all.

It can be seen from this brief discussion that price redetermination when product differentiation is weak and/or sellers are few is quite a touchy task. This is because price moves by the firm are closely related to reactions by rivals. In like manner, price moves by rivals have an important effect on any firm in the industry. In many situations, therefore, price redetermination by a firm is forced upon it by competition. When a firm itself initiates a price change, especially in an oligopolistic industry, it is actually proposing a readjustment of the relative importance of price in the *industry's* marketing mix.

Pricing a new addition to the product line

The problem of pricing a new product is compounded when the new product is to be part of an existing group or line of products. The products involved may be physically distinct or they may be physically similar but sold under different demand conditions reflecting value-in-use, seasonal, or life cycle variations.

Cost interdependence

In many situations prices for new additions to the product line are made on the basis of costs. Dean reports that common policies include, among others, setting price proportional to full cost, setting price proportional to incremental costs, or setting price to provide profit margins proportional to conversion costs.[7]

Using cost as the sole basis by which to set the price for a new addition to the line can be dangerous. Many of the costs of producing and marketing the new product are overhead costs or joint costs. Allocation or separation of these costs may be impossible and, therefore, any attempt to determine the full-cost floor for the new addition will require

---

[7] Joel Dean, "Problems of Product Line Pricing," *Journal of Marketing*, vol. 14 (January 1950), pp. 519–20.

that costs be applied on an arbitrary basis. Even if direct or incremental costs are used too great an orientation to the cost side can cause management to lose sight of the reasons for the introduction of the new product. Cost pricing by ignoring variations in demand or in competition faced may cause the firm to forego opportunities for market segmentation.[8]

Demand interdependence

The main economic question raised when a new product is added to the line is not usually concerned with costs. It is, rather, a question of the nature of demand interdependence. Is the new product a complement or a substitute? Can the new product be used as an instrument for market segmentation and/or price discrimination? The answers to questions such as these, which have a strong demand orientation, are useful in finding the "right" price to be placed on a new addition to an established line.

In much the same way that the pricing decision for an individual new product must be an outgrowth of overall strategy, so must it be when pricing a new member of the product line. Is the goal of the firm to increase its penetration of specific market segments? Does the firm wish to favor certain items in the line over others? Is the firm committed to a policy of "full-line" pricing in which the goal is to set an array of prices for members of the line so that the total contribution of the line is a maximum?

Given a clear understanding of the goals of the firm for the longer run, the pricing decision in the short run assumes a strategic as well as purely economic character. Perhaps a view of two diverse situations will offer a better view of the nature of the problem.

A substitute product. A large manufacturer of industrial chemicals had developed a nontoxic solvent for degreasing metal parts. The basic chemical in this product was produced as a by-product of another process and thus carried a low cost burden. The new solvent was superior to carbon tetrachloride, the currently used chemical. The manufacturer of the new solvent was one of the largest producers of carbon tetrachloride. It sold about 20 percent of its output to the solvent market and 80 percent as a raw material for the subsequent manufacture of chlorinated hydrocarbons.

The new chemical was clearly a substitute for the established product in the solvent market. If the new product were priced somewhat higher than the old, it could displace carbon tetrachloride in those applications where toxicity was a major problem. If the product were priced equal

---

[8] C. N. Davisson, "Pricing the Product Line," unpublished technical note, Business Administration Library, The University of Michigan.

to, or slightly under, carbon tetrachloride (as the cost floor readily allowed), considerable displacement would occur. In fact, preliminary market research indicated that if priced at the level of carbon tetrachloride, the new product would almost completely take over the cold-cleaning solvent market.

The question which faced the manufacturer was whether or not a relatively low price on the new product and its subsequent penetration of the cold-cleaning market would invite competitors to cut their prices on carbon tetrachloride. If this were to happen, the gains in revenues from an increased share of the solvent market would be more than counterbalanced by losses in revenues in those markets where carbon tetrachloride was purchased as a raw material.

Thus, the issue facing the manufacturer in pricing the new addition to the line concerned the cross-elasticity of demand not only between items in the line but also between the market segments served by the firm and its rivals.

A complementary product. In another situation a manufacturer of home traffic appliances found that he was losing business to competitors because his line did not include a small portable mixer. To remedy this weakness he developed a new mixer which on the basis of cost estimates would have to be sold at a price 10 percent above the price of competing products, that is, if the new product were to make an average contribution. Careful evaluation indicated that product superiority was not sufficient to warrant the price premium, and the decision was made to price the new product at competitive levels. It was felt that although the product was somewhat better than competing items, it would be sold at the price which would guarantee market acceptance, even if revenues received barely covered direct costs. The manufacturer reasoned that the new product would stimulate sales of the rest of the line and that total contribution was more important to the firm than was the contribution of any one item in the line.

Dual relationships.[9] In addition to a product being a substitute or a complement, it well may be both. For example, in the case of the solvent manufacturer we viewed the new product as a substitute for the old. If, however, the addition of the new product enabled the manufacturer to attract new customers, to strengthen his distributor organization, or to gain fuller coverage for his line, the demand interrelationship between the new product and the rest of the line would be one of complementarity. In similar fashion, if the portable mixer developed to fill a gap in the line of the home appliance manufacturer shifted sales away from the standard mixer, then a substitute relationship would exist.

---

[9] Ibid.

Implications

If a new product is added to a line to implement the firm's marketing strategy, as is usually the case, the demand factors must dominate the pricing decision. The degree of flexibility open to management is, however, limited by the extent of demand interdependence between the new product, existing products in the line, and products of competitors.

As is the case with individual products, costs set the floor for the price of an addition to a product line. Management does have considerably more discretion in defining the cost floor when adding a product to an existing line than when introducing a single product. This flexibility arises from management's ability to apportion revenues received across the line to the coverage of direct and indirect costs.

While gaining some flexibility on the cost side, the firm probably loses some on the demand side as has been noted above. As demand is probably the prime determinant of price, in most cases there is a net loss in flexibility when setting a price for a new addition to a line. This loss in flexibility, however, need not prevent a price setter from tapping specific market segments on the basis of price. Market opportunities are always present, and only a constant appraisal of demand will make their exploitation possible. A continuing process of demand appraisal is especially important when demand interrelationships change over the product's life cycle to such an extent that price redetermination might be necessary.

Conclusion

In this chapter we have considered the role of price in the marketing mix and three areas in which the pricing decision is of special importance. Attention has been paid to the need to understand the nature of the competitive environment in which the firm must set its prices as well as to the role that price determination plays in implementing the overall strategy of the firm.

Questions

1. Why is it generally suggested that the nonprice aspects of marketing strategy be determined before the pricing decision is made?
2. What is the value, if any, to a pricing decision maker of the economist's models of price determination in diverse market situations?
3. Can a firm have differing pricing objectives in the short run as opposed to the long run? Can a firm have more than one pricing objective for the same time period? Explain.

4. Why is demand estimation so vital to the process of price determination? How might one go about estimating demand for a new consumer product? A new industrial product?

5. What is meant by "cost-plus" pricing? What are the advantages and limitations of such an approach?

6. Define what is meant by a "cost floor." What is the "tier concept" and its pertinence to pricing decisions?

7. "Break-even analysis cannot determine a price." Comment on the preceding statement, and if you agree, indicate the value, if any, of such analysis to the pricing decision maker.

8. Describe those characteristics of a situation which would indicate the use of an initial strategy of pricing near the demand ceiling; of pricing near the full-cost floor; of pricing below the full-cost floor.

9. Can cost floors change over time? Explain.

10. Why must prices be redetermined on a periodic basis?

11. Union Carbide Corporation is a large producer of ethylene glycol, a chemical used as an antifreeze. It supplies this product in bulk to private labelers and packagers. Union Carbide also sells large quantities of ethylene glycol under its well-known Prestone brand.

    Wyandotte Chemical Company, which supplies ethylene glycol anti-freeze only in bulk to private branders announced an increase in price from $1.24 per gallon in truckload lots to $1.345 per gallon.

    The Wall Street Journal reported that Union Carbide as well as Olin Mathieson and Allied Chemical Company, other producers of ethylene glycol, were studying Wyandotte's move.

    a) How should Union Carbide Corporation executives reason before deciding whether or not to raise ethylene glycol prices to the level set by Wyandotte?

    b) How should Union Carbide Corporation reason if, contrary to the above situation, Union Carbide contemplates assuming the role of price leader by initiating an increase in ethylene glycol prices with Wyandotte's reaction being uncertain?

12. How does the problem of pricing a new addition to a product line differ from the problem of pricing a single new product?

13. Does each product in a product line have to cover its full costs in the short run? In the long run?

15

Price policies

THIS CHAPTER will discuss certain policy alternatives open to those in management responsible for the administration of prices. These alternatives range from immediate departure from the established price to the maintenance of the level of price over the longer run. The discussion, therefore, will cover such topics as price variation, discounts and discount policy, geographic pricing, and resale price maintenance. In each of these areas attention will be focused on the marketing significance of the policy as well as those legal constraints which are likely to be encountered.

Introduction

A central theme of this chapter is that price policies, whether aimed at price variation or maintenance, are promotional instruments and should be considered as means by which the firm attempts to implement its overall marketing strategy.

Basic policies

The administration of a price or a set of prices may be guided by certain basic policies. These include (1) the single-price policy, (2) the nonvariable price (one-price) policy, and (3) the variable price policy.

Under a single-price policy, there is but one price for all buyers regardless of the timing of the purchase, quantity ordered, or other aspects of the transaction. Such a policy may be highly discriminatory in an economic sense but, as will be discussed later, not illegal.

A nonvariable price (one-price) policy is one under which the seller charges the same price to all buyers who purchase under similar conditions. This policy should not be confused with the single-price policy, under which there is one price for *all* buyers. Under the nonvariable price policy, different prices are charged. These differences, however, reflect variations in quantities purchased, in timing, and in other pertinent conditions of purchase. Under a nonvariable price policy, terms of sale are known and are administered uniformly. Although utilizing price differentials, a nonvariable price policy may be nondiscriminatory in both an economic and a legal sense.

A third type of basic policy is that of variable pricing. Under this policy the price arrangement between the seller and each buyer is the result of direct negotiation or other means of reflecting relative bargaining power based upon the buyer's evaluation of the product's value-in-use and the availability of alternate sources of supply.

The use of a single-price policy appeals to firms selling to small customers. The policy is easy to administer and permits the emphasis of nonprice appeals over price by salesmen and in advertisements. The policy is not likely to appeal to large buyers who believe that their volume purchases entitle them to a price reduction. The large buyer feels that a single-price policy discriminates against him, and unless the seller has built a very strong selective demand for his product, the buyer will seek a source which will vary price in this favor.[1]

Because the U.S. market is so large and diverse and because a single-price policy usually limits patronage to small customers, most sellers vary their prices. The question is, therefore, not usually one of choosing between a single-price policy and a variable price policy. It is, rather, deciding what kind of a variable price policy to follow.

Variable versus nonvariable price policies

Under a variable price policy, prices are changed when such an adjustment is indicated by the nature of market conditions. These adjustments, either upwards or downwards, may reflect a change in competition, the differing elasticities of demand among potential buyers, and differing costs of production and/or marketing accruing to the seller.

The major advantage of a variable price policy is its speed and flexibility of adjustment. Competitive moves can be counteracted almost immediately. Desires for bargaining can be accommodated. The relative emphasis upon price versus nonprice promotion can be changed to suit the needs of a particular situation. In all, a variable price policy is a powerful promotional device.

---

[1] D. Maynard Phelps and J. Howard Westing, *Marketing Management,* 3d ed. (Homewood, Ill.: Richard D. Irwin, Inc. 1968), pp. 361–62.

The policy is not without its disadvantages. These include: (1) the need to delegate pricing authority to sales managers or to salesmen, thus requiring them to be skilled in negotiation; (2) the increased cost of selling due to the time taken up by the bargaining process; (3) the loss of centralized control over prices; (4) the customer ill will caused by different prices even though conditions of sale are similar; (5) the weakened sales effort caused by the substitution of price cutting for intensified personal selling; and (6) the legal complications growing out of the Robinson-Patman Act.[2]

The advantages of a nonvariable price policy include ease of administration, simplification of the selling process, and a general recognition that such a policy is, "fair to all buyers regardless of their ability to bargain or of the competitive situation surrounding the transaction."[3] In addition, a nonvariable price policy avoids many of the previously noted disadvantages of a variable price policy. Although a nonvariable price policy has been found most often in the United States at the retail level, manufacturers appear to be recognizing the advantages of such a policy and, "seem to be adopting a one-price [nonvariable price] policy to a far greater extent in recent years than in the past, although considerable price negotiation between manufacturers and their customers still takes place."[4]

Price variation

Regardless of whether the firm follows a nonvariable or variable price policy, the act of charging different prices for essentially similar products or services is one of price variation. The reasons for such variation are generally, but not exclusively, to advance the promotional strategy of the firm. Individual companies may use differential pricing to achieve goals unique to themselves. There are, however, several commonly sought after objectives, which are noted in the next section.

Goals of price variation[5]

Change of purchase pattern. Sellers use differential prices to influence or change patterns of purchase. Lower prices may be granted to induce customers to buy in larger quantities, to buy in anticipation of future need, or to concentrate their purchases among fewer sources of supply. Higher prices may be charged certain customers to discourage

---

[2] Donald V. Harper, *Price Policy and Procedure* (New York: Harcourt, Brace, & World, Inc., 1966), p. 174.

[3] Ibid., p. 175.

[4] Ibid.

[5] See Joel Dean, *Managerial Economics* (New York: Prentice-Hall, Inc., 1951), p. 515, and Phelps and Westing, *Marketing Management*, pp. 358–59.

them from carrying the line, thus reducing the intensity of competition in certain markets.

Market segmentation. Price variation can be used to tap segments of a market which differ in price elasticity of demand. These differences in sensitivity to price may come about because of differing values-in-use among various classes of buyers and/or differing competitive situations facing the seller.

Market expansion. By offering lower prices to customers who have lower values-in-use, the market for a given product or service may be expanded. Such expansion may also be accomplished by offering lower prices to present customers to gain new applications of the product or service where prior price levels made such applications uneconomic.

Utilization of excess capacity. Differential prices which gain additional volume may utilize excess productive and/or marketing capacity. If such capacity exists, a price differential which makes a sale possible and which covers direct costs may contribute to the total profits of the firm.

Implementation of channel strategy. Differential pricing is a major device by which a firm attempts to implement its marketing strategy with respect to channels of distribution. Price variations may reflect differences in marketing tasks performed by various types of resellers or differences in the competitive environments in which they operate. Price differentials may encourage certain channels to engage in vigorous promotion of the line, or they may be used to gain representation of the line in diverse channels. On the other hand, differential pricing may discourage certain channels of distribution when such a policy is deemed useful in the furtherance of overall strategy.

To meet competition. Price variation is, of course, a device which can be used to meet competition. As previously discussed, the price ceiling for a given product or service is set by the value-in-use or utility offered the buyer as well as by the alternatives open to the buyer with respect to other sources of supply. In many situations, although the utility offered is high, the options available to the potential customer are numerous. Under such circumstances, the varying of a price in favor of the buyer may induce him to become a customer. In other situations, where the seller is disadvantaged because his production facilities are located far from the potential buyer, a price differential may be used to make the delivered price competitive with that of a seller located closer to the potential customer.

Implementation of price variations

A variation in price from the established level may be the result of direct negotiation between the seller and the buyer. In many situations the transaction may reflect economic costs to the seller and economic values to the buyer better than would be the case if the sale was made at established prices. On the other hand, where the economic power or bargaining skill are markedly unequal, equity may better be served by an established price rather than by one which is negotiated.

When using established price variations, a schedule may be developed showing net prices charged to various customers or to all customers who buy in specified quantities or at special times. A more common approach, however, is to develop a schedule of discounts from the established level of price. These discounts reflect the extent of variation in price offered to those who represent a given class of customer or who buy under certain specified conditions.

Whether or not prices are stated as net, or gross less a discount, some variation from the established level must be specified. If discounts are used by a seller to implement his policy of price variation, they must not only offer the price concession needed to attract patronage but they must operate in a manner consistent with the overall marketing strategy of the firm.

Discount policy

The discounts most commonly used to implement a policy of nonvariable pricing include quantity discounts, trade-functional discounts, and promotional discounts and allowances. Cash discounts, although widely used for financial purposes or because they have become trade practice, will not be discussed here. Discounts in the other three categories, will, however, be examined in some detail in terms of how they are used to achieve certain marketing goals as well as the degree to which specific discounts reflect cost savings accruing to the seller. This latter point is especially important when considering the defensibility of a particular discount in terms of the Robinson-Patman Act.

Quantity discounts

The quantity discount is the most widely used instrument for establishing price variations among customers. There are two types of quantity discount: the cumulative and the noncumulative. Each has different purposes and different capacities to reflect seller cost differentials.

Noncumulative quantity discounts (NCQD). This type of discount provides a reduction from the established or the list price for those customers buying in specified quantities. An NCQD is applied on a per order basis, and the principal goal of the user is to effect some change in the purchase pattern of the buyer. This change may be in the direction of larger but less frequent orders, buying in anticipation of demand, and purchasing the full line.

Larger, less frequent orders allow more efficient scheduling of production and provide economies of scale with respect to billing, physical distribution, and selling activities. Cost savings, therefore, do accrue to the seller who can gain such orders through the use of NCQDs. Whether these savings are sufficient to cover the revenues foregone by the discount is one question. Another question, and one which appears to be more important from the marketing point of view, is whether or not the discount offered is large enough to compensate the buyer for

FIGURE 15–1
Relationship between buyer and seller costs as order size increases

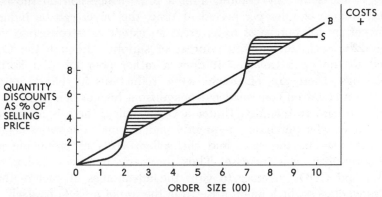

B represents increased buyer inventory holding costs with quantity purchases.
S represents seller's cost savings with quantity sales.

Source: Adapted from J. L. Heskett, Robert M. Ivie, and Nicholas A. Glaskowsky, Jr., *Business Logistics—Management of Physical Supply and Distribution*, p. 238. © 1964 The Ronald Press Co., New York.

the increase in his inventory holding costs occasioned by his purchasing in larger quantities. Given today's legal environment, the second question cannot be considered alone. Figure 15–1 graphically indicates how the two questions pertaining to the use of NCQDs are interrelated.

The shaded areas in the above illustration show that there are certain instances when the discount required to induce buyers to purchase in larger quantities can reflect the seller's cost savings. In other cases (unshaded areas) seller cost savings are insufficient to fully reflect the discounts needed to change buyer behavior.

Although NCQDs are used primarily to implement marketing strategy by getting customers to buy in larger quantities, they may have a secondary application. An NCQD can be used to satisfy the demands of larger buyers for price concessions without the need to identify these customers by trade status, industry grouping, or other criteria. NCQDs can thus be used to reflect variations in price elasticity of demand among firms of varying size and bargaining power without regard to arbitrary and often difficult classification procedures. The discount approach essentially attempts to formalize price adjustments which might be brought about by interfirm bargaining and negotiation.

Cumulative quantity discounts (CQD). This variant of the quantity discount is also used to change purchase patterns. The CQD differs from the NCQD, however, in that it is granted on the basis of total purchases over a specified period of time. For example, a discount of 2 percent might be granted a buyer purchasing at least 100 units per year.

The basic marketing goal of a CQD is to tie the customer more closely to the seller. By granting him a price concession on the basis of total volume of sales per period of time, the buyer can be induced to concentrate his purchases to as great an extent as is consistent with his needs to maintain multiple sources of supply. Although the CQD is used to "tie up patronage," it does a rather poor job of reflecting cost savings. There are, of course, some reductions in selling costs if a seller can count on continued patronage from his customers, but such savings are hard to quantify. Under a CQD policy, there is no penalty to the buyer who purchases frequently and in small quantities. Therefore, such may be the case, and the seller's costs of producing and distributing may well increase. Thus, in many instances, sellers use NCQDs and CQDs together to gain the advantages of each without the disadvantages which might arise from the use of a CQD by itself.

Regardless of the behavior of seller's costs in any specific case, CQDs can never be easily defended on the basis of cost savings. This is what might well be expected, because the objective is using a CQD is not to save on per unit production and marketing costs but rather to hold on to customers. When the pressure for justification of discounts is great, the seller is on much firmer ground with a noncumulative rather than a cumulative quantity discount.

Trade discounts

A reduction in price given to a buyer because of his position in a channel of distribution is called a trade discount. If the discount is granted to compensate customers who are resellers for their performance of certain marketing functions, perhaps a better name for the trade discount would be a "trade-functional" or "functional" discount. If the trade discount were granted to gain entry to a channel or to stimulate the resellers in the channel to provide promotional support for the product, a better name for the trade discount would be a "competitive-functional" discount.

Trade-functional discounts. As noted above, this type of discount compensates resellers for performing such marketing functions as holding inventory, engaging in sales promotion, and offering credit. Because so many resellers today have mixed trade status, i.e., wholesalers who engage in retailing and vice versa, the concept of paying resellers on the basis of functional performance has become more meaningful than paying them on the basis of their trade classifications. If the seller's objective in using a trade-functional discount is to compensate for functions performed by channel intermediaries, variations in discounts offered to customers in competition with one another may be defensible under the Robinson-Patman Act. This is especially true when variations in discounts offered reflect variations in the cost savings accruing to the seller because of customer assumption of a greater part of the marketing task.

Competitive-functional discounts.[6] When a seller is desirous of gaining entry into a channel of distribution or wants a certain level of marketing effort from his resellers in established channels, he finds that compensation for functional performance is not enough. The discounts which he offers must also take into account the competitive pressures under which the resellers operate. These pressures include the rivalry faced from other sellers for channel support, the rivalry which resellers face from other resellers within their own channels, and the competition among all resellers for patronage in the end market. Thus, an effective discount policy needed to gain channel access or support requires that payments be in excess of that required to compensate resellers for their functional performance. When such payments are made, the seller is said to be "buying distribution." Under such a discount policy, payments reflect the competitive as well as the functional needs of resellers and thus the name competitive-functional discounts. Unfortunately, these discounts which are used to buy distribution do not reflect variations in the seller's costs of serving different customers except by coincidence and are, therefore, difficult to defend under current price discrimination legislation.

Trade discount strategy

The development of a trade discount structure to implement marketing strategy is not a simple process. The objectives of the seller may vary, the needs of resellers are diverse, and competition impinges unequally on different parts of the distribution structure.

If the seller's objective in using trade discounts is to pay for functions

---

[6] For a more complete discussion of competitive-functional pricing, see Charles N. Davisson, *The Marketing of Automotive Parts* (Ann Arbor: Bureau of Business Research, Graduate School of Business Administration, The University of Michigan, 1954), pp. 910–17.

performed by resellers, his discount structure must be oriented to the costs incurred by these resellers in providing a given level of functional performance. Discounts must be set sufficiently high to gain the support of those marginal resellers whose costs are higher than average but who are needed in each geographic area to provide the intensity of distribution required by the seller. Finally, the discount schedule must reflect the seller's cost of using alternate channels of distribution (including the direct channel) to reach the market.

If the seller's strategy is aimed at buying distribution, the demand factors become more important. Questions to be considered include: (1) the discount structure of competitors, (2) the value of gaining entry to a new channel or of getting increased promotional support from an existing channel, and (3) the ability to sell to market segments of varying price elasticity of demand.

Trade discount schedules set to implement overall marketing strategy are usually discriminatory in that they favor some customers over others. Yet, these discounts are means of engaging in price competition and, as such, are of economic value to our society. From the seller's point of view the use of varying trade discount schedules, although resulting in different net prices from customers in different channels, increases total revenues and, hopefully, total profits.

Promotional discounts and allowances

Price reductions or payments granted by sellers to buyers in return for promotional services rendered by the buyer are called promotional discounts or allowances. An example of such a discount is one in which a buyer is offered a 2 percent discount on his purchases if he will give prominent window display space to the seller's product for a specified period of time. An example of an allowance is a payment to a buyer for the services of an in-store demonstration program featuring the seller's product. Other types of promotional discounts or allowances may be made to support a cooperative advertising program or to furnish incentive payments to sales personnel.

The marketing objective of these discounts or payments is to gain the promotional cooperation of the reseller. Variations in these discounts or allowances among customers may represent differences in seller's costs, but as will be noted later, a cost defense is not generally applicable when discrimination is charged on the basis of seller's use of varying promotional discounts or payments. When promotional discounts or allowances exceed the costs of services performed by buyers, they may be considered to be disguised quantity discounts or just simple price variations.[7]

---

[7] Phelps and Westing, *Marketing Management,* p. 370.

Price variation—legal issues

Whether implemented by negotiation or a discount policy, price variation is a form of price discrimination. The object of price variation is to adapt price to the requirements of a given market situation. In some cases prices may be lowered to reflect a lower value-in-use in a specific application. In other cases price may be raised to reflect increased costs of serving a customer and/or the absence of a competing source of supply. Regardless of why a price variation is used, it is almost inevitable that two or more customers will pay different prices for essentially similar products or services. When such a practice occurs, it is price discrimination, and the legal constraints relating to such discrimination must be noted by those responsible for pricing policy. Further consideration of the legality of specific price variations must await a brief discussion of the Robinson-Patman Act, which is the principal federal law relating to price discrimination.

The Robinson-Patman Act[8]

In 1936, Section 2 of the Clayton Antitrust Act of 1914 was amended by the Robinson-Patman Act. The amended section dealt with price discrimination, and the amendment sought to strengthen its provisions and extend its jurisdiction. At this time the Robinson-Patman Act has survived more than 35 years of administration by the Federal Trade Commission and continuous judicial review by the federal courts. To understand the act, which is the major legal constraint facing those sellers who use differential prices, is not an easy task. This is because the Robinson-Patman Act is not in the form of a traditional antitrust law. It is, rather, a law which attempts to redress imbalances in economic power. It is a creature of the depression years of the 1930s—a politically motivated response to the growing power of the corporate chain stores in relation to the smaller and economically weaker independent wholesalers and retailers.[9]

The Robinson-Patman Act itself is composed of six sections. Because it amended Section 2 of the Clayton Act, these sections are denoted

---

[8] This discussion is very much condensed and the intent of its presentation here is to give the reader a general overview of the act and its marketing and legal implications. Three sources which explain the act in greater detail are: Brian Dixon, *Price Discrimination and Marketing Management* (Ann Arbor: Bureau of Business Research, Graduate School of Business Administration, The University of Michigan, 1960); Phelps and Westing, *Marketing Management*, pp. 386–400; and W. David Robbins, "A Marketing Appraisal of the Robinson-Patman Act," *Journal of Marketing*, July 1959.

[9] See Joseph C. Palamountain, *The Politics of Distribution* (Cambridge, Mass.: Harvard University Press, 1955).

as 2a through 2f. Sections 2a and 2b deal with price discrimination and certain defenses available to those charged with the offense. Section 2c deals with allowances in lieu of brokerage commissions, Section 2d and 2e cover the granting of promotional services and allowances, and Section 2f holds that buyers accepting or inducing illegal price reductions are in violation of the act together with the grantor of the discriminatory price.

Injunctive or punitive action under the act may be initiated either by an FTC examiner or by a private complainant. If the presumed violation is one of price discrimination under Section 2a, a prima facie case must be shown to exist. The elements which must be present to make such a case should be fully understood by pricing executives. They include: (1) a sale at different prices, (2) by a seller engaged in interstate commerce, (3) to two or more competing customers, (4) of commodities of like grade or quality, (5) with a tendency to injure competition.

Faced with such a case, the respondent may avail himself of several defenses. These include: (1) that not all of the elements of a prima facie case were actually present as charged, (2) that variations in prices charged competing customers reflected seller cost differentials in producing, selling, or delivering goods to these customers, (3) that a price reduction was granted to one customer "in good faith" to meet the lower price offered the customer by a competitor, and (4) that there was a change in market conditions or in the goods being sold which required a distress sale at lower prices.

The respondent may avail himself of these defenses, and if he is not satisfied with the findings of the FTC in his case, he may appeal the Commission's findings to the federal courts. If found guilty of a Robinson-Patman violation, the respondent may be required to cease and desist from current pricing activities, to pay a fine, or to be imprisoned for up to one year. Customers or competitors who claim injury by the respondent's price discrimination may sue him for treble damages in federal court.

Implications for discount administration

What types of price variations are allowed under the Robinson-Patman Act? What types are patently illegal? Which pricing policies appear safer than others? These are some of the questions for which pricing executives need answers.

First, the act allows price differentials to customers who are in competition to the extent that these differentials reflect the seller's cost differences in manufacturing, selling, and/or delivery to the specific customers.

Second, under the "good faith" defense a seller may lower the price to one customer while keeping the price at former levels to competing customers if such a low price was necessary to meet a price offered the customer by a competitor.

Third, price reductions may be granted to some customers and not to others in response to "changing market conditions," such as deterioration or obsolescence of the commodity being sold or a licensed discontinuance of business by the seller.

The wording and the intent of the act does not seek to outlaw any specific type of discount or discount policy. It only says that price discrimination under certain specified conditions is illegal. A single-price policy, although discriminatory in that it penalizes customers who buy in large quantities, is not illegal under the act because the difference in price, which is the first element of a prima facie case, is missing. Likewise, a nonvariable price policy under which all customers of similar class, or who buy under the same conditions of sale, receive the same discounts is easier to defend under the act than is a variable price policy.

In terms of a cost defense, it is clear that noncumulative quantity discounts reflect seller cost savings better than do cumulative quantity discounts, and trade-functional discounts reflect variations in seller's costs better than do competitive-functional discounts.

The good-faith defense as stated in Section 2b was originally a procedural defense or a rebuttal to a prima facie case. A Supreme Court decision in 1951 in the *Detroit Gasoline* case held that the good-faith defense was an absolute defense.[10] To utilize this defense the seller must be able to prove that a customer was actually offered a lower price by a competitor and that the meeting of said price was necessary to retain the customer. Any use of a lower price to gain a customer, a partial meeting of a lower price, or an undercutting of a competitor's price will invalidate the defense.

Section 2c is concerned with the granting of price reductions to those buyers who perform their own brokerage services. The law simply states that such payments or allowances are illegal. The political basis of this section of the act was the desire to keep the large integrated chain from gaining a price advantage over their smaller and nonintegrated competitors. There are no defenses to the charge that a seller gave a buyer an allowance to reflect nonuse of a broker except proof that such was not the case.

Sections 2d and 2e cover the granting of promotional allowances or the offering of promotional services. These sections were placed in the act to prevent discrimination in the disguised form of supplementary payments or services offered to selected buyers and not to others. Two

---

[10] *Standard Oil Co. v. FTC,* 340 U.S. 231, 71 S.Ct. 240 (1951).

guidelines govern the use of promotional allowances and services under current FTC rulings.

First, payments or services must be granted on a *proportionately equal* basis. This means that competing buyers can receive payments or services which are roughly proportional to their dollar purchases from the manufacturer. For example, a buyer of $100,000 worth of goods may receive 10 times the dollar value of services and/or allowances from a manufacturer than a buyer whose purchases total $10,000 during the same period.

The second guideline is that all competing buyers must be able to *participate* in the manufacturer's program. The concept of participation covers both the informing of all buyers by the manufacturer of the allowances and services available and the designing of a program sufficiently flexible so that all buyers can benefit from the involvement. In other words, the program of the manufacturer must not be tailored solely to the needs of the larger buyers.

There are no absolute defenses to a Section 2d or 2e violation except proof that the allowances and services were properly offered and were distributed in a nondiscriminatory manner. Although in a very few isolated cases defenses available under Sections 2a and 2b have been attempted, the results are inconclusive.

Section 2f, which holds a buyer who knowingly induces or receives a discriminatory price, allowance, or service equally guilty with the grantor, has no specific defense. The best course of action for a buyer charged with a 2f violation is to help the grantor prove that there was no illegal discrimination. Another and more difficult approach for the buyer is for him to prove that he was unaware that the price, allowance, or service received was illegal.

Geographic pricing policies

In addition to the development of price differentials reflecting variations in quantities purchased, the trade status of the buyer, and the extent of the marketing job performed by him, the seller must also consider price policies which concern the relative geographic location of the seller and the buyer. These policies range from those under which the seller absorbs the varying costs of transportation to arrive at a uniform delivered price for all customers to those under which the seller passes all freight costs on to the buyer. In between these extremes are other policies which attempt to simplify the administration of price variations imposed by location or which seek to improve the position of the seller when he is faced with competition from rivals located nearer to a customer than is he.

F.o.b. factory. The first policy to be considered is that of "free on board" at the seller's factory or warehouse. Under this arrangement the customer assumes title to the goods when they are turned over to a common carrier and in addition assumes the costs of transport and insurance. The delivered price varies in relation to the distance between the factory and the customer, while prices at the factory net of transport costs are constant for all customers served unless some other type of price variation is operative.

Uniform delivered price. Under this policy the seller assumes all of the costs of delivery in order that all of his customers pay a single, delivered price. Such a policy is often called "f.o.b. customer's place of business," "freight allowed," or "postage stamp" pricing. Although the delivered prices which customers pay are equal regardless of their location, the net prices received by the seller at the factory differ in relation to the location of the customer served.

Freight equalization. A seller engaged in f.o.b. factory pricing often discovers that his market is limited geographically because competitors located closer to customers than is he have an advantage in that they can quote lower delivered prices. In order to extend his market, the seller may absorb some of the freight costs, so that his delivered price is equal to or less than that of rivals located closer to the customer. Such a practice is called freight equalization and involves the absorption of different amounts of freight costs resulting in varying net receipts for the seller.

Zone pricing. When the costs of freight are too high to allow a uniform delivered price over the entire market area, the seller may compromise by establishing a uniform delivered price for a given geographic area or zone. In so doing he may gain some of the promotional and billing advantages of a uniform delivered price policy without having to assume all of the freight costs. A policy of zone pricing should not be undertaken lightly by management because of certain associated results of such a policy which may be illegal. Perhaps the following illustration will indicate the nature of price behavior under zone pricing.

Assume the following attributes for the zone system pictured in Figure 15–2: (1) the firm (A) located in Ann Arbor sells a single product with a factory price of $100; (2) delivery costs are linear with distance and are $0.10/mile; and (3) zonal boundaries are 100 miles apart. The problem facing the seller using a system such as illustrated above is how to set the price for each zone. If the price is determined on the basis of factory cost plus delivery cost to the leading edge of the zone (for example, x_1 in zone II), then the delivered price for all customers in zone II will be $100 + $0.10/mile (50 miles) or $105. If the seller sets the price to reflect costs to get to the far side of the zone (x_2 in zone II), then the zone price is $100 + $0.10/mile (150 miles) or $115.

FIGURE 15–2
A zone pricing system (single firm)

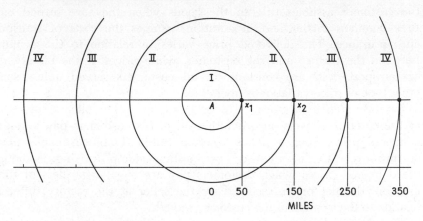

In the first case the seller is absorbing varying amounts of freight costs for customers in the zone located beyond the leading edge; in the second case he is charging customers located nearer to A than x_2 for freight costs which do not exist. This practice results in customers paying what has been called "phantom freight."

If the seller sets his zone prices on the basis of the average cost of delivery to the zone, all customers located before the zonal midpoint will be charged phantom freight, and all customers located beyond the zonal midpoint will have some of their freight charges absorbed by the seller. The legal implications of these happenings will be discussed at the end of this section.

Basing point pricing. The last type of geographic pricing method to be discussed is one in which delivered prices are quoted by adding to the f.o.b. factory price the delivery cost from a specific geographic location to that of the customer regardless of whether or not the shipment was made from that point. The specific location so chosen is called a basing point.

If there is but one location from which all sellers quote delivered prices, the industry is said to use a single basing point system. The steel industry's "Pittsburgh Plus" was the prime example of the use of a single basing point from which to set prices.

When more than one geographic location is used from which to calculate delivered prices (either by a firm or a group of firms in an industry), a multiple basing point system is said to exist. These systems are not illegal per se, but certain attributes associated with their use may run afoul of the law.

In Figure 15–3 a situation is illustrated in which three selling points, S_1, S_2, and S_3, serve three customers, B_1, B_2, and B_3. The prices at

FIGURE 15–3
A multiple basing point system with two base mills

	Price (at destination) −	Delivery cost =	Factory net (price at origin)
Seller 1 (base mill) sells to:			
Buyer 1................	$103	$ 3	$100
Buyer 2................	104	10	94
Buyer 3................	107	7	100
Seller 2 (nonbase mill) sells to:			
Buyer 1................	103	5	98
Buyer 2................	104	5	99
Buyer 3................	107	6	101
Seller 3 (base mill) sells to:			
Buyer 1................	103	9	94
Buyer 2................	104	4	100
Buyer 3................	107	10	97

PRICE AT BASE MILL = $100/UNIT

S_1 and S_3 are $100 per unit. These locations are designated as basing points while S_2 is a nonbase mill or point of origin. Distances between these points are as noted on the connecting lines.

From an examination of the behavior of individual transactions, it can be seen that when a seller is serving a customer located closer to a base mill than to the seller's mill, freight charges must be absorbed by the seller. Such absorption occurs when seller 1 ships to buyer 2. Although freight costs are $10, the customer is located sufficiently close to the basing point at S_3, so that the seller must absorb $6 in freight costs.

In other cases the seller is forced to raise his price above that which would be expected based on actual cost of delivery. For example, seller 2 charges buyer 3, $107, although the actual freight costs are $6. The added charge of $1 is phantom freight assessed because the price the buyer pays is related not to the point of origin of the shipment but to the location of the buyer in relation to the nearest base mill. That mill in this case is S_1.

Geographic pricing—legal constraints[11]

Many of the geographic pricing policies described above have run into legal difficulties over the past 50 years. In 1921, for example, the FTC complained that the single basing point system used by the steel industry discriminated in price in violation of Section 2 of the Clayton Act. The FTC claimed, in addition, that the "Pittsburgh Plus" method of quoting delivered prices violated Section 5 of the FTC Act. It held that the steel industry was engaged in a collusive attempt to fix prices and that such activity was deemed an "unfair method of competition" under the law. By 1924, the Commission ordered the steel industry to cease using a single basing point system. The industry obeyed without going to court and changed to a multiple basing point system. For the ensuing 16 years, all was relatively peaceful, but in 1940 the FTC opened a new attack on basing points which was to last a decade. The various rulings of the FTC and the subsequent support of the FTC by the courts resulted in a substantial limitation of the use of multiple basing points as a means of implementing a delivered-price policy.

The two major questions raised by the use of basing points are: (1) Is the system a method by which competing sellers attempt to fix prices? (2) Does the system discriminate in price to such an extent that competition is diminished among buyers? At present, it appears that if a basing point system does not result in price fixing through the systematic absorption of freight, if it does not contain nonbase mills which give rise to phantom freight, and if it does not result in different factory nets being received from competing buyers, then the user has a good chance of avoiding legal difficulties. The design of such a system is so difficult and the assurance that present FTC policy will hold for the future so tenuous that most sellers formerly using basing points have changed to straight f.o.b. factory pricing.

Individual sellers who want to engage in freight equalization on an *ad hoc* basis have had very little trouble with the law. Uniform delivered prices also seem to be quite acceptable to the FTC because under this policy all delivered prices are equal. The irony of the situation is that in the case of basing points, the FTC defines price as mill or factory net. Under a policy of uniform delivered price, the opposite definition prevails: that the price is the amount which is paid at the destination. Legislative change or judicial review is sorely needed to clarify the question of whether price is that which is received by the seller at

---

[11] See Phelps and Westing, *Marketing Management*, pp. 400–407, for a most complete treatment of this subject.

the point of shipment or paid by the buyer at the point of receipt.

Zone pricing by members of an industry has run into legal difficulties when all members of the industry have used identical zonal boundaries and identical zonal price differentials. The charge was one of violation of Section 5 of the FTC Act. The courts have held that in these cases evidence of collusion is not necessary if the results of a pricing system are the same as if there had been an actual meeting of the competitors or communication among them.

Section 5 is not violated by an individual firm's use of a zone system. Problems can arise, however, when customers located near zonal boundaries who are in competition pay different prices. In these situations the seller may be in violation of the Robinson-Patman Act.

Resale price maintenance

As stated in the introduction to this chapter, a seller may choose from pricing policy alternatives ranging from those which entail variation of price from an established level to those which are aimed at the maintenance of such a level. The latter policies are especially difficult to implement when the seller uses independent resellers in his pattern of distribution and when the title to the goods being sold passes to these middlemen.

When the seller decides to follow a policy of resale price maintenance, commonly called RPM, it is because the advantages to be gained from such a course of action outweigh the disadvantages. These advantages are diverse, but like those sought by the user of a policy of price variation, are essentially promotional. They arise out of the ability of a properly executed RPM policy to eliminate or control price rivalry among resellers in the channels of distribution. When price rivalry is diminished, certain benefits may accrue to the seller. These include the following.

Protection of product image. The reduction of price rivalry at the retail level may protect the consumer image of a product or a brand. The stabilization or control of resale price is especially important when the buyer associates quality with price as in the case of a luxury good or prestige item. Stabilization or maintenance of retail price is also of value when consumers purchase the product as a gift item.

Reduce interchannel rivalry. The use of an RPM policy can restrict price competition among different channels of distribution, thus protecting the margins of those resellers in high-cost channels. The promotional advantage sought is the added market coverage gained through the seller's ability to distribute through a variety of channels which differ in their average costs of operation.

Reduce intrachannel rivalry. The use of RPM to reduce price competition among competing resellers in the same channel of distribution is aimed at protecting reseller margins from erosion. If RPM can preserve margins, the seller may be able to gain the support of the resellers in terms of higher levels of nonprice promotion and service to the consumer.

Implementing a policy of resale price maintenance

If development of overall marketing strategy indicates that a price maintenance policy is desirable, there are several ways in which such a policy might be implemented. Sellers might, for example, become sufficiently selective in their distribution so that the line becomes important to the reseller. Then a franchise agreement might be negotiated with each reseller, specifying the price and discount schedule which would govern the resale of the product line. Failure to comply with this agreement would be grounds for its possible termination. Where the product line requires more intensive distribution to gain market coverage, the manufacturer's bargaining power is diminished. Selling to specific market segments which do not overlap at prices which reflect elasticity of demand in each segment may keep prices stable both within the segment and among segments. Finally, before turning to legal means of implementing an RPM policy, the seller might consider reducing his discounts so that margins are not so wide that they induce price cutting.

In many situations the only recourse left to the seller is to enter into price-setting contracts with resellers. These contracts are "price-fixing" agreements and, therefore, need federal and state enabling legislation to exist. These laws are commonly called "fair trade" laws, and the policy of engaging in an RPM policy using the contract approach under these laws is called "fair trading." The so called "fair trade" contract to be effective requires a nonsigner clause. This allows a contract made between a seller and one of his reseller customers to be legally binding on all other resellers of the line in the state when they are formally notified of the existence of the original agreement. Because of the controversial nature of the nonsigner clause, many states, including Michigan, have ruled such fair trade laws to be unconstitutional. It has been estimated that less than 30 of the 50 states have effective fair trade laws.[12]

A recent analysis of methods used to encourage stability of retail prices by manufacturers of consumer goods seems to indicate that the use of fair trade laws, promotional allowances, and moral suasion were relatively ineffective ways of attaining RPM goals. The author of the

---

[12] William J. Stanton, *Fundamentals of Marketing*, 2d ed. (New York: McGraw-Hill Book Co., 1967), p. 470.

study suggests that restricting the intensity of distribution, market segmentation, and reductions in discounts and allowances are more effective
and less controversial ways of gaining stability of price at retail levels.[13]

Analysis suggests that a policy of RPM is too intimately related to
product, channel, and promotional strategy to be applied by law. It
appears that successful application of RPM is more dependent on the
overall program of the manufacturer (or other seller) than upon the
legal environment in the existing market area.

Implications

The basic questions to be asked by a seller in attempting to decide
whether or not to follow an RPM policy might include: (1) Will the
revenue gains from an RPM policy cover the costs of policing the dealer
organization? (2) Will most of the resellers stay loyal to the seller's
policy in the face of a few recalcitrant price cutters? (3) Are stable
and relatively high prices needed to support the prestige image of the
product or product line? (4) Does the amount of aggressive selling
required from resellers require an RPM policy to protect their margins?
If the answer to most of the above queries is positive, RPM becomes
a viable policy alternative.

In contrast to a policy of price variation, RPM attempts to reduce
the influence of price in the marketing mixes of the members of the
reseller organization. Thus, if price variation aimed at gaining greater
volume from various resellers results in a mix of both price channels
and channels which do not emphasize price in their promotional strategies, the seller will have great difficulty in implementing an RPM policy.
Price variation and RPM policies appear to work in opposite directions,
and the wise manufacturer will decide in which direction he wants
to go and will develop a policy which is consistent and which will
lead him to his goals. Only if the market is clearly segmented can the
seller use both policies with some hope of success. Here an RPM policy
may be used in one market segment while a policy of price variation
may be used to tap another and more price sensitive market segment.

Conclusion

This chapter concludes the sequence on pricing. In the preceding
chapter, the discussion centered on the problems of determining a price
or a basic level of price. This chapter has attempted to illustrate how
variations from the established level or maintenance of levels of price

---

[13] See Louis W. Stern, "Approaches to Achieving Retail Stability," *Business
Horizons* (Fall 1964), pp. 75–86.

may be used for promotional purposes. The coverage of topics was highly selective and of necessity brief. The purpose of the two-chapter sequence has been to provide an overview of pricing in the context of the marketing mix.

Pricing in all of its various nuances is more of an art than a science. But in the same manner in which an artist improves his work by studying the principles of composition, perspective, and color, the executive can improve the quality of his pricing decisions by understanding more thoroughly the economic, psychological, and legal forces which impinge upon price determination and administration.

Questions

1. Why do most American business firms follow a variable price policy rather than a single-price policy?

2. How does price variation relate to the development of an overall marketing strategy? Specifically, how does price variation facilitate the achievement of product, channel, and nonprice promotional objectives?

3. "Discounts differ in terms of the marketing goals they seek to achieve as well as in their ability to reflect differences in sellers' costs." Explain the promotional and legal implications of this statement.

4. Compare and contrast trade-functional discounts and competitive-functional discounts.

5. What is the difference between a promotional discount and a simple price variation? Is this difference as clearly defined in practice as in theory?

6. What types of price variations are allowed by the Robinson-Patman Act? What types are illegal?

7. What is the "good faith" defense to a Robinson-Patman Act violation? Trace the evolvement of this defense from its initial interpretation to its present interpretation.

8. What is a basing point? A basing point system? Are all basing point systems illegal?

9. In commenting on proposed federal "fair trade" legislation the Council of Economic Advisers to the President said, in a special report: "For many types of goods, the total demand by consumers is sensitive to the number of retail outlets which handle them, and manufacturers, therefore, like to have as many outlets as possible." How do you reason concerning the outlet coverage implications of a policy of resale price maintenance?

10. What are some of the ways in which a seller may implement a policy of resale price maintenance? What legal restrictions must he be aware of in designing his program?

cases for part six

Trolex Sales Company*

Price determination and pricing strategy

A group of several young men in Detroit, Michigan, developed and patented a device called the "Trolex." The device could be used to measure the speed of a boat in water so that a fisherman could select and maintain the proper speed to troll for fish (see Exhibit 1).

Trolling is the art of dragging a fishing lure through the water at a slow speed so that the lure resembles a small fish, thus attracting the desired game fish. To be effective the lure must be drawn through the water at an appropriate and constant speed.

The Trolex

The Trolex consisted of a weight on a string, attached to a spring, which in turn was attached to a pivoted pointer. The pointer rotated on the face of a dial. The Trolex was clamped to the side of the boat, and the weight was allowed to drag in the water. The faster the boat moved, the greater was the drag on the string, as indicated by the pointer on the dial. If a constant speed was maintained, there was a constant drag on the line, and the pointer remained on the same number.

To make use of the device, the fisherman dropped the lure in the water near the side of the boat so that he could observe it. He then moved the boat at the speed at which the lure made the proper motions, and he noted the position of the pointer on the dial of the Trolex. Then he could let his line out, maintain the proper speed by watching the dial setting, and be sure that his lure was moving in the proper manner and at the desired depth.

Control of the depth and action of the lure was important to the serious troller. Control was particularly important immediately following

---

* Written by Gordon E. Miracle, Professor, Department of Advertising, Michigan State University. Although the general background of the case is essentially accurate, many of the specific facts of the case have been disguised.

EXHIBIT 1

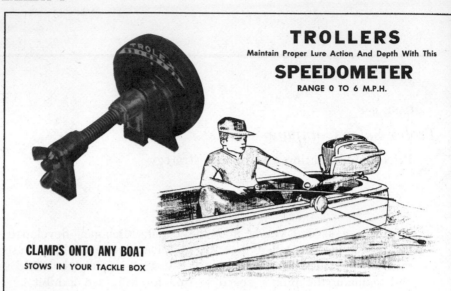

TROLLERS

Maintain Proper Lure Action And Depth With This

SPEEDOMETER

RANGE 0 TO 6 M.P.H.

CLAMPS ONTO ANY BOAT
STOWS IN YOUR TACKLE BOX

INSTALLATION AND OPERATION INSTRUCTIONS

Your TROLEX speedometer comes to you in convenient take-down form for easy carrying and storage in your tackle box. It can be installed on any boat in a matter of seconds.

To Install TROLEX, Follow These Simple Steps.

1. Squeeze two clamp fingers together. Insert bolt head into square hole in dial head. Rotate bolt ⅛ turn to engage internal recess. Release pressure on fingers and engage square end of clamp in square hole in dial head with finger extended straight down from dial.

2. Clamp TROLEX on left side of boat. One or both clamps can be turned end for end on the bolt to accomodate boats having a side thickness from ⅞″ to 2⅝″.

3. Insert wire strut thru hole in sinker with small end of sinker toward loop. Bend over end of wire to keep sinker from sliding off.

4. Attach one end of line to loop in wire strut. Thread other end of line thru hole on dial assembly marked "L". Adjust length of line so that sinker is approximately 10″ below the surface of the water. This is the setting for the average small boat which has sides 10 to 12 inches above the water line.

5. When using TROLEX on larger boats with greater free board, determine correct line length as follows: for calibration purposes power your power up to the highest speed you expect to troll (normally 4 to 5 M.P.H.). Let

out enough sinker line to enable the sinker to remain slightly below the surface of the water at that maximum speed.

Hints for Choosing the Best Speeds for
Trolling Your Favorite Lures

Few manufacturers of artificial bait specify, in miles per hour, the best speed or speeds at which to troll their lures. Many manufacturers, however, do emphasize slow speeds for maximum action. Therefore, the surest plan is as follows:

1. Troll selected lure alongside boat and observe the reading on TROLEX speedometer dial when desired lure action is obtained.

2. Let out line until the desired trolling depth is reached. Then regulate boat speed as necessary to maintain speedometer reading at same value as observed in item 1 above.

This procedure will insure your lure maintaining the desired action and running depth regardless of wind and wave action.

TROLEX SALES CO.
P. O. BOX 53
ANCHORVILLE, MICHIGAN

a strike, when the fisherman wished to get his lure back to the same place as soon as possible. The path of the lure depended upon two factors: (1) the amount of line out, and (2) the speed of the lure. An accurate speedometer such as the Trolex was especially valuable, since a difference of as little as one-half mile per hour could mean that the lure was 4 or 5 feet lower or higher than desired.

Forming a partnership

The group of men that developed the Trolex decided that it might be profitable to form a partnership to produce and sell it. They noted that fishermen often spent considerable sums of money on fishing gear and accessories. For example, a rod and reel might cost $20 to $50. A tackle box typically retailed at $8 to $10 and often was filled with $30 to $40 worth of accessories. Lures and baits usually sold in the $0.75 to $2 range. Boat speedometers sold for $8 and up, although they were not a good substitute for Trolex because they usually were inaccurate from 0 to 10 miles per hour. A minnow bucket could be purchased for about $2.50, and a landing net typically cost about $3.75.

The founding group included several engineers and men with business experience. They all held full-time jobs, and each partner expected to spend only a few hours of his spare time monthly on the business unless it should turn out to be highly successful.

Initial cost estimates indicated that the partnership needed a total of about $3,500 for dies, materials, and other "start-up" costs. This amount was easily raised by the prospective partners. Furthermore, one of the members of the group owned a garage which provided suitable space to assemble and pack the Trolex.

The device was simple and inexpensive to manufacture. The cost of materials varied somewhat (see Exhibit 2). Purchased piece parts cost about 30 cents per unit if ordered in lots of 144 or more. The five castings, which could be made by other firms using the partnership dies, cost 64 cents per unit if purchased in lots of more than 500.

On the average it took a man three minutes to assemble one unit and pack it for shipment. The cost of labor, whether performed by the partners or by hired employees, was approximately $2.50 per hour. The package consisted of a plastic box with styrofoam in the bottom. The costs of the packaging materials were included in the material costs shown in Exhibit 2. Shipping costs were about 6 cents per unit in lots of 100 or less and 3 cents per unit in larger lots. The cost of carrying an inventory of materials and finished units was considered to be insignificant. The dies and patterns, which cost about $3,000, were estimated to have a useful life of about three to four years. Rent on the garage in which the Trolex units were assembled was $300 per year.

EXHIBIT 2
Material costs

Castings	Quantity ordered			Piece parts	Quantity ordered	
	50–100	101–500	501–Up		12–144	144–U
1—Back plate w/dial, plastic..........	$0.30	$0.24	$0.20	1—Stove bolt.....	$0.10	$0.08
1—Front plate, plastic.	0.26	0.20	0.18	2—Metal washers..	0.02	0.01
2—Metal plates.......	0.32	0.25	0.20	1—Rubber washer.	0.02	0.01
1—Pointer, plastic.....	0.09	0.07	0.06	1—Wing nut......	0.11	0.07
	$0.97	$0.76	$0.64	1—Spring.........	0.06	0.04
				1—Weight........	0.02	0.02
				4 foot—String.....	0.01	0.01
				1—Plastic box.....	0.05	0.04
				Styrofoam........	0.02	0.02
				Glue.............	*	
				Paint............	*	
					$0.41	$0.30

* Insignificant.

The group felt that administrative work could be handled by one of the partners. He would be expected to perform the following duties:

1. Determine the quantity of the product to be produced each month,
2. Order sufficient materials periodically to produce the desired quantity,
3. Inform the others in the group as to when and how long they would be required to work,
4. Keep the books.

It was estimated that for the first year this administrative time would amount to about 80 hours and would be fairly constant regardless of the number of units produced. This time was valued at $5 per hour.

Marketing plan

Members of the group felt that the market for Trolex would be large and spread throughout much of the United States, since there were more than 20 million fishermen who purchase licenses, permits, and stamps in the United States (see Exhibit 3). In Michigan alone there were nearly one million fishermen (see Exhibit 4).

Although they felt that the market could be reached through sporting goods stores, department stores, hardware stores, and perhaps even drug stores, the partners were not in a position to contact all appropriate middlemen in the country. Therefore, they planned to try to achieve distribution in selected sporting goods stores in locations where fishing was quite popular, such as northern Michigan and Wisconsin. They also decided to take several advertisements in *Field and Stream,* hoping that it would bring in orders by mail.

EXHIBIT 3

Summary of the number of paid fishing license holders, license sales and the cost to fishermen, fiscal year 1962

State	Paid Fishing License Holders*	Resident Fishing Licenses, Tags Permits & Stamps Issued	Nonresident Fishing Licenses, Tags Permits & Stamps Issued	Total Fishing Licenses, Tags Permits & Stamps Issued*	Gross Cost to Fishermen
Alabama................	413,159	518,284	27,659	545,943	$ 786,820
Alaska.................	53,583	42,015	14,783	56,798	343,156
Arizona................	212,266	245,560	37,265	282,825	807,707
Arkansas...............	456,663	298,841	157,822	456,663	1,183,070
California..............	1,485,809	3,192,002	303,740	3,495,742	6,247,472
Colorado...............	413,525	296,628	120,556	417,184	1,501,931
Connecticut............	107,545	104,172	3,373	107,545	414,522
Delaware...............	11,141	10,226	915	11,141	18,396
Florida.................	502,610	385,704	135,223	520,927	1,068,498
Georgia................	495,882	484,040	13,241	497,281	588,994
Hawaii.................	4,209	4,190	19	4,209	8,824
Idaho..................	239,374	159,730	80,673	240,403	1,007,136
Illinois................	700,654	683,964	21,813	705,777	1,487,023
Indiana................	754,431	726,290	34,209	760,499	1,013,848
Iowa...................	414,215	405,840	13,688	419,528	963,041
Kansas................	271,362	261,919	9,857	271,776	827,360
Kentucky..............	316,090	247,257	69,713	316,970	1,021,961
Louisiana..............	223,031	202,297	22,304	224,601	272,429
Maine.................	229,019	153,647	76,545	230,192	758,381
Maryland..............	111,741	97,101	14,640	111,741	339,390
Massachusetts.........	183,924	140,957	4,946	145,903	578,165
Michigan..............	927,627	888,508	226,628	1,115,136	2,712,551
Minnesota.............	1,287,947	1,091,131	217,720	1,308,851	2,494,789
Mississippi............	285,898	211,022	81,116	292,138	542,780
Missouri...............	691,005	746,863	137,903	884,766	2,509,597
Montana...............	235,709	183,594	47,544	231,138	459,883
Nebraska..............	221,301	204,919	16,382	221,301	468,054
Nevada................	63,098	49,237	22,845	72,082	227,801
New Hampshire........	121,192	83,029	45,933	128,962	444,981
New Jersey............	138,950	205,850	9,894	215,744	758,066
New Mexico...........	142,168	98,745	46,111	144,856	547,061
New York..............	727,246	678,346	48,900	727,246	2,379,985
North Carolina.........	319,277	433,336	44,067	477,403	933,267
North Dakota..........	72,719	50,194	4,076	54,270	125,411
Ohio...................	821,452	802,427	19,395	821,822	1,683,303
Oklahoma..............	462,695	381,957	83,459	465,416	1,036,088
Oregon................	436,407	636,157	29,826	665,983	1,577,943
Pennsylvania...........	602,323	578,235	24,088	602,323	2,013,633
Rhode Island..........	15,207	21,315	505	21,820	51,555
South Carolina.........	272,192	281,892	21,382	303,274	599,124
South Dakota..........	148,443	109,075	43,226	152,301	293,822
Tennessee.............	649,743	708,714	179,573	888,287	1,128,527
Texas..................	832,913	832,913	...†	832,913	1,790,763
Utah..................	172,762	169,429	16,207	185,636	527,958
Vermont...............	101,028	70,107	32,004	102,111	240,066
Virginia................	324,165	475,425	32,970	508,395	883,209
Washington............	377,546	358,942	18,679	377,621	1,639,052
West Virginia..........	160,051	238,651	12,497	251,148	555,862
Wisconsin..............	1,060,000	693,615	377,854	1,071,469	3,620,729
Wyoming..............	132,168	70,899	65,655	136,554	679,179
Totals............	19,403,465	20,015,191	3,069,423	23,084,614	$54,163,163

* A paid license holder is one individual regardless of the number of licenses purchased. Data certified by State fish and game departments.

† Same license issued to both residents and nonresidents.

Source: Michigan Department of Conservation. Compiled by the Bureau of Sports Fisheries and Wildlife from information furnished by the State fish and game departments.

EXHIBIT 4
Fishing license sales in Michigan 1948–61

Year	Resident Fish	Temporary Nonresident Fish	Annual Nonresident Fish	Trout Stamps
1948..........807,911	160,245	121,745	169,498
1949..........819,702	154,740	127,430	182,058
1950..........789,382	136,302	130,376	170,773
1951..........841,913	141,838	140,587	186,138
1952..........848,659	141,007	156,720	193,744
1953..........852,788	142,342	164,795	208,497
1954..........878,668	153,246	156,220	216,774
1955..........876,670	130,379	143,613	226,824
1956..........852,440	128,563	138,654	234,009
1957..........854,775	123,197	131,461	233,417
1958..........837,877	101,547	117,038	202,572
1959..........756,132	94,525	113,816	192,580
1960..........752,806	88,916	111,130	190,246
1961..........739,063	83,413	105,151	187,509

Source: Michigan Department of Conservation, *1895–1961 History of Fishing and Miscellaneous License Sales*, p. 2.

EXHIBIT 5
Reasons for purchases of outboard motorboats

Primary reasons	*Percentage of purchases in 1959*
Hunting....................................	6.9
Fishing....................................	42.1
Racing....................................	2.9
Cruising....................................	28.0
Water skiing................................	19.6
Rental....................................	0.2
Commercial................................	0.3
	100.0

Source: Outboard Boating Club of America and National Association of Engine and Boat Manufacturers, published in Milton P. Brown, Wilbur B. England and John B. Matthews, Jr., *Problems in Marketing* (New York: McGraw-Hill Book Co., 1961), p. 123. Used by permission.

The partners selected a number of sporting goods stores in Michigan and Wisconsin and sent each of them four free samples of the Trolex. They hoped the item would catch on and generate mail orders. In order to get an idea of the proper price for the Trolex, the partners divided the selected dealers who received the free samples into five test groups. Each group was quoted a different wholesale price. The intention was to try to estimate the total quantity which would be sold at each price. The groups were offered the Trolex at the following prices: Group A: $4.75; Group B: $4.00; Group C: $3.35; Group D: $2.65; and Group E: $2.00.

EXHIBIT 6

Selling price to retailers	Expected annual sales (units)
$4.75	400
4.00	500
3.35	1,000
2.65	1,600
2.00	1,800

Based on the size of the initial orders by the selected retail sporting goods stores, and on the reactions of some of the store owners, estimates were made of the total number of units that would be sold if the price to all retailers in the test groups were set at each of the levels shown in Exhibit 6. Sporting goods stores require approximately a 40 percent markup; thus if the sporting goods store purchased the Trolex at $3, the fisherman would pay about $5.

In the first few advertisements in *Field and Stream,* the Trolex was priced at $7.95. Although the advertisement attracted few orders from ultimate consumers, it did bring in a number of inquiries from sports dealers, and even one from a New England sports broadcaster. In response to these inquiries, a wholesale price of $4.75 was quoted.

CASE QUESTION

Considering the various aspects of demand and cost, what retail price for the Trolex do you recommend? Explain your reasoning.

CASE 6–2

Pop-Tent (B)*

Pricing a new product

Some years ago, the management of the Pop-Tent Corporation of Ann Arbor, Michigan, was reviewing the pricing of its basic product, the "Pop-Tent Camper."

---

* Written by Ross J. Wilhelm, Professor of Business Economics, Graduate School of Business Administration, The University of Michigan.

The Pop-Tent Corporation was formed to conduct the business of manufacturing and selling camping and outdoor recreational equipment. Among the principal assets of the firm were the inventory of and an exclusive license to manufacture, sell, and to use the trademark "Pop-Tent." The Pop-Tent was based on a new concept of tent design and erection which had been invented and developed by Henry Stribley and William Moss of Ann Arbor.[1] The promoters of the Pop-Tent Corporation, Clifford G. Baker and Oscar W. Haab, had joined with Messrs. Stribley and Moss after the invention of Pop-Tent to help them produce and market the then existing line. A year later Mr. Baker and Mr. Haab, along with other investors, had bought out the interests of Mr. Stribley and Mr. Moss, both of whom wanted to devote themselves to other activities, and subsequently the corporation was formed.

During the period they were associated with Pop-Tent, Mr. Baker and Mr. Haab had encountered all of the problems of launching and operating a new and inadequately financed business. They had raised funds from friends and other persons in the area. They had established channels of distribution, expanded the line, and had organized and trained a work force to manufacture their basic products.

Line of products

At the time the pricing of the product was under review, the firm's line included 22 different items, 11 of which they manufactured, and the remainder of which were produced by other firms but sold by and under the Pop-Tent name.

Of the tents produced by the company, three embodied the design and mechanical principles of Pop-Tent. These were called "Pop-Tent Camper," which was the basic tent; "Pop-Tent Beach Cabana," a colorful version of the camper designed especially for waterside use; and the "Pop-Tent Sportsman's Shelter," which was a smaller adaptation of the camper and cabana for use as a portable duck-blind or as an ice-fishing shelter.

The other products manufactured and sold by the firm were:

1. "Para-Wing"—A portable, outdoor tarpaulin, supported by two poles and four stakes which was so designed that it could be erected for outdoor shelter without any center poles and without the canvas sagging. This product was designed by Mr. Moss and was manufactured in a 12′ × 12′ size and in two colors: yellow and white stripes and green and white stripes. It was designed to provide shade and privacy for backyard, patio, or picnic use by consumers or for temporary shelter for advertising or display of merchandise.
2. "Wing-Tent"—A large camping tent formed by sewing vertical side

---

[1] See "Pop-Tent (A)," p. 59, for the history of this invention and these products.

panels, together with a sewn-in floor panel, to the "Para-Wing," the enclosure thus serving as a large recreational tent. This was the largest tent sold by the firm.

3. "Para-Wall"—A colorful canvas wall panel, held up by poles and staked ropes for use as protection against wind and to provide some privacy on outdoor picnics or camping trips.

4. "Tour-A-Tent"—This was a tent which was carried on and erected on the top of a station wagon. It was large enough to sleep two adults. To use the tent, the campers climbed up a ladder to get to the top of the wagon and could easily erect the shelter, which provided ample sleeping room although it was not large enough to stand in. A zippered screen door prevented anyone from falling out. Also, an overhead shelter extended out from the side of the tent and provided shelter on the side of the station wagon.

Other items designed, manufactured, and sold by the firm at this time included: car window screens tailored for car or station wagon windows to allow sleeping or sitting in the car on trips or at drive-in theaters, etc.; toy Para-Wing and Pop-Tents large enough for youngsters to play in; a "Breeze-Wing Screened House," which was of the same design as the "Wing Tent" except that the four walls were screened for use as a summer house or for backyard sitting; "Station Wagon Boot," which was a canvas device designed to convert the wagon into sleeping quarters by closing off the windows and back tail gate for privacy.

The other items sold by the firm but not manufactured by them included air mattresses, sleeping bags, various knapsacks, and a line of conventionally designed tents.

During the period December 1, of the year after incorporation, to June 30, the company's sales totaled $188,063.01. These sales, by product, are shown in Exhibit 1.

EXHIBIT 1
Pop-Tent Corporation, sales by product, December 1–June 30, of the year after incorporation

Product	Actual sales	Percent of total
Pop-Tent Camper.............	$ 48,335.07	25.6
Wing-Tent....................	29,620.11	15.8
Tour-A-Tent..................	26,756.36	14.3
Station Wagon Boot...........	25,756.36	13.7
Air Mattresses...............	17,702.74	9.5
Para-Wing...................	10,270.99	5.5
Screens.....................	8,068.85	4.1
Breeze-Wing.................	5,869.25	3.1
Other.......................	15,683.28	8.4
	$188,063.01	100.0

EXHIBIT 2
Pop-Tent Corporation, sales by month,
December 1–June 30

Month	Actual sales	Percent of total
December.........	$ 2,202.59	1.2
January...........	1,664.29	0.9
February..........	1,268.46	0.7
March............	43,146.21	22.9
April.............	51,270.69	27.2
May.............	44,053.25	23.5
June.............	44,457.52	23.6
	$188,063.11	100.0

EXHIBIT 3
When do camping equipment dealers buy?

Month of purchase	Percent of stock
January................................	8.6
February...............................	10.9
March..................................	16.0
April...................................	15.4
May....................................	16.6
June....................................	13.7
July....................................	7.5
August.................................	4.7
September..............................	2.2
October................................	1.5
November..............................	1.5
December..............................	1.4

The sales of the company by month, during this period, are shown in Exhibit 2.

According to a survey of 8,774 sporting goods dealers who sell tents, conducted by *Sporting Goods Dealer Magazine,* the breakdown of when camping equipment dealers buy was as shown in Exhibit 3.

Of the dealers surveyed, 72.6 percent bought their stock during the months of February through June. It was also estimated by another sporting goods trade journal that of 23,974 sporting goods retailers, subscribing to the magazine, 51.7 percent carried tents and camping equipment.

The Pop-Tent Camper

The Pop-Tent Camper was designed to be a light, compact, easily erected shelter. It was made of high-quality canvas in a dome shape that required no poles for its erection and contained no inside poles.

The tent was 7 feet in diameter and 58 inches high. It folded into a 30-inch carrying bag which weighed only 13 pounds.

The Camper had a sewn-in floor, a zipper door, and a small rear window, and came equipped with a nylon mosquito netting. The material used was 7.68 ounce twill and was treated with a special dry water repellent. The tent could be erected by anyone in 90 seconds with a few simple movements.

The basic frame of the tent was provided by a fiberglass rod rib frame which could be folded down and whose tension provided the force for the erection. When erected, the tent literally "popped out," and thus the name of the product was descriptive of one of its principal features. The tent was produced in a grey-green color.

The company's list price on the tent in the summer after incorporation was $79, and its discount policy was:

1. 50 percent discount and freight prepaid on orders of $300 or more retail list.
2. 5 percent advertising allowance on orders of $1,500 or more retail list (50–5).
3. 40 percent discount and f.o.b. factory on orders less than $300 retail list.
4. Terms 2/10, net 30.

From the beginning the company had employed manufacturers' agents instead of a sales force, and it had 14 such agents who employed on the average four salesmen each. The company had salesmen in most areas of the country, except for eastern Michigan, where the officers of the firm did the selling. The agents were paid a commission of 10 percent on sales and had exclusive territories.

Initially, the firm had attempted to sell through wholesalers to retailers; however, it soon felt that it was not receiving promotional support from the wholesalers. As a result, it had its agents stop attempting to sell to wholesalers and to concentrate on direct sales to retailers, offering them the same discounts as had been originally offered to the wholesalers. After this change the company's sales were highly concentrated among large department stores, mail-order houses, retail chains, and large sporting goods dealers.

The company also had made a large number of sales to Ford dealers, who had bought the Tour-A-Tent, air mattresses, and window-screens in large quantities for use as promotional aids to sell automobiles. The sales of these items to these outlets were not expected to be continuous over time, however, in view of their promotional nature.

The retailers who sold the Camper had a wide variety of initial markups on the retail price. The markups ranged from a low of 20 percent on special sales to 40 percent or more, which were the "traditional" markups on such items. Characteristically, it was the smaller retailers who took the larger initial markups.

While there were no tents on the market at this time which had the same features as the Pop-Tent Camper, the officers of the firm felt that the tent best served the needs of the camper who was traveling on a trip in either a car, station wagon, or canoe and who had to set up and take down the tent a number of times during the trip. The management felt that the tents which were the best alternatives to Pop-Tent for the purchaser who had a need for such a shelter were pup tents, umbrella tents, and lean-to canvas shelters. The firm felt that wall tents better served the needs of the camper who went to one place and stayed there for a period of time and to whom the erection ease and portability were of lesser importance as compared to living comfort in the tent. The Wing-Tent served this need in the Pop-Tent line.

The catalog of one of the major mail-order houses for the spring-summer season of this year listed four umbrella tents which were in the same class (not scouting or children's tents) as the Pop-Tent Camper. This house did not carry or offer Pop-Tents. These four tents were:

1. $11\frac{1}{3}' \times 11\frac{1}{3}'$—four-way ventilation with sewn-in nylon screening 3 feet wide on each side. Material 7.68 ounce drill,[2] each side panel and the door having full-length zippers to seal out rain and wind. The tent had a center height of $7\frac{1}{2}$ feet, 6-foot wall height, and a front awning. This tent also had a sewn-in floor, an aluminum frame, and telescoping aluminum canopy poles, which were included along with ropes and steel stakes. The shipping weight was listed at 67 pounds and the retail price was $89.95. Color, forest green.

2. $9\frac{1}{2}' \times 11'$—in either forest green or blue spruce colors. This had three nylon screen windows plus a large nylon screen door. The walls and canopy were of 7.68-ounce drill, all water repellent and mildew retardent. This tent also had a sewn-in floor with zippers on the sides of the windows for a flap, tied at top, and the on-the-door flap had zippers at the sides and top and snaps at the bottom. Its height in the center was $7\frac{1}{2}$ feet at the peak, 6-foot high at the eaves, and it had a front awning. Its shipping weight was 54 pounds, and the retail price was $69.95. There was a $9\frac{1}{2}' \times 9\frac{1}{2}'$ variety of this also, with the same features, and it weighed 52 pounds and retailed for $62.95. Both included poles, ropes, and stakes.

3. $9' \times 9'$—with a large nylon screen rear window for two-way ventilation. This tent was made of 6.74-ounce drill (a less expensive material) which was water repellent. The door and window flaps were snap or tie fastened. The tent also included a front canopy,

---

[2] 7.68 ounce drill is a less expensive material than 7.68 ounce twill.

poles, stakes, and a sewn-in duck floor. This tent differed from the preceding two, however, in that it had an inside center pole and it was 7½ feet high in the center, with a 6-foot wall height. Its shipping weight was 50 pounds, and its retail price was $38.74. There was also a 9′ × 11′ variety with the same other dimensions and features for $44.94. Color, forest green.

4. 7′ × 7′—of 6.74 ounce water-repellent drill with a screened rear window and door-tie flaps, canopy, center pole, sewn-in floor of duck, color forest green, with a center pole and a center height of 5 feet 9 inches, and wall height of 4 feet. The unit included wood stakes, wood poles, wire, and guy ropes. Its shipping weight was 23 pounds, and its price was $18.66.

This same house also offered two-man, screened, pup tents for $25.97.

Canvas and better lean-tos sold for prices from $22.50 and up, depending on size and quality, from other mail-order houses.

While the company knew the total camper market at this time was estimated at 22 million persons and growing, it had no data on the size of the market for the Camper, nor of the sales of tents by sizes, types, prices, or even total sales of the industry.

From an appearance viewpoint the Pop-Tent Camper was generally considered to be more attractive than any other tent type.

Pop-Tent expenses

The company estimated that the direct labor and direct material costs to produce a Pop-Tent Camper (in lots of 100) were:

Direct labor............	$ 2.50
Material...............	17.34

The company also estimated that its total fixed expenses for the current year (December 1 to November 30) would be $73,688.

It was estimated that the other variable expenses which could be charged to Pop-Tent production other than materials and direct labor amounted to $6.82 per unit. This estimate was made by summing the other variable costs for the period December through June, of the current year, multiplying this figure by the proportion that Pop-Tent sales were of the total sales for the period and dividing the remainder by the number of units of Pop-Tent which were produced. This figure includes the 10 percent commission to its agents. During the period December through June, the company produced 1,790 Campers. In July, 166 Campers were produced.

Since its inception the company had been plagued by capital problems, and the firm was seriously undercapitalized. This handicap hampered the firm's operations and raised its production costs, since the company was not able to take advantage of cash discounts (around 2 percent) on its purchases, nor was it able to take advantage of excellent material-buying opportunities which periodically were presented on a cash basis.

On reviewing its experience on the cost of producing a Pop-Tent Camper, the company believed that while the material cost would remain the same, the direct labor cost would drop to $1.50 per unit if production lots of 500 units were run.

Retail sales at various prices

While the company had no information on the number of units that were sold at the various retail prices in all stores during this period, it did have the experience of the sales through its factory outlet in Ann Arbor, Michigan, to retail customers, as well as some information as to the experience of various large-scale retail outlets which had run the Camper as a sale item during the spring and summer of that year.

The cash sales of the Pop-Tent Camper to retail customers through the factory outlet during the period of January, through August, of the year after incorporation are shown below in Exhibit 4. The units sold through this outlet included items which were new and which were sold at the regular retail price indicated, as well as returned, worn,

EXHIBIT 4
Retail sales through factory outlet, Pop-Tent Camper, January–August, year after incorporation

January	(Regular retail price $79.95) Sales—none.
February	(Regular retail price $79.95) Sales—seconds:
	3—$30
	1—$25
	New—none
March	(Regular retail price $79.95) Sales—seconds:
	3—$63–$68
	1—$45
	1—$32
	New—1 unit
April	(Regular retail price $79.95) Sales—seconds:
	1—$60
	2—$49
	1—$45
	New—1 unit
May	(Regular retail price $48) Sales—seconds:
	1—$25
	1—$30
	New—1 unit

and damaged items which were sold at lower prices. The company also ran three advertised sales during this period from its outlet which were at the prices indicated. These sales were advertised in the Ann Arbor newspaper and, while advertised in two cases as "seconds," consisted of new items as well.

During May the company also ran a sale in which it advertised seconds for sale at $29.95. All 11 units which they had on hand at this price were sold out in the first two days. The company also offered its regular (new) units to these customers at a price of $39.95 each, and during the week of this sale it sold 45 units at this price.

June (Regular retail price $48)
Sales—seconds:
4—$45
3—$43
2—$39
1—$30
New—11 units

The company also ran a sale on June 30 of its regular units at a price of $44. Five units were sold during this sale.

July (Regular retail price $48)
Sales—seconds:
3—$46.00
2—$43.00
5—$41.00
4—$29.95
New—6 units

August (Regular retail price $48)
Sales—seconds: 0 units
New: 7 units

On August 14–18, the company ran a sale of seconds of which it had a large supply (many of which were, for all intents, new items) at a price of $29.95. It also offered new items at the $39.95 price. The results of this sale were:

$29.95—54 units sold
$39.95— 2 units sold

During the remainder of the month, it sold five additional units at $29.95 and one unit at $39.95.

Experience of other stores

1. A large department store in the western part of the lower peninsula of Michigan ran a sale of the Camper on May 26 at a price of $69.99, the regular price being indicated at $79. The net cost price to this store was $35 per unit. The store had six Campers on hand, and the sale was completely unsuccessful. At the $69.99 price it took this store six weeks to sell the six items.

This same store ran another sale of the Camper at a price of $49.99 on July 23. The cost was $35 per unit again. The store had 25 units on hand and sold them all out during the sale period.

2. A major department store in Cleveland ran a sale of the Camper in early June at a price of $69. The net cost per unit to the store was $47.40. The store had six units on hand, and a Pop-Tent representative reported that the store sold none of the items the first day. The sale was considered unsuccessful.

3. In mid-August a major department store in a large, southern Michigan city ran a sale of the Camper at a price of $44.50. It had 68 units on hand at a net cost of $32 per unit (a special deal). It sold 60 of the units during the four days of its sale.

4. A hardware store in a small southern Michigan town ran a sale of the Camper in early August at a price of $49 each. The net cost per unit to the store was about $36. The store had ten units on hand and sold two. A special demonstrator from Pop-Tent was in the store during this sale to sell the item.

CASE QUESTIONS

1. At what price should the Pop-Tent Camper be offered to the trade during the coming season, assuming costs given?
2. How would you recommend your hypotheses and conclusions be tested for verification?

CASE 6–3

Monson Die Casting Company°

Pricing policy of a metals fabricator

Monson Die Casting Company (hereafter referred to by the initials MDC) was organized some years ago in Detroit, Michigan, to manufacture zinc alloy die castings. Initially, it produced items for manufacturers in a variety of industries, but as time passed, its customers were primarily from the automotive industry. The company grew steadily,

---

° Written by A. R. Krachenberg, Professor of Marketing, Dearborn Campus, The University of Michigan.

and at the time of this case its annual sales were approximately $2.5 million, and its replacement value was estimated at $1.5 million.[1]

Product characteristics

Die casting is a process whereby molten metal is put into a die or form, under pressure. When the metal has cooled, it retains the shape of the form. Die casting is done with nonferrous metals. By far the greatest amount of nonferrous die casting is with zinc alloys, although there is some die casting of aluminum, magnesium, and brass.

Zinc alloy diecast parts find their greatest applications in the automobile industry, although they are also used in home appliances, plumbing and heating parts, and a variety of industrial machine applications. Zinc alloy parts were first used on autos for interior trim. As techniques improved, applications in dashboard instruments followed. As larger and more intricate shapes became possible, die castings began to be used in a number of decorative hardware items on the exterior of the car: radiator grills, door and trunk handles, and a variety of trim situations, including nameplates and letters.

MDC specialized in the relatively smaller items of automobile trim and had a reputation for being able to cast the more intricate items. The company also built a reputation for filling rush jobs on short notice without sacrificing quality.

Over the span of any one year, the company manufactured approximately 100 different items. Of these, 75 were usually new items, while 25 were so-called service jobs. Service jobs consisted of rerunning an additional quantity of an item that had been manufactured in a prior year. In the die-casting business it was standard practice for the automobile manufacturers to become the owners of the dies and special equipment necessary for any given job. These items physically remained in the possession of the individual die-casting firm, however. At any time, this firm faced the possibility of being requested to make a rerun on any given job, at which time it would be expected to have the old dies still available or stand the expense of making a new set.

In addition to the storage expense of an ever increasing number of dies, another costly feature of the service job was that it usually involved a relatively small-volume run per month. Nevertheless, being able to rapidly produce a previously manufactured item was an important patronage appeal which most die casters offered to the automobile manufacturers.

A job averaging around 100,000 pieces a month, or approximately 5,000 per day, was considered to be good business. This, of course, was based on a 9-month to 10-month year, since, on the average, two

---

[1] These figures have been multiplied by a constant; the name of the company has been disguised.

months during the summertime were devoted to changeover. Anything averaging 5,000–10,000 a month was considered small. Such runs were relatively undesirable jobs primarily because of the time and cost required to set up and tear down the equipment.

Industry competitive structure

The zinc die-casting industry was located primarily in the Detroit–Toledo area, since it depended so heavily on the automobile industry. Approximately 50 companies were active, all of whom were regarded as competitors of MDC in some degree or other. MDC was considered to be a medium-sized company for this field. Only two or three companies were of a larger size, namely Grand Rapids Die Casting with annual sales of about $12 million to $15 million and Doehler-Jarvis with annual sales of about $20 million to $30 million. There were many small companies[2] in this industry with sales averaging less than $1 million annually.

Competition within the industry was keen. It was relatively easy to enter the business, for capital requirements were small (basic capital goods requirements were a manually operated die-casting machine and a small melting furnace). "Alley shops" had very low fixed overhead and thus were able to price low on the smaller, relatively simple items. The major competitive factors favoring the larger companies on these items were their reliability regarding schedules and consistency of quality.

While competition hinged primarily on price, other factors were important. Efficient automobile production required continuous assembly; no parts delay was tolerated that could possibly cause a shutdown of a line or a plant. Therefore, reputation for prompt deliveries and for being able to meet an increased delivery schedule when necessary was most important. Also, quality level and consistency of quality were considered in making a source selection.

In addition to competition from other independent die casters, MDC, as others, faced competition from the die-casting shops owned by the automobile manufacturers, primarily those operated by General Motors. GM owned and operated rather substantial die-casting plants which produced a variety of items for use on GM autos. The major GM plants were Bay City Chevrolet and Brown-Lipe-Chapin. These shops provided not only competition for selected jobs but also provided GM buyers with a double check on prices submitted by outside die casters.

While the other automobile manufacturers were not as active as GM in die casting their own parts, there was always the possibility that

---

[2] Small firms were frequently referred to as "alley shops," a term used in the industry to denote a small 5- or 10-man operation with work often performed in a garage.

they might make their own die-cast requirements. Make versus buy evaluations were a never ending process with the automobile manufacturers, and as competitive circumstances varied, as technology improvements took place, present policies could change.

Bidding and pricing

Business was obtained by MDC through bids submitted to the automobile manufacturers. The request to bid was obtained either through personal solicitation or, once the reputation and high quality level of the company had been established, requests to bid were automatically sent to MDC from the automobile manufacturers on a variety of selected parts.

The bid requests received from an automobile company usually included the following information: (1) a blueprint and specification sheet of the part needed, (2) the maximum required number of pieces needed monthly, with some indications of possible variations that may be anticipated, (2) what percentage of the total requirements MDC was being requested to bid on, or whether this was a "sole supplier" item, and (4) when the part was needed.

In responding, MDC usually provided the following standard information: (1) the unit price of the article, (2) total charge for special tools, dies, jigs, and fixtures, and (3) a statement indicating ability to meet required schedule or an indication of alternate dates.

Since the company dealt almost entirely with the automotive industry, its work schedule throughout the year was dependent upon that of the new-car manufacturers. By late fall of each year, bids were already submitted on parts that would be used on cars to be introduced in the fall of the following year. Since the automobile manufacturers were usually prompt in awarding contracts, by early December MDC had firm knowledge of the approximate level of operations it would start the new-model year with. Manufacturing operations for the new models started in midsummer at the same time as the automobile assembly plants were switching over to the new models. July and August of each year were rather hectic, then, in that this was the time when the items of last year's model were being finished and the new dies were being tested and parts' samples being sent to the automobile companies for final approval.

Pricing procedure

MDC used a standard-volume concept in establishing bid prices, predicated primarily upon the preceding year's volume and costs. In this sense, MDC utilized a form of cost-plus pricing.

When the request to bid was received by MDC, the part's blueprint was studied by engineers, and an estimate of manufacturing cost was prepared. Total cost was estimated on the basis of cost per 100 pieces and developed by estimating separately the cost of each major manufacturing step involved in producing a given part. Exhibit 1 below presents in columns (1) through (6) a cost estimate on a nameplate made by MDC for one of the major lines of automobiles for the current model year. The cost estimate was derived as follows:

1. Column (2): The labor time required to process 100 pieces was calculated for each operation.
2. Column (3): The average prevailing hourly direct labor rate adjusted to anticipate known or considered changes in the future was determined for each operation.
3. Column (4): Total dollars overhead per hour of direct labor, also adjusted to anticipate future changes, was calculated. This overhead included all fixed and variable items for the whole company except selling costs, that is, it was not just factory overhead but included as well administrative and management costs.

   This overhead figure was determined from an analysis of the prior year's activity and was also adjusted to anticipate any changes during the coming year.
4. Columns (5) and (6): The sum of the hourly direct labor cost plus the hourly overhead allocation (column 3 and column 4) was then multiplied by the estimated hours required to produce 100 pieces for each operation. This is presented in column 5. Column 6 presents a cumulative estimated cost figure. In Exhibit 1 the cumulative, estimated, total cost of the first five operations is $10,801.
5. Metal & dross[3] costs, a scrap factor not included in the overhead calculations, and packing and shipping cost estimates, were then added to the cumulative labor and overhead costs. The result was a total cost including all company costs except selling;[4] that is, both manufacturing and administrative. In Exhibit 1 this total, estimated cost is $15,436.

A percent was then added to this total cost to arrive at the price quoted to the buyer. The percentage added for profit was not a fixed amount but varied depending on a variety of circumstances. The owners of the company had a minimum desired rate of return on the company's investment, which, in turn, was translated into a profit margin necessary to meet this standard. To obtain this required profit margin, the company

---

[3] Dross is the scum which forms on the surface of metal, especially lead, zinc, and aluminum, when molten or melting. It is due both to oxidation and the rising of dirt and impurities to the surface.

[4] Selling costs were included in the markup applied to costs when a price was being determined.

EXHIBIT 1
Auto nameplate—estimated and actual costs

(1)	(2)	(3)	(4)	(5)	(6)	(7)	(8)
Operation	Direct labor hours per 100 pieces	Direct labor rate per hour	Overhead per hour	Estimated cost per 100 pieces	Cumulative estimated cost per 100 pieces	Actual cost per 100 pieces	Cumulative actual cost per 100 pieces
1. Cast.................	0.3333	$2.35	$6.25	$2.866	$.....	$2.783	$.....
2. Trim.................	.2500	1.70	3.10	1.200	4.066	0.980	3.763
3. Buff.................	.1250	3.40	7.25	1.331	5.397	....	3.763
4. Plate................	.340	2.813	1.820	4.973	10.370	3.614	7.377
5. Pack.................	.1250	1.70	1.75	.431	10.801	0.273	7.650
6. Metal and Dross......				3.336	14.137	2.646	10.296
7. Scrap (5 percent).....				.707	14.844	0.515	10.811
8. Carton...............				.260	15.104	0.097	10.908
9. Shipping (2.2 percent)...				0.332	15.436	0.240	11.148

first estimated a normal rate of production and its attendant standard costs based on the preceding year's actual cost experience. From the (1) desired rate of return, (2) the standard cost data, and (3) capital turnover rates which were also obtained from past experience, there was then no problem to calculate the markup figure needed.[5]

A variety of factors beyond the minimum desired rate of return on investment was also considered. Intensity of competition varied so the company necessarily considered the number of, and the quality of, its competitors on each individual bid. In addition, the time of the season was a crucial consideration, especially in relation to operating level of the plant at any given moment. The particular characteristics of the part being bid on the MDC's past experience with this or a similar item were also noted. Finally, there was the consideration of MDC's past relations with this customer as well as the past competitive experiences in relation to this customer.

A detailed record was also kept of actual costs on all jobs by the company by the same breakdown as the cost estimate. In Exhibit 1, columns (7) and (8) present the actual cost data for this job. MDC relied heavily on these actual cost records to aid them both in making more effective future quotes on similar items and in establishing a standard-volume cost level for each new year.

Special tooling charges

All special tools belonged to the customer. It was standard procedure to submit a total tool charge in a lump-sum figure along with the per piece price of the item. On the first delivery of parts the tooling costs were then paid for in full by the automobile manufacturer. When bidding any job, these tool charges were important for several reasons. First, when the automotive manufacturer's buyer received the bid, the standard practice was to calculate the tool cost on a per piece basis, that is, to amortize the tool charge over the total number of pieces to be purchased from the vendor, coming up with a price per piece which included tool costs. Thus, tool charges were not simply a matter of figuring cost only, or cost plus a fixed percent; rather some degree of latitude existed on the possibility of skimping on cost so as to have a lower total cost per piece.

A second aspect of tool charges concerned the pricing of low-volume jobs. Here the tendency was to "load" tool charges, hence include a factor to cover the nuisance aspect inherent in low-volume jobs. Since the total tools charge was paid for with the first delivery of parts, this would also mean a fast return of cash.

---

[5] See Joel Dean, *Managerial Economics* (New York: Prentice-Hall, Inc., 1951), p. 448, including footnote 26.

Specific product pricing

Ornamental trim item. In late fall of the current model year, MDC was requested to bid on a piece of ornamental trim for one of the more expensive makes of automobiles. The company manufacturing the car was one of the Big Three auto makers and was a major customer of MDC. It had taken MDC some five years to become a regular supplier of this company, becoming so only after having thoroughly proven itself to be (1) an efficient and low-cost producer, (2) a consistently high-quality producer, and (3) a producer capable of expanding production schedules on short notice.

Exhibit 2 presents the cost estimate that was made on this part. In trying to develop a price, MDC officials noted the following factors peculiar to this specific item. They knew that several other companies had also been requested to bid on this part, although they did not know specifically which ones. They knew also that the part involved intricate casting considerations, hence they were certain that the other sources requested to bid would not include alley shops. They felt that since this was a type of part at which they were highly skilled in casting, and had the reputation of being able to handle well, they had some slight edge over their competitors. Finally, it was an item that would give them a fairly substantial volume for nine to ten months of the year. All things considered, the bid was submitted at a price of $1.33 each, which was equivalent to a markup on selling price of 24.9 percent.

Within a very short time, MDC was informed by the automobile manufacturer that further negotiations were being initiated on this item, and a rebid was requested from them. Through various trade and industry sources, MDC learned that if they could reduce their price to $1.17 (which is equivalent to a 14.6 percent profit margin), they could have the business.

Nameplate. Late in May of the same model year as above, MDC received a call by phone from one of the major three auto makers saying that a blueprint was on its way by special messenger on a nameplate which spelled out the name of a new-car model in script. The automobile manufacturer wanted a price on this part within two days. It seemed that the auto manufacturer's styling department had made an abrupt decision to come out with a new model and production was to start with all haste. Samples were to be ready within six weeks, whereas the normal lead time averaged four to five months. All overtime required to prepare the job was chargeable to the buyer.

MDC knew here also that they were not the only company bidding, but since it was a rush job, there would probably be no more than two or three bidders. This was an item on which the successful bidder was to be the sole source of supply.

EXHIBIT 2
Ornamental trim piece—estimated and actual costs

(1)	(2)	(3)	(4)	(5)	(6)	(7)	(8)
Operation	Direct labor hours per 100 pieces	Direct labor rate per hour	Overhead rate per hour	Estimated cost per 100 pieces	Cumulative estimated cost per 100 pieces	Actual cost per 100 pieces	Cumulative actual cost per 100 pieces
1. Cast.	0.500	$ 2.35	$ 6.25	$ 4.300	$ —	$ 2.996	$ —
2. Trim.	0.333	1.70	3.10	1.600	5.900	2.909	5.905
3. Polish.	0.500	1.85	1.90	1.875	7.775	2.907	8.812
4. Buff.	0.333	3.40	8.25	3.883	11.658	4.814	12.626
5. Buff.	—	—	—	—	—	1.311	14.937
6. Plate.	0.425	11.250	17.080	28.755	40.513	26.429	41.937
7. Paint.	1.250	1.70	3.35	6.313	46.726	5.941	47.937
8. Pack.	2.000	1.70	3.10	9.600	56.326	6.316	53.623
9. Metal and Dross.	—	—	—	30.300	86.626	19.782	73.405
10. Scrap (5 percent).	—	—	—	3.851	90.477	3.788	77.193
11. Special pack.	—	—	—	2.310	92.787	2.345	79.538
12. Carton.	—	—	—	5.000	97.787	2.417	81.955
13. Shipping (2.7 percent).	—	—	—	2.151	99.938	1.803	83.758

The cost estimate for this job was shown in Exhibit 1. The company submitted a price of 0.1704 cents each, and they were awarded the business. Columns (7) and (8) in Exhibit 1 suggest that the actual costs were much lower than the estimates and that a substantial profit margin thereby resulted.

CASE QUESTIONS

1. Would you have accepted the suggested price reduction to $1.17 and taken the business of manufacturing the trim item? What factors were pertinent to making this decision?
2. Compare and contrast the situation regarding the pricing of the ornamental trim piece (question 1 above) with the pricing of the nameplate. What specific factors were pertinent in reaching a decision in each case?
3. Evaluate MDC's general pricing policy. What are its strengths and weaknesses? Can you justify their approach?

CASE 6–4

Shell International Chemical Company, Ltd.*

Market development and pricing of an industrial solvent

In November 1963, the marketing executives of Shell International Chemical Company, Limited, were faced with the problem of planning the market development for Sulfolane—its pricing and the additional manufacturing capacity which would be needed, in view of this planning, and the marketing activities to follow.

Background

Sulfolane had first been developed in the United States by Phillips Petroleum Company in the late 1940s. Shell Chemical, a subsidiary in the United States, also produced small quantities of Sulfolane in the early 1950s and test marketed the product there as a general, high-per-

---

* Written by D. Maynard Phelps, Professor Emeritus of Marketing, Graduate School of Business Administration, The University of Michigan. Used by special arrangement with the Netherlands School of Economics, Rotterdam.

formance industrial solvent. However, the product achieved little success in the market at that time. Another solvent was used in the "Udex" process, which was the established one for the manufacture of BTX products (benzene, toluene, and xylene), a process developed by an American chemical manufacturer. At that time the Udex process was the accepted one. It was successful, and the chemical industry was hesitant to shift to a new and less established process, even though it might be technically superior.

Shell International first became interested in Sulfolane in the late 1950s when BIPM, the Production Division of Shell, was investigating alternative processes for the production of aromatics (petroleum by-products used to increase the octane rating of motor fuels) by the Udex process. In these investigations BIPM found Sulfolane to be a better solvent than the one previously used. BIPM therefore developed a new process for the manufacture of BTX products using Sulfolane as the solvent. They called it the Shell Sulfolane Extraction Process. In the opinion of Shell International executives the process was a completely viable and proved process and one which could be licensed, at a substantial fee, to third parties. An arrangement was made with Universal Oil Products Corporation to negotiate licenses in Shell's behalf.

In 1961, plans were made for converting one Shell plant which used the Udex process to the new Sulfolane process. Also, construction of a new Sulfolane extraction unit, and a small plant for the manufacture of Sulfolane at 1,200 tons per year capacity was planned for Stanlow in England.

Importance of Sulfolane

Sulfolane is considered by Shell executives to be a much more selective solvent than the ones previously used. It breaks down the chemical mixtures in which it is used better, more quickly, and at lower cost than other solvents. Less heat is needed in the manufacture of BTX products when Sulfolane is used, and this lowers costs. Thus the new process lowers capital costs, since equipment is used more economically. The significance of this fact is obvious in a capital intensive industry such as chemicals. The importance of even moderately lower costs per unit of output is apparent when it is recognized that the quantities of these chemicals produced are very large. In fact, some plants have capacities of 400,000 to 500,000 tons annually.

The market for Sulfolane

The principal market, at least immediately, was in the manufacture of the BTX products by the newly developed process. Initially, the research was in relation to the production of aromatics, but this was only one end-product, and probably, in the long run, not the most important one. All BTX products and their final derivatives were, in a sense, the market for Sulfolane; and many other uses might subsequently be found for a solvent with its properties. For instance, it was thought that Sulfolane could compete in the general solvent field with established, highly polar solvents used in a wide range of industries, including insecticides, dyes, general reaction media, and specialized solvent extraction (see Appendix). But these other uses of Sulfolane might be *less economic* in the sense that the importance of the use, the availability, and relative effectiveness of substitutes for it might make necessary a lower price for Sulfolane than for the initial uses. It was estimated that the United States would become the biggest consumption area for Sulfolane, as a solvent for aromatics extraction, by 1967.

Prices and price determinants

Sulfolane is used in relatively small quantities in the Shell Sulfolane Extraction Process, but it is the key element and, therefore, its value or contribution is out of all proportion to the quantity used. In this particular application its contribution is so significant that the price charged for it, within reason, could be high; in other words a high-value use will command a high price. Other uses may have different probable values.

It should be recognized that the values of Sulfolane in these other uses are still a matter of conjecture; that is, they can only be roughly estimated at present. The present supply of Sulfolane is not sufficient to make possible the cultivation of other possible markets representing other uses. When a supply becomes available more than sufficient for the production of BTX, market research will be undertaken to appraise opportunities for profits through sale of Sulfolane for other uses and to determine the other solvents now being used for them and their prices. Then a decision can be made in regard to the next area of market development. Thus there are questions of economics of use, market potentials of solvents presently being used and their prices, and the difficulties which are likely to be encountered in inducing substitution of Sulfolane for other solvents. In this connection it should also be noted that the replaced solvents might be products of Shell or of its competitors. In aromatics production, Sulfolane has been used as a substitute for another Shell product, diethylene glycol (DEG) which was the solvent for the Udex process.

The price of Sulfolane for sales in the United States market was established at £500 ($1375) per metric ton (2200 pounds).[1] As far as the economies of the process are concerned, this price could be continued at least until 1970. Other solvents which might be replaced by

---

[1] At the time of this case, one £ sterling = $2.75.

Sulfolane were selling at various prices ranging from £240 ($660) to £440 ($1210) per metric ton. If there were an attempt at replacement, these prices of substitutes would serve as guides for the pricing of Sulfolane, but only in view of different product attributes and possible economies in use.

As in all situations of this character, another price determinant was the possible emergence of competition in the manufacture and sale of Sulfolane. The basic patents on the Sulfolane manufacturing process had expired; therefore, all companies were free to attempt the manufacture of this product. But Shell still had a significant advantage, which was recognized in the chemical industry. This advantage was a compound of experience, know-how, lead time, and the fact that Shell is willing to license the Sulfolane process for the manufacture of BTX products to other companies. The purchase of Sulfolane then becomes almost a secondary consideration. Also, in view of present demand, it is questionable whether many companies would wish to consider its manufacture. However, there were rumors of possible production by other concerns in the United States, and this might be an important consideration in pricing in the future.

The supply situation

In 1963, the Shell Group requirements for BTX exceeded the capacity, and negotiations were opened with a third party who was interested in building a very large BTX complex. A deal was concluded whereby Shell supplied feed stocks of naphtha, etc. to this party and purchased back large quantities of aromatics. The third party was to use the Shell Sulfolane Extraction Process and would require 700 tons in the first quarter of 1965. This plant was to be the largest aromatics production unit in the world. The use of the Sulfolane process in it established that process as the one most likely to be used for manufacturing facilities for all BTX products in the future.

By 1963 it had become apparent that the demand for Sulfolane, just for the Sulfolane extraction process alone, would exceed the production at the Stanlow plant by 1965. Therefore, plans had to be made for the construction of additional capacity. As the procurement time for the necessary plant equipment was approximately 18 months, the creation of new capacity would take at least two years. Shell International was thinking in terms of a plant of 7,000 tons capacity under continuous process at some future date. In the meantime requirements would be fulfilled from the Stanlow plant.

There were a number of rumors of third party production in the United States, mainly from Phillips Petroleum and other U.S. chemical producers. Pressing this decision was the fact that some 700 tons were required in the first quarter of 1965 for the third party plant involved in the processing deal. It also had to be considered that the use of Sulfolane as a solvent for aromatics production is at the expense of another Shell-produced chemical—diethylene glycol (DEG)—which is the solvent for the Udex process and which sells at around £120 ($336) per metric ton.

APPENDIX

Sulfolane as a general solvent

Sulfolane could compete in the general solvent field with the established highly polar solvents listed below. The uses of these solvents

EXHIBIT 1
Market prices for highly polar solvents

Solvent	Cents per pound	$per ton	£per ton
Acetonitrile (methyl cyanide) (B.P. 82° C.)			
Drums, carload............................	34½	759	275
Drums, LCL..............................	36	792	288
Tank cars................................	32	704	256
Dimethyl sulphoxide (B.P. 189° C.)			
Drums, carload............................	35	770	280
Drums, LCL..............................	37–38	814–836	296–304
Tank cars................................	33	726	264
N, N-dimethyl formamide (B.P. 153° C.)			
Drums, carload............................	32½	715	260
Tank cars................................	30	660	240
N-methyl 2-pyrrolidone (B.P. 202° C.)			
Drums, LCL..............................	55	1210	440
Tank cars	49½	1089	396

are highly specialized in a wide range of industries, including insecticides, dyes, general reaction media, and specialized solvent extraction. It has not been possible to make a detailed survey of these outlets, but it is estimated that the total market in 1964 for the free world outside of the United States is some 15,000 metric tons.

Since Sulfolane would have to compete on price with these solvents, 1964 U.S. market prices for some highly polar solvents are given, for guidance, in Exhibit 1.

There are clearly many possibilities for Sulfolane to replace solvents of the above type on a long-term basis, and those that seem to be of immediate and active interest include the replacement of dimethyl formamide in the manufacture of sucrose esters, in polyether production. or in the dry spinning of polyacrylonitrile fibers.

We may also mention that N-methyl pyrrolidone, which is produced by General Aniline & Film Corporation in the United States and by B.A.S.F. in Germany, is said to be an excellent solvent for aromatics extraction; but in Shell's opinion, based on K.S.L.A tests, it is less effective than Sulfolane because of lower selectivity, poorer stability, and possibly higher corrosivity.

Sulfolane has also been mentioned as being of possible interest in dielectric fluids and hydraulic fluids, as a plasticizer in cellophane and similar films, a flexibilizer in water-soluble cellulose esters, and as a printing and dyeing aid.

CASE QUESTIONS

1. What factors must be considered by Shell before a decision can be reached on whether or not to reduce the price of Sulfolane?
2. How does management relate the impact of a price reduction to needs for new capacity? Is this a purely "marketing" case?
3. Why is it usually easier to analyze a pricing situation in the industrial market than in the consumer market?

CASE 6–5

The Borden Company*

Price discrimination and the Robinson-Patman Act

In 1967, the Borden Company ranked as the second largest domestic company specializing in dairy products. Operations included the manufacture, processing, distribution, and sale of food, dairy, and chemical products—for sales totaling $930 million.

Since 1938, Borden had been selling both nationally advertised Borden brand evaporated milk and the same milk bearing any customer label. In 1956 and 1957, Borden expanded its private label operations to its two southern plants which had not previously packed private label milk. The milk packed under the Borden and private labels was physically and chemically identical.

In 1957, Borden sold 4,300,000 cases of its premium brand evaporated

---

* Written by Ivan Velan, Research Assistant, under the supervision of Professor Stewart H. Rewoldt. The material presented in this case was derived from Supreme and Appeals Court rulings in regard to practices of the Borden Company and from related articles.

milk and 1,100,000 cases of its private label milk for net sales of $27.6 million and $5.7 million respectively. During July of the same year, Borden label milk was sold at a uniform delivered price of $6.45 per case from all plants, whereas the private label milk was sold f.o.b. plant at prices ranging from $5.01 to $5.59 per case. The average price differential between the differently labeled milk was $1.19 per case.

As a result of Borden's expansion of private label operations, some private label business which had been served by other canners shifted to Borden. It is estimated that about 7 percent of the sales of 7 midwestern canners, or roughly 240,000 cases, were lost to Borden and it was this diversion of private label sales which precipitated the FTC complaint against Borden. While Borden gained sales in the south, it lost sales amounting to 250,000 cases in the northeast, primarily to its two largest competitors—Pet and Carnation. Also, while Borden took over some of their market in the south, the testifying competitors from the midwest gained enough sales (525,000 cases) from other sources to achieve an increase in absolute sales.

Overall from 1955 to 1957, Borden's market share increased from 9.9 percent to 10.7 percent, while the share of the midwestern group increased from 6.3 percent to 6.8 percent, or roughly in the same proportion.

A major source of Borden's private label business was provided by cooperative associations of wholesalers and retailers. One such group, whose purchases accounted for 11 percent of Borden's private label volume in 1957, had more than 1,000 retail members. Not all retailers in the group availed themselves of the opportunity to market private label milk, however.

Original ruling of the Federal Trade Commission

In 1962, the following news item appeared in *The Wall Street Journal:*[1]

The Federal Trade Commission ruled that Borden Co. was engaging in unlawful price discrimination when it charged substantially higher prices for its Borden brand evaporated milk than for milk of identical quality it packaged for sale under private label. . . .

Writing for the majority, Mr. Dixon, Chairman of the FTC . . . suggested the commission won't accept . . . an attempt to attach an estimated "value" to consumer preference for the branded, advertised product over the private label product.

Section 2(a) of the Clayton Act, as amended by the Robinson-Patman Act, reads, in part, as follows:

It shall be unlawful . . . to discriminate in price between different purchasers of commodities of like grade and quality, . . . where the effect of

[1] *The Wall Street Journal,* December 12, 1962.

such discrimination may be substantially to lessen competition or tend to create a monopoly in any line of commerce, or to injure, destroy, or prevent competition with any person who either grants or knowingly receives the benefit of such discrimination, or with customers of either of them: *Provided,* that nothing herein contained shall prevent differentials which make only due allowance for differences in the cost of manufacture, sale, or delivery resulting from the differing methods or quantities in which said commodities are to such purchasers sold or delivered. . . .

Borden promptly appealed the cease and desist order and prepared a defense which differed from previous defense attempts in similar cases in that, while it also sought a cost justification for its differentiated pricing, it was willing to make an issue of the like grade and quality test as it applied to identical products sold under different labels and to challenge the premise that a difference in brands, alone, is not enough to justify different prices.

On December 4, 1964, the U.S. Fifth Circuit Court of Appeals granted Borden's petition. Judge J. C. Hutcheson held that:[2]

manufacturer's evaporated milk which bore manufacturer's own label and manufacturer's evaporated milk which bore private brand labels were not products of "like grade and quality," within Robinson-Patman Act provision prohibiting price discrimination between different purchasers of commodities of like grade and quality, where manufacturer's brand name had demonstrable commercial significance.

* * * * *

In determining whether products are of "like grade and quality," within Robinson-Patman Act, consideration should be given to all commercially significant distinctions which affect market value, whether they be physical or promotional.

* * * * *

Manufacturer's evaporated milk which bore manufacturer's own label and manufacturer's evaporated milk which bore private brand labels were not, although physically identical, products of "like grade and quality," within Robinson-Patman Act provision prohibiting price discrimination between different purchasers of commodities of like grade and quality, where manufacturer's brand name had demonstrable commercial significance.

Judge Hutcheson further stated that:

The basic issue presented here, then, is whether the demonstrated consumer preference for the Borden brand product over the private label product is to receive legal recognition in the "like grade and quality" determination.

[2] *The Borden Company* v. *Federal Trade Commission*, 339 F.2d 133, (5th Cir. 1964).

His concluding remarks summarized the Appeals Court position:

Since the Commission's erroneous determination that the products were of like grade and quality was an essential element of its cease and desist order, the petition to set aside the order is granted. We do not render any decision on the other questions presented in the case. The Petitioner's arguments concerning injury to competition and its cost justification defense seem to have considerable merit, but we do not pass on them here. The holding that the products were not of like grade and quality requires us to set aside the Commission's order and makes it unnecessary for us to consider the other points raised.

The Supreme Court decision

Due to the importance of the Court of Appeals' decision in December of 1964, the Department of Justice intervened and appealed the case to the Supreme Court. In the ruling delivered on March 23, 1966, the majority opinion, written by Justice White, upheld the views of the FTC. A dissenting opinion was presented by Justice Stewart, who was joined by Justice Harlan. The net effect of the judgment was that the decision of the Court of Appeals was reversed and the case remanded to the Court of Appeals for further proceedings consistent with the ruling of the Supreme Court.

The majority opinion

The following exerpts from the majority ruling represent their position:[3]

The position of Borden and of the Court of Appeals is that the determination of like grade and quality, which is a threshold finding essential to the applicability of Sec. 2(a), may not be based solely on the physical properties of the products without regard to the brand names they bear and the relative public acceptance these brands enjoy—consideration should be given to all commercially significant distinctions which affect market value, whether they be physical or promotional. 339 F.2d, at 137. Here, because the milk bearing the Borden brand regularly sold at a higher price than did the milk with a buyer's label, the court considered the products to be "commercially" different and hence of different "grade" for the purposes of Sec. 2(a), even though they were physically identical and of equal quality. Although a mere difference in brand would not in itself demonstrate a difference in grade, decided consumer preference for one brand over another, reflected in the willingness to pay a higher price for the well-known brand, was, in the view of the Court of Appeals, sufficient to differentiate chemically identical products and to place the price differential beyond the reach of Sec. 2(a).

We reject this construction of Sec. 2(a), as did both the examiner and the Commission in this case. The Commission's view is that labels do not

---

[3] *Federal Trade Commission* v. *The Borden Company*, 383 U.S. 637, 86 Sup. Ct. 1092 (1966).

differentiate products for the purpose of determining grade or quality, even though the one label may have more customer appeal and command a higher price in the marketplace from a substantial segment of the public. That this is the Commission's long-standing interpretation of the present Act, as well as of Sec. 2 of the Clayton Act before its amendment by the Robinson-Patman Act, may be gathered from the Commission's decisions dating back to 1936.

* * * * *

Obviously there is nothing in the language of the statute indicating that grade, as distinguished from quality, is not to be determined by the characteristics of the product itself, but by consumer preferences, brand acceptability, or what customers think of it and are willing to pay for it. Moreover, what legislative history there is concerning this question supports the Commission's construction of the statute rather than that of the Court of Appeals.

* * * * *

The Commission's construction of the statute also appears to us to further the purpose and policy of the Robinson-Patman Act. Subject to specified exceptions and defenses, Sec. 2(a) proscribes unequal treatment of different customers in comparable transactions, but only if there is the requisite effect upon competition, actual or potential. But if the transactions are deemed to involve goods of disparate grade or quality, the section has no application at all and the Commission never reaches either the issue of discrimination or that of anticompetitive impact. We doubt that Congress intended to foreclose these inquiries in situations where a single seller markets the identical product under several different brands, whether his own, his customers', or both. Such transactions are too laden with potential discrimination and adverse competitive effect to be excluded from the reach of Sec. 2(a) by permitting a difference in grade to be established by the label alone or by the label and its consumer appeal.

* * * * *

Our holding neither ignores the economic realities of the marketplace nor denies that some labels will command a higher price than others, at least from some portion of the public. But it does mean that the economic factors inherent in brand names and national advertising should not be considered in the jurisdictional inquiry under the statutory "like grade and quality" test.

The dissenting opinion

Justice Stewart expressed views which differed from those of the majority. The following passages, quoted from his statement, give the substance of his argument:[4]

I cannot agree that mere physical or chemical identity between premium and private label brands is, without more, a sufficient basis for a finding

---

[4] *Federal Trade Commission* v. *The Borden Company,* 383 U.S. 637, 86 Sup. Ct. 1092 (1966).

of "like grade and quality" within the meaning of Sec. 2(a) of the Robinson-Patman Act. The conclusion that a product that travels at a premium in the marketplace is of "like grade and quality" with products of inferior commercial value is not required by the language of the Robinson-Patman Act, by its logic, or by its legislative history.

It is undisputed that the physical attributes and chemical constituents of Borden's premium and private label brands of evaporated milk are identical. It is also undisputed that the premium and private label brands are not competitive at the same price, and that if the private label milk is to be sold at all, it must be sold at prices substantially below the price commanded by Borden's premium brand. This simple market fact no more than reflects the obvious economic reality that consumer preferences can and do create significant commercial distinctions between otherwise similar products. By pursuing product comparison only so far as the result of laboratory analysis, the Court ignores a most relevant aspect of the inquiry into the question of "like grade and quality" under Sec. 2(a)—whether the products are different in the eyes of the consumer.

* * * * *

An important ingredient of the premium brand inheres in the consumer's belief, measured by past satisfaction and the market reputation established by Borden for its products, that tomorrow's can will contain the same premium product as that purchased today. To say, as the Court holds, that these and other intangibles, which comprise an important part of the commercial value of a product, are not sufficient to confer on Borden's premium brand a "grade" or "quality" different from that of private label brands is to ignore the obvious market acceptance of that difference. Commercially the "advertised" brands had come in the minds of the public to mean a different grade of milk. The public may have been wrong; . . . it may have been right; . . . But right or wrong, that is what it believed, and its belief was the important thing.

* * * * *

The Commission's determination of like "grade and quality" under Sec. 2(a) in this case is seriously inconsistent with the position it has taken under Sec. 2(b) in cases where a seller has presented the defense that he is in good faith meeting the equally low price of a competitor. The Commission decisions are clear that the "meeting competition" defense is not available to a seller who reduces the price of his premium product to the level of nonpremium products sold by his competitors. The Commission decisions under Sec. 2(b) emphasize that market preference must be considered in determining whether a competitor is "meeting" rather than "beating" competition.

* * * * *

The Court gives no substantial economic justification for its construction of Sec. 2(a). The principal rationale of the restriction of that section to commodities of "like grade and quality" is simply that it is not feasible to measure discrimination and injury to competition where different products are involved. That rationale is as valid for economic as for physical variation between products. Once a substantial economic difference between products is found, therefore, the inquiry of the Commission should be ended, just as it is ended when a substantial physical difference is found.

Justice Stewart's closing remark related to the practices of the Federal Trade Commission in general.

In the guise of protecting producers and purchasers from discriminatory price competition, the Court ignores legitimate market preferences and endows the Federal Trade Commission with authority to disrupt price relationships between products whose identity has been measured in the laboratory but rejected in the marketplace. I do not believe that any such power was conferred upon the Commission by Congress, and I would, therefore, affirm the judgment of the Court of Appeals.

Reaction to the Supreme Court ruling

Immediately following the Supreme Court decision, *Advertising Age* conducted a survey of agency men, association leaders, and marketing men at major advertisers, to gauge the reaction of the business community.[5]

Robert Young, vice president of corporate marketing for Colgate–Palmolive maintained that the decision "leaves manufacturers vulnerable to the trade, which has great power in the private label business. Big retailers can put manufacturers off the shelves with their private labels if they put their minds to it."

A marketing man at a major soap company stated that "the thing I think is bad is the court's judgment that advertising doesn't contribute to the product's worth. This is a failure on the part of the whole industry to tell our story. Government, educators, and consumers just don't understand how business works."

E. B. Weiss, vice president and special merchandising consultant for Doyle, Dane, Bernbach, commented that "it would be foolish, at this point, for a marketing man to comment on the legal aspects of the decision; however, one point I would emphasize is that there is no reason to assume that all private brands are identical with national brands. I see an accelerating trend to ordering by large retailers and wholesalers of brands made to their own specifications. These companies will assure a continuing difference between national and private, or controlled, brands."

In a prepared statement, the Grocery Manufacturers of America said that they didn't believe that the Court's ruling would do serious injury to anyone. They felt that "while the decision forbids use of brand differences to achieve price discrimination, it also gives due recognition to genuine consumer preferences for manufacturers' advertised brands."

---

[5] *Advertising Age,* March 29, 1966, p. 3.

The second decision of the Court of Appeals

Following the Supreme Court decision, the Borden case was returned to the Fifth Circuit Court of Appeals to resolve the remaining issues. In his opening remarks on July 14, 1967, Judge Hutcheson summarized the proceedings to date:[6]

The threshold inquiry concerning a violation of Sec. 2(a) is whether the goods are "of like grade and quality." In our previous decision, we held that the marked consumer preference for the Borden brand was sufficient to differentiate the products and to place the price difference beyond the reach of Sec. 2(a). The Supreme Court reversed, holding that the economic factors inherent in brand names should not be considered in the jurisdictional inquiry under the "like grade and quality" test, but rather under the more flexible "injury" and "cost justification" provisions of the statute. For that purpose, the case was remanded for a resolution of the remaining issues which had been raised before us by Borden. These included challenges to (a) the Commission's finding of injury to competition, (b) the Commission's rejection of the cost-justification defense, and (c) the scope of the order.

The passages which follow are taken from the Appeals Court decision and adequately represent the position of the Court.

It is not disputed that a price discrimination, within the meaning of the statute, is present. However, we should point out that no overtones of business buccaneering are intended in the phrase "discriminate in price." In the context of Sec. 2(a), price discrimination means only a price difference, not an invidious price structure. Once the fact of a price difference is established, other provisions of the statute must be applied to determine whether the price difference is legal or illegal.

* * * * *

This distinction is important to the instant case because, although there is a price difference, Borden is not in any sense guilty of predatory behavior similar to that which may accompany territorial pricewars. Borden did not subsidize below-cost of unrealistically low prices on its private label milk with profits received from sales of the Borden brand. Nor does this case involve any device similar to the conventional volume discount. All of Borden's customers, large and small alike, paid the same prices for the Borden brand milk or for the private label milk.

* * * * *

There is no evidence in the record that Borden refused to sell private label milk to any customer who specifically requested it.

* * * * *

---

[6] *The Borden Company* v. *Federal Trade Commission*, 381 F.2d 175 (5th Cir. 1967).

In any event, it is plain that Borden's practices did not lead to a substantial increase in Borden's market position at the expense of these competitors. Borden's share of the market increased only from 9.9 percent in 1955 to 10.7 percent in 1957. During the same period, the total market share of the competitors increased in about the same proportion, from 6.3 percent to 6.8 percent.

We conclude, for two reasons, that the record does not contain substantial evidence to support a finding that there may be a substantial injury to competition at the seller's level. The first is that we think it significant that the testifying competitors have experienced an increase in absolute sales volume and have bettered their market position in approximately the same proportion as has Borden.

The second reason is the absence of the necessary causal relationship between the difference in prices and the alleged competitive injury. The Commission's position is that the competing sellers may be hurt because Borden sells its private label milk cheaper than its Borden brand milk. But none of the evidence adduced by the testifying competitors relates to the price difference between the milks marketed by Borden; instead it relates to the price difference between their own private label milk and Borden's private label milk. The competitors actually assert only that Borden was able to sell private label milk for a lower price than they could, and regarding that assertion, the price of Borden brand milk is immaterial in this case. In short, the evidence simply does not support the precise price discrimination alleged in the complaint.

* * * * *

It is easily understood why the private label milk is sold at all levels of distribution for substantially less than Borden brand milk. By increased advertising and promotional efforts over the years, Borden has created a decided consumer preference for milk bearing a Borden label. The label has come to represent a value in itself.

* * * * *

There has been no doubt that the economic factors associated with a premium brand would receive recognition under Sec. 2(a), the only question being the appropriate provision. Upon reversing this case, the Supreme Court made it clear that these factors should be taken into consideration under the injury and cost provisions.

The Court of Appeals summarized its findings as follows:

We are of the firm view that where a price differential between a premium and nonpremium brand reflects no more than a consumer preference for the premium brand, the price difference creates no competitive advantage to the recipient of the cheaper private brand product on which injury could be predicated. Rather, it represents merely a rough equivalent of the benefit, by way of the seller's national advertising and promotion, which the purchaser of the more expensive branded product enjoys.

* * * * *

We conclude that there is no substantial evidence to support a finding that Borden has violated Sec. 2(a). The price difference does not create a competitive advantage by which competition could be injured, and, furthermore, no customer has been favored over another.

Our holding on the injury issue again will make it unnecessary for us to reach other issues concerning cost justification and the scope of the order.

Epilogue

The FTC was not yet satisfied and asked the Justice Department to appeal the case back to the Supreme Court. This was not done and no explanation for this decision was offered.

CASE QUESTIONS

1. Is the reasoning contained in the majority opinion of the Supreme Court sound?
2. Was the Court of Appeals correct in ruling that the difference in price between Borden and private labelled milk did not injure competition?

part seven

INTEGRATED
MARKETING
PROGRAMS

A FIRM's overall marketing program is a composite of many bits and pieces. Parts three through six of this text treated, in depth, specific decision areas in the development of an overall marketing program. The success of this program, however, is not only a function of the wisdom of these specific decisions but also depends on: (1) how these decisions are integrated into a total program, and (2) how effectively both specific decisions and the overall program are implemented. If these two things are accomplished well, the resultant marketing program will be, in a very real sense, more than the sum of its parts.

The following cases are broad in scope and permit consideration of a firm's total marketing strategy. They provide an opportunity to synthesize what has been covered previously in this text and to perceive how decisions in one area of marketing strategy affect decisions in other areas of marketing strategy. The marketing planning process outlined in Chapter 1 provides a useful framework for their analysis.

cases for part seven

Merrill, Inc. (A) *

Marketing program for a new product

Merrill, Inc., of Syracuse, New York, one of the world's largest manufacturers of circuit breakers for aircraft and other electrical appliances, developed Mini-Breaker, a household circuit breaker that could be screwed into a fuse socket.[1] Although there appeared to be a profitable potential market for Mini-Breaker, sales and promotional efforts during the first three years were not successful. In the fall of the third year, accordingly, the sales manager faced the task of diagnosing reasons for failure and of working out a marketing program which would result in a profitable sales volume.

DEVELOPMENT OF PRODUCT

Some years ago, W. H. Bell, president of Merrill, Inc., engaged a very able engineer named J. W. Trask. His job was to devise a product which Mr. Bell, with his long business experience and great skill, could manufacture and develop into a profitable item. In carrying out his assignment, Mr. Trask experimented with a new principle for a circuit breaker that would make it possible to design the mechanism in a size small enough to be contained in a regular screw-based fuse case. It was thought that such a device would have certain outstanding advantages. Heretofore, it was necessary to have an electrician rewire the house in order to install one of the many types of circuit breaker boxes then on the market. In contrast, the home owner merely had to screw Mr. Trask's device into each receptacle in his fuse box in order to convert to "push to reset" circuit protection for the life of the home. The breaker, as visualized, would interrupt service on any overload and could be reset to restore service when the overload had been removed by merely

---

* Written by Peter A. Repenning, Research Assistant, Bureau of Business Research, and James D. Scott, Professor of Marketing, Graduate School of Business Administration, The University of Michigan.

[1] The location and identifying names have been disguised.

pressing a button. This could be done over and over again without damaging the device in any way.

Experimental work proved Mr. Trask's new principle to be sound. Since there was a more pressing need for such a mechanism in aircraft than in the home, company officials decided to produce first for the aviation market. This was done, and after six years Merrill, Inc. had secured a substantial portion of the aircraft circuit breaker business and was a highly successful company. After ten years, Merrill Inc. had captured an even larger proportion of the aircraft circuit breaker business, and had developed a large business in original equipment circuit breakers which were installed on heavy appliances to protect house lines from overloads originating in these appliances.

After six years of developing the industrial market, the success achieved by the company gave Mr. Trask more time to improve his original development—the household circuit breaker that could be screwed into a fuse socket. He set about to develop such a device, and when he had a working model, he took it to Underwriters' Laboratories, Inc. for approval. There he found that his idea had been far from unique. Many people had tried the same thing, and Underwriters' Laboratories, Inc. officials had been plagued with a constant stream of inventors asking them to test such inventions. The technicians took his sample and put it to the initial test—a 5,000-amp., 125-volt direct current short circuit. As with all other such screw-based circuit breakers tried in the past, the Trask model exploded violently.

Mr. Trask then went back to his laboratory and undertook further developmental work. Some time later he returned to Underwriters' Laboratories, Inc. with 12 new model household circuit breakers. This surprised the technicians, since no inventor, faced with the results of the rugged initial test, had ever tried again. The first circuit breaker not only did not blow up, but it adequately interrupted the circuit. Further, it did not set the cotton wrapped around it on fire. It did not work thereafter, but because of the violence of the test, continued operation was not a requirement to pass the test. While the first of the 12 had passed the initial test, Underwriters' Laboratories, Inc. men, in their disbelief, went through the other 11 samples and, to their surprise, all 12 passed the test. Mr. Trask was then sent home to make more samples while the testers thought about what kind of test they would give next. Previously it had not been thought necessary to develop further tests, since no applicant's device had ever passed the first one. After considerable argument as to what classification should be given the device—i.e., whether the device was considered sufficiently good not to require further tests while using the U.L. label on a tentative basis—full approval was finally given, and Mini-Breaker was ready for marketing.

Ten years after Mr. Trask began his developmental work, Merrill, Inc. had many models of circuit breakers on the market for industrial uses. For household use they had, however, only one type of Mini-Breaker in four values—10, 15, 20, and 30 amps. When qualification was imminent, the standard for fuses was introduced. To comply necessitated additional length and because of this, fuse boxes containing Mini-Breakers could not be closed. This was not a drawback if all fuse receptacles contained Mini-Breakers, but if Mini-Breakers were to be used only on trouble circuits, electrical codes in most cities required that boxes be closed to protect against flash from any of the old type fuses that might blow. Utilities were interested in the product but would not endorse it. Later, Mr. Trask redesigned the Mini-Breaker short enough to be accommodated in any fuse panel with the cover closed. After this development the short Mini-Breaker that allowed fuse box doors to be closed was the only model being manufactured.

During the initial distribution of the product, Sears, Roebuck became interested in having Merrill, Inc. supply the device for distribution under the Sears private brand. Because Merrill, Inc. executives wished to exploit the consumer market themselves, they wanted all prestige from sales to accrue to their own brand name, Mini-Breaker. They were very much against manufacturing under any but their own brand.

INITIAL MARKETING PROGRAM

Before the product had gotten final U.L. approval, the Hawley Advertising Agency was retained to help promote it. The Hawley agency was a very small one, but it had had good experience in the promotion of electrical goods. Mr. Hawley's first move was to prepare an editorial for the McGraw-Hill trade journal *Electrical World*. Soon after that, he prepared two full-page spreads on Mini-Breaker for the same magazine. The response to these two advertisements was excellent, and in a market which is not usually inquiry minded, it was phenomenal. There were hundreds of replies and many sample orders. Because of delay in getting a final decision on the proper U.L. classification for Mini-Breaker, however, it was some time before advantage could be taken of the interest shown in the product by those sending in inquiries.

Many of the inquiries were from manufacturers' agents wishing to represent Merrill, Inc. in their areas. At first, C. P. Jacobs, who preceded O. W. Greaves as sales manager of Merrill, Inc. was against the use of manufacturers' agents in the distribution of Mini-Breaker. Mr. Hawley, however, convinced him that with a single-item line of low unit value, it would be unwise for Merrill, Inc. to set up its own sales organization as a means of getting distribution. In spite of the initial rebuff, manufacturers' agents were still very anxious to get a franchise for their areas. Accordingly, after U.L. approval, 24 agents located throughout the United States were selected to handle the sale of Mini-Breaker.

These agents sold to hardware and electrical supply houses primarily, although some of the agents sold directly to industrial users in large lots.[2] The aim of Merrill, Inc. was intensive distribution in all retail outlets where consumers would think of buying a fuse. After three years, however, only spotty distribution had been achieved in hardware stores and appliance shops throughout the country. Most hardware stores could produce a Mini-Breaker from some hidden shelf if they were asked to do so. None of the agents attempted to sell Mini-Breakers to utilities.

The initial price of Mini-Breaker was set at $1.50 to a consumer, $1 to the retailer and 75 cents to the wholesaler because of manufacturing cost and distributor and dealer markups. The wholesaler was also allowed a 2 percent cash discount. From the remainder was deducted a 5 percent commission to the manufacturers' agents. After three years of experience with this price schedule, the commission of the manufacturers' agents was increased to 10 percent. This was done in order to induce greater push by the agents. Eight months after the change, however, there was no evidence that the increase in commission had had any effect upon sales.

At this time, after discounts, the company received $0.66 per Mini-Breaker sold. At this figure there was available considerably less than $0.05 per unit for administration and promotion expense.

In planning the initial promotional strategy for Mini-Breaker, the Hawley Advertising Agency recommended only a modest consumer advertising program, but suggested that real efforts should be directed to utilities which have free fuse replacement service. Toward this end, Mr. Hawley designed an animated cartoon figure of a girl with a Mini-Breaker body. This, it was hoped, would be used along with "Reddy Kilowatt," the trade character already featured in the promotion of many utilities. All utilities watch the advertising of others to see how they may effectively use this figure, and it was thought that if one utility could be induced to use the two figures together, all would soon take notice of it.

Mr. Hawley's recommendations were not accepted by the executives of Merrill, Inc. They were more interested in selling to consumers than to utilities. As a means of introducing Mini-Breaker to the consumer market immediately in a big way, company executives considered buying

---

[2] It was found that industrial users liked Mini-Breaker because a workman could restore his machine to service without violating electrical union rules by replacing a fuse without the aid of an electrician. A minor disadvantage was the pilferage of Mini-Breaker units which resulted because of the ease with which they could be removed.

a 26-week participation on Arthur Godfrey's radio program. Approval was given to show filmed commercials on television in New York, Chicago, and Syracuse. Even these programs were canceled after three weeks of broadcasts when it became apparent that the distribution pattern was not sufficient to warrant such expenditure. Later, the representative of a national magazine bypassed the Hawley agency and sold Merrill, Inc. some expensive advertisements.

Neither of these attempts was successful in building a profitable consumer demand for Mini-Breaker. Late in the first year after U.L. approval, field contacts with jobbers and manufacturers' agents provided Mr. Hawley with evidence that these middlemen were becoming dissatisfied with the apparent unpopularity of Mini-Breaker and with what they believed to be inconsistent and faulty sales policies of the company. Influenced by these findings, and by the fact that few of his suggestions were followed by Merrill, Inc. executives, Mr. Hawley resigned from the account in December of that year.

ANALYSIS AND RECOMMENDATIONS OF JOHNSON AND BAKER

In May of the following year, the executives of Merrill, Inc. appointed Johnson and Baker as the advertising agency to handle the promotion of Mini-Breaker. Johnson and Baker was a large, well-known advertising agency located in Chicago. In accepting the appointment, Johnson and Baker emphasized the need for three to four months to study the market, existing distribution methods, basic sales appeals, and other important factors before any plans were submitted for consumer advertising.

Preliminary report

On August 6, after six weeks of preliminary research and study, Johnson and Baker submitted the following preliminary report dealing with four major topics: the product, sales management and distribution, promotion, and research. Under each of these broad categories, Johnson and Baker presented a brief analysis of existing conditions, including both favorable and unfavorable factors. Recommendations then followed.

The Product

Positive factors:

1. It is a quality, precision-made product.
2. It eliminates "fussing with fuses."
3. It has the approval of Good Housekeeping and Underwriters' Laboratories, as well as many utilities.
4. When properly used, it is practically never defective—it carries a lifetime guarantee.

5. It appeals strongly to people who are uncertain and a little afraid of electricity, as well as those who like convenience and lack of trouble.

6. Its built-in "time-lag" feature is excellent for larger appliances.

7. It is unique in its field, well protected by patents.

Negative factors:

1. Although it meets code requirements in a strict sense, it has been attacked by fuse manufacturers for two reasons: (*a*) some fuse box doors won't close properly. This is being corrected. (*b*) Lack of tamperproof characteristic. Easily fixed, if necessary, by liquid solder.

2. The price to consumers at $1.50. This is not necessarily a bad feature. The Mini-Breaker is a quality item, and people appreciate the fact when its advantages are explained to them. The price seems high when people are introduced to the product because the Mini-Breaker has the outward appearance of an ordinary fuse. The prospect instinctively compares the Mini-Breaker with a fuse, and then compares their prices. He thinks of the Mini-Breaker as a fuse rather than as a circuit breaker or circuit protector.

3. The name itself is confusing to many people. It is, of course, a diminutive for "miniature circuit breaker" (although strictly speaking it is not a circuit breaker). While the name has been used effectively with an animated figure, it still does not get across quickly the product's primary function, which is to protect electrical circuits.

4. The Mini-Breaker unit is poorly packaged, and externally there are some minor criticisms of the unit itself. (*a*) The line around the plunger which shows when tripped, is hard to find. (*b*) The labels are crowded and cluttered with textual matter. (*c*) When the labels become dirty, sun-faded, or defaced, there is no easy way to determine amperages.

Recommendations:

Obviously, the good characteristics of Mini-Breaker greatly outnumber the bad. We are all agreed that this is a very fine product, well designed and well manufactured. Tentatively, we would offer these recommendations:

1. Keep the present unit price until more evidence that it is too high is forthcoming . . . we believe people will always claim the price is too high, because they compare Mini-Breaker with a fuse. People must be sold on its advantages . . . on "you can't afford

not to have a Mini-Breaker." With respect to price, we must face the fact that soon a new, improved Mini-Breaker will be ready, and that there are still hundreds of thousands on dealers' shelves. The raising of the price for the new model to about $1.69, therefore, merits consideration. It would permit more money for promotion and discounts. There is some evidence to the effect that the item could be priced higher without affecting sales adversely. Lowering of the unit price with the appearance of a new model is also a possibility, although it is difficult to see that it would increase sales volume appreciably.

2. We don't advise changing the Mini-Breaker name, but we do recommend that the designation of the item, "circuit-protector," and its functions, "ends fuse problems forever," be given greater prominence.

3. We are currently still studying the packaging of Mini-Breaker, along with point-of-sale material. We intend to recommend a packaging consultant at a future date.

Sales Management and Distribution

Positive factors:

1. The client is well established in the airplane circuit breaker market and its product is of unquestionable quality. So is its companion product, Mini-Breaker.

2. The client enjoys an excellent reputation as a soundly financed business concern with high credit rating.

Negative factors:

1. The sales and distribution problems involved in the marketing of a primarily consumer product are vastly different and more complex than those encountered in a captive market such as the aircraft industry.

   Apparently no established overall sales policy exists. The product is sold through various channels of distribution ranging from house accounts (Sears, Roebuck), manufacturers' agents, and direct distributors to house-to-house retail salesmen.

2. The sales department currently consists of a sales manager and a secretary. The very nature of such a diversified program makes it impossible at present for the sales department to cover all the facets adequately.

3. The client is interested in the widest possible distribution ranging from hardware and electrical retailers to department stores, to-

bacco stores, country stores, drugstores, food chains, and gas stations. The leading manufacturers' agents (Chicago and New York)
maintain that servicing their established wholesale accounts (primarily hardware, electrical, and housewares, selling in turn to
their retail outlets) takes a great percentage of their time and
thus they cannot go farther afield. Additionally, most want exclusive rights in their territories. The wholesalers are dissatisfied with
"spread distribution," and many maintain they will not exert extra
effort as long as this condition exists.

4. Utility cooperation in the marketing of such a product is vitally
important. Even if the utility does not actively merchandise it,
approval is almost mandatory. In some instances utilities have
given the impression they did not receive the utmost in
cooperation.

5. There does not seem to be close enough liaison between the factory and field representatives. It is not easy to master-mind a
nationally distributed product operation from a single office. Experienced representatives on the local scene, familiar with changes
in buying attitudes, distributive methods, etc., can be most helpful
to the manufacturer, if given encouragement, and reasonable attention paid to his suggestions.

6. Though it is difficult to maintain "fair-trade" prices, there are
evidences of price cutting by door-to-door salesmen, by dealers
dissatisfied with the slow turnover of their stocks, and, of course,
by Sears, Roebuck.

7. Wholesalers are discontented with the client's freight policy of
charging freight on shipments of 1,000 units or less. One quoted
Bussman's policy of shipping orders of $60, minimum freight
prepaid.

Recommendations:

1. We suggest that the client settle upon a definite sales policy and
maintain it. Whatever this policy turns out to be, if the manufacturer stays with it, the field representatives, distributors and dealers will develop greater confidence in the future of Mini-Breaker
and their stake in it. This policy should include advertising and
promotion activities. In order to build and maintain the confidence
of the sales team (distributors and dealers), any proposed promotion program should be carried through to completion.

2. To strengthen sales management, we recommend more assistance
for the sales manager.
   a) Appoint an assistant sales manager to relieve Mr. Greaves of
   much routine detail.

    b)   Begin the establishment of a group of regional sales managers (four to eight) who will report to Mr. Greaves and will maintain close contact with the manufacturers' agents, direct distributors and wholesalers in their respective areas.

3.   We agree in principle with "spread distribution." We agree that Mini-Breaker should be sold wherever fuses are sold. Today, the hardware and electrical wholesalers (via the manufacturers' agents) seem to be the strongest link in the sales chain. Though the number of their retailers is much smaller than the potential, this method seems to be best in view of the relatively short time the product has been on the market. It would appear that the soundest procedure, in the long run, would be to build upon this base and later strengthen the overall distribution picture with other types of outlets. Summarizing the distribution problem and possible solution, we recommend retaining the present manufacturers' agents, adding to them and gradually replacing those who stick to one or two fields of distribution with established agents who will aggressively increase the distributive channels.

4.   The client should do more and more to make the manufacturers' agents a part of the first-string sales team. As this group is developed and strengthened, the small direct distributors should be absorbed or dropped. We have given a good deal of thought to all methods of distribution. We do not believe that a product such as Mini-Breaker can be sold in sufficient volume by mail. We do not feel that bypassing the wholesaler is the answer either. The problems of contacting, shipping, and credit checking on dealers would offset the cost of wholesaler's discount.

5.   Price cutting should be policed and every effort made to stop it.

6.   The discount structure should be carefully reviewed. There have been complaints on the present structure. Discounts within a trade should be in line with the discount structure of other comparable lines. Otherwise, the client's sales staff will be spending time selling the discount structure—time which could be more profitably spent selling the product and the client behind it. We recommend quantity discounts be given on orders of 5,000 units and up.

7.   House accounts should be eliminated in favor of the aforementioned regular channels of distribution. The subject of house accounts includes a discussion of private labels. Sears and one or two direct selling organizations have requested private labels. We are opposed to this policy for several reasons. No customer will furnish guarantee of *continued* business. The client *cannot* control the price factor. The loss of national recognition of the trademark (M–B) is an important consideration. The only possible reason

for resorting to private label would be to reach a channel of distribution that could not otherwise be reached and that would not conflict with present channels. Sometimes, too, manufacturers use this procedure to pick up slack in production—but it seldom proves profitable.

Potential Market for Mini-Breaker

This investigation has revealed that a sizable market exists for Mini-Breaker. This potential may be divided into five classifications: (1) original equipment, (2) utility free fuse replacement market, (3) industrial and institutional market, (4) new construction market, and (5) the residential replacement market. While a brief evaluation is made below of each of these markets, our research efforts have been concentrated on the residential replacement market.

I. *Original equipment market*

Reliable figures show that the size of the original equipment market is nearly 6 million fuses per year. Further, this market exhibits a long-term growth pattern.

II. *Utility free fuse replacement market*

It is known that a sizable number of fuses are replaced free each year by certain utilities. It is not believed, however, that the free fuse replacement policy in operation by certain utilities will reduce materially the potential market for Mini-Breaker. There are indications that more and more utilities are educating their customers in how to replace fuses and thus eliminate insofar as possible the service call.

III. *Industrial and institutional market*

The industrial and institutional market consists of factories, stores, office buildings, hospitals, schools, and similar buildings. Relatively little evidence has been obtained to indicate the size of this market. It is, however, believed to be much larger than the new construction market.

IV. *New construction market*

Evidence obtained from contractor supply houses, publishing houses and utilities suggests that approximately 80 percent of homes *currently* being erected are equipped with fuse boxes. It is unlikely that contractors can be sold Mini-Breaker for original installation of residential circuit breakers. It should be noted, however, that all new homes which are built with fuse boxes do enlarge the residential replacement market for Mini-Breaker. To illustrate, this year there will be 1.5 millon new homes constructed, and

1.2 million (80 percent) will be equipped with fuse boxes. With an average of four fuses per home, the ultimate potential for Mini-Breaker has been increased by 4.8 million.

New industrial construction is not an important market for Mini-Breaker. Practically all new construction of this type is using circuit breaker installations.

V. *Residential replacement market*

    A. *Market potential*

        The purely theoretical potential residential market for Mini-Breaker equals household replacement fuse consumption. No precise figures have been obtained to show the exact size of this market. However, the following carefully considered estimates are offered.

        (1) Sears, Roebuck claims that its sale of 6 million fuses annually equals 5 percent of the total replacement fuse market. On this basis, the total market would be 120 million fuses.

        (2) The consumer survey in Springfield, Ohio, revealed that the average household contacted replaced 2.85 fuses in the past 12 months. When this figure is multiplied by the total number of households (47.5 million) the total fuse replacement market annually would equal 135,375,000. This estimate is based, of course, on an extremely limited sample.

        (3) There is strong evidence to suggest that the primary market for Mini-Breaker is in *owner-occupied residences.* Since there are 27 million such residences with an average of four fuses per home, the theoretical potential among home owners would be 108 million. The above computations do not consider the present percent of homes equipped with residential circuit breakers which has been authoritatively estimated at less than 2 percent.

    B. *Summary of market potential*

        On the basis of the above conservative estimates, the potential for Mini-Breaker would seem to exceed 100 million. This figure would be slightly reduced when homes served by direct current and by utilities offering free fuse service are considered. More important, the estimated figure may be reduced more significantly when consideration is given to the number of circuits in each home which are completely trouble free. Our later research might reveal, for example, that 25 percent of the electrical circuits account for 75 percent of fuse consumption. If this *hypothetical* case were true, the potential for Mini-Breaker would be reduced considerably.

C. *Characteristics of the ultimate consumer market*

On the basis of the consumer interviews conducted in Springfield, Ohio, the following facts have been tentatively established:

(1) The average urban home has four fuses installed. Farm homes, however, tend to have a larger number of fuses as more electrical circuits are needed.

(2) Men do most of the fuse buying and installation. This situation may not be entirely true on farms as farm women are apparently more self-reliant in this regard.

(3) People are accustomed to buying fuses in boxes of four or five. Relatively few persons buy fuses individually.

(4) Consumers are unaware of what brand of fuses exist and therefore exhibit no brand preference.

(5) Few people have an intelligent appreciation of fuse prices. Estimates ranged from 5 cents to 50 cents. Farmers were more precise in their estimates of fuse prices.

(6) When shown Mini-Breaker, approximately one third of the respondents expressed sincere interest.

(7) From the nature of the comments made, tenants are not an important market for Mini-Breaker.

(8) Estimates given with reference to the price people would be willing to pay for Mini-Breaker ranged from 25 cents to several dollars. $1, $1.50, and $1.98 were suggested several times.

Recommendations:

1. Further research should be sponsored in connection with the residential replacement market to expand and verify information gained from consumer interviews conducted in Springfield, Ohio. Specific points which warrant considerably more investigation include:

   a) The relative importance of men versus women in making the Mini-Breaker buying decision.

   b) The characteristics of the farm market for Mini-Breaker.

   c) The best retail outlets for Mini-Breaker.

   d) General fuse buying and installation practices and their relation to the sale of Mini-Breaker.

   e) The extent to which one or two circuits in the average home tend to cause most of the fuse trouble.

   Such research should be conducted on the basis of a carefully constructed nationwide sample which includes an adequate proportion of farmers and urban residents, and high-, middle-, and low-income groups. It is recommended that personal interviews be used to obtain this information and that the actual investigation be made by a national survey organization such as Market Opinion Research, Inc. or A. J. Wood, Inc. A minimum of 5,000 interviews should be conducted to make the findings reliable. Approximate cost of this undertaking will be $15,000. Actually, this will be a very economical measure, for on the basis of the facts uncovered, selling appeals and advertising media can be selected much more carefully with the result that the entire sales effort will be more effective.

2. Additional research is needed to determine with more precision the trend and regional sales pattern of circuit breakers versus fuse box installations in new home construction. This will be extremely helpful in predicting the long-run market potential for Mini-Breaker.

3. It is recommended that carefully planned and controlled research be used to determine the effects of the first advertising campaigns which were discussed elsewhere in this report. Such research will enable the agency to determine more clearly the nature of the advertising to be used in national or regional sales campaigns.

Promotion

Our preliminary investigations indicate very little organized and *sustained* promotional effort has ever been put behind the product. Consequently, we can draw no real conclusions from either the previous trade paper or consumer advertising or from sectional promotions such as that started by Sears in Chicago.

To date our research indicates that Mini-Breaker is a sound product with good sales potential. However, we have no reliable basis on which to judge just how effective *real* advertising support of the product can be . . . to what extent we can arouse interest, create consumer demand, increase sales, and facilitate distribution.

An important consideration we cannot overlook is that, at present, Merrill, Inc., has a national sales organization operating entirely without advertising support. Some sales literature, mailers, countercards, displays, ad-mats, etc., are available, but no direct consumer or trade advertising is working for your sales organization to help build consumer demand and trade support.

A limited amount of such advertising was done at one time, but this apparently was done without the full support and cooperation of your sales and distributor groups and was more a sectional than a national promotion. In a few instances we know that there was strong resentment on the part of a few distributors because they were not fully informed of these sectional promotions . . . what they would consist of, when they would start and stop, and how tie-ins could be used effectively.

For these reasons we believe it absolutely essential that we start at once on a limited, but national, advertising program which as a minimum, would be a token advertising program supporting your sales and distributor groups. Such a program would immediately start building consumer interest and demand for Mini-Breaker (urgently needed) and would be a moral and physical encouragement for your agents, distributors, and dealers to renew their enthusiasm and sales efforts.

This national program should be built around small space ads in both consumer and trade publications, maintained on a regular schedule, and fully merchandised to your sales agents, wholesalers, and dealers.

For maximum effect we believe this national program should be carried out over a 12-month period. Estimated costs would be between $35,000 and $50,000, or roughly, $4,000 monthly.

To help determine what this national effort should be, we recommend that several localized, carefully controlled sales promotions be given serious consideration. If carried out effectively, these promotions would be fairly accurate yardsticks by which we could measure consumer acceptance; distributor and dealer cooperation and the most effective distribution channels; importance of TV versus newspaper and radio as Mini-Breaker advertising media; the type of sales tools most useful; the most logical Mini-Breaker prospects; etc. In other words these local promotions would indicate who we want to sell, how we should try to sell them. By projecting these results we could estimate our national market and what it might cost to sell it.

Conclusion

On the previous pages we have condensed our findings, and given you recommendations. These can be summarized as follows:

1. *Strong sales management is necessary*
   Additional personnel should be provided; regional managers methods for getting maximum out of these personnel must also be provided. A program for utility sales should be set up.
2. *Consistent sales policy is necessary*
   This includes determining the best distributive channels and protecting and encouraging them. It includes decisions on pricing, discounts, and house accounts.
3. *Consumer advertising is necessary*
   This includes a modest but consistent magazine campaign, which will later be expanded. It also includes a definite coopera-

tive advertising program for use as desired. Additionally, individual markets should be tested and their results carefully noted.

4. *Packaging and point-of-sale material should be expanded*

   Our advertising must be carefully carried to the point of ultimate purchase. The product must be displayed, and a sales message given.

5. *Continued market research is necessary*

   At the earliest possible time, we should obtain a definite, realistic figure on the market potential. We should learn more about our prospects, and how to fit our product to their buying habits.

If Merrill, Inc. agrees to these recommendations, we are ready to serve you.

CASE QUESTION

Should the management of Merrill, Inc. accept the recommendations of Johnson and Baker? Why or why not?

CASE 7–2

Merrill, Inc. (B) *

Advertising and promotional program

Johnson and Baker, an advertising agency, took over the Mini-Breaker account in May of the second year after this product had received approval by Underwriters' Laboratories, Inc. In August, after six weeks of preliminary research and study, the agency submitted a series of recommendations outlining a program designed to develop a market for this new product.[1]

After thorough analysis and discussion by the management of Merrill, Inc., the preliminary report was approved. Johnson and Baker then continued its survey of the product, its market, and its distribution. Later in August, Merrill executives agreed that the appearance of the new model Mini-Breaker, which was shorter, would provide an excellent op-

---

* Written by Peter A. Repenning, Research Assistant, Bureau of Business Research, and James D. Scott, Professor of Marketing, Graduate School of Business Administration, The University of Michigan.

[1] See "Merrill, Inc. (A)" for this report.

portunity to change the product's price, packaging, external appearance (label, etc.), discount structure, and to perfect advertising and merchandising plans. Executives of Merrill, Inc. also agreed that sales management should be strengthened and improved as an indispensable part of retail selling.

In September of this same year, Johnson and Baker submitted a second report making definite recommendations for the advertising and promotion of Mini-Breaker during the last quarter of the current year. A condensed version of this report is reproduced below:

I. National Consumer Magazine Program

Agency previously recommended a limited, but national advertising program which, as a minimum, would be a token advertising effort to support your sales and distributor groups. This program is to start as soon as possible (earliest editions are November) and will begin immediately to build consumer interest and demand for Mini-Breaker (urgently needed) and will encourage your agents, distributors, and dealers to renew their enthusiasm and sales efforts.

Recommendations:

1. *Good Housekeeping* (circ. 3,000,000)

   One of the best read and circulated shelter books, but selected primarily for the merchandising value of the "Good Housekeeping Seal of Approval." We suggest minimum space necessary to obtain the Seal and use it over a 12-month period.

   6⅓ col. B&W ads @ $22.27 line[1] $6,413.76

2. *Household* (circ. 2,250,000)

   A popular, young and relatively inexpensive "home" magazine which claims the largest "home owner" readership of all the shelter books. Primarily a female audience, but with appeals to both sexes. Has large farm circulation.

   12⅓ col. B&W ads @ $15.75 line[2] $9,072.00

3. *Better Homes & Gardens* (circ. 3,780,000)

   The largest and best accepted shelter book with home ownership almost equal to *Household* but with primarily an urban audience.

   12⅓ col. B&W ads @ $21.50 line.........................$13,674.00

4. *True* (circ. 1,750,000)

   Largest selling men's magazine. Audience median age, 33.3 years; median income, $8,690. Selected for strictly male audience.

   12⅓ col. B&W ads @ $14.70[3] $8,467.20

---

[1] Effective February next year, $24.50/line.

[2] Effective February next year, $17.00/line.

[3] Effective January next year, $16.00/line.

5. *Popular Mechanics* (circ. 1.5 million)

Selected for the "do-it-yourself" audience and also on the basis of previous good returns from ads and publicity in this book. Primarily male readership.

12⅓ col. B&W ads @ $8.93 line..............................$4,072.08

6. *Rotarian* (circ. 275,000)

Economical space, read by good prospects, with excellent ad visibility. A fraternal magazine selected primarily for good circulation at minimum costs. High home ownership probable.

12⅓ col. B&W ads @ $3.45 line..............................$1,945.80

(Alternate space, 6½ col. B&W ads)

7. *Moose* (circ. 850,000)

Selected on the same basis as *Rotarian*, but with slightly different class readership.

12⅓ col. B&W ads @ $4.00 line..............................$2,256.00

(Alternate space, 6½ col. B&W ads)

Total space costs..................	$48,510.84
Total preparatory costs............	2,000.00
Total...........................	$50,510.84
Total circulation.................	13,809,778

Agency will contact all magazine representatives and make arrangements, if possible, for photos and description of Mini-Breaker to be used in "new product" or "retail selling" columns or sections of these magazines.

As important as the ads themselves is a *sustained* advertising program that is continued without interruption for the 12-month period. An incidental benefit is reduced space rates, but more important is the fact that we *consistently* show our product, tell our sales story, and point out the benefits of having Mini-Breaker in the fuse box. This is particularly true of small space advertising where we benefit largely from cumulative effect of repeated exposure to our sales story and where our objective is slow but progressively increasing sales to a national market.

II. Localized Promotions

Several localized, concentrated promotions were included in our previous recommendations. We believe these promotions should still be carried out, but in view of our recent findings in New York and Atlantic City, we highly recommend Atlantic City and Rockford, Illinois, as the promotion cities. If carried out effectively, they would be fairly accurate yardsticks for measuring consumer acceptance; distributor and dealer cooperation and the most effective distribution channels; importance of TV versus newspaper and radio as advertising media; the types of sales tools most effective; the most logical Mini-Breaker prospects, etc. By projecting the results from these two cities we can better estimate our national market and what it will cost to sell it.

1. *Atlantic City, New Jersey* (44,500 families). Recommendations (for promotional program): (1) Continuing spots on radio station WOND on present basis of six times daily, five times a week, for six weeks. (2) Adding spots on radio station WMID for six times daily, five times a week, for six weeks. (3) Place fractional page ads in *Atlantic City Press* to tie in with radio spots and reach new audience. (4) A close check of distribution and promotional efforts will be made by agency representative with evaluation of results at frequent intervals. Total (estimated expenditure) $1,697.00.

2. *Rockford, Illinois* (34,900 families). We propose different distribution and different advertising media in Rockford, in order to contrast results with Atlantic City procedures. Whereas in Atlantic City all "fuse selling" retailers are used, we suggest distribution in Rockford only through normal hardware and electrical retail outlets, and services through their normal wholesalers. As advertising media, we recommend the use of TV alone for the first three weeks, with small newspaper ad tie-ins and support for the balance of the promotion. As in Atlantic City, we believe close agency check of the promotion will be necessary. Recommendations: (1) Distribution to be effected and support of local utility to be solicited before promotion gets under way. (2) Station WREX–TV (CBS–ABC Network) four spots daily, five days a week, for three weeks. (3) Place small space ads in *Rockford Star* and *Register-Republic* to tie-in with TV for the first three weeks and to carry promotion alone for another six weeks after end of TV promotion. Total (estimated expenditures) $4,505.00. Both the Atlantic City and Rockford promotions should be started as soon as practical. . . . These promotions should include every effort to push the product at the point of purchase.

III. *Newspaper Ads and Dealer Ad Mats*

Newspaper ad mats should be made available for dealers, or distributors, or for use by Merrill, Inc., in any localized promotion in a metropolitan area. Layouts are included with this presentation, and proof sheets of mat ads should be made available to distributors, dealers, and agents. An opportunity to determine how well this material will benefit us is available right now in Pittsburgh. This city has been developed to a point where it needs consumer promotion. . . . We therefore recommend that $1,000 be allocated for consumer newspaper advertising in Pittsburgh during the remainder of the current year. Most of this will be cooperative, although some may be factory advertising. Increase in number of outlets and sales volume will be carefully watched. The advice of the manufacturers' agent will be solicited.

IV. Trade Campaign

A limited trade campaign is recommended to help attract new dealers and distributors and to remind the hardware and electrical trade that Mini-Breaker is a very active high-profit item that shouldn't be overlooked. Primary purpose is to attract new dealers and encourage new dealer enthusiasm. . . .

Recommendations:

Hardware Age (circulation 34,861), *Hardware and Housewares* (circulation 46,871), six one-half pages in black and white in each publication, estimated total cost $3,110.

(The second report also contained a suggested advertising by direct mail campaign to be tested in Rockford, Illinois, and Atlantic City, New Jersey, at an approximate cost of $900 and $450 respectively. Suggestions were also made for continued marketing research.)

V. Conclusion

Let's briefly review the recommendations made in this report to Merrill, Inc. and what we think they will accomplish. We have chosen five basic media—magazines, both consumer and trade; radio; TV; direct mail; and newspapers, both co-op and direct factory.

A minimum of point-of-purchase material (window streamers) and a revision of the present convention booth are also recommended. Other media, transportation and outdoor advertising, for instance, have been considered but are not recommended at this time.

We have proposed limited national campaigns, and localized promotions in several areas with these media. An estimate of their costs for the balance of the current year is shown in Exhibit 1.

The object of this advertising is to encourage the existing sales force (agents, wholesalers, retailers), to increase distribution and to learn more about our problems with specific relation to announcement of a new model next year.

Very importantly, the localized promotions should help us determine the cost per unit of promotion. Checks should be maintained in Atlantic City, Rockford, and Pittsburgh, as well as our direct-mail locations, on promotion costs versus sales. This should be of great value in determining a price for the new model.

EXHIBIT 1

Consumer magazines......................	$ 8,000*
Trade magazines.........................	0,100†
Radio...................................	1,100
TV.....................................	3,000
Direct mail.............................	1,100
Newspapers.............................	3,700‡
Point-of-purchase.......................	750
Display booth...........................	825
Total............................	$19,575

* 3-month share of 12-month schedule.
† 3-month share of 12-month schedule.
‡ Atlantic City, Rockford, and Pittsburgh.

Work on this new model must be carried on this fall. For this reason, a continuing research program should be begun and a packaging consultant retained. We estimate the costs of these activities to be $4,000 and $5,000 respectively.

Adding $7,000 for contingencies, travel expenses, etc., we recommend that Merrill, Inc., budget approximately $37,000 for promotion and allied research in the last quarter of the year. This total presupposes that we will use existing literature, displays, and TV commercials. It does not include production work on items which will be used with the new model. From time to time, during the balance of the year, we may make other recommendations. The $37,000 is a basis point only.

One approval is given to this interim program of research, national advertising, and localized promotion, it is our intention to develop point-of-sale material for the new model. This will include packaging, unit redesign, counter cards, streamers, decals, cartons, etc. All of our other material, advertisements, literature, sales aids, commercials, display booth, etc., will then be integrated with the point-of-sale material.

As soon as the skeleton framework of the consumer promotion for next year is set, and work begun on its details, we should begin development of integrated campaigns aimed at the important groups which influence the ultimate consumer. These influence groups include utilities, the REAs, the electrical inspectors, the contractors, and various trade associations. Methods of reaching them will include motion pictures, slide film and flip chart presentations, special ads, booth displays, publicity stories, etc.

Much care must also be given to the launching of the new model with the maximum impact on the public and on the trade. It is anticipated that this will take place in January. Once the new model is on the market, we can take up other problems, namely, commercial and industrial sales, the original equipment market, the cartridge breaker, and the motor protector.

This, then, is our basic blueprint for Mini-Breaker promotion in the months ahead. We hope that affirmative action will be taken on our immediate recommendations. But we reiterate that advertising and promotion will not achieve the desired results unless the sales organization is strengthened and the distribution improved. If necessary, we are willing to defer our fourth-quarter activities to accomplish this. Once begun, the timetable will be difficult to change, and Mini-Breaker cannot afford a false start. Once begun, everyone must be in complete agreement with our program.

CASE QUESTION

Should the executives of Merrill, Inc. approve the advertising and promotional program recommended by its advertising agency? Why or why not?

CASE 7–3

Merrill, Inc. (C)*

Strategy for long-range market development

During September of the second year after Mini-Breaker had received Underwriters' Laboratory approval, the Johnson and Baker advertising agency submitted recommendations for an interim program of advertising and promotion to carry the product through the last quarter of that year. This was the second report submitted to the management of Merrill, Inc., and the proposals that it contained were based upon preliminary studies just completed.[1]

Action taken on recommendations

After considering the agency's recommendations, the executives of Merrill, Inc. authorized Johnson and Baker to go ahead with the national advertising campaign in the magazines recommended. These advertisements ran for 12 months, at which time they were not renewed. Merrill,

---

* Written by Peter A. Repenning, Research Assistant, Bureau of Business Research, and James D. Scott, Professor of Marketing, Graduate School of Business Administration, The University of Michigan.

[1] See "Merrill, Inc. (B)" for information on these recommendations.

Inc. officers also authorized the agency to conduct a test campaign in Rockford, Illinois. The test campaign was personally supervised by Mr. Greaves, sales manager of Merrill, Inc. Under his direction a more efficient distribution system was set up for the test, and missionary salesmen were hired to help get intensive distribution in the area. Advertising and promotion were carried out on the basis recommended by the agency. While window streamers were available to be placed in stores which carried Mini-Breaker, difficulty was experienced in getting store owners to make use of such material. They were not willing to take window space for signs promoting a $1.50 item when there were many higher priced, higher profit items which they wished to promote in the same space. Sears, Roebuck did not take part in the campaign, but at the end of the eight-week test the local Sears store had sold 59 Mini-Breakers, more than any other retail store in Rockford.

Not only were results in the Rockford test campaign discouraging but also there was no noticeable effect during the last quarter of the current year from any of the consumer advertising which was undertaken.

Recommended promotional program for third year after U.L. approval

By December of the second year after U.L. approval, Johnson and Baker had completed its research on possible advertising themes and on the potential market for Mini-Breaker. Accordingly, a presentation was made to Merrill executives on December 3, entitled "The Outlook Today for Mini-Breaker." The essential points from this presentation are outlined in the following pages.

What We Are Selling

Mini-Breaker stands alone in: (1) personal safety . . . no danger of injury; (2) household security . . . real protection against fires; (3) convenience . . . simple, quick way to restore power; (4) home efficiency . . . household duties resumed quickly, no need to wait for husband or serviceman; (5) modernization . . . simplest, most economic way to modernize electrical panel systems; (6) economy to utilities . . . Mini-Breaker can eliminate three out of five service calls.

Potential Market

How big is the market for Mini-Breaker in American homes? Of the 45 million homes in America, 90 percent, or 40,500,000 have fuse boxes. Of those with fuse boxes, surveys indicate that 72 percent, or 29,200,000, would be interested in Mini-Breakers, 60 percent of this number of 17,500,000 would replace existing fuses 100 percent with Mini-Breaker units. The remaining 11,700,000 or 40 percent would partially replace existing fuses on selected trouble circuits (see Exhibit 1).

The 40,500,000 homes with fuse boxes average 5.7 fuses per home . . . therefore they hold 231 million fuses. The 72 percent of the homes interested in Mini-Breaker hold 167 million fuses. Those likely to replace existing fuses 100 percent with Mini-Breaker units hold 100 million fuses. Partial replacement of fuses among the 11,700,000 interested homes might be expected to add another 12 million units to the immediate potential thus giving a total of 112 million Mini-Breakers (see Exhibit 2).

EXHIBIT 1
Potential market for Mini-Breaker (number of homes)

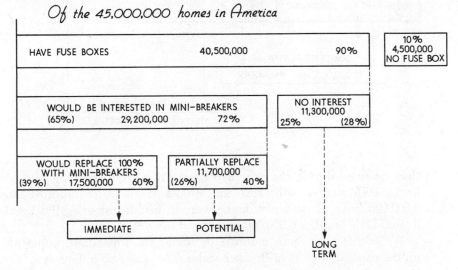

Of the 45,000,000 homes in America

In addition to the immediate potential, it is estimated that partial replacement homes plus noninterested homes provide a long-term potential market of an additional 119 million Mini-Breakers.

What does this mean in relation to (the established sales goal of) 25 million Mini-Breakers in five years? The immediate potential of 112 million units plus one sixth of the long-term potential of 119 million units, or 20 million Mini-Breakers, adds up to a total potential for the next five years of 132 million units. The sales goal of 25 million units in the next five years is 18½ percent of the very real potential calculated above.

In addition, there are 1,300,000 new homes with fuse box protection systems being built each year. This building rate will increase rather

EXHIBIT 2
Potential market for Mini-Breaker (number of Mini-Breaker units)

The 40,500,000 homes with fuse boxes average
5.7 fuses per home... *therefore, they hold*

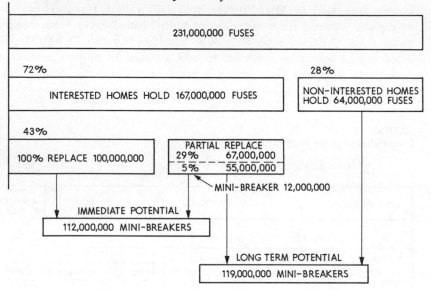

than decrease during the next five years. At current building rate, new home construction will add an annual demand of approximately 7,500,000 fuses. If each new home were to install just one Mini-Breaker it would add another 6,500,000 in the next five years.

We couldn't be more enthusiastic about the immediate opportunity for the expansion of Mini-Breaker scales. The goal of 5 million is:

. . . Only 4 percent of the estimated Mini-Breaker potential based on expressed interest for buying Mini-Breaker.
. . . Only 2.1 percent of the estimated fuse population.
. . . Only one Mini-Breaker cash register sale in every 33 fuse purchases (based on current total industry production estimate).
. . . Only one fuse in every seven homes that have an interest in Mini-Breaker (based on expressed interest for buying Mini-Breaker).

Twenty-five million in five years? Five million per year? Yes, definitely.

Recommended Marketing Program

What must we do to sell 5 million units per year? The most practical approach is a market-by-market development. Hitting few markets at a time . . . building distribution, and consumer recognition. Then moving to the next group of markets.

We suggest a three-pronged approach to each market: (1) building distribution, (2) cultivation of electric utilities, (3) building consumer recognition and demand.

Utilities play a fantastic part in the fuse business. Two thirds of residential electric meters are serviced by electric utilities without charge. Three out of five utility service calls require only the replacement of a fuse. The average utility service call costs $2 to $3. Utilities replace over 4 million fuses annually.

Why should electric utilities be interested in Mini-Breakers? (1) There are real economic pressures working in our favor to have Mini-Breaker be the standard replacement in fuse trouble calls by electric utilities. (2) Quality and standards of product are exclusively in keeping with the aim of electric utilities. (Only utility objection has now been eliminated.) (3) Personal safety and household security are in common with the major electric utilities' public relations purpose. And . . . of major importance to us is the fact . . . a very small number of utilities handle the lion's share of the business. Out of 3,300 electric utilities, 200 or 6 percent service 75 percent of the meters.

The electric utility is potentially Mini-Breaker's number one salesman. Cultivation of electric utility is a very important second prong in the marketing plan.

Prong No. 3 in the market plan: The tremendous market potential that has just been shown for Mini-Breaker is conclusive evidence for the opportunity of immediate expansion of the program to other markets. The plan for expansion, market by market, is currently being tested in Atlantic City and Rockford. We are uncovering in these two cities many of the problems that will be encountered as new markets are added. So far we see no reason to increase the rate of advertising that has been established in Atlantic City . . . rate of $8 per $1 million of consumer buying power in the market area. If we were to have national distribution this would mean an advertising budget of $1,950,000. However, we cannot build national distribution overnight. (This is one of the basic reasons for city by city recommendation.) We do recommend the development of 12 markets during the next year entailing an additional advertising expenditure of $250,000. We strongly recommend that the plan start immediately in six more markets. These markets should be small markets as there are several other combinations of media and methods of using media that need testing. Such as . . . eight-second TV spots; coupon selling in printed media to compensate for inadequate distribution; direct TV and/or radio selling for the same reason.

The cost of this advertising should be added to the manufacturer's

EXHIBIT 3

Current manufacturer's selling price.....................	$0.70
Cost of advertising (Atlantic City plan).................	.39
Total manufacturer's selling price.......................	$1.09
Manufacturers' agents commission (10 percent)...........	0.11
	$1.20
Wholesaler's mark-up (20 percent)......................	0.24
	$1.44
Retail mark-up (37½ percent)..........................	0.54
Consumer selling price.................................	$1.98

selling price. We see no indication that this increase will in any significant way affect the goal of 25 million Mini-Breakers in five years. Based on the information available to us on Mini-Breaker costs, the composition of the *consumer selling price* would be as presented in Exhibit 3.

A plan of 12 markets during the coming year, involving an additional $250,000 advertising budget would need a production volume increase next year of 650,000 or 54,000 on top of current production.

In summary:

1. Outstanding, exclusive product . . . "The one white pea in a pod."
2. Tremendous residential market potential.
3. Great opportunity through electric utilities.
4. Enthusiastic, aggressive, persistent, determined belief in the ability of the product to succeed.
5. Market by market approach . . . 12 during the coming year.
6. Build distribution . . . heavy trade relations activity in each market.
7. Additional consumer advertising in next year: $250,000.
8. Additional production in next year: 650,000 units.

The product is ready, the market is ready, the plan is ready. Your OK is all that is needed.

CASE QUESTIONS

1. If you were the sales manager of Merrill, Inc. would you accept the goal of selling five million units per year for five years as an attainable objective? Explain.
2. Would you approve the proposed three-pronged approach to each of the 12 markets which the agency proposes to develop during the coming year? Explain.
3. Would you approve an additional advertising appropriation of $250,000 as a part of the program of developing 12 additional markets during the coming year? Why or why not?

CASE 7–4

Merrill, Inc. (D) *

Reappraisal of marketing strategy

In December of the second year after U.L. approval, the Johnson and Baker advertising agency completed its research on the potential market for Mini-Breaker and on possible advertising themes. Representatives of the agency then presented recommendations to executives of Merrill, Inc., identifying an objective of selling five million units of Mini-Breaker per year for five years and proposing a three-pronged strategy for achieving this goal. A key recommendation involved establishing an advertising appropriation of $250,000 for the coming year.[1]

Action taken on agency recommendations

In reaching a conclusion on the foregoing recommendations, the officials of Merrill, Inc. kept clearly in mind the fact that the firm was already obligated to continue the magazine advertising campaign previously approved until the completion of the schedule in the fall of the coming year (a nine-month period). Moreover, at the time Johnson and Baker's recommendations for the coming year were under consideration, there was no evidence that the advertising program of the last quarter of the current year was producing any results at all. Accordingly, Merrill, Inc. officials were reluctant to approve the additional expenditure of $250,000 on the recommended advertising program. The magazine advertising was the only promotional effort which continued, and even this was canceled in June of the third year after U.L. approval.

Introduction of models MP–252 and MP–600

Due to the discouraging results from previous efforts, management and sales officials had agreed in March of the third year after U.L. approval that all marketing effort should be directed to the new MP–252 and MP–600 models of Mini-Breaker, which were designed primarily for use on electric ranges, built-in ovens, and automatic washers and dryers. This effort proved fruitful. In less than nine months, 28 original-equipment manufacturers were using the MP–252 or MP–600 models.

---

* Written by Peter A. Repenning, Research Assistant, Bureau of Business Research, and James D. Scott, Professor of Marketing, Graduate School of Business Administration, The University of Michigan.

[1] Refer to "Merrill, Inc. (C)" for this report.

Results of the 12-month campaign

By August of the third year after U.L. approval, it had become clear to the executives of Merrill, Inc. that the attempt to develop a consumer market for Mini-Breaker was a complete failure. Sales of Mini-Breaker units had not increased during the 12-month campaign starting in September of the second year after U.L. approval. Indeed, sales volume remained at about the same level as when no advertising was being done. By this time, only 8 of the original 24 manufacturers' agents were still handling Mini-Breaker. Only spotty distribution had been achieved in hardware stores and in appliance shops throughout the United States.

Diagnosis of reasons for failure

In view of these disappointing results, both Mr. Greaves, the sales manager, and the representatives of the Johnson and Baker advertising agency, faced the problem of diagnosing the causes for the lack of success and/or working out a program which would result in a profitable sales volume in the future. In the discussions which followed, David Hunter, the head of the research department of Johnson and Baker, argued that the difficulty could not properly be traced to the product. He pointed out that several major concerns were interested in the product from a functional standpoint and presumably because of the undeniable success Mini-Breaker was bound to enjoy. Sears, Roebuck was very much interested in the product and had initially made an attempt to get Merrill, Inc. to produce it for Sears exclusively. Moreover, the ease of getting manufacturers' agents to handle the product when it was first introduced was attributed by Mr. Hunter to its very great appeal. As evidence of the promise of Mini-Breaker, he pointed out that 80 percent of the homes in the United States had inadequate wiring, as of the current year, and that in the next five years the average home would have a $5,000 investment in electrical appliances as compared with the current figure of $1,300.

In Mr. Hunter's opinion the reason for the failure of the product, in spite of its appeal, was that Merrill, Inc. had not followed through on any consistent plan of promotion which it had begun. The Rockford test campaign, for example, was permitted to continue for only eight weeks, and Mr. Hunter argued that this was not a long enough period to provide a fair test of the promotional program. Moreover, he pointed out that the television spots were also discontinued after only a few weeks of broadcasting. In fact, he said, only the magazine advertising had been done consistently for any period of time.

Jack Ross, assistant to the head of the Johnson and Baker research department, held a somewhat different view from that expressed by

Mr. Hunter. While Mr. Ross admitted the high quality of Mini-Breaker, he did not believe that there was any strong appeal available which could satisfactorily be used to sell it. Mr. Ross admitted that the findings of the consumer research seemed to run counter to his opinion. Thus, it had been found that of the families living in homes with fuse boxes, 72 percent had expressed an interest in, and a definite desire for, Mini-Breaker. (See Exhibit 1 in "Merrill, Inc. [C].") Careful analysis of this survey, however, had led Mr. Ross to question its validity. Thus, he pointed out that of the homes with a fuse box under the control of the inhabitant, 45 percent were rented, and renters are not interested in buying permanent fixtures for the homes they occupy. Although renters may be interested in the product, Mr. Ross argued, they are not likely to become buyers.

Analysis of the nature of the need for Mini-Breaker, furthermore, had convinced Mr. Ross that the product could be better characterized as a necessary evil (as are ordinary fuses) rather than as a product in which consumers can be expected to develop a strong interest. As evidence to support this point of view, Mr. Ross cited the consumer response to an attempt to get consumers to fill out questionnaires giving their reactions to Mini-Breaker. This study involved two parts. In the first, a coupon and a questionnaire were enclosed in 500 Mini-Breaker packages. An offer was made to refund 50 cents of the purchase price to the consumer if the enclosed coupon were returned with a completed questionnaire. Of 500 offers made, only 50 were returned. In the second part of the study, 500 questionnaires were enclosed in Mini-Breaker packages with a request that they be filled out and returned, but in this case the company did not offer any compensation for cooperating with the request. Out of 500 questionnaires enclosed in the packages, none was returned by consumers.

With reference to the appeals which had been used in the advertising campaign, Mr. Ross argued that none was strong enough to stimulate a profitable volume of sales. The only emotional appeal that could be used was to personal safety, but Mr. Ross believed that the strength of this appeal was doubtful, since those who are afraid to replace a fuse were getting fewer and fewer in number. Except in rare cases where chronic trouble was experienced on an electrical circuit, he argued that the benefits to be derived from using a $1.50 Mini-Breaker were not great enough to justify its purchase as compared to a 7 cent ordinary fuse.

Mr. Greaves, the sales manager, took a somewhat different view from those expressed above. He claimed that the benefits of using Mini-Breaker were great enough so that he could sell the product door-to-door without the slightest difficulty. Indeed, he explained that 6 national direct-selling organizations, who maintain 100 to 150 salesmen, were handling Mini-Breaker currently. These salesmen sold lighting fixtures, lamps, starters, fuses, etc., direct to industrial and commercial establishments for their own use, not for resale. As of the current year, these 6 groups had sold more Mini-Breakers than the 1,200 wholesalers distributing the product. According to Mr. Greaves, this indicated that the product could be sold if its advantages were explained to the customer through personal contact. (These firms had maintained that even larger sales would result if they were given larger discounts and if they were permitted to distribute under private labels.) Mr. Greaves went on to say, however, that he was only too aware of the fact that Mini-Breaker looked very much like an ordinary fuse. When the consumer saw the two side by side, the ordinary fuse priced at 7 cents and Mini-Breaker priced at $1.50, he was likely to take the 7 cent item, unless he was acquainted with the advantages of the more expensive one. In the opinion of Mr. Greaves this indicated the necessity for consumer advertising.

Then, too, Mr. Greaves argued that consumer advertising was made necessary by the impossibility of getting middlemen to give aggressive support to Mini-Breaker. Thus, Mini-Breaker was sold to 1,200 hardware and electrical supply houses by manufacturers' agents. In Mr. Greaves's opinion, the reasons for their failure to market Mini-Breaker in greater volume included (a) retail price too high, (b) lack of consistent consumer advertising, and (c) discount of 25 percent of selling price too low to stimulate interest in the item. Wholesalers of this type carry thousands of items, according to Mr. Greaves, and they could therefore only be expected to serve as order takers. To expect aggressive sales help from such firms is futile, in Mr. Greaves's opinion. Thus, if retailers are to stock Mini-Breakers, the pressure of consumer demand must be such as to lead them to ask specifically for the item when ordering from supply houses.

Moreover, in Mr. Greaves's opinion, aggressive selling was not to be expected from hardware stores and appliance outlets under normal circumstances. Experience had indicated that it was difficult indeed to get dealers to push Mini-Breaker when sales might occur only once a month and when the gross margin per unit was less than 50 cents. Competing with Mini-Breaker for the retailers' sales support were items worth several hundred dollars on the floor which carried a relatively large dollar gross margin. Experience had shown that to get such a dealer to make room for a Mini-Breaker counter display was indeed a triumph.

Subsequent to March of the third year after U.L. approval, during the introduction of models MP–252 and MP–600 to original equipment manufacturers, Mini-Breaker promotion was dormant. By the fall of that year, only eight manufacturers' agents were still handling the product.

Except for two of the agents, there was very little sales activity on the part of these firms. All advertising of Mini-Breaker units had been stopped in June of that year. Nevertheless, Mini-Breaker sales continued, increasing during August, September, and October. In the opinion of company officials, this proved that the complaints of manufacturers' agents and wholesale distributors were merely excuses for poor performance rather than real reasons for failure.

At the same time, Mr. Greaves was aware of the fact that sales of Mini-Breaker by Sears, Roebuck and Company had been consistent and profitable to that firm. Sears officials, however, continued to press Merrill, Inc., for permission to sell the product under the Homart private label and for a buying price which would permit Sears to retail the item at 98 cents.

Although Mr. Greaves could see that the situation appeared to call for consumer advertising, he had serious doubts as to whether such advertising could be done cheaply enough to result in a profitable sales volume on Mini-Breaker. At the current volume of 25,000 units a month, Mr. Greaves estimated that the margin available for sales and administrative expenses was somewhat less than 5 cents per unit. It was estimated that if sales volume could be increased to 500,000 units per month, a modest profit could be made with a $300,000 per year advertising budget. But Johnson and Baker had recommended an advertising appropriation for national coverage based on a volume of 500,000 per month of six times $300,000, or $1,800,000. Thus, even though consumer advertising through mass media seemed to be highly desirable, it did not appear to Mr. Greaves that Mini-Breaker could support an advertising appropriation large enough to accomplish the necessary task.

The problem involved in developing the consumer market profitably led Mr. Greaves to consider the alternative of selling through public utilities. Mr. Hunter, of Johnson and Baker, quoted figures indicating that Mini-Breaker could save public utilities a substantial sum of money on free fuse replacement calls. Mr. Ross, however, expressed some doubts as to the appeal of this proposal to public utility managers. First, the expense of replacing fuses with Mini-Breakers in boxes served by public utilities would be sizable. Second, such replacements, together with the time which would be required to educate consumers in the operation of Mini-Breaker units, would require a great deal of time on the part of servicemen. On balance, therefore, Mr. Ross was of the opinion that public utilities would not save money by installing Mini-Breakers.

In spite of the negative arguments of Mr. Ross, Mr. Greaves was beginning to favor the suggestion of selling Mini-Breaker through the public utilities market. By this time, Mini-Breaker had been shortened to comply with electrical codes, and thus would meet the original objections which public utilities had to the substitution of Mini-Breaker for the ordinary fuse. Moreover, it appeared that profitable volume of business could be secured through the public utilities without incurring large selling expenses. Since Mr. Greaves believed that all other alternative approaches to the development of a market for Mini-Breaker had been adequately tested, he felt that sales through public utilities was the only promising path which was open to him.

CASE QUESTIONS

1. What is your diagnosis of the failure of the marketing program for Mini-Breaker?

2. What further marketing action, if any, should be taken by executives of Merrill, Inc. to develop a profitable sales volume for this product?

CASE 7–5

Wolverine World Wide, Inc.: Ski Division (A) *

Promotional strategy for new line of skiing equipment

Wolverine World Wide, Inc., of Rockford, Michigan, a manufacturer and distributor of shoes, most notably the "Hush Puppies"® line, was given the opportunity in 1970 to be the exclusive distributor of Rossignol Skis and Le Trappeur Ski Boots in the United States. Since these lines appeared to offer a promising potential for increasing the firm's sales and profits, the challenge was accepted and a Ski Division was organized to administer this segment of the business. An introductory program was developed to get distribution for the new line and to stimulate a consumer demand for it during the winter sports season of 1970–71. In March 1971 Thomas Maguire, sales manager, Ski Division, reviewed the preliminary results of the first season's campaign. He then began consultations with MacManus, John & Adams, Inc. (the advertising agency handling the account), for the purpose of developing marketing and promotional strategy for the 1971–72 winter season which would increase brand recognition, sales, and profits for that period.

---

* This case was prepared by Jay D. Lindquist, Research Assistant, and James D. Scott, Professor of Marketing, Graduate School of Business Administration, the University of Michigan.

Background

As of 1969, Wolverine World Wide, Inc. manufactured and imported a broad line of medium- and high-grade footwear for men, women, and children in a variety of materials and styles. Included in this line were the following:

1. The well-known "Hush Puppies" brand of shoes in both "breathing brushed pigskin" and smooth leather
2. Bates and Phi Bates quality men's dress shoes
3. Frolic medium-priced women's fashion footwear for private label brands
4. Trendsetter imported women's fashion boots, sandals, and volume-priced footwear for men, women, and children
5. Tru-Stitch soft-soled slippers and hand-laced moccasins
6. Verde imported men's fashion footwear
7. Wolverine brand boots and shoes for climbing, hiking, agricultural, and service use

The firm also produced Wolverine gloves for industrial and outdoor uses; protective headgear for policemen, cyclists, and people on snowmobiles; and Wolverine pigskin leather for sale to other shoe and leather goods manufacturers. Additionally, the firm was licensed to distribute Clarino, a synthetic leatherlike material used for shoe uppers (similar to DuPont's Corfam).

The line of footwear described above was sold directly to selected shoe stores, specialty shops, and department stores throughout the United States. As a means of developing the international market, the Hush Puppies brand was produced and distributed by licensees in 45 countries.

As a result of an aggressive marketing program, Wolverine achieved sales of $101 million in 1969, an increase of 11 percent over the previous year, with earnings after taxes of $3.7 million. Licensees operating in foreign markets sold 8 million pairs of Hush Puppies in this same year. Employment was provided for 5,686 people.

Addition of skiing equipment to the product line

In seeking ways of increasing sales and profits, Wolverine executives recognized the potentialities of products which could be marketed for use in connection with the leisure-time activities of consumers. Initially, gloves and mittens were produced for sale to people engaged in skiing. With this experience, management decided to seek other products which could be added to the line to serve this fast-growing market.

As a means of minimizing the capital investment involved in the development of a ski-products line, Wolverine sought opportunities to distribute established products manufactured by other firms. Activities involved in seeking foreign licensees to produce and market Hush Puppies in Europe provided an opportunity for Wolverine executives to survey interesting product possibilities in that area. Thus, arrangements were made to import from France a high-fashion line of boots to be worn after skiing (après-ski boots). The firm purchased the endorsement of Jean Claude Killy, Olympic skiing champion, for its après-ski boots, ski gloves and mittens, and protective ski headgear. A salesforce was recruited from among the ski-instructor group in the United States to get distribution for the Wolverine/Killy line of après-ski boots, gloves, mittens, and headgear during the 1969–70 skiing season. Limited success was experienced; sales of approximately $250,000 were achieved. The salesmen gained useful information and valuable experience, however, in the marketing of this limited line.

Arrangements were also made to obtain the exclusive U.S. rights for marketing the famous Rossignol Skis and Le Trappeur Ski Boots beginning with the 1970–71 ski season. The contract with Rossignol called for the minimum purchase of 50,000 pairs of skis in the 1970–71 winter season. Additionally, the contract stipulated that WWW must spend a minimum of 7 percent of the factory sales price for promotion of the product lines. The agreement could be renegotiated every two years and called for payment, in full, to Rossignol within 30 days after ski delivery to the WWW facilities in the United States.

With regard to the Le Trappeur boot line, Wolverine estimated sales of between 25,000 and 30,000 pairs in the 1970–71 season. A 5 percent minimum stipulation for promotional expenditure was included in the contract in a manner similar to the Rossignol agreement.

Characteristics of the Ski Division line

The Rossignol ski line was known the world over as being at or near the top in quality and performance. The Strato 102 ski had been raced by more ski champions and had won more prizes and medals than all other ski brands combined. The Strato 102 was a fiberglass ski that had been perfected with the aid of top French ski racers under actual competitive conditions. Rossignol was the first company to produce such a high-quality, fiberglass ski product.

Until the 1970–71 season the line had been quite narrow, but the desire to penetrate the recreational skiing market in addition to the intermediate, advanced, and racing groups triggered line expansion and cosmetic changes. This, of course, was a product plus for Wolverine to exploit.

"Rossies," as they were often called, were in the over-$50 class and generally sold at a retail price in excess of $100.

The 1970 lines of skis offered are listed in Exhibit 1. Briefly, the major products were the Strato 102 for the best of skiers, the GTA and the Strato AR for advanced skiers and the Stratix 112, the Stratoflex, the Concorde, and Strato Junior for the recreational portions of the ski market. The skis were generally a dull blue, black, or maroon in color with the exception of the Stratoflex which was orange and the GTA which was a bright red, white, and blue.

The 1970 Le Trappeur boot line is listed in Exhibit 2. It essentially consisted of noncustom-fitted boots and two custom-fitted styles (the PRO and Slalom) that used the "inject-elast" system for custom molding.

When the company came to the dealer ski show in early 1970, it did not have a custom-fitted injected boot. However, because of the "custom-fitted fever" that was apparent, Wolverine sought out, and was

EXHIBIT 1
Rossignol 1971 line

Model	Size	Dealer cost	Retail
GTA..............	190–195–200–205–210–215	$132.00	$240.00 +
Strato 102..........	180–190–195–200–207–210–210	102.00	170.00 +
Strato AR..........	180–185–190–195–200–205–210	99.00	165.00 +
Allais Major SG.....	190–195–200–205–210–215	87.00	145.00 −
Allais Major DH.....	205–210–215–220–223	87.00	145.00 −
Stratix 112.........	180–185–190–195–200–205–210	84.00	140.00 +
Stratoflex..........	180–185–190–195–200–205–210	72.00	120.00 +
Allais GP..........	180–185–190–195–200–205–210	60.00	100.00 −
Strato Junior.......	140–150–160–170–175	60.00	100.00 +
Concorde............	180–185–190–195–200–205–210	57.00	95.00 +
Rossignol Short......	160–175	57.00	95.00 −
Stratix Junior.......	140–150–160–170–175	45.00	75.00 +

Note: GTA guaranteed unconditionally for two years. All others guaranteed unconditionally for one year.

EXHIBIT 2
Le Trappeur ski boots—1970 line

Model	Size	Width	Dealer cost	Retail
PRO D..............	6 to 13	Ex W	$90.00	$165.00
Slalom D.............	6 to 13	Ex W	72.00	135.00
PRO (men's).........	6 to 13	M–W	72.00	120.00
Slalom (men's)........	6 to 13	M–W	54.00	90.00
Femina (ladies').......	5 to 9½	Ex N–N	51.00	85.00
Appollo (men's).......	6 to 13	M–W	48.00	80.00
Appollo (ladies')......	5 to 9½	Ex N–N	48.00	80.00
SM (men's)..........	6 to 13	M–W	42.00	70.00
SM (ladies')..........	5 to 9½	Ex N–N	42.00	70.00
Quick V (men's)......	6 to 13	M–W	30.00	50.00
Quick V (ladies')......	5 to 9½	Ex N–N	30.00	50.00
Junior..............	3 to 6	Medium	21.00	35.00
Junior..............	11 to 2	Medium	18.00	30.00

able to acquire, the rights to a process that Trappeur could use for injection molding. This process allowed the skier to have boots whose interior was injected with a liquid plastic foam that could set to the shape of the foot within 25 minutes after injection. The process was revolutionary and allowed for elimination of the normal "break-in" period for ski boots. Wolverine's competitors also came out with similar processes for their products. The company moved cautiously on this boot, which sold for $165 a pair. However, WWW estimates that it could have doubled its sales of the item during the 1970–71 ski season.

Distribution

When WWW began marketing ski gloves, après-ski boots and protective ski headgear in the 1969–70 season, the firm hired professional ski instructors to act as salesmen. Although this effort was not too successful, the salesmen did acquire valuable selling experience and dealer contacts that proved advantageous in the 1970–71 season.

This group of people was chosen to sell the line because of the type of dealers through whom the product would be retailed. The technical expertise of these salesmen and the similarity of interests between them and the dealers were projected as essentials for Wolverine success in acquiring outlets for its Ski Division merchandise.

These salesmen were paid an $18,000-per-year salary and expenses with a bonus for all sales over $400,000. The territorial assignments described in Exhibit 3 were used in the 1970–71 season. The territories had been established after taking into account the potential market for ski products in various parts of the country, but only nine salesmen had been hired because of the limited funds available to support the marketing effort.

1970–71 strategy

Before development of a concrete plan of action, Wolverine was faced with the problem of identifying the target market and then weighing

EXHIBIT 3
Salesmen territorial assignments

There is one man assigned to each of the following geographical regions:
1. New York State.
2. Eastern Massachusetts and Vermont.
3. Western Massachusetts, Maine, and New Hampshire.
4. Washington, Oregon, and northern California.
5. Indiana, Ohio, Michigan, Illinois, Wisconsin, and Minnesota.
6. Southern California.
7. Colorado, Texas, New Mexico, and southern Wyoming.
8. Utah, Idaho, Montana, Nevada, and northern Wyoming.
9. Connecticut, New Jersey, Delaware, Rhode Island, Maryland, and the Carolinas.

alternative distributional and promotional methods to reach these prospects.

The two major sources used by the firm for consumer profile assessment were "The Skier Market in Northeast North America," a study conducted under the auspices of the U.S. Department of Commerce during the 1962–63 season, and "The *Skiing* Subscriber: Phenomenal," a research survey done in 1968 by the Ziff-Davis Publishing Co. and Erdos and Morgan, Inc. Excerpts from the latter study may be found in Exhibits 4, 5, and 6. Additionally, Exhibit 7 gives a growth projection of the skiing population through the 1971–72 season.

The results showed that the typical skier was well educated, above average in income, an owner of luxury items, a consumer of alcoholic beverages, and a person who identified with the "beautiful people." He also sought excitement, adventure, and a little danger.

As far as a self-classification by ability was concerned, 47.2 percent of the *Skiing* subscribers saw themselves as expert or advanced, 38.2 percent considered themselves intermediate, 5.0 percent as racers, and 11.8 percent as beginner-novices.

It was noted that word of mouth was a primary interpersonal source of information within this group, particularly with regard to ski equipment and ski areas.

It was also noted that, if this group's equipment expenditures over the past 12 months could be projected to the entire skiing populace, in 1968 the level would have been about $54 million.

Having tentatively identified the total skiing public, Wolverine executives now had to decide which segment's needs were most closely met by the ski product lines available. Because of the quality image of both the Rossignol ski line and the Trappeur boot line, the target market was established as serious skiers in the intermediate and above skill levels. Some penetration into the recreational ski market was believed to be desirable, but for the 1970–71 season the other, more advanced group received the primary promotional consideration.

How to reach this target market was a multifold question. A primary consideration was what distribution policy would be most appropriate. In securing initial distribution of Wolverine ski products, salesmen had been instructed to limit their calls to professional ski shops, of which approximately 2,000 were available. A leading competitor, with a broader coverage of different price-quality levels, had distributed not only through professional ski shops, but also through sporting goods stores and the ski departments of department stores.

After careful consideration, Ski Division executives decided to limit distribution to the professional ski shops during the 1970–71 ski season. There were two reasons for this action: (1) these shops would tend to reach the target market most effectively; (2) the people who operate

EXHIBIT 4
"The *Skiing* Subscriber: Phenomenal"—Excerpts from the research conducted by Erdos and Morgan Research, Inc.

Skiing *subscribers* rate themselves	Percent	Travel method to ski area	Percent
Expert/advanced	47.2	Auto	91.0
Intermediate	38.2	Train	4.0
Racer	5.0	Plane	17.7
Beginner–novice	11.8	Bus	16.4

Note: figures add up to more than 100 percent because some expert/advanced are also racers.

Note: figures add up to more than 100 percent because some people use more than one mode of transportation.

39.4 percent skied more than 20 days last season
46.2 percent took a skiing vacation

During the skiing season 44.5 percent are asked for their opinion or advice once a week, or more, on matters relating to skiing.

The *Skiing* subscriber estimates that, on the average, he gave advice to 16.7 percent of the people during the 1969–70 season.

Most advice was given to friends or neighbors and topics of advice were heavily weighed toward equipment and ski areas.

Market dimensions

Projected U.S. purchasing patterns based upon *Skiing's* circulation of 400,000 (1969–70 season) are:

Items purchased (past 12 months)	Amount spent
Skis	$22,338,000
Boots	9,398,880
Bindings	4,553,600
Apparel	17,865,200
	$54,155,680

Other general facts:

Club membership	Percent
Skiing clubs	54.2
Country clubs	30.8
Auto clubs	18.5

Beverage use
93.3 percent drink or serve soft drinks
90.8 percent drink or serve alcoholic beverages

Radio audio equipment ownership
74.8 percent own an FM set
63.3 percent own a table model or console hi-fi

Boat ownership
31.6 percent own a pleasure boat

Flying interest
50.3 percent are interested in learning how to fly
16.9 percent have a pilot's license

Age
Median age 27.8 years

Education
73.3 percent are college educated

Annual income
Median income of *Skiing* subscriber household—$15,033
21.5 percent earn $25,000 or more
$25,000–$49,000 · · · 13.8 percent
$50,000 or over · · · 7.7 percent

Results of a questionnaire designed and mailed out by Ziff-Davis Publishing Company and tabulated by Erdos and Morgan, Inc.
Data are based upon a survey of 1,382 *Skiing* magazine subscribers and is a 55.4 percent response rate, based upon a mailing of 2,493 questionnaires.

EXHIBIT 5
The serious skier, one of the best educated and affluent customers in America (by percent)

	Serious skiers (Skiing *magazine* subscribers)*	All skiers (*respondents to* Farwell Survey)†
Education level‡		
Grade school only......................	.4	.5
High school only........................	13.7	15.7
College and post graduate...............	85.9	83.8
Total.............................	100.0	100.0
Occupation		
Professional, technical, & kindred........	26.4	28.7
Managers, officials, proprietors...........	22.2	6.6
Sales................................	3.6	4.3
Skilled, semi-skilled, unskilled...........	4.1	9.6
Government, military....................	6.0	.8
Clerical...............................	4.1	11.6
Students..............................	26.6	28.8
Housewives...........................	2.0	7.4
Other................................	1.0	.1
No answer............................	4.0	2.1
Total.............................	100.0	100.0
Household income		
Under $10,000........................	22.5	57.0
$10,000–$14,999......................	21.2	21.8
$15,000–and over.....................	43.9	18.1
No answer...........................	12.4	3.1
Total.............................	100.0	100.0
Median household income.................	$15,033	$8,550
Median age.............................	27.8 years	24.7 years

* *Skiing* Subscriber Survey, Erdos and Morgan, Inc., 1968.
† The Farwell Report, U.S. Dept. of Commerce, Area Redevelopment Administration, 1965 edition.
‡ Exact comparisons between surveys not available. Education level for *Skiing* is for subscribers age 25 and over; for Farwell Survey respondents, age 23 and over.

Skiers, as a whole, are an elite market, with extraordinary demographic characteristics that represent enormous buying power. In comparison, the marketing qualifications of serious skiers are almost unbelievably high.

The audience of serious skiers assembled by *Skiing* Magazine is the "cream of the cream"—nearly 9 out of 10 have a college education . . . almost half are in professional or managerial positions . . . and they have achieved a median household income of nearly $15,033 at a median age of only 27.8.

What a market!—the very best customers for skiing clothing, equipment, and ski resorts—fantastic customers for all quality products and services that fit into the skiing way of life.

these outlets could do the most effective job of fitting skiing equipment to the prospect, taking into account his ability and size. In executing this policy, Ski Division salesmen were able to acquire 1,070 dealers for the Wolverine line during the 1970–71 ski season (see Exhibit 8).

Three constraints had to be applied to the overall program. These restrictions were placed upon the Ski Division by the corporation and

EXHIBIT 6
The serious skier, his equipment/apparel purchasing habits (by percent)

Month of purchase	Skis	Boots	Ski parkas	Ski pants
January	15.4	8.3	13.5	12.0
February	10.3	8.3	3.8	4.0
March	7.7	11.1	5.9	8.0
April	—	2.8	1.9	2.0
May	—	—	—	—
June	—	—	—	—
July	2.6	2.8	1.9	—
August	5.0	2.8	1.9	—
September	—	5.6	3.8	4.0
October	20.5	13.9	9.6	12.0
November	20.5	13.9	26.9	24.0
December	15.4	27.8	28.8	30.0
No answer; don't know	2.6	2.7	2.0	4.0
Total	100.0	100.0	100.0	100.0

Note: The majority of purchases were made at the beginning of the season or during pre-Christmas periods. However,
—of all *skis* purchased during the year, *one third* were purchased during the three-month period, January thru March.
—Of all *boots* purchased during the year, 30.5 percent were purchased during the months January thru April.
—Of all *parkas* purchased during the year, 25.1 percent were purchased during the months January thru April.
—Of all *ski pants* purchased during the year, 26 percent were purchased during the months January thru April.
Between one fourth and one third of equipment and apparel purchases were made during the latter part of the ski season—*after* self-generating holiday business, peak-season, and late-season sales which manufacturers and retailers must get in order to have successful seasons.
Source: Skiing Equipment Purchasing Survey, Ziff-Davis Publishing Company, 1967.

EXHIBIT 7
The dynamic growth of skiing in North America

Season	Number of skiers
1962–1963	1,500,000
1963–1964	1,650,000
1964–1965	1,815,000
1965–1966	1,996,000
1966–1967	2,196,000
1967–1968	2,416,000
1968–1969	2,657,000
1969–1970	2,923,000
1970–1971	3,215,000
1971–1972	3,537,000

Source: Ziff-Davis Research Department projections based on the Farwell Report, U.S. Department of Commerce, Area Redevelopment Administration, 1965 edition.
The Farwell Report has given the skiing industry its first accurate picture of the skiing market. For these projections, a minimum growth rate of 10 percent is used, applying the figures from northeast North America, as described in the Farwell Report, to the entire market.

EXHIBIT 8
Dealer locations 1970–71 season

State	Number of dealers	State	Number of dealers
New York	151	New Mexico	14
California	118	Wyoming	12
Colorado	78	Texas	12
Massachusetts	78	Virginia	9
Michigan	69	Rhode Island	7
Vermont	62	Washington, D.C.	6
Minnesota	45	Maryland	5
Connecticut	40	Georgia	5
Washington	39	Indiana	4
New Jersey	39	North Carolina	4
New Hampshire	39	Iowa	3
Pennsylvania	34	Kansas	3
Utah	33	Arizona	3
Maine	26	Nevada	2
Illinois	25	Nebraska	2
Oregon	24	North Dakota	2
Wisconsin	23	Missouri	2
Ohio	18	Tennessee	2
Montana	16	Oklahoma	1
Idaho	14	Delaware	1
		Total	1,070

pertained to funds expenditures. First, the sales manager, Mr. Maguire, was told that he could not spend more than the contractual minimum on promotion of the Rossignol and Trappeur lines (i.e., 7 percent and 5 percent of factory sales, respectively). Second, he was allowed to establish only two ski repair centers each costing about $200,000; and finally, he was constrained to use the existing nine-man sales force.

A budget of approximately $312,000 was established for the promotional efforts to be undertaken and was allocated as shown in Exhibit 9.[1] In general, the areas of effort included dealer shows, consumer shows, "racer chasers," demonstrations, consumer advertising, cooperative advertising, and equipment loans, among others.

The dealer shows were held in March 1970 in New York, Chicago, and Los Angeles and involved booth costs ($3600.00) plus personnel, product-in-place, and transportation costs. Additionally, the costs of giveaways were incurred. Consumer shows were similar to the trade shows and were held later in the year. The "racer chaser" program consisted of three vehicles that travelled the major ski areas to promote Rossignol skis. The "chasers" were manned by French skiers who followed the skiing circuit from resort to resort with the objective of getting as many ski instructors and professional ski shop operators as possible to try

[1] Advertising and sales figures of the Ski Division have been multiplied by a constant throughout this case to avoid disclosure of actual data.

EXHIBIT 9
Promotional budget—actual 1970–71 season*

I.	*Media space costs*			
	A. Consumer			
	Ski Magazine............	$ 16,200		
	Skiing Magazine........	134,500		
	Ski racing, etc..........	5,000		
	Miscellaneous..........	4,000		
	Consumer total.......	$159,700		
	B. Trade			
	Ski Trade Magazine.....	$ 13,000		
	Trade total..........	$ 13,000	Media total........	$172,700
II.	*Production costs*			
	Art and Mechanical.....	$ 24,000		
III.	*Direct mail, brochures, catalogs*			
	Direct mail............	2,000		
	Printing...............	45,000		
IV.	*Point-of-purchase†*			
	POP...................	3,000		
V.	*Miscellaneous (pins, signs, etc.)*			
	Miscellaneous..........	12,000		
	Total...............	$ 86,000	II. to V. total.......	86,000
VI.	*Non-advertising items*			
	Consumer and trade			
	shows...............	$ 33,000		
	Racer chasers..........	5,000		
	Demonstrations........	5,000		
	Ski loans..............	10,000		
	Total...............	$ 53,000	VI. total...........	53,000
			Total advertising budget..........	$311,700

* Note: These figures have been multiplied by a constant.
† Cooperative dealer advertising is not shown, since only 6 claims were returned—$200 at most.
Source: Company records.

"Rossies" out on the slopes. Wolverine sees itself as having been the most successful exploiter of this technique.

A similar scheme, called "demo days," was used to reach as many skiers as possible. These "days" consisted of opportunities, at specific resort areas, for anyone to try Rossignol skis on the slopes.

Consumer advertising was confined almost entirely to two magazines, *Ski* and *Skiing,* for the 1970–71 season (see Exhibit 9). Because of editorial content and reach, *Skiing* magazine absorbed about three times as much in advertising funds as *Ski.* The total circulation, with about 25 percent overlap, for these two publications was about 900,000 people. McManus, John & Adams, the firm's advertising agency, estimated total readership of these publications at two and one-half to three million skiers.

EXHIBIT 10
Cooperative advertising plan

Wolverine World Wide will offer a co-op advertising program on Rossignol skis and Killy line only.

Wolverine World Wide will pay one half (½) of your advertising costs in newspapers and broadcasting media up to a total of 2 percent of your Wolverine World Wide ski products purchases.

We will furnish ad mats and recordings for news and radio broadcasting ads. However, you will not necessarily have to use these ads.

Wolverine World Wide will not pay any share of an ad showing a competitive product.

Co-op claims will be honored and paid by check upon proof of ad, and invoice covering ad, and after your Wolverine World Wide invoices have been paid to substantiate a proper accumulation of purchases.

Though cooperative advertising was offered to the dealers (see Exhibit 10), only six of the 1,070 retailers took advantage of the opportunity.

The final two promotional tools used were ski loans, to professionals and prominent members of the skiing public, and special discounts, the year round, to ski instructors. The latter of the two efforts was done so that as many students as possible would see their instructors wearing Rossignol skis.

The decision to establish only two repair centers—one in Clearfield, Utah, and the other at the home facility—was dictated by funds availability, as mentioned above. However, the firm felt it could meet the service needs of the eastern United States through its daily trucking schedule between Rockford, Michigan, and Newark, New Jersey.

Another strategy policy concerned dealer payment for products received from Wolverine. The firm decided to follow industry practices in this matter. That is, even though Wolverine had to pay within 30 days of its July, August, September receipt-of-merchandise from France, the firm allowed the dealers until January or February of the following year to settle accounts. Cash and quantity discounts were offered.

The resulting low-budget campaign for 1970–71 produced advertising copy that capitalized on the racing image of Rossignol skis and then tied this racing theme in with the Le Trappeur boot line.

The "Racing Machine" theme was the underlying thought to all ski advertising messages, and the types of skis were classed and promoted on the basis of the skier's perceived proficiency—"for the guy who hates to lose" (Strato 102), "if you're skier enough" (GTA and Strato AR), and "four speeds forward" (Stratix 112, Stratoflex, Concorde, and Strato Junior). The approach to the Trappeur promotion was essentially the same—"This one wins the race" (the PRO), "These have all the fun" (remaining models).

Promotional strategy for 1971–72

In March 1971, Thomas Maguire, sales manager, Ski Division, reviewed the preliminary results of the 1970–71 campaign as the initial step in making plans for the coming winter season.[2] He found that as of December 31, 1970, 48,000 pairs of Rossignol skis had been sold, at a dollar value of $3,401,165. Since the sales goal for the entire season was 55,000 pairs, it appeared that this objective would be reached. Sales reports also indicated that 30,000 pairs of ski boots had been sold as of December 31, at a value of $750,000. Since Wolverine executives had only expected to sell from 20,000 to 25,000 pairs, this was regarded as exceptionally strong performance. Finally, sales of other products in the line (gloves, mittens, après-ski boots, protective headgear) amounted to $330,000 as of December 31. Total sales as of December 31, therefore, amounted to $4,481,365.

As mentioned earlier, the Ski Division had secured 1,070 dealers for its line out of approximately 2,000 potential outlets. At the trade shows during the spring of 1971, company officials found that there was strong interest on the part of other dealers in taking on the Ski Division line.

With this background, Mr. Maguire and his associates then turned to the task of establishing objectives for the 1971–72 winter season. They had available to them results of a market survey made by Ernst & Ernst for the Ski Industries of America which reported industry sales by product types as of the year ended May 31, 1970 (see Exhibit 11). The results of this survey had not been reported until September 30, 1970, and thus were not available when sales goals were being set for the 1970–71 winter season. After taking into account anticipated growth in the market for various ski products, the following goals were established for the 1971–72 winter season:

Skis—20 percent of the over-$50 market—67,000 pairs.....	$4,857,000
Ski boots—45,000 pairs.................................	1,611,000
Ski poles—8,000 units...... ́............................	100,000
Other products (gloves, mittens, après-ski boots, protective headgear, among others)............................	400,000
Total..	$6,968,000

Several changes in the product line were planned for the 1971–72 winter season, and these had to be taken into account in making plans. (See Exhibit 12 for a brief description of the 12 models included in the 1971–72 line.) In the Rossignol ski line, new models described in Exhibit 13 were to be offered.

[2] Sales figures, advertising expenditures, and budget cost figures reported by the Ski Division have been multiplied by a constant throughout this case to avoid disclosure of actual data.

EXHIBIT 11

Product market survey—Ski Industries of America, 1970 (these totals and averages are based on the 109 participating member companies of 165 members solicited who submitted information for the year ended May 31, 1970)

Product	Number reporting	Total units	Total dollars wholesale	Percent of total	Wholesale unit price
Ski sweaters.	23	353,115	$ 5,729,558	3.8	$16.23
After-ski boots.	24	433,305	4,895,032	3.2	11.30
After-ski clothing.	12	37,593	1,176,853	0.8	31.31
Turtlenecks.	25	1,076,743	3,862,594	2.5	3.59
Windshirts.	14	346,498	1,231,755	0.8	3.55
Ski socks.	18	838,150	1,241,162	0.8	1.48
Ski underwear.	11	507,245	1,710,254	1.1	3.37
Ski goggles and ski glasses.	23	676,765	1,647,860	1.1	2.43
Leather ski gloves and mittens.	21	1,143,430	4,752,151	3.1	4.16
Accessories.	50	(Insufficiently reported)	8,512,592	5.6	—
Ski poles.	29	576,782	3,061,486	2.0	5.31
Bindings.	24	933,193	11,435,593	7.5	12.25
Ski boots.	34	812,349	28,662,608	18.9	35.28
Warmup pants.	18	211,938	2,512,548	1.7	11.86
Ski pants below $40 retail.	22	583,494	8,148,927	5.4	13.97
Ski pants, $40 retail and above.	18	206,743	5,505,889	3.6	26.63
Ski parkas below $40 retail.	24	866,509	11,245,752	7.4	12.98
Ski parkas, $40 retail and above.	35	463,311	13,049,133	8.6	28.16
Skis below $50 retail.	21	256,907	4,172,839	2.7	16.24
Skis, $50 retail and above.	27	401,094	29,406,959	19.4	73.32
1969–70 Total dollar volume, all categories.	109	—	$151,961,545	100.0	—

EXHIBIT 12
Brief description of Rossignol ski line, 1971–72*

Rossignol skis for 1971–72 come in your choice of twelve models. Whether for slalom or downhill racing—whether for intermediate or beginning skiers—each has been painstakingly engineered and built to deliver the ultimate in satisfaction.

The unique Rossignol design provides a relatively soft flex on the front part, so that the ski tracks well over bumps and uneven terrain—with damped vibration. Yet the flex is torsionally rigid enough so that a skier can accurately establish turning radius by the amount of edge set.

The tail of the ski is quite different in flex, to permit holding well on ice and hard-pack, but is relatively soft in torsion to allow it to conform to terrain changes.

For this skillful combining of different ski qualities—and for many other reasons—Rossignol skis are "something very special." To be sure you get the right model for your kind of skiing, rely on your experienced, authorized Rossignol dealer.

Rossignol racers

Strato 102. Proved by its record to be world's finest racing ski. Grips on ice, easy in powder. By using varying proportions and weaves of fiberglass, Rossignol designers have achieved ideal combination of torque resistance, flex, camber, and side-cut. One-piece bonded metal edge. Molded in a single operation—no rivets or screws. Tip and tail protected by bonded-in aluminum. Guaranteed one year.

ROC 550. This new, injection-molded, plasticometal ski presents the performance of fiberglass with the durability of metal. Side-cut, torque resistance, general flex and side camber engineered carefully as a combination to give ROC 550 superb carving and turning qualities. Molded in one piece—no rivets or screws to let in moisture. One-piece, bonded metal edge. Handles beautifully in powder and on ice. Guaranteed for one year.

Strato 102, Jr. Here again is the world's best racing ski—but sized and formulated especially for the younger, lighter competitor. Manufactured exactly like the champion Rossignol Strato 102. Molded in a single piece, without screws or rivets. One-piece, bonded metal edge. Bonded-in aluminum to protect tip and tail. Equally at home on ice or powder. Just the right combination of torque resistance and flex for *avalement*. Guaranteed for a full year.

Advanced performers—for intermediate skiers

GTA. World's finest all-fiberglass ski. Low swing weight, great for jetting. Provides solid support on ice or hardpack and plenty of mobility in powder. Excellent torque resistance and flex, GS side-cut. Guaranteed one year.

ROC 520. A new, all-around metalloplastic Rossignol model especially created for the intermediate or advanced skier who wants a champion-quality recreational ski. Injection-molded core for longer life and to prevent moisture seepage. Unconditionally guaranteed for one year.

Strato AR. Rossignol racing machine in a modified version for all-around use. Like the Strato 102, but with slightly different side-cut and softer torque and flex. Top metal edges for extra scrape protection. Built to take it! Guaranteed for one year.

AR, Jr. Enables young experts to enjoy same kind of outstanding ski performance as adults do with Strato AR. Combi side-cut. Softer torque and flex than pure racer. Specifically designed, sized, and formulated to needs of skilled juniors. Guaranteed for one year.

All-purpose models (advanced, intermediate, beginning skiers)

Stratix 112. Called by impartial experts "the best dollar-value fiberglass ski in America." Ideal for those advanced and intermediate skiers seeking an incomparable recreation ski at an in-between price. Built much like the famous Rossignol Strato models, so you know it's top quality all the way. Metal upper edges. Guaranteed for one year.

EXHIBIT 12 (continued)

Stratoflex. An outstanding all-purpose ski—excellent on ice, easy on powder snow. Durable, too, due largely to its special sandwich construction with top metal edges. Though intermediate in price, the Strato-Flex is a champion in delivering satisfaction and dependability in performance. Guaranteed for one full year.

M120. A brand-new recreational model with a metal sandwich design. Performs well under all conditions, but is super excellent in deep snow, because its very soft, very thin tip emerges easily from powder. Torsional rigidity permits outstanding carved turns. Easily handled, even by not-so-advanced skiers. Guaranteed one full year.

Concorde. Wishing for top ski quality at about $100? This is your baby. Low cost, but in the full tradition of Rossignol excellence. Great all-around ski. Perfect for beginners, intermediates, and good, occasional skiers. Has the versatility to perform in great style whether on bumpy hills or in powder. Guaranteed one full year.

Stratix, Jr. Well suited to the needs of young beginners and intermediates. Stylish. Easy to handle. Versatile. Built to take a lot of punishment. Though a junior model, this epoxy-fiberglass reinforced plastic ski is top quality in every detail. Guaranteed one full year.

---

* Source: Excerpts from consumer leaflet, "Rossignol—The Racing Machine," 1971.

The modifications in the Rossignol line for 1971–72 provided the Ski Division with skis adapted to the needs of beginners, intermediates, and advanced skiers. In the previous season, Wolverine had aimed its promotional effort primarily at serious skiers in the intermediate and advanced skill levels. Purchases of skis from Rossignol, accordingly, were especially heavy in the racing models such as the Strato 102, described as "the world's finest racing ski." Advertising and promotional effort had emphasized the racing image. In planning for the 1971–72 winter season, however, Ski Division executives were especially concerned with the question of how to get greater penetration into the recreational ski market. They anticipated the greatest potential for increased sales in this area. This line of thinking led Wolverine executives to increase the proportion of ski models purchased to meet the needs of the recreational segment of the market by offering models for beginners and intermediate skiers. Models were purchased to meet the requirements of skiers interested in competitive racing, of course, since Ski Division executives did not want to neglect this important segment of the market. The 1971–72 line, accordingly, was a balanced offering of 12 models designed to meet these various needs.

While the 1970–71 creative theme, "Rossignol—The Racing Machine," had served its purpose well, it was recognized that the plan to seek greater penetration into the recreational market would require the development of a new basic theme for the 1971–72 campaign. This matter had been discussed with the account executive, MacManus, John & Adams, and the agency creative staff was working on proposed new advertising theme lines.

EXHIBIT 13
New models added to Rossignol ski line for 1971–72

Racers (for advanced skiers):

ROC 550—New, injection-molded, plasticometal ski presents the performance of fiberglass with the durability of metal. Has
superb carving and turning qualities. Handles beautifully in
powder and on ice. Retail price $195.00.

(In addition, Strato 102 and Strato 102, Jr. were continued from the
previous year's line.)

For intermediate skiers:

ROC 520—New, all-around metalloplastic Rossignol model especially
created for the intermediate or advanced skier who wants a
champion-quality recreational ski. Injection-molded core for
longer life and to prevent moisture seepage. Retail price
$160.00.

AR, Jr.—A new ski that enables young experts to enjoy the same kind
of outstanding ski performance as adults do with Strato AR.
Combi side-cut. Softer torque and flex than pure racer.
Specially designed, sized, and formulated to needs of skilled
juniors.

(Continued from the previous year's line were the GTA and Strato AR.*)

All-purpose models for all kinds of skiing:

M120—A brand-new, recreational model with a metal sandwich design. Performs well under all conditions, but is super excellent in deep snow, because its very soft, very thin tip emerges
easily from powder. Torsional rigidity permits outstanding
carved turns. Easily handled, even by not-so-advanced skiers.
Retail price $120.00.

(Continued from the previous year were *Stratix 112,* Stratoflex, Concorde,* Stratix, Jr.**)

---

* Cosmetic changes had been made in the models starred (i.e., they had been given a new paint job).

With respect to ski boots, Wolverine executives had come to the
conclusion that the new custom foam-fitted boots were being accepted
so widely that at least 50 percent of sales for 1971–72 would be in
this category. Accordingly, Wolverine contracted with Le Trappeur for
a 50–50 split between the new custom-fitted models and the traditional
designs popular in the past. Specifically, the ski boots to be offered
during 1971–72 are listed in Exhibit 14 and are described in Exhibit 15.

As mentioned earlier, the 1970–71 advertising of Trappeur ski boots
tied in closely with "The Racing Machine" theme line. The rapidly growing popularity of foam custom-fitted ski boots and the changes in the
Trappeur line to cater to this trend, however, suggested the wisdom
of seeking a new, creative approach for the 1971–72 ski boot advertising.

EXHIBIT 14
Trappeur ski boot line, 1971–72

	Retail price
Foam custom-fitted models:	
Pro (for professional racers)....................	$145.00
Cosmos I (for advanced skiers).................	120.00
P150 (advanced and recreational skiers).........	90.00
GP foam (intermediate to good skiers)...........	65.00
Jr. Racer foam (young racer)...................	80.00
Traditional models:	
Cosmos I (for advanced skiers).................	$ 90.00
P150 (advanced and recreational skiers).........	80.00
Quick V (intermediate to good skiers)...........	55.00
Slalom II (intermediate skiers).................	80.00
Classic V (beginning skiers)...................	40.00
Trappeur, Jr. (beginners)......................	$35–40.00

Note: See Exhibit 15 for a description of the features of the various ski boots listed above.

The desire of Wolverine management to penetrate the recreational-skier market provided another reason for taking a fresh approach in planning this advertising. Accordingly, the creative staff of the advertising agency was actively working on this task in March 1971.

Executives of the Ski Division had also decided to carry a quality line of French-manufactured ski poles in 1971–72, the Kerma line. Seven different models were available to meet the needs of both recreational and advanced skiers, as well as special models for women and children. Each type of ski pole was available in several different sizes to match the height of the skier. Suggested retail prices ranged from $12.00 to $30.00.

The 1971–72 line of Wolverine ski gloves included 11 styles for men, ranging in retail price from $7.50 to $16.00; 9 styles of gloves and mittens for women, priced from $7.00 to $15.00; and 3 styles for children, ranging from $2.75 to $6.00. The line of après-ski boots for both men and women included 18 different styles and colors, ranging in retail price from $17.00 to $30.00. Additionally, a limited line of French ski clothing was to be tried out on an experimental basis in 1971–72.

Then too, the idea of selling a quality line of rental skis had been approved. Wolverine was planning to offer ski slope operators the Rossignol M–120 ski, a recreational model with a metal sandwich design, in a dark green color, with the name "Rossignol" in gold lettering and the word "rental" discreetly displayed. The shop, or area, name was also to be added in gold lettering on the tail of the ski. Rental skis were to be offered to dealers at a price of $72.00, less 30 percent, with a minimum order of 150 pairs. The ideas here were to introduce new

EXHIBIT 15
Brief description of Trappeur ski boot line, 1971–72

It's no coincidence that Trappeur, the boot of the French ski team has won more medals in international competition than all other ski boots combined. Behind this accomplishment is a history of old-world craftsmanship and painstaking care stretching way back to 1936. It assures every owner of Trappeur boots—be he novice or champion—that he will get full value for his money in quality, in features, and in performance.

Boots that successfully combine comfort, support, and control contribute a great deal to greater skiing enjoyment and skill. And those are precisely the qualities that are very carefully engineered and built into every Trappeur boot.

You can be sure that all Trappeur boots incorporate the latest thinking and advancements from the very finest ski-boot craftsmen. Which is to say that these boots are better values than ever.

How can you determine exactly which Trappeur boot is the one for you? We suggest you consult your authorized Trappeur dealer.

Why Trappeur Custom Foam-Fitting Is So Important
to Skiing Comfort and Performance

First, inside of boot can be molded to the exact shape of its owner's foot. So, even people with hammer toes, bone spurs, or other irregularities can find complete foot comfort. The aggravation of "breaking in" new boots disappears, too. And the surrounding foam insulation helps keep feet warm. From the performance standpoint, Trappeur foam-fitted boots anchor the heel snugly, making it much easier for foot, boot, and ski to perform as a single unit. Custom-fitting can also compensate for the fact that most people (three out of four) don't have straight legs, and so have trouble properly edging both skis in unison. Sure, foam-fitting costs slightly more. But it's well worth it in benefits. And it only takes a few minutes!

PRO–custom-fitted choice of champions

This new, custom foam-fitted model is the finest Trappeur ever built for professional racers, ski instructors, and hotshots. New injection-molded polyurethane shell is, we believe, the toughest boot shell on the market. Special hinged upper combines strong lateral support with controlled forward flex. Built-in 27° forward lean plus high racing back provides strong support for acceleration through gates and the firm backward support and forward responsiveness for *avalement*, jet turns, "wheelies," and other far-out maneuvers. Special innersole construction raises heel, puts ball of foot closer to ski for more sensitive "feel." New buckles feature easy, precise micro-adjustment.

Cosmos I, Cosmos I Foam—for advanced skiers

For 1971–72, Trappeur presents its new Cosmos I in a choice of custom foam-fitted or traditional models. Both feature the "sculptured" look in a high back with a new, molded polyurethane shell that stands up to hard wear better than any other plastic boot on the market. Carefree, too. To clean, just wipe it off—that's all! For extra lateral support, the Cosmos I has a special upper section hinged to give the skier completely controlled forward flex. Innersole is raised at heel, and puts ball of foot closer to ski for perfect "feel." Buckles feature precise micrometric adjustment.

P150, P150 Foam—top values at intermediate cost

The P150 Foam and the P150 traditional are new boots designed at Trappeur— the "choice of champions"—to bring advanced and recreational skiers competition quality at moderate prices. One-piece, injection-molded, elastomer outer shell is stiff enough to prevent lateral deflection, yet flexible enough to allow just the right amount of forward movement . . . and rugged enough to take long, hard use. These boots have been designed with the correct degree of forward lean for intermediate and ad-

EXHIBIT 15 (continued)

vanced skiers. New, micro-adjust buckles. Narrow, torsion-proof racing sole. New low-friction, jersey-neoprene inner lining prevents foot irritation.

Quick V GP Foam—budget beauties born of champions

Intermediate-to-good skiers, who are looking for Trappeur quality at modest prices, will like these two stylish boots. The GP Foam is a custom-fitted model with a surprisingly low price tag. The Quick V offers the same kind of quality in a traditional boot for slightly less. Many features you wouldn't expect in this cost range. Trappeur's extra-durable, plastic-bonded-to-nylon shell with built-in forward lean. Narrow, torsion-proof racing sole for positive edge control. New, adjustable, cam action, swivel, buckles, plus fast- and easy-adjusting, plastic-bonded upper straps. Contoured, extra-padded, reinforced tongue. Soft, durable inner boot with low-friction, jersey-neoprene lining. Superb Trappeur craftsmanship in every detail.

Slalom II, Classic V—best all-purpose boots going

Classic V is ideal for beginning skiers, since it combines many features of the more expensive Trappeur boots with the extra comfort and low price most beginning skiers want. Smart, metallic finish Slalom II is ideal—both in price and performance—for intermediate skiers. Both boots offer typical Trappeur advantages, including rugged, plastic-bonded-to-nylon shell; "just right," built-in, forward lean (more in Slalom II than Classic V); narrow, torsion-proof racing sole; special innersole construction, that puts ball of foot closer to ski, for better "feel"; wide, Martin buckles on Slalom II, Toba swivel buckles on Classic V; and soft, comfortable inner boot linings (leather in Classic V and full shearling lining in Slalom II).

Trappeur, Jr., Jr. Racer Foam—for young experts and beginners

Good ski boots for youngsters are not so easy to come by. But here are two such— Jr. Racer Foam with high back and forward lean for the young racer; Trappeur, Jr., an all-purpose model. Besides being designed for the specific needs of the very young, these boots are built with the same care and quality that have made Trappeur adult boots the "choice of champions." Both have the Trappeur-quality, plastic-bonded-to-nylon shell that is lightweight, but highly durable, with strong, lateral support. Narrow, torsion-proof racing sole. Wide, quick-adjust buckles on Jr. Racer; easy-adjusting Toba swivel buckles on Trappeur, Jr.

Source: Excerpts from consumer leaflet, "Trappeur—The Boot of the French Ski Team," 1971.

skiers to the feel of a quality ski, to cut down on rental losses, and to offer a durable product to the rental agency.

In addition, Rossignol had provided Wolverine with a metal ski to be sold under distributors' private brands in the United States during 1971–72. Leading retailers, such as Macy's and Gimbels' in the East, were to be contacted to determine their interest in such a product. Since the skis made available were quality items, they would not be sold for less than $50.00. It was thought that a ski of this quality would probably be of interest to potential private branders.

Since the line of products offered by the Ski Division included skis, ski boots, ski poles, après-ski boots, ski gloves and mittens, protective headgear, as well as ski clothing, the question was raised as to whether a blanket promotional theme could be developed which would serve to tie the entire line together in the minds of prospective buyers. In discussions between Mr. Maguire and the advertising agency, the possibility of developing a theme related to "The French Mystique" was considered because of the expertise which the French skiers had demonstrated in world competition. A competitor which imported a French ski into the U.S. market had relied heavily on the French origin of the product in his 1970 promotional effort. In fact, this firm invited the French ambassador to take part in some commercials featuring this line. People who observed these commercials, however, asked the question, "What does that have to do with skis?" This led Mr. Maguire to ask, "Where do you draw the line between the idea of 'The French Mystique' and the idea of skiing itself? What is the proper balance between these two ideas? Indeed, should the agency continue to pursue the idea, developing a theme based upon 'The French Mystique' to tie the line together, or should this concept be discarded in favor of some other common characteristic of the line?"

In planning the promotional mix for 1971–72, one of the questions under consideration was whether to increase the size of the Wolverine sales force. During the previous year the firm had used nine salesmen to call upon dealers; the cost of this organization amounted to $320,000. Although Wolverine had secured 1,070 dealers for the ski products line, Mr. Maquire felt that additional high-quality dealers would be necessary if the firm were to achieve the desired penetration of the recreational market. The questions which Mr. Maguire was pondering, accordingly, included the following:

1. Should Wolverine seek distribution through sporting goods stores and the ski departments of department stores?
2. Should the firm modify its past, highly selective distribution policy and sell through more than one dealer within a given geographic area—assuming that study of the potential market indicated that the area could support more than one dealer?
3. Since a portion of the remaining potential dealers who might be interested in the line were discounters, how could Wolverine handle the expansion of its dealer organization without creating undesirable price competition triggered by discount operators?
4. In short, how many additional dealers should Wolverine aim to secure during 1971–72, and what types of retail outlets should the Ski Division seek?

An answer to this final question would, of course, provide Mr. Maguire with a basis for deciding upon how many additional salesmen to hire for 1971–72. This, in turn, would make it possible for him to work out the size of the budget for the direct sales force expense for the coming year.

A second important question relating to the character of the promotional mix for 1971–72 was how much to appropriate for consumer advertising. If Wolverine limited its expenditures to the contractual minimum of 7 percent on sales of skis and 5 percent on sales of ski boots, this would provide approximately $425,000 on projected sales of $6,968,000. The agency account executive had suggested, however, that an increase to $600,000 would provide for a more effective advertising campaign. Wolverine executives faced the question, accordingly, of how the advertising budget should be determined and whether an amount in excess of the contractual minimum would enable Wolverine to achieve its stated promotional goals.

Still another type of promotional effort used in 1970–71 was the consumer show. Such shows enable consumers to compare different brands of skiing equipment. They tend to stimulate word-of-mouth comment by skiing friends of the prospective buyer. Wolverine had spent $8,000 to provide exhibits at leading consumer shows in 1970–71. Should this effort be maintained, increased, or decreased in 1971–72?

"Demonstration Days" had also been used as a promotional tool in 1970–71. Here Wolverine would send out a representative to a popular ski slope with about 20 pairs of Rossignol skis. An announcement would be made that on a specified date a Rossignol representative would be at the resort and that anybody who wanted to ski on a set of "Rossies" could do so just to get the feel of the equipment. During the past season $5,000 had been spent on "Demo Days," and the account executive characterized it as "very lucrative promotional effort." Should "Demo Days" be stepped up in 1971–72? How much should be budgeted for this effort?

A third decision area related to the amount of emphasis which should be given to stimulate the sales and promotional efforts of Ski Division dealers during 1971–72 and to support sales force efforts to sign up additional quality dealerships. It was argued that the dealer played a highly significant role in influencing the purchase of the products of the Ski Division. Yet it was recognized that the proprietors of ski shops were most generally skiers whose "hearts were out on the slopes." Accordingly, business-building opportunities were often neglected. How to get them to carry an adequate inventory of Ski Division products, as well as to promote and sell the line actively, was thus a real challenge. During 1970–71, for example, only six of the Wolverine dealers had taken advantage of the cooperative advertising allowances which Wolverine offered to encourage them to promote the firm's line aggressively. Wolverine's share of this expenditure amounted to not more than $200.00.

In making plans for dealer stimulation in 1971–72, therefore, one approach was to consider whether the promotional activities of the previous winter season should be continued. Specifically, should expenditures for the following items be continued, increased, or eliminated:

Advertising in ski trade papers		$ 13,000
Exhibits at six major trade shows		25,000
Point-of-purchase displays	$ 3,000	
Direct mail to dealers	2,000	
Catalogs, brochures	45,000	
Miscellaneous (signs, pins, etc.)	12,000	62,000
Total		$100,000

In addition, should expenditures be approved for the following new dealer stimulation activities suggested by the advertising agency, salesmen, dealers, reports of competitive action, or other sources:

1. A special brochure for dealers in color emphasizing the strong points of the Rossignol skis, Trappeur ski boots, and other products, as well as the service rendered by Wolverine as the distributor of these products was proposed. Emphasis to be placed on size of dealer's markup and the retail salability of the product lines which results in lower end-of-season inventories. The purpose of the brochure would be to get more dealers to visit the Wolverine booth at the trade shows; also to assist in interesting quality retailers in taking on the Wolverine Ski Division line. Estimated cost for 2,000 units, color, 8 pages $10,000.

2. A pilot program of three "shop seminars," a distant cousin of the trade shows attended in 1970–71, was proposed. Dealers would be invited to central locations, such as New York, Rockford, and Utah (ski resorts could be substituted). Here Wolverine would present a two- or three-day series of seminars, lectures, and presentations designed to explain the benefits of Wolverine equipment and service, as well as to provide dealers with tested suggestions on promotion, selling, and other key business problems commonly encountered by the manager of the typical professional ski shop. Seminars might be held at a convenient time after the new line was available and during the ordering period. Estimated cost of three experimental shop seminars $10,000. A full-scale program offered on a broader scale would probably run from $25,000 to $30,000 per year.

3. Another idea was to encourage dealers to plan and promote local ski shop shows where consumers are invited to come and examine skiing equipment. After examining how successful ski shop shows had been planned and promoted, develop suggestions and materials to help retailers do a good job of planning and promoting the show. Suggest advertisements to be placed locally, offer to share the cost of advertising on a 50–50 basis under the cooperative plan. Arrange to schedule a Wolverine salesman to be present to assist in explaining

and demonstrating the line. Since dealers should be able to see immediate sales benefits from such a show, the provision of planning and financial help in running the promotion would tend to stimulate dealers to give more active support of the line. Asking visitors to the shop to sign name and address in a guest register to qualify for a door-prize drawing would provide a good mailing list for retail, direct-mail promotion later. Estimated cost $10,000.

An important buying influence is the ski instructor. During 1970–71 Wolverine loaned skis and other equipment to instructors at a cost of $10,000. In addition, the firm had three "racer-chasers" visiting ski resorts for the purpose of getting as many ski instructors and professional ski shop operators as possible to try out Rossignol skis on the slopes. This effort cost $5,000. Instructors were also given special discounts to encourage them to use Rossignol skis. Mr. Maguire had to decide whether these programs should be maintained, increased, or reduced for 1971–72.

In short, after the objectives for the 1971–72 winter season had been established, the task of planning promotional strategy for the products of Ski Division involved making decisions on the following key questions:

1. What creative themes should be used in the consumer advertising of Rossignol skis, Trappeur boots, and Kerma ski poles—each of which was to receive separate emphasis in the campaign?
2. What blanket promotional theme or slogan should be used in the promotion of the entire line of the Ski Division, if such an approach appears to be feasible?
3. How many retail dealers should Wolverine strive to add during 1971–72, and what types of retail outlets should the firm seek?
4. How many additional salesmen should be hired, and thus, how much should be provided for total, direct, sales-force expense for the coming year?
5. How should the advertising budget be determined for 1971–72? Should the firm increase its consumer advertising appropriation to $425,000, to $600,000, or to some other figure?
6. How much should be provided for exhibits at consumer shows of skiing equipment; for demonstration days on the ski slopes?
7. What amount should be appropriated to stimulate the sales and promotional activities of Ski Division dealers and to support sales force efforts to sign up additional quality dealerships?
8. What funds should be provided to direct promotional effort at ski instructors?
9. In short, how much should be appropriated, in total, to provide for an effective sales and promotional program in 1971–72, and how

should this amount be divided among efforts directed at prospective buyers, dealers, ski instructors, and other key buying influences?

CASE QUESTION

What recommendations would you make on the various questions raised above concerning 1971–72 promotional strategy? Be prepared to support your proposals.

CASE 7–6

Wolverine World Wide, Inc.: Ski Division (B)*

Advertising strategy for skiing equipment

The Ski Division of Wolverine World Wide, Inc., of Rockford, Michigan, distributed a high-quality line of skis, ski boots, après-ski boots, gloves, and protective headgear throughout the United States. An introductory program was developed to get distribution for the new line and to stimulate a consumer demand for it during the winter sports season of 1970–71. National distribution for the line was achieved, and, as of December 31, 1970, total sales of the division were approximately $4.5 million.[1] In March 1971, Wolverine Ski Division executives and their advertising agency, MacManus, John & Adams, Inc., were planning the promotional strategy for the 1971–72 winter season.[2] In this connection, George Sorenson, account executive, was working with his associates at the advertising agency to develop recommendations for the 1971–72 advertising campaign.

---

* This case was prepared by Jay D. Lindquist, Research Assistant, under the direction of Professor James D. Scott, Graduate School of Business Administration, The University of Michigan, Ann Arbor.

[1] Sales figures, advertising expenditures, and promotional budget costs have been multiplied by a constant to prevent disclosure of actual data. In addition, the account executive has been given a fictitious name.

[2] See "Wolverine World Wide, Inc.: Ski Division (A)" for background on marketing and promotional strategy.

MacManus, John and Adams, Inc. took over the Ski Division account for Wolverine World Wide in late spring of 1970. Wolverine had previously engaged another advertising agency, but the latter firm had proposed an increase in fee based upon the projected risk of the new account. The increase in charges was more than Ski Division executives wished to pay, so they turned to MacManus, John & Adams, Inc.—the agency that was handling their Hush Puppies® advertising.

George Sorenson was assigned as the account executive, not only because of his advertising experience, but also because of his background as a professional ski instructor, the agency feeling that his experience in the skiing area would be an invaluable aid in developing an advertising campaign for promoting the sales of skiing equipment.

1970–71 SEASON

Mr. Sorenson faced two basic constraints as he accepted the account responsibility. These were, first, a three-week deadline to have advertising prepared for publication; and second, an initial funding level of $75,000 to be spent through December 31, 1970.

The steps to be undertaken, as he perceived them, were to identify the target markets for the various product lines, to create images for the ski division line as a whole and then for distinct product groups, to develop appropriate themes for the advertising, to recommend priorities between trade and consumer efforts, to allocate funds between production and space costs, to create advertisements, to select media vehicles, and to determine the advertising spending cycle.

The target

The agency was faced with a lack of demographic information on people who had purchased Rossignol skis and Trappeur boots in the past. Data were available on the ski purchasers because each one sent in a warranty card. However, the information had not been compiled into a usable form. Other methods had to be considered to get this information.

Using the findings from two basic studies, "The Skier Market in Northeast North America" (1962–63) and "The *Skiing* Subscriber: Phenomenal" (1968), Mr. Sorenson developed a series of profiles on potential Ski Division prospects. This information was shared with the client and a joint agreement on buying targets was reached. (See Exhibits 4, 5, 6, and 7 in "Wolverine World Wide, Inc.: Ski Division (A)" for information on buyer characteristics.)

Since the Rossignol line of skis was in the over $50 price class and since the products were top quality with a racing image, the decision was reached to aim promotional effort at the serious skier in the United States. Another fact that reinforced this plan was that the skew of ski models to be sold in the 1970–71 season was toward the Strato 102 which was the ski that had won more racing championships than all other competitive skis combined.

The serious skiers classified themselves by skill level as follows:

Percent of serious skiers	Skill level
47.2	Expert/advanced
38.0	Intermediate
5.0	Racers
11.8	Beginner–novice

The Rossignol line could also be divided in approximately the same manner. The Strato 102 would fill the needs of the racer or the expert/advanced skier. The Strato AR and GTA lines closely aligned themselves with the intermediate skier, the Strato Junior for the better-than-average youth skier, and the group of three skis that would suit the beginner–novice included the Stratix 112, the Stratoflex, and the Concorde.

With regard to the Le Trappeur boot line, a more gross categorization was made. In this case the Pro boot was seen as meeting the needs of the racer, the expert/advanced, and probably the intermediate skier, while the remainder of the line would suit all other skiers.

The image problem

Thomas Maguire, sales manager, Ski Division, suggested to Mr. Sorenson in light of the proven racing performance of the Strato 102 that this be the foundation for the campaign planning. In fact, he suggested that the Strato 102 be called "The Racing Machine."

After considerable concerted effort to compare this idea with other potential image descriptors, the agency recommended to the client that "The Racing Machine" image be attached specifically to the Strato 102. Also recommended was that the idea of various levels of "detuning" be attached to the remainder of the Rossignol line[3]—i.e. that other models in the line were specifically designed to fit the skiing ability of less advanced and intermediate skiers.

Since Jean Claude Killy had won the Olympics on Rossignol skis and Le Trappeur boots, the racing image was also attached to the Pro model in the ski boot line.

The rationale for the racing image was further fortified in the minds of the Wolverine World Wide and MacManus, John & Adams executives because of the success of Chrysler Motor Co. with attaching a racing image to the Dodge automobile. Also, the general appeal of all types

---

[3] Here an analogy is being made to automobile racing cars. If it is desired to operate a "hot" racing car at less than top speed it is "detuned" so that it is better adapted to running effectively at lower levels of speed.

of racing and all that the word connotes was felt to have specific impact on potential ski products purchasers.

The themes

The themes to both capitalize on the racing image and to associate specific products with the needs of specific target-buying segments were then developed. The theme for the Strato 102 was, "For the guy who hates to lose." "If you're skier enough" was attached to the GTA and Strato AR. The grouping of the Stratix 112, the Stratoflex, the Concorde, and the Strato Junior was blanketed with the theme, "Four speeds forward."

When considering the Le Trappeur boot line, only the Pro was seen as the racing ski boot and the rather straightforward theme applied to this product was, "This one wins the races." Because of the breadth of the remaining boot lines, Mr. Sorenson recommended that "These have all the fun" be used for them.

These themes were accepted by the client and incorporated in magazine advertising during the winter season of 1970–71.

Trade versus the consumer emphasis

Because of the haste with which the campaign had to be developed and because of the dollar constraint, Mr. Sorenson was unable to carry out an extensive trade versus consumer advertising priority study. While he was aware of the unique position of the professional ski shop operator in the channels of distribution, the dealer trade shows were over when the account was accepted and the consumer awareness level had to be raised. Therefore, for the 1970–71 winter season it was decided to give consumer advertising paramount emphasis in the promotional program. Spending reflects this decision in that only about 10 percent of media expenditures went to trade advertising.

Media space costs versus production costs

Mr. Sorenson knew that to produce a four-color advertisement would cost anywhere from $2,500 to $6,000. This involved the costs of photography, retouching, color separations, and platemaking. As far as the latter expense is concerned, it is a function of the type of book (magazine) selected. Some books use the offset method while others use the letterpress method when printing the ads. The letterpress method is the more expensive since one must produce four separate plates that, in combination, look like the original photograph.

Then the question of "bleed" or "non-bleed" ads had to be addressed. There is usually a 5 to 10 percent premium paid for the "bleed" advertisement that goes beyond the gutter, that is, to the edge of the page.

Also the question of color versus black and white was considered. The cost of the latter is about one fourth the cost of the former. Though theory states that in many cases the impact of color is greater than black and white, Mr. Sorenson was not convinced that the impact gain would be four times that achieved with black and white advertisements.

In this case, however, the agency recommended placing the majority of the advertisements in four-color, bleed, both for the favorable effect this would have on the consumer image of the line and for the impression this might make on dealers. The ratio of funds for production costs versus space charges for the entire season was about one to five. (See Exhibit 9 in "Wolverine World Wide, Inc.: Ski Division (A).")

Advertisement creation

A series of themes had been developed, as previously stated, and now the creation of the ads themselves had to be accomplished. The advertising agency realized that if it were not for the cosmetics (i.e. appearance) of the various ski manufacturers' products, the skiing public, with few exceptions, would not be able to tell one ski or boot from another. Therefore, it was assessed that the appearance of a ski had a lot to do with getting the product off of the merchant's shelves. Hence it was agreed that one must tie-in a product's cosmetics with its image to gain consumer awareness and acceptance.

The typical ski advertisement used by Rossignol's competitors showed a skier coming down the slopes on powdery snow and included a cross section of the product somewhere on the ad with appropriate copy. In contrast, MacManus, John & Adams recommended a new creative scheme based upon the racing image theme and taking into account the dollar constraints which eliminated an expensive photography trip outside the United States for powder snow ski shots.

The "Racing Machine" idea combined with the red Rossignol script letter, *R*, and the themes previously mentioned, produced the ski advertisements shown in Exhibits 1–3. Because of the three-to-one split in advertising dollars between Rossignol skis and Le Trappeur ski boots, the boot lines were shown in one standard format, as seen in Exhibits 4–5. The "For the guy who hates to lose" was run about as frequently as the two other Rossignol ads combined, since that was the approximate ratio of the Strato 102 inventory to that of the other skis in the line.

Media vehicle selection

In working out media recommendations, the agency analyzed many consumer magazines as well as other media forms such as television, radio, and trade publications. Because of budget constraints and high levels of potential waste, both radio and television were early omitted from further consideration. Additionally, certain well-known publications

EXHIBIT 1

The Strato 102.
For the guy who hates
to lose.

Let's face it. You enter competition to win.
After all, that's what makes it a race.
But victory isn't easy. It takes things like
agility, determination and confidence.
Confidence both in your ability and
your equipment.

With the Strato 102 you can be
confident. It's the world's finest racing ski.
And the record shows it. Last season
Strato 102 took medals in every event at
Val Gardena (10 in all). Stole the show at
the World Cup. Won more races in
international competition than all other skis
combined. But that's not all. It's used by
more competitive skiers than any other.
It's endorsed by the French National
Team. And by medal winners from
Switzerland, America, Canada and Poland.

Why such a heavy following? Because
this one's got a racing personality all its
own. A one-piece, bonded, metal edge
gives it better flex. So it's great in
powder. Varied-weave fiberglass provides
ideal torque resistance. So it grabs on
ice. And over sixty years of racing
technology does the rest.

Strato 102. The racing machine.
For the guy who hates to-lose.

ROSSIGNOL™
the Racing Machine

Distributed in Canada by Raymond Lanctot. Ltd., Montreal

EXHIBIT 2

The GTA and Strato AR.
If you're skier enough.

Maybe you're not ready for these racing machines. But then, maybe you are. You don't have to be an olympic champ. But, these Rossignols are for experts. For the recreational skier who really appreciates the way a ski performs. Wants a racing capability. Knows how to use it.

Take the GTA. Your penchant for the avant garde couldn't ask for more. Because this racing machine unfurls your true colors. Hot red, white and blue stripes for show. And a revolutionary new construction—a hollow core structure creates a homogeneous bond between fiberglass and metal. So it skis like fiberglass. Lasts like metal. Tested and proved by the Swiss National Ski Team. The GTA. It skis even better than it looks.

Or, ski Strato AR, the full race all-round. Built to take all you can give. Like the Strato 102, but softer torque and flex. Top metal edges for scrape protection, and a combi side-cut.

The GTA and Strato AR. Two more racing machines from Rossignol. If you're skier enough, one should have your name on it. Why not take a test drive soon?

ROSSIGNOL™
the Racing Machine

EXHIBIT 3

Stratix 112, Stratoflex, Concorde, Strato Junior.
Four speeds forward.

You'd rather have a more popularly priced racing machine? Then one of these Rossignols is just your speed.

Stratix 112. "The best dollar value fiberglass ski in the U.S.," says a leading ski magazine. We'll buy that. Stratix captures much of the agility and responsiveness that make the Rossignol Strato what it is today: *The* racing ski to own.

Stratoflex, too, offers the muscle and grace of more expensive Rossies. It's a great recreational ski. Racy orange. It looks it. Excellent on ice. Easy on powder. It skis it. Sandwich construction and top metal edges provide brute-strength durability.

Concorde. New name. New ski. An economy racing machine made possible only by Rossignol's increased production capacity. Ideal for beginners, intermediates.

Strato Junior. The youth ski with construction identical to the famous Rossignol Strato 102. Unique ratio between torque and flex makes it the ultimate racing machine. Easy in powder. Gripping on ice. Impossible? Not for the Strato Junior. Ski it and you could be ticketed for speeding on the slopes.

ROSSIGNOL™
the Racing Machine

Distributed in Canada by Raymond Lanctot, Ltd., Montreal

EXHIBIT 4

This one wins the races.

If you were in the French ski team's boots, this is the boot you'd wear.

Trappeur Pro. High-back support makes it ideal for tireless hours of skiing. A natural, too, for the new *avalement* technique. Or, with top buckles undone, it becomes *the boot* for ski instructors and intermediates. Comfortable, leather-lined polyurethane shell. Low damping shock absorber molding foam. Built on American lasts. New Martin buckles for easy adjustment.

For the French ski team, it all adds up to a boot so well-engineered it can help steer their skis through the gates til the rushing wind sounds like wild applause at Val d'Isere. And monsieur,

if that's your kind of skiing, then the Trappeur Pro is your kind of boot.

Does Trappeur offer custom foam-fitted boots? You bet. Only don't say "foam." Say "Inject-Elast." It's better. It comes to you in the finest shell possible. Controlled forward flex. Strong back support. New Martin "70" buckles. Torsion-proof racing sole. So if you're thinking foam-fitted, we say, great. Only say "Inject-Elast" instead.

Great recreational skier or beginner on a budget, Trappeur has a boot for you.

The Lady Trappeur. Maximum lateral stiffness. Rigid-as-possible injected sole. Lamb's wool lining for soft, soft comfort. Arch supports teamed with new American lasts. Now that's what Trappeur calls a top-notch recreational ski boot. So do the girls on the French ski team. They helped us design it.

EXHIBIT 5

These have all the fun.

Slalom for men. Your feet don't tell your skis where to go. Your boots do. With that in mind, consider the incredible control of Slalom. It's Trappeur's finest recreational men's ski boot. Built like a precision instrument, Slalom gives you the best of function and comfort. Very stiff. Very comfortable, thanks to American lasts and polyurethane shell lined with leather. Shearling up front for extra warmth.

Trappeur SM. (men's shown) Maximum comfort. Maximum support. Shearling-lined polyurethane shell. American lasts. Narrow racing soles. Martin buckles. Put it all together and what do you get? The best dollar value in recreational ski boots.

Trappeur Quick V. If you think a budget boot has to feel like one, you haven't tried the Trappeur Quick V. Compare stiffness, comfort and finish with any other budget boot. Vullcollan shell boasts leather and wool lining. Five pivotal buckles for exact adjustment. Easy-to-move clips on two straps. Men's in blue. Women's in red.

TRAPPEUR™

the boot of the French ski team

Distributed in Canada by Raymond Lanctot, Ltd., Montreal

like *Sports Illustrated, Redbook, Seventeen,* and *Time* were eliminated for the same reasons.

The agency finally limited itself to a media decision among the following books: *Ski, Skiing, Snow, Western Ski Time,* and *Colorado.* Also considered, was a new tabloid called the *Student Skier.* The latter was almost immediately eliminated, however, after it was learned that it was to be published for the first time in the 1970–71 season.

The two magazines that seemed to be able to reach the target market most effectively were *Ski* and *Skiing.* The two publications had guaranteed circulations of 350,000 and 425,000 respectively. It was estimated, however, that the combined circulation of these publications was actually about 900,000, with approximately 20 percent overlap in readership. An additional plus for these two magazines was that they both provided demographic breakdowns of their readers as an aid in media planning.

The decision was made not to attempt to go into both books with equal schedules, because the color, multiple-page spreads required for the desired level of impact were beyond the budgetary capability of the client.

After comparison of the editorial quality and interest of the two publications, it was the agency's opinion that *Skiing* provided a content which would probably attract a larger percentage of the serious skiers than would *Ski.* Therefore, it was proposed that the majority of the advertising thrust be put into this skiing publication and this was approved by the client. The split in media space expenditures between *Skiing* and *Ski,* accordingly, was approximately $134,500 to $16,200.

In order to publicize the continued racing superiority of Rossignol skis, an agreement with the newspaper, *Ski Racing,* was negotiated for 20 ads during the 1970–71 season. This publication reached just about everybody associated with the U.S. Ski Association, as well as all the racers. The ads run were black and white and included the traditional ski racer coming down the slopes. Also included in a circle in the lower left hand corner of the full-page ad was an up-to-date tabulation, as of the date of publication, showing the number of victories which racers on Rossignol skis had achieved during the 1970–71 winter season.

Expenditure timing

The multiple-page Rossignol and Le Trappeur ads were run in September 1970, in *Skiing,* and the Rossignol ads were also run in *Ski* magazine. Additionally about $4,000 worth of black-and-white ads were placed in miscellaneous publications. *Ski Racing* also received two advertising pages. A complete resume of all media expenditures is shown in Exhibit 6. Note that the approximate cost for one ski ad was $5,400 and for one boot ad about $10,700. Each page of advertising in *Ski Racing* ran $250.

EXHIBIT 6
Media schedule—1970–71

		Skiing	Ski	Ski racing	Miscellaneous
September 1970.........	Skis				$4000
October 1970..........	Skis	$16,200	$ 5,400	$ 500	
		3*	1	2†	
	Boots	10,700			
		1			
November 1970.........	Skis	16,200	5,400	500	
		3	1	2	
	Boots	10,700			
		1			
December 1970..........	Skis	16,200	5,400	1000	
		3	1	4	
	Boots	10,700			
		1			
January 1971...........	Skis	10,800		1000	
		2		4	
	Boots	10,700			
		1			
February 1971..........	Skis	10,800		1000	
		2		4	
	Boots	10,700			
		1			
March 1971.............	Skis	10,800		1000	
		2		4	
Totals.................	Skis	$81,000	$16,200	$4000	$4000
		15	3	16	
	Boots	53,500		1000	
		5		4	

* Indicates number of ads.
† Funds split 80/20, ski ads/boot ads.

Campaign results

Sales of Rossignol Skis as of December 31, 1970, amounted to 48,000 or approximately $3.4 million.[4] At this rate it was anticipated that the sales goal of 55,000 pairs of skis for the entire 1970–71 season would be reached. Sales of Trappeur Ski Boots as of the same date had reached 30,000 pairs, or $750,000, well above the target figure of from 20,000 to 25,000 pairs. Sales of other products in the Ski division line (gloves, mittens, après-ski boots, and protective headgear) amounted to $330,000 as of December 31. Total sales for the Ski Division as of December 31, therefore, amounted to $4,480,000.

Fragmentary indications as of March 1971, were that "Rossignol" and "Racing Machine" were becoming synonomous, and that brand awareness was increasing.

While advertising alone could not take full credit for the above results,

[4] Sales figures have been multiplied by a constant.

Mr. Sorenson was convinced that the 1970–71 campaign played an important part in the Ski Division's success during the first season.

1971–72 SEASON

As of March 1971, the account group at MacManus, John & Adams was developing the advertising strategy recommendations for the next season. It was estimated that a working budget of some $300,000 would be available for the winter season 1971–72. In considering the job to be done, Mr. Sorenson voiced the opinion that about double this amount should be made available, if possible.

The definition of the target market had been altered, since the Ski Division was interested in reaching a larger proportion of the recreational skiers during 1971–72. In recognition of this goal, the quantities of Rossignol skis ordered for the coming season were more nearly balanced, as models for advanced, recreational, and beginning skiers, than in 1970–71.

The question of whether or not to de-emphasize the racing images of Rossignol skis and the Pro line of Trappeur boots was being pondered. What adverse effects, if any, the racing image might have on the recreational market was unknown, as promotional plans were being developed.

Copy themes for 1971–72 lines of skis and ski boots were being developed by the agency creative staff. As of March 1971, a blanket theme of "The other French ski team" was the front runner under consideration, as a unifying concept to be used in tying together all of the products of the Ski Division (skis, ski boots, après-ski boots, gloves, and ski poles, among others).

The creative staff also had to decide whether or not to recommend the continuance of last year's creative themes for specific subgroups of products such as skis and ski boots.

Mr. Sorenson estimated that the budget for 1971–72 would be allocated, 77 percent for consumer advertising and 23 percent for dealer advertising.

Considering media vehicle selection, the agency media department was looking at other publications besides *Ski* and *Skiing*, but no firm decision had been made as to what additional books should be used. A special opportunity had been offered to the agency by *Snow* magazine. The representative of this publication was keenly interested in the Rossignol/Le Trappeur business and was having some special articles written by Patrick Rosel and Elaine Pence, two top French skiers. The articles were to appear in the September and October 1971 issues of the magazine. The book goes to all ski instructors, ski patrol members, and all racers. The circulation was about 125,000 copies in 1971 and the cost would be $4,000 per page. Also the agency was again considering one or two issues of *Western Ski Time* and *Colorado* as part of next year's campaign.

The question of whether to continue with full-page spreads or to go with half-page spreads and get twice as many pages was also being discussed. For the cost of two pages, Wolverine would have what looks like a four-page spread. Inserts in magazines were also being considered, where the agency could run eight pages for the cost of four.

Radio commercials were also under consideration. MacManus, John & Adams could produce about 300 tapes for $2,000.

Continuation of the cooperative advertising approach, with newspaper mats supplied to the dealers, was also under scrutiny. A whole program of ad mats could be produced for about $1,000.

Television advertising had not been discounted and neither had the idea of outdoor advertising.

Advertising to the trade was also under serious consideration. It was thought that a doubling of the trade advertising budget would be desirable to achieve adequate impact on the dealers.

CASE QUESTION

What campaign of advertising and promotion would you recommend to Wolverine World Wide, Inc.: Ski Division for the winter 1971–72 season? Support each recommendation briefly.

INDEXES

Index of cases

801

Index